The Enforcement of Competition Law in Europe

In the debate on the enforcement of competition law, many take the view that Europe should avoid the traps US law has fallen into by admitting excessive litigation. European law should not pave the way for judicial proceedings which ultimately serve the interests of lawyers or other agents rather than injured parties.

This inquiry describes the state of remedies in competition law in fifteen European countries, analyses the underlying determinants, and proposes ways of improving the enforcement of competition law. The international and European legal frameworks are presented, as is the approach of US-American law. It is argued that efforts to strengthen private enforcement of antitrust law should benefit from the rich European experience in unfair competition law. The divergence between the two fields of law is not so huge that a completely different treatment is justified. Thus, a specifically European way of competition law enforcement could be developed.

THOMAS M.J. MÖLLERS holds a Chair in Civil Law, Business Law, European Law, Comparative Law and International Private Law at the University of Augsburg.

ANDREAS HEINEMANN is Professor of Commercial and Economic Law at the University of Zürich.

CONTRIBUTORS TO THE VOLUME:
Antti Aine, Jesús Alfaro Aguila-Real, Torbjörn Andersson, Lia Athanassiou, Katalin Cseres, Rikard Englund, Sofia Englund, Helmut Gamerith, David Gerber, Ariënne Gommers, Andreas Heinemann, Sarah Johnson, Luís Menezes Leitão, Adelaide Leitão, Zsófia Lendvai, Fayna León, Cornelia Marin, Thomas M.J. Möllers, Siún O'Keeffe, Sune Troels Poulsen, Izabela Raiwa, Giuseppe Rossi, Peter Rott, Jeremy Scholes, Manola Scotton, David Townend, Pertti Virtanen.

The Common Core of European Private Law

For the transnational lawyer the present European situation is equivalent to that of a traveller compelled to cross legal Europe using a number of different local maps. To assist lawyers in the journey beyond their own locality *The Common Core of European Private Law Project* was launched in 1993 at the University of Trento under the auspices of the late Professor Rudolf B. Schlesinger. This is its seventh book published by Cambridge University Press.

The aim of this collective scholarly enterprise is to unearth what is already common to the legal systems of European Union Member States. Case studies widely circulated and discussed between lawyers of different traditions are employed to draw at least the main lines of a reliable map of the law of Europe.

Books in the Series

The Enforcement of Competition Law in Europe
Edited by Thomas M. J. Möllers and Andreas Heinemann

Commercial Trusts in European Private Law
Edited by Michael Graziadei, Ugo Mattei and Lionel Smith

Mistake, Fraud and Duties to Inform in European Contract Law
Edited by Ruth Sefton-Green

Security Rights in Movable Property in European Private Law
Edited by Eva-Maria Kieninger

Pure Economic Loss in Europe
Edited by Mauro Bussani and Vernon Valentine Palmer

The Enforceability of Promises in European Contract Law
Edited by James Gordley

Good Faith in European Contract Law
Edited by Reinhard Zimmermann and Simon Whittaker

The Enforcement of Competition Law in Europe

Edited by

Thomas M. J. Möllers
and
Andreas Heinemann

With an essay by

David J. Gerber

CAMBRIDGE
UNIVERSITY PRESS

CAMBRIDGE UNIVERSITY PRESS
Cambridge, New York, Melbourne, Madrid, Cape Town, Singapore, São Paulo, Delhi

Cambridge University Press
The Edinburgh Building, Cambridge CB2 8RU, UK

Published in the United States of America by Cambridge University Press, New York

www.cambridge.org
Information on this title: www.cambridge.org/9780521881104

First published 2007

Printed in the United Kingdom at the University Press, Cambridge

A catalogue record for this publication is available from the British Library

ISBN 978-0-521-88110-4 hardback

Contents

Preface

From the very beginning the Treaty of Rome included basic rules on competition law. However, these rules only covered restraints of competition ('antitrust law'), not unfair competition law. Since then, the situation has considerably changed. The fundamental freedoms of the treaty as well as secondary community legislation have heavily influenced both fields of law. Even if this development led to an important harmonization of competition law in the Member States, one aspect has stayed rather untouched: the legal consequences of a competition law violation have been left to a large extent to the disposal of the national legislature. As far as the legal consequences in private law are concerned every national legal order has tried to integrate competition law violations into its national tort law (or in some respects contract law) system. In this process, private remedies for violations of unfair competition law have gained a greater practical importance in Europe than those for violations of antitrust law. But even in the latter branch of law, public enforcement is increasingly complemented by private law mechanisms.

The wide variety of solutions which are proposed by national law were the reason for the editors to start the comparative venture within the Trento project on the *Common Core of European Private Law*. Based on the Common Core methodology (elaborated by Ugo Mattei and Mauro Bussani in the tradition of Rudolf B. Schlesinger and Rodolfo Sacco), i.e. on a questionnaire containing several cases which are discussed and answered by national reporters pursuant to their respective national legal systems and taking into account all legal and extra-legal formants, we have compared the state of the law in fifteen EU Member States. Based on the weak points and gaps resulting from the comparative analysis, we submit proposals which could lead to an improvement of private remedies in unfair competition law (Thomas M. J. Möllers) as well as in private antitrust enforcement (Andreas Heinemann). Recent initiatives on the European level for the improvement of European antitrust law triggering corresponding reforms in many member states were taken into account.

The project that has been running several years would not have been possible without the support of so many colleagues and friends. First of all, we would like to thank Wolfgang Fikentscher, who at the Trento annual meeting in 2000 inspired the birth of the competition law project. Walter van Gerven, the author of a draft EC regulation on private remedies, supported the project with his invaluable advice. David Gerber, the leading scholar in comparative competition law, drew our attention to so many aspects of the subject and contributed to this volume a comparative essay on private remedies in antitrust law. We would like to thank the country reporters for their constant engagement and the patience with which they responded to the numerous questions we had. And finally, we are deeply indebted to the participants of the Trento torts group (subsequently chaired by Mathias Reimann and Franz Werro) with whom we intensively discussed the questionnaire and the comparative details. The Common Core project has thus become a forum for us which has produced intercultural insights far beyond law.

We would also like to thank James Faulkner, Matthew Firth, Jacques Großkreuz, Thomas Wenninger and Georg S. Münzenrieder for their support in the preparation of the manuscript.

Finally, we are very grateful to Cambridge University Press for its tremendous contribution in presenting the Common Core project to the interested public.

Thomas M. J. Möllers
University of Augsburg

Andreas Heinemann
University of Zürich
October 2006

Contributors to the volume

The case studies and other parts of the book have been prepared by:[1]

ANTTI AINE, Researcher LL.Lic., University of Turku (report Finland)

JESÚS ALFARO AGUILA-REAL, Professor Dr, Universidad Autónoma de Madrid (report Spain)

TORBJÖRN ANDERSSON, Professor Dr, University of Uppsala (report Sweden)

LIA ATHANASSIOU, Assistant Professor, University of Athens, Faculty of Law, Greece (report Greece)

KATALIN CSERES, Assistant Professor of Law, University of Amsterdam (report Hungary)

RIKARD ENGLUND, EKN – The Swedish Export Credits Guarantee Board, Stockholm (report Sweden)

SOFIA ENGLUND, Lawyer – Senior Associate, Hammarskiöld & Co, Stockholm (report Sweden)

HELMUT GAMERITH, Professor Dr, former Vice-president of the Austrian Supreme Court and Professor at the University of Innsbruck (report Austria); in collaboration with Univ.-Ass. Dr KATHARINA MURSCHITZ, LL.M., (King's College London)

DAVID GERBER, Distinguished Professor at Chicago Kent College of Law, USA (essay antitrust law)

ARIËNNE GOMMERS, LL.M., Senior Member of Staff, Netherlands Competition Authority (report Netherlands)

ANDREAS HEINEMANN, Professor Dr, University of Zürich (editor, comparative part antitrust law, report Germany)

[1] The contributions reflect the personal opinions of their authors and are not necessarily the views of their employers or institutions.

SARAH JOHNSON, LL.B. (Trinity College), LL.M. (Bruges), Solicitor, Dublin (report Ireland)

LUÍS MENEZES LEITÃO, Professor Dr, University of Lisbon (report Portugal)

ADELAIDE LEITÃO, Lisbon (report Portugal)

ZSÓFIA LENDVAI, Ministry of Justice, Budapest (report Hungary)

FAYNA LEÓN, LL.M. (Bruges), Lawyer, CMS Albiñana & Suárez de Lezo, Madrid (report Spain)

CORNELIA MARIN, Ass. iur., Compiègne (report France)

THOMAS M.J. MÖLLERS, Professor Dr, University of Augsburg, Institute of European Legal Orders (editor, comparative part unfair competition law, report Germany)

SIÚN O'KEEFFE, B.C.L., LL.B. (N.U.I.), LL.M. (Bruges), Barrister, Senior officer, Netherlands Competition Authority (report Ireland)

SUNE TROELS POULSEN, PhD, Associate Professor, Department of Public and International Law, University of Aarhus (report Denmark)

IZABELA RAIWA, LL.M. (Berkeley), PhD Student, University of Amsterdam (report Poland)

GIUSEPPE ROSSI, Professor of Comparative Law, University of Turin Law School (report Italy)

PETER ROTT, Professor Dr, University of Bremen (report unfair competition law England)

JEREMY SCHOLES, Solicitor, Lecturer, Department of Law, University of Sheffield, Director of Competition Law, Walker Morris, Solicitors, Leeds (report antitrust law England)

MANOLA SCOTTON, Attorney, PhD Student, University of Amsterdam (report Italy)

DAVID TOWNEND, Lecturer, University of Sheffield (report unfair competition law England)

PERTTI VIRTANEN, Judge in the Finnish Market Court (report Finland)

Abbreviations (including legislation)

General (including European and international law)

CFR	Common Frame of Reference
CMLR	Common Market Law Review (law journal)
CPL	Competition Policy Newsletter
EIPR	European Intellectual Property Review (law journal)
EC	(Treaty of the) European Community
ECHR	European Convention on Human Rights
ECJ	European Court of Justice
ECR	European Court Reports (official journal of the ECJ)
EEC	European Economic Community
EP	European Parliament
EU	(Treaty of the) European Union
GATT	General Agreement on Tariffs and Trade
ICC	International Chamber of Commerce
ICLQ	International and Comparative Law Quarterly (law journal)
IIC	International Review of Intellectual Property and Competition Law (law journal)
lit.	Litera
PC	Paris Convention for the Protection of Industrial Property of 1883/1984
TCE	Treaty of a Constitution of Europe
TRIPS	Agreement on Trade-Related Aspects of Intellectual Property Rights
WTO	World Trade Organisation

Austria

ABGB	Allgemeines Bürgerliches Gesetzbuch (Civil Code)
BB	Betriebsberater (law journal)

BGBl	Bundesgesetzblatt
BMJ	Bundesministerium für Justiz (Ministry of Justice)
BWG	Bankwesengesetz
ecolex	Fachzeitschrift für Wirtschaftsrecht (Law Journal)
EO	Exekutionsordnung (rules on execution)
EvBl	Evidenzblatt
GRUR Int.	Gewerblicher Rechtsschutz und Urheberrecht Internationaler Teil (law journal)
JBl	Juristische Blätter (law journal)
KartG 1988	Kartellgesetz 1988 (Antitrust Code 1988)
KartG 2005	Kartellgesetz 2005 (Antitrust Code 2005)
KOG	Kartellobergericht (Superior Cartel Court)
KWG	Kreditwesengesetz
MR	Zeitschrift für Medien und Recht (law journal)
MSchG	Markenschutzgesetz (Trademark Code)
ÖBl	Österreichische Blätter für Gewerblichen Rechtsschutz und Urheberrecht (law journal)
ÖBl-LS	ÖBl-Leitsätze
ÖJZ-LSK	Österreichische Juristenzeitung – Leitsatzkartei (law journal)
OGH	Oberster Gerichtshof (Highest Supreme Court)
RdW	Recht der Wirtschaft (law journal)
StGB	Strafgesetzbuch (Criminal Code)
StPO	Strafprozeßordnung
SZ	Amtliche Sammlung von Entscheidungen des OGH in Zivilsachen (official journal of decisions of the Highest Supreme Court, civil cases)
UWG	Bundesgesetz gegen den unlauteren Wettbewerb 1984 (Federal Act against Unfair Competition)
WBL	Wirtschaftsrechtliche Blätter (law journal)
WRP	Wettbewerb in Recht und Praxis (law journal)
ZPO	Zivilprozessordnung (Code of Civil Procedure)

Belgium

cc	Code civil
LPC	Loi sur les practiques du commerce et sur l'information et la protection du consommateur

Denmark

CA	Competition Act
DKK	Danish Kroner (currency)

DRN Dansk Reklame Neve (council for advertising self-regulation)
FO Forbrugerombudsmand (consumer ombudsman)
MFL Lov om Markedsføring / Markedsføringslov (Marketing Practices Act)

England

AC Appeal Cases
ADR Alternative Dispute Resolution
All ER All England Reports
ASA Advertising Standards Authority
CA Competition Act 1998
CAP Committee of Advertising Practice
CAT Competition Appeal Tribunal
CMAR Control of Misleading Advertisements Regulations 1988/2000
Code British Codes of Advertising and Sales Promotion
CPA Consumer Protection Act 1987
DGFT Director General of Fair Trading
EA Enterprise Act 2002
EAT Employment Appeal Tribunal
ECLR European Competition Law Review
EHRR European Human Rights Reports
EMLR Entertainment and Media Law Reports
EWCA England and Wales Court of Appeals Decisions
EWHC England and Wales High Court Decisions
FSR Fleet Street Reports
FTA Fair Trade Act 1973
IRLR Industrial Relations Law Reports
ITC Independent Television Commission
JCP Journal of Consumer Policy (law journal)
OFT Office of Fair Trading
QB Queen's Bench Division
RA Radio Authority
RTR Road Traffic Reports
SI Statutory Instrument
TDA Trade Descriptions Act 1968
TLR Times Law Reports
TMA Trade Marks Acts 1994
UKHL United Kingdom House of Lords
UTCCR Unfair Terms in Consumer Contract Regulations 1994/1999
WLR Weekly Law Reports

Finland

KSL	Kuluttajansuojalaki (Finnish Consumer Protection Act)
MC	Markkinatuomioistuin (Market Court)
MCA	Laki markkinatuomioistuimesta (Market Court Act)
SopMenL	Laki sopimatoomasta menettelystä elinkeinotoiminnassa (Finnish Unfair Trade Practices Act)

France

Bull.civ.	Bulletin des arrêts des chambres civiles de la Cour de Cassation
BVB	Bureau de Vérification des Publicités
BVP	Bureau de Vérification de la Publicité
Cass.	Cour de Cassation
cc	Code Civil
CCons	Code de la Consommation
CNP	Conseil National de Publicité
CP	Code Pénal
DGCCRF	Direction Générale de la Concurrence, de la Consommation et de la Répression de Fraudes
Fasc.	Fascicule
ICC	Chambre internationale du commerce
NCPC	Nouveau Code de Procédure Civile
PIBD	Propriété industrielle – Bulletin documentaire (law journal)
RTDcom	Revue de droit commercial (law journal)
TGI	Tribunal de grande instance
Trib	Tribunal
Trib.com.	Tribunal commercial
UDA	Union National des Annconceurs

Germany

AcP	Archiv für die civilistische Praxis (law journal)
BB	Betriebsberater (law journal)
BGB	Bürgerliches Gesetzbuch (Civil Code)
BGBl.	Bundesgesetzblatt (official journal of the Federal Legislature)
BGH	Bundesgerichtshof (Federal Supreme Court)
BGHSt	Amtliche Sammlung des Bundesgerichtshofs (official journal of the Federal Supreme Court, criminal cases)

BGHZ	Amtliche Sammlung des Bundesgerichtshofs (official journal of the Federal Supreme Court, Civil cases)
BKartA	Bundeskartellamt (Federal Cartel Office)
BR-Drs.	Bundesrat-Drucksachen (official journal of the Federal Council)
BT-Drs.	Bundestag-Drucksachen (official journal of the Federal Parliament)
BVerfG	Bundesverfassungsgericht (Federal Constitutional Court)
BVerfGE	Amtliche Sammlung des Bundesverfassungsgerichts (official journal of the Federal Constitutional Court)
EuR	Europarecht (law journal)
EuZW	Europäische Zeitschrift für Wirtschaftsrecht (law journal)
EWS	Europäisches Wirtschafts- und Steuerrecht (law journal)
FCO	Federal Cartel Office (Bundeskartellamt)
GG	Grundgesetz (Fundamental Law)
GPR	Zeitschrift für Gemeinschaftsprivatrecht (law journal)
GRUR	Gewerblicher Rechtsschutz und Urheberrecht (law journal)
GRUR Int.	Gewerblicher Rechtsschutz und Urheberrecht, Auslands- und internationaler Teil (law journal)
GWB	Gesetz gegen Wettbewerbsbeschränkungen (Act against Restraints of Competition – Antitrust Code)
JZ	JuristenZeitung (law journal)
NJW	Neue Juristische Wochenschrift (law journal)
NJW-RR	Neue Juristische Wochenschrift – Rechtsprechungsreport (law journal)
OLG	Oberlandesgericht (Court of Appeals)
PreisAngV	Preisangabenverordnung
RabelsZ	Rabels Zeitschrift (law journal)
StGB	Strafgesetzbuch (Criminal Code)
StPO	Strafprozessordnung (Criminal Procedure Code)
UWG	Gesetz gegen den unlauteren Wettbewerb von 1896/2004 (Act against Unfair Competition – Unfair Competition Code)[2]
Ex-UWG	Gesetz gegen den unlauteren Wettbewerb (UWG until 2004; earlier version)
WRP	Wettbewerb in Recht und Praxis (law journal)

[2] A synopsis of the old UWG and the UWG 2004 may be found in Begr. RegE, BT-Drs. 15/1487, p. 13.

WuW Wirtschaft und Wettbewerb (law journal)
ZEuP Zeitschrift für Europäisches Privatrecht (law journal)
ZGS Zeitschrift für das gesamte Schuldrecht (law journal)
ZHR Zeitschrift für das gesamte Handels- und Wirtschaftsrecht (law journal)
ZPO Zivilprozessordnung (Civil Procedure Code)
ZWeR Zeitschrift für Wettbewerbsrecht (law journal)

Greece

AK Astikos Kodikas (Civil Code)
Arm. Armenopoulos (law journal)
CC Civil Code
CCP Code of Civil Procedure
CFI Court of First Instance
DEE Dikaio Epicheirisseon kai Etairion (law journal)
EEmpD Epitheorisis Emporikou Dikaiou (Commercial Law Review)
EllDni Elliniki Dikaiossini (Greek Justice)
L. Law
NoV Nomiko Vima (law journal)
PD Presidential decree

Hungary

CPA Törvény a fogyasztóvédelemr (Act CLV of 1997 on Consumer Protection)
HAA Reklámörveny (Act LVIII of 1997 on Business Advertising Activity)
HCA Versenytörvény (Hungarian Competition Act: Act No. LVII of 1996 on the Prohibition of Unfair and Restrictive Market Practices)
HCC Hungarian Civil Code: Act IV of 1959
HCP Hungarian Civil Procedure: Act III of 1952
OEC Gazdasági Versenyhivatal (Office of Economic Competition)

Ireland

IAC Irish Appeal Cases
App. Cas. Appeal Cases
ASI Code of Advertising Standards for Ireland
EIPR European Intellectual Property Review
FSR Fleet Street Reports
Ir Jur Rep Irish Jurist Reports

ILRM	Irish Law Reports Monthly
IR	Irish Reports
ODCA	Office of the Director of Consumer Affairs
SGSSA	Sale of Goods and Supply of Services Acts 1893 and 1980
TMA	Trade Marks Act 1996

Italy

App.	Court of appeal
Arch. civ.	Archivio civile (law journal)
art.	Article (in a piece of legislation)
Autorità Garante	Autorità Garante della Concorrenza e del Mercato (Antitrust authority)
CAP	Codice dell'autodisciplina pubblicitaria (Code of Self-Control of Advertising)
cass.	Corte di Cassazione (Highest Court)
cc	Codice civile (Civil Code)
c.p.	Codice penale (Criminal Code)
Cons. Stato	Consiglio di Stato (highest administrative court)
cpc	Codice di procedura civile (Code of Civil Procedure)
Danno e resp.	Danno e responsabilità (law journal)
d.lgs.	Decreto legislativo (legislative decree)
Foro it.	Il Foro italiano (law journal)
Giur.ann.dir.ind.	Giurisprudenza annotata di diritto industriale (law journal)
Giur. it.	Giurisprudenza italiana (law journal)
Giurì	Giurì dell'Autodisciplina Pubblicitaria (panel of Self-Control of Advertising)
Giust. civ.	Giustizia civile (law journal)
IAP	Istituto dell'autodisciplina pubblicitaria (Institute of Self-Control of Advertising)
l.	Law
Riv.dir.ind.	Rivista di diritto industriale (law journal)
TAR	Tribunale Amministrativo Regionale (administrative tribunal)
Trib.	Tribunale (tribunal)

Netherlands

BRv	Burgerlijke Rechtsvordering (Code of Civil Procedure)
BW	Burgerlijk Wetboek (Dutch Civil Code)

DCA	Dutch Competition Act
RCC	Reclame Code Commissie (Advertising Code Commission)
NCA	Netherlands Competition Authority
NRC	Nederlands Reclame Code (Dutch Advertising Code)
Sr	Wetboek van Strafrecht (Penal Code)

Poland

k.c.	Kodeks Cywilny (Civil Code)
k.p.c.	Kodeks Postepowania Cywilnego (Code of Civil Procedure)
k.p.k.	Kodeks Postepowania Karnego (Criminal Procedure Code)
OCCP	Office of Competition and Consumer Protection
p.p.	Prawo prasowe (Press Law)
u.o.k.k.	Ustawa o ochronie konkurencji i konsumentow (Act on Competition and Consumer Protection of 2000)
u.z.n.k.	Ustawa o zwalczaniu nieuczciwej konkurencji (Act on Fighting Unfair Competition of 1993)

Portugal

CC	Código Civil (Civil Code)
CP	Código Penal (Criminal Code)
CPC	Código de Processo Civil (Code of Civil Procedure)
CPI	Código de Propriedade Industrial (Industrial Property Code)
CPP	Código de Processo Penal (Code of Criminal Procedure)
CPub	Código da Publicidade (Advertising Code)
DGCC	Direcção Geral do Comércio e da Concorrência
Instituto do Consumidor	Instituto Nacional da Defesa do Consumidor (National Consumer Protection Institution)
LAV	Lei 31/86 de Arbitragem Voluntária (Voluntary Arbitration Law)
LDC	Lei de Defesa da Concorrência (Antitrust Code)
LDCons	Lei de Defesa do Consumido (Consumer Protection Act)

Spain

AAP	Asociación de Autocontrol de la Publicidad (Association for the Self-Regulation of Commercial Communication)
CC	Código Civil (Civil Code)
CC.AA.	Communidades Autonómas (autonomous regions)
CP	Código Penal (Criminal Code)

LCD Ley 3/1991 de Competencia Desleal (Unfair Competition Act)
LDC Ley 16/1989 de Defensa de la Competencia (Act for the Defence of Competition)
LEC Ley de Enjuiciamiento Civil (Code of Civil Procedure)
LECr Ley de Enjuiciamiento Criminal (Code of Criminal Procedure)
LGDCU Ley 26/1984 General para la Defensa de los Consumidores y Usarios (Act for the Defence of Consumers and Users)
LGP Ley 34/1988 General de Publicidad (Advertising Act)
LMa Ley de Marcas (Spanish Trademark Act)
LOCM Ley de Ordenación del Comercio Minorista (Act of Retail Organization)
SDC Servicio de Defensa de la Competencia (Service for the Defence of Competition)
TDC Tribunal de Defensa de la Competencia (Competition Court)

Sweden

ARN Allmänna Reklamationsnämnd (Public Complaints Tribunal)
KL Konkurrenslagen (Competition Act)
KO Konsumentombudsmannen
MD Swedish Market Court
MFL Marknadsföringslagen 1995:450 (Act on Marketing)

Switzerland

BBl. Bundesblatt der Schweizerischen Eidgenossenschaft (official journal of the Legislature)
OR Obligationenrecht (contract and torts law)
SJZ Schweizer Juristenzeitung (law journal)
UWG Lauterkeitsgesetz (Unfair Competition Law)

USA

BBB Better Business Bureau
C.F.R. Code of Federal Regulations
FTC Federal Trade Commission
FTCA Federal Trade Commission Act
H.R. House of Representatives
ITC International Trade Commission
NAD National Advertising Division
RICO Federal Rackeeter Influenced and Corrupt Organzisation provisions of the Organzied Crime Control Act of 1970

TCPA	Telephone Consumer Protection Act 1991
U.S.C.	United State Code
U.S.C.A.	United States Code Annotated
U.S.P.Q.	United States Patent Quarterly
UDAP	Unfair and Deceptive Acts or Practices (abbreviation for State Unfair Trade Act)

Introduction

In December 2005, the European Commission published a Green Paper on Damages Actions for Breach of the EC Competition Rules. This document has provoked a discussion on the role of private actions which goes far beyond competition law. Many take the view that Europe should avoid the traps into which US law has stepped by admitting excessive litigation due to a system of class actions, punitive damages, pre-trial discovery and contingency fees. European law should not pave the way for judicial proceedings which ultimately do not serve the interests of the injured parties but rather those of their lawyers, consultants or other agents. According to the methodology of the Common Core of European Private Law project, this inquiry gives a description of the state of remedies in competition law in fifteen European countries and analyses the underlying determinants. On this basis, proposals are developed showing how the enforcement of competition law could be improved. The flaws can be fixed without running the risk of abusive litigation. To this end, it has been instructive to include two fields of law which are normally treated separately, i.e. unfair competition law and antitrust law. Although the two branches share common goals, their enforcement has taken completely different paths. Whereas in many reporting countries unfair competition law is endowed with effective private law (and in some countries also with public law) remedies, the implementation of antitrust law is in practice almost completely entrusted to administrative enforcement. This is not so much a question of legislative principles - all reporting countries provide for private remedies for violations of antitrust law - but of certain legal and factual obstacles and of a lack of incentives.

The present inquiry aims at analysing the enforcement components and the different weight given to them in both fields of law. The legal framework on the international and European level is presented, as is the approach of US-American law. The cases are structured in groups concerning on the one hand the sanctions available and on the other hand the potential plaintiffs and defendants. Eight cases concern unfair competition law, seven are on antitrust law. All cases are solved according to the fifteen legal systems involved. After a comparative analysis, shortcomings and strengths are analysed. Reform proposals are based upon this result. It will be shown that efforts to strengthen private enforcement of antitrust law should benefit from the rich European experience in unfair competition law. The divergence between the two fields of law is not so huge that a completely different treatment is justified. Thus, a specifically European way of competition law enforcement could be developed.

PART I. REMEDIES IN UNFAIR COMPETITION AND CONSUMER PROTECTION LAW

THOMAS M.J. MÖLLERS

A. Setting the basics – the legal framework

I. Approach of this comparative study

1. *The status quo of legal harmonization in unfair competition law*

a) Lack of a 'European unfair competition law'

European integration is making progress; the European Constitution Treaty has been passed[1] and scholars are discussing a European Civil Code.[2] In the field of unfair competition law only few directives exist and one is tempted to use F. Rittner's words which he once used to describe the law of contract: European directives create only 'islands' of harmonized law[3] within each national law that exist without any connection between them.[4] Accordingly the law of unfair competition is still based on many origins and very often overlaps with the law of consumer protection, contract and intellectual property.

Nowadays all modern legal systems offer protection against unfair competition, i.e. against 'any act of competition contrary to honest

[1] Draft Treaty Establishing a Constitution for Europe, adopted by consensus by the European Convention on July 18, 2003, OJ C 169, 1. The negative referenda in France and the Netherlands led to immediate frustration again. In the following the terms of the TCE are cited in parenthesis.

[2] European Parliament of June 26, 1989, OJ C 158, 400, (1992) 56 RabelsZ 320, (1993) 3 ZEuP 613 et seq. as well as European Parliament of May 6, 1994, OJ C 205, 518, (1995) 3 ZEuP 669, (1994) 3 EuZW 612; Commission of July 11, 2001, COM (2001), 398 final, cf. europe.eu.int/comm/off/green/index_de.htm; cf. H. Schulte-Nölke, (2001) 56 JZ 917 et seq.; T. Möllers, *European Directives on Civil Law – Shaping a new German Civil Code*, (2003) 18 Tulane European & Civil Law Forum 1, (2002) 57 JZ 121; W. Wurmnest, *Ansätze zur Privatrechtsvereinheitlichung* (2003) 11 ZEuP 714 et seq. See Action Plan of the European Communities COM (2003), 68 final.

[3] F. Rittner, *Das Gemeinschaftsprivatrecht und die europäische Integration* (1995) 50 JZ 849 (851).

[4] This is the analysis for the law of unfair competition of the European Commission in its Green Paper on EU Consumer Protection of October 2, 2001, COM (2001), 531 final.

practices in industrial or commercial matters',[5] in short against 'dirty tricks'.[6] Because of the differing traditions in the Member States the enforcement of infringements of unfair competition law has only been harmonized marginally. In the different European directives courts and administrative agencies are equally named as competent for enforcement. Moreover, an additional self-control is allowed.[7] This form of harmonization leaves everything as it was before. The sanctions are numerous and as disparate as the provisions dealing with material aspects.[8]

b) Shortcomings in the enforcement against unfair advertisement

In everyday life it is common to be without protection against unfair measures: deceptive prize draws, direct marketing of bogus slimming agents, deceptive advertisements for summer resorts are only some examples. Sweepstakes that convey that the addressee has already won and only has to invest a small handling fee, wholehearted advertisement for panaceas that promise to reduce the gasoline consumption by 40 per cent or make your hair grow again are examples taken from everyday life.[9] Lately the opinion arguing that the system of remedies instituted in art. 4–6 Misleading and Comparative Advertising Directive 84/450/EEC is 'insufficient' is becoming stronger. Because of the different bodies that are competent to deal with infringements, legal scholars raised the reproach that in some Member States no sufficient legal protection is offered. This has been explicitly stated for English law because the Office of Fair Trading hardly ever brings proceeding against infringements.[10]

An example: in Germany over the last few years consumers have been flooded by unwanted fax machine messages; cold-calling is widespread

[5] For art. 10bis Paris Convention see below A.II.1(a).

[6] Z. Chaffee, *Unfair Competition* (1940) 53 Harv. L. Rev. 1289; see below for the attempts to develop a definition, A.I notes 74 et seq.

[7] See for the status quo of the European law of unfair competition A.III.

[8] A. Beater, *Unlauterer Wettbewerb* (2002), § 8 note 104.

[9] Green Paper on EU Consumer Protection of October 2, 2001, COM (2001), 531 final at 2.1; J. Glöckner, in H. Harte-Bavendamm and F. Henning-Bodewig, *UWG* (2004), Einl B note 203.

[10] G. Schricker and F. Hennig-Bodewig, *Elemente einer Harmonisierung des Rechts des unlauteren Wettbewerbs in der Europäischen Union*, comparative law research on behalf of the Ministry of Justice, July 2001 (2001) 47 WRP 1367 (1375). Unfortunately, the authors do not follow up this thesis.

and the abuse of 190-numbers is common. Even the federal government conceded when it amended the German Unfair Competition Act in 2004 that there are some minor infringements that will not be penalized.[11] German consumers' associations ascertain that they are able to record up to 80 per cent of the relevant cases;[12] this figure is likely to be too positive. This strongly opposes the widely held view that in Germany infringements of unfair competition law will always be stopped by competitors or by associations. That view is, at least in cases of nuisance or misleading advertising, not completely true.

The principle that 'An infringement of unfair competition law reaps rewards'[13] proves true. All legal harmonization remains *l'art pour l'art* if it remains 'law in the books'[14] and only pretends to harmonize this area of law. Actions for an injunction are directed towards the future.[15] This indicates that it will be worthwhile to examine whether further remedies should be introduced that sanction the first infringement. One will also have to discuss whether it is reasonable to institute an exclusive means of legal recourse, either through a public agency or the courts.

c) Creation of an internal market

This study examines the law of unfair competition in Europe (with some remarks concerning the law of the USA). To an extent it intends to pay heed to the demands of a European theory of legislation. The European Union is aiming towards the abolition of borders, an internal market as it is defined in art. 14 para. 2 EU (art. I-3 para. 2 TCE). For the purpose of harmonization it has developed different measures: either the approximation of law or mutual recognition. The principle of subsidiarity in art. 5 para. 1 EU (art. I-9 para. 3 TCE) burdens the EU with the proof that the measure is necessary for the completion of the internal market. Legal harmonization is thus no aim in itself. If the

[11] See below B.II.4(c) and Begr. RegE, UWG, BT-Drs. 15/1487, for § 10 p. 23.

[12] Statement of the Federal Association of Consumers' Assoctions (Verbraucherzentrale Bundesverband e.V.) before the Committee on Legal Affairs of February 19, 2004; See www.thomas-moellers.de/materialien.

[13] See G. Schricker (1979) 81 GRUR 1; R. Sack, *Der Gewinnabschöpfungsanspruch von Verbänden in der geplanten UWG-Novelle* (2003) 49 WRP 549, 554.

[14] R. Pound, *Law in Books and Law in Action* (1910) 44 American L. Rev. 12. The Commission also emphasizes that clear and reliable provisions have to be enforced effectively, Green Paper on EU Consumer Protection, COM (2001), 531 final at 5.

[15] Begr. RegE, UWG, BT-Drs. 15/1487, § 10 p. 23.

measure is not necessary for the completion of the internal market the competition between the different legal systems of the Member States is preferable.[16]

The euro as a common currency has deepened the internal market since it creates price transparency. The advent of e-commerce has facilitated cross-border trade. Different legal systems and different enforcement of provisions could result in the consumer abstaining from cross-border transactions since he is unable to enforce infringements of his rights.[17]

In a market economy, advertisement is of greatest importance for a company to survive competition or to enter into competition with other companies. As the ECJ has stated, advertisement fulfils an essential function in the 'opening of markets'.[18] Failing to implement European unfair competition provisions restricts competition as it has the same effect as state aid. It gives the Member State's companies an advantage over foreign companies that have to obey the implemented rules. If companies are forced to develop different marketing concepts because of varying legal requirements this results in additional costs.[19] Ultimately, differences in the legal requirements can even bar companies from entering a market altogether.[20] Consequently, small and medium-sized companies are still excluded from cross-border trading.[21]

[16] A. Ogus, *Competition Between National Legal Systems. A Contribution of Economic Analysis to Comparative Law* (1999) 48 ICLQ 405; P. Glenn, *Comparative Law & Legal Practice. On Removing the Borders* (2001) 75 Tulane L.Rev. 977; P. Neuhaus and J. Kropholler, *Rechtsvereinheitlichung – Rechtsverbesserung* (1981) 45 RabelsZ 73; H. Kötz, *Rechtsvereinheitlichung – Nutzen, Kosten, Methoden, Ziele* (1986) 50 RabelsZ 1; E.M. Kieninger, *Wettbewerb der Privatrecthsordnungen im Europäischen Binnenmarkt* (2002).

[17] Studies show that consumers are less confident when entering into cross-border transactions, see follow-up Communication to the Green paper on Consumer Protection, COM (2002), 289 final 25; Regulation (EC) No. 2006/2004, OJ L 364, 1, 2nd reason for consideration.

[18] ECJ C-34/95, C-35/95 and C-36/95, (1997) ECR I-3843 note 43, (1997) 45 GRUR Int. 912 (917) – 'De Agostini and TV-Shop'; ECJ C-405/98, (2001) ECR I-1795 note 21, (2001) 49 GRUR Int. 553 – 'Gourmet'. See also A. Wiebe, *Die 'guten Sitten'im Wettbewerb – eine europäische Regelungsaufgabe*? (2002) 48 WRP 283 (284).

[19] See e.g. ECJ C-30/89, (1990) ECR I-691 – 'GB-INNO-BM'; ECJ C-315/92, (1994) ECR I-317, (1994) 76 GRUR 303 – 'Clinique'; ECJ C-470/93, (1995) ECR I-1923, (1995) 41 WRP 677 – 'Mars'.

[20] A. Wiebe, (2002) 48 WRP 283 (284).

[21] Green Paper on EU Consumer Protection, COM (2001), 531 final at 3.1; Regulation (EC) No. 2006/2004,OJ L 364, 1, 2nd rationale.

d) Reactions to these shortcomings

The European Union has offered three new acts to harmonize the law of unfair competition.[22] Surprisingly, these new acts did not attempt to harmonize the sanctions against infringements.[23] The Directive 2005/29/EC concerning Unfair Commercial Practices does not introduce any previously unknown remedies.[24] Only the Regulation on Consumer Protection Cooperation No. 2006/2004 is more courageous in demanding an agency that is competent to sanction cross-border infringements.[25]

In recent years many member states have developed their law of unfair competition; very often blanket clauses have been introduced. And there are good reasons why Member States such as the United Kingdom,[26] Germany[27] or Portugal have amended and modernised their law of unfair competition. The German legislature amending its UWG in 2004 to make it 'fit for Europe' has also refrained from harmonizing its sanctions.[28] It even claims its legislation to be a 'model for a future European law of unfair competition'.[29] If confidence in this claim can be sustained, one will have to examine it by comparing the different legal systems.

In the last few years a couple of studies have been devoted to a comparison of the substantive provisions in the law of unfair competition.[30] The legal consequences are either excluded[31] or dealt with

[22] See Directive Proposal Concerning Unfair Commercial Practices, COM (2003), 356 final and Regulation Proposal concerning Sales Promotions, COM (2001), 546 final; amended in COM (2002), 585 final; see below A.III.2(c), 3(d) and (e).

[23] For the European law see below A.III.

[24] Directive 2005/29/EC of the European Parliament and of the Council concerning Unfair Business-to-Consumer Commercial Practices in the Internal Market and amending Directives 84/450EEC, 97/7/EC and 98/27/EC, of May 11, 2005, OJ L 149, 22.

[25] Regulation (EC) No. 2006/2004 of the European Parliament and of the Council of October 27, 2004 on Cooperation between National Authorities Responsible for the Enforcement of Consumer Protection Laws (Regulation on Consumer Protection Cooperation), OJ L 364, 1; see A.III.3(g).

[26] Enterprise Act 2002 and below A.II.2(o).

[27] Amendment of the UWG in 2004 and below A.II.2(e).

[28] This is especially emphasized by H. Köhler, J. Bornkamm and F. Henning-Bodewig, *Vorschlag für eine Richtlinie zum Lauterkeitsrecht und eine UWG-Reform* (2002) 48 WRP 1317; K.H. Fezer, (2001) 47 WRP 989 and below A.III.

[29] See E. Keller, in H. Harte-Bavenkamm and F. Henning-Bodewig, *UWG* (2004), Einl. A note 11; cf. http://www.bmj.bund.de/enid/fad884c433728e8a7d340bfd7b6efd49,0/al.html.

[30] Deserving special mentioning for its unique scope are the country reports by G. Schricker (ed.), *Recht der Werbung in Europa*, vol. 2 (supplement 1995). But some parts of the book are already ten years old and some important Member States like Spain or Portugal are still missing.

[31] Remedies are completely left out by H.-W. Micklitz and and J. Keßler (eds.), *Marketing Practices Regulation and Consumer Protection in the EC Member States and the US* (2002); very

summarily.[32] In scholarly writing, proposals for the legal consequences are rare or rather short. Thus one can find the demand to introduce on the European level an action for the confiscation of unlawful gains,[33] the right to sue for consumers or associations,[34] a harmonization taking the TRIPS-Treaty as a role model[35] or in general to 'clearly define the borderline of unlawful and lawful behaviour where administrative and penal sanctions are conceivable'.[36]

e) Methodical requirements of comparative law and the European harmonization of law

The Common Core Project

This study would like to examine the different remedies in European unfair competition law on a comparative law basis and deliver answers to the above-mentioned questions. Its ultimate aim is thus to remedy the above-mentioned shortcomings.

The starting point is the law of the individual Member States. Before any proposals are made the state of the law in fifteen different states is examined. Originally, comparative law aimed at introduction of a universal law.[37] The same underlying idea can be found if one examines which provisions of another state can be introduced in one's own state.[38] The Common Core Project follows the approach of Schlesinger

short even in its most current parts F. Henning-Bodewig, in H. Harte-Bavendamm and F. Henning-Bodewig, *UWG* (2004), Einl. E.

32 Only a short summary is offered by R. Schulze and H. Schulte-Nölke, *Analysis of National Fairness Laws Aimed at Protecting Consumers in Relation to Precontractual Commercial Practices and the Handling of Consumer Complaints by Businesses* (2003); J. Maxeiner and P. Schotthöfer (eds.), *Advertising Law in Europe and North America* (2nd edn 1999).

33 H. Köhler and T. Lettl, *Das geltende europäische Lauterkeitsrecht, der Vorschlag für eine EG-Richtlinie über unlautere Geschäftspraktiken und die UWG-Reform*, (2002) 48 WRP 1019 (1047).

34 See art. 7 of the draft of H.-W. Micklitz and J. Keßler (2002) 50 GRUR Int. 885 (901).

35 G. Schricker and F. Hennig-Bodewig, (2001) 47 WRP 1367 (1375), and H. Köhler and T. Lettl (2002) 48 WPR 1019 (1047).

36 F. Bultmann, G. Howells, J. Keßler, H.-W. Micklitz, M. Radeideh, N. Reich, J. Stucek and D. Voigt, *The Feasibility of a General Legislative Framework on Fair Traiding, Proposal for a General Legislative Framework on Fair Trading* (2000), p. 68; H.-W. Micklitz and J. Keßler (2002) 50 GRUR Int. 885 (896 et seq.) demand European mechanisms for supervision.

37 E. Lambert, *Opening address*, in: *Congrès international de droit comparé – Procès-verbaux des séances et documents*, vol. I, 26 (40) (1905); R. Saleilles, *Conception et objet de la science du droit comparé*, in *Congrès international de droit comparé – Procès-verbaux des séances et documents*, vol. I, 167; R. Michaels, *Im Westen nichts Neues* (2002) 66 RabelsZ 97 (101).

38 K. Zweigert and H. Kötz, *Einführung in die Rechtsvergleichung* (3rd ed. 1996), p. 43, translated as *Introduction to Comparative Law* (3rd edn 1998 – translation by T. Weir).

by first analysing without any prejudice the different solutions offered in the Member States (Level 1: Operative Rule). The search for an ideal system of regulation is thus not the ultimate purpose.[39] This approach sheds light on the different legal traditions with its legal formants[40] and its cultural diversity.[41] Other comparative law scholars also emphasise the necessity to heed the mentality and the underlying decisions of what is considered fair and just.[42] In the summary the reasons for a certain solution are given (Level 2: Descriptive Formants), as well as policy considerations, economic and social factors (Level 3: Metalegal Formants).[43]

This is also aimed at refraining from the temptation to overstretch the possibilities of a common European law of unfair competition.[44] In this context it will be shown that the remedies in the law of unfair competition could not be more diverse. Though an overlap between civil law, public law, penal law and mechanisms for out-of-court settlements[45] can be found in all Member States, the details vary significantly from state to state: civil law is preferred by Germany and Austria, public law by Scandinavian countries like Sweden, Finland and Denmark, penal law by France, Ireland and earlier by Portugal and out-of-court settlements are favoured by England. Great differences can also be found in the objectives of claims and the parties to these claims.

Comparative law can thus, especially for international and supranational organizations, offer a possible mean of coordination.[46]

39 See for this distinction (with reference to the Lando Commission), M. Bussani and U. Mattei (1997/98) 3 Colum.J.Eur.L. 339 (347).

40 In order to know what the law is, it is necessary to analyse the entire complex relationship among the legal formants of a system, i.e. all those formative elements that make any given rule of law amidst statutes, general propositions, particular definitions, reasons, holdings, etc.; see M. Bussani and U. Mattei (1997/98) 3 Colum.J.Eur.L. 339 (344).

41 Ibid. (346); based on R. Sacco, *Legal Formants. A Dynamic Approach to Comparative Law*, (1991) 39 Am.J.Comp.L. 1.

42 P. Legrand, *Le droit comparé* (1999); K. Zweigert and H. Kötz, *Einführung in die Rechtsvergleichung* (3rd edn 1996), translated as *Introduction to Comparative Law* (3rd edn 1998 – translation by T. Weir); recently H. Kötz, *Alte und neue Aufgaben der Rechtsvergleichung* (2002) 57 JZ 257 (263).

43 M. Bussani and U. Mattei, (1997/98) 3 Colum.J.Eur.L. 339 (354 et seq.); see below Part II A.I.3.

44 See A.I.2(a). 45 See below Graphic 1.

46 R. Buxbaum, *Die Rechtsvergleichung zwischen nationalem Staat und internationaler Wirtschaft* (1996) 60 RabelsZ 201 (211 et seq).

f) Purpose and examined questions in this comparative law study

The status of common remedies in the Member States of the EU

In accordance with the approach of Schlesinger, this study will start with a description of law as it is applied now, the status quo on a European and a national level. The starting point will be the directives in force since 1984 that set the aims of protection and their enforcement. Common remedies of European law were either introduced by legal harmonization or exist independently from legal harmonization by the European legislature. Therefore we will have to examine whether the claim is true that in some Member States insufficient remedies exist. This means that deficits of implementation shall be made clear.[47]

Possible legal harmonization – in small steps

For both the substantive law and remedies in the law of unfair competition, only a minimum harmonization can be found. This naturally leads to the question as to whether this status quo should be altered and in which areas further harmonization is desirable. This will include the search for a way between the maintenance of the status quo and a full harmonization.[48] Some argue that the problems occurring in some member states could be remedied if a full harmonization is achieved, since a minimum harmonization still allows for more stringent national rules. The new approach of the Commission aims at full harmonization[49] including, as demanded in the literature, remedies for infringements. This study tries not to evaluate the problems from a national point of view and to offer the export of one's own national law as the sole solution. The study rather asks whether there is enough common ground justifying further harmonization. Legal harmonization in small steps is feasible if the Member States possess different remedies that are nevertheless comparable. Under these circumstances harmonization is possible by giving the Member States the possibility to choose between two alternatives. Furthermore, cautious steps towards further harmonization can be taken if, for example, all Member States, except for one or two, favour one solution. Legal harmonisation is normally adopted according to the rules in art. 95 EC (art. III-65 TCE). This allows a majority vote. Harmonization is thus also achievable if a specific solution is favoured by a majority of Member States.

[47] For the consequences see below notes 218 et seq. [48] See below C.I.
[49] See below A.III.2 (a).

Legal traditions too diverse
Finally, some areas of the law of unfair competition are too diverse to be harmonized. In this case any further attempts at harmonization are doomed to fail.

2. *The 'Network of Excellence' and the development of a 'Common Frame of Reference' for European contract law*

On a European level, for more than fifteen years efforts have been made to develop proposals for a harmonized European contract law. By now many study groups are working on this subject. The Lando Commission has drafted the Principles of European Contract Law[50] which, similarly to the American Restatements, are not a precise codification but rather an attempt to draft principles of European contract law.[51] Further endeavours are afoot to formulate these principles as a code.[52] These include the Unidroit Principles of International Contract Law[53] which correspond significantly with the results of the Lando Commission, the Common Core Project inspired by Schlesinger,[54] which meets annually in Trento,[55] and the initiatives of the Pavia Academy[56] and the newly created Society for European Law of Obligations.[57] The most comprehensive initiative was started by the

50 O. Lando and H. Beale, *Principles of European Contract Law*, Part 1 (1995), translated in: (1995) 3 ZEuP 864 et seq.; O. Lando and H. Beale, *Principles of European Contract Law*, Part 1 and Part 2 (2000) translated in: (2000) 8 ZEuP 675 et seq. = R. Schulze and R. Zimmermann, *Basistexte zum Europäischen Privatrecht* (2000), III.10; also available under http://www.jura-uni-augsburg.de/moellers.

51 On the task of the Lando Commission see O. Lando, (1983) 31 Am.J.Comp.L 653 et seq.; O. Lando, (1992) 56 RabelsZ 261 et seq.; H. Beale, in G. Weick (ed.), *National and European Law on the Threshold to the Single Market* (1993), p. 177 et seq.; O. Remien, (1988) 87 ZvglRWiss. 105 et seq.; J. Basedow, (1996) 33 CMLRev. 1169 et seq..

52 A.S. Hartkamp and M.W. Hesselink et al., *Towards a European Civil Code* (2nd ed. 1998).

53 Unidroit, International Institute for the Unification of Private Law (ed.), *Principles of International Commercial Contracts* (1994), translated in: (1997) IPRax 205 et seq. = (1997) 5 ZEuP 890 et seq. = R. Schulze and R. Zimmermann, *Basistexte zum Europäischen Privatrecht*, (2000), III.15; see A. S. Hartkamp, (1994) 2 Eur.Rev.Priv.L 341 et seq.; R. Zimmermann, *Konturen eines Europäischen Vertragsrechts*, (1995) 45 JZ 477 et seq.

54 M. Bussani and U. Mattei, (1997) 3 Columbia J.Eur.L. 339 et seq.; see http://www.jus.unitn.it/dsg/common-core.

55 A first volume has been published, others to follow: R. Zimmermann and S. Whittaker (eds.), *Good Faith in European Contract Law* (2000); see also the Common Core-Projekt von Hinteregger, *Environmental Liability and Ecological Damage*.

56 Accademica dei giusprivatisti europei (ed.), *Code européen des contrats* (1999); see G. Gandolfi, Rev. trimistrielle de droit civil (1992) 707 et seq.

57 S. Grundmann/G. Hirsch, *SECOLA: Erste Diskussions- und Informationsplattform für das Recht des Binnenmarkthandels* (2001) 54 NJW 2687; http://www.secola.de.

European Commission in 2003[58] that resulted in the creation of the 'Network of Excellence' to which the Common Core of European Private Law is a party. This work is supported by the 6th EU Framework Programme for Research and Technological Development. The aim is to develop a 'Common Frame of Reference' (CFR) which can be used as a so-called 'optional instrument' for contracting parties who can choose it as applicable law.[59]

This study has numerous points of contact with the project for a European contract law. It is not without reason that in many Member States, e.g. France and Italy, competition law is considered to be a part of consumer protection law and is thus codified together.[60] Actually advertisement is very often the first step in entering a contract, so that precontractual obligations and tort law claims are very often involved. The Study Group on a European Civil Code[61] under its chairman C. von Bar has drafted principles of tort law which also briefly address unfair competition law. But von Bar does not provide any material rules, only proposing that infringements of unfair competition rules can constitute a damage for consumers if European or national law so provides.[62]

Competition law as well as classic contract law intend to protect the free decision making of the consumer.[63] Consequently in European directives the same problems are regulated in directives dealing with consumer protection and in directives dealing with competition law. This is the case with, for example, the regulation of cold-calling.[64]

58 European Commission, *A More Coherent European Contract Law – an Action Plan*, COM (2003) 68 final; European Commission, *European Contract Law and the Revision of the Acquis: the Way Forward*, COM (2004) 651 final; a first progress report has now been published: European Commission, *First Annual Progress Report on European Contract Law and the Acquis Review*, COM (2005) 456 final.

59 European Commission, *A More Coherent European Contract Law – an Action Plan*, COM (2003) 68 final; European Commission, *European Contract Law and the Revision of the Acquis: the Way Forward*, COM (2004) 651 final.

60 See below for France A.II.2(e) and for Italy A.II.2(j).

61 www.sgecc.net.

62 Article 2:208: Loss upon Unlawful Impairment of Business
(1) (...)
(2) Loss caused to a consumer as a result of unfair competition is also legally relevant damage if Community or national law so provides.
For download under: http://www.sgecc.net/media/downloads/text_of_articles_final.doc

63 H. Köhler, in H. Hefermehl, H. Köhler and J. Bornkamm, *Wettbewerbsrecht* (24th ed. 2006), § 1 notes 14 et seq.

64 See Art. 10 Directive 97/EC on the protection of consumers in respect of distance contracts; Art. 10 Directive 2002/65/EC on the distance marketing of consumer financial service and Art. 5 and Annex 1 no. 26 Directive 2005/29/EC on unfair commercial practices.

In European consumer protection provisions and in competition law a typical mechanism of regulation is the duty to provide information. In competition law a claim for deception is given if insufficient information is provided.[65] Another link can be found between competition law and the sales of goods law. The directive on the sale of consumer goods defines the specific characteristics of a good. Here again a claim for deception under competition law can be brought if false information is given.[66]

In both areas of law the legal consequences can be claims for elimination and for injunctive relief. The specific competition law claims can regularly be traced to their general civil law roots. But very often consumer protection law provides for a right of withdrawal without any reason,[67] which is unknown in unfair competition law.[68] Apart from civil law claims many Member States provide for further legal remedies both in classic contract law and in unfair competition law such as mechanisms for out-of-court settlement.[69] In competition law as well, consumer associations are important in enforcing the law. The directive on injunctions has brought a harmonization for many directives on consumer protection.[70] Finally supervision by public authorities is common in both areas of law.[71] All in all from the perspective of the EC and of many Member States unfair competition law is very often part of consumer protection law, and thus of contract law.[72] The German and Austrian approach with its strict separation is rather the exception.

This study has thus many points of contact with the work of the Network of Excellence. But one must be cautious in drawing the

[65] Art. 6 Directive 2005/29/EC on unfair commercial practices; BGHZ 105, 277 et seq. – 'Umweltengel'.

[66] For a discussion of this aspect cf. below Case 5 (Discontinued models).

[67] For a detailed discussion see T. Möllers, *European Directives on Civil Law – Shaping a New German Civil Code* (2003) 18 Tulane European & Civil Law Forum 1 (26 et seq.).

[68] For the reasons why such a right of withdrawal is unnecessary under unfair competition law see H. Köhler, *UWG-Reform und Verbraucherschutz*, (2003) 105 GRUR 265 et seq, who argues that the protection under civil law including consumer law is sufficient. Differing K.-H. Fezer, *Das wettbewerbsrechtliche Vertragsauflösungsrecht in der UWG-Reform – Zur Notwendigkeit eines wettbewerbsrechtlichen Vertragsauflösungsrechts wegen Vorliegens verbraucherschützender Regelungslücken und Durchsetzungsdefiziten bei bestimmten Fallkonstellationen unlauteren Wettbewerbs* (2003) 49 WRP 127 et seq.

[69] See below Case 8 (Watch Imitations II) and C.I.3.

[70] Art. 1 et seq. Directive 98/27/EC on injunctions for the protection of consumers' interests; cf. below Case 4 (Children's swing) and B.II.2.

[71] See e.g. situation in France, below A.I.2(e), Italy, below A.I.2(j) and Spain, below A.I.2(n); comprehensively for the law of unfair competition Case 4 (Children's swing) and the discussion under B.II.4.

[72] See below A.I.3(a) and A.II.3(a).

conclusion that the results can be transferred without modifications because of the specific competion law background. If in the near future the CFR is agreed upon, the next step could be to study the relationship between the results of this study and the CFR.

3. *Structure and clarification of terms*

Before one can compare the remedies in the law of unfair competition one has to clarify the meaning of the terms 'unfair competition' and 'remedies'.

a) Unfair competition law and remedies in other areas of law

Remedies and substantive law

Even the term 'law of unfair competition' seems to have various meanings.[73] As a result, it has a different scope in the various Member States. Countries with a blanket clause and its own substantive provisions normally give the law of unfair competition a broader scope; whereas for the United Kingdom and the USA it is rather restricted. Moreover, in many Member States some typical classes of case are attributed to the law of consumer protection.[74] In addition, the law of unfair competition overlaps with the law of intellectual property and other public law provisions aiming at the protection of specific branches of trade.

The topic of this study is necessarily complex since the remedies very often depend on the substantive provisions in question. Therefore, in half of the case studies a common basis of substantive provision is examined. On the other hand it is not suggested that the common basis in the law of unfair competition is broader than it actually is. In the other case studies the lack of a common basis is not denied but rather highlighted by the individual contributors. These cases are then analysed on the assumption that there is an infringement under the particular national provisions. This approach should make clear that the main emphasis of these case studies is not the substantive provisions but the law concerning the available remedies.

Common features of the substantive law

Common features of the substantive provision are discernible in the law treating comparative advertisement that has been harmonized in Directive 97/55/EC (Case 1 – Risky bread). Deceptive offers of products are dealt with in Directive 84/450/EEC (Case 4 – Children's swing).[75]

[73] For attempts to define the term see A.I above notes 6 et seq.

[74] See below A.II.3(b).

[75] Art. 3 lit. (a): 'features about availability and quantity'.

Moreover, the deception concerning the recency of a product does not only concern the law of unfair competition but also the Sale of Consumer Goods Directive 99/44/EC[76] (Case 5 – Discontinued models). Deceptive advertisements are also considered to be illegal (Case 7 – Recycled paper). The degradation of a competitor is considered inadmissible in all Member States (Case 6 – Child labour) though there has not been any harmonization on a European level so far. But the act of denigration has been introduced in art. 10bis para. 3 of the Paris Convention for the Protection of Industrial Property (PC).[77] Moreover, this case study highlights that both civil and criminal law can be applicable.

Differences

(1) Remedies in intellectual property law

(a) Trademark law was harmonized throughout the whole of the European Union. The main provisions can be found in the Trademark Directive 89/104/EEC[78] and in the Trademark Regulation (EC) 40/94.[79] According to the traditional view, the only function of the trademark is to show which undertaking a product comes from. Therefore, protection was limited to cases in which imitation of trademarks may lead to confusion of consumers as to the source of origin of products. If the products bearing the imitated trademark were so different from those of the trademark owner (as in Case 3 of cars and whisky) that nobody can be misled as to the source of origin of such products, no protection ought to be granted.[80]

After the implementation of the Trademark Directive 89/104/EEC, it was acknowledged that 'famous' trademarks deserve a wider protection

[76] Art. 2 para. 2 lit. (d). See now also art. 7 para. 1 lit. (a) and annex 1 no. 5 of the directive 2005/29/EC concerning unfair commercial practices.

[77] See below A.II.1(a).

[78] First Council Directive 89/104/EEC of December 21, 1988 to approximate the laws of the member states relating to trade marks, OJ L 40, art. 5 para. 1 Trademark Directive 89/104/EEC: The registered trademark shall confer on the proprietor exclusive rights therein. The proprietor shall be entitled to prevent all third parties not having his consent from using in the course of trade:
a) any sign which is identical with the trademark in relation to goods or services which are identical with those for which the trademark is registered;
b) any sign where, because of its identity with, or similarity to, the trademark and the identity or similarity of the goods or services covered by the trademark and the sign, there exists a likelihood of confusion on the part of the public, which includes the likelihood of association between the sign and the trademark.

[79] Council Regulation (EC) No. 240/94 of December 20, 1993 on the Community trademark, OJ L 11, 1.

[80] See e.g. Cass., October 21, 1988, note 5716, in Giur. ann. dir. ind., 1988, 109.

against attempts by third parties to benefit from their power to attract customers;[81] nevertheless, there are still doubts as to when a trademark may be considered 'famous' (not always clarified by the hesitant case law from the ECJ), and as to when the use of a famous trademark by a third party may constitute an infringement, particularly when, as in the case in question, the famous trademark is used with reference to genuine products by a third party which tries to benefit from its good reputation. The case law of the ECJ is not conclusive concerning the question as to when remedies under trademark law should be granted.[82] This leads to the paradoxical situation that trademark law has been harmonized, while it remains unclear when remedies may be awarded: consequently, the question of the use of somebody else's goodwill (Case 2 and 3) is resolved differently.[83]

(b) In the United Kingdom these cases are governed by the Trade Marks Act 1994. In Austria, trade mark law is also applied. Though A is not using somebody else's trademark for his own product, this is no longer relevant if §§10, 10a MSchG are interpreted in a way conforming with the directive. That is because the exclusive right of the trademark owner also allows him to forbid *any* business use of his trademark, including non-trademark specific usages, according to art. 5 para. 1 Trade mark Directive 89/104/EEC.[84] Contrary to this, in most states (Germany, Sweden and Italy) the use of somebody else's goodwill, for example, the reputation of a famous brand of cars is not covered by trademark law but by the law of unfair competition since the trademark is not used as a trademark. Sweden and Denmark apply the law governing comparative advertisement. In Germany the case of fake watches, as in Case 2, would be governed by §§3, 4 no. 9b UWG and would be illegal,[85] whereas in the Whisky case (Case 3) there are different opinions as to whether only

[81] For Germany cf. A. Beater, *Wettbewerbsrecht* (2002), § 22 notes 87 et seq., for Italy see art. 1, para. 1, lit. (c) of the Italian Trademark Act. Comments emphasizing the change with reference to the function of trademarks in A. Vanzetti, *La funzione del marchio in un regime di libera cessione*, Riv. dir. ind., (1998) I, 71 et seq.; A. Vanzetti, *I marchi nel mercato globale*, Riv. dir. ind., (2002) I, 92; C. Galli, *Funzione del marchio e ampiezza della tutela* (1996), p. 109.

[82] A. Beater, *Wettbewerbsrecht* (2002), § 22 notes 90 et seq. But cf. ECJ C-408/01, (2003) ECR I-389, (2003) 105 GRUR 240 – 'Davidoff v. Gofkid'.

[83] The violation of trademark law was partly answered affirmatively, partly denied, and in part legal protection was offered by unfair competition law.

[84] R. Schanda, *Markenschutzgesetz in der Fassung der Markenrechtsnovelle* (1999), p. 61.

[85] T. Sambuc, in H. Harte-Bavenkamm and F. Henning-Bodewig, *UWG* (2004), § 4 no. 9 notes 130 et seq.; H. Köhler in: W. Hefermehl, H. Köhler and J. Bornkamm, *Wettbewerbsrecht* (24th edn 2006), § 4 notes 9.55, 9.59.

trademark law would be applicable.[86] In Italy, neither trademark law nor the law of unfair competition would be applicable since the manufacturer of whisky and the car producer are not competitors. In Portugal no remedies at all are available: only if we considered the act of competition such as those which can cause economic damage to another or if we admit that this kind of advertising implies economic parasitism, can we establish in this case a competition relationship. No remedies are available in Case 3 in Finland, since product imitation is permissible as long as there is no risk of confusing the consumer.

(2) Remedies in specialized acts

Some Member States apply more stringent provision than others in some areas of the law of unfair competition. Since the Misleading Advertisement Directive 84/450/EEC only sets a minimum standard, this is permissible.[87]

(a) Protection from harmful products

Commercial advertisements, as in Case 2 (in print, radio or television) promoting the consumption of spirits (e.g. whisky), are prohibited in Sweden,[88] Finland and France.[89] Recently, a case was pending before the Market Court, in which the Consumer Ombudsman brought charges against a Swedish magazine claiming advertisements promoting quality wines were infringing this prohibition. The magazine *Gourmet* claimed that the Swedish prohibition was in breach of EC rules on free movement of services (art. 28 EC, art. III-42 TCE) and thus void. So, under Swedish law, advertisement, with or without connection to a particular car brand, would be clearly prohibited. The ECJ decided that the total ban on advertisements for alcohol infringes the free movement of goods and of services but that this infringement is justified on grounds of protecting health.[90] Whether such a prohibition is disproportionate because less stringent means are available is something that has to be decided by the national courts. The national courts are better able to examine whether according to the actual facts a more lenient means is available.[91]

[86] See Cases 2 (Watch imitations I) and 3 (Whisky). [87] See below A.III.2.

[88] Act on alcohol 1994:1738, see below A.III.3.

[89] Evin Act of January 10, 1991. For details cf. G. Raymond, in Juris-Classeur, *Concurrence, Consummation* (1998), Fasc. 900, *Publicité commerciale et protection des consommateurs*, notes 81 et seq.; for the prohibition to advertise for tobacco and its products, cf. note 121.

[90] ECJ C-405/98, (2001) ECR I-1795 note 21, (2001) 49 GRUR Int. 553 – 'Gourmet'.

[91] ECJ C-405/98, (2001) ECR I-1795 note 33, (2001) 49 GRUR Int. 553 – 'Gourmet'.

(b) Protection of specific branches

The baguette is part of French cuisine and thus part of French culture. Apart from the prohibition of illegal comparative advertising, Case 1 has another especially French dimension, because the use of the title of 'baker' and the use of the 'baker's sign' have been regulated,[92] providing that these titles or signs or a name likely to cause confusion, at a place of sale of the bread to the consumer or in advertising, may not be used by businesses who do not themselves knead dough from selected raw materials, leave it to rise, shape it, and bake the bread at the place of sale to the end user. In the United Kingdom, the problem of selling old models of a car as in Case 5 would probably not arise since cars get their number plates once they leave the factory and the first letter(s) of the registration number pinpoints the year of registration.

b) Remedies in unfair competition law – claims, parties, competent authorities for sanctions

Enforcement deals mainly with legal proceedings. Structurally speaking one has to distinguish between claims, parties and legal proceedings. The examination becomes more complicated since these three topics are very often interdependent. For example, disclosure of information or the imposition of fines is normally only found in pubic law, but not in criminal or civil law. In the case studies this can result in overlaps or in gaps since each contributor answers the questions on the basis of his own national legal order. Nevertheless, the structure of claims, parties and competent authorities for sanctions should be taken as the underlying basis of this examination.

Objective of claims

The Misleading and Comparative Advertising Directive 84/450/EEC deals with prohibitions, discontinuations and injunctions. This includes preliminary rulings and pre-emptive court decisions. In this context the main focus will be on the question as to whether legal harmonization has been actually achieved. Apart from prohibition, publication and elimination are also of great interest. The Misleading and Comparative Advertising Directive 84/450/EEC did not prescribe the publication of decisions; it only allowed the Member State to include this duty in its acts. Elimination is not regulated at all in the above-mentioned directive. There are no guidelines for the calculation of

[92] By the Act of May 25, 1998, inserted as art. L 121-80 to L 121-82 CCons.

damages.[93] If infringements are to become unattractive,[94] further harmonization ought to be considered. But very often a claim for damages fails because the plaintiff is unable to prove his loss and causality. To avoid this problem some Member States and the USA offer interesting solutions. The details of collecting unlawful gains, abstract calculation of damages, and estimation of damages, treble damages or punitive damages will be considered later on.[95]

The parties – plaintiffs, defendants and competent authorities

In the past it was normally the competitor (or a competent authority) who took actions against the infringement of unfair competition law. But it is general knowledge by now that the law of unfair competition not only protects the competitor but also protects competition in general, as well as consumers. The leads to the question as to whether the consumer ought to be able to sue.[96] The Injunction Directive 98/27/EC has harmonized the claim for an injunction brought by consumer associations. But here the question also remains as to how the right to sue is used by consumer associations in practice. In England court actions initiated by consumer associations are very rare. In Germany consumer associations have the right to claim the collection of unlawful gains on behalf of the state. A class action is also a feasible possibility. In the northern countries, in the United Kingdom and the USA, supervision lies in the hands of public authorities like the Consumer Ombudsman, the Office of Fair Trading or the Federal Trade Commission. If one institutes public authorities one will have to weigh up public and civil law against each other. The advantages and disadvantages will have to be examined later on. In the past (this is true for Germany as well), it was normally considered to be a choice between either public or civil law. Instead of this approach we will examine whether public and civil law are able to operate smoothly alongside each other. This leads to different types of legal proceedings such as those already customary in Italy, Spain, Portugal and the USA.[97]

In considering defendants we will have to examine who, besides the competitor, can be held responsible for advertisements. This could include the marketing agency and the publishing house that publishes an advertisement.

[93] For European law, see below A.III. [94] See A.I above note 13. [95] See below B.I.6.
[96] See below B.II.6. [97] See below B.II.8.

Out-of-court settlement of disputes

Besides the classical legal proceedings one also has to consider out-of-court settlements of disputes. In this respect some states like the United Kingdom and Italy are very successful. This includes not only the out-of-court settlement by third parties but also settlements within self-regulating organizations. Here too, the northern states offer interesting solutions. Apart from this, a reprimand directly between the parties involved is another means of solving disputes. Germany correctly offers the competitor a claim to recover the costs for a reprimand. Nevertheless, this has been the exception so far.

c) Concept of Part I of this book

After dealing with the methodological foundations (Part I), Part A.II will provide an overview of the state of the legal regulation in the different Member States. The study covers fifteen Member States including all the large and medium-sized ones. Besides thirteen old Member States it was possible for the first time to include the law of two new Member States (Poland and Hungary). Thus all important legal systems are included. Since the remedies in the law of unfair competition could not be more differently regulated, the European legislature reacted with different directives and recommendations. This development will be described as well as the latest proposals on the European level (Part III). The USA is one of the biggest market economies in the world; many results that the EU still wants to achieve have already been realized in the US. Moreover, in recent years many directives have been directly influenced by US-American law.[98] It was therefore only natural to include an overview[99] of the US-American law and again to take it into consideration when analysing the case studies in part three. Some part of the analysis also covers Belgium.

The eight case studies of Part B deal with the different claims, the plaintiffs, the competent authorities to impose sanctions and the out-of-court settlement of disputes. Each case study will provide an answer according to the law of fifteen Member States.[100]

[98] W. Wiegand, *The Reception of American Law in Europe*, (1991) 39 Am.J.Comp.L. 229; R. Stürner, in F.S. Rebmann, *Die Rezeption U.S.-amerikanischen Rechts in der Bundesrepublik Deutschland* (1989), p. 839; U. Mattei, *An Opportunity Not to be Missed. The Future of Comparative Law*, (1998) 46 Am.J.Comp.L. 709.

[99] See A.IV. [100] For this methodical approach see A.I above note 41.

In contrast to other studies[101] in this series, the results are included in Part C. This is due to the complex interdependence between substantive law and remedies and the different legal proceedings and claims. Therefore, the results are combined with the conclusions to be able to give a better and more coherent description. Again, we distinguish between claims, parties, competent authorities and the out-of-court settlement of disputes. For each point we try to answer, first, to what degree harmonized European law exists, second, where a cautious further harmonization is possible and, third, in which areas a further harmonization is not possible because of legal cultures that are too disparate. Theses and proposals for regulation[102] are offered for all problems.

d) Legal orders and legal groups (*Rechtskreise*)

We had to decide in which order to present the contributions from the member states: either in alphabetical order or, ideally, ordered systematically. The scholarly discussion of comparative law propagates the theory of legal groups; it aims at structuring the similarities and differences of different states. Classically, one distinguishes the Anglo-American, the German, the French and the Nordic legal groups.[103] The constitution of a legal group is a common historical development, a defined way of legal reasoning, shared solutions to legal problems and common sources of law. This seems to speak against an alphabetical order since it would result in separating countries belonging to one legal group (e.g. Denmark and Sweden or Ireland and England).

But in the field of unfair competition law most Member States cannot be clearly allocated to one of the legal groups; they are rather 'hybrid' in nature. In order not to yield to common prejudices about how the Member States should be legally grouped they will be presented in alphabetical order. At the end an attempt will be made to allocate the different states to certain groups.

[101] R. Zimmermann and S. Whittaker (eds.), *Good Faith in European Contract Law* (2000); J. Gordley (ed.), *The Enforceability of Promises in European Contract Law* (2001); M. Bussani and V. Palmer (eds.), *Pure Economic Loss in Europe* (2003); E. M. Kieninger (ed.), *Security Rights in Movable Property in European Private Law* (2004).

[102] See at the end of C.I.–II.

[103] K. Zweigert and H. Kötz, *Einführung in die Rechtsvergleichung* (3rd edn 1996), p. 68 – translated as: K. Zweigert and H. Kötz, *Introduction to Comparative Law* (3rd edn 1998, translation by T. Weir); cf. also P. Arminjon, B. Nolde and M. Wolff, *Traité de droit comparé I* (1950); R. David, *Les grands systemes de droit contemporains* (10th edn 1992), p. 16, (ed. by C. Jauffret-Spinosi) translated as R. David and G. Grasmann, *Einführung in die großen Rechtssysteme der Gegenwart* (2nd edn 1988).

e) Language in Europe – a legal lingua franca

Fortunately, jurists seem to agree on English as a common language on the international level.[104] Only in this way will permanent understanding in Europe be achievable.[105] The working language of the Common Core Project is English. All other works of this series have also been written in English with the exception of the activities of the Max-Planck Institute in Munich (G. Schricker and F. Henning-Bodewig).[106]

But this is as far as the similarities hold. Apart from the primary and secondary law of the EU and the decisions of the ECJ there are no common substantive provisions. Common standards are missing: the way of legal reasoning and the handling of citations differ throughout Europe.[107] A major problem is the lack of common understanding of certain terms. In the USA and the United Kingdom the scope of unfair competition law is much more restricted than in Germany and Austria. In many states certain aspects of unfair competition are part of the law of consumer protection.

Taking the reprimand as an example it can be shown that the understanding of a term in the different Member States is closely related to the underlying national law. Thus a reprimand in most Member States only fulfils a minor role in unfair competition law. In some it eases the proof that the infringer acted intentionally if he continues his behaviour after being reprimanded (Denmark, Finland, France and Sweden). In Spain it is under certain circumstances a prerequisite for being able to sue. And in Germany finally the notion of a reprimand is closely connected to certain specified legal consequences as, for example, a claim to recover the costs for the reprimand or certain procedural modifications.[108]

104 Against English as the European legal language see A. Flessner, *Rechtsvereinheitlichung durch Rechtswissenschaft und Juristenausbildung* (1992) 56 RabelsZ 243 (257); A. Flessner, *Juristische Methode und europäisches Privatrecht* (2002) 57 JZ 14 (22); O. Remien, *Illusion und Realität eines europäischen Privatrechts* (1992) 47 JZ 277 (282), which do not consider the cultural embedding of the second language.

105 I. Pernice, *Recht in einem mehrsprachigen Raum* (1998) 6 ZEuP 1; D. Martiny, *Babylon in Brüssel?* (1998) 6 ZEuP 227; T. Möllers, *Die Rolle des Rechts im Rahmen der europäischen Integration* (1999), translated as *Role of Law in European Integration* (2003), § 4.II; recently again C. Luttermann and K. Luttermann, *Ein Sprachenrecht für Europa* (2004) 59 JZ 1002.

106 See A.I above notes 41 et seq.

107 H. Kötz, *Die Zitierpraxis der Gerichte, Eine vergleichende Skizze* (1988) 53 RabelsZ 644 et seq.

108 See for the details Case 8 (Watch imitations II).

One has to note that even if the same language is spoken, the understanding of the terms used is dependent on the cultural background of the speaker. The development of a legal lingua franca is thus not finished by deciding which language to use. The next step will be a discussion as to what the specific terms actually mean. For the law of unfair competition this study aims to contribute to that discussion.

II. The legal background in the different Member States in unfair competition law

1. *Back to the roots – international law*

a) Paris Convention for the Protection of Industrial Property

Already more than 100 years ago the law of unfair competition was dealt with in one of the great international treaties for the protection of intellectual property: the Paris Convention for the Protection of Industrial Property of 1883 (PC).[1] In the PC, which has been adopted by more than 160 states so far (among them all Member States of the EU) each signaturary nation binds itself to assure the members of other parties of the treaty 'effective protection against unfair competition'.[2] In art. 10bis para. 2 of the PC unfair competition is described as 'any act of competition contrary to honest practices in industrial or commercial matters'. The same article prohibits three specific types of unfair competition: all acts of such a nature as to create confusion with the company, goods or activities of a competitor; false allegations that discredit the competitor; and indications or allegations that are liable to mislead the public as to the nature or qualities of the goods. But this is not further elaborated in the treaty. The remedies stay vague as well since art. 10ter PC only binds the states to implement 'appropriate legal remedies to effectively repress' all acts of unfair competition. The PC had enormous influence on the blanket clauses of some countries such as Belgium, Luxembourg, Portugal, Finland, Italy or Spain. Since the Convention only forces the parties to the treaty to offer foreigners the same protection as their own nationals[3] and since the description of the acts of unfair competition was not further elaborated the hoped for effect of harmonization was not achieved.[4]

b) Trade-Related Aspects of Intellectual Rights (TRIPS)

Alongside the foundation of the World Trade Organization the Agreement on Trade-Related Aspects of Intellectual Property Rights

[1] For further information cf. www.wipo.int/treaties/en/index.html.

[2] See art. 10bis of the current Version of the Paris Convention for the Protection of Industrial Property, above A.II.1(a).

[3] F. Hennig-Bodewig, (2002) 104 GRUR 389 (390).

[4] F. Hennig-Bodewig, in G. Schricker, T. Dreier and A. Kur (eds.), *Geistiges Eigentum und Inovation* (2001), p. 125 (133); H. Köhler and T. Lettl (2002) 48 WRP 1019 (1020).

(TRIPS)[5] was adopted. Though TRIPS refers several times to the PC, its main focus is not the law of unfair competition. Only the protection of geographical indications[6] and the protection of undisclosed information[7] could be allotted to the law of unfair competition.[8] Consequently, the common basis in international law is rather narrow in the field of unfair competition.

2. *The law of the member states*[9]

a) Austria

In Austria, protection against acts of unfair competition has been traditionally very strong. Austrian law of unfair competition is heavily influenced by German law.[10] The Federal Act against Unfair Competition (*Bundesgesetz gegen den unlauteren Wettbewerb* – UWG) dates back to 1923 and was again promulgated in 1984.[11] It compromises forty-four paragraphs. The UWG contains provisions of a civil, criminal or public law nature. Like German law, the Austrian UWG contains, as well as the big blanket clause in § 1 UWG, provisions dealing with certain infringements of competition.[12] In Austria it is accepted that the UWG not only protects the competitor but also the consumer.[13]

Apart from the UWG other acts are also relevant, such as the Consumer Protection Code. For certain professions, for example physicians or lawyers, independent rules of professional conduct have evolved. Legal proceedings can be initiated by competitors and by associations via the civil law courts. Consumers are generally not allowed to sue. But contrary to German law, the provisions of the UWG are construed to contain implied remedies that can be invoked by consumers.[14]

[5] See the website of the World Trade Organisation on www.worldtradelaw.net.

[6] Art. 22 et seq. TRIPS. [7] Art. 39 TRIPS.

[8] F. Hennig-Bodewig (2002) 104 GRUR, 389 (390); G. Reger, *Der internationale Schutz gegen unlauteren Wettbewerb und das TRIPS-Abkommen* (1999); The question whether the legal consequences of TRIPS may be called on for further legal harmonization will be answered below.

[9] The surveys about the law of the Member States mostly came from the referees. They were clearly revised and enlarged by the responsible editor.

[10] S. Kofler, in: J. Maxeiner and P. Schotthöfer, *Österreich*, p. 3; W. Loacker, *Österreich*, in *Heidelberger Kommentar zum Wettbewerbsrecht* (2000), IV.11 note 3.

[11] BGBl I 185. [12] § 2 UWG e.g. prohibits misleading advertisement.

[13] H. Gamerith (2003) 49 WRP 143 (144); H. Gamerith (2005) 51 WRP 391 (392 et seq.).

[14] See Case 4 (Children's swing).

b) Denmark

The *Lov om markedsføring* – MFL (Marketing Practices Act) – was introduced in 1973,[15] amended in 1994[16] and the previous rules on illegal competition were included in the law. The Act was last amended in 2003.[17] Within the framework of the MFL consumer interests, trade interests and more general public interests are protected. The MFL has a general clause and a clause against misleading advertisement, §1 and §2.[18] For the interpretation of the blanket clause the principles of the International Chamber of Commerce (ICC)[19] are used and for the consumer protection law the guidelines of the Consumer Ombudsman are applied.[20]

Alongside specialized laws, others exist such as the *Bekendtgørelse af Lov om mærkning of skiltning med pris* (Price Marketing and Display Act)[21] or the Doorstep Sales Act. Banks are excluded from the scope of the MFL. They are governed by their own rules.

The protection of consumers' interests is according to §15 MFL safeguarded through a Consumer Ombudsman.[22] The Consumer Ombudsman protects the interests of consumers, but he is also empowered to intervene in conflicts involving so-called 'B2B' (business-to-business) transactions.[23] According to §17 sec. 1 MFL the Consumer Ombudsman is empowered to make out and publish marketing *guidelines* in order to influence the conduct of persons carrying on a trade and business within specified areas considered important, especially to the interests of the consumers. According to §17 sec. 1 MFL the guidelines are made upon negotiations with the relevant trade and consumer organisations.

According to §14 MFL legal proceedings in civil and public affairs on contravention of the MFL shall be brought before the *Sø-og Handelsretten* (Maritime and Commercial Court) in Copenhagen, which is an ordinary court specializing in trade and commercial cases. The consumer is allowed to sue.

[15] No. 297 of June 14, 1974. [16] No. 428 of June 1, 1994.

[17] See the website of the ombudsman www.forbrugerstyrelsen.dk and www.fs.dk/uk/acts/ukmfl.htm.

[18] J. Keßler and A. Bruun-Nielsen, *Denmark*, in J. Keßler and H.-W. Micklitz, p. 43 (44).

[19] See www.icc.wbo.org.

[20] J. Keßler and A. Bruun-Nielsen, *Denmark*, in J. Keßler and H.-W. Micklitz, p. 43 (46); M. Eckardt-Hansen, *Denmark*, in J. Maxeiner and P. Schotthöfer, p. 97.

[21] No. 209 of March 28, 2000, see www.fr.dk/uk/acts/ukpml.htm.

[22] M. Koktvedgaard, *Lærebog i Konkurrenceret* (4th edn 2000), pp. 53 et seq.; P. B. Madsen, *Markedsret*, del 2 (4th edn 2002), pp. 330 et seq.

[23] P. Møgelvang-Hansen and K. Østergaard, *Denmark*, in R. Schulze and H. Schulte-Nölke, p. 3, names cases of discrimination.

c) England[24]

In England, neither a general codification of the law of unfair competition exists nor has a blanket clause been developed by the courts.[25] Consequently, in English law there is no general principle to abstain from engaging in unfair competition or to act fairly. The scope of common law, for example, contractual remedies (e.g. deception or illegitimate pressure to lure a party into a contract) or tort remedies (e.g. malicious falsehood or passing off), is rather restricted since the intentional behaviour very often cannot be proven.[26] Still, the law of intellectual property rights is partly available to award a remedy.

Apart from the rules of common law, acts have been passed that regulate some narrow questions of unfair competition.[27] They are very

[24] The findings of the UK report are not applicable in all respects throughout the UK. They deal only with English law (being the law applicable in England and Wales). Scotland and Northern Ireland each have their own separate laws and legal systems, including their own private laws, their own courts systems and their own rules on civil procedure (although the Judicial Committee of the House of Lords is the highest appellate court for all the legal systems).

The key UK competition law statutes, the Competition Act 1998 and the Enterprise Act 2002 are applicable throughout the UK, and the Office of Fair Trading has enforcement jurisdiction throughout the UK. Competition law-based private law actions are brought and defences are raised, on the other hand, under the private law of England and Wales, Scotland or Northern Ireland as the case may be.

The higher courts in each legal system have stressed that judicial interpretation of statutes which apply across the whole of the UK should be uniform in each legal system (see, for example, *Jamieson v. Jamieson* [1952] AC 525 (HL)). Private law rights and remedies and the court procedures for dealing with them will, on the other hand, vary. However, where there is no local case law on a point, the courts in Scotland and Northern Ireland would normally regard a judgment of an English court on a similar point (particularly a judgment of a higher court in England and Wales) as very strongly persuasive, and, if it is a judgment of the House of Lords on broad issues of principle in an English case (such as the House of Lords judgment in *Crehan v. Inntrepreneur Pub Company* [2006] UKHL 38), as in practice binding upon them (see *Re Tuck's Settlement Trust*, [1978] Ch. 49, 61). Equally, English courts, where there is no decided English case-law on a point, would generally regard judgments of the Scottish and Northern Irish courts on a similar point (particularly unanimous judgments of the higher courts there), whilst not creating judicial precedent technically binding upon them, as providing very strong persuasive authority which they normally ought to follow. In a case on private enforcement of competition law, one would accordingly expect the overall outcome to be very similar whether the case was brought under English, Scots or Northern Irish law, although the routes for getting to the outcome would be likely to be somewhat different.

[25] For an overview of the consumer protection law see the report of the Department of Trade and Industry (DTI) on www.dti.gov.uk/ccp/topics1/pdf1/benchuk.pdf.

[26] Illustrated by S. Weatherill, *United Kingdom*, in R. Schulze and H. Schulte-Nölke, I.2(b).

[27] Acts and Regulations can be found on the website of Her Majesty's Stationary Office (HMSO), www.hmso.gov.uk.

often narrower in their application than their title indicates.[28] Examples of these acts are the Trade Descriptions Act 1986 (TDA), the Fair Trading Act 1973 (FTA), the Unfair Contract Terms Act 1977 (UCTA), the Consumer Protection Act 1987 (CPA), the Control of Misleading Advertisements Regulations 1988 (CMAR),[29] the Competition Act 1998 and most recently the Stop Now Orders (EC Directives) Regulations 2001 and the Enterprise Act 2002 (EA).[30] Some of these have been adopted in order to implement EC Directives;[31] sometimes the scope of application overlaps.

In particular in the field of consumer protection, the Office of Fair Trading (OFT),[32] a public corporate body, is the predominant enforcer of the law of unfair trading. Specialized enforcers deal with specific fields of trade. Part II of the FTA 1973 empowered the Director General to issue orders dealing with particular consumer trade practices. Since these provisions did not have much practical relevance in the past they have been supplemented in 2003 by Part 8 of the EA.[33] The Director General was abolished and its functions are now exercised by the OFT. The local weights and measures authorities can, for example, enforce the TDA 1968.

Consequently, the available remedies largely depend on which particular piece of substantive law applies. Whilst tort law is, of course, actionable by private parties, some of the statutory provisions are not. For this reason, the analysis of remedies in unfair competition law is closely linked to the substantive law of which the trader might be in breach. Each of the various pieces of substantive law has its own particular remedies system in place.

But in general it can be stated that in unfair competition law the decisions of the courts are of minor importance. With the introduction of sec. 124 FTA the role of self-regulation has become the main focus of interest. In the past the Director General of Fair Trading supported associations issuing Codes of Practices. Self-regulation plays an important role in advertising law. More than 40 Codes of self-regulation have been passed by these associations. The Committee of Advertising Practice (CAP) is a self-regulatory body that creates, revises and enforces

28 See the wording of S. Weatherill, *United Kingdom*, in R. Schulze and H. Schulte-Nölke, I.2(b).

29 SI 1988 No. 15 implemented Directive 84/450/EEC; in addition there is the Control of Misleading Advertisments (Amendment) Regulations 2000 (SI 2000/914).

30 SI 2001 No. 1422, implemented Directive 98/27/EC.

31 In particular the CMAR and the Stop Now Orders (EC Directives) Regulations 2001.

32 www.oft.gov.uk/default.htm.

33 S. Weatherill, *United Kingdom*, in R. Schulze and H. Schulte-Nölke, I.1(a).

the British Codes of Advertising and Sales Promotion. These are in parts more stringent than the requirements of the corresponding acts.[34] The Advertising Standards Authority (ASA) is the independent body that endorses and administers the Codes, ensuring that the self-regulatory system works in the public interest. ASA is a purely self-regulatory organisation, not a public authority. This means that it does not enforce any acts but only its own code of practice. Up to its 10th edition the British Codes of Advertising and Sales Promotion comprised the Advertising Code, the Sales Promotion Code and the Cigarette Code. Since March 4, 2003 this tripartition was abandoned and since the 11th edition there is only one British Code of Advertising, Sales Promotion and Directing Marketing.[35]

d) Finland

The Finnish legal system is a Nordic one and in certain respects different from those of Central Europe. It is described as efficient but complex.[36] Unfair trade practices are divided into two categories: cases between businesses and consumer interest cases. *Laki sopimattomasta menettelystä elinkeinotoiminnassa* 1978/1061 of December 22, 1978 – SopMenL 1978/1061[37] (Unfair Trade Practices Act) – covers disruptive competition between businesses while *Kuluttajansuojalaki* 1978/38 of January 20, 1978 – KSL (Consumer Protection Act)[38] – covers those cases where consumer interests are involved. In both fields the subject matter can be the same – unfair methods of trading. It is not uncommon that even a tradesman would point out consumer interest while trying to prove that, for example, an advertisement is misleading. Both acts have a general clause[39] and clauses against misleading advertisement. For the interpretation of the act the principles of the ICC International Code on Advertising Practice and the practice of the Business Practice Board of the Central Finnish Chamber are applied.[40] In practice, the directives of the Consumer Ombudsman are very important.[41]

[34] M. Jergolla (2003) 49 WRP 431 (432).
[35] www.cap.org.uk; M. Jergolla (2003) 49 WRP 606 (607).
[36] K. Fahlund and H. Salmi, *Finland*, in J. Maxeiner and P. Schotthöfer, pp. 127 et seq.
[37] *Laki sopimattomasta menettelystä elinkeiotoiminnassa* 1978/106; changed by law no. 461 of June 5, 2002; cf. www.finlex.fi.
[38] Kulutajansuojalaki 1978/38; changed by law no. 741 of August 15, 2003.
[39] Chap. 2 sec. 1 Consumer Protection Act and sec. 1 Unfair Trade Practices Act.
[40] T. Majuri, *Finland*, in R. Schulze and H. Schulte-Nölke, I.1.a).
[41] F. Henning-Bodewig, in H. Harte-Bavendamm and F. Henning-Bodewig, *UWG* (2004), Einl E note 95.

There are additional acts dealing with acts of unfair competition, for example the *Alkoholilaki 1994/1143* (Alcohol Beverage Act) or the *Laki toimenpiteistä tupakoinnin vähentämiseksi 1977/225* (Tobacco Act).[42] In the field of unfair trade practices, a very strong position is granted to the Consumer Agency and the Consumer Ombudsman (Ombudsman).[43] The Consumer Agency is the official organization that safeguards the rights of consumers. The Consumer Ombudsman surveys market behaviour.[44] He has the right to be heard in unfair trade practices cases in the Market Court as well as the right to make claims himself. Consumer associations are mainly active in the field of information only.

e) France

French competition law (*droit de la concurrence*) is composed of unfair competition law (*concurrence déloyale*), prohibited competition practices (*concurrence interdite ou illégale*) and antitrust law (*droit de la concurrence*). Unfair competition law as concurrence déloyale is common law developed around the basic civil law tort in the articles 1382 and 1383 *Code civil* – cc (French Civil Code). Thus, according to French law only the following acts are considered to be unfair competition: imitation (*l'imitation*), denigration (*dénigrement*), competition aimed at obstructing other competitors (*désorganisation*) and the exploitation of somebody else's efforts (*parasitisme*). But apart from these acts of unfair competition in a stricter sense behaviours presenting a specific danger for the consumer but still having a relation namely with advertising practices are regulated by newer national legislation that in some cases has either been created or modified under European influences. All these cases fall under the prohibited competition practices (*concurrence interdite ou illégale*).[45] The main examples are the provisions of the *Code de la consommation* – CCons (Consumer Code).[46] It is dealing with prohibited advertising practices such as comparative and misleading advertising. Thus art. L 121.1 CCons forbids as a so-called small general clause misleading advertising.[47] But it also deals with lotteries for

[42] T. Majuri, *Finland*, in R. Schulze and H. Schulte-Nölke, I.1(a).

[43] See www.kuluttaja-asiamies.fi and www.kuluttaja.kuluttajavirasto.fi.

[44] Chap. 2 §10 para. 1 s. 1 KSL; K. Kaulamo, *Finland*, in G. Schricker, note 310 (318).

[45] This differentiation is very common: J. Passa, in Juris-Classeur, *Concurrence, consommation* (1998), Fasc. 240, 'Domaine de l'action en concurrence déloyale', note 81.

[46] Code de la Consomation, Law 93–949 of July 26, 1993; cf. www.legifrance.gouv.fr.

[47] Art. L 121.1. CCons. forbids: '... any advertising which in any form contains assertions, information or representations which are false or apt to give rise to errors if they

advertisement purposes regulated by art. L 121-36 CCons. In addition to the Consumer Code the *Code du commerce* (Commercial Code) includes some provisions in relation to unfair competition such as the legislation on final sales. Other possibilities of price reduction, for example in case of liquidation, are regulated by art. L 310-3 of the Commercial Code. The *Code du commerce* in its articles L 442-1 and following also prohibits a certain number of competitive restrictive practices such as sales or services with bonuses and refusals of sales and services fixed by art. L 121-35 and L 122-1 of the consumer code. These apply also to traders.[48] Art. 442-1 of the Commercial Code prohibits the resale with loss (*revente à perte*). Other prohibited competitive practices can be merely contractual, such as competition clauses or other legal non-competition obligations.[49]

Concerning the enforcement of unfair competition law in a stricter sense as quoted above, the *Nouveau code de procédure civile* – NCPC (New code of civil procedure) – applies containing general provisions on summary and common judicial procedures.

Concerning the *concurrence interdite* (for a great part French advertising law) a peculiarity lies in its criminal character, which figures prominently both in legislation and legal practice. Actually, nearly all legal prohibitions of advertising in the Consumer Code are stated in criminal law terms and are regularly brought before the criminal courts, even when competitors institute prosecutions. As French law permits private parties to assert civil claims in criminal prosecutions (*action civile*), private parties frequently do so in order to avoid the burden of investigation and trial.[50]

In addition, compliance with the articles of the Consumer Code and in some cases of the Commercial Code is supervised by the *Direction Générale de la Concurrence, de la Consommation et de la Répression de Fraudes – DGCCRF*[51] (General Office for Competition, Consumer Protection and Fraud Prevention) – and by the food directorate general of the Ministry

concern one or more of the following elements: the existence, the nature, the composition, essential properties, content or mode of operation, kind, origin, quality, mode and time of production, advantages, price and conditions of sale of the goods and services to which the advertising refers, conditions of use, advantages to expected from the use, reasons for and methods of the sale or the services, content of the obligations assumed by the advertiser; identity, characteristics and skills of the producer, the advertiser or the performer of the services.'

48 Thus in French Law there still remains legislation as there has been with the German regulation dealing with give-aways.

49 M. Malaurie-Vignal, *Droit de la concurrence* (2nd edn 2003), pp. 73 et seq.

50 F.O. Ranke, in J. Maxeiner and P. Schotthöfer, p. 153 (154).

51 www.finances.gouv.fr/DGCCRF.

of Agriculture and by the metrology department of the Ministry of Industry.[52]

It might be explained historically (as some writers do), on the basis that although the price control legislation adopted in 1945 to combat rampant inflation was abolished in 1986 its spirit gave to French competition law its fundamental orientation;[53] and that this traditional 'paternalism' leads to continued control by government authorities which now supervise the observance of advertising regulations instead of the former price control.[54] Another explanation might be seen in the French concept of separating unfair competition law amongst competitors only left to pure civil law, on the one hand, from consumer protection under special governmental protection, on the other hand, regulated in more obliging terms. However infringements of art. 1382 cc have necessarily to be prosecuted in civil courts by the competitor (*action en concurrence déloyale*) as they are based on general civil tort law.

f) Germany

Germany traditionally offers strong protection against acts of unfair competition. The relevant legal text in Germany concerning unfair competition law is the *Gesetz gegen den unlauteren Wettbewerb – UWG* (Law against Unfair Competition) from 1896. A general clause was implemented in 1909.[55] Originally, the UWG only aimed at the protection of market participants against acts of unfair competition by their competitors.[56] Meanwhile, the courts also accepted, besides the protection of competitors and the general public, the protection of consumers as an equally important aim.[57]

[52] They are authorized to establish breaches of the Art. L 121–8 and L 121–9 CCons., cf. Art. L 121–2 of CCons.

[53] F.O. Ranke, in J. Maxeiner and P. Schotthöfer, p. 153; M. Radeideh and J. Frank, *France*, in H.-W. Micklitz and J. Keßler, p. 75 (76); T. Dreier and S. von Lewinski, *Frankreich*, in G. Schricker, notes 5, 361.

[54] F.O. Ranke, in J. Maxeiner and P. Schotthöfer, p. 153 (154).

[55] Law against Unfair Competition of June 7, 1909, RGBl. 499. Former §1 UWG read: 'According to this provision any person who, in the course of business activity for purposes of competition committs acts against public morals, may be ordered to desist from these acts and be liable for damages'.

[56] See A. Beater, *Wettbewerbsrecht* (2002), §13 notes 10 et seq.

[57] BGH (1999) 101 GRUR 751 – 'Güllepumpen'; BGHZ 140, 134 (138) – 'Hormonpräparate'; BGH (2000) 53 NJW 864 – 'Giftnotrufbox'; BVerfG (2001) 46 WRP 1160; BVerfG (2002) 104 GRUR 455.

In 2004 the German legislature passed a major amendment of the UWG.[58] This amendment pursued several aims: the general clause was concretized by incorporating in the UWG examples for its application.[59] The aim of consumer protection was explicitly included in the text of the UWG.[60] By repealing several prohibitions the UWG was liberalized.[61] Finally an attempt was made to create a role model for a European Unfair Competition Law.[62] Furthermore, there are clear tendencies for liberalization in the adjudication of the *Bundesgerichtshof* (BGH).[63]

Trade regulations and other rules of professional behaviour also regulate practices of business. Infringements of these provisions can be sanctioned according to §§ 3, 4 no. 11 UWG[64] (ex-§ 1 UWG). Apart from this, the protection of consumers is guaranteed by the *Bürgerliches Gesetzbuch* – BGB (Civil Code) – and the *Zivilprozessordnung* – ZPO (Code of Civil Procedure).[65]

Legal proceedings can be initiated by competitors and associations of consumers in front of the civil courts. In Germany, 90 per cent of infringements are stopped after a reprimand. Consumers are not allowed to sue; supervision by public authorities is very rare.

g) Greece

Greek law has adopted a special legislative framework on unfair competition that is distinct from the framework providing restrictions under antitrust law. Thus, on the one hand, Law 146/1914 on unfair

58 UWG of July 3, 2004, BGBl. I 1414; cf. the prior history in H. Köhler, J. Bornkamm, and F. Henning-Bodewig, *Vorschlag für eine Richtlinie zum Lauterkeitsrecht und eine UWG-Reform*, (2002) 48 WRP 1317 and the two expert's opinions that were initiated by the Ministery of Justice in the 14th session of parliament in K.H. Fezer, *Modernisierung des deutschen Rechts gegen den unlauteren Wettbewerb auf der Grundlage einer Europäisierung des Wettbewerbsrechts v. 15.6.2001* (2001) 47 WRP 989, as well as G. Schricker and F. Henning-Bodewig, *Elemente einer Harmonisierung des Rechts des unlauteren Wettbewerbs in der Europäischen Union v. Juli 2001* (2001) 47 WRP 1367; E. Keller, in H. Harte-Bavendamm and F. Henning-Bodewig *UWG* (2004), Einl A notes 11 et seq.

59 See §§3 and 4 UWG (2004). 60 See §1 UWG.

61 The rules on end of season sales, anniversary sales, and clearance sales, §§6, 6a, 6b UWG, were deleted without replacement, cf. Begr. RegE, UWG, BT-Drs. 15/1487, p. 13.

62 See A.2 note 58.

63 For an overview see V. Emmerich, *Unlauterer Wettbewerb*, in *50 Jahres BGH*, vol. 2 (2000), p. 627.

64 C. von Jagow, in H. Harte-Bavendamm and F. Henning-Bodewig, *UWG* (2004), §4 no. 11 notes 18, 65 et seq.

65 See below Case 5 (Discontinued models) as well as H. J. Ahrens, in H. Harte-Bavendamm and F. Henning-Bodewig, *UWG* (2004), Einl F notes 347 et seq.; H. Köhler, in: W. Hefermehl, H. Köhler and J. Bornkamm, *Wettbewerbsrecht* (24th edn 2006), Einl 7.1 et seq.

competition prohibits and imposes sanctions on unfair trade practices, while Law 703/1977 provides for the control of monopolies and oligopolies and the protection of free competition.[66] Law 703/1977, although introduced at a later date, intervenes logically at the first stage, in order to ensure the right of unhampered access to the relevant market. Law 146/1914 intervenes at a second level, in order to protect the exercise of economic freedom from eventual unlawful practices committed by competitors.

According to the philosophy of Law 146/1914, the functioning of the market should be based on the principle of the best offer (qualitative competition), in order for the consumers to make their choice using objective criteria, such as the better quality, better price, better service, more efficient distribution network etc.[67] When a competitor tries to prevail upon his competitors by using other methods (i.e. misleading consumers), there then arises the possibility of applying Law 146/14. However, given the difficulty of predicting in a legislative instrument all possible unfair practices, the above law provides in its first article a general clause aiming at covering most of the unacceptable methods. Thus, according to art. 1, introducing a specific civil tort offence, 'any act for purposes of competition in commercial, industrial and agricultural transactions that is contrary to good morals is prohibited'. The general clause of 'good morals' provides for delegation to the courts to elaborate it further by levelling the various interests in each particular case.[68] However, the provision of art. 1 is currently criticized because of the restrictive nature of the 'good morals' criterion, the limited number of transactions involved and the requested purpose of competition.[69] Additional legal provisions stipulate specialized prohibitions covering concrete forms of illegal competition practices. Thus, for example, art. 3 prohibits inaccurate declarations, while art. 11 provides for the liability of any person propagating damaging information on his competitors

[66] Government Gazette, issue A 278, 1977, as repeatedly amended by laws 1943/1991, 2000/1991, 2296/1995, 2741/1999, 2837/2000, 2941/2001 and more recently by law 3373/2005 introducing mainly the provisions of Council Regulation (EC) 1/2003 (OJ L 1, 4-1-2003 1-25).

[67] N.K. Rokas, Industrial Property (Athens 2004) [in Greek], p. 175.

[68] For the interpretation of 'good morals' clause, see A. Liakopoulos, *Industrial Property*, (Athens 2000), [in Greek], p. 414 et seq, D. Tsimbanoulis, *Article 1*, in N.K. Rokas (ed.), *Unfair Competition* (1996), p. 51 [in Greek] and references therein, also Athens single member court of first instance [hereinafter: CFI], decision 6317/2000, 6 *Dikaio Epixeirision kai Etairion* [hereinafter: DEE] (2000) 998 [in Greek].

[69] See inter alia, N.K. Rokas, Industrial Property, n. 67 above, p. 176.

and for their right to seek reparation for damages. Additional provisions on illegal competition may be found in other legal instruments, mainly in Law 2251/1994 on consumer protection which regulates misleading, comparative and otherwise unfair advertisement. Art. 9 of the said law provides for protection against misleading, comparative and unfair advertising.[70]

In its primary conception, Law 146/1914 was considered to protect only competitors. Now, it is progressively accepted that it also directly aims at protecting consumers, the welfare of the society as well as the institution of competition itself.[71] Infringements of the above law's provisions are mainly sanctioned through civil law claims (to cease the violation, to desist from it in the future, as well as claim for reparation of damages: see for example art. 1 para. 2). For some cases of illegal competition (not for unfair practices covered by art. 1), criminal sanctions are also provided.[72] Only competitors and/or commercial and professional associations[73] may initiate legal proceedings before the civil courts; consumers and/or consumer associations may seek protection by invoking the provisions of Law 2251/1994. Supervision by public authorities or other form of public enforcement and involvement is limited to the rare cases stipulated by explicit provisions.[74]

[70] Article 9(8) of law 2251/1994 on consumer protection stipulates: 'An advertisement identifying directly or indirectly or suggesting the identity of a specific competitor, or of the goods or services that he is providing (comparative advertisement) is allowed provided it compares in an objective manner the main, related and verifiable features of competitive goods or services that have been impartially selected and which: a) is not misleading, b) does not cause confusion in the market between the advertised person and a competitor or between competitors of the advertised person or between the trademarks, other distinctive signs, goods or services of the advertised person and one of his competitors or more than one competitors between them, c) is not degrading, defamatory or contemptuous to a competitor or to the trademarks, goods, services or activities thereof, d) does not aim mainly at profiting from the well known name of the trademark or other distinctive sign of a competitor, e) regarding products with appellations of origin, it refers to products of the same appellation of origin in any case and f) does not present a good or service as the imitation or copy of a good or service having a registered trademark or trade name.' See Government Gazette, issue A 191, 1994. This law incorporates the provisions of Dir. 84/450/EEC, 97/7/EC, 97/55/EC). This article was amended by Min. Dec. Z-1496/2000.

[71] N.K. Rokas, *Industrial Property*, n. 67 above, p. 175, A. Liakopoulos, *Industrial Property*, n. 68 above, pp. 410–413.

[72] E.g. for infringements of art. 4, 11, 14, 16, 17.

[73] See art. 10 of L. 146/1914.

[74] See e.g. art. 24 of L. 2941/2001 authorizing the Minister of Development to inflict a fine in case of sales to consumers below the purchase price.

h) Hungary

In the Hungarian legal system, primarily, Act LVII of 1996 regarding the Prohibition on Unfair and Restrictive Market Practices (hereinafter HCA) contains the provisions concerning competition law.[75] It covers both unfair competition and cartel law. Unfair competition law as well as antitrust law is legislated within this single act. The HCA regulates the following practices: prohibition of unfair competition, prohibition of the unfair manipulation of consumer choice, prohibition of agreements restricting economic competition (antitrust rules), prohibition of abuse of dominant position and controlling the concentration of undertakings.[76] The Act LVIII of 1997 on Business Advertising Activities (*Reklámtörvény*, HAA) is in compliance with Directive 97/55/EC of the European Parliament and of the Council dated October 6, 1997 amending Directive 84/450/EEC concerning misleading advertising so as to include comparative advertising.

The *Gazdasági Versenyhivatal* (Office of Economic Competition, OEC) is a public, budgetary institution of national competence. The OEC is independent of government, but controlled by parliament. It is responsible for the supervision of competition as defined in the Competition Act and the Act on Business Advertising Activity. The competence of the OEC extends to the HAA. However, certain matters of competition supervision such as the injury of reputation and business secrets, boycott and imitation are within the competence of the courts. The Competition Council is the decision-making body of the OEC. It reaches its determinations on the merits of the case and can take decisions concerning enforcement. On the basis of sec. 44 HCA and unless otherwise provided in the HCA, economic competition supervision proceedings are governed by the provisions of Act CXL of 2004 on the General Rules of Public Administrative Proceedings and Services. On the basis of sec. 86 (1) HCA proceedings in cases of violation of the provisions contained in sections 2–7 HCA (prohibition of unfair competition)

[75] One can find the law in English on the website of the GVH under www.gvh.hu.

[76] The HCA was largely in compliance with the basic rules of EU competition law when it entered into force in 1997. Amendments to the act in December 2000 resulted in further harmonization. The next step in the harmonization process was Act X of 2002, based on sec. 62(3) of the Treaty on the Accession of Hungary to the European Union. Further to these harmonization measures, the Hungarian Parliament passed amendments to the HCA on May 26, 2003, Act XXXI of 2003. The amendments aim to bring the act fully into line with EU competition law. The new provisions entered into force on May 1, 2004, the date of Hungary's accession to the European Union.

belong to the competence of the courts and they are therefore governed by Act III of 1952 on Civil Procedure.

i) Ireland

In Ireland, there is no specific legislation dealing with unfair behaviour by undertakings that fall outside antitrust/competition legislation. As is the case in England, there is neither a general prohibition against trading unfairly, nor a general obligation to trade fairly. Unfair competition, in the sense in which the term is used in this publication, is dealt with under the general concept of tort, or with legislation concerned with specific torts, trademark infringement, or consumer protection. This is contrary to the situation in, for example, Germany, where competition law incorporates the concept of unfairness outside of the antitrust context. This type of unfair competition by an undertaking may affect the consumer and it may affect the undertaking's competitors.

The consumer affected by an undertaking that is behaving unfairly may contact the Office of Consumer Affairs for advice and assistance. The distinction in Irish law between competition legislation and legislation dealing with consumer protection is reflected at institutional level. Unlike in England, where competition law and consumer law are enforced by the same institution, the OFT, in Ireland consumer protection law is enforced by the Office of Consumer Affairs, a separate body from the Competition Authority, though both are ultimately connected to the Government Department of Enterprise, Trade and Employment. Irish consumer protection law is contained in a myriad of statutes, heavily influenced by EC law, and in the common law (in case law).

The principal functions of the Director of Consumer Affairs include the functions to inform the public of their rights as consumers, to conduct investigations under consumer protection legislation, to prosecute offences as provided for by statute such as breaches of the Consumer Credit Act, 1995, false or misleading advertising under the provisions of the Consumer Information Act, 1978, food labeling regulations and general product safety legislation, to keep under general review practices or proposed practices by business generally which could impact negatively on the rights provided by statute for the consumer, to seek High Court orders in certain circumstances and to promote self-regulatory codes of practice. Competitors of an undertaking that is behaving unfairly may take court action against the undertaking for various torts, such as the tort of passing off or the torts of defamation and injurious falsehood. Competitors may also have recourse to legislation to prevent misleading advertising and trademark infringement. The absence of a distinct authority or code to protect the rights of (small) undertakings reflects the legal distinction made in Irish commercial law, between consumers on the one hand, and those acting in the course of a business on the other. The former group is deemed worthy of special protection, while the latter is presumed to have consented to the risks of unfair competition inherent in commercial trade. The remedies sought in cases of unfair competition, whether taken by consumers or competitors are the same: injunctions and damages. A report, published in 2005, by the government-sponsored Consumer Strategy Group, proposes the establishment of a new consumer body, along the lines of the Irish Competition Authority. The proposed national consumer agency, NCA, would replace the Office of the Director of Consumer Affairs and would be independent of the Ministry. It would carry out research, disseminate information, enforce legislation and be responsible for both education and raising awareness of consumer issues. It is envisaged that the agency would be a powerful advocate for consumers and reverse the apathy that traditionally characterizes the consumer lobby in Ireland.

j) Italy

Under Italian law, unfair competition is prohibited by art. 2598 *Codice civile* of 1942 – cc (Civil Code). No specific rules were provided for by previously issued codes; competitive torts were regulated by the general rules of torts, and by art. 10bis PC.[77] Art. 2598 cc is a blanket clause; it begins with the statement that the prohibition of unfair competition will not prejudice the application of the law of trademarks and of patents. Afterwards, three categories of unlawful behaviour ('by any person'), which amount to unfair competition, are listed.[78]

The last category of acts of unfair competition has an open nature: it is up to the courts to state in which cases behaviour by the defendant is

[77] See above A.II.1(a).

[78] Art. 2598 cc regulates:

- No. 1: Use of trade names or signs which may induce confusion with names or signs lawfully used by another; dully imitation of a competitor's products; any kind of behaviour which, by any means, may cause confusion with a competitor's products and business;
- No. 2: spreading news or opinions on a competitor's products or business, which may disparage such products or business; usurpation of merits of a competitor's products or business;
- No. 3: using directly or indirectly any other means inconsistent with fairness in the course of business (*correttezza professionale*) which may harm competitors.

'unfair', with reference both to specific usages accepted within a given business community, and to objective criteria stated by the courts themselves, having regard to the need to prevent business conduct not compatible with the interest of businesses that consumers should not be misled, and, indirectly, with the general interest that the market is not disturbed by business conduct which may impair its efficiency and/or lead to socially undesirable outcomes. Further provisions on unfair competition, also with specific reference to remedies, are stated by arts. 2599–2601 cc. EC Directive 84/450 on misleading advertising, was implemented in Italy by legislative decree of January 25, 1992, d.lgs. 74/1992.[79] In 2000, provisions relating to comparative advertising were inserted in the decree, implementing EC Directive 97/55.[80]

There are three ways of imposing remedies. As a matter of principle private parties have to take action against infringements. As a general principle, in Italian law no public authority is entitled to take action against unfair competition. Nevertheless, d.lgs. 74/1992 is a public law piece of legislation. According to sec. 7, the *Autorità Garante della Concorrenza e del Mercato* (Italian antitrust authority) – is competent to apply the prohibition of misleading advertising and to ban unlawful comparative advertisements. The authority is an independent public agency and owner of discretionary powers, whose decisions may be appealed in front of the *Tribunale Amministrativo Regionale per il Lazio* – TAR Lazio – in Rome (administrative court). Decisions by the TAR Lazio may be appealed in front of the *Consiglio di Stato*, which is the highest administrative court. (A recent decision by the Consiglio di Stato changed the prior case law, stating that appeals in front of TAR Lazio may be filed not only by the undertakings whose advertisements were banned by the Authority – as previously held by courts – but also by the complainant, in case of dismissal of complaints by the Authority: Cons. Stato, December 17, 2005, n. 280, *Codacons v. Autorità Garante della Concorrenza e del Mercato)*. In addition, public authorities may take action if the illegal behaviour infringes further statutory provisions which protect public interests. Finally, the advertising industry has

[79] Comprehensive comments in: V. Meli, *La repressione della pubblicità ingannevole* (1994); M. Fusi, P. Testa and V. Cottafavi, *La pubblicità ingannevole* (1996).

[80] The complete legislative texts may be found on the website of the Italian antitrust authority: www.agcm.it. A detailed review of the authority's powers with reference to misleading and comparative advertising is offered by P. Auteri, *I poteri dell'Autorità Garante in materia di pubblicità ingannevole e comparativa*, in Riv. dir. ind. (2002), I, 265 et seq.

promulgated its own voluntary regulations in the *Codice dell'autodisciplina publicitaria* – CAP (Code of Self-Regulation of Advertising), which provides a far more detailed and structured system of regulation than any binding law. Adopted by the members of the industry's national umbrella organisation, *Istituto di autodisciplina pubblicitaria*, the CAP has been in force in its present form since May 1, 1966, and has been amended many times since.[81]

k) Netherlands

The Netherlands does not have specific legislation concerning unfair competition. Law enforcement occurs mainly through civil law.[82]

(1) Unfair competition is dealt with under the general concept of tort as laid down in the *Burgerlijk Wetboek* – BW (Dutch Civil Code), in particular in art. 6:162 BW.[83] The proceedings of an action based on art. 6:162 BW are conducted in accordance with the Dutch Code of Civil Procedure – BRv. One of the important procedural issues is the allocation of the burden of proof. The basic rule is laid down in art. 150 BRv, according to which the burden of proof is placed on the party that alleges a claim, which in principle will be the plaintiff. The plaintiff therefore has to prove the following elements necessary to establish tortious liability (cf. art. 6:162 BW): the existence of a wrongful act. Except where there are grounds for justification, the following acts are deemed wrongful: the violation of a right and an act or omission breaching a duty imposed by law or a rule of unwritten law pertaining to proper social conduct (requirement of carefulness). The wrongful act is imputable to the defendant. A wrongdoer is responsible for the commission of a wrongful act if it is due to his fault or to a cause for which he is accountable by law or

[81] F. Hofer, S. Lösch, A. Toricelli and G. Genta, *Italy*, in J. Maxeiner and P. Schotthöfer, p. 285 (287).

[82] F. Henning-Bodewig, in H. Harte-Bavendamm and F. Henning-Bodewig, *UWG* (2004), Einl. E note 441.

[83] The fundamental statutory basis for unfair competition litigation is found in art. 6: 162 BW:

(1) A person who commits an unlawful act against another which is attributable to him, must repair the damage suffered by the other in consequence thereof.

(2) Except where there are grounds for justification, the following are deemed unlawful: the violation of a right and an act or omission breaching a duty imposed by law or a rule of unwritten law pertaining to proper social conduct.

(3) A wrongdoer is responsible for the commission of an unlawful act if it is due to his fault or to a cause for which he is accountable by law or pursuant to generally accepted principles.

pursuant to generally accepted principles. The existence of damage is a prerequisite. The damage incurred has to be caused by the wrongful act.

It is noted that art. 6:163 BW provides that an obligation to pay damages does not exist if the standard breached does not serve to protect against damage such as that suffered by the person suffering the loss. In principle the burden of proof in this respect lies with the defendant. He has the burden of proof that this should not be the case. The second phrase of art. 150 BRv formulates an interesting 'escape' in the sense that the court may decide to lighten the burden of proof or even reverse it if reasonableness and fairness so require.[84]

The normal rules of evidence are not applicable in interlocutory proceedings.[85] The standard of proof as such is not lowered but the court is free to shift or reverse the burden of proof in a manner it feels appropriate for the case.

(2) The Dutch Civil Code has a special section on misleading and comparative advertising: art. 6:194–196 BW. These provisions must be regarded as a further substantiation of the general rule on tortious liability of art. 6:162 BW. Art. 6:194[86] and 194a[87] BW specify the circumstances in

[84] Art. 150 DCCP reads: The party that appeals to the legal consequences of the facts or rights it submits, carries the burden of proof for those facts or rights, unless another division of the burden of proof follows from any particular rule or from the requirements of reasonableness and fairness.

[85] See Supreme Court 29–01–1943, NJ 1943, 198; Supreme Court 16–02–1962, NJ 1962, 142 and Supreme Court 31–01–1975, NJ 1976, 146.

[86] Art. 194 BW reads: A person who makes public or causes to be made public information regarding goods or services which he, or the person for whom he acts, offers in the conduct of a profession or business, acts unlawfully if this information is misleading in one or more of the following respects, for example as to;

a) the nature, composition, quantity, quality, characteristics or possibilities for use;
b) the origin, the manner and time of manufacture;
c) the volume of stocks;
d) the price or its method of calculation;
e) the reason or purpose of the special offer;
f) the prizes awarded, the testimonials or other opinions or declarations given by third persons, or the scientific or professional terms used, the technical results or statistical data;
g) the conditions under which goods are supplied, services are rendered or payment is made;
h) the extent, content or duration of the warranty;
i) the identity, qualities, skills or competence of the person by whom, or under whose management or supervision or with whose cooperation the goods are or have been manufactured or offered or the services rendered.

[87] Art. 194a BW reads:

(1) 'Comparative advertising' means any advertising which, explicitly or by implication, identifies a competitor or goods or services offered by a competitor.

which advertising may be regarded as wrongful. Art. 6:195 BW[88] addresses the burden of proof and art. 6:196[89] addresses specific actions available in case of misleading or illegal comparative advertising.

(2) Comparative advertising shall, as far as the comparison is concerned, be permitted if the following conditions are met:
a) it is not misleading;
b) it compares goods or services meeting the same needs or intended for the same purpose;
c) it objectively compares one or more material, relevant, verifiable and representative features of those goods and services, which may include the price;
d) it does not create confusion in the market place between the advertiser and a competitor or between the advertiser's trade marks, trade names, other distinguishing marks, goods or services and those of a competitor;
e) it does not discredit or denigrate the good name or trade marks, trade names, other distinguishing marks, goods, services, activities or circumstances of a competitor;
f) for products with a designation of origin, it relates in each case to products with the same designation;
g) it does not take unfair advantage of the reputation of a trade mark, trade name or other distinguishing features of a competitor or of the designation of origin of competing products; and
h) it does not present goods or services as imitations or replicas of goods or services bearing a protected trade mark or trade name.

(3) Any comparison relating to a special offer shall indicate in a clear and unequivocal way the date on which a special offer ends or, where appropriate, that the special offer is subject to the availability of the goods and services, and where the special offer has not yet begun, the date of the commencement of the period during which the special price or other specific conditions shall apply.

[88] Art. 195 BW reads:

(1) If, pursuant to article 194 or article 194a, legal action is taken against the person who himself, in whole or in part, has determined or has caused to be determined the content and presentation of the information, the burden to prove the accuracy or completeness of the facts contained in the information or suggested by it and on which the alleged misleading nature of the information is based, or, as the case may be, on which the fact that the comparative advertising is not permitted, is based, falls on such persons. In the case of comparative advertising the person who himself, in whole or in part, has determined or has caused to be determined the content and presentation of the information must furnish such evidence in a short period of time on which the accuracy of factual claims in the advertising is based.

(2) If, according to article 194 and article 194a, there has been an unlawful act of a person who, in whole or in part, has himself determined or has caused to be determined the content and presentation of the information, this person is liable for the damage resulting therefrom, unless he proves that it is neither his fault nor that he is responsible for it for another reason.

[89] Art. 196 BW reads:

(1) If a person has caused damage to another or is likely to do so by making information public as described in article 194 or by making any unpermitted comparative advertising or by causing it to be made public, the court, on the

(3) In the Netherlands one finds self-regulation on advertising. Advertising is supervised by the RCC - *Reclame Code Commissie* (Advertising Code Commission). This Commission is not a formal regulatory organization but it is an important body to which the most important advertisers and media are affiliated.[90] The purpose of the RCC is to ensure that advertising in the Netherlands is responsible. To

demand of that other person, may not only order the cessation by such person from making such information public and from causing it to be made public, but also order him to publish a correction of that information or of such unpermitted comparative advertising or to have it published, in the manner indicated by the court.

(2) Article 167 paragraph 3 applies, mutatis mutandis, if an action, referred to in the preceding paragraph, is allowed against a person who is not also liable for the damage referred to in article 195, paragraph 2.

[90] The following organizations are affiliated with the Stichting Reclame Code and have approved and accepted the Advertising Code:

(1) BVA/Association of Dutch Advertisers (BVA);
(2) Consumers' Association (CB);
(3) Netherlands Publishers Union: Netherlands Daily Newspaper Press, Public Magazines, Professional and Science Magazines;
(4) VEA Association of Communication Consultancies;
(5) RMB Nederland B.V. (cinema advertising);
(6) Foundation for Ether Advertising (STER) (national public broadcasters);
(7) Regional Broadcasting Consultative and Cooperative Board (ROOS);
(8) Association of Local Dutch Broadcasters in the Netherlands (OLON).

Special Advertising Codes of the Advertising Code are drawn up in consultation with the following organizations:

(1) The Information Centre Foundation of the Bakery and Sugarindustry - Vereniging voor de Bakkerij en Zoetwarenindustrie (VGZ);
(2) The Cigarette Industry Foundation - de Stichting Sigaretten Industrie (SSI), the Association of the Dutch Shag Tobacco Industry - de Vereniging Nederlandse Kerftabakindustrie (VNK) and the Dutch Association for the Cigar Industry - de Nederlandse Vereniging voor de Sigarenindustrie (NVS);
(3) The Foundation for the Moderate Use of Alcohol - de Stichting Verantwoord Alcoholgebruik (STIVA);
(4) The National Foundation for the Exploitation of Casino Games - De Nationale Stichting tot Exploitatie van Casinospelen;
(5) (5) VAN Slot Machine Sector Organization - VAN Speelautomaten branche organisatie;
(6) Council of the Dutch Retail Trade - De vereniging Nederlandse Vereniging 'de Rijwiel- en Automobielindustrie', afdeling Auto's (RAI);
(7) Vereniging mailDB;
(8) Platform Behoud Zelfregulering Telemarketing;
(9) Thuiswinkel.org;
(10) Dutch Dialogue Marketing Association (DDMA);
(11) Email Marketing Associatie Nederland (Emma.nl).

this end the Commission has drawn up rules with which advertising[91] is required to comply, the so called *Nederlands Reclame Code* – NRC (Dutch Advertising Code).[92] Generally speaking the NRC applies to all advertising regardless of the medium used. Anyone who feels that advertising violates the NRC may submit a complaint to the Commission.

If an advertisement is found to infringe the Advertising Code, the RCC will recommend the advertiser to stop using it in its current form. In the event of a repeat offence or a serious violation of the Code, the media will be asked to stop publishing the advertisement concerned. The organizations which are affiliated to the RCC have the duty to reject advertisements against which such a type of ban has been issued pursuant to the Netherlands Media Act.[93]

As mentioned, these rules must be characterized as self-regulation. Therefore they do not have a legally binding status as such. However, the conclusion of the RCC can have an important impact in law on the question whether a specific action can be characterized as a wrongful act. The conclusion of the Commission must after all be regarded as an expression of what in the socio-economic field is considered as reasonable and fair in advertising, from a competition or consumer protection point of view.[94]

[91] The term advertising is defined as any public commendation of goods, services and concepts.

[92] See www.reclamecode/nl/pdf/DAC.pdf. The most important rules of the Advertising Code are the following:

(1) Advertising shall conform to the law, the truth and the requirements of good taste and decency.
(2) Advertising shall not contravene the public interest, public order or morality.
(3) Advertising shall not be misleading, in particular about the price, contents, origin, composition, properties or effectiveness of the products concerned. Advertising shall be as clear and complete as possible in terms of such factors as its nature and form and the public at which it is aimed. The party selling the products shall also be indicated clearly.
(4) Testimonials, commendations or statements by experts that are used in advertising shall be based on the truth and tally with the latest accepted scientific views.

[93] When the complaint is allowed by the Advertising Code Commission, the Commission can moreover:
(i) stipulate for the party whose advertising is found to violate the Code a term during which the recommendation of the Commission is to be complied with; and
(ii) impose measures (e.g. fines) as described in the contracts concluded between the Stichting Reclame Code and the organizations in consultation with which a Special Advertising Code was laid down.

[94] See Parliamentary proceedings II, 2000/2001, 27.619, no. 3, pp. 9–10.

l) Poland

The Polish system of protecting competition and preventing unfair competition is based on two acts. The Polish statute against unfair competition was enacted in 1926[95] and remained in force until 1993. Because of Poland's centrally planned economy the act was not in use and no jurisprudence was developed on its grounds. The act was replaced by the *Ustawa o zwalczaniu nieuczciwej konkurencji* of 1993 – u.z.n.k.[96] (act on fighting unfair competition). The act on fighting unfair competition is rooted in the previous legislation (general clause in art. 3 u.z.n.u.), being at the same time strongly influenced by the European legislation (chap. II, art. 5 et seq. u.z.n.u. naming particular acts of unfair competition). Consequently, the Act ensures the same level of protection as the European legislation. The *Ustawa o ochronie konkurencji i konsumentow* of 2000[97] – u.o.k.k. (act on competition and consumer protection) replaced the Antimonopoly Law of 1990. It is a complex piece of legislation forbidding acts limiting competition as well as introducing detailed antitrust provisions. Since both acts were introduced recently, limited jurisprudence and literature concerning the subject are available. Frequently, European jurisprudence is quoted in the commentaries to interpret particular provisions.

For problems which are not specified in u.z.n.k. or u.o.k.k. the general codes apply i.e. for questions in material law the *Kodeks Cywilny* – k.c. (Polish Civil Code) and for procedural law the *Kodeks Postepowania Cywilnego* – k.p.c. (Polish Code of Civil Procedure). Normally, the civil courts are competent for legal proceedings.[98]

m) Portugal

Portuguese law is characterised by a certain complexity. As in French law a distinction is drawn between unfair competition (*concorrência desleal*) and illegal competition (*concorrência illicita*).[99] The relevant text in Portugal concerning unfair competition (*concorrência desleal*) was the *Código de Propriedade Industrial* of 1940/1995 – CPI (Industrial Property

[95] Dz.U.1930 Nr. 56 Pos. 467.

[96] Dz. U. z dnia 8 czerwca 1993 r. Nr 47, poz. 211; zm. Dz. U. z 1996 r. Nr 106, poz. 496; z 1997 r. Nr. 88, poz. 556; z 1998 r. Nr 106, poz. 668; z 2000 r. Nr 29 poz. 365, Nr 93, poz. 1027; DzU z2003 Nr. 153; zm DzU z2002 Nr. 197, poz. 1661.

[97] Dz.U. z 2000 r. Nr 122, poz. 1319; zm 2001 r. Nr. 110 poz. 1189; DzU z2003 Nr. 86 poz. 804; zm DzU 2003 Nr. 60 poz. 535 oraz 2003 Nr. 170 poz. 1652.

[98] I. Wiszniewska, *Polen*, in G. Schricker, note 373.

[99] G. Schricker (1994) 42 GRUR Int. 819 (820).

Code).[100] Art. 260 CPI included a general rule based on art. 10bis PC.[101] In the meantime the CPI was repromulgated by decree no. 36/03 of March 3, 2003. The provisions concerning acts of unfair competition can be found in art. 317, 318 and 331 CPI.[102] The CPI originally only included penal actions for infringements. Following the amendment, infringements are considered to be misdemeanours. But according to art. 483 para. 1 CC the awarding of damages is possible.[103]

The specific context of misleading and comparative advertising as part of the concorrência illicita is regulated by the *Código da Publicidade* of 1990 – CPub (Advertising Code).[104] Art. 11 CPub forbids misleading advertisement. The protection of consumers is regulated by the *Lei de Defesa do Consumidor* – LDCons (Consumer Protection Act).[105] Art. 9 LDCons incorporates the fundamental principle of truth in advertising.[106] Finally, Decree 43/2001 of April 26, 2001 regulates inter alia distance selling and pyramid schemes.[107]

There are specific codes forbidding misleading advertising, namely statutes concerning labels on food and labels on washing and cleaning products. Concerning private remedies the *Código Civil* – CC (Civil Code) is normally applied and for procedural aspects, the *Código de Processo Civil* – CPC (Code of Civil Procedure). Concerning criminal aspects, the relevant texts are the *Código Penal* – CP (Criminal Code) and the *Código de Processo Penal* – CPP (Code of Criminal Procedure).

Since unfair competition is a misdemeanour, the codes are interpreted by criminal and civil courts. In addition, a General Inspector of Commercial Activities is authorised to impose administrative fines.[108] The acts are supervised by the *Direcção Geral do Comércio e da Concorrência* – DGCC (General Authority of Trade and Competition)

[100] Decreto-Lei n. 16/95 of January 24, 1995 (art. 260); see www.inpi.pt.

[101] J. Möllering, *Das Recht des unlauteren Wettbewerbs in Portugal* (1991) 37 WRP 634 (635).

[102] F. Henning-Bodewig, in H. Harte-Bavendamm and F. Henning-Bodewig, *UWG* (2004), Einl E note 514.

[103] G. Schricker (1994) 42 GRUR Int. 819; J. Möllering (1991) 37 WRP 634 (635).

[104] Decreto-Lei n. 330/90 of October 23, 1990, latest amendment n. 332/2001 of December 24, 2001.

[105] Law 29/81 of August 21, 1981; amended by Decreto Lei n. 24/96 of July 31, 1996.

[106] I. Jalles and C. Dein, *Portugal*, in J. Maxeiner and P. Schotthöfer (eds.), *Advertising Law in Europe and North America* (2nd edn 1999), p. 393 (394).

[107] F. Henning-Bodewig, in H. Harte-Bavendamm and F. Henning-Bodewig, *UWG* (2004), Introd. E note 516.

[108] I. Jalles and C. Dein, *Portugal*, in J. Maxeiner and P. Schotthöfer (eds.), p. 393 (405).

and the *Instituto Nacional da Defesa do Consumidor* (National Consumer Protection Institution).[109]

n) Spain

The Spanish law of unfair competition is characterized by a high degree of complexity. The reasons for this are the competing authorities involved in the passing of legislation of the federal parliament and the autonomous regions (*Comunidades Autonómas*, called CC.AA.).[110] On top of that, the law of unfair competition overlaps with the law of consumer protection. The relevant legal text in Spain regarding unfair competition law is the *Ley de Competencia Desleal* – LCD[111] (Unfair Competition Act). The *Ley General de Publicidad* – LGP (General Publicity Act)[112] implements the directives 84/450/EEC, 97/55/EC and 98/27/EC.[113] General clauses can be found in both codes, in art. 5 LCD and art. 6b LGP.[114] In addition there is a *Ley General para la Defensa de los Consumidores y Usarios* – LGDCU (General Consumer Protection Act)[115] dealing with the protection of consumers. It regulates, apart from prohibitions of certain unfair acts, duties to give information.[116]

For problems which are not specified in the LCD, the general codes apply, i.e. for questions in substantive law the *Código Civil* – CC (Spanish Civil Code), for procedural aspects the *Ley de Enjuiciamiento Civil* – LEC (Code of Civil Procedure), the *Código Penal* – CP (Criminal Code) and the *Ley de Enjuiciamiento Criminal* – LECr (Code of Criminal Procedure). In the *Ley de Ordenación del Comercio Minorista* – LOCM (Code of the Organization of Retailing)[117] the central state provides rules for the retail business. Alongside this one finds the Autonomy Statutes of the CC.AA.[118] An act

[109] Art. 21 LDCons and art. 1 Decreto-Lei n. 234/99 de 25 de Junho; art. 38 CPI.
[110] One can find the Spanish codes on www.noticias.juridicas.com.
[111] Ley 3/1991 de Competencia Desleal of January 10, 1991.
[112] Ley 34/1988 General de Publicidad of November 11, 1998.
[113] P. Gullién and D. Voigt, *Spain*, in H.-W. Micklitz and J. Keßler, p. 301 (310); C. Marti and K. Schmidt, *Spanien*, in *Heidelberger Kommentar zum Wettbewerbsrecht* (2000), IV.15. note 6.
[114] E. Arroyo i Amayueals and N. Navarro, *Spain*, in R. Schulze and H. Schulte-Nölke, I.2 (b). These rules were based on the former § 1 UWG of Germany, see W. Nordemann, *Das neue spanische Werbegesetz im Vergleich zum deutschen Werberecht*, FS O. von Gamm (1990), p. 109 (113).
[115] Ley 26/1984 General para la Defensa de los Consumidores y Usarios of July 19, 1984.
[116] P. Gullién and D. Voigt, *Spain*, in H.-W. Micklitz and J. Keßler, p. 301, (317).
[117] Ley 7/1996 de Ordenación del Comercio Minorista of January 15, 1996.
[118] P. Gullién and D. Voigt, *Spain*, in H.-W. Micklitz and J. Keßler, p. 301 (304).

of unfair competition can thus infringe the LCD, the LGP and the LGDCU simultaneously.[119]

In some cases the civil courts are competent (art. 22 LCD and art. 28 LGP) and in some cases public authorities (art. 63 LOCM, art. 32 LGDCU). Conflicting decisions are therefore very common.[120] It is for this reason that the status quo in Spanish law has been described as complex.[121]

o) Sweden

In Sweden in the past it was difficult to say that there was a particular field of law called unfair competition. The leading expert of questions relating to unfair competition claimed that it was a 'forgotten area of law'.[122] Since January 1, 1996, unfair competition is now regulated by the *Marknadsföringslag* – MFL (Act on Marketing).[123] According to sec. 1 the MFL protects the consumer as well as the competitor. It contains a general clause in sec. 4, a clause on misleading advertising (sec. 6) and special provisions against unfair competition. The MFL encompasses provisions ensuring that all statements and promises made in advertising are truthful, that particularly important facts are included in ads and that companies must be able to substantiate their claims. Misleading or otherwise unacceptably unfair advertising may be prohibited.

There are a number of laws whose object is to ensure that consumers are not subject to misleading advertisements, to unfair sales methods, dangerous products or unfair contract terms. These acts implement European directives.

In Sweden the state is responsible for observing market behaviour.[124] A *Konsumentverket* (Consumer agency) with a *Konsumentombudsmannen* – KO (Consumer Ombudsman) supervises compliance with these acts in the interest of consumers (sec. 10 MFL). The *Konsumentverket* has the power to issue guidelines for marketing.[125] The administrative part of the MFL is exclusive to the special proceedings in the Stockholm District

[119] See Case 4 (Children's swing).

[120] P. Gullién and D. Voigt, *Spain*, in H.-W. Micklitz and J. Keßler, p. 301 (317); E. Arroyo i Amayuelas and N. Navarro, *Spain*, in R. Schulze and H. Schulte-Nölke, I.2.h).

[121] P. Gullién and D. Voigt, *Spain*, in H.-W. Micklitz and J. Keßler, p. 301 (317).

[122] U. Bernitz, *Otillbörlig konkurrens mellan näringsidkare – det bortglömda rättsomradet*, in: Festskrift till J. Hellner (1984), p. 115.

[123] Marknadsföringslag 1995: 450; cf. www.konsumentverket.se/mallar/sv/artikel.asp?IngCategoryId=490.

[124] U. Bernitz (1976) 40 RabelsZ 593; U. Bernitz, *Sweden*, in R. Schulze and H. Schulte-Nölke, p. 1; L. Olsen, *Konsumentskyddets former* (1995), p. 17.

[125] U. Bernitz, *Sweden*, in R. Schulze and H. Schulte-Nölke, p. 2.

Court and the Market Court. In cases, in which the plaintiff is suing for imposition of a market disruption fee and/or damages, the Stockholm District Court acts as a court of first instance. Such cases can be appealed to the Market court. In cases in which the plaintiff is suing only for a prohibition or information order, the Market Court acts as first and final instance.[126] To concretize undefined legal terms the rules of the Code of Advertising of the International Chamber of Commerce (ICC)[127] are used.[128]

3. *First assessment*

a) The law of unfair competition as an independent area of law

In most Member States the law of unfair competition is considered to be an independent area of law. In Germany, in 1907, a blanket clause was introduced into the UWG because the courts refused to apply the general tort claim in §823 BGB to curb acts of unfair competition.[129] Many countries adopted this 'big blanket' clause as a role model. It can be found in the law of Germany,[130] Austria,[131] Denmark,[132] Finland,[133] Sweden,[134] Belgium,[135] Luxembourg,[136] Spain,[137] Portugal,[138] Greece[139] and Switzerland.[140] Such a general clause allows the courts to concretize the remedies against acts of unfair competition. For the last 100 years this has been done by the development and definition of typical cases of unfair competition.[141] In France,[142] Belgium[143] and the

[126] U. Bernitz, *Sweden*, in R. Schulze and H. Schulte-Nölke, p. 6. [127] www.icc.wbo.org.

[128] A. Kur, *Schweden*, in G. Schricker, note 52; U. Bernitz (1996) 44 GRUR Int. 433 (434); U. Bernitz, *Sweden*, in R. Schulze and H. Schulte-Nölke, p. 2.

[129] The Supreme Court of the German Reich reasoned that the legislation had established trademark law and therefore only those affected by it had to be protected against unfair competition, RGZ 3, 67 (68) – 'Apollinaris'; RGZ 18, 93 (99) – 'Van Houten'; RGZ 20, 71 (75) – 'Benecke'.

[130] Former §1 UWG; now §3 UWG. [131] § 1 UWG. [132] § 1 MFL.

[133] Chap. 2 1 para. 1 § KSL and 1 § SopMenL. [134] Sec. 4 para. 1 MFL. [135] Art. 93, 94 LPC.

[136] Art. 16 Loi du 27 novembre 1986 réglementant certaines pratiques commerciales et sanctionnant la concurrence déloyale.

[137] Art. 5 LPC, art. 6 b LGP. [138] Former art. 260 CPI.

[139] Art. 1 Law of Unfair Competition. [140] Art. 2 UWG.

[141] One can find examples in A. Baumbach and W. Hefermehl, *Wettbewerbsrecht* (22nd edn 2001), on several hundred pages. These annotations will clearly change beccause of the regulation of typical cases in §4 UWG. In the new edition the annotations to §3 are reduced to 20 pages, cf. H. Köhler, in W. Hefermehl, H. Köhler and J. Bornkamm, *Wettbewerbsrecht* (24th edn 2006), §3.

[142] Art. 1382 code civil.

[143] Art. 93 et seq. Loi sur les pratiques du commerce et sur l'information et la protection du consommateur.

Netherlands[144] cases of unfair competition are solved by applying the general civil law provision for torts. Italy has introduced a separate general clause for unfair competition in its *Codice civile.*[145] Meanwhile a blanket clause has also been introduced to the European level.[146]

England and Ireland do not have a codification or a blanket clause covering acts of unfair competition. Both legal systems only know a series of individual provisions dealing with certain acts of unfair competition (e.g. 'passing off' or 'libel and slander'[147]).

Advertisers in England pride themselves on having fought and won the battle against excessive legal controls. They see the system of voluntary codes set up over the last thirty years as their most potent weapon. It is true to say that England has fewer laws which impinge directly on marketing than many countries. Time will tell, however, whether the same can still be said in, say, ten years' time.[148]

b) Fragmentation of the substantive provisions

One has to be aware that even in countries with one big blanket clause the similarities in the law of unfair competition are rather limited. Only very few Member States have their own codification for unfair competition law (Germany, Austria, Sweden, Denmark). And even in these states general civil and criminal law provision have to supplement the codification. In most other states the law of unfair competition is spread over several acts. Some countries restrict the scope of unfair competition law to widen the scope of consumer protection law. So, for example, in most Anglo-American states (UK and USA) and in the French legal system (France,[149] Belgium, Italy and the Netherlands) the competitor is protected by some limited tort provisions, while consumers are protected by elaborated codifications (France, Italy, Finland, Spain, Portugal, Hungary, UK and USA).

[144] Art. 6:162 BW. [145] Art. 2598 no. 3 Codice civile.

[146] See Art. 5 of Directive 2005/29/EC see of the European Parliament and of the Council concerning unfair business-to-consumer commercial practices in the Internal Market and amending Directives 84/450/EEC, 97/7/EC and 98/27/EC of May 11, 2005, OJ L 149, 22.

[147] See below Case 2 (Watch imitations I).

[148] S. Groom, *United Kingdom*, in J. Maxeiner and P. Schotthöfer, p. 469.

[149] C. Monfort, *France*, in R. Schulze and H. Schulte Nölke, p. 1.

c) Different remedies

Remedies are influenced by the substantial provisions of a legal system. In the various Member States the remedies are very different and can be divided into four groups. Remedies in the law of unfair competition can be enforced by civil law, criminal law, by public law authorities or by out-of-court settlements. The analysis will have to show if these four ways of enforcement are equally effective.

III. The European context of unfair competition law

The national law of unfair competition can be relevant on the European level. The national law of unfair competition can infringe European primary law (1.) and the European legislature can try to harmonize the law of unfair competition of the Member States (2.).

1. *European primary law*

a) General foundations in European primary law

The EU-Treaty and the EC-Treaty are the main sources of law in the European Union. This so-called European primary law is directly applicable in all member states. Consequently, any conflicting national provision is not applicable.[1] Apart from that the EU is able to harmonize the law of the Member States by the use of regulations and directives. Principally, directives have to be implemented into national law before they can become binding between private parties.[2] This raises the question to what extent a directive has to be observed that has not been implemented or has been implemented incorrectly by the national legislature (directive-conform interpretation).[3] The preliminary ruling procedure according to art. 234 EC (art. III-274 TCE) allows national courts to submit questions of interpretation of European law to the ECJ. The national courts are bound by the interpretation given by the ECJ.[4]

b) The scope and restrictions of the basic freedoms

National law of unfair competition can infringe the free movement of goods (art. 28 EC, art. III-42 TCE) and the free movement of services (art. 49 EC, art. III-29 TCE). Thus direct and indirect discrimination against foreign goods or services are illegal. But according to the rule in 'Dassonville' of the ECJ, any restrictions are forbidden as well. According to this rule the Member States have to refrain from any

[1] ECJ C-26/62, (1963) ECR 1, (1963) CMLR 105 – 'van Gend & Loos'; ECJ 6/64, (1964) ECR 1251 (1269) – 'Costa/ENEL'.

[2] ECJ 152/84, (1986) ECR 723 note 46, (1986) 1 CMLR 688 – 'Marshall I'; ECJ C-91/92, (1994) ECR I-3325 notes 20, 24 et seq., (1994) 49 NJW 2473 – 'Faccini Dori'.

[3] ECJ C-106/89, (1990) ECR I-4135 – 'Marleasing'; ECJ 14/83, (1984) ECR 1891 – 'von Colson and Kamann'; T. Möllers, *Role of Law in European Integration* (2003), p. 79, *Rolle des Rechts im Rahmen der europäischen Integration* (1999), p. 70.

[4] ECJ 283/81, (1982) ECR 3415, 3430, BGH (1994) 96 GRUR 794 (795) – 'Rolling Stones'.

measures which are capable of hindering, directly or indirectly, actually or potentially, intra-Community trade.[5] This broad scope of application has been reduced by the 'Keck' decision. All selling arrangements, i.e. measures regulating who, where, when and how a product is sold, fall outside the scope of the free movement of goods. This includes, for example, the prohibition on resale at a loss[6] or the prohibition on selling goods on Sundays. Unacceptable annoyances like cold-calling or disguised advertisement should also be covered by the principle in 'Keck' and thus fall outside the scope of the free movement of goods.[7] Therefore national prohibitions on these practices can lawfully restrict the free movement of goods and services. Vice versa national prohibitions on advertisement can be subject to the free movement of goods if certain names[8] or ways of packaging[9] are banned. A total prohibition on the sale of certain products can also be illegal since it may have an effect on foreign products.[10]

Restrictions on advertisements that fall within the scope of the free movement of goods and services can be justified. Justifying reasons can be found in art. 30 EC (art. III-43 TCE), for example the protection of public health. Furthermore the ECJ has developed the possibility to justify restrictions on the basis of so-called mandatory requirements. These mandatory requirements include, for example, the fairness of commercial transactions[11] and consumer protection.[12] But justification on these grounds is subject to a test of proportionality which means that these measures may only restrict the free movement of goods and services so far as is necessary to achieve a certain aim.

[5] ECJ C-8/74, (1974) ECR 837, (1974) 76 GRUR Int. 467 – 'Dassonville'.

[6] ECJ Joined Cases C-267/91 and C-268/91, (1993) ECR I-6097, (1995) 1 CMLR 101, (1994) 49 NJW 121, (1994) 49 JZ 358 with comments K.H. Fezer 320 – 'Keck'.

[7] R. Sack (1998) 100 GRUR 871 (872); H. Köhler and H. Piper, *UWG* (3rd edn 2002), Introd. note 70.

[8] ECJ C-315/92, (1994) ECR I-317, (1994) 76 GRUR 303 – 'Clinique'.

[9] ECJ C-470/93, (1995) ECR I-1923, (1995) 41 WRP 677 – 'Mars'.

[10] Also discriminating sales modalities fall within the scope of application of the freedom of movement of goods, ECJ joined cases C-34/95 to C-36/95, (1997) ECR I-3843 note 42, (1997) 45 GRUR Int. 912 (917) – 'De Agostini and TV-Shop'; ECJ C-405/98, (2001) ECR I-1795 note 21, (2001) 49 GRUR Int. 553 – 'Gourmet'.

[11] ECJ 120/78, (1979) ECR 649, (1979) 3 CMLR 494, (1979) 32 NJW 1766 – 'Cassis de Dijon'.

[12] ECJ 120/78, (1979) ECR 649, (1979) 3 CMLR 494, (1979) 32 NJW 1766 – 'Cassis de Dijon'; ECJ 178/84, (1987) ECR 1227, (1988) 1 CMLR 780, (1987) 40 NJW 1133 – 'Purity requirements for beer'.

2. *Harmonization by secondary European law*

a) Foundations and concepts of harmonization

National law of unfair competition is allowed to restrict the import of goods and services if the measures fall outside the scope of the basic freedoms or if they are justified. If intra-community trade is not concerned at all the basic freedoms are per se not applicable. In these cases a harmonization could be sensible. The EU is empowered to do so if the harmonization serves the creation of an internal market, art. 95 para. 1 EC (art. III-65 TCE).

The European Commission does not adhere to a stringent concept of harmonization. The standardization of law by the EU creates one fixed set of rules for all Member States; stricter national rules are no longer permissible (full harmonization). In contrast legal harmonization only aims at creating a minimum level of common rules. So-called 'opening clauses' or 'minimum clauses' allow each Member State to pass stricter national rules e.g. for the protection of consumers. Alongside, so-called 'optional clauses' are sometimes used that allow the Member State to choose whether to implement a provision of a directive or not. Finally the European Commission can dispense with harmonization and only apply the principle of origin. According to it each Member State has to accept the law of the other member states. If a service or good can be legally marketed in one member state, another Member State is not allowed to forbid the import into its territory because it considers the service or good to be illegal. In practice, the principle of mutual recognition results in a widening of the scope of art. 4 Injunction Directive 98/27/EC.[13]

b) Directives and regulations regulating the law of unfair competition

Until recently there has been no common European law of unfair competition. Only some areas have been harmonized. Three directives have a strong impact on the law of unfair competition. The Misleading Advertising Directive 84/450/EEC sets forth rules for misleading advertisements but only sets a minimum standard of harmonization.[14] Therefore in this area the law of the Member State still has the most important relevance. The Misleading Advertising Directive 84/450/EEC was supplemented by the Comparative Advertising Directive 97/55/EC.

[13] See 11th reason for consideration of the Injunction-Directive 98/27/EC.

[14] Art. 7 para. 1 Directive 84/450/EEC, modified by Directive 97/55/EC.

One has to note that this directive does not allow for deviating national provisions.[15] These directives[16] protect the interests of consumers as well as competitors and the general public (art. 4 para. 1). In 1998 the Product Price Directive 98/6/EC[17] was introduced. The Injunction Directive 98/27/EC[18] regulates the possibility of consumer associations to sue.

At the same time there are directives that have some relevance for the law of unfair competition such as Directive 97/36/EC amending Directive 89/552/EEC concerning the pursuit of television broadcasting activities,[19] Directive 92/28/EC on the advertising of medicinal products for human use,[20] Directive 99/44/EC on the sale of consumer goods,[21] Directive 97/7/EC on distance contracts and Directive 2000/31/EC on e-commerce.[22] The latter makes use of the principle of mutual recognition.[23]

On June 18, 2003 the Directorate-General for Health and Consumer Protection issued a proposal for a directive concerning unfair commercial practices.[24] This proposal makes use of the ideas developed in the Green Paper on EU Consumer Protection of October 2, 2002.[25] In the

15 Art. 7 para. 2 Directive 84/450/EEC, modified by Directive 97/55/EC. See ECJ C-44/01, (2003) 105 GRUR 533 (536) notes 43 et seq. – *Pippig v. Hartlauer*.

16 Council Directive of September 10, 1984 concerning misleading and comparative advertising, OJ L 250, 17, amended by Directive 97/55/EC of European Parliament and of the Council of October 6, 1997, L 290, 18, corrected by Corrigendum OJ L 194, 54.

17 Directive 98/6/EC of the European Parliament and of the Council of February 16, 1998 on consumer protection in the indication of the prices of products offered to consumers, OJ L 80, 27.

18 Directive 98/27/EC on the European Parliament and of the Council of May 19, 1998 on injunctions for the protection of consumers' interests, OJ L 166/51; for an analysis of the first case under this directive see P. Rott and A. von der Ropp, *Stand der grenzüberschreitenden Unterlassungsklage in Europa* (2004) 9 ZZPInt 3.

19 Directive 97/36/EC of the European Parliament and of the Council of June 30, 1997 amending Council Directive 89/552/EEC on the coordination of certain provisions laid down by law, regulation or administrative action in member states concerning the pursuit of television broadcasting activities, OJ L 202, 60.

20 Council Directive 92/28/EEC of March 31, 1992 on the advertising of medicinal products for human use, OJ L 113, 13.

21 Directive 1999/44/EC of the European Parliament and of the Council of May 25, 1999 on certain aspects of the sale of consumer goods and associated guarantees, OJ L 171, 12, (1999) 52 NJW 2421; regarding art. 2 para. 2 lit. (d) Directive 1999/44/EC cf. below Case 5 (Discontinued models).

22 Directive 2001/31/EC of the European Parliament and of the Council of June 8, 2000 on certain legal aspects of information society services, in particular electronic commerce, in the Internal Market, OJ L 178, 1.

23 Art. 3 para. 1 Directive 2000/31/EC. 24 COM (2003), 356 final.

25 Green Paper on EU Consumer Protection of October 2, 2002, COM (2001), 531 final, BR-Drs. 851/01; Follow-up Communication to the Green paper on Consumer Protection of June 11, 2002, COM (2002), 289 final.

area of business-to-consumer (B2C) transactions it intends to protect consumers by introducing clearly defined prohibitions and a general clause (art. 5). Moreover, art. 4 para. 1 introduces the principle of mutual recognition. And Directive 2005/29/EC concerning unfair commercial practices has now been passed.[26] German scholars welcome the introduction of a general clause.[27] Finally, one has to take into consideration the Regulation (EC) No. 2006/2004 on consumer protection cooperation.[28]

c) Proposal for amendments

On October 2, 2001 the Internal Market Directorate-General issued a proposal for a regulation concerning sales promotions in the internal market.[29] This proposal considers it sufficient to harmonize protection in the field of sales promotions like rebates, free of charge give-aways or prize draws by introducing duties of transparency and information. Consumers shall, for example, be protected against faked rebates by introducing the duty to indicate the former price and the duration of its application.

3. *The enforcement of European law*

In its decisions the ECJ has always emphasized that the enforcement of duties based on European law has to be 'effective, proportional and act as a deterrent'.[30] Directives very often include no[31] or only very

[26] Directive 2005/29/EC of the European Parliament and of the Council concerning unfair business-to consumer commercial practices in the Internal Market and amending directives 84/450EEC, 97/7/EC and 98/27/EC, OJ L 149, 22.

[27] F. Hennig-Bodewig and G. Schricker (2001) 47 WRP 1367 (1378); H.-W. Micklitz and J. Keßler (2002) 50 GRUR Int. 885 (895); F. Hennig-Bodewig (2002) 50 GRUR Int. 389 (396); H. Köhler, J. Bornkamm and F. Henning-Bodewig (2002) 48 WRP 1317 (1325); K.H. Fezer (2001) 47 WRP 989 (994); O. Sosnitza, *Das Koordinatensystem des Rechts des unlauteren Wettbewerbs im Spannungsfeld zwischen Europa und Deutschland* (2003) 104 GRUR 739; H. Gameritz (2003) 49 WRP 143 (161).

[28] Regulation (EC) No. 2006/2004 of the European Parliament and of the Council of October 27, 2004 on cooperation between national authorities responsible for the enforcement of consumer protection laws (the Regulation on consumer protection cooperation),OJ L 364, 1.

[29] Proposal for a European Parliament and Council Regulation concerning sales promotions in the Internal Market (presented by the Commission pursuant to art. 250 para. 2 of the EC Treaty), COM (2001), 546 final; amended in COM (2002), 585 final.

[30] ECJ 68/88, (1989) ECR I-2965 note 22 – 'Commission/Greece'; ECJ C-326/88, (1989) ECR I-2911 note 17 – 'Hansen'. See before already ECJ 14/83, (1984) ECR 1891 notes 23 et seq., 28 – 'von Colson'.

[31] Art. 10 Timeshare Directive 94/47/EC: 'The Member States shall make provision in their legislation for the consequences of non-compliance with this Directive'.

vague[32] provisions concerning the enforcement of duties. The formulation of the ECJ can be found in different directives.[33] In some respects the enforcement is regulated in more detail as with the supervision by public authorities[34] or provisions concerning damages.[35] Modern directives normally include the possibility to seek relief in front of the courts or public authorities[36] or through effective complaints procedures.[37]

a) Misleading and Comparative Advertising Directive 84/450/EEC

Directive 84/450/EEC includes provisions concerning enforcement. But because of the different legal systems, only a minimum harmonization is introduced. Because of that there is widespread doubt whether the directive has actually contributed to a marked harmonization.[38] Moreover the directive allows for choosing between different options.

Objects of claims

(1) Under Directive 84/450/EEC the Member States shall confer upon the courts or administrative authorities the powers enabling them to order the cessation or the prohibition of misleading advertisement.[39] The courts must be able to order the cessation or the prohibition pre-emptively if the publication is imminent. This decision has to take into account all relevant interests including the interests of the public.[40] The introduction of this option is obligatory. Furthermore the Member States have to introduce a summary procedure. They are free to decide whether decisions in a summary procedure only have preliminary or permanent effect.[41]

(2) The publication of the decision as a further remedy can be chosen by the Member States. They 'may' make use of this option.[42] The right to require the publication of a corrective statement is also formulated as a optional clause.[43]

[32] E.g. art. 4 para. 3 Doorstep Directive 85/577/EEC: 'appropriate consumer protection'.

[33] The starting provision in art. 4 para. 1 84/450/EEC, changed by Directive 97/55/EC, reads: 'adequate and effective means exists to combat...' and art. 13 s. 2 proposal for Council Directive: 'These penalities must be effective, proportionate and constitute a deterrent'.

[34] Art. 12 Consumer Credit Directive 87/102/EEC.

[35] Art. 5 Package Tour Directive 98/314/EC.

[36] Art. 11 of the Distance Contract Directive 97/7/EC; art. 7 para. 2 Unfair Terms Directive 93/13/EEC; art. 6 76/207/EEC: 'to pursue their claims by judicial process'.

[37] Art. 10 Cross Border Credit Transfer Directive 97/5/EC.

[38] A. Beater (1996) 3 ZEuP 200 (227).

[39] Art. 4 para. 2 indent 1.

[40] Art. 4 para. 2 indent 2.

[41] Art. 4 para. 2 subpara. 2.

[42] Art. 4 para. 2 subpara. 3 indent 1.

[43] Art. 4 para. 2 subpara. 3 indent 2.

(3) Neither damages nor administrative fines are regulated.

(4) Furthermore the directive eases the burden of proof for the plaintiff. First the prohibition or the order of cessation can be issued without proof of actual loss or damage or of intention or negligence on the part of the advertiser.[44]

Second courts or administrative authorities are enabled 'to require the advertiser to furnish evidence as to the accuracy of factual claims in advertising, if, taking into account the legitimate interest of the advertiser and any other party to the proceedings, such a requirement appears appropriate on the basis of the circumstances of the particular cases' (art. 6 lit. (a)). If these proofs are insufficient, the factual claims can be deemed incorrect (art. 6 lit. (b)).

Plaintiffs and the authorities to impose sanctions

(1) Persons or organizations having a legitimate interest in prohibiting misleading advertisement shall be able to take legal action against such advertising.[45] Already this directive introduces the right to sue for associations with the formulation of legitimate interest.[46]

(2) The Member States are free to decide whether legal action shall be pursued before the courts or before administrative authorities.[47] The directive includes further details concerning the control of misleading advertisement by administrative authorities. Administrative authorities have to be impartial and have to be vested with appropriate powers to exercise their control.[48] Decisions of administrative authorities have to include the reasons for the decision.[49] A judicial review must be possible for improper or unreasonable exercises of its power by the administrative authority or improper or unreasonable failure to exercise the said powers.[50]

Self-control

Finally, the directive allows for the introduction of mechanisms of self-control. But such institutions can only be introduced in addition to legal proceedings before the courts or administrative authorities (art. 5).[51]

[44] Art. 4 para. 2. [45] Art. 4 par. 1 subpara. 2.

[46] A. Beater, *Europäisches Recht gegen den unlauteren Wettbewerb – Ansatzpunkte, Grundlagen, Entwicklung, Erforderlichkeit* (2003) 11 ZEuP 11 (36).

[47] Art. 4 para. 1 subpara. 2, 3. [48] Art. 4 para. 3 lit. (a) and (b).

[49] Art. 4 para. 3 subpara. 2 s. 1. [50] Art. 4 para. 3 subpara. 2 s. 2.

[51] Concerning the recommendation 98/257/EC about the principles of extrajudicial dispute settlement, cf. below B.III.1.

b) Injunction directive 98/27/EC

The Injunction Directive distinguishes between objects of claims and parties. This directive also includes several optional clauses that allows the Member States to decide whether to implement some measures or not. Furthermore the directive allows for more stringent national law; it therefore only intends to establish a minimum harmonization (art. 7). The main purpose of the directive is to facilitate cross-border legal action by associations within the European Union. Accordingly, qualified associations of one Member State whose legitimate interests have been infringed are allowed to sue in another Member State where the infringement has its origin (art. 4 para.1). This would, for example, allow the Swedish Ombudsman to sue in Germany or a German consumer association to take legal action in England although there may be no such possibilities for local associations in those Member States.[52]

Objects of claims

The objects of claim are either the cessation or the prohibition of the infringement.[53] This has to be possible with all due expediency, where appropriate by way of summary procedure.[54] The publication of the decision and of corrective statements can be introduced where appropriate.[55] In this regard the Member States are free to introduce this remedy. Damages are not regulated in general. An order against the losing party for payments into the public purse or to any other beneficiary in the event of failure to comply can be issued insofar as the legal system of the Member State concerned so permits.[56] Class actions are not regulated in the directive.

Plaintiffs and the authorities to impose sanctions

(1) The directive names as possible plaintiffs independent public authorities. This includes, for example, the Swedish Ombudsman or the UK

[52] D. Baetge, *Das Recht der Verbandsklage auf neuen Wegen* (1999) 112 ZZP 329 (345 f.); R. Greger, *Neue Regeln für die Verbandsklage im Verbraucherschutz- und Wettbewerbsrecht* (2000) 53 NJW 2457 (2461); for an analysis of the first case under this directive see P. Rott and A. von der Ropp, *Stand der grenzüberschreitenden Unterlassungsklage in Europa* (2004) 9 ZZPInt 3.

[53] Art. 2 para. 1 lit. (a).

[54] Art. 2 para. 1 lit. (a).

[55] Art. 2 para. 1 lit. (b).

[56] Art. 2 para. 1 lit. (c).

Office of Fair Trading.[57] Apart from this organizations are allowed to sue according to the criteria laid down by national law (art. 3 lit. (a), (b)). But this only includes associations aiming at the protection of consumers' interests (art. 1).

(2) The Member States shall designate the courts or the administrative authorities competent to rule on the proceedings brought by qualified associations (art. 2 para. 1). Further requirements are not regulated.

Self-control

According to art. 5 Injunction Directive 98/27/EC the Member States may introduce provisions whereby the party that intends to seek an injunction can only start this procedure after it has tried to achieve the cessation of the infringement in consultation with the defendant. The role model for this provision seems to be the German consultation procedure.[58] But the directive only regulates the relationship between infringer and administrative authorities or associations. The relation between two competitors is not touched upon.

c) Recommendations on the out-of-court settlement of consumer disputes 98/257/EC and 2001/310/EC

Finally, the Out-of-Court Settlement Recommendation 98/257/EC[59] and 2001/310/EC[60] are of special importance. Though recommendations are not binding,[61] they are nevertheless of practical relevance since the member states actually adhere to them. In Recommendation 98/257/EC the out-of-court settlement is defined as the active intervention by a third party who proposes or imposes a solution.[62] Recommendation 2001/310/EC also applies its principles to independent institutions

[57] D. Baetge (1999) 112 ZZP 329 (337).

[58] See D. Baetge (1999) 112 ZZP 329 (346), with the pointer that the proposal of the Council Directive still talks about a 'warning', cf. OJ C 107 of April 13, 1996, p. 5.

[59] 98/257/EC: Commission Recommendation of March 30, 1998 on the principles applicable to the bodies responsible for out-of-court settlement of consumer disputes, OJ L 115, 31.

[60] 2001/310/EC: Commission Recommendation of April 4, 2001 on the principles for out-of-court bodies involved in the consensual resolution on consumer disputes (notified under document C (2001), OJ L 109, 56.

[61] Art. 249 para. 3 EC.

[62] The warning of the injured person against the infringer thus does not belong to it, see 9th reason for consideration.

which induce the parties to reach a consensual solution. Both recommendations name independence, transparency and efficiency as guiding principles.

d) Directive 2005/29/EC concerning unfair commercial practices

In its articles 11 to 13 Directive 2005/29/EC concerning unfair commercial practices adopts nearly word by word the remedies of art. 4 to 6 of the Misleading and Comparative Advertising Directive 84/450/EEC.[63] Voluntary self-policing by means of rules of conduct are mentioned in art. 10. In general terms art. 13 demands that remedies have to be effective, proportionate and deterrent. Incidentally, it is the task of the Member States to constitute and enforce these sanctions.[64]

e) Proposal for a regulation concerning sales promotions

In art. 6 the proposal lists remedies. According to art. 6 para. 1 the defendant has to prove the accuracy of the information at the request of a court or an administrative authority. The promoter shall provide, free of charge, an address to which complaints can be directed to him (para. 2). A promoter shall respond to an initial complaint within four weeks of the receipt of that complaint (para. 3). This instrument has so far been in the Misleading and Comparative Advertising Directive 84/450/EEC. Deviating from the Directive Concerning Unfair Commercial Practices the promoter has to agree to an out-of-court settlement procedure or a code of conduct (para. 4). This provision of the proposal was heavily criticized.[65] The amendment of the proposal now regulates that out-of-court settlements are only obligatory if national law provides so.

f) Proposal for a European directive – the German perspective

The proposal for a directive by the Directorate-General for Health and Consumer Protection was heavily criticized by German scholars because the proposal only regulates the relationship between businesses and consumers whereas the Misleading and Comparative Advertising

[63] Directive 2005/29/EC of the European Parliament and of the Council concerning unfair business-to consumer commercial practices in the Internal Market and amending directives 84/450EEC, 97/7/EC and 98/27/EC of May 11, 2005, OJ L 149, 22.

[64] See recitals 22 and 9 of Directive 2005/29/EC.

[65] Begr. RegE, BT-Drs. 15/1487, p. 12; H. Gameritz (2003) 49 WRP 143 (154 et seq.); S. Göhre, *Frischer Wind aus Brüssel?* (2002) 48 WRP 36 (39) lists the rejecting member states Germany, Belgium, Denmark, Austria, Finland, and Sweden.

Directive 84/450/EEC also protects the competitor.[66] To remedy that German legal scholars and judges drafted their own proposal. In accordance with the amendment of the German UWG in 2004 the proposed European directive shall also protect the competitor and the general public. Moreover, the introduction of a general clause that is further partitioned into typical cases is favoured.[67]

The proposal served as a role model for the amendment of the German UWG in 2004. Whereas the proposal for the German UWG elaborates on the remedies it explicitly refrains from any recommendations concerning remedies for a European directive. It only refers to the status quo that has been reached by art. 4 of the Misleading and Comparative Advertising Directive 84/450/EEC. Thus the different competent authorities to impose sanctions (see art. 4 Directive 84/450/EEC) and the widespread optional clauses are not further questioned.[68] Nevertheless, the German legislature hails its amendment of the German UWG as a 'reference model for a future harmonized European law of unfair competition'.[69] Whether or not these high aspirations can come to fruition will have to be examined on a comparative law basis.

There exists a further proposal by H.-W. Micklitz and J. Keßler. They would like to vest consumer and professional associations with the right to take legal action.[70]

g) Regulation (EC) No. 2006/2004 on consumer protection cooperation

Regulation (EC) No. 2006/2004 on consumer protection cooperation is of special importance.[71] It is based on the assumption that there are deficits in the enforcement of the law of unfair competition and of

[66] See art. 1 of the Misleading and Comparative Advertising Directive 84/450/EEC, as well as F. Hennig-Bodewig and G. Schricker (2002) 50 GRUR Int. 319 (320); H.-W. Micklitz and J. Keßler (2002) 50 GRUR Int. 885 (895); F. Hennig-Bodewig (2002) 50 GRUR Int. 389 (396); H. Köhler and T.Lettl (2002) 48 WRP 1019 (1033, 1051); O. Sosnitza (2003) 104 GRUR 739 (741); cf. now also J. Glöckner, in H. Harte-Bavenkamm and F. Henning-Bodweig *UWG* (2004), Einl B. notes 151 et seq.

[67] H. Köhler, J. Bornkamm and F. Henning-Bodewig, *Vorschlag für eine Richtlinie zum Lauterkeitsrecht und eine UWG-Reform* (2002) 48 WRP 1317.

[68] See the missing explanation in the notes, in H. Köhler, J. Bornkamm and F. Henning-Bodewig (2002) 48 WRP 1317 (1324, 1327).

[69] See speech by the German Minister of Justice, Brigitte Zypries, in front of the Deutsche Bundestag, September 25, 2003, Minutes No. 15/63, p. 5363.

[70] See art. 7 of their draft in: H.-W. Micklitz and J. Keßler (2002) 50 GRUR Int. 885 (901).

[71] See 2nd reason for proposal.

consumer protection.[72] Therefore the Member States have to institute a public authority that is competent to take actions against cross-border infringements.[73] Authorities from other Member States shall be able to address their complaints to this public authority. This regulation applies to many consumer protection directives.[74] In contrast to Directive 84/450/EEC respectively 98/27/EC the Member States are bound to introduce such a public authority. The regulation has been in force since October 2004, becoming applicable on December 29, 2005.[75]

4. *Assessment*

a) Status quo of harmonization

Concerning the European law of unfair competition, it is definitely a step forward that enforcement is regulated in more detail than in many other areas of European law. The harmonization of provisions governing injunctions have made great progress. Another positive aspect is that the principle of mutual recognition[76] laid down in art. 4 Injunction Directive 98/27/EC has broadened the ability to sue. Legal scholars hope that this will put pressure on some member states further to harmonize their national law. This happened in England where, paradoxically, foreign consumer associations, for example, were able to sue whereas English consumer associations were not allowed to take legal action in English courts.[77]

b) Defects

Taking into consideration Graphic 2 one realizes that in the area of objects of claims, the introduction of certain remedies is left open to the member state (e.g. publication of decisions or duty to publish corrective statements). This has not changed with the introduction of Directive 2005/29/EC concerning unfair commercial practices. Regulation (EC) No. 2006/2004 on consumer protection cooperation only applies to

[72] Green Paper on EU Consumer Protection, COM (2001), 531 final; Follow-up Communication to the Green paper on Consumer Protection, COM (2002), 289 final.

[73] See art. 3 lit. (b); art. 4 para. 6 Regulation (EC) No. 2006/2004.

[74] It is therefore comparable with the Injunction Directive 98/26/EC.

[75] See art. 22 Regulation (EC) No. 2006/2004.

[76] See 11th reason for consideration of the Injunction Directive 98/27/EC.

[77] J. Dickie (1997) 16 Civ.Just.Q. 91 (92); D. Baetge (1999) 112 ZZP 329 (344); for an analysis of the first case under this directive cf. P. Rott and A. von der Ropp, *Stand der grenzüberschreitenden Unterlassungsklage in Europa* (2004) 9 ZZPInt 3.

cross-border infringements.[78] The common basis of European unfair competition law is therefore rather small.

On issues concerning plaintiffs, competent authorities to impose sanctions and the burden of proof only a minimum harmonization has taken place. Either the implementation is left to national law or due to the different legal traditions in the Member States, legal proceedings have not been harmonized. The directives state that courts and administrative authorities are on an equal footing. On top of this, voluntary self-policing is possible. Euphemistically this could be called 'an elastic treatment of enforcement'.[79] Actually, remedies are polymorphic and unsystematically regulated, as is the case with the substantive provisions of the law of unfair competition.[80] Taking this into consideration, it is astonishing that up to now there have not been any detailed proposals for a further harmonization of the system of remedies. The above-mentioned criticisms[81] that the existing law has not been properly implemented and still hinders competition have thus not been refuted and need to be further examined in more detail.

[78] See art. 3 lit. (b); Art. 4 para. 6 Regulation (EC) No. 2006/2004.

[79] G. Schricker and F. Hennig-Bodewig (2001) 47 WRP 1367 (1369, 1375); H. Köhler and T. Lettl (2002) 48 WRP 1019 (1047).

[80] A. Beater, *Unlauterer Wettbewerb* (2002), § 8 note 104.

[81] See A.2 note 58.

IV. Enforcement and sanctions under US - American unfair competition law

1. *Material provisions*

a) The legal background

In the Anglo-American legal system unfair competition law has developed slowly. Originally there was only common law that aimed primarily at protecting competitors. Over the last century these principles have been supplemented by statutory regulations. These regulations are monitored on the state and federal level since both have legislative competence. Moreover, constitutional law can be involved: the Supreme Court has stated that truthful advertising is protected by freedom of speech.[1]

The search for unfair competition law is made difficult by the fact that in the Anglo-American legal system infringements of competitors[2] are regarded as falling under unfair competition law whereas infringements of consumers' rights are often considered as unfair and deceptive practices, covered by recently developing consumer law.[3] Sec. 5 FTCA thus distinguishes between 'unfair methods of competition' and 'unfair or deceptive acts or practices'.[4]

In the USA 'unfair competition' is considered to be a commercial tort[5] that has its roots in general tort law but has to be separated from it. Consequently, separate Restatements for this area have been developed.[6] It is generally agreed on that the term 'unfair competition' is

[1] *Central Hudson Gas & Elec. Corp. v. Public Service of New York*, 447 U.S. 557, 100 S. Ct. 2343, 65 L. Ed. 2d 341 (1980); *Virginia State Board of Pharmacy v. Virginia Citizens Consumer Council, Inc.*, 425 U.S. 748, 96 S. Ct. 1817, 48 L. Ed. 2d 346 (1976).

[2] Unfair competition law is often regarded as an annex to trademark law, see e.g. B. Pattishall, D. Hilliard and J. Welch, *Trademarks and Unfair Competition* (4th edn 2000), p. 4; J. Ginsburg, J. Litman, D. Goldberg and M. Kevlin, *Trademark and Unfair Competition Law, Cases and Materials* (1996, Supp. 1998); J. McCarthy, *McCarthy on Trademarks and Unfair Competition*, vol. 6 (4th edn Supp. 2000), pp. 1–16; *Restatement (Third) of Unfair Competition* (1995), §§ 1–49.

[3] See e.g. H. Alperin and R. Chase, *Consumer Law. Sales Practices and Credit Regulation*, vol. 2 (1986, Supp. 2004); D. Pridgen, *Consumer Protection and the Law* (2003); M. Greenfield, *Consumer Transactions* (4th edn 2003).

[4] See the definition in A.4 note 9; regarding this differentiation cf. N. Allen, *North Carolina Unfair Business Practice* (3rd edn 2000, Supp. 2004), 24–2 et seq.

[5] *Fry v. Layne-Western Co.*, 282 F.2d 97, 126 U.S.P.Q. 30, 126 U.S.P.Q. 423 (8th Cir. 1960).

[6] *Restatement (Third) of Unfair Competition* (1995), §§ 1–49; H. Perlman, *The Restatement of the Law of Unfair Competition: A work in Progress* (1990) 80 Trademark Rep. 461.

hard to define: unfair competition is 'too hard'[7] or 'unfair competition consists in selling goods by means which shock judicial sensibilities'.[8] While the FTCA tries to define unfair methods of competition[9], the Restatements abstain from such a definition.[10] Though the Restatements of Unfair Competition refer to typical cases as deceptive marketing, infringement of trademarks and appropriation of intangible trade values, they generally only refer to state and federal legislation.[11] Apart from unfair competition law in consumer fraud cases the RICO[12] can, for example, be applied.

Common law

Just as in English law, the common law mainly gives private remedies for various types of interference with trade relations. The competitor is protected in cases of palming off, misappropriation and malicious competition.[13]

(1) One area of unfair competition law is constituted by deceptive marketing. In the early common law, unfair competition was often equated with 'passing off' (or 'palming off'). That is, 'passing off' one's product as the product of another seller by means of similar labelling, packaging or advertising.[14] Cases of deceptive imitation are mostly sanctioned by trademark law. Palming off can also occur in cases of deceptive product substitution or alteration. This particular form of palming off might be accomplished by deceptively substituting less well-known or inferior goods for better known or higher quality

[7] J. McCarthy, *McCarthy on Trademarks and Unfair Competition*, vol. 6 (4th edn Supp. 2000), pp. 1–16.

[8] *Margarete Steiff, Inc. v. Bing*, 215 F. 204 (D.N.Y. 1914).

[9] Sec. 5 (a) FTCA, Title 15 U.S.C. § 45 reads: 'Unfair methods of competition in or affecting commerce, or unfair or deceptive acts or practices in or affecting commerce, are hereby declared unlawful.'

[10] In *Restatement (Third) of Unfair Competition* (1995), § 1.

[11] See the same result in J. McCarthy, *McCarthy on Trademarks and Unfair Competition*, vol. 6 (4th edn Supp. 2000), pp. 1–23.

[12] Federal Rackeeter Influenced and Corrupt Organization provisions of the Organized Crime Control Act of 1970, 18 U.S.C. §§ 1961–1968.

[13] C. McManis, *Intellectual Property and Unfair Competition* (5th edn 2004), p. 9.

[14] *International News Service v. Associated Press*, 248 U.S. 215, 63 L. Ed 211, 39 S. Ct. 68, 2 A.L.R. 293 (1918); *Sears, Roebuck & Co. v. Stiffel Co.*, 376 U.S. 225, 232, 84 S. Ct. 784, 789, 11 L. Ed. 2d 661 (1964); J. McCarthy, *McCarthy on Trademarks and Unfair Competition*, vol. 6 (4th edn Supp. 2000), pp. 1–29; *International News Service v. Associated Press*, 248 U.S. 215, 63 L. Ed 211, 39 S. Ct. 68, 2 A.L.R. 293 (1918).

goods. It might also be accomplished by selling goods as new or adulterated goods as the original.[15]

(2) Malicious competition occurs if the business can be shown to have been operated purely for the purpose of causing economic harm to another business and with the intention of terminating the business after that purpose is accomplished.[16]

(3) Also the tort of defamation can be resorted to with possibility of seeking injunctive relief and damages. But one has to be aware that the courts have set a higher standard for proving defamation. One needs to prove 'actual malice' which the court defines as knowledge or reckless disregard of the statement's falsity.[17]

Federal statue law – FTCA and Lanham Act § 43 (a)

The Federal Trade Commission[18] has monitored unfair methods of competition since 1914. It derives its competence from the FTCA.[19] Sec. 5 FTCA states: 'Unfair methods of competition in or affecting commerce, or unfair or deceptive acts or practices in or affecting commerce, are declared unlawful.' One has to ask whether the practice offends public policy as it has been established by statutes, common law or otherwise, whether it is immoral, unethical, oppressive or unscrupulous and whether it causes substantial injury to consumers or competitors or other businesses.[20] Moreover, the FTC also monitors infringements of common law if this is required by 'public interest'. This is the case if it causes substantial injury to consumers or other businessmen. The consumer is only protected against very obvious abuses which come close to common law fraud or are regarded as a direct intrusion into his or her privacy.[21]

[15] C. McManis, *Intellectual Property and Unfair Competition* (5th edn 2004), p. 216; see also Case 2 (Watch imitations I) and Case 3 (Whisky).

[16] *Beardsley v. Kilmer*, 236 N.Y. 80, 140 N.E. 203 (N.Y. 1923); C. McManis, *Intellectual Property and Unfair Competition* (5th edn 2004), p. 11; See Case 6 (Child labour).

[17] *New York Times Co. v. Sullivan*, 376 U.S. 254, 84 S. Ct. 710, 11 L. Ed. 2d 686 (1964); *Gertz v. Robert Welch Inc.*, 418 U.S. 323, 94 S. Ct. 2997, 41 L. Ed. 2d 789 (1974); C. McManis, *Intellectual Property and Unfair Competition* (5th edn 2004), p. 360.

[18] www.ftc.gov. [19] Title 15 U.S.C. § 45 (a) (1).

[20] *FTC v. The Sperry & Hutchinson Co.*, 405 U.S. 233, 92 S. Ct. 892, 31 L. Ed. 2d 170 (1972); *In re International Harvester Co.*, 104 FTC 949 (1984); *Orkin Extermination Co., Inc. v. FTC*, 849 F.2d 1354 (11th Cir. 1988).

[21] The competence of the FTC was strongly restricted. The FTC could not regulate an 'unfair' act or practice unless it 'causes or is likely to cause substantial injury to consumers that is not reasonably avoidable by consumers themselves and not

The Lanham Act was passed as a federal act. § 43 (a)[22] has two separate general provisions of use of false or misleading representations of fact. Subsec. 1 is a general prohibition of statements that are likely to cause confusion as to the origin, sponsorship, approval of goods or services or commercial activities of two different persons. Subsec. 2 only applies to commercial advertising or promotion; it prohibits statements that misrepresent the nature, characteristics of another person or the maker of the statement. It is applied to almost all types of false advertising, trademark infringement and trade dress simulation.[23] Finally, there exist various specialized acts such as the Federal Cigarette Labelling and Advertising Act.[24]

State law – unfair and deceptive acts and practices (UDAP)

The FTC does not have exclusive jurisdiction to combat unfair practices;[25] it shares this competence with the states where the Attorney Generals enforce state law. For this purpose the FTC has developed a model act.[26] In all states acts exist which prohibit 'unfair and deceptive acts or practices' these are the State Unfair Competition Acts,[27] sometimes referred to as 'baby unfair competition acts'.[28] For these the FTCA, the FTC Rules and Guidelines are used for orientation.[29] Besides unfair competition through advertisements, these acts also cover deceptive acts in connection with credits, debt collection, real property, insurance etc.[30]

outweighed by countervailing benefits to consumers or to competition', H.R.2243; see R. Moore, R. Farrar and E. Collins, *Advertising and Public Relations Law* (1998), p. 139.

22 Lanham Act § 43a, 15 U.S.C.A. § 1125 (a).

23 C. McKenney and G. Long III, *Federal Unfair Competition: Lanham Act § 43 (a)* (1993); J. McCarthy, *McCarthy on Trademarks and Unfair Competition*, 6 vol. (4th edn supplement 2000), pp. 1–35.

24 Title 15 U.S.C. § 1331 et seq.

25 The FTC is competent as far as commerce is concerned. There is a wide understanding of it as interstate commerce, but it may concern purely local questions, cf. *Federal Trade Commission v. Bunte Bros.*, 312 U.S. 349, 61 S. Ct. 580, 85 L. Ed 881 (1941); D. Pridgen, *Consumer Protection and the Law* (2003), p. 550.

26 Unfair Trade Protection Act, 29 Suggested State Legislation 141 (1970).

27 J. Sheldon and C. Carter, *Unfair and Deceptive Acts and Practices* (5th edn 2001), p. 1.

28 See the evidence for the different states, in: *Restatement (Third) of Unfair Competition* (1995), § 1.

29 Regarding North Carolina cf. N. Allen, *North Carolina Unfair Business Practice* (3rd edn Supp. 2004), p. 4 et seq.

30 See e.g. North Carolina General Statute § 75–1.1.; N. Allen, *North Carolina Unfair Business Practice* (3rd edn Supp. 2004), p. 1–1.

b) Selected examples

Misleading – deceptive pricing inducements

(1) Unavailability of advertised items

Advantageous offers used as a decoy are forbidden. In US-American law two typical groups of cases are distinguished: in 'bait and switch' cases the seller lures the customer to his company to then sell him another product different from the one that has been advertised ('switch'). The FTC has prohibited various forms of this practice in numerous individual cases and through an official FTC Guide.[31] Furthermore, it is illegal if the seller does not have sufficient quantity to meet anticipated demand. The FTC's Retail Food Store Advertising and Marketing Practices Rule[32] prohibits advertised offers of retail food when the store does not have the product readily available or has not ordered enough items in adequate time to meet reasonably anticipated demands.[33] This rule is applicable in general to the advertising of other commodities.[34] A number of state UDAP regulations also prohibit the advertising of unavailable items.[35]

The enforcement of these provisions seems to be effective in respect of the generous damages awarded by the courts: some courts are willing to recognize inconvenience, travel expenses, lost time, and loss of the opportunity to purchase as compensable loss.[36] But the seller is able to rule out his responsibility for the unavailability of advertised items by using an appropriate statement of disclosure: advertisements can and must disclose all limitations as to the product, when sold in certain stores or for a certain period of time.[37] In newspaper advertisements one very often finds these restrictions. Cars whose price has been reduced are sold '2 for this price – with ID number', attractive designer clothes 'not available in all stores'[38] or 'limited for the next 72 hours'. The FTC decided that disclosures of limited supply are permitted in order to avoid discouraging the advertising of closeout specials, seasonal products, products of interest only in certain neighbourhoods,

31 *Tashof v. FTC*, 437 F2d. 707 (D.C. Cir. 1970); Guides against Bait Advertising, 16 C.F.R. part 238; S. Kanwit, *Federal Trade Commission*, vol. 2 (Supp. 2003), pp. 22–68.

32 16 C.F.R. part 424. 33 *Kroger Co.*, 90 FTC 459 (1977).

34 *General Motors Corp.*, 93 FTC 860 (1979).

35 J. Sheldon and C. Carter, *Unfair and Deceptive Acts and Practices* (5th edn 2001), p. 177.

36 *Brashears v. Sight N Sound Appliance*, 981 P. 2d 1270 (Okla. App. 1999); *Geismar v. Abraham & Straus*, 109 Misc. 2d 495, 439 N.Y.2d 1005 (Dist. Ct. 1981).

37 J. Sheldon and C. Carter, *Unfair and Deceptive Acts and Practices* (5th edn 2001), p. 177.

38 Robinson & May, *LA Times*, April 23, 2004, A 27; cf. Case 4 (Children's swing).

and of perishable items that would be too expensive to stock in large quantity.[39]

(2) Deceptive pricing

In the USA it is remarkable how often sellers use price reductions in their advertisements: on a daily basis sellers of food or clothes advertise that they have reduced their prices by 30, 40 or even 70 per cent. The slogan 'Buy 1, get 1 free' is also very common.[40] On the first day of sales the autobiography of Bill Clinton was sold at 30 per cent under the official retail price by two large chains of book sellers, Barnes & Noble and Borders.[41] The book was never sold at the suggested retail price. This creates the risk that consumers are lured into retail premises believing they are getting a bargain when they are not. In German law these are called 'moon prices'.[42] Such sales violate the general prohibition of deceptive conduct in the FTCA[43] and state UDAP statutes. The most relevant question here is whether the former price is a bona fide price. This is not always easy to determine. For example, in the jewellery industry it is common to mark prices up as much as five times the cost, and at a later date to discount those regular prices.[44] In the field of cars the Arizona Attorney General has issued that the use of the Manufacturer's Suggested Retail Price in comparative advertising is deceptive when neither the advertiser nor its competitors have made substantial or regular sales at that price.[45] The opinion relies heavily on an FTC guide that sets forth the same principle.[46]

But here also retailers try to avoid responsibility by the use of disclosure statements. The following slogans can often be found in advertisements: 'Original prices are offering prices only and may or may not have resulted in sales. Advertised merchandise may be available at these or

[39] Federal Trade Commission, Amendment to Trade Regulation Rule Concerning Retail Food Store Advertising and Marketing Practices, 54 Fed. Reg. 35456, 35463 (August 28, 1989).

[40] 'Buy 1, get 1 Free, Jockey for men, starts tomorrow', Robinson & May, *LA Times*, April 20, 2004, A 21.

[41] 'Instead of $35 for $24.50', cf. *LA Times*, June 23, 2004, A 10.

[42] Völker, in H. Harte-Bavendamm and F. Henning-Bodewig, *UWG* (2004), § 5 note 554.

[43] *Giant Food, Inc. v. FTC*, 322 F.2d 977 (D.C. Cir. 1963).

[44] See in detail J. Sheldon and C. Carter, *Unfair and Deceptive Acts and Practices* (5th edn 2001), p. 412; There are big differences between a non-binding price recommendation and the actual sales price, e.g. for suitcases.

[45] Arizona Attorney General Opinion I95-16 (R95-33), Clearinghouse No. 51.269 (12-12-95).

[46] 16 C.F.R. § 233.3 (f).

similar sale prices in upcoming sales events this season. Original prices are used for merchandise with permanent price reductions. Interim markdowns have been taken. Selections vary.'[47] Or: 'Save 45–75 per cent on clearance men's fashion' and in the small print one finds: 'Excludes men's designer sportswear collection.'[48]

In addition to the concrete price one also regularly finds the price per measuring unit. This corresponds to art. 3 para. 1 Product Price Directive 98/6/EC. But in the USA it is allowed and therefore common to give the price without the value added tax or any other taxes. The rate of the value added tax differs from state to state and ranges from 0 per cent in Texas to nearly 10 per cent in California. By excluding the value added tax it is possible to devise advertisements for all 50 states uniformly without being forced to change the content for every state. In contrast to this the Product Price Directive 98/6/EC requires the display of the retail price including the value added tax and all other taxes.[49]

Harassment – telemarketing fraud

(1) On the federal level the Telephone Consumer Protection Act of 1991 (TCPA)[50] was passed. It only allows telephone calls between 8.00 a.m. and 9.00 p.m. and obliges the caller to identify himself and to name the purpose of the call. Additionally, he is forced to keep a 'do-not-call' list for at least ten years. Advertisement via fax machines and the use of artificial or pre-recorded voices is prohibited. Congress revisited the area of telemarketing fraud in 1994 with the Telemarketing and Consumer Fraud and Abuse Prevention Act.[51] The statute requires the FTC to issue regulations prohibiting deceptive and abusive telemarketing acts and practices. It does not intend to regulate the telemarketing as such, but only to curb obvious misrepresentations and abuses which are specified in the rule.[52] The telephone company has to give the consumer a lot of information but cold-calling is not forbidden.[53]

[47] Robinson & May, *LA Times*, April 20, 2004, A 21.

[48] Macy's, *LA Times*, June 25, 2004, A 7.

[49] Art. 3 para. 1, 2 lit. a) Price Indication-Directive; implemented in Germany e.g. in § 1 PAngV.

[50] 47 U.S.C. § 227. [51] 15 U.S.C. §§ 6101–6108.

[52] See in detail J. Sheldon and C. Carter, *Unfair and Deceptive Acts and Practices* (5th edn 2001), p. 412; D. Pridgen, *Consumer Protection and the Law* (2003), pp. 937 et seq.

[53] N. Reich, *United States of America*, in H.-W. Micklitz and J. Keßler, p. 432.

The FTC adopted the Telemarketing Sale Rule of 1995.[54] The FTC's Rule goes well beyond these mandated provisions. The rule is not applicable to e-mail spam,[55] unlike the regulations in the E-commerce Directive 2000/31/EC.[56] In addition, the FTC adopted the Mail or Telephone Order Merchandise Rule of 1993.[57] The rights of the buyer are limited to receiving reliable information on the shipping date of the products ordered, and on eventual impediments, revisions and delays.[58] There is no right of withdrawal as in Directive 97/77/EC.[59]

(2) Most states have enacted their own protections against telemarketing fraud. A number of states prohibit telemarketers from calling people who have listed themselves on a state-wide database as not wanting to receive telephone solicitations.[60] The possibilities for consumers to sue are interesting.[61]

Seasonal close-out sales

There is no regulation in the United States of close-out sales or clearance sales remotely comparable to the rigid regulations of some European countries.[62]

Deceptive non-disclosure

The FTC has never posited an affirmative duty on the part of advertisers to 'tell all'. Deceptive non-disclosure thus has generally consisted of the omission of those facts that are necessary to make other express or implied representations not misleading.[63] The common element of unfairness consists in consumers not being adequately informed about risks involved in the transaction and therefore being unable to avoid them.[64]

54 16 C.F.R. § 310, published at 60 Fed. Reg. 43842. 55 § 16 C.F.R. § 310.2 (u).
56 N. Reich, *United States of America*, in H.-W. Micklitz and J. Keßler, p. 432.
57 § 16 C.F.R. § 435.
58 J. Sheldon and C. Carter, *Unfair and Deceptive Acts and Practices* (5th edn 2001), p. 416.
59 N. Reich, *United States of America*, in H.-W. Micklitz and J. Keßler, p. 431.
60 Ark. Stat. Ann. § 4–99–401; Tenn. Code Ann. 47–18–1526; Calif. Bus.and Professions Code § 17511.3 (a).
61 See below IV.2(e).
62 J. Maxeiner and F. Kent, *United States*, in J. Maxeiner and P. Schotthöfer (eds.), *Advertising Law in Europe and North America* (2nd edn 1999), p. 513 (526).
63 C. McManis, *Intellectual Property and Unfair Competition* (5th edn 2004), p. 407.
64 N. Reich, *United States of America*, in: H.-W. Micklitz and J. Keßler, p. 435.

'Deceptive non-disclosure' can occur if foreign goods are not marked as foreign because consumers prefer American merchandise.[65] But there is a strong opinion that argues that this obligation infringes art. IX GATT.[66] In the *Budget Rent-a-Car* case the unfairness consisted in renting out cars without informing consumers about prior recall actions.[67] Another case of deceptive non-disclosure was investigated by the FTC when Camel played down the risks of smoking using the cartoon character 'Joe Camel'.[68] Finally, a Becks advertisement was also censured showing people on a boat drinking beer. The Commission charged Becks with dismissing the risks associated with such activities, which are substantially increased by the consumption of alcohol.[69]

2. *Remedies – objective of claims*

Whenever an advertising suit comes into consideration, the potential plaintiff should be aware of the different proceedings: both on federal and on state level, legal proceedings can be based on civil and on public law. Apart from that the NAD can be appealed.[70]

The claims based on common law that can be brought by a competitor include damages, restitution and injunctive relief. Comparable claims exist on the basis of both the federal and state Unfair Competition Acts.

a) Injunctive relief

Orders to cease and desist

Orders to cease and desist are most easily obtained. Traditionally, where an award of monetary relief will not adequately protect the plaintiff, injunctive relief may be granted. Damages only undo past harm; they are therefore inadequate to prevent future illegal behaviour. Thus, an injunction is the standard remedy in unfair competition cases.[71] The

[65] Tariff Act of 1930, U.S.C.A., § 1304.

[66] Art. IX (Marks of Origin) (1) reads: 'Each contracting party shall accord to the products of the territories of other contracting parties treatment with regard to marking requirements no less favourable than the treatment accorded to like products of any third country'; see C. McManis, *Intellectual Property and Unfair Competition* (5th edn 2004), p. 408.

[67] *Budget Rent-a-Car*, 113 FTC 1109 (1990).

[68] The proceeding was discontinued because of the lack of evidence, see R. Moore, R. Farrar and E. Collins, *Advertising and Public Relations Law* (1998), p. 140.

[69] N. Reich, *United States of America*, in H.-W. Micklitz and J. Keßler, p. 436.

[70] J. Maxeiner and F. Kent, *United States*, in J. Maxeiner and P. Schotthöfer, p. 513 (542).

[71] *National Football League Properties, Inc. v. Wichtia Falls Sportswear, Inc.*, 532 F. Supp. 651, 215 U.S.P.Q. 175 (W. D. Wash. 1982); *Century 21 Real Estate Corp. v. Sandlin*, 846 F.2d 1175, 6 U.S.P.Q.2d 2034 (9th Cir. 1988).

attractiveness of injunctive relief is that it can be shaped and conditioned so as to balance the conflicting rights of the litigants in a way that money damages can never do.[72] Injunctions require an extensive weighing of the different interests.[73]

At the moment, claims for an order to cease and desist can be brought in thirty-three states by private parties.[74] The FTC is allowed to formulate its own rules to punish infringements of unfair competition law. Because of the complicated procedure to promulgate these rules the FTC hardly uses this competence.[75] Because of this, administrative actions, injunctions and mechanisms to seek consumer redress are more important. Equitable relief has become important for FTC law and rule enforcement.[76] The commercial victim may obtain a cease and desist order from the Federal Trade Commission or a cease-and-desist order from the International Trade Commission.[77] The Lanham Act also explicitly provides for an injunction as a remedy.[78]

Contempt – violation of injunction

The federal courts may punish as contempt the disobedience or resistance to its lawful writ, process, order, rule, decree or command.[79] The violation of an injunction issued by the FTC can be sanctioned by civil penalties.[80] Similar statutory provisions exist in every state, so that there

[72] J. McCarthy, *McCarthy on Trademarks and Unfair Competition*, vol. 6 (4th edn Supp. 2000), p. 30–37.

[73] Restatement (Third) of Unfair Competition (1995), § 35 para. 2 reads: 'The appropriateness and scope of injunctive relief depend upon a comparative appraisal of all factors of the case, including the following primary factors: (a) the nature of the interest of be protected; (b) the nature and extent of the wrongful conduct; (c) the relative adequacy to the plaintiff of an injunction and of other remedies; (d) the relative harm likely to result to the legitimate interests of the defendant if an injunction is granted and to the legitimate interests of the plaintiff if an injunction is denied; (e) the interests of third persons and of the public; (f) any reasonable delay by the plaintiff in bringing suit or otherwise asserting its rights; (g) any related misconduct on the part of the plaintiff; and (h) the practicality of framing and enforcing the injunction.'

[74] D. Pridgen, *Consumer Protection and the Law* (2003), p. 391.

[75] See *National Petroleum Refiners Ass'n v. FTC*, 482 F.2d 672, 157 U.S.App.D.C. 83 (D.C. Circ. 1973) and Magnussion-Moss-Warranty – FTC-Improvement Act 1975; C. McManis, *Intellectual Property and Unfair Competition* (5th edn 2004), p. 398; N. Reich, *United States of America*, in: H.-W. Micklitz and J. Keßler, p. 430.

[76] Sec. 5 (l, m), 13 (b), 19 (b) FTCA, 15 U.S.C. §§ 45, 53, 57.

[77] C. McManis, *Intellectual Property and Unfair Competition* (5th edn 2004), p. 228.

[78] Lanham Act § 34, 15 U.S.C.A. § 1116. [79] 18 U.S.C.A. § 401 (3). [80] Sec. 5 (l) FTCA.

is no doubt that the violation of an injunction against unfair competition constitutes contempt punishable by fine or imprisonment.[81]

b) Preliminary injunction

Preliminary injunctions are also possible.[82] This normally requires the plaintiff to show a probability of success at the ultimate trial on the merits, to show that he will suffer 'irreparable injury' without the preliminary injunction, and to show that the preliminary injunction preserves the 'status quo' which preceded the dispute and that a preliminary ruling is necessary to protect third parties.[83]

Injunctive relief may be obtained even before the defendant actually opens for business, if the threatened act of the defendant is imminent and impending. One does not have to await consummation of the threatened injury to obtain preventive relief.[84] Injunctive relief may even be obtained before the defendant has sold a single infringing product. For this purpose the requirement 'use of commerce' is construed extensively. The court noted that the Lanham Act does not require that the allegedly infringing merchandise be available to the consuming public.

c) Elimination

It is also possible to bring a claim for elimination. A defendant was ordered to send corrective information to those who had previously received his false advertising.[85] The court may order that the defendant be required to advise distributors to withdraw infringing products from the market.[86] Under the Lanham Act the courts are given discretion to issue the order that labels and advertisements bearing the infringing mark be delivered up and destroyed.[87]

[81] *Richardson v. Thomas*, 257 So. 2d 877, 173 U.S.P.Q. 237 (Miss. 1972); J. McCarthy, *McCarthy on Trademarks and Unfair Competition*, vol. 6 (4th edn Supp. 2000), pp. 30–39.

[82] J. Sheldon and C. Carter, *Unfair and Deceptive Acts and Practices* (5th edn 2001), p. 656.

[83] See J. McCarthy, *McCarthy on Trademarks and Unfair Competition*, vol. 6 (4th edn Supp. 2000), pp. 30–61 including the differentiations of the different Circuits.

[84] *Cleveland Opera Co. v. Cleveland Civic Opera Ass'n*, 22 Ohio App. 400, 5 Ohio L.Abs. 297, 154 N.E. 352 (Cuyahoga County 1926); *Standard Oil Co. v. Standard Oil Co.*, 56 F.3d 973 (10th Cir. 1932); J. McCarthy, *McCarthy on Trademarks and Unfair Competition*, vol. 6 (4th edn Supp. 2000), pp. 30–21.

[85] *Thomas Nelson, Inc. v. Cherish Books, Ltd.*, 595 F.Supp. 989, 224 U.S.P.Q. 571 (S.D.N.Y. 1984).

[86] *Gaylord Products, Inc. v. Golding Wave Clip Co.*, 161 F.Supp. 746, 118 U.S.P.Q. 148 (W.D.N.Y. 1958).

[87] Lanham Act § 36, 15 U.S.C.A. § 1118.

On the state level, the deceptive acts can be used to order corrective advertising, where necessary to eliminate the lingering effects of past deceptions.[88]

d) Publication

The publication of judgments as a sanction is not known in American law.[89]

e) Damages of private parties

Concrete damage

Where the extent of past pecuniary injury can be established with sufficient certainty, compensatory damages may be recovered. A number of courts follow the common law rule that the damage must be a foreseeable consequence of the deception.[90] Some courts use a wide range of descriptions, ranging from deliberate and knowing to wilful and fraudulent.[91] Difficulties of proof constitute the biggest hurdle to damage awards. The proof of damages does not require mathematical precision, but it must be based on more than mere speculation.[92]

Benefit of the bargain and licence fee

The profits made by the infringer can be claimed if the actor engaged in the conduct with the intention of causing confusion or deception and if the award of profits is not prohibited by statute. Moreover, the courts must extensively weigh the different interests to determine whether the award of profits is appropriate.[93] Finally, the compensation of the

[88] C. McManis, *Intellectual Property and Unfair Competition* (5th edn 2004), p. 402.

[89] J. Maxeiner and F. Kent, *United States*, in J. Maxeiner and P. Schotthöfer, p. 513 (544).

[90] *Dimarzo v. American Mutual Ins. Co.*, 389 Mass. 85, 449 N.E.2d 1189 (1983); *Witters v. Daniels Motors, Inc.*, 524 P. 2d 632, 635 (Colo. Ct. App. 1974); J. Sheldon and C. Carter, *Unfair and Deceptive Acts and Practices* (5th edn 2001), p. 613; D. Pridgen, *Consumer Protection and the Law* (2003), p. 378.

[91] J. McCarthy, *McCarthy on Trademarks and Unfair Competition*, vol. 6 (4th edn Supp. 2000), pp. 30–121.

[92] *Hall v. Lovell Regency Homes Ltd.*, 121 Md. App. 1, 708 A.2d 344 (1988); J. Sheldon and C. Carter, *Unfair and Deceptive Acts and Practices* (5th edn 2001), p. 619.

[93] Restatement (Third) of Unfair Competition (1995), § 37 para. 2 reads: 'Whether an award of profits is appropriate depends upon a comparative appraisal of all the factors of the case, including the following primary factors: (a) the degree of certainty that the actor benefited from the unlawful conduct; (b) the relative adequacy to the plaintiff of other remedies, including an award of damages; (c) the interests of the public in depriving the actor of unjust gains and discouraging unlawful conduct; (d) the role of the actor in bringing about the infringement or deceptive marketing, (e) any unreasonable delay by

damage caused by the 'harm to the market reputation of the plaintiff's goods, services, business, or trademark' can be claimed.[94]

Estimation of injury

Analogous to antitrust law it is assumed that a higher level of proof of the fact of damage is required than for the proof of the extent of the injury.[95] If the parties are competitors, the rise in profits of the defendant can be assumed to be the loss of the claimant.[96] To some extent the courts award very generous compensation for abstract damages; some courts are willing to recognize inconvenience, travel expenses, lost time, and the loss of the opportunity to purchase as compensable loss.[97]

Minimum damage

Partly there is a minimum damage set by the law. Consumers do not have to prove any monetary loss or actual damages in order to recover the statutory minimum damage. Statutory minimum damages are intended to encourage private litigation, and courts should award such damages whenever authorized to do so. About half the states authorize private litigants who have proven a UDAP violation to obtain minimum damage awards ranging from $25 to $5000, even if actual damages have not been proven. A statutory penalty is necessary to motivate consumers to enforce the statute.[98] Thus, $3000 minimum damage provisions have been awarded where the actual damages were only $200.[99] For instance, a New York plaintiff was lulled to a store by an advertisement offering to sell a $280 set of dishes for $39.95, only to find that the store claimed the advertisement was a mistake. She was entitled to recover the minimum $50 in damages, without having to prove

the plaintiff in bringing suit or otherwise asserting its rights; and (f) any related misconduct on the part of the plaintiff.'

94 See Restatement (Third) of Unfair Competition (1995), § 36 para. 2 lit. (c) and comment (e).

95 S. Oppenheim, G. Weston and J. McCarthy, *Federal Antitrust Laws* (4th edn 1981), pp. 1100–1105; J. McCarthy, *McCarthy on Trademarks and Unfair Competition*, vol. 6 (4th edn Supp. 2000), pp. 30–144.

96 Restatement (Third) of Unfair Competition (1995), § 37 comment (b).

97 *Brashears v. Sight N Sound Appliance*, 981 P. 2d 1270 (Okla. App. 1999); *Geismar v. Abraham & Straus*, 109 Misc. 2d 495, 439 N.Y.S.2d 1005 (Dist. Ct. 1981).

98 *Kaplan v. Democrat & Chronicle*, 698 N.Y.S.2d (App. Div. 1999).

99 J. Sheldon and C. Carter, *Unfair and Deceptive Acts and Practices* (5th edn 2001), p. 621.

the amount in which she was actually damaged.[100] The infringement of the TCPA can also result in a minimum damage of $500 per violation.[101]

Treble damages

The Lanham Act explicitly allows treble damages[102] which are regularly awarded in the practice of the courts.[103] In case of an infringement of the TCPA, the court may treble the damages if it finds that the defendant wilfully or knowingly violated this section. Some states also allow treble damages. Where an individual consumer's actual damages are nominal, three times this amount will still be nominal. The underlying idea is to award the claimant his damages, to deter infringers and to encourage out-of-court settlements.[104] A number of UDAP statutes limit multiple damage awards to situations where intent, wilfulness or bad faith is shown.[105]

Punitive damages

The federal Lanham Act 1946 does not specifically allow for the recovery of punitive damages apart from the judicial power to increase damages or profits.[106] But punitive damages can be awarded under common law. Where the interference was malicious, either *punitive damages* or restitution of the defendant's profits may be allowed. Because plaintiffs' damages and defendants' profits may be particularly difficult to prove in product restitution and alteration cases, the availability of injunctive relief and punitive damages is all the more important.[107]

UDAP statutes explicitly authorize punitive damages.[108] Common criteria are malice, wilful or wanton conduct, ill will, or reckless indifference to the interests of others.[109] If a UDAP statute does not authorize

[100] *Geismar v. Abraham & Strauss*, 109 Misc. 2d 495, 439 N.Y.S.2d 1005, 1008 (Dist. Ct. 1981); D. Pridgen, *Consumer Protection and the Law* (2003), p. 393.

[101] 47 U.S.C. § 227 (b) (3), (c) (5).

[102] Lanham Act § 35(a), 15 U.S.C.A. § 1117 (a).

[103] *Stuart v. Collins*, 489 F. Supp. 827, 208 U.S.P.Q. 657 (S.D.N.Y. 1980).

[104] *Refuse & Environmental Sys., Inc. v. Industrial Services*, 932 F.2d 37 (1st Cir. 1991).

[105] J. Sheldon and C. Carter, *Unfair and Deceptive Acts and Practices* (5th edn 2001), p. 624; D. Pridgen, *Consumer Protection and Law* (2003), pp. 397 et seq.

[106] *Stone v. Lozos*, 223 U.S.P.Q. 201 (N.D.Ill. 1983).

[107] C. McManis, *Intellectual Property and Unfair Competition* (5th edn 2004), p. 228.

[108] California, Connecticut, District of Columbia, Georgia, Idaho, Kentucky, Missouri, Oregon and Rhode Island.

[109] J. Sheldon and C. Carter, *Unfair and Deceptive Acts and Practices* (5th edn 2001), p. 636; *Boyes v. Greenwich Boat Works, Inc.*, 27 F. Supp. 2d 543 (D.N.J. 1998) (actual malice or wanton and wilful disregard).

punitive damages, the plaintiff can add a common law fraud count to their UDAP action and seek punitive damages under the common law fraud claim.[110] In a case involving the sale of a used car with concealed wreck damage and a rolled-back odometer, the Oregon Supreme Court upheld a jury award of $1 million in punitive damages where compensatory damages were $11,496.[111] But punitive damages violate constitutional law if they are disproportionate.[112]

Attorney's fees

Principally in the USA the claimant and defendant have to bear their attorney's fees themselves independent of the result of proceedings. In unfair competition proceedings this principle is very often not applied. According to the Lanham Act, the costs for legal counsel can be recovered from the losing party if it has acted wilfully.[113] According to the UDAPs the attorney's fees can also be recovered.[114]

f) Civil penalties of public bodies

According to federal law the FTC may apply for judicial imposition of civil penalties of up to $10,000 per day for violation of FTC Trade Regulation Rules or FTC cease and desist orders (15 U.S.C. § 45(m)). Statutory minimum damages for a consumer litigant must be distinguished from civil penalty provisions that allow the state Attorney General to seek civil penalties ranging from $500 to $25,000 for initial UDAP violations.[115]

3. *The parties: plaintiffs and defendants*

In the USA both civil law and public law proceedings are possible. The Lanham Act and common law are enforced by civil law on the federal level; the FTCA is monitored by means of public law.[116] The supervision of the UDAP is enforced by private and by public parties.

[110] *Aronson v. Creditrust Corp.*, 7 F. Supp. 2d 589 (W.D.Pa. 1998); *Drucker v. Oakland Toyota, Inc.*, Case. No. 83-04569 'CR' (Fla. Cir. Ct Broward Cty. Dec. 1984).

[111] *Parrot v. Carr Chevrolet*, 331 Or. 573, 17 P. 3d 473 (2001).

[112] *BMW of North America v. Gore*, 517 U.S. 559, 134 L. Ed. 2d 809, 116 S. Ct. 1589 (1996); the ratio was 500 times the compensatory of $4000; *Romo v. Ford*, 113 Cal.App. 4th 738.

[113] § 35 s. 2 Lanham Act, Pub.L. 93-600, 88 Stat. 1955; cf., comprehensively, J. McCarthy, *McCarthy on Trademarks and Unfair Competition*, vol. 6 (4th edn Supp. 2000), pp. 30-185.

[114] Comprehensively, D. Pridgen, *Consumer Protection and the Law* (2003), pp. 412 et seq.

[115] J. Sheldon and C. Carter, *Unfair and Deceptive Acts and Practices* (5th edn 2001), p. 621.

[116] There is no private remedy under the FTCA, cf. *Baum v. Great Western Cities, Inc.*, 703 F.2d 1197 (10th Cir. 1983); J. Sheldon and C. Carter, *Unfair and Deceptive Acts and Practices* (5th edn 2001), p. 699.

a) Competitor

The competitor can resort to all proceedings offered by common law. Only the FTC can challenge advertising prohibited by the FTCA, whereas an injured party may challenge advertising via the Lanham Act §43(a).[117] In addition, the state FTC Acts normally permit private parties to bring challenges.[118]

b) Consumer – class action

Consumers cannot bring a suit that is neither based on the FTCA nor the Lanham Act.[119] But many states allow private parties to bring challenges in their UDAP rules.[120] Moreover, many states assume that the violation of an FTC rule is a per se state UDAP violation.[121] The TCPA also explicitly grants consumers a right of action.

Apart from that, a class action offers the possibility to bring proceedings collectively.[122]

c) Consumer associations

On the national level many consumer organizations exist. The national consumer law centre is of particular importance.[123] Consumer organizations often restrict their activities to informing the public and lobbying. Consumers or consumer associations cannot enforce civil actions under the FTCA.[124] On the state level they only partly have a right to sue.[125] A simple step that consumers can take if they suspect

117 J. Maxeiner and F. Kent, *United States*, in J. Maxeiner and P. Schotthöfer, p. 513 (528).

118 J. Sheldon and C. Carter, *Unfair and Deceptive Acts and Practices* (5th edn 2001), p. 537 and Appendix A.

119 C. McKenney and G. Young, *Federal Unfair Competition: Lanham Act § 43 (a)* (1990), § 9.03 (3).

120 The exceptions are Iowa and North Dakota, cf. D. Pridgen, *Consumer Protection and the Law* (2003), p. 373; J. Sheldon and C. Carter, *Unfair and Deceptive Acts and Practices* (5th edn 2001), p. 608.

121 Idaho Consumer Protection Regulations, Idaho Admin. Code § 04.02.01.033; *Nieman v. DryClean U.S.A. Franchise Co.*, 178 F.3d 1126 (11th Cir. 1999, cert. denied, 528 U.S. 1118 (2000)).

122 *Miner v. Gillette Co.*, 87 Ill. 2d 7, 428 N.E.2d 478 (1981), cert. dismissed, 459 U.S. 86 (1982); for detailed and general remarks concerning consumer protection actions, see D. Pridgen, *Consumer Protection and the Law* (2003), pp. 439 et seq.

123 www.nclc.org.

124 *Baum v. Great Western Cities Inc.*, 703 F.2d 1197 (10th Cir. 1983); J. Sheldon and C. Carter, *Unfair and Deceptive Acts and Practices* (5th edn 2001), p. 699.

125 E.g. in California and New York cf. *Consumers Union of United States, Inc. v. Fisher Development, Inc.*, 208 Cal. App. 3d 1433, 1439, 257 Cal. Rptr. 151, 154 (1st Dist. 1989); *McDonald v. North Shore Yacht Sales, Inc.*, 134 Misc. 2d 910, 513 N.Y.S.3d 590 (Supp. 1987).

telemarketing fraud is to telephone the National Fraud Center, established by a coalition of groups battling telephone fraud and operating from the National Consumers League.[126]

d) Trade associations

On occasion, trade associations have been permitted to bring proceedings.[127]

e) Public enforcement of unfair competition law

FTC and International Trade commission

These proceedings normally result in a cease and desist order. A mandatory order cannot result without the consent of the party subject to investigation.[128]

In order to issue a cease and desist order without the consent of the party subject to it, the FTC must commence adjudicative administrative proceedings. Alternatively, the FTC can sue in the ordinary US district court.[129] Therefore the FTC itself is not able to issue injunctions but has to resort to proceedings at a US district court. The FTC must use these legal procedures if it seeks to impose a penalty. FTC adjudicative proceedings closely resemble proceedings before the federal courts of first instance, except that a so-called administrative judge presides instead of a federal district judge.[130] Against the final decision proceedings before a US court of appeals can be brought.

The International Trade Commission has been given authority under sec. 337 of the 1930 Tariff Act (19 U.S.C.A. § 1997) to issue exclusion orders and cease and desist orders to prevent unfair methods of competition connected with the importation of articles into the USA or their subsequent sale, where the requisite injury, including destruction of or substantial injury to or prevention of the establishment of an efficiently and economically operated industry in the USA, can be shown.[131]

[126] See www.nclnet.org and www.fraud.org.

[127] *Camel Hair & Cashmere Institute of America, Inc. v. Associated Dry Goods Corp.*, 799 F.2d 6 (1st Cir. 1986).

[128] J. Maxeiner and F. Kent, *United States*, in J. Maxeiner and P. Schotthöfer, p. 513 (549).

[129] Sec. 13 (b) FTCA, C.F.R. 1.61.

[130] J. Maxeiner and F. Kent, *United States*, in J. Maxeiner and P. Schotthöfer, p. 513 (549).

[131] C. McManis, *Intellectual Property and Unfair Competition* (5th edn 2004), p. 417.

Enforcement of the UDAP

The Attorney General can take measures if the UDAP has been infringed.[132] Consumers have the possibility to complain at the Attorney General's office. But it is emphasized that this may be an unsatisfactory alternative because these offices have limited resources, have their own priorities, and may be less interested in compensating individual complainants than in preventing wide-scale deception and punishing serious misconduct.[133] In California the possibility now exists that the 'public interest' can be enforced by private parties. This allows individuals whose own rights have not necessarily been violated to bring private Attorney General Actions to court.[134]

Besides, some states in the last years have established monitoring agencies on a local level.[135]

f) Defendants

Advertising agencies may be proper parties to FTC actions for false advertising where they actively participated in preparation of advertisements and knew or had reason to know that advertisements were false or deceptive.[136] So, for example, the FTC has issued orders against advertising agencies.[137]

In numerous decisions the Supreme Court has clarified that the freedom of speech of the First Amendment does not apply to misleading advertisement.[138] Commercial speech is thus less protected than political speech. Misleading advertisements can also result in injunctions against the press.[139] Furthermore, non-deceptive commercial speech

[132] 'Any person' also means the states, see regarding Massachusetts, *Spence v. Boston Ediscon Co.*, 399 Mass. 569, 506 N.E.2d 106 (1987).

[133] J. Sheldon and C. Carter, *Unfair and Deceptive Acts and Practices* (5th edn 2001), p. 772; D. Pridgen, *Consumer Protection and the Law* (2003), p. 513, is sceptical

[134] L. Sacks, *Unfair Competition Claims 2003: California Section 17200's Impact on Consumers & Businesses Everywhere* (2003), pp. 38 et seq.

[135] Regarding the City Commissioner of Consumer Affairs of New York, see e.g. D. Pridgen, *Consumer Protection and the Law* (2003), pp. 513 et seq.; before that already J. Sheldon and G. Zweibel, *Survey of Consumer Fraud*, by National Institute of Law Enforcement and Criminal Justice (1978), p. 133.

[136] J. Maxeiner and F. Kent, *United States*, in J. Maxeiner and P. Schotthöfer, p. 513 (545).

[137] *ITT Continental Baking Co., et al.*, 97 FTC 248 (1971).

[138] E.g. *Virginia State Board of Pharmacy v. Virginia Citizens Consumer Council, Inc.*, 425 U.S. 748, 96 Ct. 1817 (1976), 48 L. Ed. 2d 346; *Greater New Orleans Broadcasting Assn. v. U.S.*, 527 U.S. 173, 119 S. Ct. 1973, 144 L. Ed. 2d 161 (1999).

[139] *Encyclopaedia Britannica v. FTC*, 605 F.2d 964 (7th Cir. 1979); *People v. Custom Craft Carpets, Inc.*, 206 Cal. Rptr. 12 (Ct. App. 1984).

can be regulated, but injunctions should be no broader than necessary to prevent future deception or correct past deception, or they may violate the First Amendment.[140] If a publisher does not know that he is violating the law normally only an injunction is possible.[141]

It is a rare occurrence for the FTC to cite the media in a complaint. Some state laws even specifically exempt the media from liability.[142] On the state level the exemptions of most UDAP statutes specifically excludes printers, publishers, and others who disseminate advertisements in good faith.[143] The good faith exclusion does not apply, if a publisher disseminates an advertisement with knowledge that it is deceptive.[144]

In addition, many state UDAP statutes explicitly exempt only media statements where the media has no direct financial interest in the advertised product.[145]

4. *Out-of-court settlements of disputes*

a) Civil law – notice of violation and discovery

Federal law does not require a notice of violation since the Federal Rules of Civil Procedure do not make such a notice a prerequisite for bringing a claim. In eight states a notice letter[146] is necessary. These provisions aim to discourage litigation and encourage settlements of consumer complaints.[147] A notice of violation can also be helpful to prove the bad faith of the defendant. If the violation resulted in a loss the notice of violation is normally combined with a monetary settlement proposal.[148]

[140] *Central Hudson Gas & Elec. Corp. v. Public Service Commission of New York*, 447 U.S. 557, 566, 100 S. Ct. 2343, 65 L. Ed 2d 341 (1980); *Shapero v. Kentucky Bar Ass'n*, 486 U.S. 466, 108 S. Ct. 1916, 100 L. Ed. 2d 475 (1988); *FTC v. Brown & Williamson Tobacco Corp.*, 778 F.2d 35 (D.C. Cir. 1985).

[141] See Restatement (Third) of Unfair Competition (1995), § 7 para. 2.

[142] J. Maxeiner and F. Kent, *United States*, in J. Maxeiner and P. Schotthöfer, p. 513 (545).

[143] *Aequitron Medical, Inc. v. CBS, Inc.*, 964 F. Supp. 704 (S.D.N.Y. 1996); J. Sheldon and C. Carter, *Unfair and Deceptive Acts and Practices* (5th edn 2001), p. 63.

[144] *Mother & Unborn Baby Care, Inc. v. State*, 749 S.W.2d 533 (Tex. App. 1988), cert. denied, 490 U.S. 1090 (1989).

[145] *People ex rel. Hartigan v. Maclean Hunter Publishing Corp.*, 119 Ill. App. 3d 1049, 457 N.E.2d 480 (1983).

[146] Alabama, California, Georgia, Indiana, Maine, Massachusetts, Texas, Wyoming.

[147] *Barnard v. Mecom*, 650 S.W.2d 123, 127 (Tex. App. Corpus Christi 1983); D. Pridgen, *Consumer Protection and the Law* (2003), pp. 314 et seq.

[148] The lawyers of California's Governor A. Schwarzenegger point out that they will send a reminder, if a picture or the name of Schwarzenegger is used for illegal advertising,

The pre-trial discovery can take several months. Pre-trial discovery allows the gathering of all relevant facts by means of disclosure of the defendant's files or by interviewing witnesses. Evidence of deceptive or unfair acts toward others is relevant for any punitive damages claim.[149]

b) Public law

The initial phase of an investigation is conducted by the FTC subject to so-called non-adjudicative proceedings. A compulsory procedure to obtain evidence is available to obtain information.[150] Before a final order the commission should obtain voluntary compliance by entering into a part 2 administrative consent agreement, 16 CFR § 2.1–51. After that further formal proceedings according to part 3 can follow.

The Attorney General and numerous government agencies are able to seek a settlement.[151] The investigations, particularly at the FTC, often take years to complete.[152] In addition, the FTC and the Attorney General will only act if the public interest requires so.[153]

c) National Advertising Division (NAD)

It is well known that the costs of litigation are very high under the US-American legal system. Litigation costs for one side almost always exceed $20,000, may be more than $100,000 and sometimes run into millions of dollars.[154]

The Better Business Bureaus (BBBs)[155] are non-profit organizations supported primarily by local business members. The focus of BBB activities is to promote an ethical marketplace by encouraging honest advertising and selling practices and by providing alternative dispute resolution. For nearly three decades, the National Advertising Division (NAD) of the BBB has offered a private forum for resolution of advertising disputes. Participation is voluntary and the only sanctions are directions to modify advertising and publication of its decision by the NAD in its newsletter.

e.g. the beer brand 'Governator Ale', showing a body builder, *LA Times* March 30, 2004, A 1, 19.

149 *MacTools, Inc. v. Griffin*, 126 Idaho 193, 879 P. 2d 1126 (1994).

150 J. Maxeiner and F. Kent, *United States*, in J. Maxeiner and P. Schotthöfer, p. 513 (548).

151 J. Sheldon and C. Carter, *Unfair and Deceptive Acts and Practices* (5th edn 2001), p. 772.

152 Ibid., p. 772.

153 D. Pridgen, *Consumer Protection and the Law* (2003), p. 322.

154 The examples given by J. Maxeiner and F. Kent, *United States*, in J. Maxeiner and P. Schotthöfer, p. 513 (541), are impressive.

155 www.bbb.org.

These proceedings are very often used.[156] The NAD accepts complaints from any person or legal entity.[157]

5. *Summary*

a) Complexity

The US-American law of unfair competition is extremely complex. There are three reasons for this: the interrelation between common law and statutory law, the supervision of unfair competition on federal and state level and, finally, the possibility for private parties and public bodies to take actions against violations.

b) Practical relevance

Thirty years ago the private enforcement of unfair competition claims was considered insufficient.[158] The US-American advertising law is cited as a good example for the divergence between 'law in books and law in action'. On the national level infringements of the law of unfair competition are quickly recognised and public agencies and consumer association take action immediately. If the infringement happens on a local level the violator often does not have to fear any sanctions.[159]

This is no longer entirely true: it is true though that the enforcement of the FTCA is only executed by the FTC but an agency cannot only react to infringements. It can also act pre-emptively by issuing industry guides and trade regulation rules.[160]

Until quite recently attorneys refused to take consumers as clients because of the low fees involved. But the introduction of the UDAPs has made private enforcement much better at the state level. In many states the various sanctions like abstract damages, treble damages and punitive damages aim at encouraging proceedings.[161] The pre-trial discovery procedure and contingency fees also lead to more court proceedings.

156 See the overview in A. Levine, *NAD Case Reports Voluntary Self-Regulation of National Advertising*, in: J. Edelstein (ed.), *Advertising law in the New Media Age* (2000), pp. 73–158.

157 J. Maxeiner and F. Kent, *United States*, in J. Maxeiner and P. Schotthöfer, p. 513 (545).

158 D. Epstein and S. Nickles, *Consumer Law in a Nutshell*, (1981), p. 7; D. Epstein, *Consumer Protection* (1976), p. 12; R. Posner, *Economic Analysis of Law* (1973), p. 157; E. Kitch and H. Perlman, *Legal Regulation of the Competitive Process* (1972), p. 110; H. Pitofsky, *Beyond Nader: Consumer Protection and the Regulation of Advertising*, 90 Harv. L.Rev. 671 (1977) translated as *Verbraucherschutz und Kontrolle der Werbung in den USA*, (1977) 25 GRUR Int. 304 (307).

159 J. Maxeiner and F. Kent, *United States*, in J. Maxeiner and P. Schotthöfer, p. 513 (514).

160 S. Kanwit, *Federal Trade Commission*, vol. 2 (Supp. 2003), § 22–7.

161 The same way D. Pridgen, *Consumer Protection and the Law* (2003), pp. 4 et seq.

Small cases can become lucrative for attorneys if pursued as class actions.[162] Moreover, the Attorney General can be appealed. Finally, out-of-court settlements are often reached to avoid high attorneys' fees and pre-trial discovery.

If the law of unfair competition has less relevance than in numerous European states, as for example Germany or Austria, this is not a result of enforcement but of the fact that many actions that would be considered as violations in Europe are allowed in the USA.[163]

[162] See above notes 101 et seq.

[163] See e.g. above A.IV note 102.

B. Contemporary solutions: the case studies

I. Objects of claim – the sanctions

Case 1 Risky bread: order to cease and desist, elimination, publication

A is a baker. He advertises his products as being particularly environmentally friendly. At the same time he claims that his competitor B sells bread with additional ingredients whose risks have not yet been analysed sufficiently. Therefore, it would be very risky to eat the bread offered by B. A has also printed advertisements stating these claims.

In which way can one prevent A from publishing this misleading advertisement in the future?

Austria (1)

Assuming that the risks posed by the additional ingredients used by B cannot be proven, A's advertisement is a depreciatory comparative advertisement since A combined his allegations with the advertisement for his own product, allegedly particularly free from harmful substances. This advertisement can also be misleading, if A's bread is actually free from harmful substances in order to comply with law relating to food and drugs. If this is the case, it would be an advertisement stating obvious facts. Where comparative advertisement is concerned the advertiser bears the burden of proof for the statements of fact contained in the advertisement (§ 2 para. 5 UWG). This is congruent with the burden of proof in § 7 UWG: the plaintiff only has to prove the allegation (circulation) of the harmful facts, whereas the defendant – comparable to § 111 f StGB – has to prove the truth of his allegations. According to legal literature and the courts[1] it is sufficient for this that the supplied evidence in essence proves the truth.

(1) B as the party directly affected (and at the same time A's competitor) can apply for an injunction in accordance with § 2 para. 1 and § 7 para. 1 UWG because of deceptive statements of A about his business affairs (§ 2 UWG) and because of the depreciatory allegations (§ 7 UWG). Concerning the depreciatory allegations against his company, B can demand that A refrains from making and circulating these allegations.

According to the long-standing practice of the courts the risk of repetition is assumed, which means that the defendant has to prove that this risk no longer exists. It is assumed that somebody who – even if only once – infringes a norm of the UWG will be inclined to do so again in the future. The infringing party therefore has to supply those special circumstances that either completely rule out a repetition of these actions, or at least make it extremely improbable. The mere assertion of the defendant to refrain from future infringements is not sufficient, especially when facing an impending trial.[2]

The executive enforcement of the claim for an injunction is regulated in § 355 para. 1 EO which allows since the amendment of the EO in 2000 for draconian punishments in enforcing the prohibitions. Those who have to refrain from an action face a fine for each contravention. The contravention has to take place after the court's decision has become binding and requires a motion to the executive court on the occasion of the authorization of the execution. Upon application the executive court has to impose a further fine (or detainment) for each further contravention. The scope of these punishments depends on the nature and seriousness of the contravention and has to take into account the financial means of the bound party and the extent of the participation in the contravention. According to § 359 para. 1 EO the fine for each contravention may not exceed €100,000.[3]

[1] H. Koppensteiner, *Österreichisches und Europäisches Wettbewerbsrecht* (3rd edn 1997), p. 579; (1990) 39 ÖBl 18 – 'Mafiaprint'.

[2] Established case law, e.g. (2001) 50 ÖBl 105 – 'Reisebedarf'; (2002) 51 ÖBl 291 – 'Schulungsveranstaltung'; (2002) 51 ÖBl 302 – 'Alpentrio Tirol'.

[3] Compare e.g. the drastic decision OGH, 3 Ob 215/02 t, 321/02 f., (2003) MR 82 – 'Unsere Klestils', in which fines between €10,000 and €75,000 were imposed descendingly for repeated contraventions.

(2) The plaintiff can also claim the elimination of the infringing action. Here he is entitled to both a revocation (§7 para.1 respectively §15 UWG) and the elimination of the printed advertisement.

(3) Furthermore he can claim that the revocation should be published (§ 25 UWG).

Denmark (1)

The advertising is misleading in two respects. First of all, under the MFL (Marketing Practices Act) a condition for comparing one's own product with other products is that an advertiser is able to document a claim that his product possesses special advantages in comparison with the products manufactured by other companies. Secondly, it will in itself be illegal to make an undocumented claim concerning harmful effects of competitive products as such a claim will be detrimental to the competitor's sales. Comparative advertising and derogatory statements on other businessmen, considered disparaging as a whole, are the traditional main areas for the rules in MFL on illegal marketing. In connection with law no. 164 of March 15, 2000, § 2a was added which implemented EU Directive 97/55/EC on comparative advertising. To a large extent § 2a MFL codifies what was already governing law according to § 2 sec. 1 MFL. Contrary to § 2 sec. 1 MFL, there are no requirements in § 2a MFL that the marketing must be such that it influences both demand and supply. Comparative advertising is subject to §§ 1, 2 and 2a MFL. § 1 MFL concerning the actions of enterprises, which have been carried out contrary to good marketing practice, will not be applied as the matter is subject to the special rules in § 2 and § 2a. A's statements concerning his own products must be considered contrary to § 2a MFL, as the comparison does not comply with the requirements of the rule: A's statements regarding B's products must be assumed to be contrary to § 2 sec. 1 MFL as the statements are not properly and objectively documented. The statements must be supposed to have a demonstrably harmful effect on sales, and A's statements are based on incorrect – or at least incomplete – statements concerning B's products.[4]

(1) Violation of §§ 2 and 2a MFL can be prohibited by a judgment (§13 para.1 MFL). According to § 19 para. 1 MFL anyone with a necessary legal interest may bring an action before the ordinary courts with the

[4] See on this matter P.B. Madsen, *Markedsret*, vol. 2 (4th edn 2002), p. 269; B. von Eyben et al., *Karnovs lovssamling* (2001), p. 5698; E. Borcher and F. Bøggild, *Markedsføringsloven* (2001), p. 100.

aim of prohibiting such marketing that is contrary to the law. As B is directly mentioned in A's advertising, B will have the necessary legal interest in getting a court to assess the case. According to § 14 MFL, any action shall be brought before the Maritime and Commercial Court. Violation of an injunction issued by a court is – according to § 22 para. 1 MFL – sanctioned by fines. An interim prohibition can be issued by the Consumer Ombudsman if there is a risk that a prohibition by a court will fail in its impact (§21 para.1 MFL).

(2) The injunction can be combined with positive rulings that aim at the elimination of the infringement.[5] As a supplement to the injunction the court may include the destruction or withdrawal of products and the publication or correction of indications or statements.[6] A competitor might also request that the court orders the publication of supplementary information or of corrections.

(3) According to § 19 MFL the Consumer Ombudsman can bring an action before the courts with a claim of having an injunction issued against the marketing. According to § 15 sec. 1 MFL the Consumer Ombudsman assesses himself whether a case is of sufficient interest for the protection of the consumers before he decides to enter into the matter.[7] If the conflict mainly concerns the relation between traders the Consumer Ombudsman cannot be expected to investigate and prosecute the case. The Maritime and Commercial Court of Copenhagen as a civil court has jurisdiction for the MFL.

England (1)

In English law one has to distinguish between statutory law that is enforced by means of public law and the case law which is enforced as civil law. There is also a lot of self-regulation.

(1) In England, comparative advertisement comes under the Control of Misleading Advertisements Regulations 1988 (CMAR 1988)[8] as amended by the Control of Misleading Advertisements (Amendment) Regulations 2000,[9] where the latter have implemented Directive 97/55/EC on comparative advertisement. A's advertisement would not be permitted since it does not meet the requirements of reg. 4A(1)(c)

[5] A. Kur and J. Schovsbo, *Dänemark*, in G. Schricker, note 257.

[6] § 13 para. 1 note 2 MFL. S.P. Møgelvang-Hansen and K. Østergaard, *Denmark*, in R. Schulze and H. Schulte-Nölke, p. 3.

[7] E. Borcher and F. Bøggild, *Markedsføringsloven* (2001), p. 375.

[8] S.I. 1988 no. 915.

[9] S.I. 2000 no. 914.

and (e) since A refers to unverifiable features and discredits his competitor B.

The enforcement of the CMAR 1988, as amended, was laid in the hands of the Director General of Fair Trading (DGFT).[10] His office was, however, abolished by sec. 2 of the Enterprise Act 2002 (EA 2002),[11] and his competences were transferred to the OFT as a corporate body. B's only remedy under the CMAR 1988 is a complaint to the OFT, under reg. 4(1), which the OFT has the duty to consider unless the complaint appears to be frivolous or vexatious and unless the advertisement was broadcast via radio or television. Before considering any complaint, the OFT may require the complainant to convince him that such established means of dealing with such complaints as the OFT may consider appropriate have been invoked, that a reasonable opportunity has been allowed for those means to deal with the complaint in question, and that those means have not dealt with the complaint adequately, reg. 4(3). In exercising these powers, the OFT shall have regard to all the interests involved, and in particular the public interest, and the desirability of encouraging the control, by self-regulatory bodies, of advertisements, reg. 4(4).

The OFT is the only real enforcer of the CMAR 1988 (outside radio and broadcasting). However, to keep complaints away from the OFT, reg. 4 (3) CMAR has been introduced, which means that consumers have to try alternative complaint mechanisms such as a complaint to the ASA or to the trading standards authorities first. In practice, reg. 4 (3) CMAR establishes the priority of complaints to the local trading standards authority[12] and of the self-regulatory mechanisms of the Advertising Standards Authority (ASA)[13] that have traditionally played an important role in the control of advertisement in England.[14] In fact, the standards applied by the ASA are regarded as higher than the legal requirements. Comparative advertisement is dealt with in no. 18(1) British Code of Advertising, Sales Promotion and Direct Marketing (Code), according to which comparisons are permitted in the interests of vigorous competition and public information. However, comparisons should be clear and fair. The elements of any comparison should not be selected in a way that gives the advertisers an artificial advantage. Under no. 20(1) on

[10] See e.g. *Director General of Fair Trading v. Planet Telecom plc and others* [2002] E.W.H.C. 376.
[11] Ch. 40 of 2002. [12] S. J. Macleod, *Consumer Sales Law* (2002), p. 268. [13] Ibid., p. 3.
[14] *Director General of Fair Trading v. Tobyward Ltd. and another* [1989] 2 All ER 266; see also C. Scott and J. Black, *Cranston's Consumer and the Law* (3rd edn 2000), p. 61.

denigration, advertisers should not unfairly attack or discredit other businesses or their products. The only acceptable use of another business's broken or defaced products in advertisements is in the illustration of comparative tests, and the source, nature and results of these should be clear. A's advertisement is therefore in violation of the Code.

Thus, a complaint that is rejected by the ASA as unfounded will not succeed in the OFT. The only cases that reach the OFT are those of traders that continue to violate the CMAR 1988 despite a negative decision by the ASA. Such cases appear to be very rare.[15]

(2) (a) Reg. 4(3) also allows the OFT to seek an undertaking from the person who is alleged to be in breach of the CMAR 1988. If these means have proved unsuccessful, the OFT may bring proceedings for an injunction in the High Court if it thinks it appropriate to do so (reg. 5). Thus, it has a margin of discretion. Complainants can challenge a negative decision of the OFT by way of judicial review. However, in such proceedings the courts can only consider the lawfulness of the decision, i.e. whether the OFT was acting within his competence. They cannot control the merits of his decision. Experience under the FTA 1973 as well as in the field of unfair contract terms shows that the OFT has concentrated its activities on *negotiation* until now.[16] Court action is seen as a last resort.[17] OFT can only sue for an injunction. In case a court order is breached, this would constitute contempt of court which can result in a fine or even imprisonment.

The local weights and measures authorities can bring proceedings for an injunction in the High Court as well, under sec. 213(1) EA 2002. However, they have to consult with the OFT before taking action (sec. 214(1) EA). The OFT can then take over. This allows the OFT to keep its central role in enforcing consumer law. Details have been laid down in The Enterprise Act 2002 (Part 8 Request for Consultation) Order 2003.[18] Apart from this the local weights and measures authorities also have the power to bring public charges themselves. They are able to do this independently from the OFT.

[15] One such case was *Director General of Fair Trading v. Tobyward Ltd. and another* [1989] 2 All ER 266.

[16] See R. Ellger, *Die Bündelung gleichgerichteter Interessen im englischen Zivilprozeß*, in J. Basedow, K. Hopt, H. Kötz and D. Baetge, *Die Bündelung gleichgerichteter Interessen im Prozeß* (1997), p. 103 (125).

[17] See also C. Scott and J. Black, *Cranston's Consumer and the Law* (3rd edn 2000), p. 61, concerning misleading advertisement.

[18] S.I. 2003, 1375.

If the advertisement were broadcast via radio or television, the authority to address a complaint to would be the Radio Authority (RA) or the Independent Television Commission (ITC), under reg. 8 CMAR 1988. As with the OFT, these authorities shall have regard to all the interests involved, and in particular the public interest. The RA and the ITC would not need to bring proceedings in the High Court but can take action themselves under the Broadcasting Act 1990.[19]

(b) According to reg. 4A(3) CMAR 1988 as amended, the provisions of these regulations do not confer a right of action in any civil proceedings in respect of comparative advertisement.[20] However, they do not derogate from such a right either. A's conduct might come under the tort of malicious falsehood, which may be remedied by means of an injunction. The preconditions for this tort are that one party has published words which are false about the other party, that they were published maliciously and that special damage has followed as the direct and natural result of their publication. With regard to sec. 3(1) of the Defamation Act 1952, it is sufficient if the words published in writing are calculated to cause pecuniary damage to the rival. Malice will be inferred if it be proved that the words were calculated to produce damage and that the party publishing the words knew that they were false or was reckless as to whether they were false or not.[21] Malicious falsehood can also be used in comparative advertisement, where the calculation to cause pecuniary damage to the rival is plain.[22] Even though courts tend to be reluctant to treat all advertisements as actionable,[23] they may treat a situation as malicious falsehood where a trader is not only puffing his own goods, but also denigrates those of his rival.[24] The malicious element means that there must be no just cause or excuse for the falsehood. So the tort is rarely shown to have been committed.[25] The facts of the case at present are too unclear (with

[19] Ch. 42 of 1990. [20] See *British Airways Plc. v. Ryanair Ltd.* [2001] FSR 32, para. 27–28.

[21] *Kaye v. Robertson* [1991] FSR 62, per Glidewell L.J.; *DSG Retail Ltd. v. Comet Group plc* [2002] FSR 58, at para. 13.

[22] *Emaco Ltd. and Aktiebolaget Electrolux v. Dyson Appliances Ltd.* [1999] E.T.M.R. 903 (904); *DSG Retail Ltd. v. Comet Group plc* [2002] FSR 58, para. 37.

[23] See e.g. *White v. Mellin* [1895] A.C. 154 (167) per Lord Watson.

[24] See *DSG Retail Ltd. v. Comet Group plc* [2002] FSR 58, para. 16–20; see the overview of previous case law in *De Beers Abrasive Products Ltd. v. International General Electric Co.* [1975] FSR 323.

[25] S. Weatherill, *United Kingdom*, in R. Schulze and H. Schulte-Nölke, I.2(b). The court dismisses the complaint in *British Airways v. Rynair* [2001] FSR 541.

respect to A's knowledge and intentions) to finally decide whether the tort of malicious falsehood applies.

(3) An application for an interlocutory injunction does not involve a full trial of all the issues: there is not sufficient time for either side to prepare its evidence.[26] Interlocutory injunctions are issued if the claimant can set forth that the case is worthy of a judicial decision and that the payment of damages would not be a sufficient compensation for the claimant. In these cases the court very often issues the order that the case will be heard as soon as possible.[27] In cases involving passing-off such claims are rather frequent in practice.[28]

(4) Discovery obliges the parties to proceedings to disclose to each other all documents including papers, drafts, diary entries, notes, software, tapes or film, which are in any way relevant to the matters in issue in the action and are or have any time been in the possession, custody or power of the parties to the proceedings.[29]

Finland (1)

According to the § 2 SopMenL (Unfair Trade Practices Act) an untruthful or misleading statement about one's own or another's trade which is likely to affect the demand of a product or to injure the trade of another is forbidden. Thus, if the expressions used by A are false he is using an advertisement which is contrary to SopMenL's rules. In this case A also breaches the general clause (§ 1 SopMenL) as this covers all cases of actions of a tradesman or business that are contrary to good business practices or otherwise unfair to other tradesmen. The expression used by A could be untruthful or misleading in two senses: (1) his bread may not be particularly environmentally friendly, and (2) the statement made about B's bread could be false. Even if the statements were correct they could be contrary to § 1 SopMenL if the information is given in a manner that is overbearing (e.g. if there were untested ingredients in the bread, but which are very unlikely to be hazardous to consumers' health, and the advertising points these out as major hazards) and is likely to injure the trade of another.

(1) B can prevent A's misleading advertisements by asking the Market Court to grant an injunction under §§ 6 and 7 SopMenL, whereby the

[26] S. Groom, *United Kingdom*, in J. Maxeiner and P. Schotthöfer, p. 469 (508).

[27] D. Alexander, *Unlauterer Wettbewerb in Großbritannien*, in *Heidelberger Kommentar zum Wettbewerbsrecht*, IV.6 note 13 et seq.

[28] A. Ohly, *Vereinigtes Königreich von Großbritannien und Nordirland*, in G. Schricker, note 175.

[29] S. Groom, *United Kingdom*, in J. Maxeiner and P. Schotthöfer, p. 469 (509).

tradesman is enjoined from continuing or repeating a practice violating §§ 1–3 of SopMenL. The burden of proof is basically on the side of the claimant. Thus B would have to show that the advertisements have been untruthful or misleading and that they have affected his trade. As 'can affect' is enough, no proof is required for individual harm or damages caused by the actions of A. In this case it would be enough to prove that the advertisement might include false statements, which will possibly increase the sales of A and decrease the sales of B and other bakers. The tradesman using the advertisements then has a duty to show that any statement on environmental issues is true and also that the statement on B's bread is true. Anyone using environmental issues or comparison in advertising must be sure that the facts are correct. Usually both sides will use expert witnesses or other materials in order to prove the validity/incorrectness of the statements.

Temporary orders are not widely used and they will only be used if the harm caused to the claimant will be greater than that caused to the defendant. The claimant must ask for this order. The Market Court will grant such an order if there are objective reasons to do so.[30] For example, the product in question is a seasonal one and a final decision of the Court would be meaningless if no temporary order were granted. An example from older cases involves the advertisement for rice before Christmas (as a lot of rice is used in porridge during this season). The injunction is reinforced through the threat of a fine unless, for special reasons, this is deemed unnecessary. This kind of fine can be unnecessary, for example in cases where the practice has been discontinued as soon as the tradesman was notified of the possibility of violation (most often a fine is set). The order can be made temporarily for the duration of the proceedings in the Market Court.

(2) B can even ask that A will be obliged to correct his false statements by publishing the order of the court or other suitable information in one or more newspapers or magazines. Orders to correct have not been used very often as preventing the use of misleading advertisement has been deemed to be enough to correct the situation. If false information is widespread and only correct information would stop its effect an order under § 8 SopMenL is possible. An example is a dangerous drill, which had caused some injuries in Sweden. The company in question was asked to publish a warning. As the decisions of the Market Court are public the claimant can probably reach the same end by ensuring that

[30] Chap. 2 sec. 8 KSL; § 7 SopMenL.

the court order is published (which might even be costfree if there is enough public interest and the media takes on the case).

(3) The case discussed here is likely to be published as it has consumer implications. Even other actions of this kind could be demanded, § 8 SopMenL.

(4) If the untruthful or misleading expressions have been used wilfully A can even be fined under § 8 SopMenL. This is a criminal law sanction, which will be decided in the ordinary lower courts.

(5) In Finland the Consumer Ombudsman (Ombudsman) has a right to be heard in unfair competition cases. The Ombudsman rarely uses this right if there are no direct consumer implications. In this case there might be a reason to participate as the product is probably sold to consumers. If the actions of A are contrary to chap. 2 secs. 7 or 2 KSL (Consumer Protection Act) the Ombudsman can bring the case into the Market Court. If both Ombudsman and tradesman have made a claim in the Market Court these will be handled together. The Consumer Ombudsman has priority to institute a prohibitive action in a matter concerning marketing targeted at consumers.[31]

(6) Under chap. 2 sec. 2 KSL the Consumer Ombudsman can require that further information be included in advertisements.[32]

France (1)

A's comparative advertising violates articles L 121-8 n° 3 and L 121-9 n° 2 CCons (French Consumer Code). Thus art. L 121-8 n°3 of CCons prohibits any comparative advertising making a comparison between goods by identifying, implicitly or explicitly a competitor or his goods if it does not objectively compare one or more essential, pertinent, verifiable and representative characteristics of these goods. For the present case it was not legal to base the advertising on non-verifiable characteristics. Furthermore, the advertising violated L 121-9 n°2 CCons as it led to the discrediting and the denigration of B's goods, of his activity and his situation as a competitor. French law in the case of comparative advertising is now based on European Law.[33] There are several consequences of such advertising. It can in the first place lead to a claim for damages

[31] K. Fahlund and H. Salmik, *Finland*, in J. Maxeiner and P. Schotthöfer, p. 127 (148).

[32] S.K. Kaulamo, *Finland*, in G. Schricker, notes 112 et seq.; J. Keßler and H.-W. Micklitz, *Die Harmonisierung des Lauterkeitsrechts in den Mitgliedstaaten der Europäischen Gemeinschaft und die Reform des UWG* (2003), p. 56.

[33] Here the comparative advertisement is prohibited according to art. 3a para. 1 lit. (c) and (e) Misleading and Comparative Advertising Directive 84/450/EEC.

according to general civil tort law under art. 1382 and art. 1383 cc, art. L 121-14 CCons.

(1) An injunction can be ordered by the *juge d'instruction* or by the court to which the proceedings have been referred. The order taken in this way is enforceable, notwithstanding all rights of appeal (art. L 121-3 CCons). In order to take immediate measures against the advertising and in order to prevent further damages, a summary interlocutory procedure according to art. 808, 809, 872, 873 of the *Nouveau code de la procédure civile* – NCPC (New code of civil procedure) can be engaged.[34]

In the event of failure to adhere to decisions ordering the injunction of the advertising or the non-performance within the appointed deadline of corrective statements the penalties provided for in the first paragraph of art. 121-6 CCons are applicable (art. L 121-7 CCons). This provision points to the provisions of art. L 213-1 CCons. There the penalties range from a fine of €37,500 to two years' imprisonment.

(2) As well as injunctions of forbearance there can be injunctions to modify, as well as injunctions concerning the activity itself.[35] As an example of an injunction 'to modify' the destruction of the products and objects constitutive for the unfair competition act can be ordered.[36]

(3) In the event of sentencing, the court orders the publication of the judgment and it may in addition order the publication of one or more corrective statements (art. L 121-4 CCons). It is usual in unfair competition matters that the tribunal prescribes, in addition to compensation, special publicity measures in order to inform the clients of the unfair behaviour. The costs of this advertising are met by the defeated party. It generally consists in a press release or a notice on the competitor's premises.[37] Another quite efficient sanction consists in the posting of the judgment, but the judge has to specify where (shop, doors, etc.), at what size, with what kind of characters and how long this posting has to last.[38] Finally, even more efficient is the actual publication of the judgment in a newspaper. Generally this 'social punishment' is an accessory of the damage allocation, even in cases where the unfair competition practice has not been perpetuated via such media.[39]

[34] N.-F. Alpi, in Juris-Classeur, *Concurrence, consommation* (2003), Fasc. 245, *Action en concurrence déloyale – éléments de procédure*, note 112.

[35] Ibid., notes 113 et seq. [36] Cass. Com. of March 6, 1991 in RJDA 1991, note 571.

[37] N.-F. Alpi, in: Juris-Classeur, *Concurrence, consommation* (2003), Fasc. 245, *Action en concurrence déloyale – éléments de procédure*, notes 119 et seq.

[38] Ibid., note 119.

[39] TGI de Paris, 3rd chamber, June 15, 1999 in PIBD 1999, note 685, III, p. 457.

(4) Otherwise prohibited comparative advertising is punishable by the penalties provided for, on the one hand, in articles L 121-1 to L 121-7 CCons and, on the other hand, in articles 422 and 423 of the *Code Pénal* (Penal Code) according to art. 121-14 CCons.

On behalf of these provisions agents from the DGCCRF and those from the food directorate general of the Ministry of Agriculture and those from the metrology department of the Ministry of Industry are authorized to establish breaches of the articles L 121-8 and L 121-9 CCons (art. L 121-2 CCons.).

Germany (1)

Comparative advertisement violates §§ 3, 6 para. 2 no. 2 UWG (ex-§§ 1, 2 para. 1 UWG) as the requirements of comparative advertisement are not met. Comparative advertisement is unlawful pursuant to § 6 para. 2 no. 2 and 5 UWG (ex-§ 2 para. 2 lit. (c) and (e) UWG) if it is not based on verifiable features of those goods and if it discredits the competitor. This is the case here. These defaults are based on European law.[40] Besides the infringement of the UWG a claim could also be based on the tort law regulation of § 826 BGB for intentional infliction of harm *contra bonos mores*. Since damages can be claimed under the UWG in the case of slight negligence, § 826 BGB has only gained a marginal importance in unfair competition law.[41]

(1) A claim for an order to cease and desist thus arises from § 8 para. 1 UWG in connection with § 3 UWG (ex-§ 1 UWG in connection with § 2 UWG). The action for injunction requires an action inflicting harm and the risk of repetition.[42] The application for the action has to describe the action that inflicted the harm, i.e. the description has to be concrete enough.[43]

As in general procedural law, the principle applies that the party who seeks to gain a benefit from the favourable circumstances will bear the burden of proof.[44] This means that the claimant has to establish the

[40] Art. 3a para. 1 lit. (c) und (e) Misleading and Comparative Advertising Directive 84/450/EEC.

[41] A. Beater, *Wettbewerbsrecht* (2002), § 28 note 24.

[42] Now explicitely § 8 para. 1 UWG. For the former law see O. Teplitzky, *Wettbewerbsrechtliche Ansprüche und Verfahren* (8th edn 2002), chap. 5 note 1.

[43] Regarding § 254 para. 2 lit. 2 ZPO cf. Köhler/Pieper, *UWG* (3rd edn 2002), vor § 13 notes 279 et seq.; H. Brüning, in H. Harte-Bavendamm and F. Henning-Bodewig, *UWG* (2004), vor § 12 notes 75 et seq.; W. Büscher, in: K.H. Fezer, *Lauterkeitsrecht* (2005), § 12 note 234.

[44] BGH (2000) 46 WRP 724 (727) – 'Space Fidelity Peep-Show'; H. Köhler and H. Piper, *UWG* (3rd edn 2002), vor § 13 note 333; G. Dreyer, in H. Harte-Bavendamm and

misleading circumstances. He bears the entire burden of proof. The court helps the claimants by easing the burden of proof. If the claimant applies for an injunction the courts will assume the risk of repetition.[45] This is possible if the facts to be established are within the scope of responsibility of the defendant.[46]

§ 12 para. 2 UWG (ex-§ 25 UWG) provides for the issuing of a preliminary injunction under §§ 935, 940 ZPO for cease and desist claims under the UWG, in our case for the infringement of § 3 UWG (ex-§ 1 UWG). For this preliminary injunction the requirements of §§ 935, 940 ZPO do not have to be fulfilled. In contrast to other interim injunctions under the civil code a danger of a loss does not have to be substantiated. The urgency is assumed.[47] Consequently, preliminary injunctions are of paramount importance in the law of unfair competition.[48] The application for an injunction can be combined with a motion for administrative action. In case of non-compliance A may be liable to pay an administrative fine of up to €250,000 pursuant to § 890 para. 1 s. 2 ZPO or to be sentenced to up to six months' coercive detention pursuant to § 890 para. 1 s. 1 ZPO.

(2) Moreover, the claimant can resort to the claim of restoration of the status quo which means he is entitled to demand the revocation of the previous unlawful assertions[49] and the removal of the advertisement. This claim does not require any fault on the side of the defendant and is

F. Henning-Bodewig, *UWG* (2004), § 5 note 860; H. Köhler, in W. Hefermehl, H. Köhler and J. Bornkamm, *Wettbewerbsrecht* (24th edn 2006), § 12 notes 2.89 et seq.; W. Büscher, in K.H. Fezer, *Lauterkeitsrecht* (2005), § 12 note 275.

[45] Thus the prevailing case law, see BGH (1955) 57 GRUR 342 (345) – 'Holländische Obstbäume'; BGH (1989) 91 GRUR 445 (446) – 'Professorenbezeichnung in der Arztwerbung I'; O. Teplitzky, *Wettbewerbsrechtliche Ansprüche und Verfahren* (8th edn 2002), chap. 6 note 9.

[46] BGH (1963) 65 GRUR 270, (1962) 15 NJW 2149 – 'Bärenfang'. The jurisdiction has developed various categories of cases. These include internal processes of the defendant, prominent advertising or advertising with factually disputed representations, see H. Köhler and H. Piper, *UWG* (3rd edn 2002), vor § 13 notes 336 et seq.; H. Harte-Bavendamm and F. Henning-Bodewig, *UWG* (2004), § 5 notes 861 et seq.; J. Bornkamm, in W. Hefermehl, H. Köhler and J. Bornkamm, *Wettbewerbsrecht* (24th edn 2006), § 12 notes 2.92 et seq.; K. H. Fezer, *UWG* (2005), § 12 note 276.

[47] BGH (2000) 102 GRUR 151 (152) – 'Späte Urteilsbegründung'; H. Köhler and H. Piper, *UWG* (3rd edn 2002), § 25 note 13; H. Harte-Bavendamm and F. Henning-Bodewig, *UWG* (2004), § 12 note 301; K. H. Fezer, *UWG* (2005), § 12 note 54.

[48] H. Köhler and H. Piper, *UWG* (3rd edn 2002), § 25 note 1; I. Beckedorf, in H. Harte-Bavendamm and F. Henning-Bodewig, *UWG* (2004), § 8 note 1.

[49] Revocation is a special type of abolition, see H. Köhler and H. Piper, *UWG, Kommentar* (3rd edn 2002), vor § 13 note 52; H. Harte-Bavendamm and F. Henning-Bodewig, *UWG* (2004), § 8 note 88, vor § 12 note 135; K. H. Fezer, *UWG* (2005), § 8 note 22.

based on customary law (now § 8 UWG).[50] The defendant has to bear the costs of revocation and removal.

(3) In addition to a restraining injunction the plaintiff can file a motion for publication of the decision. In Germany there is no right to publish the decision. Rather, the court is allowed to grant a power of publication after taking into consideration the interests of the parties, § 12 para. 3 UWG (ex-§ 23 para.2 UWG). This is in accordance with a general legal consideration that publication is a suitable way to remove an infringement that is also known in claims for elimination and for damages.[51]

Greece (1)

For a comparative advertisement to be considered lawful, it has to meet the conditions set out in art. 9(8)[52] of L.2251/1994 on consumer protection; in such a case, it falls neither under the general prohibition of art. 1, nor under the specialized prohibitions of other articles of L.146/1914.[53] With regard to the present case, the method of comparative advertisement selected by A does not meet the conditions stipulated under art. 9(8)(a) and (c) and 9(2) of L. 2251/1991, since the advertisement is not (presumably) based on objective and verifiable features and is defaming B's competitive products. A has compared his products with the products of B without following the relevant legal provisions. If A's

[50] H. Köhler and H. Piper, *UWG* (3rd edn 2002), vor § 13 note 33; H. Harte-Bavendamm and F. Henning-Bodewig, *UWG* (2004), § 8 notes 94, 123; K. H. Fezer, *UWG* (2005), § 12 note 22; O. Teplitzky, *Wettbewerbsrechtliche Ansprüche und Verfahren* (8th edn 2002), chap. 22.

[51] H. Köhler and H. Piper, *UWG* (3rd edn 2002), § 23 notes 18 et seq; H. Harte-Bavendamm and F. Henning-Bodewig, *UWG* (2004), § 12 note 776.

[52] Article 9(8) of L. 2251/1994 on consumer protection is based on Community Law (directives 84/450/EEC, and 97/55/EEC; in order to incorporate the provisions of the latter, the above article was amended by Min. Dec. Z1-496/2000). It stipulates: 'An advertisement identifying directly or indirectly or suggesting the identity of a specific competitor, or of the goods or services that he is providing (comparative advertisement) is allowed provided it compares in an objective manner the main, related and verifiable features of competitive goods or services that have been impartially selected and which: a) is not misleading, b) does not cause confusion in the market between the advertised person and a competitor or between competitors of the advertised person or between the trademarks, other distinctive signs, goods or services of the advertised person and one of his competitors or more than one competitors between them, c) is not degrading, defamatory or contemptuous to a competitor or to the trademarks, goods, services or activities thereof, d) does not aim mainly at profiting from the well-known name of the trademark or other distinctive sign of a competitor, e) regarding products with appellations of origin, it refers to products of the same appellation of origin in any case and f) does not present a good or service as the imitation or copy of a good or service having a registered trademark or trade name.'

[53] *Athens single member CFI*, decision 4995/2001, 52 *EEmpD* (2001) 595.

assertions do not correspond to the truth, the advertisement is unfair and misleading;[54] however, even assuming that the said assertion of A is true, his conduct is unlawful since it constitutes prohibited and wrongful comparative advertisement.[55] By asserting that B sells bread with additional ingredients whose risks have not yet been analysed sufficiently, A is denigrating the quality of goods of his competitor in order to promote his own products.

Moreover, A's behaviour may also fall under the scope of L. 146/14 on *unfair competition*, as it is accepted that Unfair Competition Law may be applicable in parallel with Consumer Protection Law (mainly in the field of advertisement).[56] Art. 3 of L.146/1914 prohibits inaccurate assertions, especially those related to the quality, the origin and the method of production, which may create the impression of a particularly favourable offer. A's assertions that his products are particularly environmentally friendly, while also asserting that B's products contain 'risky' ingredients, constitute prohibited propagation of false facts. Additionally, art. 11 prohibits the propagation of harmful facts that are damaging to competitive enterprises, provided that such facts are not easily provable as true. It may also be considered that A's conduct violates the general prohibition of art. 1 of L. 146/1914 if it is committed with the intent to compete and is contrary to 'good morals' (i.e. especially if his assertions are false), although one should not deduce that any illegal competition practice, prohibited by a specialized provision of L. 146/1914, falls automatically under the scope of the blanket clause of art. 1.[57] If the conditions of all three articles (i.e. 1, 3 and 11) are met, they will be cumulatively applied to produce the same single legal effect.[58]

(1) L. 2251/1994 expressly sets out the classes of claimants and the nature of claims to be raised for violation of its provisions. Thus, it grants claims (a) to consumers associations for the protection of their

[54] Art. 9(8)(a) and 9(2) of L. 2251/1992. The last provision considers as misleading any advertisement which may deceive the persons to whom it is addressed and thus affect their financial conduct.

[55] E. Panayotidou, *Comparative Advertisement* (2000), pp. 274–275.

[56] See Art. 14 (2) L. 2251/1994, E. Perakis, *General Commercial Law* (1999) [in Greek], p. 56, E. Perakis, The relationship between the Consumer Protection Law and the Unfair Competition Law, *DEE* 1996, pp. 113, 115, 117, L. Kotsiris, Unfair Competition and Antitrust Law, 4th edn (2001), [in Greek], p. 198.

[57] M.-Th. Marinos, *Unfair Competition* (Athens 2002) [in Greek], p. 267.

[58] A. Sinanioti-Maroudi, *Article 3*, in N. Rokas (ed.), *Unfair Competition* (1996), 269; G. Michalopoulos, *Article 11*, in: N. Rokas (ed.), *Unfair Competition* (1996), p. 317.

members,[59] (b) to a number of consumer associations fulfilling specific criteria[60] for the protection of general interest, and (c) to commercial, industrial and professional chambers for the protection of their interests. Although competitors are not expressly recognised as potential claimants, the prevailing doctrinal view accepts that affected competitors are also entitled to raise claims for violation of L. 2251/1994 provisions.[61] Thus, B will be entitled to demand that A's competitive conduct cease and not be repeated in the future (i.e. removal and non-repetition of the unlawful advertisement). Provisional measures (preliminary injunctions) are also available according to the general rules of procedural law; in every case, the burden of proof lies on the claimant.

(2) Besides, B may found his claims on L. 146/1914. Thus, he may seek:

(a) For an order to cease and desist;[62] for those claims, B will not be burdened with either proving A's fault or the specific damage incurred as a result of the latter's conduct, since such elements are not prerequisites of his liability.[63] Art. 19 provides for a six-months' prescription period which commences from the day the claimant was informed about the offence and the offender, and in no case will be longer than three years from the unlawful act.

(b) In accordance with art. 20 of L.146/1914, B may additionally seek for the non-repetition of the same act in the future by requesting provisional measures (which are very common in the field of unfair competition).

(c) B may also request reparation in damages, according to the civil law rules regarding fault, causality and damage (CC 914, 919[64]), unless otherwise stipulated in the law.[65] For an indemnification claim, the prescription period cannot commence before the day when the damage was suffered by the claimant. Claims for moral damage in case the unlawful behaviour constitutes an offence against the competitors' right of personality are not excluded (CC 58, 932). Given that the calculation of damages in unfair competition cases is highly complicated,

[59] Art. 10(1) and (8) L. 2251/1994. [60] Set out in art. 10(9).

[61] M.-Th. Marinos, *Unfair Competition*, note 57 above, p. 36, D. Tzouganatos in Y. Karakostas and D. Tzouganatos *Consumer Protection; the Law 2251/1994*, 2, (2003), p. 299 et seq.

[62] Art. 1(2), 3(2) and 11(1).

[63] See D. Tsimbanoulis, *Article 1*, in N. Rokas (ed.), *Unfair Competition* (1996), 68.

[64] M.-Th. Marinos, Unfair Competition, note 57 above, p. 300.

[65] E.g. art. 11(2) requests as a condition for the claim for damages, that the defendant was aware or ought to be aware of the inaccuracy of his statements.

modern doctrine proposes to apply the three-axes method provided for in the patent law (L. 1733/1987, art. 17[66]).

(d) Finally, according to art. 22(4) L. 146/1914, B may accompany his claim for omission with a claim for publication of the judicial decision. The competent tribunal has the possibility (but not the obligation) to allow the claimant to proceed with the publication of the relevant decision; the costs of such publication are met by the losing party.

Hungary (1)

This kind of comparative advertisement does not meet the requirements set out in sec. 7A of the HAA (Hungarian Act on Business Advertising Activity) and therefore it violates sec. 7 HAA. At the same time it falls under the competence of the OEC as misleading advertising according to sec. 15(2) HAA. In this case the advertisement has already taken place, and the aim is to prevent further future misleading advertisement. According to sec. 19(1) HAA the body responsible for the proceedings may issue a temporary injunction prohibiting any further violating conduct, or may order in such injunction that the violating status be terminated, if such action is urgently necessary for the protection of the legal or economic interests of the parties concerned.

(1) According to the Hungarian civil law this can be best achieved by the preliminary injunction provided for by sec. 156 HCP (Hungarian Civil Procedure Act) to prevent further damage. Besides this, the HAA helps the plaintiff by stating, that if justified, the advertiser may be compelled - with due observation of the applicable circumstances and the legitimate interest of the advertiser and other concerned parties - to supply evidence in support of any facts stated in its advertisement, sec. 17(3) HAA. This shifts the burden of proof from the claimant, as established by the general rules of procedure, to the defendant.

(2) According to sec. 14(3) HAA the advertiser shall bear responsibility for violation of the provisions of sec. 7 HAA. Furthermore, according to sec. 15(3) HAA proceedings in accordance with the HAA shall not preclude the possibility that the injured party, in case his personal rights are infringed, may enforce his claim directly before the court in accordance with the general rules of civil law. Should the amount of the possible indemnification under the rules of civil liability not be

[66] The claimant may request (a) reparation in damages according to civil law rules, (b) the amount gained by the defender, or (c) an amount equivalent to the price of an agreed licence.

commensurate with the severity of the misconduct, the court may also impose a penalty to be devoted to public purposes.

(3) On the basis of sec. 80 HCA the Competition Council bringing proceedings shall publish its decisions and it may also publish its injunctions. This shall not be prevented by applications initiating a court review of the resolutions; however, the fact that a court review was initiated shall be indicated when the publication is made. If the injunction ordering the opening of an investigation has been published, the resolution concluding the proceedings shall also be published.

But there is no explicit right of publication (Note the following section is relevant to court proceedings, but misleading advertising falls within the competence of the OEC).

(4) On the basis of an allegation of unfair market practices in the statement of claim, the injured party may request the following according to sec. 86 (2) HCA:

(a) that the violation of the law be established;
(b) the termination of the violation of the law and the prohibition of the party violating the law from any further violation of the law;
(c) that the party violating the law give satisfaction (make an apology) by making a statement or in another appropriate manner, and, if necessary, that sufficient publicity be given to the satisfaction (apology) on the part or at the expense of the party violating the law;
(d) the termination of the unlawful situation, the re-establishment of the state of affairs prior to the violation of the law, and the deprivation of the goods manufactured or placed on the market through the violation of the law of their offending character, or, if this is not possible, the destruction thereof, and the destruction of any special devices and facilities used for the manufacture thereof;
(e) compensation for damages in accordance with the rules under civil law, and
(f) [Repealed by Act LXVIII of 2005]
(g) that the offender supply information about the persons who participated in the production and distribution of the goods concerned by the infringement and about the business relations created for the dissemination of such goods.

Ireland (1)

(1) Under sec. 8 of the Consumer Information Act 1978, it is an offence for anyone to publish an advertisement which is likely to mislead and as a result cause material loss, damage, or injury to the public. One option

for B is to complain to the Director of Consumer Affairs, and hope that the Director chooses to request A to cease the advertising or to prosecute A, but it is to be noted that the Act requires loss, damage or injury to members of the public to a material degree before an offence is committed. On summary conviction, the court has the power to impose a fine of up to €635 and/or six months' imprisonment. On conviction on indictment, higher penalties may be imposed.

Sec. 17 of the 1978 Act enables a court, on imposing a fine for an offence under the Act, to order that the whole or part of the fine be paid as compensation to a witness for the prosecution who suffers a personal injury, loss or damage as a result of the offence. While the Act does not specify that the witness in question must be a consumer rather than a competitor, the 'personal injury' wording implies that the witness will only be compensated if not acting in a business capacity. Sec. 17(3) of the Act makes clear that this remedy only applies if the witness has not instituted proceedings for damages for the injury, loss or damage. If the witness is subsequently awarded damages in civil proceedings, the award made under sec. 17(1) will be deemed to be in full or part satisfaction of that award.

(2) The EC (Misleading Advertising) Regulations 1988 implement the EC (Misleading Advertising) Directive and are to be interpreted in the light of the Directive 84/450.[67] Under sec. 3 of the EC (Misleading Advertising) Regulations 1988, the Director of Consumer Affairs may, following a complaint or on his own intiative, discontinue or refrain from such advertising. If the request is not met, the Director can apply to the High Court for an order prohibiting the publication of the advertisement. Under sec. 4 of the same Regulations, the Director, or any other person may request the High Court for such an order of prohibition, even if no prior request has been made. Where either the Director or any other person makes an application, they are not required to prove either actual loss or damage or recklessness or negligence on the part of the advertiser.

(a) One option for B is to complain to the Director of Consumer Affairs, and hope that the Director chooses to request A to cease the misleading advertising, or even to prosecute A. If A is prosecuted, he will be liable (on summary conviction) to pay up to €1,270. B could then claim damages from A.

[67] Directive 84/450 as amended by Directive 97/55, 1997, OJ L290/18.

(b) A second option for B is to take an action personally against A under sec. 4(1) of the Misleading Advertising Regulations.

Comparative advertising is not per se illegal in Ireland. In the case of *O'Connor (Nenagh) Ltd. v. Powers Supermarkets Limited*, the Regulations were successfully used in the Irish High Court to restrain the defendant from publishing misleading, comparative advertising regarding the plaintiff's supermarket business. Keane J noted that the defendant was perfectly entitled to mount legitimate comparative advertising campaigns but stated, 'if they elect to include comparisons with a named competitor, they must ensure that they are accurate, both in fairness to the competitor and in the public interest'.[68] The Irish Supreme Court has held that an application to restrain publication of an advertisement pursuant to sec. 4(1) of the Regulations cannot be brought by way of interlocutory application as the Regulations only allow for the application to be a full and final hearing.[69] Arguably, this limits the effectiveness of the Regulations, and makes a civil action for defamation a more attractive option for B.

(3) There is also the possibility that A is infringing B's trademark. Sec. 14(6) of the Trade Marks Act 1996 provides that the use of a registered trademark by any person for the purposes of identifying goods or services as those of the proprietor of the trademark is not to be considered an infringement of that trademark if done in accordance with honest practices in industrial and commercial matters. However, it will be considered an infringement if it is not so done and if the use, without due cause, takes unfair advantage of, or is detrimental to, the distinctive character or reputation of the trademark. Accordingly, B could seek relief by way of an injunction and/or by seeking damages in accordance with sec. 19(2) of the Trade Marks Act 1996.

An injunction is a legal order issued by a court, ordering someone to cease a particular activity, and/or ordering someone to desist from a particular activity in the future. Damages is the legal term used to describe a monetary award made by a court to a successful litigant. The Irish Courts enforce the general principle of *restitutio in integrum*.[70] The intention underlying the damages award is thus to restore the injured party to the situation he was in before the loss occurred, insofar as financial compensation allows. The court will only award compensation where it is reasonable in all the circumstances of the

[68] *Joseph O'Connor (Nenagh) Ltd. v. Powers Supermarkets Limited*, March 15, 1993 (unreported).
[69] *Dunnes Stores Ltd v. Mandate* [1996] 1 IR 55. [70] See Case 10.

case. Damages awarded may be general damages, special damages (relating to specific items of expense), exemplary (punitive) damages or nominal damages.[71]

In *Vodafone Group Ltd and Vodafone Ltd v. Orange Personal Communications Services Ltd*, Orange advertised as follows: 'on average, Orange users save £20 every month in comparison to Vodafone's equivalent tariffs'.[72] The court, in applying the English law provision equivalent to sec. 19 of the Trade Marks Act 1996, acknowledged that the law permits comparative advertising provided that advertisers do not use their competitor's trademark where such use, without due cause, would take unfair advantage of, or be detrimental to, the distinctive character or reputation of their competitor's trademark. Vodafone was ultimately unsuccessful as it failed to demonstrate that the advertisement was not an 'honest practice' or that it took unfair advantage or was detrimental to the distinctive character of the trademark.

(4) B could prosecute A in the civil court for the torts of defamation and injurious falsehood. Defamation is committed by the wrongful publication of a false statement about a person, which tends to lower that person in the eyes of right-thinking members of society, or tends to hold that person up to hatred, ridicule or contempt, or causes that person to be shunned or avoided by right-thinking members of society. The tort of defamation encompasses the torts of libel and slander. The difference between libel and slander is narrow, but generally, libel refers to defamation in a more permanent, i.e. written, form. In serious cases, defamatory libel can also be prosecuted as a criminal offence, in which case justification or truth is not a total defence, save in cases where the libel is made for the 'public benefit' under sec. 6 of the Defamation Act 1961. Trial for defamation, both civil and criminal, is by judge and jury. A defamatory statement is only actionable if it is published, so a statement in a private letter could not be held to be defamatory, but a statement in an advertisement could be held to be defamatory. In this case, A's statement about the risky ingredients could reasonably be claimed to be defamatory of B's reputation as a baker and to be calculated to cause him pecuniary damage. Under sec. 21 of the Defamation Act 1961, if A has innocently published defamatory matter about B, he is given an opportunity to make an offer of amends. This would apply if A did not realise the words were defamatory and exercised all reasonable care in relation to the publication. If the words were

[71] See Case 2 (Watch imitations I) and Case 10. [72] [1996] 10 EIPR D-307.

in fact true, A could plead the total defence of justification under sec. 9 of the Defamation Act 1961. The offering of an apology would mitigate damages under sec. 17 of the Act.

In the tort of defamation, the defendant's statement concerns the plaintiff, whereas in the tort of injurious falsehood, it concerns the plaintiff's goods. As this can be a difficult distinction to draw, it is preferable for the plaintiff to base his case on both grounds. Unlike the situation that pertains in relation to defamation, in an action for injurious/malicious falsehood, the onus is on the plaintiff to prove that the defendant's statement was false. The plaintiff must also prove malice. The common law position is that that the plaintiff must show that he has suffered actual loss; sec. 20(1) of the Defamation Act 1961 provides that it is not necessary to allege or prove special damage, (a) if the words on which the action is founded are calculated to cause pecuniary damage to the plaintiff and are published in writing or other permanent form, or (b) the words are calculated to cause pecuniary damage to the plaintiff in respect of his business.[73]

Italy (1)

Disparagement of a competitor's goods in advertising infringes art. 2598, n. 2 codice civile – cc; misleading advertising amounts to a violation of n. 3 of the same art. 2598. In the present case, there is no doubt that A's comparative advertising will be considered as unfair competition, since the requirement of truth, provided for by art. 3bis of d.lgs. 74/92, as amended by d.lgs. 67/2000, implementing EC directive 97/55, is not met. The CAP (Code of Self-Control of Advertising) is relevant as a means for interpreting the general provision of art. 2598, n. 3 cc:[74] comparative advertising may be considered 'fair', according to that provision, only if requirements provided for by the CAP are met (as confirmed by many judicial decisions. (Among recent cases, see e.g. Trib. Torino, May 6, 2004, *Hewlett Packard Development L.P. v. Recycler Component*, in *Giur. it.* (2004), 1892). In the case in question, A's advertisement

[73] *Kaye* v *Robertson* [1991] FSR 62.

[74] See Trib. Torino, November 11, 1998, *Kimberly Clark Italia s.p.a. v. Procter & Gamble Italia s.p.a.*; Trib. Torino, October 29, 1998, both in *Riv. dir. ind.* (1999), II, 61 et seq.; Cass., February 15, 1999, note 1259, *RCS Editori s.p.a. v. Il Giornale di Sicilia Ed. s.p.a.*, in *Riv. dir. ind.* (1999), II, 193 et seq.; App. Milan, July 30, 1999, *Federpietre v. Majorca*, in *Gius* (1999), 2968 et. seq.; App. Milan, February 2, 2001, *Bayer v. Sirc Natural*, in *Gius* (2002), 197 et seq.; Trib. Modena, August 19, 2002, *Meeting v. Prominter*, in: *Riv. dir. ind.* (2003), II, 347 et seq.

amounts to a breach of art. 15, since it is false and misleading; therefore, it may never be considered 'fair' under n. 3 of art. 2598 cc.

(1) According to art. 2599 cc, the judicial decision which finds an infringement of art. 2598 cc may order the defendant to desist from the illegal behaviour, and issue any further measure necessary to eliminate its effects.

B may also claim an *interlocutory injunction* preventing A from publishing his misleading advertisement, according to art. 700 of the CPC (Code of Civil Procedure). The interlocutory injunction may be claimed before litigation is started, and it may also be granted *inaudita altera parte*, according to art. 669 para. 2 CPC, if the summoning of the other party in front of the court may prejudice the fulfilment of the interlocutory measure. In a subsequent hearing, which will take place within fifteen days, the court may affirm or reverse the interlocutory order. If the interlocutory injunction is granted before litigation on the merits is started, such litigation will have to be started by the plaintiff within thirty days (or any shorter time period fixed by the court); otherwise, the interlocutory injunction will cease to be effective.

In order to be granted an interlocutory injunction, the claimant will have to prove that the advertising is actually misleading, since it contains false information concerning his products, which may divert trade from his business in favour of the defendant, and that continuation of the advertising campaign, pending litigation, may cause him serious and irretrievable loss. According to most decisions in case law, such latter requirement may be considered *in re ipsa* in claims for injunctions based on unfair competition, since any illegal behaviour of a competitor on the market has the unavoidable effect of diverting trade in favour of the defendant, therefore causing a loss to the plaintiff (which may be very difficult to prove during the trial on the merits, and this is a further ground for granting the interlocutory injunction). Some minority decisions and scholarly opinions[75] hold that, on the contrary, the claimant should prove that there exists a direct and immediate danger of diversion of trade.

[75] See e.g. Trib. Trieste, July 15, 1994, in *Foro it.* (1995), 351; Trib. Milan, July 24, 1995, in *Giur. ann. dir. ind.*, 3336; Trib. Catania, December 11, 1993, in *Giur. ann. dir. ind.*, 3092; Trib. Verona, July 25, 2000, *Stefcom s.p.a. v. Canguro s.p.a.*, in *Riv. dir. ind.* (2002), II, 54. Among legal scholars, see M. S. Spolidoro, *Le misure di prevenzione nel diritto industriale* (1982), 227; L. Sordelli, *I provvedimenti cautelari nel diritto industriale, nel diritto d'autore e nella concorrenza* (1998), 47.

According to the majority of decisions, forbearance by the claimant does not prevent the claim for an interlocutory injunction succeeding, and even if the illegal behaviour has already ceased, the interlocutory injunction may still be issued, in order to prevent any possible repetition of the illegal behaviour, pending litigation on the merits.

On the other hand, according to some court decisions, a significant lapse of time between the beginning of the infringement and the filing of the claim for interlocutory injunction may lead to the claim being dismissed, due to lack of *periculum in mora*;[76] furthermore, the claim should be dismissed when the unlawful conduct ceased prior to the claim being filed, and there are no elements which may lead to argue that it will start again.[77]

No evidence of the defendant's fraud or negligence is required in the interlocutory proceeding. Should the illegal behaviour continue notwithstanding the interlocutory injunction, the defendant may be held responsible of a criminal offence. In such cases, courts may also order publication of their judgments.[78]

According to art. 2600 cc, damages for unfair competition may be awarded only if the defendant acted fraudulently or negligently. According to the last paragraph of art. 2600 cc, once unfair competition is ascertained, negligence is presumed. Therefore, damages may not be awarded if the defendant proves that he did not act fraudulently or negligently.

(2) Other ways to prevent A from continuing his misleading advertising campaign are the suits in front of the *Autorità Garante della Concorrenza e del Mercato.*

Para. 6 of sec. 7 decree 74/92 states that the Authority, when it deems that the advertisement is misleading, or that a comparative advertisement is unlawful, has the power to issue a cease and desist order, preventing the advertisement being diffused, if it has not yet entered the public domain, or banning its further diffusion. Para. 4 of sec. 7 decree 74/92 states that the authority has the power to place on the undertaking involved the burden of proof that the challenged advertisement is truthful. If the burden is not satisfied, the advertisement will be

[76] See e.g. Pret. Modena, February 5, 1985, *Fonderia F.lli Perani v. Eurotherm*, in: *Giur. ann. dir. ind.* (1985), 1895.

[77] See e.g. Trib. Verona, July 25, 2000, *Stefcom v. Canguro Canguro s.p.a.*, in *Riv. dir. ind.* (2002), II, 54; Trib. Milano, December 10, 1996, in *Dir. ind.* (1997), 401.

[78] Similarly F. Hofer, S. Lösch, A. Toricelli and G. Genta, *Italy*, in J. Maxeiner and P. Schotthöfer, p. 285 (288).

considered misleading. According to para. 3 of sec. 7, decree 74/92, in cases of specific urgency the authority may issue an interlocutory order prohibiting further diffusion of the advertisement pending the procedure. Such interlocutory measures are issued quite rarely by the Authority. In the case of breach of a cease and desist order the defendant may be sentenced to up to three months' coercive detention, and be liable to pay an administrative fine of up to €2,500.

Decree 74/92 was recently amended by l. n. 49 of April 6, 2005, which added paragraph 6 bis to art. 7, dealing with administrative and judicial remedies. According to the new paragraph the Authority, when an advertisement is declared to be misleading, will impose fines from €1,000 to €100,000, depending on the importance and the duration of the infringement. Fines cannot be lower than €25,000 in cases of advertisement which might endanger consumers, or in cases of advertisements aimed at children or teenagers.

(3) The plaintiff can also apply to the panel of the CAP which has the power to issue cease and desists orders to prevent any continuation or repetition in the future of unlawful advertising. The breach of a self-disciplinary injunction may lead to an order by the panel that a notice will be published in some advertising medium, stating that the defendant infringed the CAP, and did not comply with the cease and desist order. Moreover, the breach of such an injunction may amount to unfair competition itself, since breaching the decisions of the CAP panel may not be considered compatible with 'professional fairness', according to n. 3 of art. 2598 cc.

(4) Action in front of ordinary courts is not pre-empted by such suits. On the other hand, suits in front of the public authority and/or of the advertising self-discipline panel are not requirements for the private law action in front of ordinary courts.

Netherlands (1)

The answer proceeds on the assumption that all substantive requirements for an action in tort (based on misleading advertisement) have been met. B can start interlocutory proceedings in order to obtain an interim injunction. It is sufficient for B to state that A's advertisement is misleading. Pursuant to art. 6:195 *Burgerlijk Wetbook* – BW (Dutch Civil Code), the burden of proof is reversed. It is not the plaintiff B but the defendant A who has the burden of proving that the statement in the advertisement was correct and thus not misleading. If the court concludes that A's advertisement is misleading, it may, at the request of B, order A to refrain from making such information public in the future under penalty of a fine. Furthermore, B may request the court to order A to publish a correction of the misleading advertisement on the basis of art. 6:196 BW.

Poland (1)

A misleading advertisement causing confusion and affecting consumers' purchasing decisions constitutes an act of unfair competition (art. 16.1 (2) u.z.n.k.). The same is true for an advertisement causing fear (art. 16.1 (3) u.z.n.k.). A comparative advertisement is deemed to be an act of unfair competition if it conflicts with custom and usage. A comparative advertisement does not conflict with custom and usage if it is not a misleading advertisement (art. 16.1 u.z.n.k.) and does fulfil the criteria (objective and verifiable comparison of goods and services; objective comparison of essential, typical features of goods and services) listed in art. 16.3 (2–8) u.z.n.k.

Art. 16 is the main provision of u.z.n.k. dealing with advertising. However, numerous provisions of the u.z.n.k. prohibit misleading acts and statements.[79] The cited provision aims at protecting both consumers and undertakings and should be read together with art. 10 and art. 16 u.z.n.k.[80] Art. 10 u.z.n.k. aims at protecting truthful information in general and interprets art. 16 in that respect. It points out the kinds of information – including the information given in advertisements – which can cause confusion.

Art. 14 complements art. 16 u.z.n.k. It applies in the situation when a misleading advertisement does not affect a consumer's decision, but nevertheless fulfils the conditions of art. 14. This is in the case of the distribution of untrue or misleading information about the undertaking itself or about another undertaking in purpose of gaining advantage or causing damage, art. 14.1 u.z.n.k. Untrue or misleading information regards in particular products or services, art. 14.2(2) u.z.n.k.[81]

(1) In the case of an infringement of the prohibition defined in the articles mentioned above, the undertaking whose interest is endangered or infringed may demand that the infringing party refrains from the prohibited activities, removes the results of the prohibited

[79] M. Pozniak-Niedzielska, *Przeslanka wprowdzenia w blad jako podstawa odpowiedzialnosci z tytulu nieuczciwej konkurencji. Studia Prawa Prywatnego* (1997).

[80] E. Nowinska and M. Du Vall, *Komentarz do ustawy o zwalczaniu nieuczciwej konkurencji* (2001), p. 141.

[81] See the analysis of Case 6 (Child labour).

activities, makes one or more statements (the form and content of which are agreed upon by the other party) and repairs the damage caused and returns unjustly gained benefits. If the act of unfair competition was intentional the undertaking can demand that the court imposes on the infringer the obligation to pay a sum of money to support Polish culture or to protect the national heritage, art. 18.1 (1–6) u.z.n.k.[82]

These remedies are typical for Polish intellectual property law and are also typical for international regulations on the same subject. The discussed regulation differs a little from the provisions of art. 363 of the *Kodeks Cywilny* – k.c.[83] (Civil Code). The provisions of chap. III of the u.z.n.k. constitute regulations specific to the general provisions of the k.c.[84]

The claim to refrain from the prohibited activities is of the highest importance in general and of the most relevance in the case of the baker's advertisement. Long-lasting infringement can cause an irreversible situation and irreparable damage.[85] However, this claim can only be brought if the act of endangering (real threat) or infringing has already taken place.[86] In his claim the plaintiff should specify the forbidden acts of unfair competition, which are endangering or infringing his rights.[87] The judgment and its execution will cover only the pleaded situations.[88] In the discussed case A has already advertised his products,

[82] Art. 18.1. (1–5) u.z.n.k. reads: An undertaking whose interests are endangered or violated by an act of unfair competition, is entitled to:
(1) the cessation of the inadmissible act,
(2) the removal of the consequences of the inadmissible act,
(3) one or more declarations containing due information and in due form,
(4) the compensation of losses according to general principles of law,
(5) the surrender of unjust advantages according to general principles of law.

[83] The damages should be repaired either by restoring the status quo or by way of monetary compensation.

[84] Under art. 24. 1 k.c., one of the actions required to undo the consequences of an infringement of someone's personal goods is to make a statement (with due content and in due form). In light of art. 18. 1. (2 and 3) u.z.n.k. there are two separate remedies. Similar lack of consistency can be observed in art. 18.1. (2 and 4) u.z.n.k. and art 363. 1 k.c. They overlap to a certain extent. According to art. 363. 1 k.c. a claimant may demand either to the state restore before damage took place or he can claim monetary compensation. Therefore, the provisions of chap. III u.z.n.k. constitute regulation specific to the provisions of k.c.

[85] R. Skubisz, in J. Szwaja (ed.), *Ustawa o zwalczaniu nieuczciwej konkurencji, Komentarz* (2000), p. 498.

[86] E. Nowinska and M. Du Vall, *Komentarz do ustawy o zwalczaniu nieuczciwej konkurencji* (2001), p. 189.

[87] Ibid. [88] Ibid., p. 190.

claiming that it would be very risky to eat the bread offered by B. In this situation, B can demand that A refrains from such advertisements. Art. 18a u.z.n.k. introduces a reversed burden of proof in cases regarding misleading branding and advertisement. According to art. 6 k.c. the burden of proof rests upon the person who derives legal consequences from the factual situation, i.e. on the plaintiff. The u.z.n.k. reverses the burden of proof, i.e. The defendant has to prove that his actions and statements do not infringe fair competition.

An interlocutory injunction banning certain advertising might be granted by the court within whose jurisdiction the defendant has got assets or within whose jurisdiction the act of unfair competition took place, art. 21.2 u.z.n.k. According to art. 730.1 k.p.c, the court can issue the injunction when the claim is credible and a lack of security would deprive the plaintiff of his remedies.

(2) In case of an infringement of the prohibition defined in the articles mentioned above, the undertaking whose interest is endangered or infringed may demand that the infringing person remedy the results of the prohibited activities, art. 18.1 (2) u.z.n.k.

(3) In addition, the violator may be ordered to make one or more statements the form and content of which are agreed upon by the other party, art. 18.1 (3) u.z.n.k.

Portugal (1)

In Portugal, there are few cases of comparative advertising that are decided by civil courts. In fact, comparative advertising is a type of commercial advertising that is not common, because competitors think it is very aggressive. In this case A actually performs both misleading advertising and illegal comparative advertising. He also makes false affirmations in commerce about the products of his competitor B. The advertising message is considered misleading, because it declares, in an untrue way, that the bread that competitor A sells is environmentally friendly and this may mislead consumers or harm competitors. Therefore, art. 11 CPub considers this kind of advertisement illegal. Besides, this is also an example of illegal comparative advertising, because the requirements of comparative advertising are not met (art. 16 para. 2 CPub). In fact, A's affirmation is purely generic and unsubstantiated, and declares that B's bread is risky without giving any proof or scientific reason. Art. 16 para. 2 lit. (c) CPub requires the comparison to refer to essential, objective and provable features. The comparison is also misleading because it is not based on verifiable features of those goods and it discredits the competitor, which is not permitted in comparative advertising (art. 16 para. 2 lit. (a) CPub). Finally, the affirmations in A's advertising message about his competitor also represent unfair competition under art. 317 lit. (b) CPI because they attack him unfairly.

Concerning the burden of proof, it is the competitor who makes comparisons in his advertising materials who must bear the burden of proof that the comparisons are true (art. 16 para. 5 CPub). This kind of rule prevents a lot of competitors from engaging in comparative advertising, because it is a very serious risk to pursue comparative advertising without being absolutely sure of the ability to prove the requirements of the comparison.

(1) Normally, a public agency controls the legality of advertising (Consumer Agency) on behalf of public interest, and not according to the different particular interests. The misleading advertising, under art. 11 CPub, and the comparative advertising regulated in art. 16 CPub both constitute illegal forms of advertising and may incur administrative fines. Uttering false affirmations in commerce with the intention of discrediting a competitor is an administrative tort under art. 317 lit. (b) CPI. Therefore, A may be liable to pay an administrative fine of up to €4.5 million.

(2) He can be forced to publish the administrative decision that applies the fine if the case is considered to be serious and socially relevant by the court (art. 35 para. 4 CPub).

(3) If someone wants to prevent competitors from pursuing such advertising in the future, he can use a civil action for an order to desist and the application of compulsory financial sanctions (fines) in the case of a defendant not respecting the court's decision. If B wants to prevent those acts in the future, a claim for an order to desist under art. 317 CPI would be possible. This kind of action has the purpose of ending and eliminating an illegal action that has already taken place. There is no Portuguese rule governing the claim for an order to desist, but it results from the generic rule under art. 2 para. 2 CPC: 'Every right has its own action.' But in practice the action for an injunction has not gained widespread relevance.[89]

It would also be possible to demand the application of compulsory fines (art. 829a CC) should A insist on pursuing the same type of advertising in the future.

[89] J. Möllering, (1991) 37 WRP 634 (641).

(4) Under civil law A may also be liable for any losses and damages (art. 30 CPub and 483 para. 1 CC) to his competitor B.

Spain (1)

Public comparison of activities of an individual or an establishment and those of a third party undertaking (competitor) are considered as unfair when they refer to information which is not analogous, relevant or verifiable. This comparative advertisement infringes art. 10 para. 1 LCD. Individual legal remedies are listed in art. 18 LCD.[90]

(1) B may claim for an order to desist from the unfair behaviour thus arises from art. 18 no. 2 LCD.

(2) B may also have the right to demand that A remedies the effects of his unfair behaviour (art. 18 no. 3).

(3) There is a right to publish the decision, if the judge decides so, art. 18 no. 5 LCD.

(4) B may also have the right to rectify any incorrect, false or misleading information (art. 19 no. 4 LCD) or to remedy those damages produced by the unfair behaviour when *dolus* or negligence are proven, art. 18 no. 4 LCD.

(5) Finally, an interlocutory injunction is possible, art. 25 LCD.

Sweden (1)

In Sweden, as in the rest of the Nordic countries, there was a shift towards a more permissive attitude in the use of comparisons in marketing from the 1960s onwards.[91] Thus, the Swedish MFL (Act on Marketing) is based upon the principle that all comparisons between the goods, prices and other activities of competitors are permitted.[92]

[90] Art. 18 LCD. Legal actions.
Against an act of unfair competition the following legal actions may be filed:
1. Action for a declaratory judgment on the unfairness of the act, if the interference continues.
2. Action for the termination of the act or its prohibition, if it has not yet been carried out.
3. Action for the removal of the consequences of the act.
4. Action for the compensation of the damages and disadvantages caused by the act, if there was intent or negligence on the side of the acting person. The damages may include the publication of the decision.
5. Action for the surrender of the unjustified enrichment, which is only admissible, if the act has violated a legal status protected by sole and exclusive right or another right with a comparable economic content.

[91] See U. Bernitz, *Marknadsföringslagen* (1997), p. 68.

[92] E.g. U. Bernitz, *Marknadsföringslagen* (1997), p. 69.

This permissive attitude has been made somewhat less permissive due to the influence of EC law[93] and as from 2000 there is a sec. 8a MFL providing criteria for using comparisons with the products of other undertakings in advertisement. In the preparatory documents of the MFL it is considered that a correct comparison in marketing could be of significant importance to the customer when making his choice between different products and services. However, it is stressed that the comparison must be correct and must present a complete picture of the compared products. Hence, a commercial undertaking cannot use statements that are misleading in relation to the undertakings or any one else's commercial business (sec. 6 MFL). Moreover, under the new sec. 8a.5 MFL, which more or less lays down in statutory text the previously partly unwritten meaning of the law, it is clearly prohibited to ridicule or slander the products of another undertaking.

To evade this prohibition, A must be able to demonstrate relatively strong impartial facts supporting his comparison. Should his statements include far-fetched conclusions or generalisations, he will probably have violated sec. 8a.5 MFL.

(1) Since the burden of proof lies on the undertaking responsible for the marketing, A will have to establish that his or her submissions are correct. Now, in case A cannot satisfactorily prove the facts he submits in his advertisement, there are a number of remedies available. In order to prevent A from publishing (this) misleading advertisement(s) in the future sec. 14 MFL may be used for an injunction. An injunction is clearly a remedy with particular focus.[94] Preliminary injunctions under sec. 20 MFL fall under the jurisdiction of the District Court of Stockholm.[95] Parties seeking preliminary injunctions are required to prove their claims.[96] The applicant must show probable cause and that it may be reasonably expected that the defendant by taking or omitting to take a certain act reduces the impact of the possible forthcoming prohibition.[97]

It is not clear from the wording of the act whether it is possible to seek an interim injunction before the court have considered the case and issued a final injunction; the preparatory documents (Governmental

[93] See Comparative Advertising Directive 97/55/EC, above A.III.2.

[94] This is not the place to discuss whether or not prospective legal measures may be defined as 'remedies'.

[95] M. Plogell, *Sweden*, in J. Maxeiner and P. Schotthöfer, p. 425 (443).

[96] Ibid., p. 425 (444). [97] U. Bernitz, *Sweden*, in R. Schulze and H. Schulte-Nölke, p. 6.

Bill 1994/95:123 'New Marketing Act') seem to suggest that there is such a possibility under particular circumstances (see pp. 92–97).

Under sec. 19 MFL an injunction may be combined with periodic penalty payment.

(2) Court decisions may include orders on the elimination of misleading statements on goods, packages, commercial documents etc., sec. 31 MFL.[98]

(3) Besides this, the MFL provides for administrative fines as well as damages. Such measures are generally considered to be retrospectively focused.[99] It is not only administrative fines and damages that by their very existence prevent misleading advertisements being carried out by more or less anonymous undertakings.[100] The remedies in question may also have the effect, when invoked against a particular undertaking, of preventing continuance of some particular misleading advertisement, i.e. in this case baker A's behaviour. Therefore, we will briefly mention the possibility of invoking administrative fines and damages against A.

The Consumer Ombudsman alone has the power to make a claim for a *marknadsstörningsavgift* (market distortion fine; administrative fine) when an undertaking, with intent or negligence, has acted in breach of sec. 6, sec. 22 MFL.[101] The fine may be set somewhere between €500 and €500,000, but may not exceed 10 per cent of A's revenues, sec. 22–25 MFL. This fine goes to the state.[102]

Damages based upon infringements of sec. 4, as a general rule under sec. 29 MFL, may only be claimed when an undertaking infringes an injunction already laid down. In the preparatory works it is left open to the courts to develop liability rules according to the general principles of tort law. It is considered that it would be possible under Swedish law to obtain damages by a court judgment even in the absence of a previous breach of an injunction, where the measures in question clearly come within the prohibitions of the MFL as developed by the case law of the Market Court. And in the relevant literature, it is assumed that cases

[98] U. Bernitz, *Sweden*, in R. Schulze and H. Schulte-Nölke, p. 6.

[99] And thus, in a way, they more genuinely, in some senses, remedy infringements.

[100] E.g. in Governmental Bill 1994/95:123 it is said that rules on liability should e.g. have a preventive effect.

[101] See sections 22 and 39 MFL.

[102] U. Bernitz, *Sweden*, in R. Schulze and H. Schulte-Nölke, p. 6.

of discrediting between undertakings would qualify for liability even without an infringed injunction.[103] In this case, though, it does not seem to be required that an injunction is infringed before a damage claim is brought. Under sec. 29 MFL a claim for damages founded on a breach of some of the specific prohibitions of the MFL does not presuppose an injunction. Sec. 8a.5 MFL is such a specific prohibition.

It seems possible to combine a claim for damages with a claim for an injunction.[104] But in cases where the Consumer Ombudsman brings an action concerning an administrative fine, there is no availability of interim injunction.[105]

Thus, if B were to pursue the matter on his own, the remedies available would be to claim an injunction before the Market Court and/or to claim damages from A. He could also try to persuade the Consumer Ombudsman or a consumer association to investigate the matter further and hope that they seek an injunction.

(4) A businessperson can be ordered to provide such information that is of particular importance for the consumer, sec. 4 para. 2 MFL.[106]

Summary (1)[107]

1. *Injunction or prohibition*

a) Content of the injunction or prohibition

In most Member States the most important legal remedy is that unlawful advertising is not repeated in the future. This so-called claim for an injunction is usually a civil law procedure, for example in Germany, Austria, or Poland. If there is supervision by an authority, as for example by the Consumer Ombudsman in Sweden, Finland and Denmark, or the OFT in England, then the prohibition is equivalent to the civil law injunction order.[108]

[103] U. Bernitz, *Marknadsföringslagen* (1997), p. 112.

[104] This does not follow from MFL, but from the Swedish Code of Civil and Criminal Procedure, chap. 15. In sec. 50 MFL, the Code applies if MFL does not regulate a situation differently.

[105] Sec. 20 MFL *a contrario*.

[106] U. Bernitz, *Sweden*, in R. Schulze and H. Schulte-Nölke, p. 2.

[107] For the operative and metalegal formants see M. Bussani and U. Mattei (1997/98) 3 Colum.J.Eur.L. 339 (354 et seq.) and above A.I.1(e).

[108] See Case 1 (Risky bread).

Evaluation

The cessation claim was unknown in Roman law. Until the nineteenth century the cessation claim had no practical significance in Germany because the supervision of trade was carried out by the guilds.[109] In 1905 the Reichsgericht had founded the claim for an injunction under the principle of equity.[110] The European legislature harmonized the cessation claim with the Misleading and Comparative Advertising Directive 84/450/EEC, in that it encouraged the enforcement of cessation of confusing or inadmissible comparative advertising. This can be enforced through the courts or administrative authority.[111] In this way the claim for an injunction and prohibition are aimed at the same legal remedy, that is cessation of the unlawful conduct. As a result it will be no surprise that all Member States know this legal remedy. In England for example reg. 4(3) CMAR establishes the priority of complaints to the local standards authority[112] and of the self-regulatory mechanisms of the advertising standards authority[113] that have traditionally played an important role in the control of advertising in England.[114] As the OFT surrendered the legal matter to the ASA it remains questionable how effective this legal protection is.

On the other hand it may be said that the Misleading and Comparative Advertising Directive 84/450/EEC nominates the self-regulatory bodies, but emphasizes that they may only act in addition to the court or administrative proceedings. In fact, the standards applied by the ASA are regarded as higher than the legal requirements. To the extent, however, that no further harmonization in substantive law has taken place, the self-regulatory bodies will be allowed to monitor the advertising infringement.

b) Easing of substantive burden of proof

(1) The Misleading and Comparative Advertising Directive 84/450/EEC has in addition harmonized the requirements for a claim. The cessation

[109] O. Teplitzky, *Wettbewerbsrechtliche Ansprüche und Verfahren* (8th edn 2002), chap. 2 notes 1 et seq.

[110] RGZ 60, 6 (7); O. Teplitzky, *Wettbewerbsrechtliche Ansprüche und Verfahren* (8th edn 2002), chap. 2 note 6.

[111] Art. 4 para. 2 s. 1 indent 1 Misleading and Comparative Advertising Directive 84/450/EEC.

[112] See J. Macleod, *Consumer Sales Law* (2002), p. 268. [113] Ibid., p. 3.

[114] *Director General of Fair Trading v. Tobyward Ltd. and another* [1989] 2 All ER 266. See also C. Scott and J. Black, *Cranston's Consumer and the Law* (3rd edn 2000), p. 61.

of unlawful conduct can also be required without proof of fault on the part of the advertiser or loss by the claimant.[115] This factual requirement, necessary in general tort law, is no longer necessary and thereby clearly eases the pursuit of the claim. Basically, the claim of the misleading circumstances by the advertiser is to be proven by the claimant. Art. 6 lit. (a) Misleading and Comparative Advertising Directive 84/450/EEC gives courts or administrative authorities the power to require the advertiser to furnish evidence as to the accuracy of factual claims in advertising, if, taking into account the legitimate interest of the advertiser and any other party to the proceedings, such a requirement appears appropriate on the basis of the circumstances of the particular case. Should this evidence be insufficient, the factual claim may be seen as incorrect.[116] The legal harmonization effected in this way is, however, subject to several uncertain legal concepts. The reversal of the burden of proof depends on the circumstances of the particular case; it must be reasonable and ultimately subject to a balancing of the interests of the advertiser and other participants in the proceedings. It may therefore be no surprise that harmonization has not been achieved in the implementation of easing the burden of proof in the various Member States.

(2) In Austria in cases of comparative advertising the advertiser bears the burden of proof for the correctness of the advertising (§ 2 para. 5 UWG). This also corresponds to the burden of proof under § 7 UWG. The claimant only has to prove the dispersal of the harmful fact, whereas the defendant, similarly as under §111 StGB, has to prove the truth of its representation. For this, according to doctrine and judge-made law,[117] it is sufficient that substantial evidence is provided. In Poland contrary to the general distribution of evidence the u.z.n.k. reverses the burden of proof, i.e. the defendant has to prove that his actions and statements (advertisement) do not infringe fair competition.[118] In Finland anyone using environmental issues or comparison in advertising must be sure that the facts are correct.

In comparison the requirements in Germany are noticeably narrower. There it is emphasized for example that the plaintiff must demonstrate the requirements for a claim. Accordingly, the claimant must

[115] Art. 4 para. 2 s. 1 Misleading and Comparative Advertising Directive 84/450/EEC.
[116] Art. 6 lit. (b) Misleading and Comparative Advertising Directive 84/450/EEC.
[117] H. Koppensteiner, *Österreichisches und Europäisches Wettbewerbsrecht* (3rd edn 1997), p. 579; (1990) 39 ÖBl 18 – 'Mafiaprint'.
[118] Art. 18a u.z.n.k.

prove the misleading nature of the advertisement.[119] However, the jurisdiction has admitted two exceptions. There is a procedural duty of a declaration of the advertiser pursuant to § 242 BGB in the case of disproportionate difficulty for the claimant (for example with internal business procedures of the defendant). If the claimant does not react or reacts insufficiently its behaviour may be evaluated in terms of the free evaluation of evidence as a circumstance which supports the presumption of misleading conduct.[120] In addition there is a reversal of the burden of proof in cases of scientifically disputed factual statements.[121] Apart from that it is emphasized that a directive-conform interpretation is possible.[122]

Evaluation

The easing of the burden of proof under the Misleading and Comparative Advertising-Directive 84/450/EEC was only partly implemented in Germany. In consistent jurisdiction the ECJ has required that directives must be clearly implemented, so that citizens can rely on their rights.[123] In the literature it is argued that this principle does not apply to competition, as it is not citizens, but rather competitors or associations that are subject to the legal regime and that these are normally aware of their rights.[124] The argument, however, is not convincing as this goes against the obligation of Member States to implement directives. The obligation would be limited to directives which confer rights upon the citizen. The obligation under art. 10 para. 1 EC to implement directives is, however, not limited to such directives but applies to all directives.

Another result would only be possible if the ECJ were to decide that the consideration of the individual case (and thereby the question of

[119] J. Bornkamm, in H. Hefermehl, H. Köhler and J. Bornkamm, *Wettbewerbsrecht* (24th edn 2006) § 5 note 3.23.

[120] BGH (1978) 80 GRUR 249 (250) – 'Größtes Teppichhaus der Welt'.

[121] BGH (1991) 93 GRUR 848 (849) – 'Rheumalind II'; J. Bornkamm, in H. Hefermehl, H. Köhler and J. Bornkamm, *Wettbewerbsrecht* (24th edn 2006) § 5 note 3.23 et seq.

[122] K. Tonner, (1987) 40 NJW 1917 (1922 f.); J. Bornkamm, in H. Hefermehl, H. Köhler and J. Bornkamm, *Wettbewerbsrecht* (24th edn 2006) § 5 note 1.15.

[123] ECR 28/84, (1985) ECR 1661 note 23; ECJ C-144/99, (2001) ECR I-3541 notes 17 et seq., (2001) 54 NJW 2244 – 'Unfair Terms Directive 93/13/EC'; ECR C-192/99, (2001) ECR I-541.

[124] A. Beater, *Wettbewerbsrecht* (2002), § 8 note 14; the same opinion in H. Köhler and H. Piper, *UWG, Kommentar* (3rd edn 2002), § 3 note 42a, emphasizing that all prerogatives of the Misleading and Comparative Advertising Directive 84/450/EEC are well known.

how the balancing of interests in favour of an easing of the burden of proof is to be decided) would be subject to the national courts and not the ECJ.[125]

c) Knowledge of the claim requirements through information entitlement

The requirements of a claim are also easily proved provided the claimant is aware of them. In England and the USA no easing of the burden of proof is recognized. However in both jurisdictions the pre-trial discovery procedure facilitates civil law disputes. In England discovery obliges parties to proceedings to disclose to each other all documents including papers, draughts, diary entries, notes, software, tapes or film, which are in any way relevant to the matters at issue in the action and are, or have at any time, been in the possession, custody, or power of the parties to the proceedings.

Particularly interesting are the possibilities for the administrative authorities to gain information on the conduct relevant to competition issues. Thus Swedish,[126] Finnish,[127] and Danish[128] law oblige the business party to provide information to the consumer ombudsman on request. The obligation is sanctioned by a fine should the enterprise fail to fulfil the information requirement.

Evaluation

In Germany there is no satisfactory mechanism to obtain disclosure of information about competitors.[129] However, pre-trial discovery procedure as in the Anglo-American system, should not be overemphasized. The law of unfair competition is applicable only in the narrow field of anticompetitive claims under tort law. Beyond this, civil law disputes are costly and the pre-trial discovery procedure often takes several months.

By contrast action by the Consumer Ombudsman is effective because under Swedish and Danish law he has a claim for information from

[125] See ECJ C-210/96, ECR I-4657, (1998) 46 GRUR Int. 795 (797), (1998) 44 WPR 848 (840) note 27 – 'Gut Springheide'; ECJ C-303/97, ECR I-513, (1999) 47 GRUR Int. 345 (348), (1999) 45 WRP 307 (311) note 37 – 'Sektkellerei Kessler' concerning the question whether national courts may obtain expert opinions on questions of fact concerning deceptions.

[126] § 11 MFL. [127] Sec. 4 of the National Consumer Administration.

[128] § 15 para. 2 in connection with § 22 para. 2 MFL.

[129] Critical O. Teplitzky, *Wettbewerbsrechtliche Ansprüche und Verfahren* (8th edn 2002), § 26 note 39.

advertisers. Here public law has the advantage that it need not support legal enforcement through a laborious easing of the burden of proof.

d) Threat of administrative fines or criminal fines

The threat of administrative or criminal fines is not expressly regulated by European law. However, in almost all states there are sanctions for cases where the prohibition or cessation order is not observed. In Germany, for example, the cessation claim may be supported by an administrative fine of up to €250,000,[130] and in Austria with fines of up to €100,000.[131]

Similarly in Sweden,[132] Finland[133] and Denmark,[134] an injunction may be combined with the threat of a fine. Fines are also possible in France, Italy and Portugal. By contrast in England, court action is seen as a last resort. The OFT can only sue for an injunction. In case of a breach of a court order, it would have to sue again.

Evaluation

Almost all states combine the injunction respectively the prohibition with the threat of a fine if the advertiser repeats its unlawful conduct. Only in England must the OFT again bring a claim against the infringement of his cessation order. Such an obligation to claim a second time before the courts has been known on the European level with the default proceedings under art. 226–228 EC: it proved to be highly ineffective as the delay before the legal infringement was ended tended to protect the infringer. With the Maastricht Treaty in 1992 it was therefore provided that under default proceedings the ECJ may impose a lump sum.[135] For this reason the threat of a fine should be harmonized on the European level. The general enforcement order of art. 4 Misleading and Comparative Advertising Directive 84/450/EEC, that each 'Member State shall ensure that there are adequate and effective means to combat misleading advertising', would in this way be clearly realized and thereby for the first time truly effective.

[130] § 890 para. 1 s. 2 ZPO. [131] § 355 para. 1 EO. [132] Sec. 5 MFL.
[133] § 6 para. 1 s. 2 SopMenL; Kap. 2 § 7 para. 1 s. 2 KSL. [134] § 22 para. 1 MFL.
[135] Art. 228 para. 2 subpara. 3 EC. The ECJ developed an additional state liability claim, see ECJ Joined Cases C-6/90 and C-9/90, (1991) ECR I-5357, (1993) 2 CMLR 66, (1992) 45 NJW 165 – 'Francovich'.

2. *Elimination*

A claim for elimination is recognized in almost all Member States either by statute or judge-made law.[136] This applies particularly to Germany, Austria, Sweden, Finland, Denmark, Spain and Portugal, but also to Poland and Hungary. In France the court can order the publication of the judgment and it may in addition order the publication of one or more corrective statements.[137] In Italy, according to art. 2599 cc, the judicial decision which ascertains an infringement of art. 2598 cc may order the defendant to desist from the illegal behaviour, and issue any further measure necessary to eliminate its effects.

In the USA, a defendant was ordered to send corrective information to those who had previously received its false advertising.[138] The court may order that the defendant be required to advise distributors to withdraw infringing products from the market.[139] Under the Lanham Act the courts are given discretion to order that labels and advertisements bearing the infringing mark be delivered up and destroyed.[140] On the federal state level, the deceptive acts can be used to order corrective advertising, where necessary to eliminate the lingering effects of past deceptions.[141]

Evaluation

(1) Under the Misleading and Comparative Advertising Directive 84/450/EEC the elimination claim is subject to two limitations. First, as an optional clause it is dependent on implementation in the Member States. Second, the elimination, that is the publication of a corrective declaration, is not generally expressly provided for but is only a subsidiary aspect.[142]

(2) In almost all states an elimination claim is recognized under statute or by judge-made law. The elimination may typically go further than cessation of unlawful advertising,[143] because the elimination order can remove the legal consequences of an unlawful position and

136 See Case 1 (Risky Bread). 137 Article L 121-4 CCons.

138 *Thomas Nelson, Inc. v. Cherish Books, Ltd.*, 595 F.Supp. 989, 224 U.S.P.Q. 571 (S.D.N.Y. 1984).

139 *Gaylord Products, Inc. v. Golding Wave Clip Co.*, 161 F.Supp. 746, 118 U.S.P.Q. 148 (W.D.N.Y. 1958).

140 Lanham Act § 36, 15 U.S.C.A. § 1118.

141 C. McManis, *Intellectual Property and Unfair Competition* (5th edn 2004), p. 402.

142 Art. 4 para. 2 subpara. 3 indent 2.

143 See O. Teplitzky, *Wettbewerbsrechtliche Ansprüche und Verfahren* (8th edn 2002), § 22 note 6.

thereby restore the lawful position. The publication of a corrective statement is certainly an important subsidiary aspect of general elimination, but it is merely a subsidiary element. An elimination order can for example be directed at the removal of posted brochures, the destruction of unlawfully labelled goods, or machinery produced in violation of commercial secrets. For this reason the two limitations under the Misleading and Comparative Advertising Directive 84/450/EEC should not be maintained. In this way the elimination claim would be introduced on a European level and an elimination order would generally be held admissible and not limited to the corrective declaration.

3. *Publication*

In the publication of decisions three points of view may be distinguished.[144] In Finland, publication orders have not been used very often since preventing the use of misleading advertisement has been deemed sufficient to correct the situation. If false information is widespread and only correct information would stop its effect, an order under § 8 SopMenL is possible. An example is a dangerous drill, which had caused some injuries in Sweden. The company in question was asked to publish a warning. As the decisions of the Market Court are public the claimant can probably reach the same end by ensuring that the court order is published (which might even be without cost if there is sufficient public interest and the media takes on the case). Publication as a sanction is rare in the USA.[145]

By contrast, in France it is usual in unfair competition matters that, apart from compensation, the tribunal prescribes special publicity measures in order to inform consumers of the unfair behaviour. The costs of this publicity are charged to the defeated party. It generally consists in a press release or advertising at the competitor's sales premises. Another quite effective sanction consists in the posting of the judgment, but the judge has to lay down where (shop, doors, etc.), what size, with what kind of characters and how long this posting has to last. Finally, even more efficient is the actual publication of the judgment in a newspaper. Generally, this 'social punishment' is supplementary to the damages award, even in cases where the unfair competition practice has not been perpetuated via this medium.

[144] See Case 1 (Risky Bread).
[145] J. Maxeiner and F. Kent, *United States*, in J. Maxeiner and P. Schotthöfer, p. 513 (544).

Finally there are Member States which take a middle path. In these states, such as Germany or Portugal, publication is only admissible under narrowly limited circumstances. Thus the case must be serious and socially relevant in Portugal,[146] whereas in Germany the interests of the parties must be weighed, and in Hungary the publication must be necessary.[147]

Evaluation

(1) The publication of the decision certainly has a deterrent effect. It is also partially used by self-regulation authorities of advertising agencies as the appropriate sanction.[148] It thus has a greater preventative effect than the pure injunction order, which merely ends the unlawful circumstance but does not affect consequences already suffered. Thereby publication may be particularly considered where the elimination of the unlawful circumstance is to be effective, as for example the denial of an incorrect fact. However, the publication of the decision can have an excessive and disproportionate effect. After such publication numerous consumers could decide no longer to buy the advertised product. Such turnover losses could go beyond the significance of the actual legal infringement.

(2) Thus, a compromise solution would seem to be appropriate. The Portuguese publication law generally provides that the violator can be ordered to publish the administrative decision that applies a fine if the case is considered by the court to be serious and socially relevant.[149] In German legal writing it is emphasized that the publication should be in conformity with the requirements for elimination.[150]

*(3)*The Misleading and Comparative Advertising Directive 84/450/EEC gives Member States only the possibility of publication of the decision as a sanction. They may exercise this possibility.[151] As a result of this optional clause legal practice varies widely so that further harmonization should be considered. Publication should not only serve to satisfy the injured party, but must also be an appropriate means of eliminating a persisting violation.[152]

[146] Art. 35 para. 4 CPub. [147] Sec. 86 (c) HCA. [148] See Case 3 (Whisky).

[149] Art. 35 para. 4 CPub.

[150] O. Teplitzky, *Wettbewerbsrechtliche Ansprüche und Verfahren* (8th edn 2002), § 26 note 22 including further proof.

[151] Art. 4 para. 2 subpara. 3 indent 1.

[152] H. Köhler and H. Piper, *UWG* (3rd edn 2002), § 23 note 18.

Case 2 Watch imitations I: interim injunction

Colourable imitations of a reputed mark of Swiss watch, B, are offered as genuine in a bakery belonging to the A chain. While the original B watches cost €2,000, the A imitations cost only €20. A has not only published an advertisement in a number of newspapers, but has decorated his shop display window with pictures of the imitation watch.

B happens to find out that A is planning to sell the imitation watches the following week, accompanied by an advertising campaign. The watches have already been ordered from the supplier, the advertising posters printed and TV spots booked. B wishes to prevent the advertising campaign.

Does B have material claims against A realizing his plans? To what extent can B undertake proceedings against the advertising campaign before its publication?

Austria (2)

In this case the claim for an injunction could be based on § 1 UWG because of 'immoral' imitation (preventable deception about origin). One has to differentiate between prevention of misleading advertiseming that has already taken place (adverts; advertisement in shop windows), prevention of further advertising (posters and TV spots), and the sale of slavish imitations of Swiss brand name watches: for the first phase (fully completed misleading advertiseming) B has an action for permanent injunction based on § 2 UWG (statements likely to mislead about the nature of goods), because the disturbance continues (advertising in shop windows) or because there is the danger of repetition (further adverts).

To prevent the planned advertising campaign B could resort to a preliminary injunction based on the imminent risk of damage to him. But the burden of proof for this rests with the claimant. Advertising for the future sale of imitation products is sufficient to prove the probability of imminent risk to the claimant.

The claimant is allowed – as is the case with all other claims for an injunction (§ 14 UWG) or for elimination (§ 15 UWG) under the UWG – to seek an interlocutory injunction to protect his claim. This is even possible if the prerequisite of § 381 EO, a risk of damage, is not met (§ 24 UWG). This claim is widely used in Austria. More than 50 per cent of the decisions of the OGH in cases concerning the UWG are interlocutory injunctions. And they normally lead to a quick and final resolution of the legal proceedings if the facts of the interlocutory proceedings are proven and irreversible.[1] With an interlocutory injunction B is able to prohibit the advertising campaign even before it is started but the court might impose on him the provision of security.

Denmark (2)

The controversy concerns the situation between traders where A is trying to sell copies of B's products and thus benefits from goodwill connected with B's product and trademark. The main question is whether the advertising campaign can be stopped. The marketing – and the sale – is regarded by B as contrary to § 1 MFL. B's product has a distinctive character, and A's product is presumed to be a copy whose production B has not permitted.[2] The marketing and the sale of A's product are also regarded as contrary to the Trademarks Act as an unauthorized application of B's trademark.

Under § 13 MFL an injunction may be ordered against A's sale of an unauthorized imitation product. B has an independent interest in preventing the advertising campaign as it may cause irreparable damage to his goodwill.[3] Under § 13 MFL he can bring an action before the courts having issued an injunction against A's marketing. There are no conditions of fault attached to having an injunction issued under § 13 MFL.[4] It will often not be appropriate to await such a judgment; especially in the present case where the marketing is imminent.

Based on the general rules of the §§ 641 et seq. Administration of Justice Act B can apply at the Enforcement Court for an interlocutory injunction against A's marketing.[5] Before the Enforcement Court B must render it probable that A's action will be unlawful in relation to B under the law of unfair competition and/or the Trademarks Act; that A may be expected to carry out the unlawful action, and that B's right will be prejudiced unless an interlocutory injunction is issued. According to § 644 sec. 1 Administration of Justice Act, a security must normally be provided for A's possible losses caused by the injunction, and according to § 648 sec. 2 Administration of Justice Act a claim on the legality of the injunction must be brought within two weeks after the interlocutory

[1] H. Fitz and H. Gamerith, *Wettbewerbsrecht* (4th edn 2003), p. 80.

[2] E. Borcher and F. Bøggild, *Markedsføringsloven* (2001), p. 78.

[3] M. Koktvedgaard, *Lærebog i Konkurrenceret* (4th edn 2000), p. 66.

[4] E. Borcher and F. Bøggild, *Markedsføringsloven* (2001), p. 359.

[5] E. Bruun et al., *Fogedsager* (2nd edn 2000), p. 635; B. von Eyben et al., *Karnovs lovssamling* (2001), p. 3944.

injunction has been issued. The injunction may be appealed. This rule is applied only in very rare cases.

England (2)

The imitation watches could constitute a number of intellectual property infringements in the UK: trademarks in aspects of the originals that are copied in the imitations;[6] design rights; copyright; and possibly an action for passing off may be possible.

The Trade Marks Act 1994, sec. 10(1), indicates that 'a person infringes a registered trademark if he uses in the course of trade a sign which is identical with the trademark in relation to goods or services which are identical with those for which it is registered' and, under sec. 10(2) 'there exists a likelihood of confusion on the part of the public, which includes the likelihood of association with the trademark'. 'Confusion' and 'association' have received much judicial attention in English law.[7] However, B must show that there is such a likelihood created in the mind of consumers by the advertising campaign (and the imitation watches). The advertising is caught not only by 'in the course of trade' above, but also in sec. 10(4) as 'a person uses a sign if, in particular, he (b) offers or exposes goods for sale, puts them on the market or stocks them for those purposes under the sign'. If B has trademarks in the original watch, there seems to be a strong possibility of trademark infringement, especially as the goods are offered as 'genuine'. In these circumstances, the actions of A could give rise to civil remedies[8] and criminal sanctions[9] for trademark infringement.

Equally, given the quality of B's watches, there is an argument that they are works of 'artistic craftsmanship',[10] and that a copy of such a copyright work, be it three- or two-dimensional can constitute an infringement. However, items produced on a large scale have not

[6] By the Trade Marks Act 1994, section 1(1) 'any sign capable of being represented graphically which is capable of distinguishing goods or services of one undertaking from those of other undertakings' can be a trademark. This includes 'words (including personal names, designs, letters, numerals or the shape of goods or their packaging'. Section 3 indicates exclusions from registration. A relevant element here could be if the sign was determined by the 'nature of the goods themselves' (sec.3(2)(a)), was 'necessary to obtain a technical result'(sec. 3(2)(b)) or 'gives substantial value to the goods' (sec. 3(2)(c)), see *Philips Electronics NV v. Remington Consumer Products* [1999] RPC 809.

[7] See e.g. *Wagamama Ltd v. City Centre Restaurants* [1995] FSR 713.

[8] Trade Marks Act 1994 secs. 14 to 21 [9] Ibid., secs. 92 to 98

[10] Copyright, Designs and Patents Act 1988, sec. 4. But see *George Hensher Ltd v. Restawhile Upholstery (Lancashire) Ltd* [1976] AC 64 and *Merlet v. Mothercare plc* [1986] RPC 115.

attracted such protection[11] but could attract protection through design rights[12]. In the circumstances between A and B, the possible infringements of copyright could give rise to both civil actions[13] and criminal sanctions;[14] design rights could give rise to civil actions.[15] It may also be possible to prove a civil action for passing off. The essential elements of such a claim are taken from two cases: *Erven Warnink BV v. Townend and Sons (Hull) Ltd*[16] and *Reckitt and Colman Products v. Borden Inc.*[17] The formulations are slightly different. However, the combined essential elements are that a 'misrepresentation', causing, or likely to cause, the 'prospective or ultimate' customer to believe that he was gaining the goods or services of the claimant, is made 'in the course of trade' causing injury to the 'goodwill or business of another' and causes or is likely to cause damage to the other.[18] Here, the goods are sold as 'genuine', but a difficulty could be in showing that the public is confused by the goods given the difference in price and the place of sale.

There is, therefore, scope for B to bring an action against A for the advertising campaign through breaches of intellectual property rights. A's actions may also contravene the Trade Descriptions Act 1968, as photographs of the counterfeit goods could constitute 'false description' of the goods (i.e. that they are what they are not).[19]

Once the basis for an action is identified, there are two avenues in English law for B to take in relation to the advertising: an injunction to prevent the continued advertising and proposed infringements; and, an application to the local weights and measures authority (Trading Standards) for an order under Part 8 of the Enterprise Act 2002.[20] Part 8 of the Enterprise Act 2002, 'creates a more consistent enforcement regime [. . .] giving enforcers strengthened powers to obtain court orders against businesses that fail to comply with their legal obligations to

[11] See secs. 51 and 52 of the CDPA 1988.

[12] Registered Designs Act 1949 and Copyright Designs and Patents Act 1988, Part III.

[13] Copyright, Designs and Patents Act 1988, secs. 96 to 100.

[14] CDPA 1988, secs. 107 to 110.

[15] Ibid., secs. 226 to 235, and Registered Designs Act 1949, sec. 7.

[16] [1979] AC 731. [17] [1990] 1 All ER 873.

[18] J. Philips and A. Firth, *Introduction to Intellectual Property Law* (4th edn), p. 294, (paras. 20.11, 20.12, and 20.13)

[19] Trade Descriptions Act 1968 sec. 1(1).

[20] Replacing Fair Trading Act 1973 Part III and Stop Now Orders (EC Directive) Regulations 2001 (*Enforcement of Consumer Protection Legislation: Guidance on Part 8 of the Enterprise Act*, Office of Fair Trading, 2003., paragraph 3.2)

consumers'.[21] Part 8 proceedings are taken in respect of the 'collective interests of consumers in the United Kingdom'[22] rather than a single specific consumer, and must be triggered by an infringement of a relevant statute or statutes or by another prohibited act or omission.[23] Offering counterfeit goods for sale, as A proposes, could offend a sufficient group of consumers to satisfy the collective interest requirement. The Trade Descriptions Act 1968,[24] the Trade Marks Act 1994, sec. 92, the Copyright, Designs and Patents Act 1988, sec. 107 are all relevant statutes for Part 8 proceedings. The action is taken by an 'enforcer',[25] and ideally start with 'consultation' with the alleged infringer and the Office of Fair Trading,[26] to attempt to resolve the issue without recourse to the courts for an order.[27] Reasonable consultation periods are indicated in the Act as fourteen days for an enforcement order and seven days for an interim order.[28] Immediate orders can be sought where the OFT believes that 'an enforcement order should be made without delay'.[29] The application, where necessary, is made to the High Court or county court (England and Wales) and the Court of Session or the sheriff (Scotland),[30] and the 'purpose of the enforcer'[31] must be considered. An enforcement order makes clear how the infringer must stop his conduct[32] and may require publication of either the order or a 'corrective statement' 'for the purpose of eliminating any continuing effects of the infringement'.[33] The OFT has published interesting guidance on how it sees the operation of Part 8.[34]

These measures could give an effective stop to the advertising with undertakings not to infringe the intellectual property rights in the

[21] *Enforcement of Consumer Protection Legislation: Guidance on Part 8 of the Enterprise Act*, Office of Fair Trading, 2003, para. 3.3.

[22] Enterprise Act 2002, sec. 211(1)(c) (see also sec. 210). [23] Ibid., sec. 211(2).

[24] Note that the operation of Part 8 in respect of trade descriptions and misleading advertising follow and respect the British Codes of Advertising and Sales Promotion Advertising and the Advertising Standards Authority procedures (depending on the severity of the case) – see *Enforcement of Consumer Protection Legislation: Guidance on Part 8 of the Enterprise Act* Office of Fair Trading, 2003, para. 3.77 and 3.78.

[25] Enterprise Act 2002, sec. 213 (here the most relevant is the local Trading Standards Office).

[26] Ibid., sec. 214. [27] Ibid., sec. 214(2). [28] Ibid., sec. 214(4)(a) and (b) respectively.

[29] Ibid., sec. 214(3). [30] Ibid., sec. 215(5).

[31] Ibid., sec. 215(6) and which 'must be construed with reference to the Injunctions Directive' (s. 215(8)).

[32] Ibid., sec. 217. [33] Ibid., sec. 217(8).

[34] *Enforcement of Consumer Protection Legislation: Guidance on Part 8 of the Enterprise Act*, Office of Fair Trading, 2003.

future. They depend upon a view that it is in the general consumer interest to act. B can also act through the courts to stop A's actions where an infringement of rights can be shown.[35] The starting point is, as in the case of Part 8 orders, that an agreed undertaking from A not to infringe B's rights is preferable and a first course could be to notify A of the infringement and to seek a voluntary undertaking from A. This has the advantage of avoiding the high costs of litigation. However, it has two potential problems: first, it could allow the destruction of evidence or the disappearance of an infringer rather than an end to the infringement; second, the notification of a potential breach and the request for an undertaking, unless very carefully constructed, could constitute an abuse of a trademark owner's rights by an inappropriate threat of litigation.[36]

Alternative dispute resolution (ADR) opportunities are available in the United Kingdom, where the parties need help in finding a solution but will try to avoid the costs of litigation. There are a great variety of schemes currently operating.[37] These can be voluntary and outside litigation, but under the new Civil Procedure Rules with the greater emphasis on the management of cases within proper times and costs, judges encourage parties, where appropriate, to seek ADR solutions to their difficulties.[38] This is available to B and may be a requirement of proceedings. However, the reality of the case – the need for swift action to stop a breach or to prevent the destruction of evidence, etc. – may make ADR impossible.

B can seek an injunction from the court to prevent the sale of the counterfeit goods and to end the advertising campaign. Injunctions can

[35] Patent Court within the Chancery Division or Patent County Court, depending on the scale of the case. Note, for example, that the Trade Marks Act 1994 allows for 'all such relief by way of damages, injunctions, or otherwise is available to him as is available in respect of the infringement of any other property right' sec. 14(2).

[36] See for example, Trade Marks Act 1994, sec. 21.

[37] See the Department of Constitutional Affairs website http://www.dca.gov.uk/civil/adr/ (last visited: June 10, 2005), and the National Mediation Helpline – a pilot study on mediation, from March 1, 2005 http://www.nationalmediationhelpline.com/ (last visited: June 10, 2005).

[38] See Civil Procedure Rule 1.4(2)(e) and 3.1(2)(f). The Pre-action Protocols show the importance of seeking alternative dispute resolution in the management of cases (Practice Direction – Protocols http://www.dca.gov.uk/civil/procrules_fin/contents/practice_directions/pd_protocol.htm, last visited June 10, 2005). Judges have the power under the rules to penalize those who do not follow the protocols, including participation in ADR where that has been part of the protocol (see, for example, Civil Procedure Rule 44.3 – especially 44.3(5)(a)).

be made at various points in proceedings and as part of the final remedy, depending upon the requirements of justice, operating in equity, and where common law damages will not be an 'adequate remedy'.[39] Across the chronology of the case, therefore, B may seek the following injunctions: a freezing order or search order; interim injunction; and final injunction. All these orders are made in equity, and are therefore made at the discretion of the courts and require that the claimant observes rules of fairness. Freezing orders or search orders[40] could be necessary at the outset if it is likely that evidence would be destroyed or removed, or if it is necessary to freeze assets to ensure that the defendant will not flee. Likewise, the court may make an injunction as an interim remedy before the proceedings start[41] (a) if no other 'rule, practice direction or other enactment which provides otherwise' [applies]; and (b) 'only if – (i) the matter is urgent; or (ii) it is otherwise desirable to do so in the interests of justice'.[42] These injunction and orders would be presumed to work with notice to the defendant, unless there are 'good reasons for not giving notice'.[43] Evidence to support the application must be given, including reasons why notice has not been given to the defendant where this is the case.[44] Given the power of search orders, they operate under particular safeguards for the defendant including the supervision of the search by an independent 'supervising solicitor'.[45] Beyond these specific safeguards, in almost all cases of granting interim injunctions, the claimant is required to give an 'undertaking in damages' by which 'the claimant is required to compensate the defendant for any loss incurred by the defendant during the currency of the injunction if it later appears that the injunction was wrongly granted'.[46]

The courts determine whether or not to grant an interim injunction following *American Cyanamid Co v. Ethicon Ltd.*[47] The claimant must

39 Lord Diplock in *American Cyanamid Co. v. Ethicon Ltd* [1975] AC 396, at p. 408; see the discussion at C. Plant, W. Rose, S. Sime, D. French (eds.), *Blackstone's Civil Practice 2004* (2004), p. 392, (para. 37.22).

40 Civil Procedure Rule 25.1(1)(f) (freezing order) and 25.1(1)(h) (search order – allowing access to premises).

41 Civil Procedure Rule 25.2(1).

42 Civil Procedure Rule 25.2(2)(a) and (b).

43 Civil Procedure Rule 25.3(1).

44 Civil Procedure Rules 25.3(2) and (3), 22 and 32, and Practice Direction – Interim Injunctions.

45 See Practice Direction – Interim Injunctions (especially part 7).

46 C. Plant, W. Rose, S. Sime, D. French (eds.), *Blackstone's Civil Practice 2004* (2004), p. 393 (para. 37.23).

47 [1975] AC 396.

determine 'a serious question to be tried on the merits. [...] All that needs to be shown is that the claimant's cause of action has substance and reality'.[48] Where the defendant has notice of the proceedings, this could be disputed, and the intellectual property reports show that there can be detailed arguments presented and, equally, on the strength of the outcome of the interim injunction proceedings, the case may be settled between the parties outside court. Where the case proceeds to a full hearing, an interim injunction can be made during the hearing or a final injunction can be made alongside damages or other remedy, where such an order would satisfy equity. Thus, B can seek various injunctions to stop the advertising campaign, and, indeed, to gain evidence about the supplier of the watches and also against the supplier itself (which could be B's more important concern).

Finland (2)

There might be no case at all as such product imitation is allowed in Finland. Thus the Market Court cannot order the sales of a copy to be stopped. The Court can only order that the real origin and/or quality is clearly stated in any advertising. Only when the origin of the goods could be confused (for example when the imitations are marked similarly to the 'genuine' products) could the firm whose product has been copied or the ombudsman demand the marketing to be stopped or changed. Marketing can be forbidden even if the products are clearly marked differently if the marketing could mislead consumers or other buyers. The case is different if an immaterial right has been violated (trademark etc). In such cases, even the sale of the goods can be forbidden.

The only interim measure under SopMenL and KSL is the possibility to temporarily issue an injunction for the duration of the process. But this requires a 'marketing operation' that has already started or an unfair trade practice that has already been committed. There has never been a case in the Market Court where a claimant would have even asked a forthcoming marketing campaign to be forbidden. There is a category called 'precautionary measures' in chap. 7 of the Finnish Code of Judicial Procedure. This is granted by civil law courts.[49] Sec. 1 and 2 refer to debt and rights to objects. The above-mentioned section has

[48] C. Plant, W. Rose, S. Sime, D. French (eds.), *Blackstone's Civil Practice 2004* (2004), p. 391, (para. 37.20).

[49] Chap. 7 para. 3 subpara. 1 reads: 'If the petitioner can establish a probability that he/she has a right not referred to in sec. 1 or 2, enforceable against the opposing party by a decision referred to in chap. 3, sec. 1(1) of the Enforcement Act, and that there is a

been used in connection with cases brought to the Market Court (with a local civil court deciding on the precautionary measure), but in all these cases the marketing has already been committed. In the writer's opinion the section above does not refer to future rights; there must be a right at the time when a precautionary measure is asked for. And in theses cases the right would only arise from an activity contrary to the SopMenL or KSL. So it is impossible to react in a legally binding manner to an advertisement campaign before it has begun because the SopMenL, the KSL and also the Code of Judicial Procedure only deal with actions that had already been committed.

France (2)

By intending to offer colourable imitations of a reputed mark of Swiss watch of B as genuine through his chain, A is about to violate art. 1382 and 1383 cc. Depending on how A actually argues in French law, his advertising would amount to either the promotion of a prohibited colourable imitation or parasitism; parasitism being defined as the placing one's products into the context of a competitor's products in order to profit from his notoriety without any direct competition.[50]

In the first case consumers have to believe in the genuine character of the watches, whereas in the second case, the damage suffered by B results from the depreciation of his brand mark and the effect on the brand mark image, assuming that the price difference between €20 and €2,000 suggests B's marketing to be purely a publicity gimmick. Such damage has been recently admitted by the Cour de Cassation in the famous case *Métro v. Cartier*.[51]

In both cases, however, the procedure would be the same; it would be a damage claim based on art. 1382 and 1383 cc. Due to these provisions a triple condition has to be fulfilled: fault, causality and damage have to

danger that the opposing party by deed, action or negligence or in some other manner hinders or undermines the realisation of the right of the petitioner or decreases essentially its value or significance, the court may:

(1) prohibit the deed or action of the opposing party, under threat of a fine;
(2) order the opposing party to do something, under threat of a fine;
(3) empower the petitioner to do something or to have something done;
(4) order that property of the opposing party be placed under the administration and care of a trustee; or
(5) order other measures necessary for securing the right of the petitioner to be undertaken.'

[50] Com. 22 Octobre 2002, in: *Contrats, Concurrence, Consommation* (January 2003), observations, p. 9.

[51] Ibid., p. 8. One can find the cases of the cour de cassation on www.courdecassation.fr.

be proved by the plaintiff. But this supposes the existence of certain, personal and direct damage.[52]

The simple fact that the damage is future damage does not make the action unviable but it has to be ascertained that the damage is really certain and not simply hypothetical.[53] A distinction has also been made between a merely possible damage insufficient for a damage claim and virtual damage, a case where the probability of the actual prejudice is already so high that it remains simply a matter of time until the damage is realized.[54]

A preventive action in order to cease the unfair competition had been established by art. 2 of the Act of July 2, 1963, but the executing order of the Conseil d'Etat (Estate Council) has never been voted on.[55] Fortunately, since then there has been the *Nouveau Code de Procédure Civile* – NCPC (new code of civil procedure) with its art. 808, 809, 872 and 873 giving power to the president of the Tribunal de Commerce (commercial court) to take conservatory measures in order to prevent an imminent damage or to order a cessation of activities that are obviously illegal (*trouble manifestement illicite*). The injunctions that can be ordered by a court are many and varied. The injunction concerning the partial or total cessation of activity can only be limited to a prohibition on advertising.[56] However, the difficulty of this summary procedure resides in the fact that proof of an obviously illegal activity virtually requires that the unfair competition practice be proved in itself, even if the procedure has only a provisory character.[57] However, summary procedures are very common in competition law.[58]

Germany (2)

The jurisdiction has developed a line of cases for these circumstances. The last amendment of the UWG has codified several typical groups of cases. Therefore only exceptionally does one resort to the blanket clause in § 3 UWG.[59] As a general rule it is allowed to imitate products unless

[52] J. Passa, in Juris-Classeur, *Concurrence, consommation* (1998), Fasc. 240, 'Domaine de l'action en concurrence déloyale', note 70.

[53] P. Malaurie and L. Aynès, *Cours de droit civil*, vol. 5, *Les obligations*, p. 139.

[54] Ph. Le Tourneau, *La spécificité du préjudice concurrentiel*, in RTDcom 1998, p. 83 (92).

[55] N.-F. Alpi, in Juris-Classeur, *Concurrence, consommation* (2003), Fasc. 245, 'Action en concurrence déloyale - éléments de procédure', note 111.

[56] Ibid., note 115. [57] Ibid., note 112. [58] Ibid., note 112.

[59] W. Schünemann, in H. Harte-Bavendamm and F. Henning-Bodewig, *UWG* (2004), § 3 note 48; K. H. Fezer, *Lauterkeitsrecht* (2005), § 3 note 63.

specific rights prohibit it or certain circumstances constitute an act of unfair competition.[60] According to § 4 no. 9 lit. (b) UWG it is prohibited to exploit the goodwill of the imitated product disproportionally. In this case the goodwill towards the Swiss watch is exploited by the imitated ones.[61] It is sufficient that the public in general is confused concerning the origin of the watches.[62] Thus, the requirements of § 3 UWG (ex- § 1 UWG), § 4 no. 9 lit. (b) UWG are fulfilled so that there is a valid claim for an order to desist pursuant to § 8 para. 1 UWG (ex- § 1 UWG).[63] This is the case with B's watches, since the goodwill of somebody else is exploited.[64]

The advertising campaign is still at the planning stage and has not yet begun. Thus, there has been no injury in law to B. A preventive cease and desist claim would be possible.[65] As no infringement has yet occurred, however, particular circumstances must arise which justify legal proceedings, the so-called initial risk of infringement (*Erstbegehungsgefahr*). This concerns a serious, direct and immediate future threat, and not a mere possibility of legal infringement.[66] Concrete grounds for suspicion are required.[67] We know that A ordered

[60] H. Köhler, in W. Hefermehl, H. Köhler and J. Bornkamm, *Wettbewerbsrecht* (24th edn 2006), § 4 note 9.4; T. Sambuc, in H. Harte-Bavendamm and F. Henning-Bodewig, *UWG* (2004), § 4 no. 9 note 5; H.H. Götting, in K.H. Fezer, *Lauterkeitsrecht* (2005), § 4 no. 9 note 46.

[61] H. Köhler, in W. Hefermehl, H. Köhler and J. Bornkamm, *Wettbewerbsrecht* (24th edn 2006), § 4 note 9.53; H.H. Götting, in: K.H. Fezer, *Lauterkeitsrecht* (2005), § 4 no. 9 note 62.

[62] H. Köhler, in W. Hefermehl, H. Köhler and J. Bornkamm, *Wettbewerbsrecht* (24th edn 2006), § 4 note 9.55; T. Sambuc, in H. Harte-Bavendamm and F. Henning-Bodewig, *UWG* (2004), § 4 no. 9 note 132.

[63] H. Köhler, in W. Hefermehl, H. Köhler and J. Bornkamm, *Wettbewerbsrecht* (24th edn 2006), § 4 note 9.59; T. Sambuc, in H. Harte-Bavendamm and F. Henning-Bodewig, *UWG* (2004), § 4 no. 9 note 132; H.H. Götting, in K.H. Fezer, *Lauterkeitsrecht* (2005), § 4 no. 9 note 62.

[64] BGH (1985) 87 GRUR 876 (877). Critical A. Beater, *Wettbewerbsrecht* (2002), vor § 13 note 39; opposed to it T. Möllers, (2004) 168 ZHR 225 (229).

[65] J. Bornkamm, in W. Hefermehl, H. Köhler and J. Bornkamm, *Wettbewerbsrecht* (24th edn 2006), § 8 notes 1.7, 1.15 et seq.; H. Köhler and H. Piper, *UWG* (3rd edn 2002), § 13 notes 17 et seq.; I. Beckedorf, in H. Harte-Bavendamm and F. Henning-Bodewig, *UWG* (2004), § 8 notes 23 et seq.; W. Büscher, in K.H. Fezer, *Lauterkeitsrecht* (2005), § 8 note 76.

[66] J. Bornkamm, in: W. Hefermehl, H. Köhler and J. Bornkamm, *Wettbewerbsrecht* (24th edn 2006), § 8 note 1.17; H. Köhler and H. Piper, *UWG* (3rd edn 2002), vor § 13 note 17; Harte-Bavendamm/Henning-Bodewig, *UWG* (2004), § 8 note 25; K.H. Fezer, *UWG* (2005), § 8 note 79; BGH (1993) 95 GRUR 53 (55).

[67] J. Bornkamm, in W. Hefermehl, H. Köhler and J. Bornkamm, *Wettbewerbsrecht* (24th edn 2006), § 8 note 1.17; H. Köhler and H. Piper, *UWG* (3rd edn 2002), vor § 13 note 17; I. Beckedorf, in H. Harte-Bavendamm and F. Henning-Bodewig, *UWG* (2004), § 8 note 26; W. Büscher, in K.H. Fezer, *Lauterkeitsrecht* (2005), § 8 note 79; BGH (1992) 38 WRP 706 (707).

the watches and the advertising campaign has been agreed upon in a binding agreement. The campaign's launch is just a matter of time. The infringement is not only possible but is likely to a degree bordering on certainty. The launch in one week gives a direct temporal connection. Thus, B can undertake pre-emptive measures against A and demand that he desist from his advertising campaign. If B wishes to prevent the planned advertising campaign in the short term, he can apply for a pre-emptive interim injunction.

Greece (2)

The Greek law on unfair competition fully allows the freedom of imitation.[68] On the other hand, the legislature has chosen to award special protection to certain categories of rights of intellectual property.[69] In any case, the perfect (by contrast to the simple) imitation of products of a third person may constitute an act of unfair competition covered by the general prohibition of art. 1 of Law 146/1914. In order for this to take place, the following conditions have to be met: (a) the original product must be characterized by competitive originality,[70] (b) an objective possibility of consumer confusion that usually occurs when the original products are recognizable and known through business transactions, and (c) knowledge of the imitation and simultaneous omission to take any action to avoid the possibility of confusion.[71]

The case in question, as described, does not refer to simple imitation of a third product, but rather to a direct, faithful and identical copying thereof. Thus, the condition on objective possibility of consumer confusion recedes, while the courts may even accept that the condition on competitive originality need not be fulfilled either.[72] It should be noted that A's product is inferior in quality and is sold at a substantially lower price than the original, a fact that may provide grounds for a claim for reparations of the damage caused to the reputation of the producer of the original product. Besides, protection under the trademarks Law

[68] Cf. I. Soufleros, *Article 1*, in N. Rokas (ed.), *Unfair Competition* (1996), p. 112; N. Rokas, *Industrial Property* (2004), pp. 192 et seq.

[69] See e.g. trademark law 2239/1994, intellectual property law 2121/1993.

[70] A. Liakopoulos, *Industrial Property* (2000), p. 482.

[71] *Athens Court of Appeals*, decision 447/1981, *Arm* (1982) 33; *Athens single member CFI*, decision 41435/1999, 42 *EllDni* (2001) 249.

[72] I. Soufleros, *Article 1*, in N. Rokas (ed.), *Unfair Competition* (1996), p. 123.

2239/1994 could also be envisaged, mainly under the provisions regarding the protection of reputed trademarks.[73]

B may raise against A a claim to desist from the envisaged unfair practice (sales and advertising campaign). Such a claim exists even if the defendant has not yet realized his plans, provided that there is a threat of first offence (the so-called 'first danger').[74] In the present case, B is allowed to file a preventive action, since A has already performed certain acts preparatory to the unlawful infringement of B's rights.[75]

Besides, in accordance with art. 20 of Law 146/1914, the person entitled to request the prevention of the unfair practice, may apply for provisional (interim) measures[76] (arts. 682–738 CCP), so as to protect his enterprise from the imminent danger. The general conditions upon fulfilment of which provisional measures will be awarded are: (a) ascertainment of an imminent danger of violation, and (b) prima facie proof of the existence of unfair competition practices.[77] The appropriate provisional measure to be decided by the court depends on the nature of the occurring or expected offence. Thus, the applicant may request, as a provisional remedy, the prohibition of product circulation and of the advertising materials, the publication of the interim instruction, as well as the imposition of a threat of pecuniary penalties or temporary detention of A in case of non-compliance with the decision to be rendered.[78] The decision on provisional remedies is a decision on specific performance and constitutes a provisional right.[79] It does not, however, interrupt the prescription period.[80]

Hungary (2)

According to sec. 6 HCA without the express prior consent of the competitor goods or services (hereinafter jointly referred to as goods) may not be produced, placed on the market or advertised with such typical

[73] See Art. 26.

[74] The threat must exist at the time of the case's examination by the court; see L. Kotsiris, *Unfair Competition and Antitrust Law*, *op.cit*, pp. 327–328.

[75] D. Tsimbanoulis, in: N. Rokas (ed.), *Unfair Competition* (1996), p. 68.

[76] The rather slow progression of ordinary proceedings in Greece makes recourse to provisional remedies highly desirable. See K. Kerameus in K. Kerameus/Ph. Kozyris, *Introduction to Greek Law*, 2nd edn, Kluwer/Sakkoulas, (1993), p. 290.

[77] T. Kontovazainitis, *Article 20*, in N. Rokas (ed.), *Unfair Competition* (1996), p. 432.

[78] *Patra single member CFI*, decision 868/2001, 7 *DEE* (2001) 711.

[79] The provisional right remains in force up to the issuance of the court decision following the regular procedure.

[80] Athens Court of Appeals 633/1979, *EEmpD* 1980, p. 329.

outside appearance, packaging or marking (including the indication of origin); or any such name, marking or indication of goods may not be used by which the competitor or its goods are normally recognized.

Before the advertisement is published, the party who might suffer loss can ask for a preliminary injunction under sec. 156 HCP. According to sec. 156(1) HCP a court may, upon application, issue a preliminary injunction in order to prevent imminent damage to a party, to maintain the status quo during a legal dispute, or to protect the claimant's rights should they require special recognition, as long as the burdens imposed by such a measure do not exceed the benefits that may be gained by it. The facts of the case do not have to be established; the party just has to show that it is very likely that the violation will happen. The rulings in the preliminary injunction are enforceable regardless of any appeal.

Ireland (2)

(1) Under the Consumer Information Act 1978, it is an offence to apply a false or misleading trade description to goods or to sell goods to which such a trade description has been applied. See Case 1 above. The definition of 'trade description' is very broad and includes any description, statement 'or other indication direct or indirect' as to the characteristics of the goods. Accordingly, it would include the claim that the watches are 'genuine'. One option for B is to complain to the Director of Consumer Affairs, and hope that the Director chooses to request A to cease the advertising or to apply to the court for an injunction to prevent the publication of the misleading advertisement.

(2) B can hope that the Director chooses to prosecute A under sec. 3 and 4 of the Misleading Advertising Regulations 1988.[81] Alternatively, B can take action personally against A under sec. 4(1) of the Misleading Advertising Regulations and request the court to prohibit A from starting the advertising campaign.

(3) B can take a tort action against A in the civil court for passing off the watches as B's product. In passing-off cases the plaintiff has to show that in the mind of the public his goodwill or reputation attaches to the goods because of their brand name or distinctive features, including packaging features and that the violator is misrepresenting his goods to the public in a way which is likely to lead the public to believe that the goods are the plaintiff's goods.

[81] See Case 1 (Risky bread).

In passing-off actions, the action rarely goes to full trial if the applicant has been awarded an injunction. B does not have to show that the public really was misled by the similarity between the two products. It is sufficient to show that there was a real likelihood of their being misled. If the advertising campaign has already begun before the claim is taken, and B is successful in the action, then he may claim for damage suffered. If the passing off was unintentional, he is unlikely to get more than nominal damages. The term nominal damages is used to describe the award of a very small compensatory sum. A judge sometimes awards nominal damages where the plaintiff is correct in law, but has in fact suffered little or no actual loss.

(4) Alternatively, if B's watches are trademarked, B could take an action against A, seeking an injunction and/or damages to prevent the infringement of his trademark under sec. 14 of the Trade Marks Act 1996.[82]

(5) B could attempt to take action against A in the civil court for the torts of defamation and injurious falsehood.[83]

Italy (2)

A's behaviour may amount both to trademark infringement (if the imitation watches carry B's trademark or a similar trademark) and to unfair competition.

N. 1 of art. 2598 cc is infringed since A acted in such a way as to create confusion between B's watches and the imitation watches; n. 2 may be infringed also, since A takes advantage of B's good reputation,[84] and, moreover, since the very low price advertised by A may amount to disparagement of B's watches, usually sold at a ten times higher price. Finally, n. 3 of art. 2598 is infringed, since the misleading advertising campaign, which A is planning to continue, undoubtedly amounts to a violation of 'professional fairness'.

It should be noted that it is not a valid defence to argue that while B is a manufacturer of watches, A is the owner of a chain of retail bakeries, and therefore, they may not be considered as competitors, at least in the strict meaning of this word. According to the case law, the prohibition

[82] See Case 1 (Risky bread). [83] See Case 1 (Risky bread).

[84] For a recent decision, cf. Trib. Udine, February 23, 2004, *Anese v. Nitta Gioielli*, in *Dir. ind.*, 2004, which held that the exhibition of the 'Bulgari' trademark on the window of a shop where Bulgari jewels were not actually sold amounted to a violation of art. 2958, c.c. for misleading advertising.

of unfair competition may be applied any time that the plaintiff and the defendant are (or will be) active in the same product and geographic market, even if at different levels. Moreover, art. 2598 cc will also apply when, as in this case, the defendant is a 'potential' competitor of the plaintiff, i.e. when there is an actual possibility that the defendant, though not at present active on the market of the plaintiff, is going to, or reasonably may, enter such market. Such possibility could be accepted by the judge on solid evidential grounds, provided by the plaintiff, that show how the defendant's undertaking might develop in the future.[85] In the case in question, A has clearly announced his intention to enter into the market for watches, though he does not currently sell them. Therefore, he may be considered as a 'potential' competitor of B, and art. 2598 cc will apply.

B may prevent the continuation of the advertising campaign by means of a claim for an injunction before the ordinary courts. It may be doubted whether an infringement of art. 2598 cc has already taken place at this stage, since A is not yet selling the imitation watches. The beginning of the advertising campaign, through newspapers and shop displays, may be sufficient to constitute trademark infringements. At the same time, it may constitute an actual breach of art. 2598 cc. Under that provision and art. 2600 cc, once unfair competition is ascertained the court has power to prevent its continuation. Under a generally accepted principle these provisions do not require an actual injury to the plaintiff. It is sufficient that the unfair behaviour of the defendant may potentially injure competitors, in order to obtain a judicial cease and desist order, according to art. 2600 cc.

In such a case, B may have no claim for damages. An exception is made for damages which B may have suffered as a consequence of the disparagement of his products by means of the advertising campaign already begun by A: it is likely that B may have lost customers due to such campaign, since people interested in high-quality expensive watches may no longer buy products which were advertised as sold in a chain of retail bakeries for only €20.

Also in the present case, B may seek an interlocutory injunction, prior to litigation on the merits. Even if the mere beginning of the advertising campaign should not be considered a breach of art. 2598 cc, A's behaviour leaves no doubt as to his intention to sell imitation watches, and to

[85] Among recent decisions, see e.g. Cass., sez. I, feb. 14, 2000, note 1617, *Tupperware Italia s.p.a. v. Spinelli*, in *Riv. dir. ind.* (2001), 96.

spread misleading advertisements, where such watches are offered as genuine. Therefore, unlawful behaviour on the part of A is a clear possibility; B is under an immediate future threat of a violation of art. 2598 cc. Therefore, the plaintiff's claim for an injunction is likely to succeed on the merits. The requirement of *periculum in mora* (serious and irretrievable loss to the plaintiff in case of delay) may be considered *in re ipsa*.

Netherlands (2)

B could start interlocutory proceedings to obtain an interim injunction against A. It would be sufficient if B claims that A's advertisement is misleading. Pursuant to art. 6:195 BW, A has the burden of proof that the statement in the advertisement is correct and thus not misleading. If the court holds that the advertisement is misleading and that all other substantive requirements for establishing possible tortious liability of A against B are met (e.g. B must prove that he will suffer damage as a result of A's advertising campaign), the court may issue an injunction against A pursuant to which A is prohibited from pursuing this advertising campaign and publishing the contested advertisements. If so requested by B, the court may order the prohibition under penalty of a fine.

The Advertising Code in the first place disciplines conduct that might mislead the public. Therefore, the code requires advertising to be just and complete. The Code does not discipline behaviour that may infringe rights of intellectual property as such. In this case the seller seems to give information on the imitated watches and therefore information that may be regarded as just. It depends on the further factual situation whether the information given by the seller must be characterized as misleading or unjust. The question to that answer is relevant for the question whether the Code would apply to this case.

As referred to in Case 10, according to the Code of Conduct of the Dutch Bar Association, the lawyer of a claiming party is obliged first to refer to the alleged infringer before bringing a case to court. Therefore, in practice there shall almost always be a first phase in which the claimant admonishes the alleged infringer before taking any further steps. For the Netherlands it is not possible to give any figures on the question how many cases end by a contractual settlement. It very much depends on the facts and on the proof that the claimant has against the infringer. Once parties agree on the fact that the infringement has taken place and on the responsibility of the infringer, they may, to end their dispute, set a so-called contract of settlement (*vaststellingsovereenkomst*). The Dutch civil code (BW) has a special section on the contract of settlement, 7: 900–906 DCC. In a contract of settlement, the parties bind themselves towards each other, in order to end or avoid any uncertainty or dispute in respect of what, in law, shall apply between them, to a settlement which shall also apply to the extent that it deviates from the previously existing juridical (legal) situation. Such a settlement can be established pursuant to a joint decision of the parties, or to a decision entrusted to one of them or to a third person.

The parties are in principle free to determine the issues they want to lay down in the contract of settlement. Therefore, it is not obligatory to agree on certain issues as, for example costs involved or (contractual) damages.

Poland (2)

Imitating a product with the use of technical means of reproduction constitutes an act of unfair competition if it can cause confusion about the identity of the product or its manufacturer (art. 13.1 u.z.n.k.). In general, imitating products is allowed as long as the products are not protected by the law of intellectual property and there is no risk of causing confusion.[86]

Art. 13 u.z.n.k. prohibits imitation of products only in the case in which the average customer is not able to distinguish originals and copies of the product. Therefore, only 'individualized products'[87] are protected under art. 13 u.z.n.k. Since the protection under art. 13 u.z.n.k. constitutes an exception to the general rule allowing imitation, art. 13.1 should be interpreted narrowly.[88] Art. 13 prohibits imitation but does not regulate the selling of imitated products, which is a definite shortcoming of the provision. However, art. 24 u.z.n.k. (chap. IV – penal provisions) penalizes acts of unfair competition defined in art. 13 u.z.n.k., dealing both with acts of imitation and the sale of imitated products.[89] Intentional sale/bringing into trade of imitated products

[86] E. Nowinska and M. Du Vall, *Komentarz do ustawy o zwalczaniu nieuczciwej konkurencji* (2001), p. 104.

[87] Opinion of the High Court of Germany of March 21, 1991, I ZR 158.89 IIC 1992, nb. 5 p. 701.

[88] M. Pozniak-Niedzielska and S. Soltysinski, in J. Szwaja (ed.), *Ustawa o zwalczaniu nieuczciwej konkurencji, Komentarz* (2000), p. 361.

[89] Everyone, who using technical means of reproduction imitates or introduces in the trade imitation products, causing confusion concerning identity of the producer or the product and causing serious damage to the entrepreneur shall (...) penalty (...) fine or jail up to two years.

contradicts the 'good customs' of the market and as such violates art. 13 u.z.n.k. This way of interpretation preserves the consistency of the u.z.n.k. since only acts of unfair competition are penalized. Bringing into trade colourable imitations of a reputed mark of watches would most probably cause confusion about the origin of the product or its producer constituting an act of unfair competition. B would therefore have material claims against A.

When the law of unfair competition is applicable, the undertaking whose interest is endangered or infringed may demand that the endangering or infringing party refrains from prohibited activities (art. 18.1 u.z.n.k.). However, this claim can only be brought in case the act of endangering or infringing the competition has already taken place.[90] But there are contradicting voices regarding the application of art. 439 k.c[91] to the situation under discussion. Certain opinions favour the application of art. 439 k.c.[92] The contrary view is based on the literal interpretation of the provisions of the u.z.n.k. Since the u.z.n.k. grants protection after the act of unfair competition has taken place, application of art. 439 k.c. when there is merely a likelihood of infringement of the protected rights does not seem to be justified.[93] On the other hand, the definition of an act of unfair competition (art. 3.1 u.z.n.k.) is very broad and includes preparatory activities directly endangering protected rights of undertakings.[94] Since B's interest is being endangered (or already infringed) he can demand that A refrain from the prohibited activities, i.e. stop the advertising campaign.

Portugal (2)

A's plans to sell the imitation watches, the advertising campaign and the decoration of the shop display with pictures of imitation watches are illegal according to art. 317 CPI (Industrial Property Code). In fact, all

[90] E. Nowinska and M. Du Vall, *Komentarz do ustawy o zwalczaniu nieuczciwej konkurencji* (2001), p. 104; See also Case 1 (Risky bread).

[91] One, who because of the actions of the other person becomes endangered and damage can be caused, can demand that this other person undertake an action to remove the danger. If it is necessary, security/guarantee shall be given.

[92] J. Swaja, in J. Szwaja (ed.), *Ustawa o zwalczaniu nieuczciwej konkurencji, Komentarz* (2000), p. 509.

[93] L. Gornicki, *Nieuczciwa konkurencja, w szczegolnosci przez wprowadzajace w blad oznaczenie towarow i uslug, i srodki ochrony w prawie polskim* (1997), p. 72; J. Barta and J. Markiewicz, in J. Szwaj (ed.), *Ustawa o zwalczaniu nieuczciwej konkurencji, Komentarz* (2000), p. 161.

[94] E. Nowinska and M. Du Vall, *Komentarz do ustawy o zwalczaniu nieuczciwej konkurencji* (2001), p. 188.

of those acts would represent, if they occur, unfair competition against his competitor B. The selling of an imitation watch is an act that can cause confusion and exploitation of the work and reputation of another competitor: art. 317 lit. (a) CPI. It can also be considered as counterfeiting or the selling of an imitation model without licence. The advertising campaign also implies the exploitation of reputation: art. 317 CPI. The decoration of the shop display can also cause confusion with the products of the competitor: art. 317 lit. (a) CPI. Those three situations together represent an economic parasitism that is also treated as unfair competition even in cases in which there would be no risk of confusion (such as this one, in which one competitor is a watchmaker and the other is a baker). The parasitism also requires continuity and a global action against the competitor.[95]

Unfair competition, according to Portuguese law, is considered an administrative tort that does not require a result, such as the causing of loss to a specific competitor. The mere risk of that occurrence is sufficient to consider it illegal. Therefore, B can prevent the advertising campaign with a preventive claim even before any action takes place or any publication of the illicit advertising campaign occurs. In fact the Civil Procedure Code (CPC) establishes innominate preventive claims in the case of a future injury. This provisional preventive claim only requires *periculum in mora* and *fumus boni iuris*, art. 381 CPC. Actually, there are conditions that must apply in order to bring the claim: the fear of a severe violation (injury to a right) and the difficulty of its reparation following the injury (*in casu*, the probability of the violation of the protected interest). The preventive claim is urgent (art. 382 CPC) and it is possible for the court to determine the application of a monetary compulsory sanction, art. 384 para. 2 CPC. Afterwards, the claimant must fulfil the requirement of bringing a principal action against the competitor within a month (art. 389 CPC). If a preventive order is issued, the court decision may forbid any publication in different newspapers of the illegal advertising campaign and may also order the decoration of the shop display window and the selling of the counterfeit watches to cease. The court may also order the seizing of the imitation goods and all advertising material. Those decisions are provisionary, so an action must be pursued in order to obtain a final decision.

[95] A. Menezes Leitão, *Imitação servil, concorrência parasitária e concorrência desleal*, Direito Industrial, vol. I, APDI (2001), p. 128.

B bears the burden of proof that A's actions could cause him harm, demonstrating the risk of damages. The risk has to be concrete one and may not only be abstract.[96] The action for an injunction is a preventive claim against an illegal violation that someone fears could occur, therefore the initial risk of infringement has to be proved. There are normally difficulties in proving the initial risk of infringement in claims for provisional or final preventive injunctions. This is probably the reason why these claims are so rare in Portuguese civil courts.

Spain (2)

Art. 41 *Ley de Marcas* – LMa 17/2001 (Spanish Trademark Act),[97] confers on a trademark owner the right to inform any person about the existence of that right and about the infringement and to require to desist from the infringement. The owner is also entitled to ask the civil courts to take all the necessary measures *to prevent the infringement* and, particularly, to remove from commercial trade the infringing goods.

Sweden (2)

It is not unusual that an imitation or misuse of a trademark concurrently violates both the MFL and intellectual property rights. In practice the MFL has proved to be a more extensive protection against exploitation than intellectual property rights. Violations must, however, be tried before different courts and can, consequently, not be pursued concurrently unless the claims only relate to damages, which are handled by ordinary courts. The highest instance deciding matters according to the administrative side of the MFL, the Market Court, has on numerous occasions waived jurisdiction on deciding matters relating to intellectual property rights.[98]

In Sweden the protection against exploitation is primarily established through intellectual property rights. Even though the Swedish MFL does not protect the mere use of someone else's intellectual property right, such as a trademark or a design, the act constitutes an important complement to these rights. The MFL protects rather the exploitation of rights when there is a risk of consumers being misled.

The MFL covers all forms of marketing that are carried out for commercial purposes, including public announcements as well as all other

[96] See J. Ascensão, *Concorrência Desleal* (2002), p. 258.
[97] Art. 41 Ley de Marcas o LMa 17/2001 of December 7, 2001.
[98] MD 1988:6 Klorin I, MD 1995:25 Svensk Miljöexport.

activities with the object of promoting the supply of products. Already the mere provision of a product, even though altogether passive, falls within the scope of the MFL. Consequently, both A's advertisement and the pictures in the shop display window are covered by the MFL. Although the watches are not yet for sale, the measures already taken to support the sale may be examined under the provisions in the act.

Exploitation of imitations of brand watches should be covered by the relatively recently enacted[99] sec. 8a.8 of the MFL. This provision prohibits comparative advertisements involving imitations of products protected by intellectual property rights. Moreover, exploitation of intellectual property rights is, and has been, caught by the prohibition against misleading advertisement in sec. 6 and misleading reproductions in sec. 8. In some circumstances the general clause in sec. 4 could also apply to exploitation, such as when an advertisement unjustly profits from someone else's good reputation.

Sec. 6 covers advertisements that are misleading as to the origin of the product but, more specifically the character, composition and use of the product. The misuse of a trademark, such as the use of someone else's trademark on a product, would probably be deemed misleading to the commercial origin in the sense that is covered by sec. 6. However, the reproduction of products is covered by sec. 8 if the product could be confused with someone else's products. According to sec. 8 an undertaking cannot, in its marketing, use reproductions that are misleading in a way that can be easily confused with the well-known and distinguished products of another undertaking. The use of another commercial entity's trademark would violate sec. 6,[100] while the reproduction of someone else's trademark or other design of products violates sec. 8, but the distinction between the two prohibitions is not altogether clear. At present, many of the cases formerly covered by secs. 6 and 8 will be caught by sec. 8a MFL.

As to preventing the new advertising campaign, B is in a weak position. It would probably be possible to prevent a repetition *of a previous illegal campaign* with an interim injunction. Under sec. 20 an *interim injunction* would be available, provided that certain conditions are fulfilled.[101] If

[99] See Cases 1 (Risky bread) and 3 (Whisky). [100] MD 1989:9 Svita.

[101] The conditions are that the plaintiff shows that there is a probability his claim will be upheld (which may be difficult to theoretically reconcile with the fact that the defendant in these situations has to prove that his submissions are accurate) and that it is reasonable to assume that the defendant by continuing advertising in what is presumed to be a misleading way reduces the effect of a final injunction.

solely an injunction is sought, sec. 38 provides for (1) a consumer ombudsman, (2) an undertaking concerned (that would include e.g. B), and (3) an association of consumers, undertakings or employees to be able to sue. Accordingly, single consumers are barred from using this remedy.

However, under Swedish constitutional law there is an unconditional prohibition on censorship of any publication prior to the date of its release (Freedom of Print Act of 1949). The freedom of print has actually been limited in regard to commercial announcements. The publishing of such announcements may be limited by way of governmental acts. This is the legal basis for accepting the limitations laid down in the MFL. Still, the exemption of commercial announcements from freedom of publication does not cover the prohibition against censorship prior to publishing. This constitutional right makes it impossible in Sweden for all state and governmental institutions, including the courts, to examine the content of an announcement, whatever its nature, prior to its publishing.

Summary (2)

4. *Injunctive protection*

In Germany the injunction offers extremely important legal protection. In contrast to other interim injunctions under the civil code the danger of loss does not have to be substantiated.[102] The urgency of the matter is presumed.[103]

In Italy, proceedings for an interlocutory injunction according to art. 700 of the civil procedure code is the most common way to prevent the continuation of unlawful advertising campaigns. Usually, the issuing of such an injunction will not take more than a few weeks. Case law has developed certain methods which may facilitate the claimant: for example, the opinion according to which in claims for interlocutory injunctions against unfair competition the requirement of *periculum in mora* may be considered *in re ipsa*. However, it is different when legal protection is sought through the administrative authorities. In Italy, according to para. 3 of sec. 7, decree 74/92, in cases of specific urgency, the authority may issue an interlocutory order prohibiting further distribution of the advertisement pending the procedure. Such interlocutory measures

[102] § 12 para. 2 (former § 25) UWG.

[103] BGH (2000) 102 GRUR 151 (152) – 'Späte Urteilsbegründung'; H. Köhler and H. Piper, *UWG* (3rd edn 2002), § 25 note 13.

are issued quite rarely by the authority. Injunctive protection is also possible in Sweden,[104] Finland[105] and Denmark.[106] In Denmark provisional prohibition may be imposed by the consumer ombudsman if there is the danger that the prohibition by the courts will prove ineffective. In states such as Finland where the consumer ombudsman regulates, interlocutory orders are not widely used and they will only be used if the harm caused to the claimant will be greater than that caused to the defendant. In states such as Finland the claimant must ask for this order. In England and the USA injunctive protection is only known for competition law claims under tort law. Interlocutory injunctions are only granted in England and the USA where the claimant can establish that the payment of damages would be no adequate compensation in case of an infringement. For preliminary injunctions in the USA it is required that the plaintiff shows a probability of success at the ultimate trial on the merits, and that the plaintiff shows that it will suffer irreparable injury without the preliminary injunction, that the preliminary injunction preserve the group's status quo which preceded the dispute and a preliminary ruling is necessary to protect third parties.[107] For consumer law concerns the OFT in England must apply to the courts for an injunction and this is regarded as the remedy of final resort.

Evaluation

(1) The rapid elimination of an infringing circumstance is of primary importance in restoring a lawful circumstance. The Misleading and Comparative Advertising Directive 84/450/EEC provides that Member States introduce an expedited procedure under which at the discretion of Member States the measures must contain provisional or final effect.[108] As a result injunctive protection is possible in all Member States. On the one hand some scholars take the view that should injunctions be too easily granted against alleged acts of unfair competition, absent any evidence of damage, or of an immediate danger of damage, the protection of free economic activity, granted to the defendant for example by art. 41 of the Italian Constitution may be at stake. In this way in all states there is basically a balancing of interests. Such

[104] § 20 MFL. [105] Chap. 2 8 para. 2 § KSL. [106] § 21 para. 1 MFL.

[107] Instructive is J. McCarthy, *McCarthy on Trademarks and Unfair Competition*, vol. 6 (4th edn Supp. 2000), pp. 30–61 with the differentiations between the different Circuits.

[108] Art. 4 para. 2 subpara. 2, Misleading and Comparative Advertising Directive 84/450/EEC.

a balancing of interests is also required by the Misleading and Comparative Advertising Directive 84/450/EEC, where the balancing of interests is expressly referred to in subpara. 1.[109]

(2) However, it is noticeable that the practical relevance of this legal remedy varies. In most Member States which have largely civil law remedies, the injunction is seen as the most important remedy. In contrast the authorities seem to ignore injunctive relief. In Finland and also in Italy, in the field of competence of the Autorità Garante, the injunction is only seldom applied. The same applies, for the OFT in England.

(a) In Germany and Italy, for example, no harm has to be proved in order to gain an injunction. The remedy is therefore of great importance in practice. In a large number of cases once interlocutory injunctions are granted, litigation is often ended by an out-of-court agreement. Decisions on the merits particularly with reference to damages are less important than decisions on applications for interlocutory injunctions. Once the injunction is issued, the defendant may prefer to settle the dispute, ceasing his allegedly wrongful conduct rather than facing further costs and delays of litigation on the merits. The claimant may usually waive or reduce his claim for damages.

(b) In states with public law regulatory authorities the obligation under the Misleading and Comparative Advertising Directive 84/450/EEC to introduce an expedited procedure is fulfilled in that the authority undertakes negotiations with the infringer.

(c) It is questionable whether the injunction may be classified as secondary to the compensatory claim, as is the case in England.[110] The ECJ for example in its case law has laid down that Member States may not make a compensatory claim dependent on fault.[111] This may be generalized in that it is impossible when Member States make a legal remedy dependent on additional requirements, because otherwise these means are not 'adequate and effective'. Here we have a deficit in implementation.

[109] Art. 4 para. 2 subpara. 1, Misleading and Comparative Advertising Directive 84/450/EEC.

[110] Also in the USA the preconditions for a preliminary injunction are quite strict, see above A.IV.2(a).

[111] See ECJ C-14/83, (1984) ECR I-1891 – 'von Colson and Kamann'; ECJ C-180/95, (1997) ECR I-2195, (1997) 52 NJW 1839, (1999) 62 JZ 1172 – 'Draehmpaehl'.

5. *Preventative injunction order or prohibition*

In Germany the claim for a preventive injunction[112] was developed by the courts[113] and became recognized as customary law. The threat of harm is not a requirement.[114] Under Polish law the preventive cessation claim is less clearly developed than in Germany and Austria. There are, however, authors who affirm such a claim provided there is the potential danger of a legal infringement. In France art. 808, 809, 872 and 873 NCPC giving power to the President of the Commercial Tribunal (tribunal de commerce) to take preservative measures in order to prevent imminent damage or to order conduct to cease that is obviously illegal (*trouble manifestement illicite*). In Italy the preventive cessation claim is possible, provided the potential danger of a legal infringement is imminent. The requirement of serious and irretrievable loss to the plaintiff in case of delay may be considered *in re ipsa*. In Spain the plaintiff is also entitled to apply to the civil courts to take all necessary measures to prevent the infringement, and in particular to remove from commercial trade the infringing goods. The preventive injunction claim is also known in Portugal, where there are certain conditions that must be observed in order to bring this preventive claim: the fear of a severe violation (infringement of right) and the difficulty of cure after the violation of the right. The preventive claim is urgent (art. 382 CPC) and it is possible for the court to determine the application of a compulsory monetary sanction (art. 384 para. 2 CPC). Subsequently, the claimant must fulfil the requirement of moving a principle action against the competitor after a delay of a month (art. 389 CPC). The USA and England follow a middle path. Interim actions are possible but the exception. That an exception is applicable has to be substantiated. In the USA, injunctive relief may be obtained even before the defendant actually opens for business, if the threatened act of the defendant is imminent. One does not have to wait for the threatened injury to occur before obtaining preventive relief.[115] Injunctive relief may even be obtained before the defendant has sold a single infringing product. Here the factual requirement, similarly to Poland, of

[112] Cf. Case 2 (Watch imitations I).

[113] RGZ 101, 335 (339); BGHZ 2, 394 (395), (1952) 54 GRUR 35 – 'Wida-Ardia'.

[114] O. Teplitzky, *Wettbewerbsrechtliche Ansprüche und Verfahren* (8th edn 2002), chap. 9 note 7.

[115] *Cleveland Opera Co. v. Cleveland Civic Opera Ass'n*, 22 Ohio App. 400, 5 Ohio L.Abs. 297, 154 N.E. 352 (Cuyahoga County 1926); *Standard Oil Co. v. Standard Oil Co.*, 56 F.3d 973 (10th Cir. 1932); J. McCarthy, *McCarthy on Trademarks and Unfair Competition*, vol. 6 (4th edn Supp. 2000), pp. 30–21.

commercial usage will be broadly construed. The court noted that the Lanham Act does not require that the allegedly infringing merchandise be available to the consuming public.

As a result numerous states provide for the preventive injunction claim, for example Germany, Austria, Portugal, France, Italy and Spain. The requirement is the imminent threat of unlawful anticompetitive conduct. On the other hand, in Member States in which the claim is denied there can be surprising results. Under Swedish constitutional law there is an unconditional prohibition on censorship of published announcements prior to release (Freedom of Print Act 1949). The legal position in Finland is identical; it is impossible to react in a legally binding manner to an advertisement campaign before it has begun as the SopMenL only deals with actions that have already been committed. The conflict with press freedom is also seen in England. In practice, courts have always been very reluctant to order an injunction in libel cases, at least in interlocutory proceedings, and they have not done so if the defendant intends to plead justification.[116] In fact, it is easier to obtain an injunction order in malicious falsehood cases since damages are, in such cases, inevitably difficult to calculate, follow some time after the event, and may not be adequate.[117] By contrast, the preventive cessation claim is well-known in the USA.[118]

Evaluation

(1) The Misleading and Comparative Advertising Directive 84/450/EEC requires that cessation or prohibition as a preventive measure must also be possible if publication is imminent subject to consideration of all interests concerned and in particular the public interest.[119] This also meets the interests of the claimant because one does not have to await commission of the threatened injury to obtain preventive relief. Through the plaintiff having to provide appropriate security the defendant's interests can be safeguarded, in the event that the claim is ultimately held to be unfounded.

[116] See *Schering Chemicals Ltd. v. Falkman Ltd. and Others*, [1982] Q.B. 1 (17 et seq.), per Lord Denning MR; *Kaye v. Robertson & Another* [1991] FSR 62 (67).

[117] See *Kaye v. Robertson & Another* [1991] FSR 62 (68).

[118] *Cleveland Opera Co. v. Cleveland Civic Opera Ass'n*, 22 Ohio App. 400, 5 Ohio L.Abs. 297, 154 N.E. 352 (Cuyahoga County 1926); *Standard Oil Co. v. Standard Oil Co.*, 56 F.3d 973 (10th Cir. 1932); J. McCarthy, *McCarthy on Trademarks and Unfair Competition*, vol. 6 (4th edn Supp. 2000), p. 30–21.

[119] Art. 4 para. 2 indent 2 Misleading and Comparative Advertising Directive 84/450/EEC.

(2) The introduction of this obligation is not at the discretion of the Member States. It is mandatory. Member States which deny the preventive cessation claim on grounds of press freedom may therefore be violating European law. It is difficult to take an opposing view: it could be objected that the introduction of this obligation is subject to the reservation that the preventative cessation claim is not against the public interest. The public interest requires press freedom. On the other hand the directive in principle requires such a weighing of the interests. In this context the extent of the legal infringement and threatened harm must above all be considered which justifies the preventive cessation claim. However, the Misleading and Comparative Advertising-Directive 84/450/EEC does not provide for the general priority of press freedom over other interests. Were this so, then no preventive legal protection would be possible. Finally, it may be argued that a (civil law) preventive cessation claim is not necessary as the Misleading and Comparative Advertising Directive 84/450/EEC expressly confers the supervision of unlawful conduct on the administration as well as the courts. This, however, requires that the consumer agencies in Sweden, Finland and England also take preventive measures. They do not normally do so. Thus the legal position in Sweden, Finland and England is not in conformity with European law. Member States which deny the preventive cessation claim on the grounds of press freedom thus violate the requirements of the Misleading and Comparative Advertising Directive 84/450/EEC.

Case 3 Whisky: damages and discovery

The whisky manufacturer A has engaged an advertising agency to create an advertising campaign. The agency has designed a poster with a bottle of whisky visible in the foreground and three men sitting on the wing of a very expensive English quality car manufactured by B, playing cards and drinking the whisky with evident enjoyment. Sales of A's whisky increase significantly as a result of the advertisement. B is unwilling to see A earn money on the back of his good reputation and demands compensation. Admittedly, he cannot establish a loss of earnings on his own part, but he wants a licence fee for the advertisement with his trademark and the profit from the sales increase. Because of the advertisement campaign, A has an additional profit of €10,000.

Has B a compensatory claim against A? How will the amount of the compensation be calculated ?

Austria (3)

According to the latest decisions of the courts[1] § 1 UWG can be resorted to if a competitor from another branch of trade is trying to profit from the reputation and prestige of somebody else's products bearing a well-known or famous sign for the sale of his own (different and not competing) products. By choosing the same or a resembling trademark, the notion of quality that is linked to the original product is transferred to the identical products from other industry sectors (or products with striking resemblance from other industry sectors). Protection according to § 9 UWG is not possible since the products are different and stem from different branches of trade, so there is normally no deceptive usage. However, the infringement consisting in the risk of the transferral of the reputation of the original product institutes a competitive relationship since the owner of the famous trademark and the violator compete for usage of the trademark. Therefore, § 1 UWG can be applied.[2]

Even before the introduction of the extended protection of famous trademarks according to art. 5 para. 2 Trademark Directive 89/104/EEC Austria has introduced the extended protection of famous trademarks in unfair competition law with this practice.

[1] (1997) 46 ÖBl 72 – 'Schürzenjäger'; (1997) 46 ÖBl 83 – 'Football-Association'; (1997) 46 ÖBl 225 'BOSS-Energy drink'; (1998) 47 ÖBl 182 – 'Fußballverein-Logos'.

[2] H. Fitz and H. Gamerith, *Wettbewerbsrecht* (4th edn 2003), p. 67.

(1) According to § 16 para. 1 UWG somebody who immorally exploits the reputation of somebody else's product can be held liable for damages. These damages can include the loss of profits.[3] In practice this is hard to prove.[4]

(2) Yet the courts repeatedly resort to a general concept of civil law that allows a claim without regard to fault against anybody who uses somebody else's goods to his advantage without being legally entitled to do so. In this context, the meaning of goods is understood in the extended sense of § 285 ABGB. Therefore it also includes intellectual property rights and assets resulting from the unfair competition law protection against 'immoral' imitation of one's goods and against the exploitation of one's good reputation.[5] This is even extended to the exploitation of the popularity of a person, for example, a famous sportsman, which can be measured as an asset.[6] Based on this, B is entitled to claim unjust enrichment for the infringement of the UWG if he is able to prove that the sales of A increased significantly as a result of this advertisement. Concretely, this means A could be held liable to relinquish his extra earnings of €10,000.

In Austria, a discovery claim concerning origin and distribution has been known since July 1, 2005, but only if intellectual property rights are infringed. This includes trademarks, but not claims arising out of unfair competition law. Nevertheless, the OGH has granted a claim for accounting in a case of 'immoral' imitation of somebody else's products.[7]

(3) Under the Austrian UWG there is no licence fee analogy to calculate damages.

(4) B is therefore entitled to bring an unfair competition claim because of the exploitation of his good reputation. As the producer of a 'very expensive English quality car'[8] B can also base his claim on an infringement of his trademark if the poster shows the car's trademark accordingly. This is not a trademark specific usage by A, but this is no longer relevant if §§ 10, 10a MSchG are interpreted in a way which conforms

[3] H. Koziol, *Haftpflichtrecht*, (3rd edn 1997), p. 27.

[4] P. Rummel, *Unlauterer Wettbewerb*, in H. Koziol, *Haftpflichtrecht*, (2nd edn 1984), p. 302.

[5] SZ 49/63, (1976) 25 ÖBl 124 – 'Smile'; (1981) 30 ÖBl 8 – 'Verdichterstation'.

[6] SZ 55/12, (1983) 32 ÖBl 118 – 'Fußballwerbung I'; (1991) MR 68 – 'Carreras'; (1995) 44 ÖBl 284 – 'Fußballer-Abziehbilder'; (1998) 47 ÖBl 298 – 'Hörmann'.

[7] SZ 67/207 = ÖBl 1995, 116.

[8] Concerning the exploitation of the reputation of Rolls-Royce see (1996) 45 ÖBl 35 – 'Rolls-Royce'.

with the directive since the trademark owner is allowed to prohibit any commercial usage, including non-trademark specific usages, according to art. 5 para. 1 Trademark Directive 89/104/EEC.[9] If B can also claim an infringement of his trademark rights he is entitled to claim an appropriate fee without proving fault of the defendant according to § 53 para. 1 MSchG. The appropriate fee is considered to be the fee that would have to be paid for the right to use the trademark in question (common licence fee).[10] Instead of the appropriate fee the claimant is entitled to damages including loss of profits and extra earnings which were gained by the violator, if the defendant's fault can be proven. To enable the claimant to calculate the extra earnings he can, according to § 55 MSchG, force the violator to reveal his accounting documents. An easing of the burden of proof is granted in § 53 para. 1 MSchG: independent of proof of damage, the violated party is allowed to claim two times the amount of the appropriate fee according to § 53 para. 1 MSchG if the infringement of the trademark results from gross negligence or intent. B is thus entitled to either claim damages or the relinquishing of the (higher) profits.

Denmark (3)

In this example advantage is being taken of B's trademark and product and also of B's goodwill. A's behaviour may be contrary to the Trademarks Act and the MFL (Marketing Practices Act). A sponging on the goodwill, which is part of the trademarks and product design of other firms, will be contrary to § 1 MFL, according to which a firm is not allowed to carry out actions contrary to good marketing practices. Such behaviour will probably also be contrary to the rules in § 2a para. 2 no. 7 MFL, according to which comparative advertising is not permitted if by the comparison a competitor takes an unfair advantage of the reputation related to another competitor's trademark.[11] The behaviour must also be assumed to be contrary to § 5 MFL, according to which a firm is not allowed to make use of trademarks it does not own.

Under Danish law, the main interest is related to situations where B's trademark, goodwill and reputation are damaged by A's marketing. Financial exploitation of the goodwill linked to B's trademark may, however, be contrary to MFL. B can apply to the court for an injunction

[9] R. Schanda, *Markenschutzgesetz in der Fassung der Markenrechtsnovelle* (1999), p. 61.
[10] (2002) 51 ÖBl 237 – 'Sissy-Weißwein'.
[11] E. Borcher and F. Bøggild, *Markedsføringsloven* (2001), p. 235.

to be issued against A under § 13 MFL to prevent A's unauthorised use of B's product and trademark.

(1) Damages may be awarded in accordance with the ordinary provisions for such remedies. Hence, the plaintiff must prove a loss, its size, that the loss was caused by defendant's actions and that there is a valid connection between the claim and those actions. Typically, because of the difficulty of establishing harm, damages do not fully compensate plaintiffs for their losses.[12] In connection with the marketing in question an unlawful use of B's goodwill has taken place. It is stated in § 13 para. 2 MFL, that actions in contravention of the MFL may incur a liability for damage in accordance with the general rules of Danish law. B must prove that A's behaviour constitutes a basis for liability, that a financial loss has been incurred, that there is a causal link between A's behaviour and B's loss, and that the loss flows from A's behaviour.[13] First, it must be assumed that financial compensation for the unauthorized use of B's trademark can be obtained even if there is no financial loss for B. Secondly, there may also be an actual financial loss for B because unauthorized and unlawful use of B's trademark may result in disturbances in the market and thus imply a risk of long-term damage to the value of B's goodwill.[14] Such loss is by its very nature difficult to assess and to quantify, but the courts might award damages on the basis of an estimation of the loss suffered.[15]

(2) In Danish case law one finds a number of judgments concerning the protection of the goodwill of individuals. The assessment of the compensation will – based on an analogy from these judgments – primarily include the financial value of the use of B's trademark for A. One may also take an analogy from § 43 Trademarks Act according to which unauthorized use of a trademark justifies a repayment. The assessment of the compensation will be based on estimation. It may be part of the assessment to ascertain to what extent A's sales have increased from using B's trademark, the increase in A's profits from the use, and whether there are identifiable and quantifiable disturbances of the market for B.

[12] M. Eckardt-Hansen, *Denmark*, in J. Maxeiner and P. Schotthöfer, p. 97 (116).
[13] B. von Eyben et al., *Lærebog i Erstatningsret* (4th edn 1999), p. 3.
[14] M. Koktvedgaard, *Lærebog i Konkurrenceret* (4th edn 2000), p. 274.
[15] Ibid., p. 66; P. B. Madsen, *Markedsret*, vol. 2 (4th edn 2002), p. 343.

(3) If the infringing party acted with intent, the awarding of damages can also have the character of a fine. Apart from this, the courts are relatively free in their estimation of the damages.[16]

The compensation will be assessed as a lump sum since it is assumed that the utilization of B's trademark will be stopped.[17]

(4) However, certain violations of the MFL can subject perpetrators to fines or imprisonment.[18] The Consumer Ombudsman is entitled to bring several claims against the same infringing party in one application.[19]

England (3)

If B's registered trademark is reproduced in the photograph, then an action may be possible under the Trade Marks Act 1994. As in scenario 2 above, sec. 10 is key. Sec. 10(3) indicates that an infringement occurs 'where the trade mark has a reputation in the United Kingdom and the use of the sign, being without due cause, takes unfair advantage of, or is detrimental to, the distinctive character or the repute of the trade mark'. This, arguably, covers the case in scenario 3. If the mark is not visible or reproduced, then the car manufacturer must rely on design rights, copyright, or perhaps even passing off, with the difficulties identified in scenario 2. It should be noted that the designs of whole bodyshells are routinely registered.[20]

(1) Licence negotiation. As in scenario 2, it would be preferable to find a settlement without recourse to an action for compensation. If B does not object to the continued use of the image and association of his product to A's, as is often the case in intellectual property infringements, the breach can be used to negotiate a retrospective licence and agreement for the future use of the intellectual property for a fee. This could be achieved through negotiation between the parties (taking care to avoid the problems noted in scenario 2 of using the trademark rights to threaten unfairly).

[16] A. Kur and J. Schovsbo, *Dänemark*, in G. Schricker, note 263.

[17] P.B. Madsen, *Markedsret* (4th edn 2002), pp. 343 et seq.; concerning the copying of products, B. von Eyben et al., *Karnovs lovssamling* (2001), p. 5680 on § 43 of the Trade Marks Act.

[18] M. Eckardt-Hansen, *Denmark*, in J. Maxeiner and P. Schotthöfer, p. 97 (117).

[19] A. Kur and J. Schobsbo, *Dänemark*, in G. Schricker, note 262.

[20] We thank Professor J.N. Adams for his comment on this practical aspect of IP protection.

(2) Pecuniary Damages. If B wants not only to be compensated for the infringement, but also to stop the continued use of the image and association, again negotiation is preferred, but where this fails an action can be brought before the court. Compensation is calculated in one of two ways (damages or account), at the choice of the claimant.[21] Pecuniary damages are calculated to 'compensate the claimant for measurable financial losses caused by the defendant's wrongdoing'.[22] Where there is clear evidence of loss, damages could be adequate. One could ask whether or not there is loss in one of two ways: first, is there evidence of actual losses (e.g. lost income) that can be shown to flow from the infringement; and second, at what amount would the value of a licence to do the otherwise infringing action have been calculated? The latter is exceptional,[23] but may be the easier to show for B.

(3) Account. Alternatively and often the preferred option, where the financial damage to B is less than the financial gain to A from the infringement, B can seek the equitable remedy of account.[24] A would be required to 'account' – to show its financial situation, and therefore the benefit derived from the breach, and the compensation would be awarded on that basis. Plant et al. indicate that '[p]roving damage is often extremely difficult, so that an account of the profit made by the defendant may be a more attractive remedy'.[25]

Finland (3)

The Finnish Trademark Act could be applicable if A uses B's trademark or another mark like it in his marketing if the origin of the goods could be confused (§ 4 Trademark Act). The goods in question must, however, be similar or from the same product category. As cars and whisky are not similar goods, the Trademark Act is not applicable.

The advertising of strong alcohol is not allowed in Finland, thus the example must be beer. As the advertisement does not include any false statements § 2 SopMenL is not applicable. The only rule in this law that might be used is § 1 SopMenL that forbids any activity that is contrary to

[21] C. Plant, W. Rose, S. Sime, D. French (eds.), *Blackstone's Civil Practice 2004* (2004), p. 32 (paragraph 4.17)

[22] Ibid., p. 29 (paragraph 4.12)

[23] Ibid., p. 30 and particularly *Experience Hendrix v. PPX Enterprises Inc.* [2003] EWCA Civ 323.

[24] Civil Procedure Rule 25.1(1)(o) and Practice Direction 40, see also Civil Procedure Rule 23.

[25] C. Plant, W. Rose, S. Sime, D. French (eds.), *Blackstone's Civil Practice 2004* (2004), p. 32 (para. 4.17)

good business practices or otherwise unfair to other traders. This might be possible if the advertisement shows B's product in a negative or demeaning way or with a connection to a product that might reduce the good reputation of B's product. Further, using someone's 'good reputation' might be against good business practices (for example when a cheap or non-quality product is marketed with the image of an exclusive product).

(1) However, B could not be compensated for any gains made by A in this way as the Market Court can only order the advertising campaign to be ended. B must sue in an ordinary court.

(2) As it is a case of purely economic damages the Finnish Tort Liability Act would require especially weighty reasons for a claim to be successful under this act. In any case, the claimant must prove what harm the actions of the defendant have caused him. As it is in most cases unlikely that there would be any damage (loss of good reputation etc.) there is no real possibility of success. In cases where the reputation of an exclusive product is deliberately used in such way that the good reputation of these goods will suffer, there is a possibility that such a claim could be accepted. The Finnish Supreme Court has to date not decided any such case.[26]

The interpretation of § 5:1 Tort Liability Act has become more liberal during the 1990s. In addition, there is a possibility that the law might be changed, but this is only in the preliminary stages (a report on the issue has been made but there are no concrete proposals yet and it is still unknown whether the law will be changed). If B had suffered losses that may be remedied these could have included loss of income/profit, loss of trademark value etc.

France (3)

As a matter of fact such advertising is impossible in France since the Evin Act of January 10, 1991 prohibiting any public advertising for alcoholic drinks.[27] We therefore assume the legality of advertising alcohol. There is no special legislation on unfair competition apart from cases of prohibited competition. French unfair competition law

[26] For a prediction see I. Kaulamo, *Finland*, in G. Schricker, note 353.

[27] For details on this see G. Raymond, in Juris-Classeur, *Concurrence, consommation* (1998), Fasc. 900, 'Publicité commerciale et protection des consommateurs', notes 81 et seq.; for the prohibition to advertise for tobacco and its products see note 121.

has been developed as case law around the general tort law provisions. A liability according to art. 1382 cc always requires 'faute', i.e. an attributable, illegal and culpable action. This kind of unfair competition is known in French literature as *parasitisme* and it is considered to be one type of behaviour of unfair competition falling under the art. 1382 and 1383 cc. Jurisprudence admits basically three main groups: imitation or confusion, discrediting or denigration and disorganization.[28] What all three groups, having been revealed as the triad of French unfair competition law by Roubier, have in common is that there is a competitive situation at the beginning, often also described as one of the conditions for the exercise of a judicial action.[29]

In cases, such as the present, where there is no such competitive situation it has been doubted whether there could be any damage at all, given that the classic damage in French unfair competition law is the loss of customers.[30]

Characteristic for cases of this kind is that the advertiser does not want to create a confusion concerning the origin of his products but just wants to profit from the notoriety of the other product.

Matters are different when the protection of a brand mark is concerned. In this case art. L 713-5 of the Code of intellectual property regulates that the use of a brand mark that has itself a high prestige is prohibited even for different products and services. Thus in the well-known 'Champagne' case from the Paris Tribunal on December 15, 1993 (JCP éd. E 1994 II 540), where the association of the producers of champagne wanted to prevent Yves Saint-Laurent from giving the name 'Champagne' to a perfume, the court deemed that the damage consisted in a *trouble commercial*, present or future, leading to a dilution of the value of the brand. It has been considered as development damage (*préjudice de développement*). However, this is not the present case where the product has simply been presented together with the original prestigious product of another company.

French civil law distinguishes between *dommage moral* and material damage.[31]

[28] J. Passa, in Juris-Classeur, *Concurrence, consommation* (1998), Fasc. 240, 'Domaine de l'action en concurrence déloyale', notes 31 et seq.

[29] Ibid., notes 11 et seq.

[30] Ph. Le Tourneau, *De la spécificité du préjudice concurrentiel*, in RTDcom 1998, p. 83 (86).

[31] Ibid., p. 83 (90).

(1) In French law there is the prescription of strict equivalence between damage and reparation.[32] Thus art. 1149 cc announces that damages and interests are constituted by the actual loss that the creditor has suffered or the profit that he has been deprived of. Thus in general the material damage in competition matters is calculated in reference to the turnovers before and after the unfair behaviour.[33] If this is not appropriate either because the accounts do not reflect any influence of the unfair behaviour since it is stopped at an early stage, or the accounts are otherwise of no relevance, the judges can use any other document or indication available to them in order to support a finding of the existence of damage.[34] It is also common to ask an expert for an assessment.[35] Finally, concerning the reparation of future damage, this is only possible where it is virtual damage that will very probably be realized, and not hypothetical.[36]

(2) The *dommage moral* is often assessed by the judge with an award of symbolic value (one franc or one euro).[37] In this case the damage is found in the dilution or the depreciation of a product being seen with an unbranded product or service.[38] In a more general way the damage is often seen as a *trouble commercial*, which does not, however, dispense with a plaintiff having to provide evidence of the existence and extent of damage.[39] It has in this context been considered that any sort of usurpation of an economic value can constitute damage in unfair competition law.[40]

(3) The judge has a complete discretion in the assessment of damages (*dommages-intérêts*).[41] The judge can either refer to the actual loss (e.g. on the basis of an expert opinion) or he can assess an amount having only a

[32] J. Passa, in Juris-Classeur, *Concurrence, consommation* (1998), Fasc. 240, 'Domaine de l'action en concurrence déloyale', note 75.

[33] N.-F. Alpi, in Juris-Classeur, *Concurrence, consommation* (2003) Fasc. 245, 'Action en concurrence déloyale – éléments de procédure', note 107.

[34] Ibid. [35] Ibid.

[36] Ph. Le Tourneau, 'De la spécificité du préjudice concurrentiel', in RTDcom (1998), p. 83 (92); the same way T. Dreier and S. von Lewinsky, *Frankreich*, in G. Schricker, note 375.

[37] N.-F. Alpi in Juris-Classeur, *Concurrence, consommation* (2003), Fasc. 245, 'Action en concurrence déloyale – éléments de procédure', note 108.

[38] M. Malaurie-Vignal, *Droit de la concurrence* (2nd edn 2002), p. 132.

[39] Ph. Le Tourneau, *De la spécificité du préjudice concurrentiel*, in RTDcom 1998, p. 83 (91).

[40] Ibid. [41] Cass., Com April 25, 1983 in Bull. Civ. IV, note 123, p. 104.

symbolic value.[42] Art. 700 NCPC now explicitly allows the court to assess the damage at its discretion.[43]

Germany (3)

The protection of well-known trademarks is exclusively guaranteed by the law of trademarks and the law governing comparative advertising. The law of trademarks has been harmonized by the Trademark Directive 89/104/EEC and the Trademark Regulation (EC) 40/94; their scope and boundaries are defined by the ECJ. § 14 para. 2 no.3 *Markengesetz* – MarkenG (Trademark Act) prohibits the exploitation of a well-known trademark.[44] Before the introduction of § 14 para. 2 no. 3 MarkenG these cases could only be subsumed under the blanket clause of § 3 UWG (ex-§ 1 UWG). Now recourse to the general law of unfair competition is no longer necessary.[45] A does not use the automobile brand for his own products as a trademark;[46] he only uses it as a means to transfer the goodwill towards B's products to his own products. For this way of using a trademark § 14 para. 2 no. 3 MarkenG is also applicable.[47]

B could be entitled to damages. For the claim to succeed it must be shown that A acted wilfully or negligently, § 14 para. 6 MarkenG.[48] B can

[42] Y. Guyon, *Droit des affaires*, vol. 2 (8th edn 2001) p. 876.

[43] Art. 700 NCPC, Decree No 76-714 of July 29, 1976, sec.5, OJ of July 30, 1976, Decree No 91-1266 of December 19, 1991, sec.163, OJ of December 20, 1991 in force since January 1, 1992, reads: 'As provided in I of art. 75 of the Act n. 91–647 of July 10, 1991, in all proceedings, the judge shall order against the party having the burden of taxable charges or, in default, the unsuccessful party, to pay to the other party the amount which he shall fix on the basis of the sums outlayed and not included in the taxable charges. The judge shall take into consideration the rules of equity and the economic condition of the party against whom it is ordered. He may, even *ex proprio motu*, for reasons based on the same considerations, rule that there is no need for such order.'

[44] T. Sambuc, in H. Harte-Bavendamm and F. Henning-Bodewig, *UWG* (2004), § 4 no. 9 notes 115 et seq.; P. Ströbele and F. Hacker, *Markengesetz* (7th edn 2003), § 14 note 148.

[45] T. Sambuc, in H. Harte-Bavendamm and F. Henning-Bodewig, *UWG* (2004), § 4 no. 9 note 117.

[46] The opinion of the German High Court is that this is a prerequisite for § 14, cf. BGH (2002) 104 GRUR 814 – 'Festspielhaus'; BGH (2002) 104 GRUR 818 (819) – 'Frühstücksdrink II'.

[47] P. Ströbele and F. Hacker, *Markengesetz* (7th edn 2003), § 14 note 148; T. Sambuc, in H. Harte-Bavendamm and F. Henning-Bodewig, *UWG* (2004), § 4 no. 9 note 117; J. Bornkamm, *Markenrecht und wettbewerbsrechtlicher Kennzeichenschutz – Zur Vorrangthese der Rechtsprechung*, (2005) 107 GRUR 97, (100); probably a different opinion in H. H. Götting, in H. Harte-Bavendamm and F. Henning-Bodewig, *UWG* (2004), § 4 no. 9 note 46; W. Nordemann et al., *Wettbewerbs- und Markenrecht* (9th edn 2003), note 1191.

[48] P. Ströbele and F. Hacker, *Markengesetz* (7th edn 2003), § 14 note 293.

pursue compensation of his losses in three different ways:[49] under German law the claimant can either claim his actual losses under § 249 s. 1 BGB, an appropriate fictional licence fee (licence analogy), or the surrender of realized profits by the infringing party.[50]

(1) Under § 252 s. 1 BGB he can also claim lost profits. § 252 s. 2 BGB is based on the presumption that the profit is deemed to be lost if it could have been expected as likely in the normal course of affairs. It is assumed as a matter of general experience that the injured party has been deprived of business and profit because of the infringement.[51] Calculation of the amount of losses must be substantiated by the injured party.[52] Where the injured party claims actual losses he must establish these to the satisfaction of the court pursuant to § 286 ZPO. Generally, the injured party will not be able to provide concrete evidence of financial losses. B has not suffered any concrete loss.

(2) The claimant can require surrender of profits made by the infringing party. This is based on the idea that generally losses to the injured party can be inferred from the profits of the infringing party.[53] Here, not the whole of the profits can be claimed, but only those which are attributable to the infringing behaviour. This portion of the profits must be proved within the provisions of § 287 ZPO.

Proof of the the infringing party's realized profits can be difficult. B does not know the increase in A's turnover. Thus, he cannot quantify his claim under § 253 para. 2 no. 2 ZPO, which would result in his being unable to pursue his claim in the courts. German law does not provide for a general obligation of discovery.[54] Thus, the legal basis of a claim to be entitled to discovery is the culpable relationship itself, which is founded on the unfair competition infringement together with the good faith requirement of § 242 BGB.[55] Because of the advertising

[49] H. Köhler and H. Piper, *UWG, Kommentar* (3rd edn 2002), vor § 13 note 100 et seq.; P. Ströbele and F. Hacker, *Markengesetz* (7th edn 2003), § 14 note 301.

[50] H. Köhler, in W. Hefermehl, H. Köhler and J. Bornkamm, *Wettbewerbsrecht* (24th edn 2006), § 9 note 1.38.

[51] H. Köhler and H. Piper, *UWG* (3rd edn 2002), vor § 13 note 99; A. Baumbach and W. Hefermehl, *UWG* (22nd edn 2001), Einl. note 379.

[52] BGHZ 77, 16 (19).

[53] H. Köhler, in W. Hefermehl, H. Köhler and J. Bornkamm, *Wettbewerbsrecht* (24th edn 2006), § 9 notes 1.24 et seq. with reference to BGH (1993) 95 GRUR 55 (57) – 'Tchibo/ Rolex II'.

[54] H. Köhler, in W. Hefermehl, H. Köhler and J. Bornkamm, *Wettbewerbsrecht* (24th edn 2006), § 9 note 1.45.

[55] BGH (1976) 78 GRUR 367 (368) – 'Ausschreibungsunterlagen'; BGH (1996) 98 GRUR 271 (275) – 'Gefärbte Jeans'; H. Köhler and H. Piper, *UWG* (3rd edn 2002), vor § 13 note 114;

campaign, A gains an additional €10,000. B can claim this additional amount from A. The reform of the UWG in 2004 has introduced for the very first time the sanction of disgorging profits. These can be claimed by consumer protection societies and have to be paid to the state (§ 10 UWG). They could claim the €10,000.

(3) The calculation under the licence model is intended to give the injured party compensation. It is based on the assumption that the infringing party should not be treated better or worse than a contractual licensee.[56]

The infringing party has received a monetary benefit through the illegal behaviour, the value of which can be most reliably calculated in terms of what his financial position would be if he had used the displayed car in a permissible way.[57] The level of the licence fee is determined in terms of what a reasonable party would have agreed in view of the factual circumstances and the degree of benefit at the time of conclusion of the fictional agreement.[58]

Greece (3)

The protection of the advertising function of the trademark per se remains a controversial issue under Greek Law.[59] Two points of view are developed in the legal doctrine.

According to the first one, the trademark law L. 2239/1994[60] is not applicable to the present case, as it prohibits only the trademark-specific usages made by third (unauthorized) parties. Under this restrictive approach, the provisions of the trademark law[61] award protection to the trademark owner only when the same or a similar sign is used by third parties as distinctive of origin (for that reason, the protection is granted upon condition that the use, imitation or counterfeiting of the trademark by the third party creates a risk of confusion, unless the trademark has a reputation).[62] The same condition should apply regarding famous trademarks; it means that only their naming and

H. Köhler, in W. Hefermehl, H. Köhler and J. Bornkamm, *Wettbewerbsrecht* (24th edn 2006), § 9 note 1.42.

56 BGHZ 82, 310 – 'Fersenabstützvorrichtung'; H. Köhler and H. Piper, *UWG* (3rd edn 2002), vor § 13 note 102.

57 BGHZ 77, 16 (25). 58 H. Köhler and H. Piper, *UWG* (3rd edn 2002), § 13 note 103.

59 See N. Rokas, *Industrial Property* (2004), p. 130.

60 This law is mainly based on the provisions of Directive 89/104/EEC.

61 Articles 18 (3) and 26.

62 See e.g. *Athens multimember CFI* 460/1996 (1996) 47 EEmpD 404 with comments by Chr. Chrissanthis.

informative function (distinction of origin) should be protected under the trademark law,[63] and not the advertising one. If this position is followed, the application of L. 146/1914 on unfair competition could be envisaged, in particular the provisions of art. 1.[64] The case refers to the parasitic exploitation of a distinctive sign of a third party aiming at transferring the reputation of the original product to the advantage of the whisky producer, which is an (unfair) act contrary to good morals. However, art. 1 of L. 146/1914 requires that a competitive situation exist between the involved parties A and B. It could be considered that the competitive relationship exists not through the products themselves (whisky and car) but through the market in brand-merchandising, although Greek courts do not seem inclined to accept such a wide interpretation.[65]

(1) In accordance with art. 1 of L. 146/1914, the damaged party may seek reparation. The conditions for such action are the unlawful character of the act committed by the author of the damage, fault, the existence of damage resulting from the unlawful and culpable act and a causal link between the said act and the damage. The calculation of damages in cases involving unfair competition is extremely difficult, as only damage that has actually been incurred (and proved) may be indemnified;[66] in any case damages usually include both the decrease in the existing property of the damaged party and lost profits thereof which could probably have been expected in the ordinary course of events or according to the special circumstances (art. 298 CC).[67]

In light of the difficulties in the calculation of damages, art. 17 of L. 1733/1987 on patents[68] adopts three methods for the calculation of

[63] This solution is similar to that reached by the German High Court in the *Rolls Royce v. Jim Beam* case, before the amendment of the German Law (see above). See the references on this case made by I. Soufleros, *Article 1*, in R. Rokas (ed.), *Unfair Competition* (1996), p. 170.

[64] Art. 13 of L. 146/1914 regarding the protection of distinctive signs cannot apply in the present case, as it presupposes a risk of confusion.

[65] For this difficulty, see N. Rokas, *Exploitation and protection of the advertising value* (1999) 50 *EEmpD* 6. In the positive sense, *Piraeus court of appeals*, decision 3855/1988 (1989) 39 *EEmpD* 119; see however *Athens multimember CFI*, decision 19/1982 (1983) 33 *EEmpD* 506, which in a similar case did not accept the application of art. 1 of law 146/1914 and opted for a narrower interpretation of the condition of competitive relations, thus finding that the condition was not met since the products were of different kinds.

[66] M. Stathopoulos, *General Law of Obligations*, 4th edn (2004) [in Greek], pp. 462 et seq.

[67] *Thessaloniki Court of Appeals*, decision 94/1994, (1994) ARM 953; *Thessaloniki Court of Appeals*, decision 540/2000, (2000) 6 DEE 1022.

[68] Government Gazette, issue A 171, 1987.

culpable violations of patent rights.[69] According to the said article, the bearer of the patent right 'may request the restitution of the damage or the return of any profit from the unfair exploitation of the patent or the payment of a monetary sum proportional to the price of the exploitation licence'. Legal doctrine supports the view[70] that the application by analogy of the above-mentioned method of calculations in the field of unfair competition is necessary provided that the unfair and competitive act is directed against incorporeal goods similar to the ones protected by specific statutes (i.e. patents).

Thus, if the above extensive interpretation is accepted, the automobile manufacturer B may select in the case in question one of the following: (i) to claim and prove actual and material damages resulting from A's unfair conduct; (ii) to claim and prove that A profited from exploiting the reputation of a third party and request the return of the profit, or (iii) to request the payment of a sum proportional to the licence fee. The fee will be calculated on the basis of the existing market conditions.[71] B will most probably select the second or the third option. If he chooses to request the profit from the sales increase, the question of which kind of profits should be returned to B arises, as the court will have to determine the degree to which the infringed product has contributed to the realization of the profit.

(2) In any case, B may also request pecuniary reparation for the 'moral' (non-pecuniary) harm[72] by application of the provisions on the violation of the right to personality.[73]

According to the second and progressively prevailing point of view, the trademark law should penalize violations of trademarks not only in their distinctive function, but also in their advertising function. This is now largely accepted regarding the advertising function of famous trademarks.[74] This position is closer to the letter and the spirit of the

[69] See above Case 1 (Risky bread).

[70] A. Liakopoulos, *Article 1*, in N. Rokas (ed.), *Unfair Competition* (1996), p. 145. In favour of the payment of a reasonable fee by the tortfeasor, despite the courts' reluctance, see N. Rokas, op. cit., (1999) 50 EEmpD 7.

[71] For the difficulties of such calculation, see A. Liakopoulos, *Industrial Property*, 5th edn (2000), pp. 136–137.

[72] D. Tsimbanoulis, *Article 1*, in N. Rokas (ed.), *Unfair Competition* (1996), p. 70.

[73] Articles 57–60 CC.

[74] N. Rokas, *Industrial Property*, (2004), pp. 137–138; B. Antonopoulos, *Industrial Property* (2002), p. 424; A. Psaras, *Restriction to the Protection of Trademark*, 1996 (3) DEE 227, 232 M.-Th. Marinos, *Risk of Confusion and the Field of Protection of Distinctive Signs under the New Trademark Law and the Law 146/14 on Unfair Competition*, EllDni 1995, p. 1226, *Athens*

new trademark law. Thus, if a third person uses a famous trademark for advertising purposes, thus obtaining an unfair benefit or harming the trademark's reputation, the trademark proprietor should be entitled to invoke the provisions of L. 2239/1994 (art. 26). Under this approach, B may be also entitled to damages. The conditions for compensation as well as the methods for the calculation of damages are the same as described above regarding the application of L. 146/1914. In fact, in order to overcome the difficulties related to the calculation of the concrete damage suffered, the legal doctrine proposes the application of art. 17 of L. 1733/1987 in all fields of industrial and intellectual property.[75] Theoretically, B will again have the choice to claim: (a) actual and material damages ('moral' damage is not excluded); (b) the return of profit realized by A, or (c) the payment of a fictional licence fee.

Hungary (3)

On the basis of the facts we can assume that B has a trademark protection on his cars. Accordingly, he can ask the court to prohibit the use of his trademark. Consequently, he can recover damages according to the rules of Hungarian civil law.

(1) He can recover real damages as well as unjust enrichment. There are no rules set by the courts as to the estimation of the damages. So the determination of the actual sum is left to the discretion of the court. In case of a claim for compensation the person who suffered the damages shall prove the following: the amount of his damages suffered as a consequence of the activity of the other party, and the link of causality between the activity of the defendant and the suffered damages. The responsibility of the defendant is directly linked to culpability (in contrast to the claim that aims at prohibition – when the liability of the defendant is a strict liability).

(2) In the course of litigation and the fact-finding procedure, difficulties may arise in proving the reduced turnover of the products of the plaintiff and the amount of the resulting damage (outstanding profits)

multimember CFI 9364/1994 and 8393/1995, (1995) 46 *EEmpD* 495, 497, *Piraeus single member CFI* 2400/1993, (1993) 43 *EEmpD* 650. Cf. *Athens single member CFI* 8150/1991 with the critical comments of D. Tzouganatos (under the previous legal regime), *Athens single member* CFI 1653/1999, (1999) 49 EEmpD 813.

[75] B. Antonopoulos, *op.cit.*, p. 700, contra *Athens court of appeals* 454/1990, (1991) 42 *EEmpD* 528.

or the damage arising from the infringement of the business secrets of the plaintiff, etc. Therefore, in the course of litigation, it is reasonable firstly to request the establishment of the violation and the prohibition of such violation. Any other claim (claim for compensation) shall subsequently be requested in order to avoid the continuance of the claim.

Ireland (3)

(1) B can bring a tort action against A in the civil courts for *passing off* the whisky as B's product. To be successful B would have to show the three criteria listed in Case 2 above. Generally, B would have to establish loss of earnings in order to be successful. However, even where no actual financial loss could be established, it has been held that there can be passing off where similar names are used that cause some confusion among customers.[76]

B's case may not be successful because of the degree of difference between the products concerned. A could reasonably claim honest use of B's product. Hypothetically, if a passing off was established, on the basis of the *Falcon Travel* case, the court may decide that an injunction is unnecessary under the circumstances, and use its discretion to award B an amount to enable him to mount an advertising or public relations campaign to explain that the products are not related.

(2) Alternatively, if B's car brand is trademarked, B could take an action against A, seeking an injunction and/or damages to prevent the infringement of his trademark under sec. 14 of the Trade Marks Act 1996, which applies even where a trademark is used in relation to goods or services which are not similar to those for which the trademark is registered, where the trademark has as a reputation in the state and the use of the sign, being without due cause, takes unfair advantage of, or is detrimental to, the distinctive character or the reputation of the trademark.[77] A trademark can be licensed under sec. 32 of the Trade Marks Act 1996, or assigned under sec. 28. The parties have to negotiate between them the terms of the licence fee. Following the *Vodafone* case, it would seem likely that B could show that A's use of his trademarked car was use which, without due cause, would take unfair advantage of, or be detrimental to, the distinctive character or reputation

[76] *Falcon Travel Ltd. v. Owners Abroad Group plc* [1991] 1 IR 175.

[77] See Case 1 (Risky bread).

of his trademark.[78] B's request for an injunction is more likely to be successful on this ground.

(3) A third option for B would be to sue A in the civil courts. B could try to sue A for *defamatory slander* but he would have to show that his reputation has been damaged by the innuendo in A's advertisement, implying that his car was associated with A's whisky, and that he had suffered special damages, unless he could show that the slander was intended to cause him pecuniary loss, which would seem not to be the case. It may be difficult for B to succeed because no actual statement about his goods has been made, and because he has suffered no actual loss.[79]

Italy (3)

It is debatable whether trademark law applies. It may be argued that B's trademark is very well-known, and should therefore be entitled to protection from to any kind of exploitation, including advertisements, notwithstanding the difference between the products of the trademark owner and those of the defendant, and the fact that the trademark is used with reference to the genuine product of B. It could be held that there is an actual risk of confusion of consumers, in the particular form of a risk of association, also in the narrow meaning in which the ECJ construes such notion. Consumers seeing A's advertisement may think that there is some link between A and B (for example, that they belong to the same group of companies), or simply that B authorised the use of his trademark by A, in order to testify to the particular quality of A's liquor (see now art. 20 lit. (c) d.lgs. n. 30/05, of February 10, 2005, Industrial Property Code).

Therefore, B may seek an injunction according to the law of trademarks (art. 124 Industrial Property Code), and he may also have a claim for damages (art. 125 Industrial Property Code). Such claims are quite unlikely to succeed, since it might be held that B's trademark is not violated by means of its use with reference to genuine products, notwithstanding that such products are used in the context of an advertisement by a third party.

Art. 2598 *codice civile* – cc (Civil Code) is unlikely to be applied in the case in question, since A and B may not be considered as competitors. The application of art. 2598 cc requires that the parties are undertakings

[78] *Vodafone Group Ltd and Vodafone Ltd v. Orange Personal Communications Services Ltd* [1996] 10 EIPR D-307.

[79] See Case 1 (Risky bread).

active in the same market, or, at least, that the defendant may be likely to enter the market of the plaintiff ('potential competition'). In the present case, it is likely that a car manufacturer will never be considered as a competitor to a whisky distiller. Moreover, A has never shown any intention to enter the car market: he just used the picture of B's car in order to improve the appeal of his product, one that is completely different from cars and not related to them in any way.

Finally, general tort law stated by art. 2043 et seq. cc may be applied, at least if B can offer evidence that the use of his trademark by A has injured his good reputation, for example because A's product is of a low quality. Should B's good reputation not be injured, it may be argued that B has no legal right that can be infringed by A, other than those granted by the law of trademarks, since the law, though recognising an exclusive right in pictures of physical persons, which may not be used in advertisements without their permission, does not vest anybody with exclusive rights in pictures of their own goods. In other words, everybody can freely use a picture of somebody else's goods in his own advertising.[80]

(1) A judgment can order the compensation of damage, art. 2600 cc. This requires intent or negligence. In practice, normally only a judgment concerning the prerequisites of a claim is sought, art. 278 cpc. This is then the basis for an out-of-court settlement about the actual amount of the damages.[81] To avoid difficulties in proving the actual amount of a loss the courts can estimate the actual loss if the occurrence of a loss has been proven (art. 2056 together with 1226 cc).

(2) In the event that B's claim for damages should succeed under the law of trademarks or under general tort law, the amount of damages may be calculated with reference to the fee which B might have demanded from A for a licence to use the trademark in his advertisements. Such a way of calculating damages has sometimes been applied in case law, with reference to cases in which famous people claimed their name and/or picture had been improperly used for advertising purposes; according to such decisions, the judge ought to calculate the amount of money the plaintiff might have earned from the advertising. That amount will constitute the basis for calculating the damages.

Art. 125 Industrial Property Code now states that damages arising from any infringement of industrial property rights shall be calculated

[80] See above A.IV.2. [81] E. Bastian, *Italy*, in G. Schricker, note 270.

by the court applying general provisions of the Civil Code (arts. 1223, 1226 and 1227 cc); specific reference shall be made to profits lost by the plaintiff, taking into account earnings by the defendant and costs which the latter ought to have paid to obtain a licence from the plaintiff. Alternatively, according to para. 2 of art. 125, the plaintiff may ask damages to be calculated in a lump sum, to be calculated on the basis of circumstantial evidence.

Netherlands (3)

The mere fact that one profits from the business success or the good reputation of someone else, does not in itself constitute a wrongful act. The Dutch Supreme Court has formulated the following general rule in this respect: 'That in commerce – where one continuously builds on to the achievements of others – it is not in itself a breach of rules of unwritten law pertaining to proper social conduct to benefit from the attractiveness of the products of another party, even if this leads to competition with and, consequently, a disadvantage for that other party.'[82] However, pursuant to art. 13 para. 1 lit. (c) Trade Mark Act, B may have an action against any use in commerce of his trademark. For B to successfully object against such use of his trademark, the following conditions must be fulfilled: (i) the trademark is well-known, (ii) the infringer profits unjustly from or damages the reputation of the distinguishing capacity of the trademark, and (iii) the infringer does not have a legitimate reason for using the trademark.

(1) If A is liable for damages towards B, the burden of proof with respect to the (amount of) damages suffered, lies with B. The Trade Mark Act provides that, in addition to or instead of a claim for damages, B may claim the surrender of profits gained by A as a result of the use of B's trademark, cf. art. 13 para. 4 Trade Mark Act. In many cases it will be difficult for B to establish the extent of the profits gained by A. In that

[82] 'Dat het in het economisch verkeer – waarin doorlopend wordt voortgebouwd op het door anderen tot stand gebrachte – profijt te trekken van de aantrekkelijkheid van het product van een ander op zichzelf niet in strijd is met de zorgvuldigheid die in het maatschappelijk verkeer jegens die ander betaamt, en ook dan niet als dit profijt trekken die ander concurrentie aandoet en hem daardoor nadeel toebrengt'; see Supreme Court June 23, 1961 – *'Leesportefeuille'*, NJ 1961, 423; see also Supreme Court, January 16, 1970 – *'Ja Zuster Nee Zuster'*, NJ 1970 220; Supreme Court, October 23, 1987 – *'NOS – KNVB'*, NJ 1988 310; Supreme Court, November 20, 1987 – *'Staat- Den ouden'*, NJ 1988 311.

respect, art. 13 para. 4 provides that B may also claim that A renders account of his profits.

(2) The amount of any claim shall be calculated on the basis of the information given by the parties (taking into account the rules on the burden of proof). It is at the discretion of the court to assess the evidence advanced by the parties in this respect. The court will as a rule base its decision on what it considers to be a reasonable and fair calculation of damages.

Furthermore, B has no action against A on the basis of the Competition Act.

Poland (3)

Earning money from another undertaking's reputation is not regulated *expressis verbis* as an act of unfair competition in chap. III u.z.n.k. However, the general provision in art. 3 u.z.n.k. creates a legal ground for the claim B may have against A. Acting against the law or custom and usage, if it endangers or infringes the interests of another undertaking or customer, constitutes an act of unfair competition (art. 3.1 u.z.n.k.). Art. 3.2 u.z.n.k. contains an open-ended list giving specific examples of acts of unfair competition. Consequently, various acts of unfair competition, not listed in chap. III can be 'created' on the basis of the general clause. Using another undertaking's/product's reputation and in this way building one's own reputation, gaining advantage over competitors and diluting the reputation of the original undertaking or its product would definitely constitute an unspecified act of unfair competition on the basis of art. 3 u.z.n.k.[83]

(1) The plaintiff can claim compensatory damages[84] (art. 18.1(4) u.z.n.k.) and the return of unjustly gained benefits (art. 18.1(5) u.z.n.k.) according to the general rules. The general provisions of the Kodeks Cywilny – k.c. (Civil Code) dealing with compensation of damages, in particular with rules of responsibility, extent of damages (*damnum emergens, lucrum cessans*), third parties' responsibility, and joint responsibility, and joint and several liability will apply. Because of the difficulties in calculating damages in unfair competition cases,

[83] E. Nowinska and M. Du Vall, *Komentarz do ustawy o zwalczaniu nieuczciwej konkurencji* (2001), p. 38; also J. Szwaja (ed.), *Ustawa o zwalczaniu nieuczciwej konkurencji, Komentarz* (2000).

[84] Black's Law Dictionary (2nd edn 2001).

the courts must apply art. 322 k.p.c.[85] According to this provision, the court shall assess damages according to its own views, based on careful consideration of all the circumstances of the case, if in claims for compensatory damages, unjust enrichment etc. the precise calculation of the damages is not possible, or very difficult.

(2) The general rule of unjust enrichment from art. 405 k.c. is applicable in conjunction with art. 18.1 (5) u.z.n.k.[86] The question of whether the infringing entrepreneur's enrichment should correspond with the claimant entrepreneur's damage remains open. The dominant view assumes that there is such correspondence.[87] The contrary view assumes that because art. 18.1 (5) u.z.n.k. refers to the general rules of compensation, it does not necessarily mean that the claimant does suffer such damage (as required by art. 405 k.c.).[88]

(3) There is a variety of views regarding the extent of the damages an undertaking can claim on the grounds of art. 18.1(5) u.z.n.k. in connection with art. 405 k.c. Since using the reputation of another undertaking/product constitutes an act of unfair competition similar to infringement of intellectual property rights, the jurisprudence and doctrine developed on this ground can be used.[89] The High Court in its opinion regarding unjust enrichment stated that restitution damages should equal potential licence fees.[90] Subsequently, this opinion was amended, when it was pointed out that limiting compensation to a licence fee would be too restricted since the infringer would not bear the risk of illegal exploitation of another undertaking's reputation.[91] Since the dominant doctrinal view presumes that damages should be determined by the extent of the damage suffered,[92] B will not be able to

[85] E. Nowinska and M. Du Vall, *Komentarz do ustawy o zwalczaniu nieuczciwej konkurencji* (2001), p. 192.

[86] J. Szwaja, in J. Szwaja (red.), *Ustawa prawa prasowe. Komentarz* (1999), p. 529; R. Skubisz, *Prawo znakow towarowych. Komentarz* (1997), p. 182.

[87] W. Czachorski, *System prawa cywilnego* t3 (1981), p. 70; E. Letowska, *Bezpodstawne wzbogacenie* (2000), p. 140.

[88] T. Knypl, *Zwalczanie nieuczciwej konkurencji w Polsce i Europie* (1995), p. 159.

[89] E. Nowinska and M. Du Vall, *Komentarz do ustawy o zwalczaniu nieuczciwej konkurencji* (2001), p. 193.

[90] SN 10 stycznia 1962 r., III CR 410/61.

[91] SN 14 lutego 1969 r., I CR 575/68.

[92] W. Czachorski, *System prawa cywilnego* t3 (1981), p. 70; E. Letowska, *Bezpodstawne wzbogacenie* (2000), p. 140; J. Sobczak, *Ustawa prawo prasowe* (1999); R. Skbisz, in J. Szwaja (ed.), *Ustawa o zwalczaniu nieuczciwej konkurencji* (2000), p. 492; contrary: L. Gornicki, *Nieuczciwa konkurencja, w szczegolnosci przez wprowadzajace w blad oznaczenie towarow i uslug, i srodki ochrony w prawie polskim* (1997), p. 113.

claim the profit A made from increased sales on the basis of the unjust enrichment laws.

Portugal (3)

This kind of advertising constitutes an illegal and unauthorized exploitation of the good reputation of the mark of B and can cause dilution of B's mark. In this case it is very difficult according to Portuguese law to admit an action based on unfair competition. In fact, A and B are not really competitors in the same market: one sells cars and the other sells alcoholic beverages. Only if we consider as an act of competition an action which can cause economic damage to another, or if we admit that this kind of advertising implies economic parasitism,[93] can we establish in this case a competitive relationship.[94] In this case, B could bring a compensatory claim against A, because his interest is protected under the unfair competition rules (art. 317 CPI and art. 483 para. 1 CC). In any case, we can only admit a compensation claim, according to art. 317 CPI, first part, if we classify this statute as a norm protective of another's interest, according to art. 483 para. 1 CC, whose specific aim is to protect competitors like B. Besides that, other requirements for civil liability must also be fulfilled such as illegality, fault, causation and damage. If B is still not able to determine and prove his damage, he can bring a generic demand, according to art. 565 and 569 CC, in which the amount of damages can be further determined.

The amount of the compensation can be calculated according to three kinds of solution: the cost of a licence from A to use his car in an advertising campaign from B, the profits A earned or the profits B lost. Moreover, in Portugal it is also possible to use the method of 'threefold calculation of damages' when the damages cannot be accurately demonstred.[95]

(1) Under art. 566 para. 3 CC the court can use equity to determine compensation even if it cannot establish with precision the exact amount of damages.[96]

[93] C. Olavo, *Propriedade Industrial* (Almedina Coimbra, 1997), p. 170; A. Menezes Leitão, Leitão, *Imitação servil, concorrência parasitária e concorrência desleal*, Direito Industrial, vol. I, APDI (Almedina, Coimbra, 2001), p. 15.

[94] O. Ascensão, *Concorrência Desleal* (1994), pp. 110 (119 et seq.), states that this case cannot be considered as unfair competition, because there is a total absence of a competitive relationship. According to this point of view, it would be only possible to admit in this case dilution of a trademark.

[95] A. Menezes Leitão, *Estudo de Direito Privado sobre a Cláusula Geral de Concorrência Desleal* (2000), p. 169.

[96] Ibid., p. 170.

(2) If there are not any damages, but only unjust profits of B, A can still restore a claim against him based on unjust enrichment[97] because in this case the generic requirements of this civil action are fulfilled (art. 473 para. 1 CC).

(3) Winning an action for compensation can be very difficult because of the burden of proof to determine the damages (so-called *probatio diabolica*). Normally, competitors do not receive any kind of compensation for the economic damage they suffer in the competition area. Therefore, some legal writers in Portugal hold the opinion that the most frequent claim against unfair competition should be the claim for an order to desist. However, others argue in favour of establishing alternative forms of computing damages and easing the burden of proof.[98] It is possible to use other forms of computing the damages, such as the price a wronged competitor would claim in order to authorize the act complained of, or the profits gained by the infringer from the illegal action, or the loss of profits suffered by the wronged competitor. The computing of the damage is really difficult, but the court has a certain freedom in evaluating the evidence and can be satisfied with a less exacting standard of proof in such civil actions.

Spain (3)

B has a compensatory claim against A before the ordinary civil courts because A has exploited B's good reputation contained in the trademark.

(1) He therefore brings an action under art. 12 LCD (Unfair Competition Act); he is legally entitled to claim damages, as provided in art. 18 LCD, including damages for unjust enrichment.

(2) In order to calculate the compensation, the courts would use art. 43c *Ley de Marcas* – LMa (Trademark Act) which entitles B to claim, at his option, the profits A has obtained because of the infringement or the price he would have obtained for the grant of a licence to use the trademark right (art. 43c LMa).

(3) B has a right to information about the profits of A.

Sweden (3)

First, it should be observed that commercial advertisements (in print, radio or television) promoting the consumption of spirits (e.g. whisky)

[97] L. Menezes Leitão, *O enriquecimento sem causa no direito civil português*, CEF (1996), p. 756.

[98] P. Costa e Silva, *Meios de reacção civil à concorrência desleal*, in Concorrência Desleal (Almedina Coimbra, 1997), p. 116; A. Menezes Leitão, *Estudo de Direito Privado sobre a Cláusula Geral de Concorrência Desleal* (2000), pp. 169 et seq.

as such are prohibited in Sweden.[99] Still, in the following we discuss Case 3 as if the Swedish prohibition did not exist.

The rules protecting B from exploitation of his car is decided by the intellectual property rights and complemented by the rules in the MFL. In Sweden 'goodwill sponging' (*renommésnyltning*) is considered to be an established type of unfair marketing.[100] It covers marketing measures whereby an undertaking unjustly makes a connection to the activities, products or commercial symbols of other undertakings, without there being a risk of confusion between their respective activities etc.[101] Under the MFL such measures are caught by the general clause in sec. 4. However, as from 2000, due to the Swedish implementation of Directive 97/55/EC, there is a specific provision in the MFL, sec. 8a. 7. The provision prohibits comparative advertisement if it leads to unfair goodwill benefits from another undertaking's brand, other specific features or mark of origin. The prohibition covers direct or indirect 'pointing out' of, for example, another undertaking's products in advertisements.

Thus, it is generally considered that it is not in accordance with Swedish law to benefit from someone else's goodwill without permission.[102] Although it may be questioned whether or not A by the advertisement 'points out' B's car in a way that is required to qualify the advertisement as 'comparative advertisement' under sec. 8a, it seems like a clear case of 'goodwill sponging', prohibited under, at the very least, sec. 4 MFL.

(1) All parties, commercial undertakings as well as consumers, have standing to sue for damages before an ordinary court if they have suffered loss as a consequence of a violation of the MFL (sec. 29). Being an undertaking B could also decide to file his claim with the Stockholm District Court and would then in addition have the option of pursuing a claim for an injunction concurrently (sec. 38 and 41) with his claim for damages. Under sec. 29 MFL, a claim for damages for breach of the general clause in sec. 4 requires a breach of an injunction

[99] Act on alcohol 1994:1738. See above A. A.I.2.b).

[100] See e.g. MD 1996:3, MD 1993:9 and MD 1988:19.

[101] U. Bernitz, *Marknadsföringslagen* (1997), p. 71.

[102] See U. Bernitz, *Marknadsföringslagen* (1997); and governmental Bill 1999/2000:40, p. 29.

order issued by the Market Court.[103] Thus, from the strict wording of the act a claim for damages under sec. 4 would probably not be upheld, although B would have standing; no injunction order has been issued and consequently no such breach has occurred.[104] This is based on the assumption that the general clause in sec. 4 MFL is not concrete enough to justify a claim for damages.[105] However, under sec. 29 again, a claim for damages is granted if the infringer violates a prohibition of a special rule. Sec. 8a. 7 as a legal basis for infringement does not require that A has acted in breach of an injunction order. Therefore, it may be vital for the success of B's claim that the court classifies A's advertisement under the specific prohibition and not under the general clause. The importance of this is due to the fact that under Swedish tort law damages for pure economic loss in non-contractual relations generally requires harm to have been inflicted by a criminal act, for example in cases of deliberate deception of others (sec. 6 MFL).[106] Thus, B may raise a compensatory claim without using the MFL as a legal basis and have standing before the ordinary courts. Such a claim will, however, not be upheld under Swedish tort law. A compensatory claim for breach of sec. 4 would be admitted before the ordinary courts, but not upheld due to the lack of a breach of an injunction. The only realistic alternative for B would be to claim damages for breach of sec. 8a. 7.

The compensation awarded is usually lower than the real losses. This is because of the difficulty of proving losses, which must be shown to have risen as a direct consequence of the challenged conduct. When calculating the damages the court may consider factors besides the injury to the plaintiff, for example profits made by the defendant and the nature of the defendant's culpability.[107]

(2) As to the calculation of the amount of the compensation, first, it seems peculiar from the point of view of the MFL to raise a claim for a

[103] See also Case 1 (Risky bread).

[104] U. Bernitz, *Marknadsföringslagen* (1997), p. 111, holds that the requirement that an injunction must have been infringed may be set aside where damages are claimed for measures recognized by case law as clearly unfair. And he submits the example of 'goodwill sponging'. Still, there is no case law supporting his view on this, at least not yet.

[105] U. Bernitz, (1996) 44 GRUR Int. 434.

[106] A. Kur, *Schweden*, in G. Schricker, note 479.

[107] M. Plogell, *Sweden*, in J. Maxeiner and P. Schotthöfer, p. 425 (442).

licence fee retroactively and, concurrently, raise a claim for A's profit from the sales increase. Since B has not suffered any economic loss, B has nothing to gain from the possibility of having loss assessed at a 'reasonable amount'.[108] However, in the second paragraph of sec. 29 it is submitted that the calculation of compensation may also include 'factors of a non-economic nature'. In the preparatory works this is specified in the following way: under Swedish law, infringements of intellectual property rights are considered to create rights of compensation. Such compensation is motivated by reference to the interest of the holder of the right that no infringement should be made and, thus, not necessarily with reference to the actual loss caused by the infringement.

Accordingly, the second paragraph of sec. 29 has as its object to compensate undertakings for direct and undue exploitation of their position in the market, exploitation which notoriously jeopardizes their goodwill.[109] This is what is called 'general damages' in Sweden.[110] As we understand the law on this point, this provision would make it possible for B to make a successful claim for compensation in a situation such as the one at hand, without proving actual economic loss. And here chap. 35 sec. 5 of the Code of Civil and Criminal Procedure would come in handy to calculate a reasonable amount.[111] It is most doubtful whether a Swedish court would consider it 'reasonable' to allow B an amount corresponding to both a 'licence fee' and profits from A's sales increase. But an exact amount is of course impossible to assess.

In the absence of case law concerning this sort of situation, it must be said that the state of Swedish law is not clear. It is difficult to say, inter alia, whether or not B will be compensated in a situation where A establishes in court that B's goodwill has benefited from the advertisement. Thus, it is not perfectly clear whether the provision primarily fulfils the object of exempting B from proving a presumed loss or of simply remedying the damage to an intellectual property interest. But our conclusion is that B under Swedish law may well be able to bring a successful claim for compensation against A.

[108] See Code of Civil and Criminal Procedure Ch. 35 sec. 5.

[109] Bill 1994/95:123 at p. 112. [110] U. Bernitz, *Marknadsföringslagen* (1997), p. 71.

[111] Bill 1994/95:123 op. cit.

Summary (3)

6. *Compensation of harm or monetary fine*

a) Enforcing the claim for damages

The claim for damages is recognised in all states.[112] The compensation of harm is accorded under the general principles of the law of obligations so that there are no peculiarities. However, in Sweden and Finland civil law damages are hardly ever awarded in practice.

Evaluation

Damages claims constitute financial detriment to an enterprise. They limit the freedom of the advertiser in a markedly stronger way than injunctions or prohibitions. This may be the reason why up until now damages claims have not been regulated on the European level. European unfair competition law admittedly names in the Misleading and Comparative Advertising Directive 84/450/EEC various forms of prohibition or cessation but not the claim for damages. Similarly, damages claims are not mentioned in the current proposals for a directive regarding a new regulation.[113] However, the damages claim can certainly help to terminate legal infringements. Whereas cessation can only stop future violations, the damages claim is directed towards compensation and thereby penalizes the existing violation.

In most jurisdictions (Germany, Austria, Portugal and Italy), however, the claim for compensation of harm fails because the loss of profit is difficult to prove. This is appropriately discussed in terms of *probatio diabolica*.[114] Even in the USA, a country known for liability in all areas of life, damages claims are still unusual. Where the extent of past pecuniary injury can be established with sufficient certainty, compensatory damages may be recovered. Difficulties of proof constitute the biggest

[112] See Case 3 (Whisky). [113] See above A.III.3.

[114] In Denmark a company was convicted due to the fact that it had marketed bookcases, which by the court was considered to be an imitation of a bookcase marketed by a competitor. As to the question of compensation/ damages, the victim sued for DKK 10 million, the High Court awarded compensation amounting to DKK 6 million, but the Supreme Court reduced the compensation to DKK 3 million – without clarifying the basis for this reduction. The profits of the wrongdoer were assumed to be approximately 20 million DKK but the Supreme Court was apparently convinced that to some extent the companies were not targeting the same group of customers and therefore there was not any direct causation between the turnover of the wrongdoer and the loss of the victim, see Danish Weekly Court reports 2004, p. 1085.

hurdle to damages awards. Until recent years, damages were rarely awarded in private Lanham Act cases for false advertising. Therefore, there have been many attempts to ease the enforcement of damages claims through additional measures.

b) Surrender of profits

(1) The surrender of profits by the infringer is recognized as the object of claims in numerous states. In Austria, Poland, Hungary, England and Spain, for example, considerations of unjust enrichment are applied to justify the surrender of profits. This route is not possible under the German jurisdiction because only the infringement of a possibility of use should justify an intervention on enrichment grounds.[115] Therefore, under the German jurisdiction one uses general considerations of equity in order to justify the claim for surrender of profits.

(2) Under German law it must be proved that the infringing conduct has led to profits for the infringer and harm to the claimant. However, the harm may be inferred generally from the infringer's profits.[116] The dominant opinion in Poland on the other hand will only allow a claim by the claimant to be entitled to the infringer's profits to the claimant where a corresponding loss is proven. In addition in Germany, for example, it is recognised that in general not all the profits can be attributed to the infringement. Therefore, the claimant has only a partial claim to the profits.[117]

Evaluation

German scholarly literature calls for a harmonization at the European level of the claim for surrender of profits.[118] However, one should not be too hopeful in this respect. In practice such claims for the surrender of profits are of limited significance. This is first of all due to the fact that either the corresponding harm must be proved (Poland) or that the profit, similarly to the harm of the injured party, is often

[115] H. Köhler, in *2. Festschrift W. Lorenz* (2001), pp. 161 (174 et seq.); H. Köhler and H. Piper, *UWG* (3rd edn 2002), vor § 13 note 107.

[116] BGH (1993) 95 GRUR 55 (57) – 'Tchibo/Rolex II'; H. Köhler and H. Piper, *UWG, Kommentar* (3rd edn 2002), vor § 13 note 105; that does not apply if also the profits of the injured party increase, BGH (1995) 41 WRP 393 (397).

[117] BGH (1993) 95 GRUR 55 (59) – 'Tchibo/Rolex II'; O. Teplitzky, *Wettbewerbsrechtliche Ansprüche und Verfahren* (8th edn 2002), chap. 34 note 33; H. Köhler and H. Piper, *UWG* (3rd edn 2002), vor § 13 note 105.

[118] H. Köhler and T. Lettl (2002) 48 WRP 1019 (1047) and above A.III.3.

difficult to establish and accordingly to quantify. In Sweden the surrender of profits is also of a theoretical nature in that the profit of the defendant is very hard to prove. Therefore, the claim for surrender of profits must usually be joined with a discovery claim in order to be effective. However, the discovery claim is also of limited use. In Greece and France it has had only limited effect until now. Until now in Germany the cartel authority under § 34 and § 81 para. 2 GWB had the possibility to claim surplus profits. Although the cartel authorities can enforce discovery, seize business documents and carry out searches, the surplus profit claim in the past had only very limited practical significance.[119]

In addition, the difficulty is of course to be sure that the profit was made entirely through the infringement alone. The profit can only seldom be explained mono-causally in terms of an unfair conduct, so that problems of evidence will persist.[120] Therefore, the claimant in England or Germany has at best only a partial claim to profits. Ultimately, the actual profit is difficult to prove. It remains unclear which heads of damages can be deducted.[121] Also, a claim to surrender of profits by associations, as under § 10 UWG, does not seem to be the ultimate solution.[122] The time-consuming nature of the procedure is correctly pointed to because the defendant's profits must first be identified in the accounts.[123]

Thus, it must be realized that gaps in the law are likely to remain regarding surrender of profits claims even if harmonized on the European level.

c) Enforcement of a comparable licence fee

The licence fee is known in a number of states (Germany, Poland, Denmark, Italy, Spain, Portugal and the USA). Also, in jurisdictions which protect injured parties through trademark law, such as for example Austria or England, there is reliance on the licence fee. In terms of

[119] R. Sack (2003) 49 WRP 549 (551). [120] R. Sack (2003) 49 WRP 549 (554).

[121] According to § 10 para. 2 UWG the claim of disgorgement of profits is reduced by the benefits that the injuring party produces to third parties. This may lead to the awkward result that a claim fails at trial, as the injuring party benefits a third party. See R. Sack, (2003) 49 WRP 549 (553 et seq.); A. Stadler and H.-W. Micklitz, *Der Reformvorschlag der UWG-Novelle für eine Verbandsklage auf Gewinnabschöpfung* (2003) 49 WRP 559 (561 et seq.)

[122] See B.II.2.c).

[123] A. Ohly, *Vereinigtes Königreich von Großbritannien und Nordirland*, in G. Schricker, *Recht der Werbung in Europa* (Supp. 1995), note 172.

the amount, under German law the court determines what the parties would have agreed in a fictitious licence agreement.[124] In the majority of cases a one-off licence is assumed. In practice the licence fee amounts to between 1 and 5 per cent, or more in individual cases.[125]

Evaluation

Calculating damages on the principle of the licence analogy is most widespread in Germany and provides the easiest means of calculation.[126] As with the surrender of profits the licence analogy is compared with the compensation for unjustified enrichment (restitution).[127] Compared with the surrender of profits the licence fee has the advantage that it is not based on concrete profits but is rather an abstract calculation for enforcing a customary licence fee.

However, jurisdictions which normally penalize infringements of unfair competition law by public law means (Sweden, Finland), have little or no legal practice based on compensatory claims. In these states the consumer ombudsman normally adopts the active role in pursuing legal claims and punishes unfair conduct through monetary fines. Ultimately, the licence fee fails if there is no customary market due to the lack of infringed trademarks. If by means of a loss-leader offer, as in Case 4, customers are lost to the competitor, it will be difficult to compensate an alleged loss through the licence fee principle.

d) Civil law fines - punitive damages

In the USA the concept of damages is markedly more flexible than under European law. It is possible not only to compensate concrete harm but to award punitive damages in cases of a particularly objectionable conduct. In addition the state attorney general may enforce civil law damages. Punitive damages are also possible in England.

Evaluation

In Germany it is an alien idea that particularly objectionable tortious conduct allows for increased damages. In Germany constitutional law objections are raised against punitive damages as known in the USA and in England. In the leading judgment the highest Federal Court has

[124] H. Köhler and H. Piper, *UWG* (3rd edn 2002), vor § 13 note 103.

[125] BGH (1991) 93 GRUR 914 (917) – 'Kastanienmuster'.

[126] H. Köhler and H. Piper, *UWG* (3rd edn 2002), vor § 13 note 102.

[127] Regarding German law see H. Köhler and H. Piper, *UWG* (3rd edn 2002), vor § 13 note 102.

emphasized that the recognition of foreign judgments based on punitive damages contradicts a number of legal principles and is therefore contrary to public order, § 328 para. 1 no. 4 ZPO. Thus, sanctions which are intended to punish and deter remain the exclusive competence of the state. This does not apply, however, to the surrender of profits.[128] Nevertheless, to the extent that the surrender of profits is exceeded in terms of punitive damages (England, USA and Denmark), the reservations of the BGH continue to apply.

e) Assessment of damages

Where civil law or criminal law fines are rejected due to their punitive nature, composite calculation of damages may instead be considered. In Poland according to art. 322 k.p.c., the court shall assess damages in accordance with its own views, based on careful consideration of the circumstances of the case, if in cases for compensatory damages, unjust enrichment etc., the precise calculation of the damages is not possible or very difficult. In France damages can be claimed at civil law under art. 1382 cc (*action en responsabilité civile*). If the infringement is also sanctioned criminally, the harm may additionally be pursued under the *action civile*. This claim may be pursued in the civil courts but also by way of a consolidated procedure in the criminal courts (*constitution de partie civile*).[129] The amount of compensation (*dommages-intérêts*) is assessed at the discretion of the judge. Analysis of some 200 decisions in unfair competition matters by the business law research Centre of the Paris Chamber of Commerce and Industry published in 2000 has shown that in most cases how the judge determined a specific amount could not be established from the judgment. There was no allusion to the method of calculation used or even the facts to which consideration had been given. In fact the assessment of a specific amount is more due to a tariff based on past awards.[130] In Italy the claimant is assisted as well. The determination of the level of damages can be done according to equity if it is established that harm has occurred, art. 2056, 1226 cc.

[128] BGHZ 118, 312 (331), (1992) 45 NJW 3096 with comment H. Koch 3073, (1993) 48 JZ 261 with comment E. Deutsch – 'punitive damages'; BVerfG (1995) 48 NJW 649, (1995) 50 JZ 716 with comment A. Stadler – 'Zustellung von Klagen auf punitive damages'. The constitutional doubts of R. Sack (2003) 49 WRP 549 (552 et seq.) thus do not hold true.

[129] T. Dreier and S. von Lewinsky, *Frankreich*, in G. Schricker, note 363.

[130] www.ccip.fr/creda, colloque organisé le 6 décembre 2000, Table ronde, *Concurrence déloyale: ammendes civiles ou 'punitive damages'*, p. 10.

Assessment of damages is also possible in Portugal, and is also known in Switzerland.[131]

Evaluation
Similarly to punitive damages, with the calculation of damages the intended preventive effect arises. In addition, calculation of damages has the advantage that it need not be linked to actual profits or actual harm, but similarly to the licence fee may be determined in terms of abstract harm. It is therefore understandable that a number of member states permit this form of calculation of damages.

Under German[132] and US-American law[133] damages calculation is normally possible only regarding the amount. It requires, however, that the harm already exists. In contrast the calculation of damages contains an arbitrary element in terms of the question of whether harm has actually occurred at all, in the same way as with punitive damages. This is shown by the statistics in France where amounts of between one to a couple of thousand francs have been awarded in damages.[134] The experience of France and Greece shows that the courts generally either dismissed[135] the claims for lack of certainty of damages or awarded the notorious token franc. Here the suspicion again arises that the infringer has to be punished.[136]

f) Public law monetary fines – the market disruption factor

In some Member States there is in addition the possibility that even the first legal infringement can incur a fine or punishment.

(1) In Sweden there is a principle that a fine is first incurred when an infringement occurs against a cessation order.[137] The background is the principle *nulla poena sine lege* (no punishment without law). The infringer should be able to foresee that his action will be illegal and subject to a penalty. The general Swedish law provision is too uncertain to allow this. However, an exception is made in two cases. First the consumer

[131] Regarding Art. 9 para. 3 UWG see R. Knaak and M. Ritscher, *Schweiz*, in G. Schricker, note 340.
[132] See §§ 286, 287 ZPO. [133] See above A.IV.2.e)cc).
[134] H. Puttfarken and N. Franke, *Die action civile der Verbände in Frankreich*, in J. Basedow, K. Hopt, H. Kötz, and D. Baetge, *Die Bündelung gleichgerichteter Interessen im Prozeß* (1999), 149 (175 et seq.).
[135] LG Athen 2960/1996, DEE 1997, 71 (73); LG Athen 3229/1996, DEE 1997, 75 (81); see A. Papathoma-Baetge, *Die Verbandsklage im griechischen Recht*, in J. Basedow, K. Hopt, H. Kötz, and D. Baetge, *Die Bündelung gleichgerichteter Interessen im Prozeß* (1999) 187 (204).
[136] Calais-Auloy, D. 1988, chron. 195. [137] Sec. 29 MFL.

ombudsman alone has standing to apply for a market distortion fine (administrative fine) to be imposed when an undertaking, with intent or negligence, has acted in breach of sec. 6 or sec. 22 MFL.[138] In these cases the infringer is aware of his legal duty. The fine may be set somewhere in the range between €500 and €500,000, but may not exceed 10 per cent of A's revenues (sec. 22 – 25 MFL). The fee paid belongs to the state.[139] Secondly, a fine is possible if the legal obligation, as with the comparative advertising, is sufficiently concrete.

(2) Member States apply monetary fines more severely where an infringement against unfair competition law is in principle seen as a penal offence. In France, otherwise prohibited comparative advertising is punishable by the penalties provided for, on the one hand, in articles L 121-1 to L 121-7 CCons and, on the other hand, in arts. 422 and 423 of the Penal Code according to art. 121-14 CCons. On the basis of these provisions agents from the DGCCRF and those from the food directorate general of the Ministry of Agriculture and those from the metrology department of the Ministry of Industry are authorised to establish breaches of arts. L 121-8 and L 121-9 CCons. (art. L 121-2 CCons.). In Portugal, too, misleading advertising, under art. 11 CPub, and comparative advertising regulated in art. 16 CPub constitute both illegal advertising forms and incur administrative fines. The making of false statements in commerce with the intention of discrediting the competitor is a crime under art. 260 CPI. Exceptionally, in Finland the violator can be fined, if the untruthful or misleading expressions have been used wilfully, § 8 SopMenL. This is a criminal law sanction, which will be decided in the ordinary lower courts. In Germany until 1974 there was even the possibility to award fines in favour of the injured party.[140] Now § 16 UWG (ex-§ 4 UWG) provides for criminal prosecution with a fine up to €1,800,000. However, the field of application is narrow insofar as it is limited due to the analogy prohibition. Only the dissemination of incorrect facts by public announcement or communication is prohibited.[141] Thus true but unfair facts are not caught by the factual requirements[142] – equally, negotiations with customers are not caught by § 16 UWG (ex-§ 4 UWG). In addition, the untrue representations must be made knowingly.

[138] See sec. 22 and 39 MFL.
[139] U. Bernitz, *Schweden*, in R. Schulze and H. Schulte-Nölke, 6.
[140] H. Köhler and H. Piper, *UWG* (3rd edn 2002), § 4 note 15.
[141] E.g. tours involving sales promotion for about €10, BGH (2002) 55 NJW 3415.
[142] See R. Sack, (1996) 98 GRUR 461.

Evaluation

(1) Public law fines are especially useful where anti-competitive conduct is sanctioned under public law (Sweden) or penal law (France and Portugal). The introduction of the administrative fine in Sweden was an orientation towards European antitrust law. In this respect one could also consider harmonization on the European level. Monetary fines have the additional advantage of allowing sanctioning of the subjective element of an unlawful act such as intention or maliciousness. Finally, monetary fines imposed by the administration or criminal courts are effective if in practice no damages may be obtained under civil law, as for example in the Nordic states.

(2) However, in many states sanction through public law or criminal law mechanisms is still the exception (Germany, Austria, England and the USA). This is for a number of reasons. The well-known principle in all member states of *nulla poena sine lege* speaks against penal sanctions. It is found not only in § 1 StGB and art. 103 para. 2 Basic Law, but in the American Federal Constitution of 1776, the French Declaration of Human Rights of 1789 and above all today in the European Human Rights Convention.[143]

The evidentiary problems in the calculation of damages are not automatically solved through the monetary fine. Rather one is compelled to consider criteria other than the loss suffered by the injured party. This renders every penal law procedure complicated and also – as with most infringements of competition law – disproportionate. If the Swedish administration fine has its origins in European antitrust law, this is not a compelling argument for the harmonization of public law monetary fines. Thus, antitrust procedures require higher degrees of unlawfulness and distortion of the market than under unfair competition. It is no accident that fines of millions of euros are awarded by the European Commission general competition directorship. Factual situations such as concerted cartels which have distorted competition over a number of decades are, however, hardly ever found in unfair competition cases. As a result unfair competition law is generally not classified as penal law.

In consequence, public law sanctions are hardly suitable for the classic violation of unfair competition law. Penalties for a first-time violation of unfair competition law would not seem therefore to be capable of finding a consensus to support them as only few states have

143 Art. 7 ECHR. See V. Krey, *Keine Strafe ohne Gesetz* (1983); C. Roxin, *Strafrecht, Allgemeiner Teil*, vol. 1 (2nd edn 1994), § 5.III, notes 13, 19.

criminalized unfair competition law.[144] The contrary only applies where hard-core unfair competition law is concerned, as for example in cases of denigration as regulated in art. 10bis Paris Convention[145] or § 16 UWG (ex-§ 4 UWG). As all member states recognise such a factual requirement, a corresponding public law or penal law fine would also be worth considering.

g) *Extension of the concept of damage*

In England with the passing-off claim, in contrast to Germany, the proof of actual property damage is not necessary. The concept of preventing harm is primary. It is assumed that harm will have occurred in that the claimant would have sold more without the misleading advertising. The general harm to the reputation of a business or a possible risk of litigation would also be recognized as justifying a claim.[146] In France in addition it is assumed that the association which pursues the claim has suffered immaterial loss in its own right.

In Italy the consumer may have a cause of action under the general discipline of consumers rights (l. 281/98), which states that consumers have, inter alia, the fundamental right to 'adequate information and fair advertising' (art. 1, par. 2, lit. (c)), as well as the right to 'fairness, transparency and equity in contractual relationships with reference to goods and services'. From such a provision it may be argued that consumers have a legal right not to be misled by advertising.[147] Both consumer associations and each single consumer may take action against infringement of such a right. The single consumer whose right not to be misled has been infringed may claim damages, according to l. 281/98 and the general discipline of torts (arts. 2043 et seq. cc).

In Portugal, consumer agencies claim compensation even if they are not directly injured (arts. 12 and 13 (b) LDCons). In Greece it is assumed that collective consumer interests are affected which gives entitlement to compensation for immaterial loss. The factors to be considered here are the gravity of the infringing conduct, the profit gained by the infringer through the infringement, the size and turnover of the defendant enterprise as well as the requirement of general and particular care. In Switzerland damages amounting to 10,000 francs have been

[144] See below B.II.8. [145] See above A.II.1.a).

[146] See A. Ohly, *Vereinigtes Königreich von Großbritannien und Nordirland*, in G. Schricker, note 113.

[147] See G. Rossi, *La pubblicità dannosa* (2000), p. 156.

awarded.[148] In some states in the USA there is a legally fixed minimum damage. With the infringement of the TCPA consumers do not have to prove any monetary loss or actual damage in order to recover the statutory penalty of $500 per violation ('minimum damage').[149] About half the states authorize private litigants who have proven a UDAP violation to obtain minimum damages awards ranging from $25 to $5,000, even if actual damages have not been proven. Thus, $3,000 minimum damage provisions have been awarded where the actual damages were only $200.[150] The Lanham Act expressly provides for treble damages,[151] and these are awarded by the courts.[152] In cases of TCPA violation, the federal court may treble the damages if it finds that the defendant wilfully or knowingly violated this section. In addition certain states allow treble damages. Where an individual consumer's actual damages are nominal, three times this amount will still be nominal. A number of UDAP statutes limit multiple damage awards to situations where intent, wilfulness or bad faith is shown.[153] Finally, in Germany one finds at the forefront of a claim a further damage concept in that the injured party may recover the costs of the proceedings.[154]

Evaluation

In Greece a damages claim aims at compensation and not sanctioning.[155] In the USA minimum damages and treble damages are also clearly distinguished from punitive damages. A statutory penalty is necessary to motivate customers to enforce the statute.[156] Statutory minimum damages are intended to encourage private litigation, and courts should award such damages whenever authorized to do so. The underlying idea is to award damages to the claimant, to deter violations and to encourage an out-of-court settlement.[157]

148 R. Knaak and M. Ritscher, *Schweiz*, in G. Schricker, note 342.
149 47 U.S.C. § 227 (b) (3), (c) (5). See Part I.IV.C.2(e).
150 J. Sheldon and C. Carter, *Unfair and Deceptive Acts and Practices* (5th edn 2001), p. 621.
151 Lanham Act § 35(a), 15 U.S.C.A. § 1117 (a).
152 *Stuart v. Collins*, 489 F. Supp. 827, 208 U.S.P.Q. 657 (S.D.N.Y. 1980).
153 J. Sheldon and C. Carter, *Unfair and Deceptive Acts and Practices* (5th edn 2001), p. 624.
154 See below B.III.2.a).
155 G. Karakostas, *Prostasia tu katanalote – N. 2251/1994* (1997) pp. 208 et seq.; A. Papathoma-Baetge, *Die Verbandsklage im griechischen Recht*, in J. Basedow, K. Hopt, H. Kötz, and D. Baetge, *Die Bündelung gleichgerichteter Interessen im Prozeß* (1999), p. 187 (202).
156 *Kaplan v. Democrat & Chronicle*, 698 N.Y.S.2d (App. Div. 1999).
157 *Refuse & Environmental Sys., Inc. v. Industrial Services*, 932 F.2d 37 (1st Cir. 1991).

On the other hand, the loss suffered by the collective consumer interest is diffuse because the construction of a collective interest liberated from individual interests can be quickly overloaded with social objectives. Also the assertion that a consumer association can suffer damage is objected to by some.[158] However, this objection cannot be upheld. It is beyond doubt that such groups are worthy of protecting. An extension of the concept of damage would have the advantage over the assessment of damages of being founded on more precise legal principles. One would not leave to the judge the rather intangible assessment of damage but link it to concrete criteria.

This would mean providing further individual criteria to justify the award of damages. Three approaches are given here.

Extension of the protection of the person

On the one hand the individualistic character of civil law could be further developed. If the loss of the claimant and the profit or gain of the infringer cannot be proven, one should check who additionally falls within the protective scope of unfair competition law. This is usually the competitor, the consumer, and competition itself.[159] Normally, it can also be determined who the intervention was against. Therefore it would be conceivable to extend the actual concept of harm and, for example, to award damages in respect of personal rights of the consumer. This would correspond to the legal position in Switzerland, where damages for immaterial loss can be awarded under art. 49 OR, for example for trade libels or imitation.[160] The German jurisdiction recognizes a violation of personal rights, for example with unsolicited telephone calls.[161] Thus would result in the circle of those entitled to protection being drawn more abstractly.

A similar approach is chosen by member states which emphasize that the consumer has a right to 'adequate information and fair advertising'

[158] K. Hopt and D. Baetge, in J. Basedow, K. Hopt, H. Kötz and D. Baetge, *Die Bündelung gleichgerichteter Interessen im Prozeß* (1999), p. 11 (45).

[159] See e.g. § 1 UWG: This law serves the protection of competitors, consumers and other participants of the market from unfair competition. It protects the interest of the public and fair competition.

[160] R. Knaak and M. Ritscher, *Schweiz*, in G. Schricker, note 341.

[161] BGH (1999) 54 JZ 1122 with comments by T. Möllers (1124); BGH (2001) 56, JZ 102 – 'Telefonwerbung VI' with comments by T. Möllers (104); W. Fikentscher and T. Möllers, *Die (negative) Informationsfreiheit als Grenze von Werbung und Kunstdarbietung*, (1998) 51 NJW 1337 (1338 et seq.).

This formulation is found in Italian law. A tort claim is considered possible for a legal infringement.[162]

Further elements in the calculation of levels of damages
Numerous authors raise the problem of how the actual level of damage is to be measured. This requires making the loss concrete. Greek courts take into account the severity of the harm to the legal order in the unlawful conduct, the size of the defendant enterprise and above all the annual turnover as well as the requirement of general and particular care.[163] In addition regard may be had to the profits gained as a result of the legal infringement. In the meantime the Greek jurisdiction has also begun to make this claim concrete.[164]

Determination of minimum damages
Finally, the US approach of minimum damages should be considered. The above-mentioned jurisdiction of the German Federal Constitutional Court would not apply in this case because the amount of damages would be noticeably less than punitive damages. If minimum damages were laid down by the legislature, as in the USA, they would be foreseeable and would act as a deterrent.

In effect the extension of the concept of damages, as with the monetary fine, offers the possibility to recognize anti-competitive conduct more clearly than is the case with a prohibition or the establishment of actual harm. In this way the criticism that anti-competitive conduct is always worth it for the infringing party could be countered. It is therefore conceivable as an additional remedy.

7. *The information order*

(1) The additional information claim is only expressly provided for in the Nordic states, through special laws in Sweden, Finland and Norway. Under Swedish law a business party can be ordered to provide such information as is of particular importance for the consumer (sec. 4 para. 2 MFL).[165] Under chap. 2 para. 2 § KSL of the Finnish law the Consumer

[162] See Case 4 (Children's swing).
[163] Art. 10 para. 9 lit. (b) Consumer protection law 2251/1994. A translation may be found in (1996) 44 GRUR Int. 897.
[164] See the pointers by A. Papathoma-Baetge, *Die Verbandsklage im griechischen Recht*, in J. Basedow, K. Hopt, H. Kötz, and D. Baetge, *Die Bündelung gleichgerichteter Interessen im Prozeß* (1999), pp. 187 (205 et seq.).
[165] U. Bernitz, *Sweden*, in R. Schulze and H. Schulte-Nölke, 2.

Ombudsman can obtain additional information on the advertisement. In Finland, on the other hand, obligations are imposed which aim at the protection of the health of the consumer, such as the notification that steel splinters may come from a drill or that a fire extinguisher is not suitable for all situations because of its limited effectiveness.[166] In the USA advertising bans have also been imposed by the FTC and not the Consumer Product Safety Commission for 'dangerous' products such as cigarettes and alcohol.[167]

(2) Most other member states do not provide for such an information claim. In Germany it is presumed only in exceptional cases that confusion may be caused by forbearance. Cases are concerned with advertising in the environmental and health fields[168] but also, for example, advertising with test results.[169] These clarification obligations only affect the economic security of the consumer. Now § 5 para. 2 s. 2 UWG prohibits the concealing of essential information.

Evaluation

(1) Some legal scholars call for the introduction of a legally prescribed information duty.[170] In fact there has been a gap in German law until now between the duty to warn under product liability law and the still rudimentary duty under unfair competition law. This applies for example to the health risks such as the electromagnetic radiation from cellular telephones.[171] Special law duties of information only existed so far in few specialized areas.[172]

(2) However, two objections must be raised to the proposal by J. Keβler and H.-W. Micklitz. From the perspective of the European law duties of product safety are methodologically above product safety law, as is made clear by the numerous directives on product safety.[173] The gap

[166] MT 1982 : 22 – 'Bohrmaschine'; MT 1985 : 11 – 'Feuerlöscher', proof at K. Kaulamo, *Finland*, in: G. Schricker, note 117.

[167] See above A.IV.1.b)dd).

[168] See the proof in K.N. Peifer, in K.H. Fezer, *Lauterkeitsrecht* (2005), § 5 notes 395 et seq.

[169] BGH (1982) 84 GRUR 437, (1982) 28 WRP 413 – 'Test gut'.

[170] J. Keßler and H.-W. Micklitz, *Die Harmonisierung des Lauterkeitsrechts in den Mitgliedstaaten der Europäischen Gemeinschaft und die Reform des UWG* (2003), p. 69 with a suggestion for wording on p. 155.

[171] T. Möllers, *Rechtsgüterschutz im Umwelt- und Haftungsrecht* (1996), p. 293 et seq.; T. Möllers and H. Schmid, 8 (1997) EWS 150 (154).

[172] E.g. in pharmaceutical law and media law including the duty to strictly identify advertisement as such.

[173] T. Möllers, *Rechtsgüterschutz im Umwelt- und Haftungsrecht* (1996), § 6.

in product safety law was also closed by the Directive on General Product Safety 92/59/EEC. A product can, for example, be seen as safe within art. 3 para. 1 Directive on General Product Safety 92/59/EEC, if it does not contain the necessary information. Art. 3 para. 2 indent 1 Directive on General Product Safety 92/59/EEC (now replaced by Directive 2001/95/EC) requires information so that the consumer may assess the danger and protect himself against it.[174] The Sale of Consumer Goods Directive is comparable under which consumer expectations and advertising terms determine the quality of goods.[175]

If supervision is left to private parties (as the competitors are), this can soon become incomplete. The public law supervision would seem to be the more secure approach. In the USA since 1972 there is the Consumer Product Safety Act (CPSA).[176] It created an independent authority,[177] which monitors the safety of consumer products. In addition motor vehicles, boats and medications are regulated by separate authorities.[178] The CPSA permits product standards to be enforced, prohibitions to be imposed and products to be recalled.[179] In France there is also the central regulation of products, unlike in Germany.[180] The security authorities would seem to be the most objectively appropriate supervisory bodies for corresponding duties of information. In this way no information duty should be imposed under competition law which affects the risks to the safety of consumers.[181]

[174] It was expressed more clearly in the Proposal for a Directive on General Product Safety: 'pointers to dangers have to occur in a manner that every potential or future consumer may examine the rest of the danger before purchasing the product or using it, if the pointers play an essential role in this decision', see art. 4 para. 2 of the Proposal for a Directive on General Product Safety, COM (1989) 162 final, OJ C 193, 1 (3). However, Council Directive 92/59/EEC was replaced by Council Directive 2001/95/EC. The new Directive on General Product Safety does not include this formulation anymore.

[175] Art. 2 lit. (d) Sale of Consumers Goods Directive 99/44/EC and Case 5 (Discontinued models).

[176] Public Law 92-573, Stat. 1207, October 27, 1972; 15 U.S.C., §§ 2051–2083, 1976.

[177] Regarding the Consumer Product Safety Commission, see www.cpsc.gov.

[178] National Traffic & Motor Vehicle Safety Act von 1966, 15 U.S.C., §§ 1411–1420, 1976; Federal Boat Safety Act von 1971, 46 U.S.C., §§ 1464, 1976; Food and Drug Administration, 42 U.S.C. § 263 (b)–263 (n), bes. § 263 (g).

[179] For an overview of the CPSA see W. Löwe, *Rückrufpflicht des Warenherstellers*, (1972) 20 DAR, p. 288; C. Joerges, *Nachmarktkontrollen im amerikanischen Recht*, in H.-W. Micklitz (ed.), *Post Market Control of Consumer Goods* (1990) p. 155 (173).

[180] C. Joerges, J. Falke, H.-W. Micklitz and G. Brüggemeier, *Die Sicherheit von Konsumgütern und die Entwicklung der Europäischen Gemeinschaft* (1988), pp. 72.

[181] See also W. Schünemann, in H. Harte-Bavendamm and F. Henning-Bodewig, *UWG* (2004), § 1 notes 46 et seq.

8. *Discovery claims*

Although under German law the principle of adducing evidence prevails and speculative investigation is inadmissible, under the principle of good faith the claimant will exceptionally be granted a right of discovery so that he can substantiate the profit of the infringer. Something similar is seen in Spain. The right to discovery in the context of pre-trial discovery is also known in England and the USA.

Evaluation

However, such right of discovery conflicts with the principle that the claimant has to establish the requirements of his claim and to prove them (so-called principle of adducing evidence). In public law the theoretical problem by contrast would not arise as the public authority is under a duty to itself establish the material facts (investigation principle).

II. Plaintiffs and defendants

Case 4 Children's swing: attracting customers – the different plaintiffs

Consumer C reads in a newspaper advertisement about the supermarket chain owned by A that A is going to sell a children's swing in his shops priced at €400, instead of the usual €500. So as to make sure he can avail himself of this attractive offer, C goes to the nearest shop next morning immediately after opening. To his disappointment he sees that all swings available have already been sold to another customer. All A's other supermarkets had only five swings each, and it was impossible to order further swings. C is angry as this is not the first time that A has had not enough of the advertised articles in his shop following an advertisement, which C has tried to purchase. To prevent this conduct, C informs a consumer association. This association requires A to desist from such advertising in the future. Because of these unfair measures the profits of A increase by €10,000.

1. Can C as a consumer take legal proceedings to force A to desist from such advertising in the future? Can he sue for damages?
2. Are consumer associations or business associations entitled or under a duty to represent the interests of consumers as a whole?
3. Can such associations sue for an injunction or the disgorgement of the extra profits?
4. Does this constitute an infringement of competition law against which B as a competitor can take action?
5. What claims can public authorities or institutions pursue against it?

Austria (4)

This is a case of deception about the availability of goods that is given as an example in art. 3 Misleading and Comparative Advertising Directive 84/450/EEC: the main feature of this illegal advertisement is that the product advertised as especially cheap is either unavailable or not available in sufficient quantities. The advertising party wants to lure customers to his premises and to induce them into buying other products.[1] This is deceptive since the customer can reasonably expect that goods advertised as especially cheap are actually available for a certain time in sufficient quantities to meet the normal demand one must

[1] (1992) 41 ÖBl 39 – 'Blaupunkt Bremen'.

expect – at least at the time the advertisement is published. There is no deception if the offered quantity met the expected demand[2] or if unexpected problems of delivery occurred, since then the original advertisement was true and the public must allow for such exceptional cases. Such mitigating circumstances have to be proven by the advertiser. In the above-mentioned case the supermarket chain obviously did not purchase a large enough quantity of the advertised product. This is at least true for those supermarkets that only offered five swings.

(1) Standing for consumers in Austria to prevent A from such advertisement in the future is restricted: a consumer claim for an injunction to prevent A's supermarket chain from such advertisement in the future is unknown to Austrian law. The OGH has already granted a consumer compensation for the loss incurred by relying on the profits guaranteed by an enterprise based on § 874, 1311 ABGB and § 2 UWG. The consumer was allowed to be compensated for the costs he incurred for legal counsel assessing his claims against the company. The court reasoned that § 2 UWG since the amendment of the UWG in 1971 also aims at the protection of consumers and that therefore the individual as victim of unfair competition must be able to bring a claim.[3]

(2) In cases of misleading advertisement regulated under § 1 UWG[4] and § 2 para. 1 UWG the *Verein für Konsumenteninformation* (§ 14 para. 1 UWG) (Association for Consumer Information) is entitled to sue. Implementing the Injunction Directive 98/27/EC standing is also granted to consumer associations located in other Member States of the EU if the origin of the infringement is in Austria in cases of misleading advertising under § 1 or § 2 para. 1 UWG, the protected interests of these associations are infringed in those Member States and their purpose justifies legal proceedings (§ 14 para. 2 UWG). Surrender of profits cannot be claimed by consumer associations in Austria.

[2] (1992) 41 ÖBl, 192 – 'Satellitenempfangsanlagen'; (2000) 49 ÖBl 259 with comment by S. Langer, ÖBl-LS 00/106, ÖBl 2000, 259 (261).

[3] OGH (1998) 47 ÖBl 193, (1999) 48 GRUR Int. 181 (182) – 'Erster Hauptpreis' with reference to R. Sack, *Schadenersatzansprüche wettbewerbsgeschützter Verbraucher nach deutschem und österreichischem Wettbewerbs- und Deliktsrecht*, in M. Kramer and H. Mayrhofer, *Konsumentenschutz im Privat- und Wirtschaftsrecht* (1997), pp. 99 et seq. and H. Koppensteiner, *Österreichisches und europäisches Wettbewerbsrecht* (3rd edn 1997), § 34 note 66.

[4] As § 2 UWG, which prohibits misleading advertisement, is very broad (a so-called 'kleine Generalklausel' of the UWG), there are only few cases left, which have to be handled according to § 1 UWG (e.g. foisting unsolicited or defective goods).

Private associations for the protection of competition concerned by the infringement in question can bring an action for an injunction according to § 2 UWG in connection with § 14 para. 1 UWG. A claim for an injunction can also be brought by the *Bundesarbeitskammer* (Federal Chamber of Labour), *the Bundeskammer der Gewerblichen Wirtschaft* (Federal Chamber of Commercial Economy), the *Präsidentenkonferenz der Landwirtschaftskammern* Österreichs (Austrian President's Conference of the Chambers for Agriculture) and the *Österreichischen Gewerkschaftsbund* (Austrian Association of Unions) according to § 14 para. 1 UWG. Of these institutions only the *Bundesarbeitskammer* has from time to time brought claims on the behalf of consumers. Under the legislation the *Österreichische Gewerkschaftsbund* ought to protect consumer's interests but has not done so yet. At least there are no published decisions showing this.

(3) Competitors are granted standing by § 2 UWG in connection with § 14 para. 1 UWG to bring an action for an injunction. This includes all procedural means and measures of enforcement.[5] Competitors have standing independently of their being affected economically by the misleading advertisement.

(4) Other agencies and public authorities have no standing.

Denmark (4)

Advertising without explicitly stating that there are limitations on quantity is contrary to § 2a sec. 3 MFL, introduced into the act by law no. 164 of March 15, 2000 with a view to implementing EU Comparative Advertising Directive 97/55/EC in Danish law.[6]

(1) According to § 19 para. 1 MFL a consumer can bring action before the courts claiming that an injunction must be issued towards A's advertising. According to § 14 MFL proceedings are instituted in the Maritime and Commercial Court in Copenhagen. The consumer will have to demonstrate that he is directly and individually affected.

(2) Based on § 19 MFL consumer associations may bring action before the courts. It follows from the drafts for the MFL that consumer associations are meant to play an important role in the enforcement of the

[5] See Case 1 (Risky Bread).

[6] P.B. Madsen, *Markedsret*, vol. 2 (4th edn 2002), p. 336; M. Koktvedgaard, *Lærebog i Konkurrenceret* (4th edn 2000), p. 52 (58); E. Borcher and F. Bøggild, *Markedsføringsloven* (2001), pp. 224 et seq.

MFL.[7] Since according to § 19 para. 1 MFL only a legal interest has to be shown, business associations are also entitled to sue in Denmark.

(3) Competitors may also bring action before the courts, as they will be directly affected by the advertising and on this basis must be supposed to have a sufficient legal interest to be able to institute proceedings at the courts.

(4) According to § 19 MFL the Consumer Ombudsman will be able to institute proceedings with the aim of having an injunction issued. Violation of § 2a sec. 3 MFL might, according to § 22 MFL, be the basis for a penalty and the Consumer Ombudsman will be able to request the public prosecutor to bring a criminal action before the courts on the matter.

England (4)

Statements about the availability of advertised products come under reg. 4A(2) of the CMAR 1988, as amended. Thus, a comparative advertisement referring to a special offer is not permitted unless it indicates in a clear and unequivocal way the date on which the offer ends or, where appropriate, that the offer is subject to the availability of the goods and services. The latter requirement appears to have been breached in A's advertisement.

In contrast, it would seem highly unlikely that a statement which induces customers to come to a shop would be actionable under the Trade Descriptions Act 1968. The only case which comes anywhere near the present case is *Westminster County Council v. Ray Alan (Manshops) Ltd.* where the Divisional Court held that an alleged 'closing down sale' where the trader in fact continued to trade did not constitute an infringement of the TDA 1968.

Under no. 16(1) of the British Code of Advertising, Sales Promotion and Directing Marketing (Code) advertisers must make it clear if stocks are limited. Products must not be advertised unless advertisers can demonstrate that they have reasonable grounds for believing that they can satisfy demand.

(1) Some regulations have been violated. However, the rights of the consumer C are very limited. The only remedy available under the CMAR 1988 is a complaint to the OFT.[8] A's repeated advertising of

[7] M. Koktvedgaard, *Lærebog i Konkurrenceret* (4th edn 2000), p. 52; B. von Eyben et al., *Karnovs lovssamling* (2001), p. 5718.

[8] See the solution to Case 1 (Risky bread).

products which are obviously merely available for a tiny number of customers may give rise to a complaint to and action by the Advertising Standards Authority – ASA.[9]

(2) In the case at stake, consumer associations would not be able to represent the collective interests of consumers. In 1999, when the Unfair Terms in Consumer Contract Regulations 1999 were adopted,[10] consumer associations obtained for the first time the opportunity of legal standing in English courts, limited to the field of unfair contract terms in consumer contracts. Only the Consumers' Association (CA) was granted legal standing. In 2001, the Stop Now Order (EC Directives) Regulations 2001[11] were adopted, implementing Directive 98/27/EC on injunctions. However, their scope was restricted to the EC Directives listed in the annex to Injunctive Directive 98/27/EC.[12] Attracting customers is not covered by any of these directives, whereas the situation of comparative advertisement is somewhat unclear.[13] On November 7, 2002, the Enterprise Act received Royal Assent. Its chap. 8, which deals with injunctions came into effect on June 20, 2003.[14] The Stop Now Order (EC Directives) Regulations 2001 were repealed.[15] According to sec. 213 (4), the Secretary of State may designate a person or body which is not a private body only if this person or body satisfies such criteria as the Secretary of State specifies by order.[16] This list of criteria has been specified by the Enterprise Act 2002 (Part 8 Designated Enforcers: Criteria for Designation, Designation of Public Bodies as Designated

[9] For details, see the solution to Cases 1 (Risky bread).

[10] The UTCCR 1999 replaced the UTCCR 1994. They have implemented Directive 93/13/EC on unfair contract terms.

[11] S.I. 1422 of 2001. [12] For details, see P. Rott, (2001) 24 JCP 401 (420 et seq.).

[13] The annex to Directive 98/27/EC merely lists Directive 84/450/EEC concerning misleading advertising but not 'as amended'. In contrast, it mentions Directive 87/102/ EEC 'as last amended by (. . .)'. In its recent proposal on codified version of the Injunction Directive, COM (2003) 241 final of 12/5/2003, Directive 97/55/EC appears in the annex.

[14] See the Enterprise Act 2002 (Commencement No. 3, Transitional and Transitory Provisions and Savings) Order 2003, S.I. 1397. For a description of the new rules, see the consultation paper 'Consumer reforms', published by the Office of Fair Trading in August 2002, available at www.oft.gov.uk. See also H.-W. Micklitz and P. Rott, *Richtlinie 98/27/EG*, in E. Grabitz, M. Hilf and M. Wolf (eds.), *Das Recht der Europäischen Union* (2005).

[15] Schedule 26 of the Enterprise Act.

[16] In addition, consumer associations are allowed to sue if they are 'Community enforcers' in the terms of sec. 213(5), i.e. if they are listed in the Official Journal of the EC in pursuance of art. 4(3) of Directive 98/27/EC. Until now, no English consumer association has been listed, see the Commission's Communication, [2002] OJ C 273 of November 9, 2002, p. 7.

Enforcers and Transitional Provisions) Order 2003.[17] As the Stop Now Order (EC Directives) Regulations 2001, chap. 8 of the Enterprise Act gives priority to enforcement of consumer law by the OFT and therefore restricts legal action by consumer associations, even if they are designated as enforcers by the Secretary of State, in many ways, in particular through consultation requirements.[18] However, comparative advertisement is still not covered by the scope of chap. 8 of the Enterprise Act. Thus, consumer associations cannot take action in the present case.

Business associations do not have any legal rights. The reason for this is that in the past if at all only the violated party was entitled to sue. Only recently were consumer associations given further rights.

(3) Like consumers, competitors only have the opportunity to file a complaint to the OFT, under reg. 4(1) of the CMAR 1988 as amended.[19] Also, they can complain to the Advertising Standards Authority.[20]

(4) The public authorities can try to implement different steps. If A's advertisement was in breach of reg. 4(2) of the CMAR 1988, the OFT could bring proceedings for an injunction in the High Court.[21]

Otherwise, the OFT cannot take action against the unfair attraction of consumers. Under the Fair Trading Act 1973[22] its competence only extended to the pursuance of business practices that were to be regarded as 'unfair to consumers', sec. 34(1). This, however, did not entail a general clause,[23] but was further defined in sec. 34(2) and (3) as contraventions to enactments which impose duties, prohibitions or restrictions enforceable by criminal proceedings, and to things done, or omitted to be done, in breach of contract or in breach of a duty owed to any person by virtue of any enactment or rule of law that is enforceable by civil proceedings.

Part III of the FTA 1973, comprising sec. 34 et seq., was then replaced by the Enterprise Act 2002. Since attracting consumers does not

[17] S.I. 2003, 1399. For details, see the Department of Trade and Industry document 'Designation as an Enforcer for Part 8 of the Enterprise Act 2002: Guidance for Private Bodies Seeking a Designation under Section 213'. Reg. 4 (2) of the Stop Now Orders Regulations (2001) had also listed a number of criteria. For details, see P. Rott (2001) 24 JCP 401 (423 et seq.).

[18] For details on restrictions under the Stop Now Orders Regulations (2001), see P. Rott (2001) 24 JCP 401 (422 et seq.).

[19] For details, see the solution to Case 1 (Risky bread) at 1.

[20] See the solution to question 1 of this Case at 3.

[21] For details, see the solution to Case 1 (Risky bread) at 1.

[22] Ch. 41 of 1973.

[23] For failed attempts to introduce a general clause in English unfair competition law, see C. Miller, B. Harvey and D. Parry, *Consumer and Trading Law* (1998), pp. 553 et seq.

constitute a community infringement, it could only be actionable as a 'domestic infringement' in terms of sec. 211 EA. A domestic infringement is an act or omission which is committed or made by a person in the course of a business, harms the collective interests of consumers in England, and is of a description specified by the Secretary of State by order, in accordance with sec. 211(2). Domestic infringements are now listed in The Enterprise Act 2002 (Part 8 Domestic Infringements) Order 2003.[24] They do not include attracting consumers.

Since there is no violation of the Trade Descriptions Act 1968, criminal prosecution cannot take place.

Finland (4)

There are no clear rules in the KSL (Consumer Protection Act) as to whether there should be a certain amount of the advertised products available in the shops. General rules of contract law and the Contracts Act governing these rules state that an offer is binding. However, advertisements are not necessarily regarded as offers as they could also be regarded as asking the public to make an offer. In the guidelines for special discounts given by the Ombudsman it is required that the product should be available during the period mentioned in the marketing, or that the limitations should be clearly stated in the marketing (even exact information can be required if the number of available products is very limited). Phrases like 'as long as the products are available in the shop' can be used if it is a question of a left over consignment or a limited consignment which is expected to be sold quickly.

Using a product in advertising which is not available in the shops, other than in very few cases, could be a violation of § 1 SopMenL or even § 2 SopMenL if the advertisement is misleading. This is clearly stated in the above-mentioned guidelines too. For § 1 SopMenL to be violated it is enough that the advertisement is contrary to good business practices.

(1) A consumer has no legal standing in the Market Court as the Ombudsman represents consumer's interests. Claims for damages by the consumer can be brought according to the general rules. Financial loss can be claimed if a penal law has been violated. In the law of unfair trading loss is presumed according to 1 § Penal Act[25] if intentionally

[24] S.I. 2003, No. 1593. [25] Rikoslaki of December 19, 1889.

untruthful or misleading statements are made that are of special importance for the target group. In practice, this claim is not used.[26]

(2) Consumer associations have a secondary right to bring a case into the Market Court if the Ombudsman refuses to do so: § 4 *Laki eräiden markkinaoikeudellisten asioiden käsittelystä* (Law on Market Court procedure regarding certain matters within the court's jurisdiction). In these circumstances, the associations represent the interests of consumers. These cases are rare as the Ombudsman will usually be the one to bring a case to the Market Court.

Even an organization representing businesses would have a right to bring this case to the Market Court. This is because a practice which is contrary to fair trade practice, can affect all businesses in the field. The competitor and the consumer associations (when the Ombudsman has refused to bring the case forward) can ask the Market Court to forbid A's marketing, and demand that it not be repeated.

(3) As neither § 1 nor § 2 SopMenL require direct interest in the matter any competitor could in theory bring a case to the Market Court. However, under § 3 of the Act on Proceedings in the Market Court only those tradesmen whose trade could be affected by the marketing or other practices have a right to bring a case to Market Court. In this case, any supermarket or swing manufacturer would probably have a sufficient interest and would have a right to demand a cease and desist order. In the first example the supermarket could be harmed as customers might go shopping in A's supermarket chain because of the advertisement. In the second example, other swing manufacturers could be harmed if consumers are seeking the competing product, which in reality is not sold as cheaply as promised. Usually cases are brought forward only by direct competitors. In the preparatory legislative documents this right has also been limited, but the interpretation has been a relatively wide one (for example an association representing supermarket and market owners had a legal standing in a case regarding marketing of soap). Thus, trade can be affected even if there is no evidence of a loss of sales etc. or any contact between the claimant and the tradesman whose practices are claimed to be contrary to the SopMenL. A word of warning: there is as yet no case law on § 3 of the Act on Proceedings in the Market Court.

[26] K. Kaulamo, *Finland*, in G. Schricker, notes 355, 360.

(4) A prohibition is principally issued by the Market Court, but the Consumer Ombudsman is also entitled to do so, § 7 SopMenL; chap. 2 § 8 KSL.

France (4)

The advertising is misleading, because the advertised article is not available or not available in sufficient quantities. This kind of advertising is prohibited by art. L 121-1 CCons., because there are insufficient quantities of the advertised products. In French procedural law legal action can only be intended by plaintiffs having the quality to act (*qualité pour agir*) as is stated by art. 31 NCPC. Considering that unfair competition behaviour does not only concern the interests of two competitors but only consumer's interests, the bilateral concept of action has been abandoned.[27] Nowadays, individual competitors and certain groups of persons are entitled to take legal action against instances of unfair competition.[28]

(1) In principle, anyone can bring a claim on the basis of art. 1382 et seq. cc if his rights are culpably and illegally violated. However, the consumer as a person does not have standing to act in cases of unfair competition comprising the classic tort found in arts. 1382 and 1383 cc. In both the literature and the jurisprudence this fact is justified by the nature of unfair competition supposing a situation of competition and having a disciplinary aspect;[29] moreover, there is no situation of competition between the consumer and the competitor.[30] In the present case, the situation is different as the misleading advertising is made a crime by the consumer code and under art. 2 of the code of penal procedure. It can be assigned to the Procureur by any person having suffered individual damage, including consumers.[31]

[27] N.-F. Alpi, in Juris-Classeur, *Concurrence, consommation* (2003), Fasc. 245, 'Action en concurrence déloyale – éléments de procédure', note 27.

[28] Ibid.

[29] G. Raymond, in Juris-Classeur, *Concurrence, consommation* (1998), Fasc. 900, 'Publicité commerciale et protection des consommateurs', note 150.

[30] Cour de Cassation chambre commerciale de 14. Octobre 1963. Misleading on the other hand T. Dreier and S. von Lewinsky, *Frankreich*, in G. Schricker, note 373.

[30] T. Dreier and S. von Lewinsky, *Frankreich*, in G. Schricker, note 373; incorrectly J. Keßler and H.-W. Micklitz, *Die Harmonisierung des Lauterkeitsrechts in den Mitgliedstaaten der Europäischen Gemeinschaft und die Reform des UWG* (2003), p. 92, answering a consumer's right of action in the affirmative.

[31] G. Raymond, in Juris-Classeur, *Concurrence, consommation* (1998), Fasc. 900, 'Publicité commerciale et protection des consommateurs', note 156.

Furthermore, consumers have extrajudicial means to restrain the infringer. C can, for example, address the Bureau of Verification of Advertising (BVP).[32] He can also address a consumers' association or communicate his disappointment to the postal box 5000 (*boîte postale 5000*), a possibility to bring complaints via the regional offices of the DGCCRF.[33]

(2) For the same reasons as have just been cited concerning the consumer as a person, that is to say the lack of supposing a situation of competition and the disciplinary aspect of the action, consumer associations are not entitled to act in matters of unfair competition.[34] Generally, actions of consumer associations have been rejected either because of the absence of damage or the absence of standing to act.[35]

The situation is radically different when provisions of the Code de la Consommation are concerned. In such cases consumer associations have been entitled, since the Act n° 93-949 of July 26, 1993, to take legal steps themselves to act in tort actions for reparation of the damage suffered by the consumers as a whole.[36] The provisions concerning their class actions are art. L 411- 1 et seq. of the CCons. The associations can thus be the civil party in criminal procedures (art. L 421-1 CCons).[37] As such, they can even obtain penalties if illicit actions are not stopped immediately (art. L 421-2 CCons). They can also defend the consumer interest by a representative action (art. L 422-1 CCons). In case of a representative action, the association may institute legal proceedings to obtain reparation before any court on behalf of the consumers.[38] However, the mandate may not be solicited by means of public appeal on radio or television, nor by way of poster, pamphlet or personalized letter as is stated by para. 2 of art. L 422-1 CCons. As the present case presents an infraction of art. L 121-1 CCons an approved consumer

[32] N.-F. Alpi, in Juris-Classeur, *Concurrence, consommation* (2003), Fasc. 245, 'Action en concurrence déloyale – éléments de procédure', note 39.

[33] G. Paisant, in Juris-Classeur, *Concurrence, consommation* (1993), Fasc. 1210, 'Moyens d'action des consommateurs et riposte des professionnels', notes 8 et seq.

[34] N.-F. Alpi, in Juris-Classeur, *Concurrence, consommation* (2003), Fasc. 245, 'Action en concurrence déloyale – éléments de procédure', note 39; misleading, on the other hand, T. Dreier and S. von Lewinsky, *Frankreich*, in G. Schricker, note 373.

[35] N.-F. Alpi, in Juris-Classeur, *Concurrence, consommation* (2003), Fasc. 245, 'Action en concurrence déloyale – éléments de procédure', note 39.

[36] Ibid., note 40.

[37] Example in *Contrats, concurrence, consommation* (2003), note 191; TGI de Nanterre June 24, 2003, *Association CLCV v. Société EMI France*; see also T. Dreier and S. von Lewinsky, *Frankreich*, in G. Schricker, note 368.

[38] L. Boré, *L'action en représentation conjointe*, in Dalloz 1995, chroniques p. 267.

association could take steps against A, once it has been informed by C. For this C has to give a written authorization to an approved consumer's association and at least one other consumer who has suffered the identical individual damage has to do so as well.

Professional associations can also bring claims for damages and for an injunction before the civil and criminal courts.[39]

(3) The civil action, according to arts. 1382 and 1383 cc, of the competitor still remains possible (art. L 121-14 CCons), but he has to prove fault, damage and causality. This seems to be very difficult in the present case.[40]

(4) Where the field of consumer protection and the provisions of the consumer code are concerned, the DGCCRF and those from the food directorate general of the Ministry of Agriculture and those from the metrology department of the Ministry of Industry are authorized to establish breaches.[41] Criminal proceedings can be brought by the agents of the DGCCRF in cases of misleading advertising.[42] There are also duties to supply information: for example, information justifying the advertisement has to be supplied (see art. L 121-7 CCons). These records are forwarded to the public prosecutor. The public prosecutor has the option of returning it with a proposal for a settlement.[43] This is the equivalent to the German *Strafbefehlsverfahren* (order for summary punishment).[44] For all other cases of the common law of unfair competition, however, there is no competent administrative authority.

Germany (4)

A's conduct could fulfil the factual requirements of § 3 UWG (ex-§ 1 UWG) and § 5 UWG (ex-§ 3 UWG). It can be misleading to advertise goods that are not available at the announced price in sufficient quantity, § 5 para. 5 UWG. With respect to these so-called 'bait offers', it is crucial to take all the particularities of the case into account. The number of swings available is an indication of unfair competition.

(1) The ultimate consumer is not named in § 8 para. 3 UWG (ex-§ 13 para. 2 UWG). § 13 para. 2 UWG is not exhaustive. On the one hand, the directly injured party is entitled to claim. A party is directly injured

[39] T. Dreier and S. von Lewinsky, *Frankreich*, in G. Schricker, note 369.

[40] Concerning the engagement of administrative and criminal procedures the reader may also refer to Case 1 (Risky bread).

[41] See above Case 1 (Risky bread). [42] Art. L 121-2 CCons.

[43] T. Dreier and S. von Lewinsky, *Frankreich*, in G. Schricker, note 384.

[44] T. Dreier and S. von Lewinsky, *Frankreich*, in G. Schricker, note 384.

when it falls within the scope of protection of the norm. That is, someone whose protection is intended by the norm. In the first place § 3 UWG (ex-§ 1 UWG) protects the general interest rather than that of the individual consumer.[45] Thus, this does not involve an individual protective norm in the interest of the consumer.[46] § 1 UWG as amended in 2004 states as its aim the protection of competitors, consumers and other market participants against unfair trading practices. On the other hand, according to German law the consumer does not have the right to bring an action before a court.[47] This meets with the approval of leading scholarly opinion. Moreover, it is held that most of the norms of the UWG cannot be qualified as protective norms in the sense of § 823 para. 2 BGB which also rules out standing for consumers. Only exceptionally is the protective character of the norm assumed, especially norms that penalize certain behaviour, for example, §§ 16–19 UWG (ex-§ 4, 17, 18, 20 UWG).[48] C is therefore not entitled to sue for an injunction or for damages. He would still be advised to encourage a consumer association to bring a claim under § 8 para. 3 no. 3 UWG (ex-§ 13 para. 2 no. 3 UWG).[49]

(2) Consumer interests may be pursued by consumer institutions under § 8 para. 3 no. 3 UWG (ex-§ 13 para. 2 no. 3 UWG), that is by associations under § 4 Forbearance Claims Law (*Unterlassungsklagengesetz*) and at the community level under art. 4 Injunction Directive 98/27/EU. For entry in the list of legal standing under § 4 *Unterlassungsklagengesetz*, only idealistic associations registered under § 21 BGB can be considered.[50] The objects in their articles must be to seek to advance consumer interests by means of information and advice. The consumer is to be understood in a collective sense, that is to say that it is not sufficient if the association represents the interests of its members who are

45 H. Köhler, in W. Hefermehl, H. Köhler and J. Bornkamm, *Wettbewerbsrecht* (24th edn 2006), § 1 notes 1 et seq, 34.

46 BGH (1974) 27 NJW 1503, (1975) 77 GRUR 150 – 'Prüfzeichen'. Consumers are only entitled to claim if the factual requirements of § 4 para. 1 UWG are met: an untrue statement that is capable of misleading is required. In contrast, see Cases 2 (Watch imitations I) and 6 (Child labour).

47 Begr. RegE, BT-Drs. 15/1487, p. 22 regarding § 8.

48 Ibid.

49 H. Köhler and H. Piper, *UWG* (3rd edn 2002), § 13 note 3; A. Bergmann, in H. Harte-Bavendamm and F. Henning-Bodewig, *UWG* (2004), § 8 note 257.

50 H. Köhler and H. Piper, *UWG* (3rd edn 2002), § 13 note 27; J. Bornkamm, in W. Hefermehl, H. Köhler and J. Bornkamm, *Wettbewerbsrecht* (24th edn 2006), § 8 notes 3.55 et seq.; A. Bergmann, in H. Harte-Bavendamm and F. Henning-Bodewig, *UWG* (2004), § 8 note 301; W. Büscher, in K.H. Fezer, *Lauterkeitsrecht* (2005), § 8 notes 219 et seq.

consumers.[51] However, it need not represent the interests of all consumers; market segment consumer interests are sufficient.[52] In view of the danger of conflict of interests, the associations may not be hybrid associations, that is to say those which also represent commercial interests.[53] In addition to the objects in the articles, the association must be adequately equipped to pursue the objects.[54] This includes financial resources and sufficiently qualified staff.

Under § 10 UWG as amended in 2004 the legislature for the first time introduced the disgorgement of profits that can be claimed by associations. The disgorged profits are to be paid to the state.

In the amendment of the UWG in 1994[55] the German legislature has curbed the standing of associations to sue that aim at furthering commercial interests. According to § 8 para. 3 no. 2 UWG (ex-§ 13 para. 2 no. 2 UWG) business organizations are only entitled to sue if the organization has a considerable amount of tradesmen as its members and if it has sufficient staff and means. The organization cannot sue abroad[56] and foreign organizations are not entitled to sue in Germany. Moreover, the action may not be frivolous; this is always the case if its main purpose is to recover the costs of the proceedings: § 8 para. 4 UWG (ex-§ 13 para. 4 UWG).

(3) Trade competitors are entitled to sue under § 8 para. 3 no. 1 UWG (ex-§ 13 para. 2 no. 1 UWG). If they are directly harmed, they are entitled to sue anyway.[57] The new UWG restricts standing to certain competitors, i.e. to companies that act on the same market as the infringer either on the supply or the demand side, § 2 no. 3 UWG. This is a restriction of the right to sue contained in the former UWG. A competitor who is 'only abstractly' concerned is no longer considered to be

[51] H. Köhler and H. Piper, *UWG* (3rd edn 2002), § 13 note 28; J. Bornkamm, in W. Hefermehl, H. Köhler and J. Bornkamm, *Wettbewerbsrecht* (24th edn 2006) § 8 note 3.56; A. Bergmann, in H. Harte-Bavendamm and F. Henning-Bodewig, *UWG* (2004), § 8 note 301; W. Büscher, in K.H. Fezer, *Lauterkeitsrecht* (2005), § 8 note 221.

[52] J. Bornkamm, in W. Hefermehl, H. Köhler and J. Bornkamm, *Wettbewerbsrecht* (24th edn 2006), § 8 note 3.56.

[53] H. Köhler and H. Piper, *UWG* (3rd edn 2002), § 13 note 28; J. Bornkamm, in W. Hefermehl, H. Köhler and J. Bornkamm, *Wettbewerbsrecht* (24th edn 2006), § 8 note 3.56.

[54] H. Köhler and H. Piper, *UWG* (3rd edn 2002), § 13 note 29; J. Bornkamm, in W. Hefermehl, H. Köhler and J. Bornkamm, *Wettbewerbsrecht* (24th edn 2006), § 8 note 3.57; W. Büscher, in K. H. Fezer, *Lauterkeitsrecht* (2005), § 8 note 221.

[55] From July 25, 1994, BGBl. I 1738.

[56] BGH (1998) 100 GRUR 419 (420) – 'Gewinnspiel im Ausland'.

[57] H. Köhler and H. Piper, *UWG* (3rd edn 2002), vor § 13 note 39; A. Bergmann, in H. Harte-Bavendamm and F. Henning-Bodewig, *UWG* (2004), § 8 note 267.

in need of protection. According to the new law such a competitor's interests have to be pursued by associations.[58]

(4) German law provides for no administrative authority to monitor observance of advertising standards.[59] But there are very often specific laws: for example, in capital market law the Bundesanstalt für Finanzdienstleistungen (German Financial Supervisory Authority) supervises fair trading according to § 23 *Kreditwesengesetz* – KWG ('German Banking Act'), § 36b *Wertpapierhandelsgesetz* – WpHG (Securities Trading Act)[60] or § 28 *Wertpapiererwerbs- und übernahmegesetz* – WpÜG (Securities Acquisition and Takeover Act). Only exceptionally is the public prosecutor able to act if the defendant acted intentionally and one of the following norms is given: §§ 16–19 UWG (ex-§§ 4, 17, 18, 20 UWG).

Greece (4)

By announcing that child swings would be sold at a lower price, without clarifying that he had a very limited stock, A deceived consumers, thereby influencing their economic behaviour; A should have referred to the quantity of available products as soon as there was a risk of there not being enough to cover the eventual demand. Such conduct is prohibited by L.2251/1994 on consumer protection, and more specifically by art. 9(2) and (3)(a) concerning misleading advertisements.[61] Moreover, A's advertisement falls into the scope of art. 3 of L.146/1914 prohibiting inaccurate declarations that may create the impression of a particularly advantageous offer. This provision is applied provided that the said declarations refer to commercial, industrial or agricultural transactions and that they become known to a wide circle of persons. Inaccurate declarations related to features of products offered to consumers[62] are specifically prohibited. In the present case, A made inaccurate declarations relating to the quantity of products offered at his stores, by creating the impression of a particularly advantageous offer, in order to

[58] Begr. RegE, BT-Drs. 15/1487, p. 22 regarding § 8.

[59] H. Köhler and H. Piper, *UWG* (3rd edn 2002), § 13 note 3; A. Bergmann, in H. Harte-Bavendamm and F. Henning-Bodewig, *UWG* (2004), § 8 note 257.

[60] T. Möllers, *Das neue Werberecht der Wertpapierfirmen: § 36b WpHG* (1999) 11 ZBB 134 et seq.

[61] The content of this article is based on the provisions for Directive 85/450/EEC.

[62] Such as quality, origin, manufacturing method, price, supply source, distinctions, quantity and reason for sale.

make consumers visiting the stores purchase goods that are irrelevant to the advertised product.[63]

The answers to the questions raised in the present case vary according to the legal basis on which claims are founded. More specifically:

(1) L. 2251/1994 expressly grants standing only to consumer associations and chambers of commerce. Whether an individual consumer has a claim against A to desist from such advertisement in the future is a controversial issue. A part of the legal doctrine considers that any consumer personally affected by a supplier's act violating L. 2251/1994 (in the present case art. 9(2) and (3)) is entitled to raise a claim for an injunction.[64] An opposite view denies the consumer's right to take legal proceedings to enforce injunction claims, arguing that such interpretation would imply the risk of contradictory judgments.[65] Nevertheless, it is unanimously accepted[66] that the individual consumer C may seek compensatory damages for any damage he may have suffered (on the basis of art. 9 L. 2251/1994 in combination with art. 914 CC). As to the possibility of consumer C taking legal action to prevent A from continuously violating the law on unfair competition, different views have also been expressed. According to art. 10 of L.146/1914, only enterprises that produce similar products, chambers of commerce and commercial associations have the right to request the cessation of such acts in the future. The wording of the law excludes such possibility for individual consumers. A rather sounder view prevails in legal doctrine, however, according to which the consumer may claim the remedy of such violation and its cessation in the future;[67] in addition, a direct claim for compensatory damages must be allowed to any consumer who has been damaged by inaccurate declarations.[68]

(2) Through a combined reading of arts. 9, 10(8), (9) and (15) of L.2251/1994, it can be concluded that each consumer association or multiple

[63] L. Kotsiris, *Competition Law* (2002) p. 198.

[64] E. Alexandridou, *Consumer Potection Law*, vol. II (1996), p. 198.

[65] Y. Karakostas and D. Tzouganatos, *Consumer Protection*; Law 2251/1994 (2002), pp. 302–304, *Athens Single Member CFI* 5874/94 (1994) 44 *EEmpD* 668 (under the regime of the previous consumer law).

[66] E. Alexadridou, op. cit., p. 198, Y. Karakostas and D. Tzouganatos, op. cit., pp. 302–304, A. Liakopoulos, *Industrial Property* (2000), p. 473.

[67] Ibid., p. 458, see *Athens single member CFI* 335/1995, (1996) 2 DEE 515, contra *Athens multi-member* 2339/1997, (1997) 3 DEE 470.

[68] A. Tsironis, *Article 3*, in R. Rokas (ed.), *Unfair Competition* (1996), p. 293; A. Liakopoulos, op.cit., p. 458; A. Stathopoulos, *Introductory Remarks to Articles 914–938, The Civil Code* (1982) p. 690.

consumer associations may through a collective action request that a supplier be ordered to end his unlawful conduct, for the protection of consumers' general interest,[69] when such conduct relates to misleading, unfair, comparative or direct advertisement.[70] It is clearly stated in art. 10(8) and (9) that consumer associations *may file collective actions*, but are under no duty to do so. In this context, the consumer associations are entitled to sue for an injunction (art. 9(9)(c)) and may also request 'collective moral damages'[71] (art. 9(9)(b)). The moral damages are calculated by the court taking into account the gravity of the offence towards legal order, the economic status of the defendant (especially the annual turnover) as well as the need for general and specific prevention of unlawful acts. No fault is required for the adjudication of moral damages.

It is suggested that the legal nature of this pecuniary compensation for non-material damages is primarily *restitutionary*,[72] aimed at the restoration of the social detriment provoked by the unlawful act. This would justify the intended use of the amount awarded;[73] according to art. 10(13), the said amount may be claimed only once and must be spent for public benefit purposes relating to the consumer's protection. However, some of the legal commentary[74] and jurisprudence accepts a different view, according to which the pecuniary compensation for moral damages is appropriate as a form of punitive (exemplary) damages, for sanction and prevention reasons.[75] This approach is grounded on the criteria for the calculation of compensation, which are similar to those met in jurisdictions that recognize the imposition of general punitive damages.

The effectiveness of this provision depends on the amounts to be awarded by the courts. Symbolic compensations may not serve the

[69] Collective actions may be exercised by consumer association(s) having, each one of them or in toto, more than 500 active members and registered to the Consumers Associations Registry for at least two years prior to exercise of such action (see art. 9(9) and (10)). Consumer associations of more than 100 members are entitled to request the protection of their members' rights (art. 9(8)).

[70] *Areios Pagos (Supreme Court)*, decision 778/2000, http://lawdb.intrasoftnet.com/ [in Greek].

[71] See A. Pouliadis, *Consumers Associations and the collective action*, (1998) [in Greek], pp. 30 et seq.

[72] Y. Karakostas and D. Tzouganatos, *Consumer Protection; Law 2251/1994*, op.cit., p. 341.

[73] Ibid., pp. 345, 348.

[74] See A. Pouliadis, *Consumers Associations and the collective action*, op. cit., pp. 32–35.

[75] *Areios Pagos (Supreme Court)* 589/2001, 7 (2001) DEE 1117, *Athens Court of Appeals* 7950/1999, (2000) 6 DEE 1121 and 1448/1998, 46 (1998) NoV 1251.

sanction and prevention objectives of the legislation.[76] Besides, art. 10(14) and (19) protects suppliers from the (rather theoretical) risk of the abusive exercise of collective actions for moral damages, providing for severe sanctions.[77]

(3) As already mentioned above, A's conduct also falls within the scope of art. 3 of L. 146/14 on unfair competition. Art. 10 of the said law provides that the cessation of A's misleading declaration may be requested by business persons engaged in the same commercial field who are thus his competitors. Any such business persons who have been damaged by his conduct may also seek damages

(4) Criminal prosecution may be sought against A in accordance with art. 4 of L.146/1914, providing that any person who intentionally makes inaccurate declarations that are capable of misleading the public in order to create the impression of a particularly advantageous offer will be punished with imprisonment of up to six months or pecuniary penalty or even both. According to art. 21(2) of the same law, this crime is prosecuted only after accusation by the persons listed in art. 10 thereof (competitors, chambers of commerce and industry, commercial, industrial and in general professional associations).

Moreover, according to art. 14(3) of L. 2251/1994, the violation of its provisions leads to the imposition by the Minister of Development of a fine of 500,000 to 20 million drachmas (equal to about €1,500 to €60,000) on the liable businesses. The maximum amount of the fine is doubled if the liable business is guilty of a previous violation. If the violation was committed repeatedly in the past, the Minister of Development may consider shutting down the business for a period not exceeding one year.

[76] That seems to be the tendency of the courts; see Pouliadis, *Consumers Associations and the collective action*, op. cit., pp. 33–34. See two cases in which the Athens multi-member CFI dismissed the association's claim for moral damages as indefinite. In the first one (2960/1996, 3 (1997) DEE 71, with note by E. Perakis), the reason was the lack of grounds for the claim; the association did not request the cessation of the unlawful conduct, but the payment of reparation in the form of marking down by 12% the bills of all consumers. The indefiniteness of the main claim led to the indefiniteness of the claim for pecuniary reparation of moral harm. In the second case (3229/1996, 3 (1997) DEE 75) the association had requested the prohibition of unlawful general terms contained in insurance contracts and the payment of moral damages caused to consumers as a whole. The court prohibited the use of those terms in the future, but dismissed the claim for moral damages as indefinite, considering that the criteria for the calculation of the reparation should have been particularized for each abusive term, in order for the compensation amount to be determined.

[77] E. Alexandridou, *Consumer Protection Law*, op. cit., p. 211.

Greek law does not provide for an administrative body entitled to monitor the observance of advertising standards in general; such committees are established in specific fields.[78]

Hungary (4)

According to sec. 8 HCA this constitutes misleading of consumers.

(1) C as a consumer cannot take legal action or commence legal proceedings to force A to desist from such behaviour. In the case of misleading of consumers, on the basis of sec. 43/G any person who observes conduct falling within the competence of the OEC and infringing sec. 8 HCA may make a formal or an informal complaint to the OEC.

Sec. 43/H declares that complaints can be made by the submission to the OEC of a properly completed form issued by the OEC. The form shall contain the important facts required for the assessment of the complaint. Within sixty days of receipt of the complaint, the investigator shall issue an order: (a) to open an investigation pursuant to sec. 70(1), or (b) to state, based on the data supplied by, or obtained in the procedure conducted on the basis of the complaint, that the conditions for the opening of an investigation set out in sec. 70(1) are not fulfilled. Furthermore, complainants shall be informed of the order made pursuant to (b) above, and they may seek legal remedy against such an order within eight days of the issue of the order (sec. 43/H 10 and 11).

Documents other than formal complaints are treated as informal complaints pursuant to sec. 43/I HCA. This is the case when a submission does not include all the necessary information. The rights of the informal complainant are more narrowly defined. In particular, an informal complainant has no right of access to the file, and no right to appeal if the complaint is rejected. A formal complaint must be dealt with by the OEC within 60 days (extendable by 60 days), whereas the deadline in the case of an informal complaint is 30 days (also extendable).

(2) Consumer associations are under no duty to represent the interests of consumers. However, according to Act CLV of 1997 on consumer protection social organizations providing representation of consumer interests may file charges against any party causing substantial harm to a wide range of consumers by illegal activities aimed at enforcing the interests of consumers, even if the identity of the injured consumers

[78] I.e. the Committee for the protection of public companies' consumers (art. 13 of L. 2251/1994).

cannot be established (sec. 39 (1)). Sec. 2h CPA defines social organizations as organizations founded on the basis of Act II of 1989 on the Right of Association, or alliances of such organizations, if one of the goals specified in the statutes is the protection of consumer interests, the organization or alliance has been operating for at least two years and has at least fifty members who are natural persons. This legal action may be filed within one year of the occurrence of the illegal activity.

Since Hungary's accession to the European Union all qualified entities established under the laws of the member states with respect to the consumer interest they represent, provided they are included in the list published in the Official Journal of the European Communities pursuant to Article 4(3) of the Injunction Directive 98/27/EC, are entitled to file a legal action, provided that the claim for which the action is filed pertains to the infringement of a legal regulation specified in other specific legislation.

Trade associations have neither under the HCA, nor under the CPA the right to sue.

(3) The trade competitor has two possible ways to take steps against the advertising. He can also notify the OEC for the purpose that the OEC commences an investigation and a procedure against the infringer.

Since, in this case, the provisions of sec. 2 HCA[79] are met, the competitor can file a lawsuit before the civil courts according to sec. 86(1) HCA. In this case, the unfair competition act violates the interest of the competitor by way of stating false facts that in turn induce consumers to favour the advertised products.[80]

(4) In a proceeding commenced before the OEC alleging the misleading of consumers, the competition council in its decision shall: (i) declare an act as illegal, shall order the termination of any illegal conduct, and shall prohibit the continuation of any illegal conduct, (ii) order the publication of a statement of correction in connection with any misleading information, and/or (iii) impose a fine on that entity who infringes the provisions of the Competition Act (sec. 77 and 78 HCA).

[79] Sec. 2 HCA reads: 'It is prohibited to conduct economic activities in an unfair manner, in particular, in a manner violating or jeopardizing the lawful interests of competitors and consumers, or in a way which is in conflict with the requirements of business integrity.'

[80] Supreme Court Nr. Pf. IV. 20.314/1998/2.

Ireland (4)

(1) C can request the High Court to order A to desist from such advertising in the future, under the Misleading Advertising Regulations. In determining whether the advertisement is misleading, account shall be taken of all its features the characteristics of the goods, their expected use, their price, conditions of supply and the nature of the advertiser, as per art. 3 of the EC Misleading Advertising Directive 84/450.[81]

Alternatively, C can request the Director of Consumer Affairs to request A to desist from such advertising in the future, and to take him to court if he declines to accede to the request under the Misleading Advertising Regulations.

Cases such as this may best resolved by the self-regulatory advertising authority (Irish Advertising Standards Authority), which in cooperation with the Director of Consumer Affairs, is in a good position to apply pressure on A to encourage him to change his advertising practice. It may be difficult to prove the charge in court unless A was systematically engaging in misleading advertising under the circumstances, as A could easily claim that there was a particular supply problem with some particular shops, or during a particular time period.

(2) Consumer associations are neither entitled nor obliged to represent the interests of consumers as a whole. No class actions are permitted in Irish courts. All cases are conducted by individual named parties. Where a group of similar actions exist, parties often agree that a small number of test cases be selected and prioritized for litigation. However, these test cases are not binding on parties in other cases. The rules of the Superior Courts provide that a plaintiff may apply to the court to unite in the same action several causes of action if they can be conveniently disposed of together by the court and they meet certain criteria. In 2003, the Law Reform Commission published a consultation paper on multiparty litigation, which recommends that Government give serious consideration to the implementation of a class action system.[82] There is no indication when, if ever, this may become law.

(3) Trade competitors can complain to the Director of Consumer Affairs and seek to have the Director take action against A under sec. 8 of the Consumer Information Act 1978.[83] Alternatively trade

[81] See Case 1 (Risky bread).
[82] Consultation Paper Multi Party Litigation – Class Actions (July 2003) (LRC CP25 - 2003).
[83] See Case 1 (Risky bread).

competitors can take action against A under the EC (Misleading Advertising) Regulations 1988.

(4) The Director of Consumer Affairs can take a criminal action against A under sec. 8 of the Consumer Information Act 1978. Alternatively, the Director could take an action against A under sections 3 and 4 of the EC (Misleading Advertising) Regulations 1988.[84]

Italy (4)

A's advertising cannot be automatically considered as misleading: the particular facts of the case will have to be taken into account (number of products stored, foreseeable number of request by consumers, duration of the special offer, and so on).

(1) C has no cause of action under the Italian law of unfair competition. According to a generally accepted principle, the ultimate consumer is not protected directly by the prohibition of unfair competition. C may signal the misleading advertisement by A to the *Autorità Garante della Concorrenza e del Mercato*, according to d.lgs. 74/1992, and ask such Authority to issue a cease-and-desist order.[85] D. lgs. no. 74/1992 provides in art. 7 that competitors, consumers and their associations, as well as the Ministry of Trade and every public administration that has an interest in the matter institutionally, can ask the antitrust authority to ban misleading advertising and eliminate its effects. Therefore, consumers do not have standing to start an action.[86] Apart from this, everyone who believes he has suffered a disadvantage through the advertisement of an advertiser that is committed to the CAP can request the review of the advertisement, according to art. 36 CAP.[87]

C may have a cause of action under the general law of consumers' rights (l. 281/98), which states that consumers have, inter alia, the fundamental right to 'adequate information and fair advertising' (art. 1 para. 2 lit. (c)), as well as the right to 'fairness, transparency and equity in contractual relationships which reference to goods and services'. From such provision, it may be argued that consumers have a legal

[84] See Case 1 (Risky bread).

[85] The same way L. Antoniolli and E. Ioriatti, *Italy*, in R. Schulze and H. Schulte-Nölke, 2(b); V. Meli, *I rimedi per la violazione del divieto di pubblicità ingannevole*, in *Riv. dir. ind.* (2000), I, 6.

[86] L. Antoniolli and E. Ioriatti, *Italy*, in R. Schulze and H. Schulte-Nölke, 3.a).

[87] C. Käser, *Effizienz des Rechtsschutzes im deutschen und italienischen Wettbewerbsrecht* (2003), p. 251.

right not to be mislead by advertising;[88] both consumer associations and each single consumer may take action against infringements of such right (art. 3 para. 1 of l. 281/98 specifies that actions by consumer associations do not preclude actions by individual consumers).

The single consumer whose right not to be misled is infringed may claim damages, according to l. 281/98 and the general law of torts (articles 2043 ff. cc): in the case in question C may only claim damages equivalent to so-called 'negative interests', i.e. compensation for loss of time and expenses in visiting A's shops. Should C have entered a contract with an undertaking, as a consequence of a misleading advertising, and should such contract be harmful to him because of the differences between what was stated in the advertisement and the actual performance offered by the undertaking, he would be entitled to compensation for any damages suffered as a consequence of the contract. Among remedies listed in art. 3 of l. 281/1998 against infringements of rights granted to consumers there are also cease-and-desist orders by courts.

It is doubtful whether such orders may be claimed by individual consumers: it seems rather that a single consumer has no actual interest in obtaining such an order, once he discovers the misleading nature of the advertisement, since such advertisement is not likely to cause him any (further) loss which may justify the cease-and-desist order. The interest of the single consumers to other consumers not being misled has no legal relevance.

(2) Consumer associations which meet the requirements set out in l. 281/1998[89] can take action against any infringement of consumer rights listed there. Only consumer associations listed in a register kept by the Ministry of Industry may take action against infringements of l. 281/1998; requirements for being included in the register aim at ensuring that the association does actually have a capacity to represent consumers. The act establishes a special procedure of conciliation for consumer disputes, whereby consumer associations can start such a procedure in front of a special panel of the Trade Chamber (*Camera di commercio*), a mechanism created by l. 580/1993 (art. 2, 4a).[90] This right to sue applies among others to misleading and comparative advertising.[91]

[88] See G. Rossi, *La pubblicità dannosa* (2000), p. 156.
[89] Amended by legislative decree no. 224/2001.
[90] L. Antoniolli and E. Ioriatti, *Italy*, in R. Schulze and H. Schulte-Nölke, 1(e).
[91] Art. 7 para. 14 D.lgs. Nr. 74/1992 in connection with art. 3 d.lgs. Nr. 281/1992; see C. Käser, *Effizienz des Rechtsschutzes im deutschen und italienischen Wettbewerbsrecht* (2003), p. 39.

Some legal scholars have proposed that the provision of art. 2601 cc, enabling trade associations to take action against unfair competition, should be amended in order also to include consumer associations, but such proposals were never followed by legislative provisions.[92]

The association will have the burden of proving that the advertisement is misleading (such burden may be facilitated by a previous decision by the antitrust authority or the *Giurì d'Autodisciplina*): then, it may claim a cease-and-desist order in front of the ordinary courts, as well as any other measure needed to eliminate the harmful effects of the infringement (e.g. the publication of the decision in a number of newspapers). Bills are now pending in the Italian parliament in order to grant consumers' associations standing for damages claims. The association may also claim an interlocutory injunction, prior to litigation on the merits, according to arts. 669 et seq. cpc. According to art. 5, last paragraph of l. 281/98, as amended by national legislation implementing EC directive 98/27, in case of infringement of cease-and-desist orders the undertaking may have to pay a fine from €516 to €1,032 for each day until the infringement ceases.

Art. 2601 cc states that in cases where acts of unfair competition are harmful towards a whole category of business, trade associations representing such businesses may take legal action against such acts. Therefore, while consumer associations are never entitled to sue under the law of unfair competition (as we have seen, a legal basis for their actions may be found elsewhere), trade associations quite often are. Moreover, trade associations are able to claim collective damages.[93]

(3) Trade competitors may claim for an injunction against A, according to arts. 2598, no. 3 and 2600 cc.

(4) The *Autorità Garante della Concorrenza e del Mercato*, which is the public body charged with the task of monitoring advertising standards, may issue a cease-and-desist order. Such an authority may not take action *ex officio*: it is necessary that an entitled person asks it to exercise its powers against a specific advertisement. The claimant has the

[92] With its decision of January 21, 1988, n. 59 the Corte Costituzionale dismissed the motion for declaration of unconstitutionality of art. 2601, for infringement of the principle of equality (art. 3 of the Italian constitution), stating that the Constitution did not bind the legislature to enable consumer associations to sue under the law of unfair competition, and that it was up to the legislature to provide for adequate alternative means of protection of consumer interests.

[93] C. Käser, *Effizienz des Rechtsschutzes im deutschen und italienischen Wettbewerbsrecht* (2003), p. 145.

burden of indicating why the advertisement, in his opinion, is misleading (see art. 2 of d.P.R. n. 284 of July 11, 2003, n. 627, implementing d.lgs. 74/92 with reference to rules of procedure to be applied by the authority), but the authority is not bound by such an indication in formulating its charges.[94]

Netherlands (4)

(1) The advertising is misleading and the plaintiff could bring an action against A based on art. 6:194(b) BW, aimed at preventing A from such advertising in the future. Whether C has a right of action must be assessed in accordance with art. 3:303 BW, pursuant to which parties have no right of action if they lack sufficient interest. C, as a consumer, will generally lack such sufficient interest. Furthermore, it is doubtful whether C suffers damage as a result of A's actions. After all, C merely misses an advantage.

C can always submit a complaint against the supermarket chain A with the *Reclame Code Commissie* – RCC (Advertising Code Commission).[95] If the advertisement is found to infringe the *Nederlands Reclame Code* – NRC (Dutch Advertising Code), the Commission will ask A to stop using this advertisement in its current form. In the event of a repeat offence or a serious violation of the Code, the relevant media can be asked to stop publishing the advertisement concerned. The organizations which are affiliated to the RCC pursuant to the Netherlands Media Act have the duty to reject advertisements against which such a type of ban has been issued. Furthermore, if a Special Advertising Code is drawn up, the Commission can impose measures (e.g. fines) as described in the contracts concluded between the *Stichting Reclame Code* and the organizations in consultation with which the Special Code was drawn up.

(2) Consumer associations may be entitled, but are never under any duty to represent the interests of consumers in legal proceedings.[96]

According to art. 3:305a BW associations or foundations with full legal capacity can institute an action to protect similar interests of other

[94] L. Antoniolli and E. Ioriatti, *Italy*, in R. Schulze and H. Schulte-Nölke, 3.a).

[95] See the preliminary remarks.

[96] Conduct cannot be the basis of an action by such association or foundation, to the extent that the person affected by such conduct, objects thereto. Furthermore, a judicial decision does not affect a person whose interest the right of action is intended to protect, and who opposes the decision's resulting effect as regards himself, unless the nature of the decision is such that its operation cannot be excluded as regards that person.

persons to the extent that its articles promote such interests. Such an association or foundation shall have no *locus standi* if, in the given circumstances, it has not made a sufficient attempt to achieve the objective of the action through consultations with the defendant. A two-week period from receipt by the defendant of a request for consultations giving particulars of the claim shall in any event suffice for such purpose. The right of action may have as its object an order against the defendant to publish or cause publication of the decision in a manner to be determined by the court and at the expense of the party or parties, as directed by the court. Its object may not be to seek monetary compensation.

(3) In civil actions the main rule of art. 3:303 BW applies, according to which a person has no right of action where he lacks sufficient interest. If it can be established that a competitor has a right of action, then the question arises whether the standard breached serves to protect against damage such as that allegedly suffered by the trade competitor (*Schutznorm*). According to art. 6:163 BW the burden of proof in this respect lies with the defendant. It is difficult to draw firm and unequivocal conclusions from existing case law; the success of legal actions brought by competitors depends very much on the specific circumstances of the case.[97] Also trade competitors can file a complaint with the RCC.

(4) The NCC is an organization that assesses complaints regarding advertisements. The Commission does not pursue claims itself. Decisions taken by the RCC can include a 'recommendation', or if the complaint concerns advertising which propagates concepts, it delivers an 'opinion without commitment'. In other words, it recommends or advises that the advertiser discontinue the placement or use of the advertising in question. A recommendation can be made in two different ways:

(a) Private, in which case the recommendation by the Commission is only made known to the parties involved.

[97] See for example, Pres. District Court, Utrecht of December 12, 1990, BIE 1991, p. 269, in which the claim of a competitor was denied and where the court stated that if the advertisement of the defendant should be considered as a misleading and therefore as a wrongful act, it was not likely to be a violation of a right which must be considered to protect the plaintiff being a competitor. See furthermore Court of Appeal Den Bosch December 8, 1995, NJ 1996/456 in which the claim of a competitor was sustained. Both parties were active as distributors of fashion-ware. The defendant bought the leftover of the summer collection 1995 from an insolvent company. The advertisement of the defendant was found misleading because of the fact that the defendant promoted the collection as 'the summer collection 1995'. The court accepted the statement of the plaintiff that (i) the advertisement was misleading and (ii) that this fact was wrongful towards the plaintiff because, due to this wrongful conduct, the plaintiff lost turnover.

(b) Public, in which case the Commission distributes a press release announcing its ruling.[98] Also an 'opinion without commitment' can be either private or public.

When the complaint is sustained by the Commission, it can moreover (i) set conditions on the broadcast time of the radio and/or TV commercial submitted for evaluation, (ii) stipulate for the party whose advertising is found to violate the NRC, a term during which the recommendation of the commission is to be complied with, or (iii) impose measures as described in the contracts concluded between the *Stichting Reclame Code* and the organizations in consultation with which a Special Advertising Code was laid down.

Poland (4)

The advertisement related to the special offer should clearly indicate the date at which the offer expires or include the information that the offer only stands as long as the offered product or service is not sold out, art. 16.4 u.z.n.k.

Art. 19.1. u.z.n.k. states the persons who can sue: (1) consumer associations, (2) business organisations, (3) the President of the Office for Competition and Consumer Protection, and (4) the consumer ombudsmen in the counties and cities. They can claim injunctions, elimination and the delivery of a statement from the infringing party, art. 19.1. u.z.n.k. However, this right to sue is restricted. Art. 19.2. u.z.n.k. regulates that the provision of art. 19.1 does not apply to the following acts of unfair competition: misleading branding (arts. 5–7 u.z.n.k.), infringement of trade secrets (art. 11 u.z.n.k.), distribution of untrue or misleading information (art. 14 u.z.n.k.) and bribery (art. 15a u.z.n.k.). Therefore, the right to sue is limited in certain cases.

(1) No individual consumer can take legal proceedings to force A to desist from such advertising.

(2) A consumer organization can bring a claim on the behalf of the consumers.[99] The other organisations listed in art. 19 can bring such an action as well. The organizations (art. 19.1 u.z.n.k.) can bring a claim against an undertaking violating competition law, art. 16.4 u.z.n.k. The consumer organizations are entitled to represent the interests of consumers as a whole

[98] However, third parties are entitled to take notice of private and public recommendations alike (including the names of the parties involved).

[99] M. DuVall, *Dochodzenie roszczen w sprawach o zwalczanie nieuczciwej konkurencji*, in T. Szymanek (ed.), *Naruszenie praw na dobrach niematerialnych* (2001), p. 330.

on the basis of u.o.k.k. Business organizations at state or regional level that aim at protecting the interests of businesses are also entitled to sue.

(3) The infringed competitor has all the above-mentioned rights.[100]

(4) In Poland there are a president of the *Urząd Ochrony Konkurencji i Konsumentów* – UOKK (Office for Competition and Consumer Protection) and a consumer ombudsman.[101] Both are entitled to sue under art. 19.1. no. 3 and 4 u.z.n.k. Title IV of u.o.k.k. regulates the organization of competition and consumer protection. Chap. I of this title regards the President of the UOKK, who is the central government administration organ competent in the protection of competition and consumers supervised by the Prime Minister. Art 26 of u.o.k.k. lists the very broad powers of the office. Joint tasks carried out by the UOKK in the field of competition, consumer and state aid policies include, for example, exercising control over the observance by undertakings of the provisions on competition and consumer protection.

The particular tasks in the field of consumer policy comprise:

- addressing undertakings and their associations in matters of the protection of consumer rights and interests;
- addressing specialized units and relevant bodies of state control about monitoring observance of consumer rights;
- surveillance over the general safety of products intended for consumer use, providing assistance and cooperating with local self-governing authorities as well as national and foreign social organizations and other institutions whose statutory tasks include protection of consumer interests;
- initiating tests of products and services carried out by consumer organizations etc.

All these powers are executed thoroughly and the UOKK has a huge practical importance.

Portugal (4)

A uses the advertisement to mislead customers, because he does not have enough products at the advertised price. Therefore, the advertisement is considered deceptive under art. 317 lit. (e) CPI.

(1) However, C has no claim against A under this rule, because he is a consumer and only competitors' interests are directly protected by unfair competition rules. Consumers as a whole group are only indirectly

[100] I. Wiszniewska, *Polen*, in G. Schricker, note 362.

[101] I. Wiszniewska, *Polen*, in G. Schricker, note 36; see Case 4 (Children's swing).

protected. According to art. 273 CPI only competitors, competitors associations or consumer associations can take criminal proceedings against competitor A. Therefore, as regards unfair competition, the consumer C can only encourage a consumer association to bring a criminal or civil claim.

However, if the advertising deceived consumer C and it was the cause of a purchase, he has a claim to defend his own interest under consumer law. As stated above, the Portuguese statute of unfair competition is not a law protective of the individual consumer.[102] However, in cases where the consumer wants to react against a misleading advertising he has a claim under the CPub, which directly protects both consumers as a whole group and the individual consumer. In fact, under art. 11 CPub the individual consumer is protected from false advertising. As art. 11 CPub is a consumer protective rule, according to art. 483 para. 1 CC it would support a claim from consumer C to obtain compensation or a claim for an order to desist if he was directly injured: art. 10 para. 1 lit. (c) and art. 13 lit. (a), *Lei de Defesa do Consumidor* – LDCons[103] (Consumers' Protection Law). Normally in cases like this, the damages caused to individual consumers are insignificant, so consumers do not want to resort to civil actions. Instead, consumers complain to the consumer associations or to the Consumer Agency.

(2) Consumer associations are entitled to represent the interest of the consumers as a whole or the interests of their members according to art. 17 LDCons. Consumer associations can sue under the art. 13 lit. (b) LDCons. They can also bring criminal proceedings as with the crime of unfair competition (art. 273 CPI). Besides that, they can bring preventive claims under art. 10 LDCons and ask for compensation even if they are not directly injured, art. 12 and art. 13 lit. (b) LDCons. Business associations can sue competitors in unfair competition cases when a whole group of competitors is affected.

(3) Individual trade competitors can take measures against misleading advertising under art. 317 (e) CPI, under which competitors as a whole and the individual competitor are directly protected. In this case, there is not only a competitor that is targeted, but also a whole group of competitors who can be reached by the deceptive message. In this case, anyone who belongs to this group can bring a preventive claim (if there is a risk of damage) or a claim for an order to desist (if there is an illegal act that continues) or a compensation claim (if he

[102] O. Ascensão, *Concorrência Desleal* (2002), p. 138. [103] Lei n. 24/96, de 31 de Julho.

suffers damage).[104] However, trade competitors could not react under the Advertising Code, which only protects consumers.[105]

(4) The public authority competent for monitoring the legality of advertising is the *Instituto Nacional da Defesa do Consumidor* (National Consumer Institution)[106] that according to the public interest protects all consumers. The *Instituto do Consumidor* is the Portuguese authority that monitors the observance of advertising standards and can apply administrative sanctions, like fines and other ancillary sanctions. The fines that can be imposed are considered to be ridiculously low.[107] It can also sue competitors claiming an injunction or prohibition.

Spain (4)

(1) C, as a consumer, is entitled to sue in respect of unfair competition acts according to art. 19 LCD[108] and art. 25 et seq. LGP. Nevertheless, if A's activity is deemed to be an act of misleading advertisement, C will be entitled by art. 25 *Ley General de Publicidad* – LGP (Advertising Act) to sue the advertiser and request the misleading publicity. For A's advertisement to be considered as misleading the requirements of art. 4 LGP must be fulfilled (i.e. that the information might mislead the public and affect its economic behaviour). If the advertiser does not desist, A would be entitled to bring an action before a civil court: art. 27 para. 4 LGP.

[104] A. Menezes Leitão, *Estudo sobre os interesses protegidos e a legitimidade na concorrência desleal*, Revista da Faculdade de Direito da Universidade de Lisboa, vol. XXXII (1996), pp. 111 et seq.

[105] O. Ascensão, *Concorrência Desleal* (2002), pp. 142 et seq.

[106] Art. 21 LDCons and art. 1 Decreto-Lei n. 234/99 de 25 de Junho; art. 38 CPI.

[107] J. Möllering, (1991) 37 WRP 634 (637); G. Schricker, (1994) 42 GRUR Int. 819 (822).

[108] Artículo 19 LCD. Legitimación activa.
1. Cualquier persona que participe en el mercado, cuyos intereses económicos resulten directamente perjudicados o amenazados por el acto de competencia desleal, está legitimada para el ejercicio de las acciones previstas en los cinco primeros números del artículo anterior.
La acción de enriquecimiento injusto solo podrá ser ejercitada por el titular de la posición jurídica violada.
2. Las acciones contempladas en los números 1 a 4 del artículo anterior podrán ejercitarse además por las siguientes entidades:
Las asociaciones, corporaciones profesionales o representativas de intereses económicos cuando resulten afectados los intereses de sus miembros.
Las asociaciones que, según sus estatutos, tengan por finalidad la protección del consumidor. La legitimación quedará supeditada en este supuesto a que el acto de competencia desleal perseguido afecte directamente a los intereses de los consumidores.

(2) A competitor of A or a consumer association will also be legally able to sue A, as far as his behaviour will directly affect consumers' interests. The consumer associations may request the advertiser to cease or rectify the illegal advertisement, art. 25 para. 1 LGP. Moreover, art. 8 para. 2 of *Ley General para Defensa de los Consumidores y Usuarios*[109] – LGDCU (Act for the Defence of Consumers and Users) declares that concerning false or misleading offers, promotion or advertisement of goods, activities or services, the consumer associations will be legally entitled to initiate and intervene in those administrative procedures tending to its cessation.

(3) In order for a competitor to bring a claim against A, his economic interests must be harmed or menaced by the unfair act, as provided in art. 19 para. 1 LCD. The burden of proof rests on the plaintiff, who must prove that the unfair act has been committed and has affected his interests.

(4) Competent administrative bodies, such as the *Instituto Nacional del Consumo* and similar organizations from the regional or local governments and the public prosecutor, are also entitled to sue the advertiser on the grounds of art. 25 LGP. They are not very active. Administrative bodies usually have the right to impose fines on firms when they behave against the general interest of consumers; so they do not apply private law.

Sweden (4)

Sec. 4 MFL contains a general clause, which encompasses a prohibition against so-called 'bait advertising', i.e. to advertise a certain product fully aware that it will be impossible to satisfy the demand. The misleading effects of this behaviour may be neutralized if the undertaking in the advertisement stipulates that there is only a certain number of products available at that price.[110]

(1) Reacting to unfair trade practices is not a civil law issue and thus consumers themselves have no standing in these cases. Under MFL C does not, as an individual consumer, have the right to take legal action in order to force A to abstain from such advertising in the future. First, a consumer does not have a claim for an injunction under the Swedish MFL and, secondly, ordinary courts are not competent to judge on such claims under general rules. It should be observed, though, that consumers, since the introduction of the act in 1995, have a right to *damages* (see Governmental Bill 1994/95:123) and consequently have standing. In

[109] Ley General para la Defensa de los Consumidores y Usarios 26/1984 of July 19; reinforced by Ley 39/2002 of october 28.

[110] U. Bernitz, *Marknadsföringslagen* (1997), p. 76.

the application of consumer rights, consumers do not always have individual standing, such as in the case of the MFL. Furthermore, for obvious reasons, the consumers in practice seldom regard ordinary courts as a real alternative to settle their disputes with commercial undertakings.[111]

(2) A consumer organization may, but is not obliged to, take legal action. Under sec. 38 subsec. 2 MFL it is perfectly possible for such an organization to claim an injunction. An injunction order is normally sanctioned by periodic penalty payments. In case an organization has applied for an injunction and periodic penalty payments, it has standing to claim that the latter be imposed in case of infringement of the injunction. There is no single recent case in which a consumer association has brought an action of its own in the courts under the MFL. The explanation is, primarily, the existence of a state system with a Consumer Ombudsman and a Consumer Agency, which normally take care of the consumer interests.[112]

On January 1, 2003 a new act came into force, which allows a group of consumers with the same interest to bring a group action.[113] This act is applicable where a group of consumers raises a number of similar claims which come within the jurisdiction of ordinary courts under the general rules of the Code of Civil and Criminal Procedure. Under the new Swedish act on group actions, it is now possible for a group of consumers, an organization or a public agency to bring a so-called group action. Such an action will require that the members of the group have similar reasons for their actions and that their claims cannot be satisfied equally well on an individual basis. Under sec. 5 it is provided that organizations may bring a group action where the organization promotes the interests of consumers or employees. We would say that applying the new act in a situation such as that in Case 4, suffers from the same problem as where a consumer organization applies for an injunction as if it were a number of consumers. A claim for injunction may not be raised by a consumer before the ordinary courts applying general procedural rules.

Individual undertakings as well as associations of undertakings have a right to do this, and they quite often make claims concerning, for example, misleading advertising. However, in Sweden it is most unusual that associations use their right to pursue such claims.

[111] Regarding the Public Complaint Tribunal, see below Case 5 (Discontinued models).
[112] U. Bernitz, *Sweden*, in R. Schulze and H. Schulte-Nölke, p. 7.
[113] Act on Group Actions (2002:599).

These organizations probably lean on the public agency, expecting it to pursue such claims. Undertakings and consumers can also claim compensation for damages if any of the articles in the act have been breached.

(3) It is expected that the competitor takes care of his rights on his own since the Consumer Ombudsman only feels responsible for consumers.[114] Competitors have a right to take steps to stop the continuance of future similar advertisements, i.e. by means of an injunction (sec. 39 MFL). To have standing, a competitor must be concerned by the action taken by A. An alternative step against the advertisement would be to obtain an order against A that A in the future must provide information in respect of the number of items for sale. Such orders are provided for by sec. 15 MFL. The requirements for bringing a claim for an *information order* are the same as for an injunction under sec. 14 and the subjects with standing are also the same; that is, the Consumer Ombudsman, undertakings concerned and organizations.

(4) In the field of unfair competition (covered by the MFL), there is a public consumer agency called *Konsumentverket*,[115] which ensures that the public policy for consumers is pursued. One of the responsibilities of the authority is to make sure that consumers have a strong position on the market. The director general for this consumer authority has another function as well, as the Consumer Ombudsman.[116] The Consumer Ombudsman represents consumer interests in relation to undertakings and pursues legal action in consumer's interest. The Consumer Ombudsman is responsible for ensuring that companies abide by the laws and rules in the consumer field and ensures that consumer rights are respected. The Ombudsman is empowered to take legal action against companies who violate market laws. The Consumer Ombudsman may bring cases to specially designated courts (special courts). The office is linked with an old tradition of ombudsmen in Sweden. The Consumer Ombudsman may bring a claim for an injunction or an information order.[117] Moreover, the Consumer Ombudsman has, according to sec. 39 MFL of the act, the primary competence to take action concerning administrative fines. The reason for this is that administrative fines are punitive in character.

In case the Consumer Ombudsman chooses not to bring an action for administrative fines, a concerned individual undertaking or an

[114] U. Bernitz, (1996) 44 GRUR Int. 433 (436). [115] www.konsumentverket.se.
[116] Konsumentombudsmannen, KO. [117] Sec. 38 MFL.

organisation of undertakings may bring such action. The latter two thus have supplementary standing.

Summary (4)

1. *Competitor*

a) Rights of claim for actual legal infringement

In Germany the UWG 2004 limits the right of claim to competitors, that is enterprises which are in competition with the infringer as suppliers or buyers of goods or services, § 2 no. 3 UWG. In this way the scope for claims is limited in comparison to the previous legal position. The so-called 'abstractly concerned competitor' no longer merits protection. In *Sweden* competitors have a right to takes steps to stop the continuance of future similar advertisements by means of injunction.[118] To have standing the competitor must be concerned by the action of the violator.[119] In Denmark competitors may bring an action before the courts as they will be directly affected by the advertising and on this basis must be supposed to have sufficient legal interest in instituting proceedings in the courts. In order for a competitor to bring a claim against the infringer, in Spain his economic interests must be harmed or menaced by the unfair act, as established in art. 19 para. 1 LCD. The burden of proof lies on the plaintiff, who must prove before the judge that the unfair act has been committed and has affected his interests. In France the competitor can only sue in cases of art. 1382, 1383 cc. He has to prove fault, damage, and causation. However claims under art. 1382 cc would seem to be rare.[120] In Italy the competitor can also pursue a tort claim under art. 2598 cc.[121]

b) Broad rights of claim

In Austria competitors are entitled to claim an injunction under §§ 2, 14 para. 1 UWG along with all other enforcement possibilities. Competitors have the right of claim independent of whether they are commercially affected by the confusing advertisement. The right to claim is similarly broad in Portugal. Individual trade competitors can take

[118] This ensues from sec. 39 MFL.

[119] Besides an order to cease and desist the competitor can sue for an information order in Sweden.

[120] T. Dreier and S. von Lewinsky, *Frankreich*, in G. Schricker, note 82.

[121] Corte di Appello di Roma, September 23, 1985.

measures against the misleading advertising under art. 260 lit. (e) CPI, whereby competitors as a whole and the individual competitor are directly protected. In this case it is not only one competitor that is harmed, but all competitors who can be affected by the deceptive message. In this case, anyone who belongs to this group can bring a preventive claim (if there is a risk of damage), or a claim for an order to desist (if there is an illegal act that continues), or a compensation claim (if he suffers damage). However, trade competitors cannot take action under the CPub, which only directly protects consumers. In Poland all claims are open to the injured competitor.

Evaluation

(1) Under the Misleading and Comparative Advertising Directive 84/450/EEC 'persons or organizations regarded under national laws as having a legitimate interest' can impose a prohibition on misleading advertisement.[122] Against this the Injunction Directive 98/27/EC designates only qualified institutions as claimants but not the competitor.

(2) In most Member States a legitimate interest or actual legal infringement must be proved (Germany, Sweden, Finland, Denmark, England, France, Italy, and Spain). This requirement corresponds to the legitimate interest of the Misleading and Comparative Advertising Directive 84/450/EEC. Such a criterion is also sensible if the rights of a competitor are directly infringed, as in cases of trade libel or imitation. In these cases there is a high likelihood that the competitor will bring proceedings against legal infringement. In the scholarly literature it is correctly emphasized that the competitor knows best what the competition is doing.[123]

The extension of claim opportunities to every competitor (formerly in Germany, now in Poland and Portugal), however, brings opportunities and risks. The competitor can, like associations or the state, become the agent of third parties. Undertakings with a strong market position could abuse the right of claim in order to further strengthen their market power.

(3) Conversely, a right of claim does not further assist in the enforcement of unfair competition law, if the legal infringement is directed at

[122] Art. 4 para. 1 subpara. 2.

[123] G. Schricker, *Möglichkeiten zur Verbesserung des Schutzes der Verbraucher und des funktionsfähigen Wettbewerbs im Recht des unlauteren Wettbewerbs* (1975) 139 ZHR 208 (233); G. Schricker, *Die Rolle des Zivil-, Straf- und Verwaltungsrechts bei der Bekämpfung unlauteren Wettbewerbs* (1973) 21 GRUR Int. 694 (697)

the consumer, as for example in cases of harassment or canvassing of customers. Not without cause therefore is the competitor's possibility of claim not seen as a complete solution. It therefore requires a sensible augmentation, for example through a right of claim for consumer associations[124] or supervision by the authorities.[125] Finally, it should be considered whether the competitor should be given more attractive claim objects, such as various forms of damages.[126]

c) Lack of right to claim or little practical relevance

In some countries the right to claim is seldom exercised by the competitor. In Finland, cases are usually brought forward only by direct competitors. In the literature this right has also been limited, but the interpretation has been relatively wide (for example, an association representing supermarket and market owners had legal standing in a case regarding marketing of soap). Thus trade can be affected even if there would be no evidence of a loss of sales etc. or any contact between the claimant and the tradesman whose practices are claimed to be contrary to the SopMenL. A word of warning: there is as yet no case law on § 3 of the Act on Proceedings in the Market Court. In addition there is no right to claim for competitors in certain areas. In the USA competitors may not claim against unconformity with the FTCA. In England competitors, to the extent that the CMAR 1988 are involved, only have the opportunity to file a complaint to the OFT, under reg. 4(1) of the CMAR 1988. Also, they can complain to the Advertising Standards Authority. Only if tort case law applies may competitors claim directly.[127]

Evaluation

(1) Under the Misleading and Comparative Advertising Directive 84/450/EEC either persons or organisations which according to national law have a legitimate interest in the prohibition of misleading advertising may claim relief.[128] The Misleading and Comparative Advertising Directive 84/450/EEC does not require that competitors should be able to claim. Regulation by administrative authorities is sufficient. If authorities do intervene it cannot be objected that in cases of misleading and comparative advertising state authorities intervene initially or exclusively. With the consolidation procedure in France and Portugal

[124] See B.II.2. [125] See below B.II.4. [126] See above B.I.6.
[127] See Case 1 (Risky bread). [128] Art. 4 par. 1 subpara. 2.

competitors have the further possibility to enforce civil law claims in criminal proceedings.

(2) In almost all states the competitor has a right of claim which is also frequently exercised. However, it is apparent that in Nordic member states competitors are usually the exception. This is explicable in terms of the active role of the consumer ombudsman and in English law in terms of alternative dispute resolution mechanisms.[129] In the USA there are comprehensive possibilities of claim for the competitor at state level.

As the competitor is the first to perceive the legal infringement, England should also introduce a right of claim for competitors for infringement of the CMAR in terms of misleading advertising. Moreover, the right of claim for competitors should be introduced at the European level.

2. *Consumer associations*

a) Reasons for lack of attractiveness – novelty, subsidiarity, lacking financial substance

In Austria the Association for Consumer Information (§ 14 para. 1 UWG) may claim in cases of misleading advertising under §1 UWG and § 2 para. 1 UWG. In the implementation of the injunction directive 98/27/EC the claim can also be brought by consumer organizations from other member states in the Union, provided the origin of the infringement of misleading advertising pursuant to § 1 or § 2 para. 1 UWG is in Austria and to the extent that the protected interests of the consumer organizations in these member states are affected and that the object of the claim is justified (§ 14 para. 2 UWG). In Germany consumer associations have enjoyed a right of claim since 1967. Since the amendment of the UWG in 2004 consumer associations may also bring a claim for surrender of profits in favour of the state. Foreign associations also have a claim if they are listed with the European commission: § 8 para. 3 no. 3 UWG (ex-§ 13 para. 2 no. 3 s. 1 UWG). In Poland consumer organizations can bring a claim on behalf of consumers. The other organisations listed in art. 19 u.z.n.k. can also bring an action. These organisations and the president of the OCCP (art. 19.1 u.z.n.k.) can bring a claim against an undertaking violating competition law. In Sweden consumer organizations can sue. In Finland consumer associations have a secondary right

[129] See below BIII.4.

to bring a case in the market court if the ombudsman refuses to do so. In these circumstances the associations represent the interests of the consumers. Based on § 19 MFL in Denmark consumer associations may bring action before the courts. It follows from the drafts to the MFL that consumer associations are meant to play an important role at the enforcement of the MFL. In 1999, when the Unfair Terms in Consumer Contract Regulations 1999 were adopted,[130] consumer associations obtained in England for the first time the opportunity of legal standing in English courts, limited to the field of unfair contract terms in consumer contracts. Only the Consumers' Association (CA) was granted legal standing. In 2001, the Stop Now Order (EC Directives) Regulations 2001[131] were adopted, implementing Directive 98/27/EC on injunctions. However, their scope was restricted to the EC Directives listed in the annex to Injunctive Directive 98/27/EC.[132] Attracting customers is not covered by any of these directives, whereas the situation of comparative advertisement is somewhat unclear.[133] On November 7, 2002, the Enterprise Act received Royal Assent. Its chap. 8 that deals with injunctions came into effect on June 20, 2003.[134] The Stop Now Order (EC Directives) Regulations 2001 were repealed.[135] According to sec. 213(4), the Secretary of State may designate a person or body which is not a private body only if this person or body satisfies such criteria as the Secretary of State specifies by order.[136] This list of criteria has been specified by the Enterprise Act 2002 (Part 8 Designated Enforcers: Criteria for Designation, Designation of Public Bodies as Designated

[130] The UTCCR 1999 replaced the UTCCR 1994. They have implemented Directive 93/13/EC on unfair contract terms.

[131] S.I. 1422 of 2001.

[132] For details see P. Rott (2001) 24 JCP 401 (420 et seq.).

[133] The annex to Directive 98/27/EC merely lists Directive 84/450/EEC concerning misleading advertising but not 'as amended'. In contrast, it mentions Directive 87/102/EEC 'as last amended by (. . .)'.

[134] See the Enterprise Act 2002 (Commencement No. 3, Transitional and Transitory Provisions and Savings) Order 2003, S.I. 1397. For a description of the new rules see the consultation paper 'Consumer reforms', published by the Office of Fair Trading in August 2002, available at www.oft.gov.uk. See also H.-W. Micklitz and P. Rott, *Richtlinie 98/27/EG*, in E. Grabitz, M. Hilf and M. Wolf (eds.), *Das Recht der Europäischen Union* (2004).

[135] Schedule 26 of the Enterprise Act.

[136] In addition, consumer associations have legal standing if they are 'Community enforcers' in the terms of sec. 213 (5), i.e. if they are listed in the Official Journal of the EC in pursuance of art. 4 (3) of Directive 98/27/EC. Until now, no English consumer association has been listed, see the Commission's Communication, [2002] OJ C 273 of November 9, 2002, p. 7.

Enforcers and Transitional Provisions) Order 2003.[137] As the Stop Now Order (EC Directives) Regulations 2001, Part 8 of the Enterprise Act gives priority to enforcement of consumer law by the OFT and therefore restricts legal action by consumer associations, even if they are designated as enforcers by the Secretary of State, in many ways, in particular through consultation requirements.[138] However, comparative advertisement is still not covered by the scope of Part 8 of the Enterprise Act. Thus, consumer associations cannot take action in cases of comparative advertising. In French literature it is always stated there can be no action by a consumer's association in unfair competition law.[139] However consumer associations can claim in cases of infringement of the consumer code. Actually, the main cases of interest to the consumer are codified in the consumer code and these are also the provisions where a representative action is possible. Nevertheless, such claims are brought in only 2.3 per cent of cases.[140]

In Italy, consumer associations which meet the requirements laid down under l. 281/1998[141] can take action against any infringement of consumer rights listed by the same law. Only consumer associations listed in a register kept by the Ministry of Industry may take action against infringements of l. 281/1998; requirements for being included in such list aim at ensuring that the association does actually have a capacity to represent consumers. The act establishes a special procedure of conciliation for consumer disputes, whereby consumer associations can commence such a procedure in front of a special panel of the Trade Chamber (*Camera di commercio*), a mechanism created by l. 580/1993 (art. 2, 4a).[142] The right of claim applies, however, only to misleading and comparative advertising[143] and not to the field of application of the cc. Some legal scholars proposed that the provision of art. 2601 cc, enabling trade associations to take action

[137] S.I. 2003, 1399. For details, see the Department of Trade and Industry document 'Designation as an Enforcer for Part 8 of the Enterprise Act 2002: Guidance for Private Bodies Seeking a Designation under Section 213'. Reg. 4(2) of the Stop Now Orders Regulations (2001) had also listed a number of criteria. For details, see P. Rott (2001) 24 JCP 401 (423–4).

[138] For details on restrictions under the Stop Now Orders Regulations (2001), see P. Rott (2001) 24 JPC, 401 (422 et seq.).

[139] M. Malaurie-Vignal, *Droit de la concurrence* (2nd edn 2002), p. 122.

[140] The study is from 1983 though, see H. Puttfarken and N. Franke, *Die action civile der Verbände in Frankreich*, in J. Basedow, K. Hopt, H. Kötz, and D. Baetge, p. 182.

[141] Amended by Legislative Decree No. 224/2001.

[142] L. Antoniolli and E. Ioriatti, *Italy*, in R. Schulze and H. Schulte-Nölke, 1(e).

[143] C. Käser, *Effizienz des Rechtsschutzes im deutschen und italienischen Wettbewerbsrecht* (2003), p. 39.

against unfair competition should be amended in order to include consumer associations, but such proposal was never followed by legislative provisions.[144] Up to now, although four years have passed since l. 281/98 was issued, and although the importance of such act has been stressed by many legal scholars, there is practically no case law applying its provisions. Though there are many consumer associations in Italy, they are still quite litigation-adverse. Possible explanations may be found in high costs and long delays in civil litigation, which make resort to administrative proceedings (and, sometimes, to out-of-court settlements) more attractive for consumer associations. On the other hand, control of misleading advertising by the *Autorità Garante*, though not inefficient as a whole, has not yet solved some quite important problems: for example, procedures are too lengthy, and usually the cease-and-desist order is issued when the advertising campaign has already reached its natural end. In Spain, the consumer associations may request the advertiser to cease or rectify the illegal publicity (art. 25 para. 1 LGP). Moreover, art. 8 para. 2 LGDCU declares that concerning false or misleading offers, promotion or publicity of goods, activities or services, the consumer associations will be legally entitled to initiate and intervene in those administrative procedures tending to its cessation (reinforced by Ley 39/2002). In Portugal, consumer associations are entitled to represent the interest of consumers as a whole or the interests of its members according to the art. 17 LDCons. Consumer associations can sue under art. 13 lit. (b) LDCons. Finally consumer association claims are possible in the Netherlands and Belgium,[145] but not in the USA.

Evaluation

(1) Already under the Misleading and Comparative Advertising Directive 84/450/EEC either persons *or* organisations could claim which had a legitimate interest under national law.[146] With the formulation of legitimate interest the possibility was already introduced that consumer associations proceed against infringements. An association claim was thereby not necessarily involved as Member States retained

[144] With its decision of January 21, 1988, note 59, the Corte Costituzionale dismissed the motion for declaration of unconstitutionality of art. 2601, for infringement of the principle of equality (art. 3 of the Italian Constitution), stating that the Constitution did not bind the legislature to enable consumer association to sue under the law of unfair competition, and that it was up to the legislature to provide for adequate alternative means of protection of consumer interests.

[145] F. Beier (1984) 32 GRUR Int. 61 (67), (1985) IIC 139 (153).

[146] Art. 4 para. 1 subpara. 2.

the possibility alongside proceedings in the court to institute an administrative proceeding against the infringements.[147] The Injunction Directive 98/27/EC designates qualified entities as entitled to claim alongside independent public bodies and also consumer associations.[148] However, legal harmonization was again undermined to the extent that member states can decide whether they include consumer associations alongside independent public bodies. They may decide between consumer associations and public bodies.[149] In addition the Injunction Directive 98/27/EC expressly does not apply to comparative advertising and the Product Price Directive 98/6/EC.[150]

(2) Although in all Member States of the European Union the legal framework for consumer association claims has been introduced, the results are disappointing. With the exception of France there is almost no member state in which consumer associations play a significant role. This has various causes. In Italy and England it may be because the right of claim for consumer associations was first introduced with the Injunction Directive 98/27/EC. In Sweden there is no single recent case in which a consumer association has brought an action of its own in the courts under the MFL. The explanation is primarily the existence of the state system of a consumer ombudsman and a consumer agency, which normally takes care of consumer interests.[151] There is a comparable situation in Finland and Denmark. In addition the right of claim is partly subsidiary, in that it only applies if the consumer ombudsman does not himself claim.[152] In Germany there has been an association claim for consumer associations since 1965.[153] Usually, only completely certain infringements are pursued.[154] Consumer claims are in part financed by competitors and in this way conceal themselves behind consumer claims.[155] According to recent data consumer associations

[147] Incorrectly A. Beater (2003) 11 ZEuP 11 (36), on the assumption that there is a duty to establish the possibility of a legal action taken by an association in the Misleading and Comparative Advertising Directive 84/450/EEC.

[148] Art. 3 lit. (a) and (b). [149] Art. 3 lit. (a) Injunction Directive 98/27/EC: ‘and/or’.

[150] See Injunction Directive 98/27/EC Annex; correctly A. Beater (2003) 11 ZEuP 11 (37).

[151] U. Bernitz, *Sweden*, in R. Schulze and H. Schulte-Nölke, 7.

[152] E.g. in Finland, see above Case 4 (Children’s swing).

[153] A. Beater, *Unlauterer Wettbewerb* (2002), § 3 note 117.

[154] K. Tonner (1987) 40 NJW 1917 (1922) referring to a study of R. von Falckenstein, *Die Bekämpfung unlauterer Geschäftspraktiken durch Verbraucherverbände* (1977), p. 506.

[155] W. Nordemann et al., *Wettbewerbs- und Markenrecht* (9th edn 2003), note 73; G. Schricker (1996) 44 GRUR Int. 473 (478) regarding trade associations; G. Jennes and P. Schotthöfer, *Germany*, in J. Maxeiner and P. Schotthöfer, p. 203.

are starting to take a more active role.[156] But the fact remains that certain infringements are still not pursued.[157]

(3) It should be questioned whether the priority of the consumer ombudsman in relation to consumer associations is in conformity with European law. For this the consumer ombudsman would have to be a person or organization pursuant to the Misleading and Comparative Advertising Directive 84/450/EEC. The concept of person could be challenged in that this means a natural person. In addition, the consumer ombudsman cannot be an organization. Such an understanding is, however, clearly too narrow as the Injunction Directive expressly designates independent public bodies as claimants. This includes the Swedish Consumer Ombudsman or the English Director of Fair Trading.[158] From the European point of view it is correct that first public law bodies proceed against the infringement and only then can consumer associations claim. Not without reason therefore in Sweden, where the Consumer Ombudsman is an active participant, the extension of competencies of consumer associations was seen as rather superfluous.[159] In addition, public law proceedings, as shown by the experience in France and Portugal, are actually successful. In Germany the limited financial condition of consumer associations is criticized.[160] To this extent the right of claim for consumer associations is not satisfactory. This constitutes an implementation deficit because the Injunction Directive 98/27/EC imposes an obligation that either consumer associations or public law bodies can proceed against anticompetitive conduct. Even less satisfactory is the legal situation in England. Consumer associations and other institutions entitled to submit cessation claims enjoy no privileges with regard to the risk of costs, which is seen as a welcome limitation on their activities by the Department of Trade and Industry.[161] There is also an implementation deficit if in England the consumer associations cannot claim or may

[156] German consumer associations claim that they record 80% of the relevant cases, see statement of Verbraucherzentrale Bundesverband e.V. in front of the law panel of the European Parliament of February 19, 2004, see www.thomas-moellers.de. The legislators point out that consumer associations only moderately used their right to sue, Begr. RegE, *UWG*, BT-Drs. 15/1487, p. 42.

[157] A.I.1(b). [158] D. Baetge (1999) 112 ZZP 329 (337).

[159] P. Doeffel and J. Scherpe, *Grupptalan – Die Bündelung gleichberechtigter Interessen im schwedischen Recht*, in J. Basedow, K. Hopt, H. Kötz, and D. Baetge, p. 429 (439).

[160] See the findings by G. Schricker, *Möglichkeiten zur Verbesserung des Schutzes der Verbraucher und des funktionsfähigen Wettbewerbs im Recht des unlauteren Wettbewerbs* (1975) 139 ZHR 208 (233).

[161] P. Rott (2001) 24 JCP 429 et seq. with further proof.

claim in a subsidiary capacity and the OFT – in contrast to the Nordic states – performs its regulatory tasks inadequately.

(4) So as to reduce the risk of liability for consumer associations, a guarantee fund has been suggested.[162] In addition a right of claim for consumer associations on the basis of the comparative advertising and the Product Price Directive 98/6/EC should be created. In its recent proposal on a codified version of the Injunction Directive, Directive 97/55/EC appears in the annex, but not the Product Price Directive 98/6/EC.[163]

b) Mistaken enhancement of attractiveness: surrender of profits

By means of the reformed UWG the German legislature intended to close a gap in the law[164] by introducing in § 10 UWG a new claim to surrender of profits. If profits are gained at the expense of a number of customers, a claim from associations may be brought in the interest of the state.

Evaluation

The claim to surrender of profits is of doubtful value to consumer associations. Extensive rights of discovery are necessary to determine the profits. In addition the consumer association bears the risks of proceedings in favour of the state. However, precisely the opposite is required in order to strengthen consumer associations. Finally, it is not apparent why in Germany the state should take the profits. This is why it has been described as a foolish act.[165]

c) Increasing attractiveness: class actions, claim for immaterial losses, consolidated proceedings

In Sweden and there is not only a right of claim for consumer associations but also class actions by consumers. In addition on January 1,

[162] G. Schricker (1975) 139 ZHR 208 (243).

[163] Proposal for a Directive of the European Parliament and of the Council on injunctions for the protection of consumers' interests (codified version) of May 12, 2003, COM (2003) 241 final, Annex I No. 1.

[164] Begr. RegE, *UWG*, BT-Drs. 15/1487, Begr. Zu § 10, p. 23.

[165] A. Stadler and H.-W. Micklitz (2003) 49 WRP 559 (562). For a contrary view see the prognosis by R. Sack (2003) 49 WRP 549 (555), fearing that professional associations for the surrender of profits might develop and assert the reimbursement of their expenses.

2003 a new act came into force which allows for a group of consumers with the same interest to bring a group action. That act, however, is applicable where a group of consumers raises a number of similar claims which come within the jurisdiction of ordinary courts under the general rules of the Code of Civil and Criminal Procedure. Such an action will require that the members of the group have similar reasons for their actions and that their claims cannot be satisfied equally well on an individual basis. Under sec. 5 MFL it is provided that organizations may bring a group action where the organization promotes the interests of consumers or employees. One could say that applying the new act in a situation such as that in Case 5, suffers from the same problem where a consumer organization applies for an injunction as if it were a group of consumers. A claim for an injunction may not be raised by a consumer before the ordinary courts applying general procedural rules.

In France these representative actions are seen in the legal literature as a form of class action. However, the French principle of procedural law is respected, that is no one can bring a claim via another person. Thus, an action always requires the mandate of at least two consumers: Art. L 422-1 et seq. CCons expands the possibility of representative claims for damages which arise for several consumers against the same enterprise for a common reason, so long as at least two of the injured parties have commissioned the action. Consumer associations can bring criminal proceedings for damages through the action civil. In 97.4 per cent of cases consumer associations have directly participated in the criminal proceedings of the authorities.[166] Often, however, only one symbolic euro is awarded.[167] In Denmark the Consumer Ombudsman can enforce different compensatory claims in one procedure. Finally, there is the consumer association claim for immaterial loss in Greece (art. 10 para. 9 lit. (b) L. 2251/1994).[168] In Portugal consumer agencies can claim compensation even if they are not directly injured. Consumer associations can also be criminal prosecutors in court

[166] H. Puttfarken and N. Franke, *Die action civile der Verbände in Frankreich*, in J. Basedow, K. Hopt, H. Kötz, and D. Baetge, p. 182.

[167] J. Keßler and H.-W. Micklitz, *Die Harmonisierung des Lauterkeitsrechts in den Mitgliedstaaten der Europäischen Gemeinschaft und die Reform des UWG* (2003), pp. 121 et seq.; H. Puttfarken and N. Franke, in *Die action civile der Verbände in Frankreich*, in J. Basedow, K. Hopt, H. Kötz, and D. Baetge, pp. 149 (152 et seq.).

[168] A. Papathoma-Baetge, *Die Verbandsklage im griechischen Recht*, in J. Basedow, K. Hopt, H. Kötz, and D. Baetge, p. 187 (201).

proceedings such as for the offence of unfair competition (art. 273 CPI). The legal position is the same in Greece. In Germany, although consolidated proceedings are possible in practice they are irrelevant.

Evaluation

(1) It is interesting that in some states consumer associations can elect whether to claim themselves or to join the public law proceedings (France, Italy and Portugal). In these states participation in the public law proceedings is significantly more attractive to consumer associations than claiming themselves. In this way they avoid the risks entailed and in addition profit from the investigation principles of public law.

(2) In order to ensure that the harm of consumers is better compensated against the unlawful conduct of the infringer, further proposals could be considered. Consumer associations should not only have cessation claims but should also be able to claim for reparation of the actual harm.

If it is true that consumers do not exercise their rights because the loss is not sufficiently great, this also applies if one attempts to solve the case through contract or tort law. If instead consumer associations were allowed to claim for the harm to a consumer, it would be effective because consumer associations are in a better position to claim for such harm than the individual consumer. This form of class action is possible in Sweden and France. Alternatively, one could consider extending to consumer associations their own compensatory claim for immaterial loss, as is the case in France, Portugal and Greece.

Therefore, the additional financing of consumer associations or the introduction of a claim for surrender of profits would seem to be of limited value in enhancing the effectiveness of legal protection. On the other hand the combination of attractive objects of claim (immaterial loss) and the public law route (consolidated proceedings) would seem to be particularly attractive for consumer associations. In Germany the MPI expertise has suggested compensatory claims. Payments should be devoted to the general public benefit after deduction of costs of the injured party.[169]

[169] See K. Hopt and D. Baetge, in J. Basedow, K. Hopt, H. Kötz and D. Baetge, p. 1 (5). According to art. 8 of their draft in H.-W. Micklitz and J. Keßler (2002) 50 GRUR Int. 885 (901) the Commission should consider the introduction of a collective claim for damages after two years.

3. *Business associations*

a) Broad rights to claim

In Austria private associations for the protection of competition can claim for an injunction: §§ 2, 14 para. 1 UWG. Pursuant to § 14 para. 1 UWG a cessation claim can also be brought by some federal organisations. Similarly, in Poland state or regional organizations may claim where their tasks under their charter include protection of the interests of undertakings. In Sweden individual undertakings as well as associations of undertakings have a right to sue. In Finland even an organization representing these businesses would have a right to bring cases to the market court. This is because a practice which is contrary to fair trade can affect all businesses in the branch. In Finland competitors and consumer associations can ask the market court to forbid certain marketing and demand that it not be renewed, only if the Ombudsman has refused to bring the case forward. As under § 19 para. 1 MFL only a legal interest has to be shown, in Denmark business associations can also claim. Under French law professional associations can bring claims for damages and injunction before the civil and penal courts. In Italy art. 2601 cc states that in cases where unfair competition is harmful towards an entire category of business, trade associations representing such businesses may take legal action against such acts. Therefore, while consumer associations are never entitled to sue under the law of unfair competition (as we have seen, the legal basis for their actions may be found elsewhere), trade associations quite often are. In addition trade associations may bring the group action.[170] The claim is also possible in the USA.[171]

b) Lack of right to claim

In England trade associations have no legal rights to claim in a representative capacity. This is because in the past only the injured party could claim, if at all, and only in recent times have consumer associations been accorded additional rights.

c) Limited rights to claim

The German legislature in the UWG amendment limited the ability to sue of associations for the promotion of trade interests. Under § 8 para. 3

[170] C. Käser, *Effizienz des Rechtsschutzes im deutschen und italienischen Wettbewerbsrecht* (2003), p. 145.

[171] *Camel Hair & Cashmere Institute of America, Inc. v. Associated Dry Goods Corp.*, 799 F.2d 6 (1st Cir. 1986).

no. 2 UWG (ex-§ 13 para. 2 no. 2 UWG) business associations can only claim if the association has a significant number of business members and sufficient personnel and material resources. The business association cannot claim abroad and foreign associations cannot claim in Germany. In addition the enforcement of the claim may not be abusive. This is the case if the principal purpose of the claim is to enable recovery of the costs of legal proceedings: § 8 para. 4 UWG (ex-§ 13 para. 4 UWG). In Portugal business associations can sue against competitors in unfair competition cases when a whole group of competitors is attacked.

Evaluation

(1) The requirements of the Misleading and Comparative Advertising Directive 84/450/EEC are vague. The circle of persons with rights to claim includes persons or organizations which have a legitimate interest in the enforcement of claims.[172] Against this the Injunction Directive 98/27/EC designates qualified entities but limits these to the protection of the collective interests of the consumer.[173] In this way the member state is free to decide whether it allows competition associations as claimants. All states with the exception of the United Kingdom have decided in favour of this.

(2) In Germany and Austria claims by trade associations are dominant.[174] Already in 1896 the possibility to claim was introduced in the UWG.[175] In 1994 the German legislature intervened to prevent a flood of claims and complaints. With the limitation of rights of claim to trade associations and the amendment in 1994 the legislature intended to abolish associations which existed only to levy fees for complaints against, for example, trivial infringements of competition law. The fee for complaints therefore obviously invited abuse. In fact, however, in so far as rights of claim have been withdrawn from serious associations there has been a failure to fulfil the requirements of § 13 para. 2 no. 2 UWG. Therefore, in the literature the abolition of fees for complaint and the extension of rights of claim under previous law have been called for.[176]

Several arguments support further rights of claim as is the case in England or Germany. If it is true that the competitor has the best

[172] Art. 4 para. 1 subpara. 2. [173] Art. 3 lit. (b) and art. 1 para. 1.

[174] K. Tonner (1987) 40 NJW 1921; A. Beater, *Unlauterer Wettbewerb* (2002), § 1 note 29.

[175] W. Büscher, in K.H. Fezer, *Lauterkeitsrecht* (2005), § 8 note 191.

[176] W. Nordemann et al., *Wettbewerbs- und Markenrecht* (9th edn 2003), note 72 criticizes a clear decline of legal actions to 20% of the previous number of cases.

knowledge of the admissibility of competition measures, then this will also apply to trade associations which thereby can in doubt react more quickly than the authorities or have perhaps more financial resources than the individual competitor or consumer associations. Moreover, a competitor will not always be willing to bring claims against an infringement.[177] If trade associations are actively engaged in alternative dispute resolution, then supplementary rights of claim are the logical consequence in order to make their actions effective. It is surprising that in England the CAP surrenders disputes to the OFT[178] rather than pursuing them itself. Decisions by administrative authorities have the disadvantage that they are subject to judicial review.[179] Thus a legal dispute can be extraordinarily complex as the regulation of the ASA often proceeds via the OFT and the courts. A degree of inefficiency is inevitable.

Therefore, on the European level in future alongside consumer associations trade associations should also be accorded rights of claim.[180]

4. *State authorities – consumer ombudsman, OFT etc.*

a) Occurrence and effectiveness

Three distinct models may be distinguished. Only a few Member States have no regulation by public law structured authorities. These include up to now, for example, Germany, Luxembourg, Austria and the Netherlands.[181] Most states on the other hand have established state authorities for the regulation of infringements of unfair competition law. These include above all the Nordic states, Sweden, Finland and Denmark, with their consumer ombudsman. In the field of unfair competition in Sweden there is a public consumer agency, *Konsumentverket*, which is to ensure that the public policy for consumers is pursued. One of the responsibilities of the authority is to make sure that the consumers have a strong position on the market. The director general for this consumer authority has another function as well, that is the Consumer Ombudsman. The Consumer Ombudsman represents consumer interests in relation to undertakings and pursues legal action

177 W. Büscher, in K.H. Fezer, *Lauterkeitsrecht* (2005), § 8 note 191.

178 See sec. 61.10 Code.

179 See art. 4 para. 3 subpara. 2 of the Misleading and Comparative Advertising Directive 84/450/EEC.

180 With the same result but without explanation see art. 7 of their draft in H.-W. Micklitz and J. Keßler (2002) 50 GRUR Int. 885 (901).

181 Regulation Proposal on consumer protection cooperation, COM (2003), 433 final in reasons 3.1.2.

in the consumer interest. The Consumer Ombudsman is responsible for ensuring that companies abide by the laws and rules in the consumer field and ensures that consumer rights are respected. The Ombudsman is empowered to take legal action against companies who violate market laws. The Consumer Ombudsman may bring cases to specially designated courts (special courts). The office is linked with an old tradition of ombudsmen in Sweden. The Consumer Ombudsman may bring a claim for an injunction or an information order. Moreover, the Consumer Ombudsman has, according to sec. 39 MFL, the primary competence to take action concerning administrative fines. The reason for this is that administrative fines are punitive in character.

In Finland, the Ombudsman can ask the Market Court to forbid the violators marketing and demand it not to be renewed. According to § 19 MFL in Denmark the Consumer Ombudsman will be able to institute proceedings with the aim of having issued an injunction. The legal position of consumer associations is therefore particularly strong in the Nordic states because the law can be enforced by competitors or consumer associations.

Finally, there are a number of Member States in which public law does not necessarily dominate but which has a field of application alongside the civil law procedure. These include Poland, United Kingdom, France, Italy, Spain, Portugal, also the USA and Switzerland. In Poland there is a president of the *Urząd Ochrony Konkurencji i Konsumentów* (Office for Competition and Consumer Protection) and a consumer ombudsman. Both have a right of claim pursuant to art. 19.1 no.3 and 4 u.z.n.k. In the United Kingdom Part II of the Fair Trading Act 1973 gives the right to the director general to issue orders dealing with particular consumer trade practices that may from time to time raise concern. In previous years, however, only three such orders of limited significance were handed down.[182] The possibility to hand down orders under Part III against individual rogue traders in cases of persistent conduct which is unfair and detrimental to the consumer were of only limited success. In practice this was only utilized if the trader engaged in conduct which was unlawful under an existing provision of civil or criminal law.[183]

In France the intervention of the state is also limited to the application of the CCons. However, this is a typical criminal proceeding.[184] For

[182] SI 1976/1813; SI 1976/1812 and SI 1977/1918.

[183] S. Weatherill, *United Kingdom*, in R. Schulze and H. Schulte-Nölke, I.1(a).

[184] See below B.II.7.

all other cases of the common law of unfair competition there is no competent administrative authority. Where the field of consumer protection and the provisions of the consumer code are concerned, again, as has already been shown in Case 1, the DGCCRF and those from the food directorate general of the Ministry of Agriculture and those from the metrology department of the Department of the Ministry of Industry are authorised to establish breaches. In Italy the powers of the *Autorità Garante della Concorrenza e del Mercato* stem from lgs. 74/1992 that is the field of application of comparative and misleading advertising. In Spain competent administrative bodies are also entitled to claim against the advertiser on the grounds of art. 25 LGP. As far as the LPG is concerned, in Spain the competent administrative body, the consumer association and the affected individual or corporation is able to request the advertiser to cease or rectify the unlawful publication. The advertiser must inform its intention to cease or rectify, so that if the advertiser does not proceed to answer the request or there is the negative answer, an action can be brought before the ordinary civil courts. In Portugal the public authority with competence for monitoring the legality of advertising is the *Instituto da Defesa do Consumidor* (National Consumer Protection Institution),[185] that according to the public interest defends all consumers. The institute is the Portuguese authority that monitors the observance of advertising standards and can apply administrative sanctions, such as fines and other ancillary sanctions. It can also sue competitors for injunctions and prohibitions. In Portugal the institute can also apply other complementary decisions such as compelling publication of corrections in the same newspaper. In the USA the FTC regulates the FTCA; at the state level the attorney general regulates the respective UDAP. In Switzerland the federation has its own right of claim.[186]

Evaluation

In the Misleading and Comparative Advertising Directive 84/450/EEC the Member States gain the opportunity, and thereby an option, to arrange legal protection through the courts or an administrative authority.[187] The requirements for regulation by administrative authorities are further defined. Administrative authorities must be independent and must

[185] Art. 21 LDCons and art. 1 Decreto-Lei n. 234/99 de 25 de Junho; art. 38 CPI.

[186] Art. 10 para. 2 lit. (c) UWG, introduced by Act of March 20, 1992, BBL 1992 II 844 et seq.

[187] Art. 4 para. 1 subpara. 2, 3.

possess sufficient powers to carry out an effective supervision.[188] Decisions of administrative authorities must in addition be reasoned, if no further legal proceedings before the courts are foreseen.[189] A judicial review must be possible in cases of improper or unreasonable exercise of its power by the administrative authority or improper or unreasonable failure to exercise the said powers.[190] The Injunction Directive 98/27/EC duplicates this option: alternatively courts or administrative authorities are nominated to take decisions on the legal remedies to be applied.[191] The Regulation on Consumer Protection Cooperation is of particular importance, which now requires, in the case of cross-border legal infringements, that Member States appoint competent authorities to give official assistance in response to requests for information by other member states.[192]

b) Potential disadvantages

From the German perspective regulation by public law authorities of infringements of the UWG have been consistently rejected.[193] In the course of the reform of the UWG in 2004 the German legislature also recently recognized that in future no public authority is necessary to enforce unfair competition law.[194] A number of familiar arguments have been advanced: courts are better able than administrative authorities to construe a general clause. In the case of the German territory with 80 million inhabitants a huge administrative machine would be necessary.[195] For this reason, ultimately, the infringements would not be eliminated.[196] The competitor would be more knowledgeable regarding the fellow competitor than any public authority. As a result public law supervision would be superfluous, as competitors and association would file claims in sufficient numbers. Consequently it would be of doubtful benefit to devote public resources to this purpose.[197]

188 Art. 4 para. 3 lit. (a) and (b). 189 Art. 4 para. 3 subpara. 2 s. 1.

190 Art. 4 para. 3 subpara. 2 s. 2. 191 Art. 2 para. 1.

192 Regulation (EC) No. 2006/2004 of 27.10.2004 on cooperation on consumer protection, OJ L 364, 1 and above A.III.3(g).

193 G. Schricker (1975) 139 ZHR 208 (234 et seq., 242 et seq.); idem (1973) 21 GRUR Int. 694; K. Kreuzer, *Behördenbefugnisse in Unlauterkeitssachen?* (1979) 27 WRP 255 (262); limited G. Schricker, 1996 44 GRUR Int. 473 (478) on condition that the association claim is appropriately handled; in disagreement E. von Hippel, *Verbraucherschutz* (1976) 40 RabelsZ 513 (522 et seq.).

194 Begr. RegE, BT-Drs. 15/1487, p. 22 for § 8. 195 G. Schricker (1975) 139 ZHR 208 (242).

196 G. Schricker (1973) 21 GRUR Int. 694 (698); K. Kreuzer (1979) 27 WRP 255 (262).

197 G. Schricker (1973) 21 GRUR Int. 694 (698 et seq.).

The administrative legal procedure would follow the court procedure, thereby prolonging a final decision.[198] In addition the legal position in USA and England is pointed to: in the USA the FTC was so unsuccessful that it had to be reformed in the mid-70s,[199] whereas in England the rules of the FTA were so lacking in practical relevance in the past that they were supplemented by Part 8 of the Enterprise Act in 2003.[200] The Director General was abolished and instead his powers transferred to the OFT.

c) The advantages of public law legal procedures

The statement of the German legislature on the reform of the UWG in 2004 that no public authority would be needed in the future to enforce unfair competition law is not true in its generality. First, there are special laws: in capital market law for example the federal authority for financial services (*Bundesanstalt für Finanzdienstleistungen*) regulates unfair competition law pursuant to § 36b WpHG[201] or § 28 WpÜG. Theses norms are not based on European requirements,[202] but rather the legislature proceeded from the position that public law supervision was necessary. Secondly, there are norms in the German UWG 2004 itself which, even if only to a restricted extent, provide for the involvement of the criminal law authorities.[203] Thirdly and finally, it is possible for public law bodies from abroad, for example the Danish consumer ombudsman, to proceed within Germany against cross-border infringements.[204] The situation is comparable in Austria. Thus at least in fringe areas of unfair competition law there are in both Germany and Austria sanctions under public law.

A number of arguments point towards a public law supervision by official bodies. Under comparative law there is in all other Member

[198] Ibid. (696); clearly presented by K. Kreuzer (1979) 27 WRP 255 (262), taking the case *FTC v. Carter's Little Liver Pills* as an example, where the bundle of documents comprised 20,000 pages.

[199] G. Schricker (1973) 21 GRUR Int. 694 (699); see also K. Kreuzer (1979) 27 WRP 255 (262).

[200] S. Weatherill, *United Kingdom*, in R. Schulze and H. Schulte-Nölke, I.1(a) and B.III.4.

[201] T. Möllers, *Das neue Werberecht der Wertpapierbörsen* (1999) 11 ZBB 134.

[202] Art. 13 Securties Firms Directive 93/22/EEC (OJ L 141, 11.6.1993, p. 27) requires no such condition, see T. Möllers (1999) 11 ZBB 134 (136).

[203] For example of an infringement of §§ 16 – 19 UWG (ex-§ 4, 17, 18, 20 UWG). The practical field of application is narrow however, see below B.II.7.

[204] § 8 para. 3 no. 3 (§ 13 para. 3 no. 3 s. 1 UWG); see H. Köhler and H. Piper, *UWG* (3rd edn 2002), § 13 note 34.

States public law supervision to a greater extent than in Germany, Austria, Luxembourg and Netherlands. This also applies under Nordic and also under Anglo-American and French law. Even states which have only recently introduced the market economy, such as Poland or Hungary, know the consumer ombudsman or the OEC. What is vehemently rejected from the German side can therefore not be so bad. The effectiveness of the consumer ombudsman in the Nordic Member States (Sweden, Finland and Denmark) is beyond question. In Sweden, for example, the consumer ombudsman has dealt with 20,000 cases in five years, including above all the possibility of an amicable settlement.[205] Legal enforcement also attracts praise in France and Italy. In addition a generalized condemnation of public law proceedings in England is inappropriate, as the local wieghts and measures authorities have the possibility of bringing proceedings against infringements before the OFT.[206] As a rule traders wish to avoid conflicts with the local weights and measures authorities or the OFT. This is not least because all judgments or other measures against traders are publicized. Thus, for example, in the monthly OFT publication the names of those whose licence to provide credit has been withdrawn are always printed. In addition, alternative dispute resolution outside the courts appears to function well.[207]

The public law authorities have in addition a range of legal measures at their disposal, which are unavailable under civil law proceedings. The principle of investigation makes possible extensive information claims by the authority. With respect to legal enforcement, administrative fines or, as in Sweden or Finland, even information orders are possible. Where there are information claims intentional acts can be better investigated and sanctioned. However, the fact that there are gaps in legal protection is a decisive point. While the competitor often seeks its own legal protection, the consumer not infrequently waives legal protection.[208] Only too often the principle applies that anti-competitive conduct is always worth it. In Germany, for example, consumers have for a number of years been inundated with unsolicited telefaxes; cold

[205] For the period from January 1, 1971 to May 1, 1976 from 20,000 complaints only 279 cases resulted in a prohibitive injunction and 153 applications to the market court, see E. von Hippel (1976) 40 RabelsZ 513 (520).

[206] For example, the local weights and measures authorities can bring proceedings for an injunction in the High Court as well, under sec. 213(1) EA 2002.

[207] See similarly B.III.4. [208] See above B.II.5.

calling exists and the 0190-telephone numbers are abused.[209] Until now nothing effective has been done about this. On the other hand under capital market law in Germany cold calling under 36b WpHG was prohibited by a public law authority.[210] Thereby at least in cases of nuisance or loss-leader offers, the thesis that in Germany infringements of misleading advertising law are always proceeded against by the competitor or associations is not persuasive.

It is significant therefore that most Member States (France, Italy, Spain, Portugal) have developed legal protection mainly through authorities, if legal interests of consumers are infringed. Interestingly, the German legislature under the reformed UWG 2004 rejected on the one hand public law protection and a right of claim for consumers,[211] but on the other hand criticized a double gap in legal enforcement: in the case of widely dispersed harm where numerous investors suffer limited losses the infringer, according to the legislator, could often retain the gains because the consumers have no right of claim under the UWG and are not motivated to pursue their own claims in view of the limited extent of the losses. The cessation claims of competitors are directed only towards the future.[212] As shown above, the legislature reacted with a claim for surrender of profit on the part of consumer associations pursuant to § 10 UWG. As conceived, however, this seems a rather ineffective measure.[213] Thus in Germany not a few gaps in legal protection remain.

d) Combination of authorities and court intervention

In the USA there is a double competence at state level. Both the Attorney General and private parties may proceed against infringements of unfair competition law. In the Member States which supervise unfair competition law through authorities there is also a double competence (Sweden, Finland, Denmark, United Kingdom, Poland, France (through criminal law), Italy, Spain and Portugal). Because of the regulation on consumer protection cooperation the Member States must establish competent authorities by December 31, 2005.[214] They should not then

[209] See above A.II.1(b). Further examples in J. Glöckner, in H. Harte-Bavendamm and F. Henning-Bodewig, *UWG* (2004), Einl B note 203.

[210] T. Möllers (1999) 11 ZBB 134 (142 et seq.).

[211] See B.II.5.

[212] Begr. RegE, UWG, BT-Drs. 15/1487, for § 10 p. 23.

[213] See above B.I.6.(b).

[214] Regulation (EC) No. 2006/2004 of October 27, 2004 on cooperation on consumer protection, OJ L 364, 1. Agreeing Verbraucherzentrale Bundesverband e.V., disagreeing BR-Drs. 589/03.

limit such authorities to cross-border matters. It would be preferable that in Germany, Austria, Netherlands and Luxembourg the public law supervision of the cases would be seen as at least secondary and subsidiary when there is a gap in the law, if private parties do not proceed in the courts against the legal infringement.[215] This would correspond with the legal position in Italy. In these states a supplementary right of claim for the cartel authorities could be considered to the extent that anti-competition infringements can be pursued neither by the competitor nor the associations. These could then, for example, make claims to the commercial chamber of the regional court.[216]

In the literature it is instead proposed to support consumer associations financially so that they may claim in these cases. This form of standing was also considered by the German legislature for claims for surrender of profits under § 10 UWG. However, to date no corresponding financial resources have been made available.

In England the OFT can only proceed at law to a limited extent. This requires a domestic infringement in terms of sec. 211 EA. A domestic infringement is an act or omission which is done or made by a person in the course of a business, harms the collective interests of consumers in England, and is of a description specified by the Secretary of State by order, in accordance with sec. 211(2) EA. Domestic infringements are now listed in the Enterprise Act 2002 (Part 8 Domestic Infringements) Order 2003. They do not include attracting consumers. In England therefore the possibility for claims by the OFT should be extended.

[215] Supporting an addition, J. Glöckner, in H. Harte-Bavendamm and F. Henning-Bodewig, *UWG* (2004) Einl B notes 204 et seq.; more far-reaching regarding state supervision, E. von Hippel (1976) 40 RabelsZ 516 (522).

[216] Regarding Polish and Hungarian law, see Case 4 (Children's swing).

Case 5 Discontinued models: misleading advertisement – the consumer as plaintiff

The car manufacturer A sells cars. He advertises his cars in the newspaper as the newest and cheapest cars in town, without pointing out that this applies exclusively to discontinued models. C buys such a car because he thought that he would buy a brand new model.

1. To what extent can consumer C take legal proceedings against A? Which claims can he pursue, which not?
2. Are consumer associations entitled or under a duty to represent the interests of consumers as a whole?
3. To what extent can trade competitors take steps against the advertising?
4. What claims can public authorities or institutions pursue against the advertising?

Austria (5)

The car manufacturer is liable according to § 2 UWG for misleading advertising even if he does not emphasize that his car are the newest and cheapest in town. Anyone who advertises goods as new causes the reasonable expectation that those products stem from the current series of models.[1]

(1) The Austrian UWG does not include civil law provisions that regulate claims arising from the contract between the advertiser and the targeted consumer. However, there are remedies in general civil law. The OGH has already granted a consumer compensation for the loss incurred by relying on the profits guaranteed by an enterprise based on § 874, 1311 ABGB and § 2 UWG. The court reasoned that after the amendment of the UWG in 1971 § 2 UWG now also aims at giving competition protection to consumers and therefore gives individual victims of unfair competition a right to sue. The contracting party also has warranty claims: § 922 para. 2 ABGB, which implements Art. 2 Directive 1999/44/EC on the Sale of Consumer Goods, determines, among other things, that the question whether goods transferred to someone for valuable consideration comply with the contract is a question that has also to be judged by expectations of the transferee caused by public remarks of the transferor or the manufacturer, especially in advertising and in written statements enclosed with the goods.

[1] (1981) 30 ÖBl 21 – 'Gartengeräte-Listenpreise'; SZ 57/117, (1984) 33 ÖBl 153 – 'Aktion Hobelmaschine'.

According to § 871 ABGB a consumer – but also every deceived entrepreneur buying goods (in this case a car) for his company – is entitled to rescind the contract because of a misconception about a main feature of the product and, under § 874 ABGB in cases of at least negligent[2] deception to claim damages incurred by reliance on the contract, i.e. the costs of entering into the contract.[3] Claims for a pre-emptive injunction prohibiting such misleading advertising cannot be brought by the consumer.[4]

(2) For questions 2–4 see Case 4.

Denmark (5)

A's marketing is contrary to § 2 sec. 1 MFL concerning misleading advertising.

(1) According to § 19 para. 1 MFL a consumer may bring an action before the courts against the trader for an injunction under § 13 MFL. A consumer may also bring an action to obtain remedies under civil law. According to the Sale of Goods Act § 76, goods are defective if the seller when advertising the goods has provided incorrect or misleading information and this information can be presumed to have influenced the consumer's buying decision. Under the Sale of Goods Act § 78 selling defective goods might have the consequence that the consumer either requests delivery of a new model, be given a reduction in the price or that he withdraws from the contract. This last option is conditioned upon the defect to be of considerable importance for the buying decision. The claim here will be cancellation of the contract because of fraudulent behaviour at the time of entering into the contract. The case has to be brought before the civil court situated in the town where the seller has his business premises.

(2) Please refer to Case 4.

(3) According to § 8 of the act a trader cannot bring legal proceedings before the courts as long as a case is pending before the Complaints Board. If a case has already been brought before the courts, the consumer may request the case be deferred.

(4) A special administrative complaints body, the Consumer Complaints Board, has been established.[5] According to § 1 of the act the

[2] The wording of § 874 ABGB requires a 'cunning'; court rulings and doctrine (e.g. P. Rummel, *ABGB* (3rd edn 2002/2003/2004) § 874 note 2) require only negligence of the contracting party.

[3] See Case 4 (Children's swing). [4] See Case 4 (Children's swing).

[5] The Consumer Complaints Board was established in 1974 and is presently empowered by consolidated Act No. 282 of May 10, 1988; S. Kristoffersen and K.V. Gravesen, *Forbrugerretten* (2001) p. 459; B. Gomard, *Civilprocessen* (5th edn 2000), p. 763.

Complaints Board can attend to complaints from private consumers concerning goods, work performances and service. According to § 6 sec. 1 of the act, a complaint may be made against any person who can be sued in a Danish court. Complaints will only be attended to if the payment amounts to at least DKK 500 and not more than DKK 24,000. For motor vehicles, however, the maximum is DKK 82,000. A fee of DKK 80 is paid for the submission of a complaint (for motor vehicles DKK 480). Decisions made by the Complaints Board are not legally binding for the parties. If a decision from the Complaints Board is not complied with, the case must be brought before the regular courts. According to the § 11 sec. 2 of the act upon the request of and on behalf of a consumer – the complainant – the Board's secretariat shall in the event of non-compliance bring the case before the courts. Decisions of the Complaints Board are not binding on the courts. The courts will often reach the same result as the Complaints Board.[6]

Cases of this kind will fall within the competence of the Consumer Ombudsman. The aim of establishing the Consumer Ombudsman was explicitly to strengthen the protection of the consumers and thus create a better balance between consumers and traders.

England (5)

In practice, this problem would probably not arise in England since cars get their number plates once they leave the factory (or once they are imported into England), and the first letter(s) of the registration number pinpoints the year of registration. Leaving this aside, A's conduct might come under the Trade Descriptions Act 1968.

(1) The consumer C has different rights. Retailers can incur civil liability when they misrepresent the quality of products and services either orally or in writing. A misrepresentation is a false statement made by one party that is intended to and does induce the other party to enter the contract. The statement does not need to be made fraudulently.[7] A mere trader's puff is not sufficient for misrepresentation. In the present case, however, the description of the car as being 'new' clearly is not a puff but a serious statement. Misrepresentation may give rise to a claim for damages or rescission. Thus, C may choose to rescind the contract. Damages can be claimed instead or on top of rescission. Damages are payable if the misrepresentation is fraudulent, negligent or contractual. In the present

[6] S. Kristoffersen and K.V. Gravesen, *Forbrugerretten* (2001), p. 463.

[7] See P. Dobson, *Sale of Goods and Consumer Credit* (6th edn 2000), para. 6-02.

case, the misrepresentation was probably fraudulent because A did not believe in the truth of his statement. However, under sec. 2(1) of the Misrepresentations Act 1967,[8] damages are also recoverable for negligent misrepresentation which A's statements at least constitutes.[9]

C might also have remedies under the Sale of Goods Act 1979[10] as amended by the Sale and Supply of Goods Act 1994[11] and by the The Sale and Supply of Goods to Consumers Regulations 2002.[12] The description of the car as 'new' would in a consumer context amount to an essential commercial characteristic and therefore to a description in terms of sec. 13(1)[13] so that there is an implied term of the contract that the car is in conformity with this description. According to sec. 13 (1A), this implied term is a 'condition' which allows the purchaser to withdraw from the contract in case of a breach. Further, C could claim damages.

In practice, however, C should probably complain to a trading standards department which may investigate the case for breach of the Trade Descriptions Act 1968, which would be an offence giving rise to criminal liability.

Under sec. 1(1) of the TDA 1968, a false trade description, including false trade descriptions made in advertisements, is an offence.[14] Trade descriptions must be false to a material degree but the prohibition extends to trade descriptions that are misleading: sec. 3(2). A false description can, amongst others, be contained in an advertisement: sec. 5. An omission may render a description misleading.[15] Thus, it would not matter whether one regarded the description of the car as 'new' as misleading or whether one expected an additional explanation on the fact that it was a discontinued model. The test for the misleading character of a description is whether ordinary consumers to whom the description is directed could be misled.[16] In *R v. Ford Motor Co. Ltd.*, where

[8] Ch. 7 of 1967.

[9] See P. Dobson, *Sale of Goods and Consumer Credit* (6th edn 2000), para. 6-03 and 6-04.

[10] Ch. 54 of 1979. [11] Ch. 35 of 1994. [12] S.I. 2002 No. 3045.

[13] Note that only few cases have been decided under the Sale of Goods Act 1979, and there seems to have been no case concerning the description of a product as 'new'; see, however, *Andrews Brothers (Bournemouth), Limited v. Singer and Company, Limited* [1934] 1 K.B. 17, which was decided under the Sale of Goods Act 1893.

[14] For the role of criminal law in English consumer protection law, see D. Parry, (2002) 25, JCP 439 et seq.

[15] See also C. Scott and J. Black, *Cranston's Consumer and the Law* (3rd edn 2000), p. 299.

[16] It is not important that anybody was actually misled, see *Stainthorpe v. Bailey* [1980] R.T.R. 7. For more details, see also C. Scott and J. Black, *Cranston's Consumer and the Law* (3rd edn 2000), pp. 296 et seq.

a car was sold as 'new' after minor repairs, the Court of Appeal held that sec. 1 of the TDA 1968 was not violated.[17] In contrast, in *R v. Anderson*, the conviction of a car dealer who had sold cars as 'new' which had been registered before in its own name in order to meet import quotas imposed on the producer, Nissan, was upheld by the Court of Appeal.[18] In the light of the latter case, it is highly likely that to sell a discontinued model as 'new' meets the requirements of a false trade description. Persons guilty of an offence under this act are liable on conviction on indictment, to a fine or imprisonment for a term not exceeding two years or both.

This might encourage A to settle the dispute, due to the threat of criminal proceedings. If the case came to court, and A was convicted for breach of the Trade Descriptions Act 1968, C could claim compensation under the procedure set out in sec. 130 of the Powers of Criminal Courts (Sentencing) Act 2000.[19]

(2) Misleading advertisement is covered by chap. 8 of the Enterprise Act since Directive 84/450/EEC is a 'listed Directive' in terms of sec. 210(7).[20] Still, consumer associations first have to be named by the Secretary of State as 'designated enforcers' in terms of sec. 213(2) and (4) before they can take legal action.[21]

Business associations cannot sue.

(3) The only mechanism available for *competitors* is a complaint to the OFT under reg. 4(1) of the CMAR 1988.[22]

(4) For public authorities there are different possibilities.

Since A's advertisement was in breach of reg. 4(2) of the CMAR 1988, the OFT can bring proceedings for an injunction in the High Court.[23] Under reg. 7 of the CMAR 1988, the OFT has the right to obtain information from the trader in order to enable the OFT to exercise or to consider whether to exercise any functions it has under the CMAR 1988.

The OFT is the central consumer protection agency, based in London. The Local Weights and Measures Authorities can be found nation-wide. If consumer protection is concerned, the OFT takes a supreme role. It has

[17] *R. v. Ford Motor Co. Ltd.* [1974] All ER 489 (CA). [18] *R. v. Anderson* (1988) 152 J.P. 373.

[19] See also C. Scott and J. Black, *Cranston's Consumer and the Law* (3rd edn 2000), p. 152.

[20] See also The Enterprise Act 2002 (Part 8 Community Infringements Specified UK Law) Order 2003, S.I. 2003, No. 1374.

[21] See the solution to Case 4 (Children's swing).

[22] For details, see the solution to Case 1 (Risky bread) at 1.

[23] For details, see the solution to Case 1 (Risky bread) at 1.

the power to order local authorities to pursue an infringement and has to be consulted before local authorities take actions independently.

At the same time, chap. 8 of the Enterprise Act 2002 applies since the misleading advertisement would, at the same time, be a 'Community infringement' in the terms of sec. 212(1) with Schedule 13 of the Enterprise Act 2002. Enforcement of Community infringements follows more formalised rules set out in sec. 214 et seq. EA 2002. Before taking action, the OFT has to consult with the trader: sec. 214 (1) EA 2002. The OFT can claim an injunction or an interim injunction: sec. 217 and 218. Moreover, the court can order the trader to publish the decision and to correct his earlier wrong statements: sec. 217 (8) EA 2002.

Finland (5)

This case would be regarded in Finland either as a purely civil law case or a case of untruthful or misleading information. The SopMenL does not cover the validity of contracts or any means of compensation under contract law. The Consumer Protection Act covers consumer contracts (both consumer goods and consumer services), their validity and generally the rights of consumers against businesses. In the case of consumer contracts, the law is binding and the legal position of a consumer may not be weakened by contract terms.

(1) The consumer C has no right to demand that A should stop using misleading advertisements in a civil law case and as stated in Case 4 a consumer has no legal standing in the Market Court. However, C can sue A and demand that A should deliver such goods, which are deemed to have been agreed on between the parties. In this case, this could mean that A would have to deliver a new model if C has been led to understand due to marketing and other sales representation that the object of the contract is a new model of the car. Under § 12:1 KSL A has a duty to deliver such goods, which correspond to what is deemed to have been agreed. C could also claim that the contract should be adjusted under § 4:1 KSL if it is unreasonable from the point of view of the consumer. This could even mean the adjustment of the price. Both these possibilities depend on the particular facts of the case. If for example the sales person gave C the correct information before the parties agreed on a sale then C's standing in the case would be weaker.

(2) Consumer associations have no standing in civil law cases. In Finland, the main purpose of consumer organizations is more in the field of giving information and advice. In this field the position of undertakings is an active one and has during past years become more

so. Unlike antitrust law, traders have a right to make claims in the Market Court themselves. In such cases, civil law proceedings are used in the Market Court.

(3) If competitors are directly affected by A's marketing (these could be other local car sales outlets) they can take the matter to the Market Court and ask for a cease and desist order. This is possible as A's marketing is misleading and thus in violation of § 2 SopMenL.

(4) Before taking the matter to the general court of first instance, A could ask for a non-binding opinion of the Consumer Complaints Board. These opinions do not bind the parties, but they carry a lot of weight as the board consists of well-known lawyers in the field of consumer affairs. The board is impartial which also gives its opinions more credibility.

There are also advisors at municipality level whose duty is to advise consumers in consumer civil law issues such as whether a complaint could be made against a seller. These advisors receive their income from the municipality and consumers receive the information for free or have to pay a small charge.

(5) The Consumer Ombudsman could demand that the entrepreneur should cease with this kind of marketing and, if A fails to do so, take the matter to the Market Court.

France (5)

In this case, there is a violation of art. L 121-1 CCons. with the same consequences already described in Case 4. Furthermore, general civil law claims have to be considered. A defect under the law of sales only exists if the goods become unusable for the consumer's purposes because of the defect.[24] The existence of a defect has to found by objective criteria. In the present case, one has to rule out a defect in the sense of art. 1641 cc since being a discontinued model does not make its use impossible for the consumer. In addition, causing a misconception or fraudulent deception about a fundamental quality (*erreur* or *dol*) could also arise. Then rescission of the contract can be claimed. In contrast to German law, where on entering the contract the seller's assurance of the absence of defects is implied, rescission makes it possible for the consumer to void the contract because of a misconception.[25] The fact that the car is a discontinued model will have to be

[24] Cass. civ. January 22, 1997. [25] Cass. civ. III, May 18, 1988 in Bull. civ. III No. 96.

considered as a substantial characteristic (*qualité substantielle*)[26] and not as an irrelevant mistake. If the seller omitted substantial facts intentionally a fraudulent deception can be assumed.[27]

Until 2004 the Sales of Consumer Goods Directive 1999/44/EC had not been implemented despite the expiration of the deadline of implementation.[28] The directive has finally been implemented (by ministerial order rather than parliamentary act) in art. L 211-1 and following the consumer and not the civil code: order n° 2005-136 of February 17, 2005).[29] The new dispositions apply to sales between a professional seller and a consumer: art. L 211-3 CCons. In this situation the A has to deliver a product in conformity to the contract (L 211-4), meaning that the product has to be employable in the usual way for the kind of product that it is (L 211-5 1°), or that the product has to have the essential qualities that the parties of the contract have agreed on (L 211-5 2°). In case of non-conformity of the product C as a consumer can either claim compensation or replacement of the product in question: L 211-9 CCons. The defect is presumed to have already existed at the delivery, when the defect shows during the first six months: L 211-7 CCons. The action (*action résultant du défaut de conformité*) has a limitation period of two years starting from the delivery of the product, L 211-12 CCons.

Germany (5)

(1) C cannot base a claim against A on § 5 para. 1 UWG (ex-§ 3 s. 1 UWG). This section primarily protects the general interest, that is the consumer as a collective,[30] not the individual consumer.[31] Thus, no individual protective norm in the interest of the consumer is involved.[32] C is

[26] Answered in the affirmative for mileage, CA Orléans, October 10, 1990, Jurisdata 050831.

[27] Cass. civ. I, November 12, 1987, J.c.Pc. 1988, IV, 25.

[28] According to a report of the Assemblée Nationale from 2003 France had already been asked on June 10, 2000 and on April 17, 2002; by decision of December 17, 2002, it was finally urged to implement the new rules.

[29] French Official Journal (J.O.), art. 1, 18/02/2005.

[30] J. Bornkamm, in W. Hefermehl, H. Köhler and J. Bornkamm, *Wettbewerbsrecht* (24th edn 2006), § 5 note 1.8.

[31] BGH (1975) 77 GRUR 150 – 'Prüfzeichen'; A. Baumbach and W. Hefermehl, *UWG* (22nd edn 2001), § 3 note 440; H. Köhler and H. Piper, *UWG* (3rd edn 2002), § 3 note 4; J. Bornkamm, in H. Hefermehl, H. Köhler and J. Bornkamm, *Wettbewerbsrecht* (24th edn 2006), § 5 note 1.9; Harte-Bavendamm/Henning-Bodewig, *UWG* (2004), § 5 note 7.

[32] H. Köhler and H. Piper, *UWG* (3rd edn 2002), § 3 note 5; Harte-Bavendamm/Henning-Bodewig, *UWG* (2004), § 5 note 52.

not a beneficiary under this claim. However, in the past C could withdraw from the contract with A pursuant to ex-§ 13a para. 1 s. 1 UWG. A would have had to fulfil the factual requirement of § 16 para. 1 UWG (ex-§ 4 UWG).[33] In the amendment of UWG in 2004 the legislature has deleted this remedy because it had not gained any significance in practice. Moreover, general contract law is able to protect consumers adequately.[34]

Alternatively C could claim general civil law remedies. Initially C could claim the special sales remedies. The Sale of Consumer Goods Directive 99/44/EC regulates that the advertisement of a product defines a product's qualities that have to be fulfilled.[35] § 434 para. 1 s. 3 BGB implements this into German law. In this case, a new car has been sold that is defective in the sense of § 434 para. 1 s. 3 BGB. The delivered car is admittedly not defective within § 434 para. 1 BGB, but is a so-called 'aliud', that is something other than the performance owed. In view of the equivalence of 'aliud' and 'peius' by the modernization of the law of obligations (§ 434 para. 3 BGB) the sales remedies pursuant to § 437 BGB also apply to an aliud-performance. C can demand a cure under § 439 BGB, pursuant to §§ 440, 323 and 326 para. 5 BGB, withdraw from the contract or demand a reduction of the purchase price under § 441 BGB, and demand compensation in place of the specific performance under §§ 440, 280, 281 BGB or under § 284 BGB compensation of the alleged expenses.

C could also claim recovery of the sales price under § 812 para. 1 s. 1 alt. 1 BGB. A has gained property and financial assets (= purchase price) through performance by C. A legal ground could not have existed from the beginning through a successful avoidance of the agreement: § 142 para. 1 BGB. A must establish the avoidance against A: § 143 para. 1, 2 BGB. Further, there must be grounds for avoidance. There is a ground for avoidance on mistake respecting quality under § 119 para. 2 BGB, as C was mistaken regarding a commercially significant attribute of the car.

In addition A has induced C to enter into the contract through an illegal misrepresentation, so that there are grounds for challenge under § 123 para. 1 alt. 1 BGB. Thus, a legal ground for the purchase price

[33] H. Köhler and H. Piper, *UWG* (3rd edn 2002), § 13a note 3 with reference to OLG Nuremberg (1990) 92 GRUR 141 (142); A. Baumbach and W. Hefermehl, *UWG* (22nd edn 2001), § 13a note 3.

[34] Begr RegE, BT-Drs. 15/1487, p. 14 et seq.

[35] Art. 2 para. 2 lit. (d) Sale of Consumers Goods Directive 99/44/EC.

performance did not exist from the beginning. Consequently, C can claim recovery of the sales price within the scope of § 812 para. 1 BGB.

He could also bring a compensatory claim for infringement of pre-contractual obligations: §§ 280 para. 1, 311 para. 2, 241 para. 2 BGB (*culpa in contrahendo*).[36] Pre-contractual liability is applicable alongside the various protective challenges.[37] A's breach of duty is to be seen in his misrepresenting the composition of the car. This happened knowingly, that is with intention, and accordingly is culpable. C can claim natural restitution to the extent of the negative interest under § 249 s. 1 BGB.[38] This means he is to be placed in the position he would have been in had he not relied on the validity of the transaction.[39] As he should not have paid the price, he can claim recovery of it.

According to § 823 para. 2 BGB you can be held liable for damages if you infringe a norm that aims at the protection of someone else. A protective norm is thus a prerequisite. According to the courts, a norm can be qualified as a protective norm if the protection of individuals is also intended even if the protection of the general public is its main concern.[40] A compensatory claim under § 823 para. 2 BGB is possible, as § 16 para. 1 UWG (ex-§ 4 UWG) is a consumer protection provision.[41] A, from a subjective point of view, wishes to give the impression of a particularly favourable offer. A promises a very cheap car.

Further, § 263 para. 1 StGB could be realized as a protective provision. As, according to the facts, performance and counter-performance are not equivalent, there is a damage to property. Thus the consumer can bring a claim on the basis of § 823 para. 2 BGB in connection with § 263 para. 1 StGB.

(2) Consumer associations can pursue claims based on the UWG. According to § 374 para. 1 no. 7 StPO (§ 22 para. 2 UWG) they are eligible to sue in the course of a public prosecution.

[36] H. Heinrichs, in O. Palandt, *Bürgerliches Gesetzbuch* (64th edn 2005), § 276 note 79.

[37] Ibid., § 276 note 68. [38] Ibid., § 276 note 100. [39] Ibid., before § 249 note 17.

[40] See BGHZ 22, 293 (297); BGHZ 40, 306 (307); BGHZ 106, 204 (206); BGH (1973) 26 NJW 1547 (1548).

[41] H. Köhler and H. Piper, *UWG* (3rd edn 2002), § 4 note 2 with reference to BGHSt 27, 293 (294); J. Bornkamm, in W. Hefermehl, H. Köhler and J. Bornkamm, *Wettbewerbsrecht* (24th edn 2006), § 16 note 29; different opinion by G. Dreyer, in H. Harte-Bavendamm and F. Henning-Bodewig, *UWG* (2004), § 16 note 22, denying the nature as protective law for the same reasons as in § 5 UWG.

Claims based on other norms than the UWG cannot be pursued by associations;[42] unless there is an explicit rule of competence, e.g. the *Unterlassungsklagengesetz*.

(3) Trade competitors could proceed under the same preconditions as under Case 4.

(4) Under German law there is in general no public authority responsible for monitoring observance of advertising standards.[43] However, only state prosecution proceedings could be brought in view of the fraudulent circumstances § 263 StGB and the criminally misleading advertising (§ 16 para. 1 UWG, ex- § 4 UWG).

Greece (5)

A has made an inaccurate declaration related to the quality of products sold by him. He has presented his products as brand new whereas in reality they were discontinued models.

(1) Consumer C may thus request the prevention of such an act, and also claim damages according to the law of unfair competition, as already illustrated in Case 4. Consumer C may also invoke the provisions of L. 2251/1994, in particular art. 9(2)–(4) on misleading advertisement[44]

Concurrently, however, A is also contractually liable to C since a contract of sale has been concluded between them. In particular, A is liable for lack of qualities agreed upon or expected by the client (taking into account the content of the advertisement)[45] in accordance with articles 534, 535 and 537 of the Civil Code. In fact A's offer invited consumers to purchase new automobiles, while in reality they could only purchase discontinued models. It should be noted that the European parliament and council Directive 1999/44/EC 'relating to certain aspects of sales and consumer goods guarantees' has been implemented in the Greek legal order by virtue of law 3043/2002.[46] In the new legal context, favourable to consumers, A is liable even if C was unaware

[42] BGH (1968) 70 GRUR 95 (97 et seq.) – 'Büchereinlass'; W. Nordemann et al., *Wettbewerbs- und Markenrecht* (9th edn 2003), note 1491.

[43] H. Köhler and H. Piper, *UWG* (3rd edn 2002), § 13 note 3; A. Bergmann, in H. Harte-Bavendamm and F. Henning-Bodewig, *UWG* (2004), § 8 note 257.

[44] See Case 4 (Children's swing); Y. Karakostas and D. Tzouganatos, *Consumer Protection. The Law 2251/1994* (2003).

[45] P.A. Papanikolaou-Kl. Roussos, *The New Law of the Seller's Liability* (in Greek) [2003], p. 334 et seq.

[46] Government Gazette, issue A 192 (2002).

of the lack of agreed upon qualities due to gross negligence or, in the present case, even if the price of the discontinued model was substantially lower, thus making evident the fact that the automobiles could not have been brand new. Art. 540 CC grants C the right to demand (a) the replacement of the product, or (b) a reduction of the price, or (c) the rescission of the contract.[47] Instead of exercising the above rights, C may claim reparation for any damage caused by the lack of the quality reasonably expected or agreed upon; he may also seek reparation, while exercising one of the above rights.[48] In the last case, the reparation will concern only the damage not covered by other available remedies. All actions on the above claims are filed before the civil courts.

(2) From a combined reading of art. 9, 10 (8), (9) and 15 of L. 2251/1994 that exclusively regulates protection of consumers in relation to suppliers, it follows that each consumer association or multiple consumer associations may request, by filing a collective action, the cessation of unlawful conduct by a supplier when such conduct relates to misleading, unfair, comparative or direct advertising. They are not, however, under an obligation to do so. It should also be stressed, however, that a consumer association could not exercise the rights of C which emanate from his contractual relation with A.

(3) Art. 10 of L. 146/1914 provides that the cessation of A's misleading declaration may be requested by business persons engaged in the same commercial field who are thus his competitors. Any business persons who have been damaged by his conduct may also seek damages. Although it is not expressly provided by L. 2251/1994, it has been suggested that not only consumers but also competitors may base claims on its provisions (see above, Case 1).

(4) Criminal prosecution may be sought against A in accordance with art. 4 of L. 146/1914, providing that any person who intentionally makes inaccurate declarations that are capable of misleading the public in order to create the impression of a particularly advantageous offer is punished with imprisonment of up to six months, pecuniary penalty or both. According to art. 21 (2) of the same law, this offence is prosecuted only after accusation by the persons listed in art. 10 (competitors, commercial and industrial chambers, commercial, industrial and, in general, professional associations).

[47] See P.A. Papanikolaou-Kl. Roussos, *The New Law of the Seller's Liability*, p. 373 et seq.
[48] Art. 543 CC.

It has to be noted that, under Greek law, no other public authority is responsible for controlling in general the kind of advertisement referred to in the present case.

Hungary (5)

*(1)*On the basis of sec. 305 HCC the act in this case is considered to be defective performance as the obligor warrants that the characteristics prescribed by law or stipulated in the contract are present in the item at the time of performance (implied warranty). According to sec. 306 HCC (1), the obligee shall be entitled to request repairs or an appropriate price reduction at his discretion in the case of defective performance.

(2) The answer of question 2, 3 and 4 are the same as in Case 4, questions 2–4.

Ireland (5)

(1) It seems unlikely that fraud could be proven in this case. A person to whom a fraudulent representation has been made, and who enters into a contract on the basis of that representation is entitled to rescind the contract, and claim damages. Where the contract is rescinded the purchaser is awarded such damages as would put him back in the financial position he was in before the contract was made, and not in the position he would be in had the representation been true.

(a) C may try to prove that A made a pre-contractual misrepresentation to him concerning the contract for the sale of the car. In that case, C would have to show that A represented the car he purchased as being an entirely different car, that A's representation operated on the mind of C when C was buying the car, and that it was reasonable for C to rely on the representation. If it can be proved that A acted fraudulently, then the court will readily order rescission of the contract.[49] However, mere non-disclosure does not constitute misrepresentation and fraud is very difficult to prove. Under Part V of the Sale of Goods Act 1980, the courts can award damages for innocent, that is non-fraudulent misrepresentation under appropriate circumstances.

(b) C can try to take legal proceedings against A under the Sale of Goods and Supply of Services Act 1893 and 1980.[50] Under sec. 13 of the 1893 Act as amended by sec. 10 of the 1980 Act, there is an implied condition in every contract of sale to a consumer that the goods

[49] *Derry v. Peak* [1889] 14 App. Cas. 337.

[50] See Cases 1 (Risky bread) and 2 (Watch imitations I).

purchased will correspond with their description. C must have relied on A's description of the goods, but such reliance is readily assumed by the court. However, the description of the goods relates to their essential characteristics, rather than their quality. Not all words will amount to a description. Mere non-contractual representations will not suffice. For there to be breach of implied condition of correspondence with description the quality of the goods sold must be fundamentally different from the quality implied by the description.[51] In this case, it seems unlikely that C would be successful in an action for damages, as the words 'newest and cheapest' would likely be interpreted by the court as a 'mere representation'.

(c) Alternatively, C could take action against A under sec. 4 of the Misleading Advertising Regulations 1988 to force A to withdraw the misleading advertisement and try to claim damages. In determining whether the advertisement is misleading, account shall be taken of all its features, the characteristics of the goods, their expected use, their price, conditions of supply and the nature of the advertiser, as per art. 3 of the EC Misleading Advertising Directive 84/450.

(2) Consumer associations are neither entitled nor under a duty to represent the interests of consumers as a whole in court.[52] However, consumer associations may exert political pressure on A on behalf of one or all consumers.

(3) Trade competitors may complain to the Director of Consumer Affairs, but they have no legal claim against A, other than an action under sec. 4 of the Misleading Advertising Regulations 1988.[53]

(4) The Director of Consumer Affairs could prosecute A under sec. 8 of the Consumer Information Act 1978 or sec. 3 and 4 of the EC (Misleading Advertising) Regulations 1988.[54]

Italy (5)

Protection of individual consumers against misleading advertisements still raises some problems under Italian law. Though many possible means of protection may be found, it is not certain that C's suit may succeed. The first problem is that of interpreting A's advertisement. It could be held that the advertisement claiming that A 'sells the newest

[51] *O'Connor v. Donnelly* (1944) IrJur Rep 1; *Ashington Piggeries v. Hill* [1972] AC 441.
[52] See Case 4 (Children's swing).
[53] See Cases 1 (Risky bread), 2 (Watch imitations I) and 4 (Children's swing) above.
[54] See Cases 1 (Risky bread), 2 (Watch imitations I) and 4 (Children's swing) above.

and cheapest cars in town' is no more than an exaggeration typical in advertisements (*dolus bonus*), which may have no specific harmful consequences for consumers, or at least cannot be considered as an actual inducement to enter the contract, which was entered by C on different grounds (after he saw the car, and after he evaluated whether the price was cheap or not). A further problem is that the plaintiff will bear the burden of proof as to whether his decision to enter the contract was actually induced by the advertisement. That very difficult matter of proof may be satisfied by means of circumstantial evidence. Third, the eventual application of the *dolus bonus* doctrine will lead to the plaintiff's claim being dismissed anyway, even if he succeeds in proving that he was actually misled by the advertising: an inference of such a doctrine is that he who recklessly believes in merchants' lies will bear the consequence of his naïvety. The *dolus bonus* doctrine has been severely criticized by legal scholars,[55] and has rarely been applied by courts. Many legislative provisions, including those implementing EC Directives (e.g. the d.lgs. 74/1992, prohibiting misleading advertisements), show that advertising can no longer be considered as irrelevant in consumer decision making.[56] On the other hand, the risk that the court may be influenced by the *dolus bonus* doctrine may not be excluded completely.

Let us suppose that C succeeds in proving that he was induced to enter the contract by A's advertisements, and that the *dolus bonus* doctrine is not applied.

A further problem would be that of the legal qualification of the advertisement: may it be considered as an actual offer to enter a contract, or is it just an invitation to treat? In the first case, the advertisement may be considered as a source of contractual obligations, as in French law (where court decisions speak of *force obligatoire des documents publicitaires*) or in English law, under the decision in *Carlill v. Carbolic Smoke Ball Company*. Therefore, C may claim that the car which was delivered to him by A does not conform with the contract, according to the Italian national provisions implementing the Sales of Consumer Goods Directive 99/44/EC on guarantees in consumer sales. Therefore, C may demand the substitution of the car with a brand new equivalent

[55] See e.g. G. Criscuoli, *La réclame 'non obiettiva' come mezzo d'inganno nella formazione dei contratti*, in *Riv. dir. ind.* (1968) II, 22; A. Vanzetti, *La repressione della pubblicità menzognera*, in *Riv. dir. civ.* (1964) 585; G. Ghidini, *Introduzione allo studio della pubblicità commerciale* (1968).

[56] See e.g. R. Sacco and G. de Nova, *Il contratto* (1993), I, p. 403.

model, or the termination of the contract, with damages, under art. 1519ter cc.

(1) C has no cause of action according to the Italian law of unfair competition, for the same reasons as mentioned above with reference to Case 4. C may have a cause of action under the law of torts, and may also rely on the general law of consumer rights, stated by l. 281/98, claiming that A infringed his rights not to be misled by advertising, and to fairness in contractual relationships. He may claim damages, whose amount may be equivalent to the difference in worth between the car which was delivered by A and a corresponding brand new model. C may sue under the law of contracts: C may claim the substitution of the car, according to national provisions implementing EC directive 99/44/EC, and the termination of the contract, with damages, as a consequence of non-performance of the seller's obligations. According to art. 1519ter cc, which reproduces the corresponding provision of the EC directive, conformity with the contract of the goods delivered to consumers must be assessed taking into account any public statement from the seller, including advertisements. According to such provision, notwithstanding that an advertisement may or may not be considered as equivalent to a contractual offer, it will always be taken into account in determining what the consumer's expectations with reference to the contract were, and what the exact features of the product to be delivered by the seller are.

Alternatively, C may challenge under art. 1439 cc, claiming that he was induced to enter the contract by fraudulent misrepresentation. C may claim the avoidance of contract, with damages, whose amount will be determined with reference to C's 'negative interest' (time loss and expenses incurred as a consequence of the contract). According to art. 1440 cc, the contract may not be avoided if, were it not for the misrepresentation, the plaintiff would have entered the contract under different terms. In such case, the plaintiff may be entitled to damages only.

(2)–(3) Same as Case 4.

(4) Same as Case 4, with reference to the powers of the *Autorità Garante della Concorrenza e del Mercato*, according to d.lgs. 74/1992.

A may be subject to criminal prosecution, for infringement of art. 640 of the Criminal code which prohibits cheating; for such article to be applied, it has to be proved by the public prosecutor that the consumer was actually misled by the advertisement, and that economic detriment was suffered as a consequence. Criminal prosecution may not be started *ex officio*, unless the amount of the damage suffered by the misled person is particularly high. Any suit by the injured person must be filed within thirty days of the fraud being discovered.

Netherlands (5)

(1) It can be argued that C has bought a new brand model which A is obliged to deliver. The answer depends on the information that both parties have provided during their negotiations. If it was clear for A that C wanted a new brand model and not a discontinued model, the claim will succeed.

Furthermore, C can base his claims on a general rule in contract law concerning error. If a contract is concluded on the basis of an error, the contract can, in accordance with art. 6:228 BW, be nullified. C may claim nullification of the contract and damages. However, the relevant question is whether C entered into the agreement under influence of an error and which he would not have concluded had there been a correct assessment of the facts. C can nullify the contract: a) if the error is due to information given by A, unless A could assume that the contract would have been entered into irrespective of such information, b) if A in view of what he knew or ought to know regarding the error, should have informed C, and c) if A in entering into the agreement made the same incorrect assumption as C unless A, even if there had been a correct assessment of the facts, did not necessarily understand that C would therefore be prevented from entering into the contract.

Given that the advertising must be regarded as misleading, C can base a claim for damages on art. 194, sec. b, BW as well. The question whether C as a consumer has a right of action must be assessed in accordance with art. 3:303 BW.

C can submit a complaint against manufacturer A with the RCC (Advertising Code Commission). If the advertisement is found to infringe the NRC, the Commission will advise A to stop using this advertisement in its current form. In the event of a repeat offence or a serious violation of the Code, the media can be asked to stop publishing the advertisement concerned. The organizations which are affiliated to the NCC pursuant to the Netherlands Media Act have the duty to reject advertisements against which such a type of ban has been issued. Furthermore, if a Special Advertising Code is drawn up, the Commission can impose measures (e.g. fines) as described in the contracts concluded between the *Stichting Reclame Code* and the organizations in consultation with which the Special Code was drawn up.

(2) Consumer associations are entitled, but never under a duty to initiate actions. According to art. 3: 305a BW these associations or foundations with full legal capacity can only institute an action if they intend to protect similar interests of other persons and to the extent that its articles promote such interests.

(3) In civil actions the main rule of art. 3:303 BW applies, according to which a person has no right of action where he lacks sufficient interest. Case law does not show a uniform line. The success is very much dependent on the specific facts of the case.[57]

All persons can file a complaint with the RCC.

(4) Art. 328bis Penal Code states that misleading the public or a specific person, with the intention to profit and with the consequence that competitors suffer damages, is guilty of unfair competition. Criminal proceedings may be based on this regulation. The RCC can take steps on the basis of the Advertising Code.

Poland (5)

Any misleading advertisement causing confusion and affecting a consumer's purchasing decision constitutes an act of unfair competition: art. 16.1 (2) u.z.n.k.

(1) C as a consumer can claim general civil law remedies based both on the Sale of Consumer Goods Act of 2002[58] (SCGA) and the general provisions of the Civil Code.

According to art. 4.1 SCGA the seller shall be liable to the buyer for any lack of conformity with the contract of sale which exists at the time the goods were delivered. Consumer goods are presumed to be in conformity with the contract if they show the quality and performance which are normal in goods of the same type and which the consumer can reasonably expect. The same applies to goods, which show the quality the buyer can expect, based on any public statements on the specific characteristics of the goods made about them by the seller, the producer or his representative, particularly in advertising or on labelling: art 4.3 SCGA.

[57] See note 319 with reference to the cases District Court Utrecht of December 20, 1990, BIE 1991, p. 269, in which the claim of a competitor was denied and Court of Appeal Den Bosch of December 8, 1995, NJ 1996/456, in which the claim of a competitor was sustained.

[58] The Polish SCGA is based on the Directive of May 25, 1999 on certain aspects of the sale of consumer goods and associated guarantees. Ustawa z dnia 27 lipca 2002 o szczegolnych warunkach sprzedazy konsumenckiej oraz o zmianie Kodeksu cywilnego, DZ.U. z 2002 r. Nr 141, poz 1176, z 2004 r. Nr 96, poz. 959.

In the case under discussion C buys a car, believing it to be a brand new model, based on the advertisement by the car manufacturer. Therefore, the goods can be considered to be not in conformity with the contract since they do not have the quality (of 'newest') that A had announced in his public statement. On the other hand, however, the seller shall not be deemed responsible if the consumer was aware, or could not reasonably be unaware of the lack of conformity: art. 7 SCGA. Here, since the subject of the sale is a car – which usually requires a more detailed investigation – A could argue that under the circumstances C could not reasonably be unaware of the lack of conformity. The seller shall not be bound by public statements, if he shows that by the time of conclusion of the contract the statement had been corrected or shows that the decision to buy the goods could not have been influenced by the statement: art 5 SCGA. The facts of the case do not mention whether the statement was corrected or not. However, the burden is placed on the seller to prove that C 'could not have been influenced' by A's advertisement. The buyer can demand to have the goods brought into conformity free of charge by repair or replacement, unless the repair or replacement is impossible or would cause extensive costs: art 8.1 SCGA. If the buyer cannot demand to have the goods brought into conformity or the seller did not comply with the demand, or bringing into conformity would cause gross inconvenience to the buyer, the buyer has the right to demand an appropriate reduction of the price or that the contract be rescinded with regard to those goods. The buyer cannot rescind the contract if the non-compliance is not substantial. In the case under discussion, it seems that the second of the remedies would be easier to enforce. However, C would probably be able to demand specific performance i.e. the delivery of the newest version of the car as advertised.

According to art. 84. 1 k.c. (Civil Code) in case of a mistake regarding the subject matter of the legal action (here a contract of sale) a party can avoid the consequences of his statement. The party can bring such a claim only in the situation where the mistake was substantial and where, if the party was not mistaken, he or she would not have made such a statement. In this case, C would not have bought the car if he had known about the mistake (non-compliance) regarding the car model. However, if one party (A) caused the mistake intentionally, the other party (C) can bring a claim even if the mistake was not substantial as well as when it was not regarding the subject matter of the legal action (contract). Here, if C could show A's bad intent, he could bring the claim under art 86.1 k.c.

(2) The claims listed in art 18. 1 (1–3 and 6) u.z.n.k. can be brought by the President of the Office for Competition and Consumer Protection if the act of unfair competition infringes or endangers consumers' interests: art 19.1 u.z.n.k.

Portugal (5)

The advertising omits relevant information to such an extent that it may mislead consumers: art. 11 CPI.

(1) Art. 12 LDCons (right to compensation) only allows a claim by the consumer if the product would be considered defective. In this case the product is not really defective.

Under the CC the contract was with erroneous understanding as to the qualities of the car. In this situation there can be argument as to the effect of the error or as to the reasons for the purchase, and whether this should lead to the cancellation of the contract (art. 251 CC or art. 252 para. 1 CC). Besides this, the car manufacturer A did not respect his duty of disclosure at the formation stage of the contract, which can justify compensation for consumer C for the damages he suffers due to lack of disclosure (*culpa in contrahendo*, art. 227 para. 1 CC).

Under the Advertising Code, consumer C could make complaints to a consumer association or to the Consumer Agency, which would *in casu* impose administrative fines on the car manufacturer A.

(2) There are no grounds for distinguishing this case from Case 4 with regard to consumer associations.

(3) Trade competitors could proceed under the same preconditions as referred to in Case 4.

(4) The Consumer Agency can impose administrative fines in this case under art. 11 and art. 34 para. 1 lit. (a) CPub and also other ancillary orders such as the compelling of publication in the same newspaper as the incorrect advertising, to include the information in clear letters that the car is not a brand model: art. 41 para. 7 CPub.

Spain (5)

(1) The consumer C could bring a legal action against A on the basis of the LGP. If A's campaign is deemed to be misleading advertising art. 27 LGP would apply.

(2) The consumer associations may request the advertiser to cease or rectify the illegal advertisement (art. 25 para. 1 LGP). Moreover, art. 8 para. 2 LDCU declares that concerning false or misleading offers, promotion or advertisement of goods, activities or services, the consumer

associations will be legally entitled to initiate and intervene in those administrative procedures tending to its cessation.

Business associations are usually able to file claims to defend collective interests.

(3) In order for a competitor to bring a claim against A, his economic interests must be harmed or menaced by the unfair act, as established in art. 19 para. 1 LCD. The burden of proof rests on the plaintiff, who must prove that the unfair act has been committed and affected his interests.

(4) As far as the LGP is concerned, the competent administrative body, the consumer association and the affected individual or corporation is able to request the advertiser to cease or rectify the illegal advertisement. The advertiser must give notice of its intention to cease or rectify; therefore, if the advertiser does not proceed to answer the request or if there is a negative answer, an action can be brought before the ordinary civil courts.

Sweden (5)

(1) Under pure private law it may be possible for C to return the car and have his money back, if the car deviates from what follows from A's offer. There is nothing preventing C from having any possible private law remedy tried before an ordinary court, although it seems unlikely that he will be successful. C cannot make a claim that A should be prohibited from selling cars or from advertising.

(2) Not only the Swedish Consumer Agency may bring cases before the court. Individual undertakings as well as associations of undertakings have a right to do this and they quite often make claims concerning, for example, misleading advertising. However, in Sweden it is most unusual that associations use their right to pursue such claims. These organizations probably lean on the public agency expecting it to pursue such claims. Undertakings and consumers also have the possibility to claim compensation for damages if any article in the act has been breached.

(3) See above Case 4(3).

(4)(a) Besides the Consumer Agency and the Consumer Ombudsman (KO) there is also a *Allmänna Reklamationsnämnd* – ARN (Public Complaints Tribunal)[59] which resolves disputes by means of issuing recommendations. The ARN has been in existence since 1968 and issues about 4,000 recommendations per year. It has therefore been

[59] www.arn.se.

established as an easy and effective form of arbitration in respect of disputes between consumers and commercial undertakings.[60] The decisions of the ARN are not legally binding, but to a great extent Swedish undertakings feel obliged to respect the tribunal's recommendations. In 75 per cent of cases undertakings comply with the recommendations.

(b) The Consumer Ombudsman may apply to the Board if a group of consumers have similar claims on the same grounds, a so-called group action. For instance, the Board decided after an application by the KO to afford financial compensation to all passengers on a summer bus trip to Spain. The bus company had promised modern buses, but the air conditioning in the bus was defective. The passengers were hence entitled to a reduction in price. In another case, a group of subscribers for a newspaper were charged for Value Added Tax without previous agreement with the seller. The Board recommended the seller to return the tax charge to the subscribers.

Summary (5)

5. *The consumer as plaintiff in general unfair competition law*

a) No right of claim

In some Member States consumers have no right of claim, for example in the United Kingdom, Poland and Hungary. In Germany a general right of claim for consumers was hotly discussed some thirty years ago,[61] but could not be agreed upon.

b) Extensive rights of claim

Numerous[62] other states however have rights of claim for consumers, such as for example Denmark,[63] Spain,[64] Italy, Greece, and the USA at state level.[65] The consumer right of claim in Denmark is surprising to the extent that there public law regulation by the Consumer Ombudsman is already highly developed. In addition there is an individual right

[60] P. Doppel and J. Scherpe, *'Grupptalan' – Die Bündelung gleichgerichteter Interessen im schwedischen Recht*, in J. Basedow, K. Hopt, H. Kötz and D. Baetge, *Die Bündelung gleichgerichteter Interessen im Prozess* (1999), p. 429 (438).

[61] See the evidence in A. Beater, *Unlauterer Wettbewerb* (2002), § 28 notes 6.

[62] Slightly misleading in this respect A. Beater, *Unlauterer Wettbewerb* (2002), § 28 notes 6, who asserts an exclusive right for consumers in Switzerland to sue.

[63] Sec. 19 para. 1 MFL. [64] Art. 19 LCD and art. 27 LGP. [65] See above A.IV.3(b).

of claim in Switzerland.[66] Under Belgian[67] and Dutch law[68] the consumer can bring claims for cessation and damages. The right of claim for consumers in France is extensive due to the special protection of the Consumer Code. It is exercised mostly in cases of illegal advertising. With criminal law claims the state prosecutor can bring a claim for infringement of the CCons and the consumer may also act as joint claimant (*action civile*).[69] But the consumer can be assigned to the prosecutor by any person having suffered individual damage, including the consumer. In Italy the consumer may have a cause of action under the general regime of consumers' rights, which states that consumers have, inter alia, the fundamental right to adequate information and fair advertising, and as well as the right to fairness, transparency, and equity in contractual relationships concerning goods and services.[70]

c) Narrowly limited cause of action – unfair competition circumstances as protective tort laws

A median approach is taken by states which regard a limited range of competition law norms as protective tort laws providing an implied right of action. The harm can then be claimed for under general tort law. In states such as France, Italy, Belgium and the Netherlands, which have a broad general clause in tort under their civil law integrating unfair competition law at least in part in general tort law, discussion on the protective extent of unfair competition norms is obviously unknown.

In Austria the OGH has relied on §§ 874, 1311 ABGB and § 2 UWG to award the consumer compensation for reliance damage suffered as a result of relying on the declared profits of an enterprise. The consumer could therefore claim expenses for the legal representation of his claim. He argued that § 2 UWG also intends competition-oriented protection

[66] Art. 10 para. 1 UWG: ' costumers are entitled to actions according to art. 9, if their economic interests are threatened by unfair competition '; see R. Knaak and M. Ritscher, *Schweiz*, in G. Schricker, notes 322 et seq.

[67] Art. 94 LCP as well as art. 1382 cc; see F. Henning-Bodewig, *Belgien*, in G. Schricker, notes 515 et seq.

[68] According to the tort law general clause art. 6: 162 Burgerlijk Wetboek – *BW* (Civil Code); F. Henning-Bodewig, W. Verkade and A. Quaedvlieg, *Niederlande*, in G. Schricker, note 619.

[69] J. Keßler and H.-W. Micklitz, *Die Harmonisierung des Lauterkeitsrechts in den Mitgliedstaaten der Europäischen Gemeinschaft und die Reform des UWG* (2003), pp. 92 et seq.

[70] l. 281/98 art. 1, par. 2, lit. (c); see Case 4 (Children's swing).

of the consumer and therefore includes individual claims by the consumer as victim of unfair competition.[71] The legal position in Sweden is similar. The requirements in Germany, Finland and Portugal are even narrower. Under German law hitherto it has been highly controversial whether the claimant can recover damages because alongside the punitive norms of the UWG the general clauses are also to be regarded as protective laws. Jurisprudence[72] and the dominant opinion in literature[73] deny such recovery because there is no competitive relationship between the consumer and the violator. The contrary opinion[74] is that as the UWG undeniably protects the consumer a corresponding protection at law is to be affirmed. The right of claim therefore exists for norms which are subject to penal law, that is normally for offences which are committed with foresight or intention.[75] The legal position in Finland is similar. In the field of unfair competition law there is an infringement of punitive norms if intentionally incorrect or misleading statements are made which are of particular importance to the target group.[76]

It remains open what effect the express inclusion of the consumer within the scope of protection of § 1 UWG 2004 on general tort law has. Whether §§ 3 et seq. UWG 2004 can be understood as a protective law in terms of § 823 para. 2 BGB depends in part upon whether the legislature intends protection of the consumer in its generality or as the actually affected consumer. The question is not easy as a matter of legal

[71] OGH (1998) 47 ÖBl 193, (1999) 47 GRUR Int. 181 (182) – 'Erster Hauptpreis'.

[72] BGH (1975) 77 GRUR 150 – 'Prüfzeichen'; BGH (1983) 36 NJW 2493 (2494).

[73] E.g. A. Baumbach and W. Hefermehl, *UWG, Kommentar* (22nd edn 2001), § 3 note 440; H. Köhler and H. Piper, *UWG, Kommentar* (3rd edn 2002), § 3 note 5.

[74] Criticism against this decision: W. Lindacher (1975) 30 BB 1311 (1312); R. Sack, *Deliktsrechtlicher Verbraucherschutz gegen unlauteren Wettbewerb* (1975) 28 NJW 1303; G. Schricker, *Schadensersatzansprüche der Abnehmer wegen täuschender Werbung?* (1975) 77 GRUR 111 (116 et seq.); G. Schricker (1975) 139 ZHR 208 (231); G. Schricker, *Soll der einzelne Verbraucher ein Recht zur Klage wegen unlauteren Wettbewerbs erhalten?* (1975) 7 ZRP 189 (195); F. Fricke (1976) 78 GRUR 680 (683); F. Traub (1980) 82 GRUR 673 (676); Recently again K. Fezer, *Modernisierung des deutschen Rechts gegen den unlauteren Wettbewerb auf der Grundlage einer Europäisierung des Wettbewerbsrechts*, expert opinion for the Ministry of Justice of June 15, 2001, p. 6; J. Keßler and H.-W. Micklitz, *Die Harmonisierung des Lauterkeitsrechts in den Mitgliedstaaten der Europäischen Gemeinschaft und die Reform des UWG* (2003), p. 77. W. Nordemann et al., *Wettbewerbs- und Markenrecht* (9th edn 2003), note 1482 wanting to answer claims from § 823 para. 2 BGB in the affirmative according to the law in force.

[75] E.g. §§ UWG 16 – 19 UWG (former §§ 4, 17, 18, 20 UWG). Regarding the former law see H. Köhler and H. Pieper, *UWG* (3rd edn 2002), § 4 note 2, § 15 note 7.

[76] Chap. § 1 StrafG.

principle. The legislature expressly designated § 1 UWG as a protective provision. The wording and legislative history indicate a protective law - otherwise the wording of § 1 UWG 2004 would be misleading. On the other hand, there are systematic arguments. There was no compensatory claim for consumers included in the new § 9 UWG 2004. In addition, the consumer right to cancel a contract under ex-§ 13a UWG was abolished.[77] Primarily natural restitution is owed as a compensatory claim under § 823 para. 2 BGB; the recognition of §§ 3 et seq. UWG 2004 as a protective law in favour of consumers would lead to the right to cancel contracts by the backdoor in the guise of a compensatory claim.

In Portugal the norms of CPub have in principle no protective function. However, if the advertising was deceptive for a consumer and was the cause of a consumer purchase, then he has a claim to defend his own interest under consumer law. As art. 11 CPub is a consumer protective rule, according to art. 483 para. 1 CC it would support a claim from the consumer to obtain compensation or a claim for an order to desist if he was directly injured.[78]

6. *The consumer as plaintiff in contract law*

The consumer is protected under general civil law against deception in all Member States.[79] In addition in many states there is liability for pre-contractual misconduct, so-called *culpa in contrahendo*. As a result most member states rely on contract law to protect the consumer in blatant cases (Austria, Finland, Germany, Greece, Italy, Poland, Portugal, Spain, United Kingdom).

In addition the Sales of Consumer Goods Directive 99/44//EC protects the buyer in that advertising can determine the concrete characteristics of a product.[80] A defect can therefore be present if the consumer has been informed of a particular characteristic of the goods through advertising. This corresponds to the European law concept of defects, which is also determined by the presentation of the product under the Product Liability Directive 85/374/EEC.[81] In some states (Germany, Italy) as a result the legal protection through the Sales of Consumer Goods

[77] See Begr. RegE UWG, BT-Drs. 15/1487, p. 14. [78] Art. 10 para. 1 lit. (c) and 13 (a) LDC.

[79] For an overview see K. Zweigert and H. Kötz, *Einführung in die Rechtsvergleichung* (3rd edn 1996), §§ 25, 28, 30, 39.III – translated by T. Weir as *Introduction to Comparative Law* (3rd edn 1998).

[80] See above Case 5 (Discontinued models).

[81] Art. 6 para. 1 lit. (a) Product Liability Directive 85/374/EEC.

Directive 99/44//EC is emphasized. Other states by contrast such as France have not yet implemented this last directive and must restrict themselves to general contract law.

Evaluation

(1) Most Member States recognize the consumer cause of action. The prolonged denial of the right to claim for consumers in Germany is therefore surprising. In the literature such a claim is often denied on the basis that §§ 1 and 3 UWG only protect the general public. Also, legal protection is relatively ineffective as the consumer is put off by the proceedings and the associated costs.[82] This corresponds to the fact that the consumer right of cancellation under § 13a UWG was abolished in Germany due to lack of practical relevance in 2004.[83]

These arguments are, however, rather sketchy and of limited persuasiveness. Numerous jurisdictions (Austria, Denmark, Netherlands[84], USA) expressly emphasize that the consumer should be protected through unfair competition law. Other jurisdictions additionally introduced special consumer protection laws (Finland, England, Belgium, France, Italy, Spain). The protection of consumers is partly expressly designated as a legal objective (Germany, Sweden, Poland).[85] Nevertheless, the legislature and the dominant opinion in Germany provide that the consumer has no right of claim.[86] To this extent the express reliance on the protection of consumers in § 1 of the German UWG seems confusing.[87] That the consumer has no right of claim because he makes no use of it anyway,[88] indicates an extremely cynical approach to the law. This mixes standing and claim objectives. If, for example, the consumer were given a more effective claim objective, such as the minimum damage provision[89] to be found in the USA, he would be more likely to exercise his right to claim. As a result the two cited arguments against a right of claim for consumers are not convincing.

[82] A. Beater, *Wettbewerbsrecht* (2002), § 28 notes 7 et seq. with pointer to the negative experiences in Switzerland.

[83] Begr. RegE UWG, BT-Drs. 15/1487, p. 14.

[84] F. Henning-Bodewig, W. Verkade and A. Quaedvlieg, *Niederlande*, in G. Schricker, note 22.

[85] E.g. § 1 German UWG 2004; § 1 MLF; § 1 u.z.n.u.

[86] Begr. RegE, BT-Drs. 15/1487, p. 22.

[87] Critical T. Möllers, *Bookreview of A. Beater, Unlauterer Wettbewerb (2002)*, 2004 (168) ZHR 225 (229).

[88] See note 82 above.

[89] See above A.IV.2.f).

In addition it is argued that no right of claim for consumers is necessary because they are sufficiently protected by general civil law.[90] This argument becomes less convincing, however, if gaps in the protection remain because general civil law does not apply. This can be the case, for example with harassment or loss-leader offers. However, the consumer right of claim should not be overestimated. For example, a compensatory claim by consumers has the disadvantage that causation between advertisement and conclusion of contract is difficult to prove.[91] In Finland, Sweden and Denmark the consumer can sue, although in general consumers are not expected to bring actions before the courts. The reasons for this are that the costs of taking legal action may be considerable, and often several years will pass before a final decision is available. In Italy and Portugal consumers normally just complain to a consumer association or the consumer agency, which after an administrative process of investigation decides on the application of an administrative fine. In the Netherlands[92] it is emphasized that the consumer right of claim is merely theoretical. In Switzerland[93] the right of claim is also of limited significance.

(2) Thus, the controversy conducted in Germany on the protective nature of UWG norms seems highly academic or like the proverbial storm in a teacup. The fear of a flood of claims,[94] which was also decisive for a decision of the BGH, is unjustified, as many Member States recognize the consumer right of claim without being overwhelmed by a flood of claims. Rather the opposite applies in that an additional right of claim merely supplements effective legal protection itself but cannot further strengthen it significantly. From this perspective the recognition of the protective nature of legal norms in the UWG or the introduction of an individual right of claim in all the states would be desirable.

[90] H. Köhler, UWG-*Reform und Verbraucherschutz*, (2003) 105 GRUR 265; H. Köhler, in W. Hefermehl, H. Köhler and J. Bornkamm, *Wettbewerbsrecht* (24th edn 2006), § 1 note 34.

[91] Regarding the German right to rescind in ex-§13a UWG see J. Keßler and H.-W. Micklitz, *Die Harmonisierung des Lauterkeitsrechts in den Mitgliedstaaten der Europäischen Gemeinschaft und die Reform des UWG* (2003), p. 76.

[92] F. Henning-Bodewig, W. Verkade and A. Quaedvlieg, *Niederlande*, in G. Schricker, note 619.

[93] A. Beater, *Wettbewerbsrecht* (2002), § 28 note 7.

[94] Begr. RegE, *UWG*, BT-Drs. 15/1487, p. 22; H. Köhler, in W. Hefermehl, H. Köhler and J. Bornkamm, *Wettbewerbsrecht* (24th edn 2006), § 1 note 34 talks about the risks of a popular action.

(3) On the European level a harmonization of the right to claim for consumers seems conceivable. Although the consumer claim for an injunction offers little incentive to claim, the compensatory claim is often incapable of proof as the claimant would have to prove to the satisfaction of the court that the unlawful advertising had caused his decision to purchase. With an extension of the concept of harm, as is the case for example in the USA,[95] the claim would be attractive to the consumer.[96] If the consumer were given a right of claim it would be consistent in that he could pursue it through the authorities or through alternative dispute resolution mechanisms.

[95] See above B.I.6(g) and A.IV.2(e).

[96] Supporting a claim for damages *de lege ferenda* already thirty years ago G. Schricker, *Soll der einzelne Verbraucher ein Recht zur Klage wegen unlauteren Wettbewerbs erhalten?* (1975) 7 ZRP 189 (194).

Case 6 Child labour: civil and criminal law

Shop owner B sells teddy bears. A intentionally spreads the untrue fact that B's teddy bears are manufactured by child labour in Africa. Through this misrepresentation, A hopes to gain a competitive advantage; B actually suffers a loss of profit amounting to €100,000; A makes an additional profit of €150,000.

1. Does this constitute an infringement of competition, which B as a competitor can take action against?

2. Can a public authority also take steps against this conduct? Can private and public law proceedings be combined?

Austria (6)

The denigration of the undertaking of another for the purpose of competition by stating or spreading facts about the undertaking, or about its owner or director, or about the goods and services of another, where those facts are of a nature to damage the company or the creditworthiness of the owner of the undertaking, constitutes under § 7 para. 1 UWG an infringement of competition law. The violator can be made subject to an injunction and liable for damages if the facts cannot be proved to be true. It is not the task of the claimant to prove that the statements are untrue. The burden of proof rests on the defendant who has to prove their truthfulness. This is especially true for the claim for damages that does not require the proof of fault.

(1) The statement that goods are produced by child labour in Africa is without any doubt of a nature to damage the company concerned and in the present case such a damage has actually taken place. A can bring a claim against his competitor B und sue for damages.[1]

The violated party is also protected by the penal law provision of defamation (§ 111 para. 1 StGB). According to that provision, anybody who accuses somebody else of contemptible qualities or attitudes or of dishonourable or immoral behaviour in a way that is perceivable to third parties, and if these accusations are of a nature to denigrate or belittle the party concerned in public, the violator can be sentenced to up to six months or fine of up to 360 days' net pay. If this is committed in a work of print or via radio or other means, whereby the defamation is perceivable by the public at large the violator can be sentenced to up to

[1] Concerning the question whether A can also demand from B the profit beyond his damages, see Case 3 (Whisky). This is not explicitely stated in the UWG.

a year in prison. Defamation of individuals will only be prosecuted at the demand of the violated party (§ 117 StGB).

An offence will be prosecuted *ex officio* only if the defamed party has been intentionally accused of committing a crime. In our case this is not the case since the sale of goods produced abroad by child labour does not constitute a crime.

(2) Private and public law proceedings cannot be combined. Every person violated in their rights by a crime or by an offence prosecuted *ex officio* can join the criminal proceeding to assert their civil law claims and thereby become a private party up to the main trial (§ 47 StPO). Claims requesting an opportunity of legal status and actions for a declaratory judgment can also be asserted.[2]

Denmark (6)

A situation of this nature is subject to § 2 sec. 2 MFL. According to § 2 sec. 2 MFL information on irrelevant matters concerning other traders with a view to achieving an advantage of competition may be improper and contrary to the act.[3] The violation of § 2 and §§ 6–9 are criminal offences.[4] Fines are possible. The violation of the general clause is not in itself a crime.[5] The reason for this is the nature of a general clause, which can be extended to cover new issues that were not foreseen either by the legislature or by traders.

A number of judgments have been given where statements have been declared to be a contravention of the act because of their irrelevant content and because they were detrimental to an undertaking.

According to § 19a MFL a competitor may institute legal proceedings against such statements with a view to obtaining an injunction under § 13 MFL. It has been explicitly stated in § 13 sec. 2 MFL, that a competitor can also bring an action before the courts with the aim of obtaining compensation for a financial loss caused by the statements. The indication in § 13 sec. 2 MFL of the possibility of liability to pay damages for violations of the Marketing Practices Act (MPA) only specifies the general rules in Danish law on liability to pay compensation.

[2] See EvBl 1970/341; ÖJZ-LSK 1981/78.

[3] P.B. Madsen, *Markedsret*, vol. 2 (4th edn 2002), p. 269; M. Koktvedgaard, *Lærebog i Konkurrenceret* (4th edn 2000), p. 268; E. Borcher and F. Bøggild, *Markedsføringsloven* (2001), p. 216.

[4] J. Keßler and A. Brunn-Nielsen, in J. Keßler and H.-W. Micklitz, p. 43 (47).

[5] Møgelvang-Hansen and Østergaard, *Denmark*, in R. Schulze and H. Schulte-Nölke, p. 3.

(1) Violation of § 2 sec. 2 MFL might be the basis for a penalty. According to § 22 sec. 3 MFL a fine may be imposed on violators of § 2 sec. 2 of the act. Violation of § 2 sec. 2 MFL, concerns relations between traders, and prosecution of violations of the rule is therefore, contrary to the other rules of the law, under § 22 sec. 2, no. 2 MFL subject to private prosecution.[6] According to legal practice, only a limited number of people/traders will be entitled to institute legal proceedings with the aim of having a fine imposed on a trader. A trade association, for example, will often not possess sufficient legal interest.[7]

(2) The Consumer Ombudsman may request that the prosecuting authorities bring a criminal case concerning violation of the MPA. A criminal case is brought before the ordinary courts. According to § 19 sec. 6 MFL the Consumer Ombudsman may request to conduct the criminal case himself.

England (6)

(1) A's conduct would be actionable under tort law. Relevant torts might be malicious falsehood, slander of goods, libel or slander, the latter relating to the defamation of persons.

A's conduct clearly satisfies all the prerequisites of the tort of malicious falsehood.[8]

Libel and slander form part of the law of defamation. The tort of defamation protects a person from untrue imputations that harm his reputation with others. Libel is defamatory material in permanent form, for example, in print, whereas slander takes a transient form. In the present case, it is unclear in which form A has spread the untrue allegations about child labour used in the production of B's teddy bears.

Defamation consists of the publication of material that reflects on a person's reputation so as to lower the claimant in the estimation of right-thinking members of society generally.[9] The test is objective so that it does not matter whether or not the defendant intended to defame the claimant. Accusing a trader of using child labour is nowadays clearly defamatory. The defamation must refer to the claimant, i.e. make him identifiable which is clearly the case since B has been named. Further, the defamation must have been communicated to some person

[6] P.B. Madsen, Markedsret, vol. 2 (4th edn 2002), p. 343.

[7] An example of this can be seen in the Danish Supreme Court judgment referred to in U 2002.1007 H.

[8] For details, see the solution of Case 1 (Risky bread) at 2.

[9] *Sim v. Stretch*, (1936) 52 TLR 669.

other than the claimant,[10] which is obvious in the present case. Libel does not require any damage to be shown by the claimant but is actionable *per se*. This is different in slander, with a number of exceptions.[11] In the present case, damage can be established by B anyway. Under both the laws of malicious falsehood and of defamation, B can obtain an *injunction* order against A, and he can also sue for damages.

(2) Libel, however, can be prosecuted as a crime if the libel was so serious that it was proper to invoke the criminal law and where the public interest required the institution of criminal proceedings. This has not occurred for a long time in practice, and it was thought that criminal libel had become virtually obsolete. However, the mere threat of proceedings by Sir James Goldsmith in 1977[12] succeeded in forcing the satirical magazine 'Private Eye' to withdraw copies from bookshops.[13] In contrast, the case of A and B would not appear to be sufficiently serious to invoke the criminal law.

(3) There is no protection available by way of the OFT since the case does not touch on the protection of consumers.[14]

Finland (6)

(1) As stated in Case 1 giving false information is a breach of § 2 SopMenL and also § 1 SopMenL. B could ask the Market Court to issue a cease-and-desist order to force A to stop spreading untrue information. As this has been done intentionally, the fine payable if the order is not followed would probably be quite considerable. Such cases are very rare in Finland and thus the possible amount of the fine cannot be stated. At the same time, B could ask A to be compelled to correct the information given. There is also a possibility to demand those working for A to stop spreading untrue information. This could include both workers and even outsiders such as a marketing company. Para. 2 of § 6 SopMenL requires special reasons if the order is to affect the above mentioned groups. When it is a question of intentionally spreading false information there might be reasons to order even workers or marketing companies etc. to cease giving this kind of information.

As the untrue information has been spread intentionally, and it is possibly a crime too, B could demand compensation under the Finnish

[10] *Powell v. Gelston* [1916] 2 KB 615.

[11] For details, see M. Jones, *Torts* (7th edn 2000), p. 511.

[12] *Goldsmith v. Pressdram Ltd. and Others* [1977] QB 83.

[13] See H. Harpwood, *Principles of Tort Law* (4th edn 2000), p. 369.

[14] See the solution to Case 5 (Discontinued models), question 4.

Tort Liability Act. Under art. 5:1 even purely economic damage can be compensated if it has been caused by a criminal act. Even if A's deed is not considered as a criminal act the damage can be compensated as it is an intentional act.

(2) As A has been intentionally spreading an untrue fact about B's teddy bears A could face prosecution by the state prosecutors. B also has the personal right to prosecute. Usually it would be B that informs the police of the possible crime (as crimes are only investigated by the police) and after the events have been investigated the prosecutor would decide whether to prosecute or not.

(3) As the Market Court has no right to decide on criminal law issues and the lower general courts have no right to decide on other sanctions which are possible under SopMenL these cases cannot be combined. If B would demand compensation this case could be combined with a criminal law case.

The Ombudsman has a right to be heard when the criminal charges are decided in the general court of first instance: § 11 SopMenL. Criminal proceedings are not common and the Finnish Supreme Court has not yet decided any such case. The problem with criminal proceedings for the injured party is that to get an injunction to end illegal marketing and forbid the renewal of this marketing one must take the matter to the Market Court.

France (6)

(1) A's behaviour constitutes an infringement of competition as it is discrediting B. B has the possibility to start a civil action for reparation of the material damage, art. 1382, 1383 cc. As has already been pointed out discrediting and denigration is an established group in jurisprudence. A second possibility consists in commencing a criminal procedure with an action for defamation (*diffamation*). It is prohibited by art. 29 of the act of July 29, 1881. But only the denigration of a person is reprehensible, not a denigration of his products.[15] Only if the denigration of the product is accompanied by statements affirming the dishonesty of the producer, is the criminal provision on defamation to be applied.[16] Thus in the present case criminal proceedings would not

[15] M. Malaurie-Vignal, in: Juris-Classeur, *Concurrence, consommation* (1996), Fasc. 210, 'Dénigrement', note 75.

[16] Ibid.; Cour de Cassation, Chambre criminelle, July 22, 1922 in Bulletin criminel note 273.

be possible. A third and final possibility could be a breach of art. L 121-1 CCons, if the denigrating purposes are also considered as misleading advertising. The misleading advertising is considered to be a criminal behaviour under art. L 213-1 CCons. This is the case if consumers are misled by the denigration. In the present case it could be considered that there has been false information on the origin of B's products. Therefore, it is sufficient that the purposes are capable of misleading the consumer.[17]

(2) Concerning the criminal action, this has to be sought from the Procureur de la République. Where the field of misleading advertisement is concerned[18] the directorate general for competition, consumer protection and fraud prevention (DGCCRF) and those from the food directorate general of the Ministry of Agriculture and those from the metrology department of the Ministry of Industry are authorized to establish breaches of arts. L 121-8, L 121-9 and L 121-2 CCons.

Apart from these public authorities, whenever advertising is concerned it would also be possible to apply to self-regulation authorities such as the *Bureau de vérification de la publicité*.[19]

(3) All actions, private, administrative and criminal, can be combined, in the sense that they can be engaged at the same time.[20] Especially, it has been decided that a summary interlocutory procedure (art. 484 of the New Code of Civil Procedure) can be pursued in parallel to criminal procedure.[21] In French law it is also possible to engage a civil law claim for damages as an accessory to the criminal prosecution, the so-called *partie civile*.[22]

Apart from cases where the competitive behaviour is explicitly subject to a criminal provision, a tort action based on unfair competition cannot be combined with a criminal procedure.[23] Thus, the defamation and insult are the only two cases where unfair denigration is penalized.

[17] M. Malaurie-Vignal, in: Juris-Classeur, *Concurrence, consommation* (1996), Fasc. 210, 'Dénigrement', note 77.

[18] See Case 1 (Risky bread). [19] See Case 2 (Watch imitations I).

[20] M. Malaurie-Vignal, *Droit de la concurrence* (2nd edn 2002), p. 281.

[21] Cour de Cassation, Chambre Commericale, October 19, 1999, in: *Contrats, Concurrence, Consommation* (2000), note 7.

[22] TGI de Nanterre of June 24, 2003, in: *Contrats, Concurrence, Consommation* (2003), note 191 (with an example of a consumer defence association being civil party in a criminal procedure).

[23] N.-F. Alpi, in Juris-Classeur, *Concurrence, consommation* (2003), Fasc. 245, 'Action en concurrence déloyale – éléments de procedure', note 71.

Germany (6)

Both competitors and the state prosecutors can take action against this type of infringement of competition. Civil proceedings and criminal proceedings can be combined.

(1) B could have a compensatory claim for disparagement under §§ 9 s. 1, 3, 4 no. 8 UWG (ex-§ 14 UWG). A has spread untrue facts for competitive purposes, that is to gain a competitive advantage. These facts were commercially and operationally harmful within § 4 no. 8 UWG (ex-§ 14 UWG), as the misrepresentation has led in the actual case to a loss of profits by B amounting to €100,000. A compensatory claim can also be based on § 823 para. 2 BGB together with § 187 StGB, provided the spreading of untrue facts was likely to endanger B's good name. This concerns the protection of a commercial reputation, so-called goodwill. The allegation that B sells teddy bears produced using child labour is likely to adversely affect this goodwill, so that § 823 para. 2 BGB together with § 187 StGB also applies. In addition, the requirements of defamation of business reputation under § 824 BGB are fulfilled.[24]

(2) Under German law, in principle there is no public authority responsible for monitoring observance of advertising standards.[25]

Criminal offences are involved in the circumstances of § 187 StGB, § 194 para. 1 s. 1 StGB. This means that the criminal prosecution authority may not be involved *ex officio*, but a criminal prosecution may be brought by the injured party under § 77 para. 1 StGB. This claim can only be brought within three months of knowledge of the act and the identity of the perpetrator: § 77b StGB. Where a criminal claim is filed, the state prosecution brings the action if there is a public interest in the claim: § 376 StPO. Otherwise, the injured party can bring a private action under § 374 para. 1 no. 7 StPO.[26]

(3) Civil proceedings can be brought within the criminal proceedings as a so-called 'joint procedure' (*Adhäsionsverfahren*) under §§ 403 et seq. StPO. Such a claim has the same effect as filing civil proceedings: § 404 para. 2 StPO. In cases falling under § 405 StPO, however, a ruling can be denied particularly if the claim is likely to delay criminal proceedings.

[24] H. Köhler, in W. Hefermehl, H. Köhler and J. Bornkamm, *Wettbewerbsrecht* (24th edn 2006), § 4 note 8.9; W. Nordemann, in K.H. Fezer, *Lauterkeitsrecht* (2005), § 4–8 note 5.

[25] H. Köhler and H. Piper, *UWG* (3rd edn 2002), § 13 note 3; A. Bergmann, in H. Harte-Bavendamm and F. Henning-Bodewig, *UWG* (2004), § 8 note 257.

[26] Until the amendment of the UWG in 2004 former § 15 UWG was additionally relevant; meanwhile former § 15 was deleted, as § 187 StGB applies in this case.

Thus, this procedure is not very effective. This is decided by a criminal judge rather than a civil judge, who under the circumstances is more familiar with the material.

Greece (6)

(1) A's conduct is prohibited by the special provision of art. 11(1) of L. 146/1914.[27] The conditions for the application of art. 11 are: (a) the intent to compete, (b) the propagation of information and (c) the evaluation of such information as harmful. Knowledge, however, by the person propagating the information as to the inaccuracy of the information is not a prerequisite. To the contrary, such information must simply not be readily provable as true.[28] Therefore, B may take legal proceedings against A and request the prevention of any repetition or further propagation of the inaccuracies. He may also request reparation of the material damages suffered, irrespective of the respondent's fault.[29] The damages shall in principle be calculated on the basis of the profit lost by B, since the adequate connection between the lost profit and A's conduct is easily established. B may seek pecuniary reparation for 'moral' (non-pecuniary) harm,[30] provided that he adduces proof that his honour or personality has been damaged by the respondent's fault (art. 57, 59 and 932 CC).

(2) Art. 12 of L. 146/1914 characterizes A's conduct as a criminal offence (misdemeanour) falling under the category of slander in the competition field (see art. 363 of the Criminal Code). The criminal act refers to the untruthfulness of facts, while its imputability refers to the offender's knowledge of the untruthfulness of the facts propagated. Intent to compete is not essential; however, the offender must be aware that the facts propagated may cause damage.[31] The offender is

[27] Art. 11(1) of L. 146/1914 stipulates: 'Any person who, with the intent to compete, alleges or propagates information on the activity or enterprise of another, the owner or director thereof and the products or the industrial works of another that may damage the activity or the commercial credibility thereof, is under obligation to repair the damage inflicted, provided that the information is not readily provable as true. The damaged party may request the omission of any repetition or further propagation of the inaccuracies.'

[28] G. Michalopoulos, *Article 11*, in N. Rokas (ed.), *Unfair Competition* (1996), p. 314; if the propagated information is proved to be true, the application of art. 1 L. 146/1914 may be envisaged.

[29] M.-Th. Marinos, *Unfair Competition* (2002), p. 194. See also *Athens Court of Appeals* 698/2003 (2004) EllDni 1064.

[30] *Areios Pagos (Supreme Court)* 849/1985, 34 NoV 836.

[31] G. Michalopoulos, Article 11, in N. Rokas (ed.), Unfair Competition (1996), p. 316.

punished with a custodial penalty of imprisonment of up to six months and a pecuniary penalty or one of the above penalties. The crime may not be prosecuted *ex officio* but only after accusation by the victim, as provided for by art. 21 of L. 146/1914. The accusation must be submitted to the competent prosecutor within three months of the criminal act and the identity of the offender being known by the victim. If the accused is found guilty, the victim may be granted permission to publish the decision in the press at the victim's expense.[32] The cumulative application of art. 12 of L. 146/1914 and of the relevant provisions of the penal code (art. 361 on insult, art. 362 and 363 on simple and defamatory slander) is not excluded as different interests are protected by the above-mentioned articles (on one hand, the trust and honour of the victim in commercial transactions, on the other hand his reputation and esteem).

(3) In any case, B may request the pressing of criminal charges against A, and may also file actions in accordance with the law of unfair competition before the civil courts.

Hungary (6)

According to sec. 3 HCA it is prohibited to violate or jeopardize the good reputation or credit-worthiness of a competitor by stating or spreading untrue facts, and by misrepresenting true facts, as well as by any other practice. Therefore, the action of A constitutes an infringement of the HCA. The prohibited action of the competitor can be twofold. It can be aimed at breaking up already existing economic relations or it can be aimed at hindering the establishment of such relations. Accordingly, the action must be intentional. It is, however, not a requirement that the competitor should be in the same economic position as the damaged party, nor is it necessary that the action has actually caused damage.[33]

(1) According to sec. 86 (1) HCA this case belongs to the jurisdiction of the courts: 'Proceedings in cases of violation of the provisions contained in sections 2 to 7 shall fall within the competence of the court.' In this particular case, public authorities cannot take steps against this conduct.

[32] See art. 22 of L. 146/1914.

[33] K. Kaszainé Mezey and P. Miskolczi Bodnár, Versenyjogi Kézikönyv, Budapest: HVG-Orac (2001) p. 75.

(2) But if the same case would harm the interest of consumers and thus violate sec. 8 HCA, then they could submit a complaint or an informal complaint to the OEC on the basis of sec. 43/G HCA to take steps against A. (See Hungary (4) on complaints and informal complaints.)

(3) Private law and public law proceedings cannot be combined with one another, but they can be brought parallel to each other if the actions violate criminal law. In this case, it could be libel or slander (sec. 179 and sec. 180 Criminal Code).

Ireland (6)

(1) This commercial slander is not in breach of Irish competition law, but is actionable by B, as a tort at civil law. Under sec. 20 of the Defamation Act 1961, B does not have to show any special damages have been suffered, because the falsehood was intended to cause him pecuniary loss.[34]

It is interesting to note that in Ireland's common law jurisdiction this type of misrepresentation is not at all viewed as relating to competition law, but is treated almost solely as a matter to be settled by tort law. While a public prosecution is technically possible in this case, it would be highly unlikely. Both the Law Reform Commission and a Government Legal Advisory Group on Defamation have made recommendations for the reform of the law on defamation but there is no indication when, if ever, these recommendations may become law.[35]

(2) A's misrepresentation is also actionable under criminal law. The Director of Public Prosecutions could take action against B under the Defamation Act 1961. The penalty is a fine and up to two years' imprisonment for conviction on indictment.

(3) Private and public law proceedings may be combined by the court. Trial in a defamation action is by judge and jury.

Italy (6)

A's behaviour amounts to disparagement breaching art. 2598, no. 2 cc. A has knowingly made an untrue statement as to a competitor's products, which has caused a loss to the plaintiff.

[34] See Case 1 (Risky bread).

[35] Report on the Civil Law of Defamation (December 1991) (LRC 38–1991); Report on the Crime of Libel (December 1991) (LRC 41–1991); Report of the Legal Advisory Group on Defamation (March 2003).

(1) B has a compensatory claim; the sum of damages should be equal to the profits lost by the plaintiff. Moreover, according to art. 2600 para. 2 cc, the plaintiff may ask the court to order that the decision, or its summary, may be published in a number of newspapers, at the defendant's expense. Such publication has a compensatory function, since it aims at restoring the plaintiff's good reputation. At the same time, through such publication consumers may learn that the defendant made false statements, thereby making him less trustworthy as a business-person for the future.

The plaintiff has the burden of proving the amount of damages: such proof may be provided in the form of abatement of sales with reference to prior periods, or to forecasts. Profits made by the infringing party may also be taken into account, though the plaintiff is entitled to claim only compensation for losses suffered, and he is not entitled to claim the surrender of profits made by the other party.

(2)(a) As a general principle, in Italian law no public authority is entitled to take action against unfair competition under the Civil Code. Nevertheless, public authorities may take action if the illegal behaviour infringes further statutory provisions that protect public interests. In the case at stake, A's conduct may amount to misleading advertising: according to d.lgs. 74/92 the *Autorità Garante della Concorrenza e del Mercato* is entitled to take action against misleading advertisements, issuing cease and desist orders.

Proceedings by the Authority may not be started *ex officio*: it is necessary that an entitled person (competitors or consumers, their associations, any interested third party) asks the Authority to start a proceeding.

(b) Furthermore, A may be held liable for an infringement of art. 595 of the Criminal Code prohibiting defamation. Criminal prosecution for defamation may not be started *ex officio*: a suit from the injured person is needed, within thirty days following the offence.

(c) Under Italian criminal procedure, it is possible to bring private claims for damages within the criminal proceeding (*costituzione di parte civile*). According to art. 75 of the Code of Criminal Procedure, it is possible to file claims for damages both in front of civil and criminal courts. As a general principle, civil litigation is not subject to stay, pending the criminal judgment.

(3) According to art. 7 par. 13 of d.lgs. 74/1992 proceedings by the *Autorità Garante* do not interfere with court litigation for unfair competition. Therefore, it is possible that the plaintiff simultaneously starts

court litigation and the administrative proceeding in front of the Autorità. The decision by the Autorità is not binding on the court, and vice-versa, though the two decisions may influence each other. According to some case law, in particular, decisions by the Autorità may be taken into account in trials at court.[36]

Netherlands (6)

(1) B may institute legal action against A based on the general rules concerning tort (art. 6:162 et seq. BW) and claim damages (as well as an injunction against such action by A). Furthermore, to the extent that A spreads this untrue fact in a way that the public can take notice of it and the information distributed by A can therefore be characterized as a misleading advertisement in the sense of art. 194a para. 2 lit. (e) BW, B can claim cessation of these actions and/or publication of a correction of that information, in the manner indicated by the court.

(2) A criminal action may be taken against A. Pursuant to art. 328bis of the Dutch Penal Code a person that misleads the public or a specific person, with the intention of gaining commercial profit, and thereby damages competitors, is guilty of unfair competition. If the information can be regarded as public information, the facts might be characterized as advertising in the sense of the Advertising Code enabling the RCC to take steps.

(3) If the public prosecutor decides to bring criminal charges against A, B may join a claim for civil damages in the criminal proceedings. However, this does not affect B's power to bring a claim for damages against A before the competent civil courts.

Poland (6)

Distribution of untrue or misleading information about an undertaking itself or with the purpose of gaining an advantage or causing damage constitutes an act of unfair competition, art. 14.1 u.z.n.k. Untrue or misleading information concerns in particular products or services, art. 14.2 (2) u.z.n.k. As mentioned earlier, numerous provisions of the u.z.n.k. protect the transparency of the market. The cited provision complements art. 10 and art. 16 u.z.n.k. Art. 14 aims to protect both undertakings and customers; anyone who defames another with the

[36] See Trib. Roma, February 25, 1998, Johson & Johnson s.p.a. v. Fater s.p.a., in Riv.Dir.Int. (1998), II, 204, according to which ordinary courts may assess the misleading nature of advertisements applying the same criteria stated by d.lgs. 74/92.

object of gaining an advantage or causing damage is deemed to be liable.[37]

'Distribution' means making the information broadly available. The information must be untrue (in case of informative statements) or misleading (might be true, but the way it is presented causes the addressees confusion).[38]

(1) The claims listed in art. 18.1 (1–3 and 6) u.z.n.k.[39] can be brought by organizations and other institutions whose statutory tasks include the protection of undertakings' interests and the President of the Office for Competition and Consumer Protection.

The provision of art. 19.1 does not apply to the following acts of unfair competition: misleading branding (art. 5–7 u.z.n.k.), infringement of trade secrets (art. 11 u.z.n.k.), distribution of untrue or misleading information (art. 14 u.z.n.k.) and bribery, art. 15a u.z.n.k. The undertaking, whose interests have been infringed or endangered can bring a claim based on art. 5–7, 11 and 14 u.z.n.k. The President of the Office for Competition and Consumer Protection can initiate an action based on art. 15a u.z.n.k. Consequently, the undertaking is the only legitimate plaintiff to bring a claim against the defamation, art. 14 u.z.n.k.

(2) Anybody who distributes untrue or misleading information about an undertaking – in particular about its management, goods, services and prices or about its economic or legal situation – with the purpose of harming the undertaking can be penalized with imprisonment or fine: art. 26.1 u.z.n.k. The same penalty applies to the person, who with the purpose of gaining a financial advantage distributes untrue or misleading information about the undertaking: art. 26.2 u.z.n.k. Action will be taken on the harmed person's request in case of crimes and on the harmed person's demand in case of misdemeanours: art. 27.1 u.z.n.k. Demand to take an action can be made by the institutions mentioned in art. 19.1 u.z.n.k. (art. 27. 2 u.z.n.k.). This is an exception to the general rule of art. 27.1 u.z.n.k. Action is taken by the police in case of serious crimes and by a special institution (*Kolegium d.s. Wykroczen*) in case of misdemeanours.

(3) According to art. 7 k.p.k. (Criminal Procedure Code) the prosecutor can demand action to be taken in every case. He can also participate in all procedures, even those already pending, if in his opinion it is

37 A. Kraus and F. Zoll, *Polska ustawa o zwalczaniu nieuczciwej konkurencji* (1929).

38 M. Kepinski, in J. Szwaja (ed.), *Ustawa o zwalczaniu nieuczciwej konkurencji* (2000), p. 368.

39 For more details on Art 18 see the analysis of Case 1 (Risky bread).

required to protect justice, citizens' rights or the public interest. He is not limited in the remedies he can demand, so he can also demand compensation.

Portugal (6)

A intentionally behaves in an unfair way in competition. Under art. 317 lit. (b) CPI these false statements made to discredit a competitor's reputation are considered an act of unfair competition.

(1) The untrue statements distributed by A have caused a loss of profit amounting to €100,000. B can sue A under art. 317 lit. (b) CPI and art. 483 para. 1 CC for the damages he has suffered. A is in fact the injured party protected under art. 317 lit. (b) CPI. A compensatory claim can also be based on the crime of defamation (art. 180 para. 1 CP) or under the civil tort of false affirmation which affects someone's good name or reputation (art. 484 CPC). B, as the injured party, can also be a party in a criminal claim.

(2) In Portuguese law, unfair competition is an administrative tort. The administrative tort is public, meaning that the public prosecution service has to commence *ex officio* an administrative proceeding against the defendant.

The injured party B can only bring a civil action to obtain compensation for his losses and damages. In fact, B can also bring a compensatory claim under art. 317 lit. (b) CPI and art. 483 CC. For this compensatory claim only the purpose of discrediting the competitor or to damage or profit from him is required.

(3) Civil proceedings, like the compensation action, have to be brought in a civil court.

The legislature has recently changed the criminal sanctions into administrative torts. Thus it is possible that in the future more fines will be applied. At present, civil sanctions are the most relevant part of unfair competition law.

Spain (6)

This is a denigrating statement, which constitutes unfair conduct forbidden by art. 9 LCD.

(1) As far as the LCD is concerned, only those competitors whose economic interests have been harmed or menaced by the unfair conduct are entitled to exercise any of the actions foreseen in art. 18 LCD as stated in art. 19 para. 1 LCD. Nevertheless, associations, professional corporations or those associations representing consumers' rights

could also bring one of these actions when defending the rights of their members or of consumers.

(2) The LCD deals primarily with private law. However, if A's behaviour severely distorts free competition in the market and affects the public interest, art. 7 LDC. Art. 7 LDC provides that the competition authorities (administrative bodies inside the Ministry of Economy) can act against unfair competition behaviour when these acts significantly affect competition in the market, usually because the firms engaging in such conduct are large firms and so their actions can have significant effects in the market. Administrative action would result in prohibitions and fines, but no damages for the victim, who should go to the civil courts to ask for them.

(3) Art. 282 CP (Criminal Code) punishes deceptive advertising when damage to consumers of special gravity results.

Sweden (6)

All statements and activities with the purpose of supporting the sale or offer of products are covered by the MFL. According to sec. 6 MFL these statements must be correct in the sense that they are not allowed to be misleading. Sec. 6 primarily covers advertisements that are misleading as to the character, composition, geographic origin and use of own and others' products. Sec. 6 MFL includes a list of the type of practices that are prohibited, but the list is not exhaustive. Among these examples are the product's effect on health and environment and other commercial businesses' qualifications. There is reason to believe that the statement from A is covered by sec. 6 MFL. If not, general misrepresentations and 'needless ridicule' of competitors and their products are covered by the general clause in sec. 4 MFL.

(1) According to sec. 38 MFL the concerned undertaking and the KO (Consumer Ombudsman), the head of the Consumer Authority, have standing to take action against violations of the rules in the MFL. The remedies available to the KO are injunctions with or without periodic penalty payments, interim injunctions, administrative fines and destruction of misleading presentations (see further Case 3). An undertaking does not have standing to make a claim for administrative fines, unless the KO has decided not to pursue the matter on its own.

KO decides on its own which matters it will investigate. In deciding whether or not to pursue a case, the KO will look at the effects of the marketing from a public point of view. This means that the KO will only pursue matters that have sufficient negative effects on consumers, thereby disqualifying matters with limited effects or effects that only affect commercial undertakings.

(2) According to the MFL the KO must first try to resolve conflicts on a voluntary basis.

Summary (6)

7. *State prosecutor*

a) The enforcement of infringements against unfair competition law through criminal law means

The criminal law is most strongly formulated in France and Portugal. In France, for the bringing of a criminal action, application must be made to the Procureur de la République. Where the field of misleading advertisement is concerned[40] the directorate general for competition, consumer protection and fraud prevention (DGCCRF) and those from the food directorate general of the Ministry of Agriculture and those from the metrology department of the Ministry of Industry are authorized to establish breaches of articles L 121-8 and L 121-9 of the CCons (art. L 121-2 CCons). In French law it is also possible to join a civil damage claim as an accessory to the criminal prosecution, the so-called *partie civile*. Abuse of someone's vulnerability in specific situations such as home visits or canvassing by telephone or fax[41] constitutes an offence punishable by imprisonment of between one and five years and/or a fine of €9,000. The criminal law nature of advertising law forces the French Parliament to adopt a multitude of individual regulations to comply with the rule of law requirement *nulla poena sine lege* (no punishment without law). In Portuguese law, unfair competition was a crime until 2003. The crime was public with the consequence that the public prosecution service had to commence *ex officio* a criminal proceeding against the agent. In this criminal proceeding the competitor can be part of it and it does not require a particular criminal complaint to begin the proceeding. It is not in fact necessary that someone brings a claim to the criminal authorities in order to begin a criminal procedure against the perpetrator. Civil proceedings, like the compensation action, could be brought within the criminal proceedings in a so-called 'joint procedure' (*processo de adesão*). Under art. 71 CPP, which applies this procedure, the civil action to gain compensation for the loss of profit must be pursued in the criminal

[40] See Case 1 (Risky bread). [41] Art. L 122-8 et seq. CCons.

action. Such a claim has the same effect as filing civil proceedings. Normally, in Portugal, the criminal law is not applied in battles between competitors. In fact, in the last decades judgments about unfair competition have not applied criminal sanctions. Therefore, there are authors who consider the criminal sanction purely symbolic.[42] Civil sanctions are in fact the most relevant part of the tort of unfair competition, which competitors can use to defend their own private economic interests. In the meantime the CPI has been reformed through the Decree No. 36/03 of March 5, 2003. The CPI provided for criminal penalties against an infringement, whereas under the reform infringements are only classified as a regulatory offence.

b) Criminal law as the exception

In most states, by contrast, intervention of the state prosecutor is the exception. In Germany, both competitors and the state prosecutors can take action against certain types of infringement of competition. Civil proceedings and criminal proceedings can be combined. Basically the intervention of the state prosecutor requires an application by the injured party. An exception is provided under § 16 UWG (ex-§ 4 UWG). In Germany, civil proceedings can be brought within the criminal proceedings as a so-called *joint procedure* (*Adhäsionsverfahren*) under §§ 403 et seq. StPO. Such a claim has the same effect as filing civil proceedings: § 404 para. 2 StPO. In cases falling under § 405 StPO, however, a ruling can be overlooked, particularly if the claim is likely to delay criminal proceedings. Thus, this procedure is not very effective. These cases are decided by a criminal judge rather than a civil judge, who under the circumstances is more familiar with the material. In Austria criminal proceedings are also possible in exceptional circumstances. Civil law proceedings can be combined with criminal proceedings in cases prosecuted *ex officio* and at the demand of the individual. However, in Greece the civil law proceedings cannot be combined with criminal proceedings.

In Poland a party who distributes untrue or misleading information about an undertaking – in particular about its management, its goods, services and prices, or about its economic or legal situation – with the purpose of harming the undertaking can be penalized with imprisonment or fine, art. 26.1 u.z.n.k. Action is taken by the police in case

[42] A. Menezes Leitão, *Estudo de Direito Privado sobre a Cláusula Geral de Concorrência Desleal* (2000), p. 170.

of serious crimes and by a special institution (*Kolegium d.s. Wykroczen*) in case of misdemeanours. According to art. 7 k.p.k. (Criminal Procedure Code) the prosecutor can demand action to be taken in every case. He can also participate in all procedures, even where pending, if in his opinion it is required to protect justice, citizens' rights or the public interest. He is not limited in the remedies he can demand, so he can also demand compensation.

In Sweden there is no actual penal law, but rather the Consumer Ombudsman prosecutes infringements. As a result there is no civil law proceeding which can be joined to a criminal proceeding. In Finland, if done intentionally the fine payable if the order is not followed would be quite considerable. If the untrue information has been spread intentionally and it is possibly a crime too then the injured party could demand compensation under the Finnish Tort Liability Act. Under art. 5:1 even purely economic loss can be compensated if it results from a criminal act. Criminal proceedings are not common and the Finnish Supreme Court has not yet decided any such case.[43] The problem with criminal proceedings for the injured party is that to get an injunction to end illegal marketing and forbid the renewal of this marketing one must take the matter into the Market Court. In Denmark, the Consumer Ombudsman may request that the prosecuting authorities bring a criminal case concerning violation of the Marketing Practices Act. A criminal case is brought before the ordinary courts. According to § 19 sec. 6 MFL the Consumer Ombudsman may request to conduct the criminal case himself. In England, libel, however, can be prosecuted as a crime if the libel was so serious that it was proper to invoke the criminal law and where the public interest required the institution of criminal proceedings. This has not occurred for a long time in practice, and it was thought that criminal libel had become virtually obsolete. However, the mere threat of proceedings by Sir James Goldsmith in 1977 succeeded in forcing the satirical magazine 'Private Eye' to withdraw copies from bookshops. In contrast, Case 6 would not appear to be sufficiently serious to invoke the criminal law. In civil disputes the principle forms of relief are awards of damages and costs, and the grant of injunction. If advertising leads to a criminal prosecution, perhaps because of an alleged breach of the Trade Descriptions Act 1968 or infringement of copyright or trademark, fines will be the sanction or, in serious cases, imprisonment.[44]

[43] See Case 6 (Child labour).

[44] S. Groom, *United Kingdom*, in J. Maxeiner and P. Schotthöfer, p. 469 (505).

As a general principle, under Italian law no public authority is entitled to take action against unfair competition under the Civil Code. Nevertheless, public authorities may take action if the illegal behaviour infringes further statutory provisions which protect public interests. In Case 6 the violator's conduct may amount to misleading advertising: according to d.lgs. 74/92 the *Autorità Garante della Concorrenza e del Mercato* is entitled to take action against misleading advertisements, issuing cease-and-desist orders. Furthermore, the violator may be held liable for infringement of art. 595 of the Criminal Code, prohibiting defamation. Criminal prosecution for defamation may not be started *ex officio*: a suit from the injured person is needed, within thirty days after the offence. Under Italian criminal procedure, it is possible to bring private claims for damages within the criminal proceeding (*costituzione di parte civile*). According to art. 75 of the Code of Criminal Procedure, it is possible to file claims for damages both before civil and criminal courts. As a general principle, civil litigation is not subject to stay, pending the criminal judgment. In Spain, the LCD deals primarily with private law. Only if the violator's behaviour severely distorts free competition in the market and affects the public interest, will art. 7 LDC apply and the infringement be prosecuted by the Spanish antitrust authorities.

Evaluation

(1) The arguments against criminal proceedings are to an extent identical with those against public law monetary fines. The principle of no punishment without law requires that the infringer knows of the legal duty and the penalty for the infringement of that duty. Unfair competition law is, however, intrinsically such that numerous forms of conduct cannot be precisely prescribed. Hence numerous Member States provide for a general clause in unfair competition law. With general clauses this legal duty can, however, often not be determined in advance. Therefore a penalty is only possible in particular cases, as demonstrated by Swedish and French law.[45] The no punishment without law principle means in addition that the extension of the scope of an offence is not possible through analogy.[46] According to BGH jurisprudence in Germany there is no harm within the scope of fraud under § 263 StGB, for example, where the purchased goods can be sensibly used by the

[45] T. Dreier and S. von Lewinsky, *Frankreich*, in G. Schricker, note 10.

[46] For § 16 UWG (former § 4 UWG) see e.g. OLG Stuttgart (1981) 83 GRUR 750 – 'statt Preise'; BGH (2002) 55 NJW 3415.

aggrieved party and where the purchase price is not excessive.[47] Criminal proceedings would also seem to be disproportionate.[48]

In Germany recently the concept of unconscionability was deleted from the UWG in favour of anti-competitive conduct, because the competitor should no longer be tainted by the charge of unconscionable conduct.[49] In France and Portugal[50] monetary fines are described as ridiculously low.

(2) However a number of arguments can be found in support of criminal proceedings. Criminal proceedings allow penalties, that is fines, which are often difficult to enforce under civil law. These administrative law proceedings must in doubtful cases be subject to judicial review. Criminal proceedings by contrast are judicial proceedings from the beginning. Therefore, they are, as a rule, shorter than administrative law proceedings. Ultimately, the inquisitorial and investigative principle of criminal law proceedings is decisive. State bodies monitor the legal infringement. If the private claimant can join in the proceedings, then enforcement for the private claimant is made significantly easier. Consolidated proceedings are known in a number of states (Germany, France, Italy and Portugal).

(3) As a result however there are more arguments against criminal proceedings than in favour. Above all, the principle of certainty and the lack of severe wrongdoing in the infringement render criminal proceedings less convincing. It is significant that in most Member States (with the exception of France) criminal proceedings have hardly any role to play. As a result the Portuguese legislature has understandably reclassified the unfair competition infringement as a breach of regulation rather than a criminal offence in its amendment of the CPI. Thus criminal law would seem to be appropriate only when the hard core of unfair competition law is concerned, for example with the defamation of competitors as provided in art. 10bis Paris Convention[51] or § 16

47 BGHSt 3, 99; BGHSt 16, 220 (221 et seq.); BGHSt 23, 300 (302); BGH (2001) 103 GRUR 1178 (1180). Therefore there have been voices asking for a change to the elements of fraud, see R. Sack, (2003) 49 WRP 549 (557).

48 Criticism from the German point of view in E. von Hippel, *Verbraucherschutz* (1974), p. 24; G. Schricker, (1975) 139 ZHR 208 (214 et seq., 230); K. Kreuzer, (1979) 25 WRP 255 (257).

49 See § 3 UWG in contrast to former § 1 UWG and Begr. RegE, BT-Drs. 15/1487 p. 16; see now W. Schünemann, in H. Harte-Bavendamm and F. Henning-Bodewig, *UWG* (2004), § 3 note 58.

50 J. Möllering, (1991) 37 WRP 634 (637); G. Schricker, (1994) 42 GRUR Int. 819 (822).

51 See above A.II.1(a).

UWG (ex-§ 4 UWG). As all Member States provide for such an offence, the corresponding public law or criminal law fine should be considered.[52] This, however, does not solve the problem to the extent that the EU is competent to impose penal sanctions.[53]

8. *The problem of divergent procedural routes*

a) The relationship between the various sanctioning bodies

On the European level administrative and court procedural routes are equally admissible and of equivalent status.[54] The relationship between them is, however, only clarified to the extent that the administrative law procedure must be followed by a civil law procedure. However, the relation between possibilities for parties under the civil law and the procedure for public authorities has not been regulated. As a result there is a variety of relationships, including priority for the public law procedure, secondary status and, finally, equivalence of the civil law and public law routes.

(1) Equivalence exists for example in France, where all actions – private, administrative and criminal – can be combined, in the sense that they can be pursued at the same time. In particular it has been decided, that a summary interlocutory procedure (art. 484 NCPC), a *référé* procedure, can be conducted parallel to criminal procedure. The situation in Spain and Portugal is similar.

(2) Other Member States on the other hand assume that the procedure in favour of the authority has priority. In Sweden if the Consumer Ombudsman chooses not to bring an action for administrative fines, a concerned individual undertaking or an organization of undertakings may bring such action. The latter two thus only have supplementary standing.[55] In Finland, the Consumer Ombudsman has priority to institute a prohibitive action in a matter concerning marketing targeted at consumers.[56]

(3) The intervention by the OFT in England is, if anything, secondary. In practice in England reg. 4(3) CMAR establishes the priority of complaints to the local trading standards authority[57] and of the

[52] See above B.I.6(f).
[53] See e.g. H. Satzger, in R. Streinz, *EUV/EGV* (2003), art. 29 EUV notes 18 et seq.
[54] Art. 4 para. 2 Misleading and Comparative Advertising Directive 84/450/EEC.
[55] See Case 4 (Children's swing).
[56] K. Fahlund and H. Salmik, *Finland*, in J. Maxeiner and P. Schotthöfer, p. 127 (148).
[57] J. Macleod, *Consumer Sales Law* (2002), p. 268.

self-regulatory mechanisms of the Advertising Standards Authority (ASA)[58] that have traditionally played an important role in the control of advertisement.[59] In Italy the *Autorità Garante* does not supervise the unfair competition law of the cc. In addition an application is required for intervention by the authority. Some claim that the authority should be entitled to take action *ex officio*, so that the authority itself may better choose which advertisements to prosecute, and take action more quickly. The situation in Hungary is similar. In the case of misleading of consumers, any party whose right or lawful interest is affected by such market behaviour may notify such market practice to the OEC for the purpose that it commence an investigation and a procedure against the infringer. The HCA thus sets a general rule that determines which parties are entitled to notify. The notification has to specify the activity or conduct which has allegedly breached the law. The notifying person shall not be entitled to the rights a party has in civil litigation and shall not be encumbered with the obligations such a party has. If the OEC finds the initiation of the investigation unjustified, the decision shall be sent to the notifying person, who may appeal against the decision: sec. 69 HCA. In Spain, art. 7 LDC provides that the competition authorities (administrative bodies inside the Ministry of Economy) can act against unfair competition behaviour when these acts significantly affect competition in the market, usually because the firms engaging in these behaviours are large firms whose actions have significant effects in the market.[60]

Evaluation

The fact that the courts and authorities simultaneously address the same conduct is less effective. To this extent regulations which provide for the priority or secondary status of authorities against the rights of claims of the third parties would seem to be preferable to an unregulated coexistence. However, specialization also has a disadvantage. Priority of the authority can lead to the need to develop a large administrative authority. Secondary status can possibly mean that the administrative authority takes no action at all. This danger can be avoided, as under Italian or Polish law, by for example obliging the authority to

[58] J. Macleod, *Consumer Sales Law* (2002), p. 3.

[59] *Director General of Fair Trading v. Tobyward Ltd. and another* [1989] 2 All ER 266; see also C. Scott and J. Black, *Cranston's Consumer and the Law* (3rd edn 2000), p. 61; see also Case 1 (Risky bread).

[60] See Case 6 (Child labour).

address the case provided a private person has filed a corresponding application with the authority.[61]

b) The binding nature of decisions by various sanctioning bodies

(1) In Sweden as a general rule, private and public law claims may not be combined in ordinary courts. Moreover, they are not reciprocally binding; an ordinary court may award damages due for a breach of the MFL, although the Market Court previously has held that the particular behaviour under consideration is not in breach of the MFL. For the purpose of avoiding diverging application of the prohibitions in the MFL there is, however, the possibility to join claims for damages and 'public claims' before the Stockholm District Court: sec. 38 MFL.

The Finnish antitrust and consumer protection systems in the case of unfair practices rely heavily on administrative systems with the Market Court[62] as the court of first instance. Any civil law issues between, for example, a consumer and a tradesman are handled in the ordinary courts, so the Market Court has no jurisdiction over criminal cases or over private claims for damages.[63] A business may bring marketing matters to the Market Court based only on unfair trade practices.

In the French jurisdiction different legal routes are the rule. This is because unfair competition law is classed as civil tort law and public consumer protection law. With infringements of art. 1382 et seq. cc in France competitors must claim in the civil courts (*action en concurrence déloyale*). In addition the articles of the CCons are supervised by the *Direction Générale de la Concurrence, de la Consommation et de la Répression de Fraudes* and by the food directorate general of the Ministry of Agriculture and by the metrology department of the Ministry of Industry.[64]

In principle private parties must proceed against the legal infringement. As a general principle, in Italian law no public authority is entitled to take action against unfair competition. Nevertheless, the d.lgs. 74/1992 is a public law piece of legislation. According to sec. 7, the *Autorità Garante* is competent to apply the prohibition of misleading advertising

[61] Also E. Bastian, in G. Schricker/F. Henning-Bodewig (eds.), *Neuordnung des Wettbewerbsrecht (1999)*, p. 199 (208); for current law see Case 4 (Children's swing).

[62] See www.oikeus.fi/markkinaoikeus/index.htm.

[63] K. Fahlund and F. Salmi, *Finland*, in J. Maxeiner and P. Schotthöfer, p. 127 (147).

[64] They are authorized to establish breaches of articles L 121-8 and L 121-9 CCons, see art. L 121-2 of CCons.

and to ban unlawful comparative advertisements. According to art. 7 para. 13 of d.lgs. 74/1992 proceedings by the Authority do not interfere with court litigation for unfair competition. Therefore, it is possible that the plaintiff simultaneously initiates court litigation and the administrative proceeding before the Authority. Its decision is not binding on the court, and vice versa, though the two decisions may influence each other. According to case law, in particular, decisions by the Authority may be taken into account as evidentiary elements in trials at court.[65] In Spain, while competition law is enforced by civil courts (art. 22 LCD and art. 28 LGP), the public authority is competent for other laws (art. 63 LOCM, art. 32 LGDCU). As a result in Spain there are frequently divergent decisions.[66]

(2) On the other hand there are only few states which attempt to combine the different legal routes. The problem does not arise in Germany and Austria because there are no authorities and criminal proceedings have no role to play. In Finland, if both Ombudsman and entrepreneur have made a claim in the Market Court these will be handled together.[67] In Denmark, according to § 14 MFL legal proceedings in civil and public affairs on contravention of MFL shall be brought before the *Sø- og Handelsretten* (Maritime and Commercial Court) in Copenhagen, which is an ordinary court specialized in trade and commercial cases.[68]

Evaluation

Different legal routes carry the danger that varying, and perhaps to an extent contradictory, decisions result. While there is an awareness of this problem (Spain), usually no action has been taken. Two solutions are possible:

(1) Consolidation is the best-known option. Consolidated proceedings give private parties the possibility to enforce compensatory claims in criminal proceedings (Germany, France, Italy, Portugal and Greece). Consolidated proceedings are known, however, in other states (Sweden).

65 See Trib. Roma, February 25, 1998, *Johnson & Johnson s.p.a. v. Fater s.p.a.*, in *Riv. dir. ind.* (1998), II, 204, according to which ordinary courts may assess the misleading nature of advertisiments applying the same criteria stated by d.lgs. 74/92; Case 6 (Child labour).

66 P. Guillén and D. Voigt, in H.-W. Micklitz and J. Keßler, p. 301 (317); E. Arroyo i Amayuelas and N. Navarro, *Spain*, in R. Schulze and H. Schulte-Nölke, I.2(h).

67 See Case 1 (Risky bread).

68 Enforcement proceedings have to be brought to one of the 82 lower courts, see P. Alsted, *Das Wettbewerbsrecht in Dänemark*, in *Heidelberger Kommentar zum Wettbewerbsrecht* (2000), IV note 29.

(2) Even more elegant is the possibility of declaring a special court exclusively competent for decisions of the civil courts and the authority. This route is followed in Finland and Denmark. Several other Member States have a court with exclusive competence in antitrust law.[69] It would also be possible to do this in the field of unfair competition law, as professional expertise would be concentrated and divergent decisions could be avoided.

[69] E.g. in Germany.

Case 7 Recycled paper: advertising agencies and the press as defendants

The paper manufacturer A, who sells his products exclusively to shops specializing in ecologically friendly products, produces papers with a maximum recycled paper content of 5 per cent. In addition, he sells this paper himself to consumers directly.

A engages D's advertising agency to create and conduct an advertising campaign for him. D conceives the advertising slogan – 'ecologically friendly recycled paper'. The paper is advertised under this slogan in E's newspaper. A, D and E are all aware that the recycled paper content is only 5 per cent.

Subject to which preconditions can D be joined in proceedings against A ? Is it possible to bring proceedings against E ? On what basis?

Austria (7)

A's remarks concerning the ecologically friendly qualities of his paper constitute a misleading advertisement falling under § 2 para. 1 UWG. The advertisement describes the product's composition and the way it is manufactured, which are specified as examples of (relevant) deception under § 2 para. 1 UWG. But that is hardly relevant since § 2 para. 1 UWG is applicable to all circumstances relating to a business, that is anything that is directly or indirectly connected with the business operations and can possibly advance the commercial activity so far as these circumstances are capable of affecting the decision to buy.[1] Ecology-related remarks are especially suitable to appeal to people's emotions; thus they have a strong attraction. An advertisement with such suggestions is only allowed if they are positively documented and if the deception of consumers is ruled out.[2] As already described in Case 1 an injunction and an order of cessation can be imposed on A and he can be held liable for damages if (as in this case) A acted culpably. A claim for publication (§ 25 UWG) for the information of consumers is also allowed.

(1) The claim for an injunction is not only directed against the immediate violator who causes the infringement and whose wilful decision

[1] Established case law, e.g. (1961) 11 ÖBl 70; (1989) 38 ÖBl 74 – 'Erlagscheinwerbung III'; (1988) 37 ÖBl 190 – 'Fahrschule A'.

[2] H. Fitz and H. Gamerith, *Wettbewerbsrecht*, (4th edn 2003) p. 19; established case law, e.g. (1995) 44 ÖBl 164 – 'Bioziegel'; (1999) 48 ÖBl 22 (Langer) – 'Stockerauer Salat-Erdäpfel'.

set it in motion[3] (in this case A, who commissioned the advertising campaign despite knowing the low content of recycled paper in his products), but it can also be directed against anybody who participates in it. Such act of participation has to advance or make possible the violation of somebody else – even if the third party acts independently.[4] The violator must at least be aware of the influence of his behaviour on the market; to this end he has to know those circumstances of his acts that cause the influence on the market. The aiders have to support the violator consciously.[5] A merely adequate causal connection is not sufficient.[6] The person assisting in the violation of competition has to fulfil all elements of the particular act of unfair competition except the act itself, which has only to be carried out by the violator.[7] Acting as an independent contractor in the course of fulfilling a commission (for reward) does not generally exclude the possibility of being held liable under unfair competition law for aiding in the violating act of the principal.[8]

The acts of the advertising agency D for the paper manufacturer obviously intend to advance somebody else's competitive position, so that this intention, contrary to the general rules,[9] does not need to be proved by the claimant.[10] The advancement of A's competitive position by creating an advertising slogan (that is suitable to mislead) is also clear. Since D is aware of the low content (5 per cent) of recycled paper an injunction can also be issued against him and he can be held liable for damages.

(2) The same applies to E. The economic self-interest in A's commission to publish an advertisement does not rule out the newspaper's liability under unfair competition law since it was aware of the falsity of the advertised statement and is thus liable as an aider. If the newspaper was not aware of these circumstances it could resort to § 3 UWG. It rules out a claim for an injunction against the newspaper (publisher or

3 Established case law, e.g. (2000) 49 ÖBl 216 – 'FORMAT-Schecks'; (2002) 51 ÖBl 297 – 'Internationales Kultur- und Filmfestival'.

4 Established case law, e.g. (2000) 49 ÖBl 59 – 'Wasserwelt Amadé'; (2001) 50 ÖBl 109 – 'cook & chill-Produktion'.

5 Established case law, e.g. (1998) 47 ÖBl 33 – 'Ungarischer Zahnarzt'.

6 (1998) 47 ÖBl 33 – 'Ungarischer Zahnarzt'.

7 Ibid.; comprehensive regarding the problem of aiders is H. Gamerith, *Wettbewerbsrechtliche Unterlassungsansprüche gegen Gehilfen*, WBl 1991, 305 et sqq.

8 (1999) 48 ÖBl 229 – 'ERINASOLUM'.

9 (2000) 49 ÖBl 109 – 'Bezirkstelefonbuch'.

10 (1998) 47 ÖBl 9 – 'SN-Presseförderung'; (2000) 49 ÖBl 109 – 'Bezirkstelefonbuch'; (2000) 49 ÖBl 213 – 'Betriebsrat aktuell'.

owner) for announcements violating § 2 UWG since it is not the newspaper (e.g. issuing a recommendation) but the advertiser who speaks to the public in these announcements. Under these circumstances a claim against the newspaper is ruled out even if the newspaper acted culpably and independently of the fact whether the advertisement was paid for.[11] § 3 UWG intends to protect newspapers against excessive duties of care when running advertisements. But it does not apply in cases of conscious violations. An advertising agency (D) cannot rely on this provision since it directly participates in the violation of unfair competition law.[12]

Denmark (7)

The action is presumed to be contrary to § 2 sec. 1 MFL, according to which one must not apply misleading information in marketing that is suited to influence demand.[13]

According to § 22 sec. 3 MFL criminal proceedings may be taken against the advertiser (A), the advertising agency (D), and the newspaper (E). Cases of violations of § 2 sec. 1 MFL are regulated by public prosecution. The advertiser (A) will be directly responsible on the basis of § 2 sec. 1 MFL.

The advertising agency (D) and the newspaper (E) may, according to § 23 of the Civil Penal Code, be subject to criminal liability for collaboration in violating § 2 sec. 1 MFL. In legal practice, judgments have been given where all three parties involved have been convicted.[14] In particular, advertising agencies risk a liability for collaboration in violating the MFL as they typically carry out marketing tasks for a large number of companies, whereas the individual advertiser is only planning marketing for himself.

The subjective conditions for punishment under the MFL indicate that negligence must have occurred. In order for it to be shown to be liable the advertising agency must probably be shown to have acted with intent and as regards the newspaper a relatively clear violation of the MFL will need to be proved.

[11] SZ 49/57 = (1976) 25 ÖBl 163 – 'Konkursverkauf II'; (1991) 40 ÖBl 267 – 'Lotto-Systemplan'.

[12] (1984) 33 ÖBl 135 – 'Superaktionsspanne'.

[13] M. Koktvedgaard, *Lærebog i Konkurrenceret* (4th edn 2000), p. 258.

[14] P.B. Madsen, *Markedsret*, vol. 2 (4th edn 2002), p. 340; E. Borcher and F. Bøggild, *Markedsføringsloven* (2001), p. 404.

England (7)

Under reg. 5 of the CMAR 1988, the OFT can bring proceedings for an injunction against any person appearing to him to be concerned or likely to be concerned with the publication of the advertisement. This may include, for example, the directors of a company,[15] and it also includes the business that has produced the advertisement, and the publisher. For the court to order an injunction it is not necessary that the person responsible was acting with intent or that he failed to exercise proper care to prevent it being misleading (reg. 6 (5)(b) of the CMAR 1988).

Under sec. 1(1) of the TDA 1968, a false trade description, including false trade descriptions made in advertisements, is an offence. Persons guilty of an offence under this act are liable on conviction on indictment to a fine or imprisonment for a term not exceeding two years or both. However, sec. 24 et seq. provide for defences. According to sec. 25 on innocent publication of advertisement, a person whose business it is to publish or arrange for the publication of advertisements has a defence if he can prove that he received the advertisement for publication in the ordinary course of business and did not know and had no reason to suspect that its publication would amount to an offence under this act. E might have a defence under sec. 25 of the TDA 1968. Furthermore, sec. 24 provides for a defence for a person who can prove that the commission of the offence was due to reliance on information supplied to him or some other cause beyond his control. Thus, if D had no reason not to rely on A, he might have a defence under sec. 24 of the TDA 1968.

Finland (7)

The advertisement is based on incorrect information and is thus untruthful and misleading, which is a violation of both § 1 and § 2 UTA.

It is possible to demand that even workers or outsiders be ordered to stop using untruthful or misleading information in marketing. According to para. 2 of § 6 SopMenL this requires special reasons if the order is to affect such groups. The only criteria for outsiders, is that they are working for the undertaking in question. When it is a question of intentionally spreading false information there might be reasons to order even marketing companies etc. to cease giving this kind of

15 *The Director General of Fair Trading v. Planet Telecom plc and others* [2002] EWHC 376.

information. Thus, D could be joined in the proceedings if this is demanded by a claimant (a competitor or the Ombudsman).

Cases in which an advertising agency has been ordered to cease advertising with untruthful and misleading information when acting for a client are very rare. Still, this can be seen as a relevant possibility.[16]

The case regarding E as the newspaper publisher is unclear because such issues as freedom of speech and press can become relevant. Even disregarding these it would require a close link between the advertising firm and the newspaper before any action against the newspaper could be considered. The case of the newspaper is not relevant in Finland, as it is almost impossible to conceive a situation where an order would also cover the publisher.

Of course, a newspaper publisher could have acted in order to further the sales of their newspaper or magazine. In this case this could be a violation of § 1 and § 2 SopMenL as incorrect information has been used as a means of competition. No such case has ever been filed in the Market Court and the likelihood of such a case is very small. In the case in question, where the advertisements are clearly only in the interest of the paper producer (and not for example in advertisements for the newspaper – such as 'We use environmentally friendly paper'), the newspaper is not a direct subject of the above-mentioned rules.

France (7)

Concerning a criminal action the main defendant is the announcer, that is to say the person on whose account or order the advertising had been done.[17] In the present case this is A.

Art. L 121–5 of the CCons declares that the advertiser on behalf of whom the advertising is circulated is principally responsible for the offence committed. However, it also says that complicity is punishable under the same conditions as in common law. That means that the responsibility of D and E could be engaged, especially when considering that both were perfectly aware of the misleading character of the advertising.

Thus, others implicated in the advertising campaign can be held responsible, such as the advertising agency.[18] The director of the

[16] But see Market Court MT 1981:1.

[17] Cour de cassation, chambre criminelle, in: *Contrats, concurrence, consommation* (1994), comm. 180.

[18] G. Raymond, in: Juris-Classeur, *Concurrence, consommation* (1998), Fasc. 900, 'Publicité commerciale et protection des consommateurs', note 162.

publication containing the advertisement can also be held responsible either for complicity or even as the author, or as both.[19] A distinction can be made as regards the intention either to mislead or to aid to mislead.[20] E in the present case could prove that he had delegated his powers for the publication in order to avoid criminal prosecution.[21]

Germany (7)

The question arises: against whom can claims be brought? Potential defendants include the competitor, the advertising agency and the newspaper that published the unlawful advertisement.

A claim against A would be possible under § 5 para. 1, para. 2 no. 1 UWG (ex-§ 3 s. 1 UWG). The requirement is that the manufacturer A is the infringing party within the UWG.[22] The infringing party is anybody who under the circumstances perpetrates an unfair competition infringement.[23] A makes misleading statements concerning the attributes of the paper in the course of commercial dealings; that is they create a false impression regarding its composition. Accordingly, it can be demanded that the advertising with this slogan be stopped and the existing advertising such as on posters be removed.[24]

Proceedings against D as an advertising agency may be successful if there is an unfair competition claim against him. It is questionable, however, whether the creation of the advertisement with the slogan is not only an unfair competition infringement by a third party. A is only outwardly involved. The wording of the liability norm of § 8 para. 2 UWG (ex-§ 13 para. 4 UWG) ('also against the proprietor') does not mean that only the proprietor of the business is liable.[25] The infringing party is anybody who willingly and causally contributed to an infringing act or who supported it, although he would legally have been in a position

[19] Ibid., note 165. [20] Ibid. [21] Ibid.

[22] A. Baumbach and W. Hefermehl, *UWG* (22nd edn 2001), Introd. note 394; A. Baumbach and W. Hefermehl, *UWG* (23rd edn 2004), § 8 notes 2.1 et seq., § 9 note 1.3; K. H. Fezer, *UWG* (2005), § 8 notes 94 et seq., § 9 note 5.

[23] H. Köhler and H. Piper, *UWG* (3rd edn 2002), § 13, note 66; H. Harte-Bavendamm and F. Henning-Bodewig, *UWG* (2004), § 8 notes 60, 62, § 9 note 7.

[24] H. Köhler and H. Piper, *UWG* (3rd edn 2002), § 3 note 502; H. Harte-Bavendamm and F. Henning-Bodewig, *UWG* (2004), § 8 notes 5 et seq., 86 et seq.; K.H. Fezer, *UWG* (2005), § 8 notes 8, 36.

[25] F. Henning-Bodewig, *Die wettbewerbsrechtliche Haftung von Werbeagenturen* (1981) 83 GRUR 164 (165), translated as: *The Liability of Advertising Agencies under German Unfair Competition Law*, (1981) 12 IIC 755 (756).

to prevent it.[26] This further requires an act for competitive purposes, i.e. an act with the intention of advancing himself or another in competitive terms.[27] The advertisement is intended objectively to increase sales of the paper and subjectively the act is intended to advance the advertising agency. Accordingly, the agency is liable for the creation and execution of the advertisement.[28] The agency is obliged to examine the legality of each advertising measure and in case of doubts it must consult legal counsel.[29]

Claims are possible against E for forbearance, removal and compensation, §§ 8 para. 1, 9 s. 1 UWG (ex-§§ 13 para. 6 no. 1, 3 s. 1 UWG). However, E could be protected under the basic principle of the freedom of the press under art. 5 para. 1 s. 2 GG. Nevertheless, this does not relieve from the duty not to publish evidently misleading advertising.[30] Because of time pressure and to ensure the freedom of the press, such a duty to monitor arises only in cases of particularly serious and easily detected infringements.[31] A claim for damages requires intentional behaviour: § 9 s. 2 UWG (ex-§ 13 para. 6 s. 2 UWG). E will only be liable if he himself commits an unfair competition infringement as the publisher of the newspaper. He might have made misleading statements in publishing the advertisement: § 5 para. 1 UWG (ex-§ 3 s. 1 UWG). E is aware of the untruthfulness of the advertised statement. He has acted to promote sales of the paper by A both from the objective and subjective points of view. In view of his knowledge, E is

[26] BGH (1994) 96 GRUR 441 (443) – 'Kosmetikstudio'; A. Baumbach and W. Hefermehl, *UWG* (22nd edn 2001), Introd. note 327; H. Köhler and H. Piper, *UWG* (3rd edn 2002), § 13 note 66; A. Baumbach and W. Hefermehl, *UWG* (23rd edn 2004), § 8 note 2.12; H. Harte-Bavendamm and F. Henning-Bodewig, *UWG* (2004), § 8 note 64; K. H. Fezer, *UWG* (2005), § 8 note 100.

[27] A. Baumbach and W. Hefermehl, *UWG* (22nd edn 2001), Introd. note 327; A. Baumbach and W. Hefermehl, *UWG* (23rd edn 2004), § 8 notes 2.12 et seq.

[28] BGH (1973) 75 GRUR 208 (209) – 'Neues aus der Medizin'; H. Köhler and H. Piper, *UWG* (3rd edn 2002), § 13 note 67a; A. Baumbach and W. Hefermehl, *UWG* (23rd edn 2004), § 8 note 2.10; F. Henning-Bodewig, (1981) 83 GRUR, 164, (1981) 12 IIC 755 (756).

[29] F. Henning-Bodewig, (1981) 83 GRUR, 164 (169 f.), (1981) 12 IIC 755 (768 et seq.).

[30] H. Köhler and H. Piper, *UWG* (3rd edn 2002), § 13 note 67a; Introd. notes 254, 223; A. Baumbach and W. Hefermehl, *UWG* (23rd edn 2004), § 8 note 2.10; H. Harte-Bavendamm and F. Henning-Bodewig, *UWG* (2004), Introd. F note 41; K.H. Fezer, *UWG* (2005), § 8 note 106.

[31] BGH (1990) 92 GRUR 1012 (1014) – 'Pressehaftung I '; BGH (1992) 94 GRUR 618 (619) – 'Pressehaftung II'; BGH (1994) 96 GRUR 454 (455) – 'Schlankheitswerbung'; BGH (1995) 97 GRUR 751 (7529) – 'Schlussverkaufswerbung I'; H. Piper, in Festschrift R. Vieregge (1995), p. 717 (721).

liable pursuant to § 5 para. 1 UWG (ex-§ 3 s. 1 UWG). Thus, this can give rise to claims for an injunction and for damages.

Greece (7)

In the case in question, A, D and E seem to have violated art. 3 of L. 146/1914 by making misleading declarations related to the composition and quality of the paper sold by A. The said legal provision does not require the inaccurate declaration to be made with the intent to compete, as long as the inaccurate fact has been widely propagated and has the ability to create the impression of a particularly advantageous offer.[32] The fact that, in order for a practice to fall under the scope of application of art. 3, the existence of competition between the injured party and the author of the damage is not necessary is further reinforced by art. 10(2)(a) of the above law on unfair competition, providing for the obligation of writers, publishers, printers and newspaper and magazine agents engaged in the propagation of the misleading declarations to repair the damage.

In the present case, the advertising agency D, acting for the account of A on a contract basis (representative of A in the broad sense of the term)[33] is considered as an infringing party, since he conceived the misleading slogan and contributed to its propagation to the general public; he can therefore be joined in proceedings against A, in accordance with art. 3 and 10 of L.146/1914. More specifically, claims for removal and cessation of the unfair practice can be brought against him. In addition, any person suffering damage may seek compensation,[34] provided that D knew or ought to have known of the unlawful character of the declaration: in other words, it is sufficient that he ignored through his fault the untruthfulness of the declaration.

By contrast, the newspaper publisher E will only be found liable if his knowledge of the untruthfulness of the declaration can be proved: in order to protect the freedom of the press, art. 10(2)(a) of L. 146/1914 stipulates that a claim for damages may be brought against writers, publishers, printers and newspaper and magazine agents only if they knew of the untruthfulness of the declarations made. Therefore, E will be liable for reparations to any person injured if it can be proven that he

[32] N. Rokas, *Industrial Property* (2004), p. 214; A. Sinanioti-Maroudi, *Art. 3*, in N. Rokas (ed.), *Unfair Competition* (1996), p. 269.

[33] L. Kotsiris, *Unfair Competition and Antitrust Law* (2001), pp. 359–360.

[34] T. Kontovazainitis, *Art. 20*, in N. Rokas (ed.), *Unfair Competition* (1996), p. 306.

was aware of the untruthfulness of the advertised statement (regarding the extent of recycled material in A's paper).

Hungary (7)

Misleading advertisement is defined in sec. 2(n) HAA as any advertising which in any way, including its presentation, deceives or is likely to deceive the persons to whom it is addressed or whom it reaches and which, by reason of its deceptive nature, is likely to affect their economic behaviour or which, for those reasons, injures or is likely to injure a competitor who is engaged in the same or similar activities. This case constitutes a misleading advertisement according to sec. 7 HAA, which states that it is forbidden to publish misleading advertisements. For the purpose of defining a misleading advertisement, the information conveyed in the advertisement, which pertains to the general characteristics of the merchandise shall be taken into consideration. In the context of sec 7(2) an HAA information pertaining to the general characteristics of the merchandise shall be understood as any facts conveyed concerning the place of origin of the merchandise, its ingredients, safety factors, its impact on health, technical features, its environmental features and energy consumption, also its availability, date of manufacture, quantity, its suitability for a given function, the expected results from its use, the way it is controlled or tested, and any other fact regarding the application, shipping, use and maintenance of the merchandise.

According to sec. 14(3) HAA (which is an exception to sec. 14(1) HAA according to which the advertiser, the advertising agency and the publisher of the advertisement are jointly liable) only the advertiser is liable for violation according to sec. 6, 7, 7 A and 7B HAA. The advertiser is the entity in whose interest the advertising is published, or which orders the publication of advertising in its own interest (sec. 2(p) HAA). Since he bears sole responsibility for the violation, it is only possible to recover damages from him.[35]

The legislature initiated the exception in sec. 14(3) HAA, as otherwise everyday business would be brought to a halt. If a newspaper would be liable for every piece of advertising they issue, they would not accept or publish advertisements at all. The idea behind sec. 14(1) and (3) is that the strict liability of advertising agencies should not apply to the press.

[35] Pázmándi (2001), p. 591.

Ireland (7)

(1) A consumer who purchases A's paper, and feels aggrieved at the low recycled content could request the Director of Consumer Affairs, or the Director could decide on his own initiative, to prosecute A under sec. 8 of the Consumer Information Act 1978, for publishing or causing to be published a misleading advertisement. E could be joined to the proceedings for publishing the misleading advertisement, but not D, unless he was responsible for causing the advertisement to be published. It is a defence for E to establish that the advertisement was accepted in the normal course of business and that the newspaper had no reason to suspect that it was in breach of the Act. It may be difficult for the Director to succeed in such an action because under the Act a misleading advertisement is one which is 'likely to mislead, and thereby cause loss, damage or injury to members of the public to a material degree'. This seems unlikely in the circumstances given.

(2) Under the Misleading Advertising Regulations, any person can take an action against 'any person proposing to engage in any advertising which is misleading'. An action could be taken under these Regulations by an aggrieved consumer, or by one of the shops purchasing A's paper or by a competitor of A. Again E could be joined in proceedings against A. D could not be joined unless D had been contracted to place the advertisement for A. Under the 1988 Regulations the definition of misleading advertising is broader and means 'any advertising which in any way, including its presentation, deceives or is likely to deceive the persons to whom it is addressed or whom it reaches and which, by reason of its deceptive nature, is likely to affect their economic behaviour or which, for those reasons, injures or is likely to injure a competitor'. A consumer, customer, or competitor of A, or the Director of Consumer Affairs would seem likely to have more success under the Misleading Advertising Regulations.

(3) A consumer who purchases A's paper, and feels aggrieved at the low recycled content could try to take action against A under the Sale of Goods and Supply of Services Acts 1893 and 1980, for breach of a trade description under sec. 13 of the 1893 Act, as amended by sec. 10 of the 1980 Act. Liability for breach of duty under sec. 13 cannot be excluded where the buyer is 'dealing as a consumer' (sec. 55 of the 1893 Act, as amended by sec. 22 of the 1980 Act). Sec. 3 of the 1980 Act defines a consumer as one where the purchaser is not acting in the course of business, the seller is, and the goods are of a type ordinarily supplied for

private use. It is an offence under sec. 11 of the 1980 Act for the seller to purport to exclude such liability.

If the plaintiff is one of the shops in this case, the sale would be one in which the purchaser is acting in the course of a business. Even in such non-consumer sales, exclusion clauses must be 'fair and reasonable' as per the schedule of the 1980 Act, so it would depend on whether or not such a clause was present in the contract, and the wording of such clause. However, a commercial purchaser may find it difficult to convince a court that he relied on such description given his presumed expertise. In any case, it would be difficult to show that there was a breach of the implied condition as to description because the words 'ecologically friendly' do not imply any specific percentage of recycled paper, and may be considered to be acceptable provided the product contains at least some recycled paper, which it does. A plaintiff would seem likely to have more success under the broader definition contained in the Misleading Advertising Regulations.

Italy (7)

A's competitors may bring claims for unfair competition against A, D and E. A made a misleading statements in advertisements concerning an important quality of his product, infringing art. 2598 no. 3 cc.

According to case law, any person who, though not being a competitor to the plaintiff, contributes to acts of unfair competition to the benefit of a competitor of the plaintiff, may be held responsible for the unfair competition infringement. Therefore, both D and E may be liable for unfair competition, provided that the plaintiff proves that they fraudulently infringed the prohibition of unfair competition to the benefit of his competitor.[36]

Such proof may be offered by means of circumstantial evidence, for example showing that there are specific relationships, such as

[36] See e.g. Cass., April 11, 2001, n. 5375, *Camera di commercio di Gorizia v. Associazione grossisti birra isontino*, in: *Danno e resp.*, 2002, 288; Cass., October 25, 1978, n. 4834, *Soc. Crippa v. Piretti*, in *Arch. civ.*, 1979, 627; Cass., February 4, 1981, n. 742, *Citti v. Isac*, in *Giur. it.*, 1981, I, 1, 720. A quite similar case was decided by Trib. Milan, December 20, 1973, *Cedit v. F.lli Crespi & C. S.a.s.*, in (1973) *Giur. ann. dir. ind.*, II, n.429, which held that the publisher of a newspaper may be held responsible for unfair competition when unfair advertising was knowingly or negligently published in his newspaper, to the benefit of a competitor of the plaintiff. See also Trib. Napoli, August 8, 1997, *Pomicino v. Geredil*, in *Giust. civ.*, 1998, I, 259, which held that the owner of a web site may be liable for damages arising from a misleading advertisement published on the site for the benefit of a third party under art. 2043 cc but not under art. 2598 cc

contracts relating to the defendant's business (employment, commercial agency), or different kinds of links (such as, in the case of legal entities, corporate control, or interlocking directorates), between the third-party infringer and the defendant. Even a single contract, such as a contract for the creation of an advertisement, may be sufficient to show the 'special relationship' between the defendant and the third party infringer.

When a claim for unfair competition is brought against a non-competitor, the burden of proof for the plaintiff is heavier, since under the law of unfair competition it would not be necessary to prove that the defendant acted fraudulently or negligently (if damages are claimed, the defendant will have to prove that he did not act negligently). Moreover, the plaintiff will have to prove that there is a 'special relationship' between the third-party infringer and his competitor who benefited from the infringement. Such 'special relationship' may be inferred even from the same advertising contract, which shows that the third-party infringers (the publisher and the advertising agency) did act to the benefit of a specific competitor of the plaintiff.

E as a publisher may be held liable for unfair competition if it can be proved that he is linked to A by a 'special relationship', and that he knowingly acted to the benefit of the defendant, and to the detriment of the plaintiff. It may not be easy to supply such evidence, since newspaper publishers are not under a general legal duty to make sure that any advertisement they publish is not misleading. Therefore, E's intent to act to the benefit of A and to the detriment of his competitors cannot automatically be inferred from the mere publication of the advertisement.

Netherlands (7)

(1) According to art. 6:196 BW claims can be brought against any person that has caused damage to another or is likely to do so by making the misleading information public. This means that it is not necessary that the person who made the information public is liable for the damage incurred. As a result, the advertising agency can be joined in proceedings against A and can be prohibited from publishing or be ordered to rectify. The plaintiff only has to prove that D has created and conducted the advertising campaign. The plaintiff does not have to prove that D was at fault or is liable for the conduct or the damage.

If an action is allowed against a person who is not liable for the damage art. 6:167 para. 3 BW applies, which means that the court can order that the costs of the proceedings shall partially or wholly be paid by the plaintiff.[37] For this reason it may be of importance that the plaintiff can prove that D was aware of the misleading advertising.

(2) Claims can be made against any person that has caused damage to another or is likely to do so by making information public. E can be prohibited from publishing or be ordered to rectify. The plaintiff does not have to prove that E was aware of the fact that the recycled paper content was only 5 per cent. If an action is allowed against a person who is not liable for the damage (art. 6:167 para. 3 BW), the court can order that the costs of the proceeding be paid partially or wholly by the plaintiff. For this reason it can be of importance that E was aware of the misleading advertisement.

Poland (7)

The act of unfair competition, as described in art. 16 u.z.n.k. is considered to be committed by the advertising agency or any other undertaking who created or fabricated the advertisement (art. 17 u.z.n.k.).

The advertising agency without regard to its legal form is considered to be an undertaking, for the purposes of the u.z.n.k.[38] A business entity is considered to be an advertising agency if it: creates the concept of the advertising campaign, or realizes the concept (production), or introduces the advertisement to the market.[39] D's advertising agency created and conducted an advertising campaign for A, therefore it should be considered liable on the ground of art.17 u.z.n.k. in connection with art. 16 u.z.n.k. The fact that the advertising agency was operating in collaboration with the undertaking and according to the latter's suggestions does not exonerate the agency from responsibility.[40]

The press announcements and advertisements cannot be deemed illegal or contrary to custom and usage, art. 36 *Prawo prasowe*[41] – p.p. (Press Law). The publisher and the editor are not responsible for the content of announcements and advertisements published according to the rule of law (art. 42.2 p.p.). The publisher and the editor are responsible only for illegal announcements and advertisements and if they are

[37] The plaintiff, for his part, may claim the costs against the person liable for the damage.

[38] E. Nowinska and M. Du Vall, *Komentarz do ustawy o zwalczaniu nieuczciwej konkurencji* (2001), p. 179.

[39] J. Solarz, *Ekonomiczne uwarunkowania reklamy* (1995), p. 44.

[40] J. Szwaja (ed.), *Ustawa o zwalczaniu nieuczciwej konkurencji, Komentarz* (2000), p. 154.

[41] Prawo prasowe of 1984.

contrary to custom and usage.[42] However, the question regarding the relation between art. 42.2 p.p. in connection with art. 36 p.p. and art. 16 u.z.n.k. arises. The u.z.n.k. was enacted later than the p.p. Moreover, the u.z.n.k. aims to protect the market from various acts of unfair competition. Consequently, distributing advertisements violating any kind of law or custom and usage should create a potential liability on the part of the press[43] provided fault can be proved.[44]

Portugal (7)

As regards the different kinds of defendants in cases of misleading advertising there are two different solutions: first, administrative proceedings that are brought by the Consumer Agency and, secondly, civil liability. The Consumer Agency can bring administrative proceedings with the aim of imposing an administrative fine against A, D and E under art. 36 CPub (Advertising Code) with the only precondition being that the advertising is misleading according to art. 11 CPub. Concerning civil liability and compensation claims the injured party can bring claims against A, D and E (art. 30 CPub). However, the advertiser A can exempt himself of liability if he proves that he did not have any knowledge of the advertising message (art. 30 CPub). The advertising agency D and the owner of the newspaper E may also be civilly liable if they cause damage.

The press is co-liable for damages resulting from any illegal advertising under art. 30 CPub. The press does not have any privileges and has a duty to monitor all advertising materials that it publishes. The press is civilly liable for any damages resulting from illegal advertising and can be subject to fines under art. 36 CPub.

Spain (7)

A's conduct could be deemed to be an act of misleading information as stated in art. 7 LCD. Therefore A's competitors whose economic interests are directly harmed or threatened by the unfair act are entitled to bring actions against him. D as an advertising agency has entered into a cooperative agreement with A and the advertising slogan is the product

[42] J. Szwaja (ed.), *Ustawa o zwalczaniu nieuczciwej konkurencji, Komentarz* (2000), p. 492; J. Sobczak, *Ustawa prawo prasowe. Komentarz* (1999).

[43] E. Nowinska and M. Du Vall, *Komentarz do ustawy o zwalczaniu nieuczciwej konkurencji* (2001), p. 179.

[44] B. Kordasiewicz, *Jednostka wobec sdroków masowego* (1991), p. 61; I. Wiszniewska, *Polen*, in G. Schricker (ed.), *Recht der Werbung in Europa* (supplement 1999), notes 259 et seq.

of its legal obligations. In this case art. 20 para. 2 LCD provides for the indemnity of the principal's employees or collaborators and both D and E could fulfil the requirements to be considered as collaborators, and they could be joined in proceedings against A.

As far as the application of the LGP is concerned, this act only refers to the advertiser's liability in cases of illegal advertisement. Such illegal advertisement must be unfair, deceptive, racist, and must contradict constitutional values. In such cases, the press can be liable for illegal advertisement if it acts with knowledge. However, advertising is considered to be a part of the freedom of expression.[45]

Sweden (7)

A's advertising campaign for 'ecologically friendly recycled paper' seems to fit well under art. 6 para. 2 MFL where it is stated that misleading submissions must not be used, particularly where submissions are misleading in respect of the 'origin, use and effect on health or environment' of the marketed product. The Market Court has applied a strict standard when considering this sort of advertisement.[46] Therefore, there would be no problem commencing proceedings against A (as to what can be done and by whom, see cases above).

Concerning D, proceedings may be brought under art. 22 para. 3 MFL. A precondition is that D may be considered to have to a major extent, intentionally or negligently, contributed to the infringement. So, prohibitions can be brought against advertising agencies.[47]

In principle, the same applies to E. However, in respect of E one must be aware of the constitutional protection afforded to printed periodicals. This protection may seem strange from an international perspective.[48] It is, for example, impossible to stop illegal information from being printed.[49] Still, the MFL applies in respect of commercial marketing, with a commercial purpose and which has as its object purely commercial relations. Although an advertisement promoting ecological paper may be said to possess some sort of political connotation, this does not seem to alter the impression that the advertisement, in the

[45] See www.uam.es/centros/derecho/privado/mercanti/; see also C. Paz-Ares and J. Aguila-Real, *Ensayo sobre la libertad de empresa*, publicado en el libro Estudios homenaje a L. Diez-Picazo, vol. IV (2003), pp. 5971–6040.

[46] MD 1990:20 - 'Norsk Hydro'; MD 1990:22 – 'Nordtend'; MD 1991:11 – 'Opel'; MD 1994:10 – 'Procter & Gamble'.

[47] U. Benritz, *Sweden*, in: R. Schulze and H. Schulte-Noelke, p. 6.

[48] U. Benritz, *Marknadsföringslagen* (1997), p. 89.

[49] See Case 3 (Whisky).

given situation, is purely commercial. Therefore, it appears to be possible, on the assumption that the preconditions mentioned above are fulfilled, to take action against E. However, the possibility of bringing proceedings against D and E in their capacity as 'contributors' is reserved for the administrative fine remedy and the Consumer Ombudsman alone.

Summary (7)

9. *Advertising agencies as defendants*

In all Member States liability of advertising agencies is relatively strict. However, the methods of allocation differ. Advertising agencies are either held liable for their own unlawful conduct, or are liable only for unlawful conduct of another.

a) Own unlawful behaviour or participation in someone else's anti-competitive behaviour

In some states advertising agencies are held liable for their own unlawful behaviour and the question is whether the appropriate requirements are fulfilled. Thus, under German law the advertising agency must be proved to have competitive purposes.[50] This is normally the case if the advertisement is intended objectively to increase sales and subjectively to advance the agency. Accordingly, the agency is liable for the creation and execution of the advertisement.[51] In Poland there is even a special regulation which applies to the conduct of advertising agencies. Also in England and in the USA the advertising agency's own conduct as a contributory factor is considered. In Portugal the advertising agency is responsible for its own unlawful behaviour.

In several states liability of the advertising agency requires a relationship to the competitor. Thus the terms used are 'contribution' (Sweden and Italy), 'collaboration' (Denmark and Spain), 'employee' (Finland) or even 'complicity' (France). Such a relation is necessary in order to establish personal liability of the advertising agency. This may be explained in terms of these states only addressing the conduct of the

50 Regarding the element 'for purposes of competition' see § 2 No. 1 UWG (former §§ 1, 3 UWG).

51 BGH (1973) 75 GRUR 208 (209) – 'Neues aus der Medizin'; H. Köhler and H. Piper, *UWG, Kommentar* (3rd edn 2002), vor § 13 note 67a; F. Henning-Bodewig (1981) 83 GRUR 164, (1981) 12 IIC 755.

competitor. Third parties are only caught as participants under the categories of contract law ('employees'), tort law ('contribution'), or criminal law ('complicity'). In addition, the advertising agency must have acted for the benefit of the competitor (Italy), or at least a claim of negligence is possible (Sweden, Denmark).

b) The strictness of allocation – strict liability versus negligence

Finally, the claims are distinguished according to the strictness of liability allocation. In some states (Sweden, Denmark and the USA[52]) liability is only incurred if the advertising agency can be held to have been at least negligent. France requires a higher standard of intention (perfectly aware). Other states (Germany and England) assume strict liability for cessation claims, i.e. no fault is required. This corresponds to the legal situation for cessation claims. In these states unfair competition law is not limited to competitors but can be enforced by anyone who participates in the competition. Also in this case the requirements are either objective (England and the USA) or subjective (Germany) in nature.

Evaluation

(1) The Misleading and Comparative Advertising Directive 84/450/EEC does not regulate those responsible for the competition law infringement. As a result advertisers, advertising agencies or the press are not designated as potential defendants by the directive. All Member States are thus free to create the possibility of proceedings against the advertising agency for a competition infringement. They are expected to know the legal basis of unfair competition law. An advertising agency is under an obligation in cases of doubt to take legal advice. This is also reasonable as it can pass the costs on to the client.[53] However, the requirements vary. On the one hand own responsibility and strict liability is presumed, on the other hand third-party conduct and own fault lead to liability. Compensatory claims in misleading advertising cases are extremely rare in Italy, Portugal and Finland, because neither competitors nor the consumers react against those situations. The damage is too anonymous and diffuse and the fulfilment of the burden of proof poses severe difficulties. In Portugal and Finland this may depend upon

[52] See above A.IV.

[53] For German law see F. Henning-Bodewig (1981) 83 GRUR 164 (169), (1981) 12 IIC 755 (767).

the relatively small jurisdictions. But there are also few decisions in larger jurisdictions such as the USA and Germany.

The plaintiff is usually interested in obtaining an injunction preventing his competitor from continuing the unlawful behaviour, even with the help of other third parties: an eventual injunction against the advertising agency will not have bound the competitor, which may continue its unlawful advertising campaign through different media. On the other hand, the plaintiff may be interested in claiming damages against third-party infringers, whose pocket can sometimes be 'deeper' than that of the plaintiff's competitors. But damages may not be awarded against third party infringers, if it is not proved that they knowingly acted to the detriment of the plaintiff: such proof may be quite difficult. Therefore, actions against third-party infringers are quite scarce in legal practice, at least before ordinary courts.

(2) In view of the fact that advertising agencies may be held liable for competition law infringements in all Member States, it would seem to be sensible to harmonize the liability of advertising agencies for unlawful competition conduct on the European level. Own contributory conduct is conceivable in Member States where the responsibility of the advertising agencies is recognized. Further requirements for liability are, on the other hand, extremely varied. It should be possible to enforce the prohibition or injunction without having to prove fault on the part of the advertising agency. This corresponds to the requirements of the Misleading and Comparative Advertising Directive 84/450/EEC,[54] so that these requirements could be harmonized. On the other hand, the requirements for further liability should remain the task of Member States.

10. *The press as defendant*

a) Privilege of the press because of press freedom

While advertising agencies are liable as a matter of principle, liability of the press for advertising infringements is significantly more limited. Numerous states (Germany, USA, Sweden, Finland, Italy and Poland) emphasize that press freedom leads to certain privileges in the publishing of advertisements. In Poland the press cannot be deemed illegal or contrary to custom and usage: art. 36 p.p. Fault on the part of press organs is necessary.

[54] Art. 4 para. 2.

This privilege leads to the situation that the newspaper – in contrast to the advertising agency – only has to check the legitimacy of the advertisement to a limited degree. As a result there is either no duty (Italy and the USA) or only a limited duty (Germany and England) on the part of the press to monitor the lawfulness of advertising. This means in addition that that the management of newspapers may trust in the legitimacy of the statements and thereby act in good faith (England and the USA). The protection of the press is most extensive in Sweden. Here injunctions are completely inadmissible. On the other hand even in the home country of basic rights, the USA, injunctions against the press are admissible,[55] although they must be reasonable.[56] In states where there is public law supervision there is control of the press through these bodies. In Sweden the possibility of bringing proceedings against the advertising agency and against the press in their capacity as contributors is reserved solely for the administrative fine remedy and the consumer ombudsman. In Portugal in the majority of cases the consumer agency brings administrative proceedings against all who interfere in the diffusion of the advertising message.

In other states such a privilege, which has constitutional implications, is not emphasized (Hungary, France, Italy, Spain and Portugal). As the addressee of unfair competition law in these countries is the competitor, however, the press as a third party is only seldom responsible for the infringement.

b) Limiting press freedom

However, there are exceptions. Freedom of the press is not unlimited (Germany, USA, Sweden, Italy and Poland). In the USA the Supreme Court has observed that the freedom of speech under the first Amendment does not apply to misleading advertisement.[57] Commercial speech is therefore in principle less protected than political speech. As with advertising agencies there is a difference between states, with some imposing a direct responsibility for their actions on

[55] *Encyclopedia Britannica v. FTC*, 605 F.2d 964 (7th Cir. 1979); *People v. Custom Craft Carpets, Inc.*, 206 Cal. Rptr. 12 (Ct. App. 1984).

[56] *Shapero v. Kentucky Bar Ass'n*, 486 U.S. 466, 108 S. Ct. 1916, 100 L. Ed. 2d 475 (1988); *FTC v. Brown & Williamson Tobacco Corp.*, 778 F.2d 35 (D.C. Cir. 1985).

[57] E.g. *Virigina State Board of Pharmacy v. Virigina Citizens Consumer Council, Inc.*, 425 U.S. 748, 96 Ct. 1817 (1976), 48 L. Ed. 2d 346; *Greater New Orleans Broadcasting Assn. v. U.S.*, 527 U.S. 173, 119 S. Ct. 1973, 144 L. Ed. 2d 161 (1999).

press organs and other states requiring third-party unlawful conduct by the advertiser.

c) Own unlawful conduct

Both objective and subjective criteria are applied to own unlawful conduct. Where a publisher has a financial interest of its own in the advertising campaign the privilege is removed (USA). In Finland the publisher must have acted in order to further the sales of its own newspaper or magazine. In Germany a distinction is drawn between the proprietor share and editorial share.[58] While press freedom applies in principle to the editorial share, the duty of supervision of the press over the proprietor share is limited to broad and easy to detect infringements against competition law. In Germany compensatory claims can only be enforced in respect of intentional conduct of the press. The USA requires knowledge for a claim against the press enterprise.

d) Allocation of third-party fault

In cases where a connection is established to unlawful third party conduct, a subjective element is required. In Italy knowledge of unlawfulness is required. French criminal law requires awareness of unlawfulness. Other jurisdictions require at least negligence. In Denmark the subjective conditions for punishing under the MFL indicate that negligence must have occurred. Concerning the press it is necessary that a relatively clear violation of the MFL exists. It is also at times necessary that the conduct was for a commercial purpose (Sweden).

Evaluation

(1) The Misleading and Comparative Advertising Directive 84/450/EEC does not regulate press responsibility for competition infringement. It is true that the freedom of the press is not expressly codified in the law of the European Union. However, freedom of expression is laid down in art. 10 para. 2 ECHR.[59] This encompasses the freedom of the press.[60] In addition the ECJ in its jurisprudence has expressly recognized press

[58] B. Jestaedt, in W. Pastor and H. Ahrens, *Der Wettbewerbsprozeß* (4th edn 1999), § 26. V.2, p. 417.

[59] European Convention for the Protection of Human Rights and Fundamental Freedoms of November 4, 1950 (www.echr.coe.int).

[60] R. Streinz, in R. Streinz (ed.), *EUV/EGV, Vertrag über die Europäische Union und Vertrag zur Gründung der Europäischen Gemeinschaft* (2003), GR-Charta, art. 10 note 9.

freedom.[61] The freedom of the media has also now been expressly mentioned in art. 10 para. 2 of the proposed Treaty establishing a Constitution for Europe.[62]

In all Member States liability of the press for competition infringements is the exception. This is because in most states press freedom leads to the requirements for liability of the press being less onerous. The likelihood is therefore low that the press can be held responsible or legally liable. The publisher must either have its own commercial interest in the publication or knowledge of the competition infringement.

(2) The freedom of the press as a European basic right is only binding on European institutions or national institutions in the application of European law.[63] Therefore, it would seem sensible in the interests of harmonization of legal consequences of unfair competition law on the European level to designate the press as responsible bodies while at the same time emphasizing the freedom of the press as the basic right. The requirements for liability would be oriented towards the respective law of the Member State. The approach requiring knowledge or own commercial advantage for liability provides a role model. However, as infringements are rare, on the grounds of subsidiarity it can also be argued that further harmonization is not necessary.

[61] ECJ C-368/95, (1997) ECR I-3689 note 26 – 'Vereinigte Familapress'.

[62] Art. II-10 para. 2 of the proposed European Constitution reads: 'The freedom and pluralism of the media shall be respected'.

[63] See art. II-51 para. 1 of the proposed European Constitution.

III. Out-of-court settlements of disputes

Case 8 Watch imitations II: pre-trial measures

In a bakery belonging to the A chain colourable imitations of a reputed mark of Swiss watch, B, are offered as genuine. While the original B watches cost €2,000, the A imitations cost only €20. A has not only published an advertisement in a number of newspapers, but has decorated his shop display window with pictures of the imitation watch.

B happens to find out that A is planning to sell the imitation watches the following week accompanied by an advertising campaign. The watches have already been ordered from the supplier, the advertising posters printed and TV spots booked. B wishes to prevent the advertising campaign.

Can or must B involve arbitrators or mediation procedures before bringing legal proceedings in pursuit of these claims? Are there any other non-trial measures which are effective?

For the substantive law see Case 2 (Watch imitations I).

Austria (8)

(1) Arbitrators or mediators normally do not have to be consulted by B before filing a suit. A proposal by the federal government dating back to the 1930s that wanted to institute arbitration panels for competition matters[1] has never been followed up. Thus, there are no relevant legal norms concerning this matter.

However, there are codes of conduct and some voluntary arbitration proceedings between competitors and consumers.[2] Specific regulations of branches, which were made by professional organizations, seem to be rare. Formerly, in the banking sector – under the scope of the KWG (Banking Act) – there had been a competition agreement to resolve such cases. The BWG now in force does not have such a provision.

In the authoritative commentary on the UWG by Wiltschek[3] the notion of 'arbitration agreement' does not appear; the notion of 'arbitral tribunal' only appears in the context of foreign tribunals. In many years working for the unfair competition chamber of the OGH this writer does not remember a single case, where in competition law

[1] *Anwaltszeitung* 1934, 43.
[2] See www.eej-net.at; A. Engel, *Austria*, in R. Schulze and H. Schulte-Nölke, 2.i).
[3] L. Wiltschek, *UWG* (2003).

matters lack of jurisdiction because of an existing or necessary prior arbitration has been relied upon.

(2) Under Austrian law, no notice of violation or other out-of-court action is required before bringing a lawsuit for a violation of competition law. Failure to notify the other party before filing proceedings has no effect on awarding costs. However, in practice, potential plaintiffs give potential defendants notice before filing suit.[4]

Denmark (8)

(1) There is no requirement for a preceding mediation between A and B, but it is quite common that B approaches A specifying his rights, and it will be an element included in the courts' assessment of whether or not there is sufficient justification for issuing an injunction.

(2) There is no board on business practices at the Chamber of Commerce. There are only some special tribunals such as the Radio and Television Advertising Board or the Medicinal Information Board, which handle advertising issues between the parties.[5] If consumers are involved, proceedings can be taken before the Consumer Complaints Board.[6]

(3) The Consumer Ombudsman can ask the trader to supply information; incorrect information can be sanctioned by a fine, §§ 22 para. 2, 15 para. 2 MFL. If a company gives a commitment to the Consumer Ombudsman concerning his marketing behaviour this commitment might, according to § 16 sec. 2 MPA, provide the necessary basis for the Ombudsman issuing an order whereby he seeks to ensure the fulfilment of such commitments. The Consumer Ombudsman shall endeavour to influence the traders and business-persons by negotiation or voluntary arrangements before he uses his more forceful powers under the MFL. According to § 16 MFL, the Consumer Ombudsman can through negotiations attempt to influence A to abstain from the advertising campaign.[7] It is, however, important here that the Consumer Ombudsman can refrain from taking up a case if, in his opinion, it is only of a minor importance. In this assessment, he will also consider whether the controversy mainly concerns the mutual relations between traders and whether B has access to alternative remedies.

[4] See S. Kofler, *Österreich*, in J. Maxeiner and P. Schotthöfer, pp. 3, 19.

[5] M. Eckardt-Hansen, *Denmark*, in J. Maxeiner and P. Schotthöfer, p. 97 (119).

[6] See Case 5 (Discontinued models).

[7] E. Borcher and F. Bøggild, *Markedsføringsloven* (2001), p. 379.

According to § 19 sec. 2 MFL if negotiations have proved to be unsuccessful the Consumer Ombudsman can issue an order to a trader to abstain from the contemplated behaviour if the latter's expected action will be clearly contrary to the law. The provision was included in the MFL by law no. 342 of June 2, 1999. It is a prerequisite for issuing an order that both the law in the particular area is certain and that – assessed on the basis of the concrete circumstances – it is beyond reasonable doubt that a violation of the Act has taken place. The rule does not appear to have been applied so far.[8]

Non-compliance with such an order shall according to § 22 sec. 1 MFL, as amended, be punishable by a fine or imprisonment of a maximum of up to four months.

According to § 21 MFL the Consumer Ombudsman can issue an interlocutory injunction if there is a reasonable possibility that the object of an injunction issued by an ordinary court according to § 13 MFL may not be achieved if the decision of the court has to be awaited. This option for the Consumer Ombudsman to issue an interlocutory injunction himself is applied only in very rare cases. One reason for this is that the application of the provision will provide the general public with knowledge of the very circumstances which the Consumer Ombudsman wishes to prohibit and this might be considered inappropriate. Furthermore, there are strict requirements concerning the application, which makes this difficult.[9] The Consumer Ombudsman is, inter alia, required to bring the case before the ordinary courts the very day after he has issued an injunction. The interlocutory injunction has to be confirmed by the court.[10]

The Consumer Ombudsman also has a series of powers with which to impose measures of his own against companies' and traders' marketing actions.

England (8)

In the law of unfair competition court decisions are of minor importance. The introduction of s. 124 of the Fair Trading Act 1973 puts its emphasis on self-regulation. The Office of Fair Trading[11] supports associations formulating codes of practice. The self-regulatory body

[8] P.B. Madsen, *Markedsret*, vol. 2, (4th edn 2002), p. 336.

[9] M. Koktvedgaard, *Lærebog i Konkurrenceret* (4th edn 2000), p. 57 (59); S. Kristoffersen and K.V. Gravesen, *Forbrugerretten* (2001), p. 476.

[10] A. Kur and J. Schovsbo, *Dänemark*, in G. Schricker, note 269.

[11] www.oft.gov.uk/default.htm.

controlling advertisements is the Advertising Standards Authority (ASA)[12] that supervises the Committee of Advertising Practice (CAP), which is composed of representatives from a wide range of bodies involved in advertising including media owners and advertisers. It publishes the British Codes of Advertising and Sales Promotion (Code)[13]. Next to the ASA exists the Broadcast Advertising Clearance Centre (BACC), which examines the commercials to ensure that they comply with the ITC Code or Radio Code, as appropriate.[14] Individual viewers or listeners who are concerned about the content of broadcasts, including advertisements, can complain to either the Broadcasting Complaints Commission (BCC) or the Broadcast Standard Council (BSC).[15]

Complaints are investigated free of charge. They must be made in writing, normally within three months of the advertisement's appearance, and should be accompanied by a copy of the advertisement or a note of where and when it appeared. The Secretariat conducts a fact-finding investigation into those complaints that are pursued; most are dealt with within six weeks, some are fast-tracked and completed within 48 hours, while others are given priority. Where necessary, the Secretariat takes advice from expert external consultants before producing a recommendation based on its findings for the ASA Council. Recommendations made by the Secretariat can, at its own request or the request of those affected, be considered by a CAP Panel. The Council will take into account the Panel's opinions. The final decision on complaints and on interpretation of the Codes rests with the Council.

Importantly, the ASA does not only control its members, or the members to the CAP, but the whole advertising sector. It can do so because all relevant distributors of advertising materials, such as the print media, the broadcasting media, and even the Royal Mail, are members of the ASA and will not publish or distribute any advertising that has been held to be in violation of the BCA. Since the ASA, in practice, exercises public functions, courts have held that the ASA is subject to judicial review, which means that traders who face

[12] The ASA was set up in 1962 to oversee the workings of the CAP, see S. Groom, *United Kingdom*, in J. Maxeiner and P. Schotthöfer, p. 469 (471).

[13] Available at www.asa.org.uk. For a comparison of the ASA rules with German law, see M. Jergolla, (2003) 49 WPR 431.

[14] S. Groom, *United Kingdom*, in J. Maxeiner and P. Schotthöfer, p. 469 (508).

[15] Ibid.

sanctions by the ASA can challenge the lawfulness of the decisions taken by the ASA.[16]

A number of sanctions exist to counteract advertisements and promotions that conflict with the Codes: the media, contractors and service providers may withhold their services or deny access to space; adverse publicity, which acts as a deterrent, may result from rulings published in the ASA's Monthly Report; pre-vetting or trading sanctions may be imposed or recognition revoked by the media's, advertiser's, promoter's or agency's professional association or service provider and financial incentives provided by trade, professional or media organizations may be withdrawn or temporarily withheld. Finally, the case can be remitted to the OFT.[17] Some hold that Code is not really complied with;[18] but the majority considers it as highly effective, since 98 per cent of the sanctions *are* complied with.[19]

Finland (8)

(1) Private dispute settlement outside the courts is possible and organizations might help by mediating. Arbitration or mediation is possible as almost any matter can be decided in this way between businesses. There are no rules about civil process or arbitration/mediation process in the SopMenL. There are no statistics about how many cases involving unfair competition might have been decided in arbitration. There have been no cases where a party has demanded the case to be dropped in the Market Court because there is an ongoing arbitration process. An educated guess would be that cases are rather rare as arbitration is used more in connection with contract law and company law matters. If the Ombudsman is the claimant she will not use arbitration, as part of consumer protection is to ensure publicity, which is not possible in arbitration.

Both the Consumer Agency and the Board on Business Practices can, however, give a non-binding opinion even before the advertisement campaign has started. The Board on Business Practices[20] is a part of the Finnish Chambers of Commerce. The Board issues statements on

[16] Established case law since *R v. Advertising Standards Authority, ex parte The Insurance Service plc*, (1990) 9 Tr. L. 169.

[17] See rule 61 of the Code.

[18] The Code of Practices is very differently taken note of, as the exclusion from an association only rarely deters, see S. Weatherill, *United Kingdom*, in R. Schulze and H. Schulte-Nölke, I.1.a).

[19] See the study of ASA on www.asa.org.uk; reproduced in M. Jergolla, 49 (2003) WRP 606.

[20] *Liiketapalautakunta*.

marketing disagreements between companies. It only deals with disputes between businesses; it is not competent if consumers are concerned. In practice, this procedure is often used as a pre-trial procedure; normally the parties accept its decisions.[21] These are not binding and the Board has no right to make claims in the Market Court.

Contacting A before the campaign or asking the opinion of the Board on Business Practices might influence the possibility of being awarded damages later on as knowingly acting contrary to § 1 and § 2 SopMenL might be regarded as a special circumstance. To be able to get compensation for purely economic damage (as in this case since there is no damage to material property or persons) there must be especially weighty reasons, according to § 5:1 Finnish Tort Liability Act.

In a case where a product had been imitated the Supreme Court decided that as no special weighty reasons had been proved the claimant had no right for damages even though § 1 SopMenL had been violated.[22] In a later case there were especially weighty reasons according to the Court and damages were awarded.[23] However, this case dealt with using teaching materials without paying royalties (the person behind these acts had purchased the right to use the materials but had after the bankruptcy of his previous companies used the materials without paying any royalties). The Supreme Court decided this was a violation of § 1 SopMenL. Thus, there is a possibility that the interpretation of § 5:1 of the Tort Liability Act will allow damages to be awarded in future.

(2) Public settlement is quite common. According to § 5 of the Act on the National Consumer Administration the Consumer Ombudsman has a duty to start negotiations with the trader who has violated the Consumer Protection Act. In the course of these negotiations, the trader is obliged to prove the truthfulness of his claims included in the advertisement. The Consumer Ombudsman has a right to information that he can combine with a fine in case of non-compliance: § 4 para. 1 s. 1 Act on the National Consumer Administration.[24] The Consumer Ombudsman ordinarily enforces the prohibition by imposing a conditional fine. The Consumer Ombudsman may issue a prohibition only if there is no significant question of law involved; he can also impose a temporary prohibition in a case requiring urgent action.[25]

[21] K. Kaulamo, *Finland*, in G. Schricker, note 372.
[22] Finnish Supreme Court judgment KKO: 1991:32.
[23] KKO: 1997:181. [24] K. Kaulamo, *Finland*, in G. Schricker, note 322.
[25] K. Fahlund and H. Salmik, *Finland*, in J. Maxeiner and P. Schotthöfer, p. 127 (149).

In practice the insightful trader commits himself in future to refrain from the reprimanded action in a written declaration. Such a declaration has no independent legal sanctions attached to it.[26] An official order to desist is regulated in chap. 2 § 7 para. 2 and § 8 para. 2 KSL. An order issued by the Consumer Ombudsman will not bind the trader if he opposes it. If these negotiations are not successful, the Ombudsman must either issue an order forbidding the offence or take the matter to the courts (in this case to the Market Court). Consumer associations are under no duty to represent consumers' interests in court.

France (8)

(1) Legally, it is not necessary to first warn the competitor. Nevertheless, it is usual to do so prior to serving him with a *mise en demeure* because it has the advantage that it either avoids legal action or at least helps to prove intent of the infringer.[27] Otherwise, there are no compulsory mediation procedures prescribed by the general civil or procedural law in cases of torts. When the conflict arises from a contract, the parties are free to determine which methods of enforcement they want to choose; usually this would be the *mise en demeure* - apart from cases where the parties have dispensed with any summons.[28] In competition matters, it is more common for individual consumers or consumer associations to start professional mediation proceedings. In consumer law, the non-mediated and the mediated resolution of conflicts can be distinguished , either via a *mise en demeure* sent directly to the infringer, or via mediation, arbitration or conciliation methods.[29]

(2) Nevertheless in matters concerning advertising, self-regulation is of supreme importance in France. There are a certain number of extra-judicial measures devised to prevent further conflict. The organizations and associations are mainly the following: the Bureau de Vérification de la Publicité - BVP (Bureau of Verification of Advertising), the Conseil National de Publicité - CNP (National Council of Advertising), the Comité de la Communication Publicitaire Radiodiffusée et Télevisée au Sein du CSA (Committee for Advertising on Radio and Television within the Council of Audiovisual Supervision), the Chambre Internationale du Commerce - ICC (International Chamber of Commerce), the Union

[26] K. Kaulamo, *Finland*, in G. Schricker, note 323.

[27] Y. Guyon, *Droit des affaires*, vol. 2 (8th edn 2001), p. 876.

[28] Cour de cassation, civ. January 27, 1949: Bulletin civil note 272.

[29] Ph. Pedrot and F. Kernaleguen, in: Juris-Classeur, *Concurrence, consommation* (1988), Fasc. 1230, 'Procédure amiables de règlements de litiges', note 4.

National des Annconceurs – UDA (National Union of Advertisers), the Conseil National de la Consommation (National Consumer Council), to cite the most important.[30]

Some of them even have the power to order injunctions in case of lack of conformity with the articles of these organizations and associations. This is the case, for instance, with the Committee for Advertising on Radio and Television, whose injunctions and penalties are regulated by the *Conseil d'État*[31] and the BVP which can summon its members to justify, or put an end to, any prohibited advertising under the threat of being excluded from the association.[32]

The BVP can give recommendations and in case of non-compliance utters a warning to the infringing party, or can even bar the enterprise from the association.[33] Since membership is often a criterion in selecting an advertising agency, expulsion from the BVP for unfair competition, including for non-observance of its recommendation, is a sanction taken seriously.[34] Finally, the BVP can also act as a joint plaintiff.[35] In 1989 for example, the BVP was involved in more than 6,000 cases.[36]

Germany (8)

(1) Pursuant to § 15 UWG (ex-§ 27 a UWG) dispute settlement centres for civil law disputes are provided. This procedure only applies in business-to-consumer (B2C) transactions. The proceeding is in principle voluntary, since the word 'can' is used in § 15 para. 3 UWG (ex-§ 27 a para. 3 UWG). The start of proceedings depends on the consensual application of the parties.[37] Above all, they are not public, and the parties are not subject to any duty of truthfulness or of discovery; evidence need not be adduced, although witnesses may be heard. Minutes will be kept of

[30] G. Raymond, in: Juris-Classeur, *Concurrence, consommation* (1998), Fasc. 900, 'Publicité commerciale et protection des consommateurs', notes 142 et seq.

[31] Ibid., note 144. [32] Ibid., note 150.

[33] T. Dreier and S. von Lewinski, *Frankreich*, in G. Schricker, note 390.

[34] F.O. Ranke, *France*, in J. Maxeiner and P. Schotthöfer, p. 153 (156).

[35] Trib. Corr. Grasse of November 30, 1976, Gaz. Pal. 1976, 1, 237; CA de Paris of January 25, 1984, B.V.P.

[36] T. Dreier and S. von Lewinski, *Frankreich*, in G. Schricker, note 391.

[37] H. Köhler and H. Piper, *UWG* (3rd edn 2002), § 27a note 7; H. Harte-Bavendamm and F. Henning-Bodewig, *UWG* (2004), § 15 note 30; with respect to form and content see A. Baumbach and W. Hefermehl, *UWG* (22nd edn 2001), § 27a note 11; A. Baumbach and W. Hefermehl, *UWG* (23rd edn 2004), § 15 note 12; K. H. Fezer, *UWG* (2005), § 15 note 49.

the proceedings.[38] The aim of the settlement procedure is an amicable settlement: § 15 para. 5 UWG (ex-§ 27a para. 6 s. 1 UWG). Nevertheless, the dispute settlement centre can make non-binding proposals for a settlement.[39] The proposal for a settlement may only be published if the parties agree: § 15 para. 5 s. 2 UWG (ex-§ 27a para. 6 s. 3 UWG). Dispute settlement did not have a very promising start in Germany; private mediation generally had not produced very many results.[40] In the meantime the results have improved: there are about 2,000 proceedings each year and about 50 per cent end with a settlement.[41] The competition centre alone initiates 1,000 proceedings.[42]

Codes of Conduct have been developed by the *Deutscher Werberat* (German Advertising Council),[43] a self-regulatory institution created by the *Zentralausschuss der Werbewirtschaft e.V.* (Central Committee of the German Advertising Industry). The *Deutscher Werberat* has developed codes for advertising concerning children, alcohol, and discrimination. Such codes play a minor role in interpreting the rules of fair trade.[44]

(2) Yet, in practice, litigation is prevented because the injured competitor admonishes the violator in advance. Of all infringements of fair trade 90–95 per cent are settled with this reprimand.[45] The reprimand asks the infringer to desist from certain infringements, to eliminate them and, if necessary, to admit claims for damages. Normally, the reprimand is combined with a contractual penalty: if there is another culpable infringement the infringer promises to pay a certain sum.[46] Where a party violates a cease-and-desist declaration that it has given, it is liable for the contractual penalty.

[38] H. Köhler and H. Piper, *UWG* (3rd edn 2002), § 27a note 9; H. Harte-Bavendamm and F. Henning-Bodewig, *UWG* (2004), § 15 note 43; H. Köhler, in: W. Hefermehl, H. Köhler and J. Bornkamm, *Wettbewerbsrecht* (24th edn 2006), § 15 note 24; K. H. Fezer, *UWG* (2005), § 15 note 69.

[39] M. Nieder, *Außergerichtliche Konfliktlösung im gewerblichen Rechtsschutz* (1999), p. 80; H. Köhler, in W. Hefermehl, H. Köhler and J. Bornkamm, *Wettbewerbsrecht* (24th edn 2006), § 15 note 25; K.H. Fezer, *UWG* (2005), § 15 notes 70 et seq.

[40] O. Teplitzky, *Wettbewerbsrechtliche Ansprüche und Verfahren* (8th edn 2002), chap. 42 note 1.

[41] H. K. Mees, in K.H. Fezer, *Lauterkeitsrecht* (2005), § 15 note 10.

[42] H. Köhler, in W. Hefermehl, H. Köhler and J. Bornkamm, *Wettbewerbsrecht* (24th edn 2006), § 15 note 2.

[43] See www.interverband.com/dbview/owa/assmenu.homepage?tid=69392&fcatid.

[44] L. Brandmair, *Die freiwillige Selbstkontrolle der Werbung* (1978), pp. 185 et seq.; H. Schulte-Nölke, C. Busch and. K. Hawxwell, *Germany*, in R. Schulze and H. Schulte-Nölke, I.1.e).

[45] O. Teplitzky, *Wettbewerbsrechtliche Ansprüche und Verfahren* (8th edn 2002), chap. 41 note 3.

[46] For an example see W. Nordemann et al., *Wettbewerbs- und Markenrecht* (9th edn 2003), note 3012.

The reprimand (*Abmahnung*) is not binding but has cost implications under § 93 ZPO. If the infringer declares that he will discontinue the practice, no further action is necessary. Without a reprimand, the legal costs will be imposed upon the claimant, provided the defendant immediately admits the claim.[47] Where prior notice is given, an immediate acknowledgment is excluded, so that the defendant has to bear all the costs if the court upholds the claim of the violated party: § 91 para. 1 s. 1 ZPO. On the other hand, a reprimand provides the claimant not with an enforceable court decision but with only a non-binding obligation on his opponent.[48]

The admonishing party is allowed to claim the costs for the reprimand on the basis of agency of necessity.[49] These principles have been developed by the courts and are now codified in § 12 para. 1 UWG.

There are no public law procedures.

Greece (8)

Although L. 2251/1994 on consumer protection provides for voluntary mediation between suppliers and consumers (the so-called 'Committees of amicable settlement'),[50] the law on unfair competition does not contain any specific provisions on alternative forms of dispute resolution. However, according to the general rules of civil procedure (art. 867–869 CCP), the parties themselves may submit, by written agreement, all private law disputes (including unfair competition claims) to arbitration.[51] The procedure of this regular arbitration, as well as the form and the effect of the award are defined by art. 870–901 CCP.[52] The arbitral award will be final and binding on the parties, having in

[47] M. Nieder, *Außergerichtliche Konfliktlösung im gewerblichen Rechtsschutz* (1999), p. 15; H. Köhler and H. Piper, *UWG* (3rd edn 2002), vor § 13 note 172; H. Harte-Bavendamm and F. Henning-Bodewig, *UWG* (2004), § 12 note 3; J. Bornkamm, in: W. Hefermehl, H. Köhler and J. Bornkamm, *Wettbewerbsrecht* (24th edn 2006), § 12 note 1.8; K. H. Fezer, *UWG* (2005), § 12 note 3; W. Nordemann et al., *Wettbewerbs- und Markenrecht* (9th edn 2003), note 283.

[48] J. Bornkamm, in W. Hefermehl, H. Köhler and J. Bornkamm, *Wettbewerbsrecht* (24th edn 2006), § 12 note 1.7; K. H. Fezer, *UWG* (2005), § 12 note 2.

[49] BGHZ 52, 393 (399) – 'Fotowettbewerb'; H. Köhler and H. Piper, *UWG* (3rd edn 2002), vor § 13 note 191; H. Harte-Bavendamm and F. Henning-Bodewig, *UWG* (2004), § 12 notes 77, 84 et seq.; K.H. Fezer, *UWG* (2005), § 12 note 49.

[50] Art. 11. The said Committees are established in each prefecture and are composed from three members (one lawyer, one representative of the local commercial or industrial Chamber and one representative of the local consumers associations).

[51] A. Liakopoulos, *Industrial Property*, 5th edn (2000), p. 122.

[52] See also L. 2735/1999 on the *International Commercial Arbitration*.

principle the effect of *res judicata*,[53] and may only be attacked and annulled on specific grounds with an application for setting aside.[54] As provided by art. 902 CCP, permanent arbitration proceedings may be established by the Chambers, the Stock Exchange and public law corporate bodies. Thus, the Greek Chambers of Commerce and Industry maintain a permanent department for the resolution of commercial disputes.[55] Another example is the arbitration tribunals constituted by the Bar Associations, in particular those established by the Athens[56] and the Piraeus[57] Bar Associations; such tribunals are competent for the resolution of all private disputes, provided that they can be decided by arbitration.

Moreover, a prior attempt to mediate is required as a condition of admissibility for certain categories of legal proceedings, although it seems to constitute a simple procedural formality. In particular, art. 214 A CCP provides that all actions falling within the jurisdiction of the multimember courts and for which an amicable settlement is allowed according to the applicable substantive law, should be preceded by an attempt to reach an out-of-court settlement on the basis of the procedure described therein. According to one point of view, all unfair competition claims based on the L. 146/1914 fall within the subject-matter competence of the multimember courts;[58] another opinion considers that the competent court should be determined on the basis of the total value of the claims. If the calculation of the amount is feasible regarding the claim for compensation of damages, it is not feasible with the injunction claim, even if it is considered as having a monetary value.[59] Proceedings for provisional measures are not subject to the condition of an attempt of prior mediation as they fall within the jurisdiction of the single-member courts of first instance.

Hungary (8)

In Hungary it is not possible for the parties to involve arbitrators or mediators, but according to sec. 121(f) HCP it is necessary to declare in the statement of claim whether there has been any kind of arbitration or mediation between the parties. Alternative dispute resolution is not

[53] Art. 896 CCP.
[54] For an overview see S. Koussoulis, *Arbitration. Article by Article Commentary* (2004) [in Greek].
[55] P.D. 31/1979. [56] P.D. 168/1983. [57] P.D. 199/1984
[58] Th.-M. Marinos, *Unfair Competition*, (2002), p. 312.
[59] L. Kotsiris, *Unfair Competition and Antitrust Law* (2001), pp. 365–366.

common, but it has been used in consumer affairs. Finally, the injured party does not have to give notice to the violating party before it may sue.

Ireland (8)

There is no requirement to involve arbitrators or mediators before bringing legal proceedings in pursuit of these claims and no legal provision relating to their involvement. The parties may choose to resolve the dispute by arbitration, but in these circumstances such a choice would be rare. However, frequently, in a commercial dispute, the action will be settled by the parties' lawyers before it reaches the courts.[60]

An aggrieved party may choose to complain to the self-regulatory advertising authority (Advertising Standards Authority of Ireland), which cooperates closely with the Director of Consumer Affairs and is in a good position to apply pressure on its members to encourage changes in advertising practice. The Advertising Standards Authority of Ireland is an independent body set up and financed by the advertising industry. The Authority enforces the rules set out in the Code of Advertising Standards and the Code of Sales Promotion Practice. The codes require that advertising and sales promotion campaigns are legal, decent, honest and truthful. If members of the Advertising Standards Authority publish an advertisement or sales promotion which is found by the Authority to break the rules, the advertisement or promotion must be withdrawn or amended. The codes envisage that the media should refuse to publish an advertisement or sales promotion, which fails to conform with code requirements. Breach of the code is not an offence in law.[61]

Italy (8)

(1) The violator may be admonished (*diffida*) in advance by the other party, prior to court proceedings being started. Such prior warning is not binding, and it has no effect on the eventual subsequent court proceeding. B is under no legal duty to resort to arbitration or mediation procedures.

(2) The *Istituto di Autodisciplina Publicitaria* (IAP) has published its *Codice di Autodisciplina Pubblicitaria* (CAP)[62] for the first time in 1966. Anyone injured or offended by an advertisement may submit a complaint to

[60] See Case 4 (Children's swing). [61] Ibid. [62] See www.iap.it.

the Advertising Code Jury.[63] It is possible to file a suit in front of the Jury as a panel of advertising self-discipline, against the misleading advertisements published by A, provided that A, and/or the newspaper publishers, accepts the self-disciplinary jurisdiction. The panel of the Code of Advertising Self-discipline is a highly qualified body of lawyers, scholars and advertising experts; it usually issues its decisions within a few weeks; costs of litigation are quite low (€1,500).

The Panel can issue orders to desist and order publication of the decision.[64] A summary of each decision is published on the Institute's website (art. 40 of the Code); the Jury may order the infringing party to give public notice of the infringement, through publication of a summary of the decision in one or more advertising media. On the other hand, the panel has no power to award damages; an action for damages may be filed in front of the ordinary courts before or after the panel issued its decision. Such decision (as well as decisions by the *Autorità Garante*) may facilitate the plaintiff in proving that the advertisement is misleading.

The claimant has no duty to start any further litigation in front of ordinary courts after the judgment is issued by the panel. Self-disciplinary judgments have quite a high degree of effectiveness, since most advertising media (including the most important publishers of newspapers and magazines, and TV and radio broadcasters), will refuse any further publication of an advertisement which has been banned by the panel.[65] Their importance is therefore great; 80 per cent of the cases are resolved by means of these self-control mechanisms. According to statistics supplied by the Institute,[66] in 2003 almost one thousand cases were managed by the self-regulatory bodies. Most of such cases were handled by the Review Board, which issued cease-and-desist orders voluntarily accepted by the advertisers concerned, which did not oppose such orders. In 2002 the Jury issued 88 decisions (21 following a complaint by a private party); in 2003 the Jury issued 60 decisions (24 following a complaint by a private party). In all cases,

[63] F. Hofer, S. Lösch, A. Toricelli and G. Genta, *Italy*, in J. Maxeiner and P. Schotthöfer (1999), p. 285 (313).

[64] C. Käser, *Effizienz des Rechtsschutzes im deutschen und italienischen Wettbewerbsrecht* (2003), p. 252.

[65] The same judgment can found in F. Hofer, S. Lösch, A. Toricelli and G. Genta, *Italy*, in J. Maxeiner and P. Schotthöfer (1999), p. 285 (288).

[66] See www.iap.it.

complainants were competitors of the infringing advertiser. More than 75 per cent of the complaints are successful.[67]

(3) Suits in front of the *Autorità Garante* are less expensive than any private law action, but the proceeding may take some months (the authority has the power to issue immediately an interlocutory cease and desist order, but it uses such power very rarely). The average length of these proceedings amounts to more than five months.[68]

Netherlands (8)

Under the present Dutch Code of Civil Procedure there is no such obligation. However, the Dutch Parliament has approved a provision according to which courts will actively refer parties to mediation. The court will have the possibility to refer parties to mediation in civil, family, administrative and tax cases if the case could be solved by mediation. However, it is essential that parties agree to such mediation, in which case the court proceeding will be suspended during the mediation efforts. Parties are never obliged to agree to or initiate mediation, as this would run contrary to art. 17 of the Dutch Constitution which determines that no one can be prevented against his will from being heard by the courts to which he is entitled to apply under the law. Therefore the parties can reject the referral and proceed with the legal proceedings.[69]

Poland (8)

(1) The u.z.n.k. does not regulate any procedures for alternative dispute resolutions, and does not impose any obligation on the plaintiff in this respect. However, the provisions of chap. III title III k.p.c allow bringing claims to the Court of Arbitrators. The parties themselves can determine the procedure according to which the case will be decided (art. 705 k.p.c.).

There is no appeal against the decision of the Court of Arbitrators (art. 711.1 k.p.c). A decision or agreement reached in the presence of arbitrators is equally binding as a decision of a national court after the national court declares that the decision can be executed (art. 711.2). A party can file for dismissal of the decision of the Court of Arbitrators (art. 712 k.p.c), if: the parties did not agree to submit the dispute to the

[67] C. Käser, *Effizienz des Rechtsschutzes im deutschen und italienischen Wettbewerbsrecht* (2003), pp. 254 et seq.

[68] Ibid., p. 279.

[69] For self-regulation see Case 4 (Children's swing).

Court of Arbitrators, such an agreement was not valid or expired, a party was deprived of due process, the court did not follow the agreed procedures or the court decision is incomprehensible.

Self-regulation is developing very dynamically. A Code concerning the Rules of Conduct in the Field of Advertising (*Kodeks Poest powania w Dziedzinie Reklamy*) has been developed. The ICC international code on advertising practice was taken as a role model in formulating the Polish code. As a sanction, a member can be barred from the association.[70]

(2) Poland has a Consumer Ombudsman and a President of the Office for Competition and Consumer Protection (*Urzd Ochrony Konkrencji i Konsumentów*).[71]

Portugal (8)

(1) B can only involve arbitrators or mediation procedures before bringing legal procedures if A consents to this kind of resolution. In fact, the proceedings of voluntary arbitration are completely optional, so they depend on the agreement of the parties (art. 1 Law 31/86, August 29, *Lei de Arbitragem Voluntária* – LAV (Voluntary Arbitration Law). If the parties agree to submitting the case to an arbitrator they can go to the existing centres of arbitration for self-regulation of advertising. The arbitrator can judge the case in law or in equity, according to the decision of the parties: art. 22 LAV. If the arbitration decision determines that A cannot advertise the imitation watch or decorate his shop window with pictures of the imitation watch, A would be obliged to cease doing so, and if he fails to carry this out, he can be condemned to pay monetary compensation to B. The arbitration decision is sufficient for the executive proceedings. Arbitration still does not play a major role in the resolution of competition conflicts, as among competitors there is no confidence in the ability of arbitration procedures to solve these kinds of problems. Therefore, arbitration is rare, as it always depends on the parties' agreement.

Competitors have a duty to collaborate, but not a duty to give notice of any violation of the Code of Good Advertising Practices.

(2) There is some self-regulation. The *Instituto Civil da Autodisciplina da Publicidade*,[72] that belongs to the European Advertising Standards Alliance, can take measures, such as the correction or elimination of the advertising when it receives complaints from competitors or from

[70] I. Wiszniewska, *Polen*, in G. Schricker, notes 393 et seq.

[71] Ibid., note 36; see Case 4 (Children's swing). [72] www.icap.pt.

consumers. The Portuguese Association of Advertising Agencies has adopted a *Código de Ética na Publicidade* (Code of Fair Practices in Advertising) that is based on the International Codes of the International Chamber of Commerce.

Spain (8)

(1) There are no special rules for mediation in Spanish unfair competition law. Arbitration is only possible with the agreement of the parties involved in the dispute (art. 1 Arbitration Act).

Art. 18 para. 2a LCD, which can also be used by the owner of the mark, gives him the right to file a claim for an order to prohibit the violator to initiate the advertising campaign. However, there is no specific obligation on the owner of the mark to previously inform the violator, but it usually makes sense to do so in order to avoid judicial expenses that cannot be recovered if the violator agrees not to initiate the campaign. Specifically, the *Ley General de Publicidad* – LGP (Advertising Act) seems to impose a duty to give notice to the person who is carrying out an illicit advertising campaign (art. 26 LGP),[73] but this duty is not imposed when it is claimed that the advertising is damaging the collective interest of consumers.

(2) It must be taken into account that in Spain the *Asociación de Autocontrol de la Publicidad* – AAP[74] (Association for the Self-Regulation of Commercial Communication) works as an extra-judicial body to settle those disputes that arise from the application of the Codes of Conduct based on the ICC International Code of Advertising Practice. It is an association that serves its members as an arbitration panel to solve disputes among its members (advertisers and media) concerning advertising and also gives advice on the legality of advertising prior to its publication. The panel applies its own code; if necessary the International Code of Advertising Practice of the ICC is applied. These proceedings are described as highly effective.[75]

Sweden (8)

(1) As regards the private part of marketing law (i.e. unfair competition), the parties to a dispute may agree that the case should be decided by

[73] See W. Nordemann, *Das neue spanische Werbegesetz im Vergleich zum deutschen Werberecht*, in *Festschrift O. von Gamm* (1990), p. 109 (115).

[74] See www.aap.es/data/frames/freng.htm and www.autocontrol.es; see A. Tato Plaza, *Das neue System zur Selbstkontrolle der Werbung in Spanien*, (1999) 47 GRUR Int. 853.

[75] A. Tato Plaza, (1999) 47 GRUR Int. 853 (864).

arbitration. In the absence of such an agreement, ordinary courts must settle the dispute. Private parties may, by mutual agreement, decide to settle their dispute by arbitration as long as it is within their power. The form and procedure for the regular arbitration is established by the Swedish Arbitration Act (1999:116). The act stipulates that arbitration can be used in all legal matters regarding disputes that, according to the law applicable, are open for settlements between the parties. The act covers all matters decided by ordinary courts under private law. The awards are binding and the principle of *res judicata* applies. The award will, however, be subject to limitations according to a general principle of *ordre public*. The general rule in Swedish law is that the courts decide legal matters. There are hardly any examples at all where statutory law provides that disputes must be decided by arbitrators.

Nevertheless, many advertising disputes are settled out-of-court.[76] There exists no Board on Business Practices in the Commerce Chamber but there is a very successful consumer complaint board.[77] In addition, many self-regulatory bodies are competent to settle advertising law disputes. These bodies are normally set up by enterprises or organization of enterprises concerned with a specific product category or service category.[78] There are a number of trade specific tribunals set up voluntarily by their trade associations, such as The Publishers' Opinion Tribunal (PO), The Publicists Partnership Tribunal, The Ethical Tribunal and others.

(2) Although prior warnings have no procedural effect and are not required, they serve the purpose of making the other side aware of the situation. Potential defendants who continue the challenged behaviour after receiving a warning risk are found to have acted intentionally.[79]

(3) Advertisers are obliged to respond to the Consumer Ombudsman's request for information and documentation etc., and are subject to fines for a failure to comply.[80] In uncontroversial cases, the Consumer Ombudsman may issue prohibition or information orders coupled with a default fine: sec. 21 MFL. If it is not approved, the Consumer Ombudsman would have to take the case to court: sec. 22 MFL.[81]

[76] M. Plogell, in J. Maxeiner and P. Schotthöfer, p. 425 (443).
[77] See Case 5 (Discontinued models).
[78] M. Plogell, in J. Maxeiner and P. Schotthöfer, p. 425 (443).
[79] Ibid., p. 425 (442). [80] Ibid., p. 425 (443).
[81] U. Bernitz, *Sweden*, in R. Schulze and H. Schulte-Nölke, p. 6; P. Doppel and J. Scherpe, *'Grupptalan' – Die Bündelung gleichgerichteter Interessen im schwedischen Recht*, in J. Basedow, K. Hopt, H. Kötz and D. Baetge, *Die Bündelung gleichgerichteter Interessen im Prozeß* (1999), p. 429 (435).

Besides the newly introduced possibility of bringing group actions the Consumer Ombudsman was, from 1997 to 2002, competent to represent individual consumers before civil courts in cases concerning financial services.[82] This was an experiment in order to bring on case law in the area; but this possibility was rarely used. The reason for this is that undertakings have been quite willing to reach different forms of settlements when the Consumer Ombudsman has been engaged in the matter. Also in the area of financial services, foreign authorities or organizations from other EEA member states are given competence to claim injunctions in Sweden under the MFL, insofar as they are pointed out in Directive 98/27/EC.[83] This is laid down by the Swedish Act 2000:1175 on standing for certain foreign consumer agencies and consumer organizations. None of this matters in situations where watches are marketed in a misleading way, of course.

Currently, in this situation there may not be any mediation, unless agreed on and organized by the parties.

Summary (8)

The various possibilities for out-of-court legal protection are often lumped together. However, one should distinguish between settlement by the parties without involvement of third parties, out-of-court dispute resolution through third parties, dispute resolution in the course of self-regulation, and finally state institutions such as the ombudsman.

1. *European law rules*

(1) Notice of violation is not provided for in the Misleading and Comparative Advertising Directive 84/450/EEC. However under art. 5 Injunction Directive 98/27/EC the Member States are at liberty to provide for regulations on consultation between the infringer and affected party. The model was the German system of warning.[84]

(2) The Out-of-court Recommendations 98/257/EC and 01/310/EC on basic principles of out-of-court dispute resolution by third parties are particularly important. It is true that a recommendation has no

[82] At the time of writing, the news is that this possibility has been extended.

[83] See also the more recent Directive 2002/65/EC concerning the distant marketing of consumer financial services amending inter alia Directive 98/27/EC.

[84] See D. Baetge, (1999) 112 ZZP 329 (346) pointing out that the proposal for the directive still talks about 'violation notice'; see ABl. No. C 107, April 13, 1996, p. 5.

binding force.[85] At the same time it is relevant to the extent that Member States in fact observe their substantive requirements. The Out-of-court Recommendation 98/257/EC defines out-of-court dispute resolution as the active intervention of a third party which proposes or prescribes a solution.[86] The Out-of-court Recommendation 01/310/EC extends the basic principles to independent institutions which the parties commission to create the consensual solution. The basic principles mentioned for the recommendation include independence, transparency and efficiency.

(3) The Misleading and Comparative Advertising Directive 84/450/EEC permits voluntary self-control through institutions for self-regulation. In England it was sought to ensure the preservation of its tradition of self regulation, albeit that it was required under the directive to supplement the self-regulation structure with an element of public control.[87] However, such institutions can only be established additionally to court or administrative proceedings: art. 5.

2. *Out-of-court settlement of disputes between the parties*

a) Notice of violation by a competitor or an association

Scope of application

The notice of violation (*Abmahnung*) has a central place in German advertising law. Approximately 90 per cent of all advertising disputes are settled by this procedure without resort to the courts.[88] The award of costs encourages parties who feel aggrieved by competitors' advertising to consult attorneys and undertake legal action. In Austria the notice of violation is sometimes directed at the infringer. However, this does not lead to the claim for recovery. The notice of violation is also known in Sweden. It serves the purpose of making the other side aware of the situation. Potential defendants who continue challenged behaviour after receiving a warning risk are found to act intentionally. In Denmark, it will be an element included in the courts' assessment of whether or not there is sufficient justification for issuing an injunction that the plaintiff has specified his rights. Under French law it is not

[85] Art. 249 para. 3 EC.

[86] A notice of violation from the injured party to the injuring party does not count as this, see reason for consideration 9.

[87] S. Weatherill, *United Kingdom*, in R. Schulte and H. Schulze-Nölke, 2(a).

[88] W. Büscher, in K.F. Fezer, *Lauterkeitsrecht* (2005), § 12 note 1; G. Jennes and P. Schotthöfer, *Germany*, in J. Maxeiner and P. Schotthöfer, p. 203 (228).

necessary first to admonish the competitor. Nevertheless, it is usual to do so prior to serving him with a *mise en demeure* because it has the advantage that it either avoids legal action or at least it assists in proving intention. In Italy, the violator may be admonished in advance by the other party, prior to court proceedings being started. Such prior warning is not binding, and it has no effect on the eventual subsequent court proceeding. Finally, the notice of violation is also seen in Spain and the USA. In Sweden and the USA, for example, it serves to facilitate proof of the intent of the infringer in legal proceedings. In Germany, Denmark and Spain it is important for legal costs whether the affected party has previously served notice of violation on the infringer.

Evaluation

Reservations against claim for recovery of expenses

(1) The notice of violation is known in a number of Member States and in the USA. In Germany it terminates over 90 per cent of all disputes. The enforcement of relief against the unfair competition methods in Germany has been described as 'probably the most effective' system of advertising control.[89] It has the advantage of enabling a rapid reaction to the legal infringement, because no third parties need be involved in the court or out-of-court proceeding. In addition legal proceedings are avoided[90] so that the conflict can be settled more quickly.

(2) However, the notice of violation and related claim for recovery of expenses is not a universal cure. The notice of violation does not apply where there is no claimant, as with the lack of rights of claim for consumers in Germany and many other states. Ultimately, it does not help the injured party but rather, in general, the attorney.[91] In Germany it has taken over thirty years to prevent abuse by professional associations. Even now the limits of admissible expenses are far from being explored to their full extent. Recently, it was pointed out what problems the disgorgement of profits claim can involve in the calculation of expenses.[92] Because of supposed abuse through associations whose sole purpose is to issue notices of violation, the legislature in 1994 strictly limited the rights of claims for associations. This led to an

[89] G. Jennes and P. Schotthöfer, *Germany*, in J. Maxeiner and P. Schotthöfer, p. 203.

[90] J. Bornkamm, in H. Hefermehl, H. Köhler and J. Bornkamm, *Wettbewerbsrecht* (24th edn 2006), § 12 note 1.5.

[91] The competitors have to self-execute their rights, see the evidence in H. Brüning, in: H. Harte and F. Henning, UWG (2004), § 12 note 85.

[92] B.II.6(b).

80 per cent reduction in claims and now unlawful practices are frequently no longer acted against.[93] Therefore, doing without the expenses claimed has been suggested. Thereby, the injured party would only have a claim if it wins its action before the court.[94] With the 2004 reform the German legislature has however expressly adopted the expenses recovery claim in § 12 para. 1 s. 2 UWG. The notice of violation only helps if the infringer stops the infringing behaviour and if possible compensates the harm.

Comparing the notice of violation under German law with out-of-court dispute settlement, what both have in common is that they consist of a procedure which precedes litigation. However, there are also differences. In practice supervision is not carried out by a neutral third party, but rather, as formerly in Germany, by professional 'notice associations' as 'quasi police' (at least in respect of certain advertising measures). The European Commission in its out-of-court recommendation 98/257/EC called for impartiality and objectivity. Logically the reconciliation of the parties must be accepted from this as the parties are not independent.[95] The notice of violation under German law invites abuse because the claim for recovery of expenses is to be seen as a form of private sanction. In contrast to this several member states exclude the compensatory claim for participation in disputes by self-regulating organizations. Thus, the notice of violation gives at once too much and too little, if it invites abuse. Too little if legal enforcement fails for lack of standing. Thus it is not particularly surprising that all other states have not chosen the path of the recovery of expenses claim through a notice of violation of anticompetitive conduct. Recovery of costs for a notice of violation exists nowhere else in the European Community.[96] If the German legislature believes that with the new UWG it is providing a model for European legal harmonization[97] this is certainly not the case regarding the recovery of expenses claim for a notice of violation. Harmonization of the notice of violation is, on the other hand, conceivable; but the claim for recovery of expenses should by contrast not be introduced in a directive.

93 Insofar critical W. Nordemann et al., *Wettbewerbs- und Markenrecht* (9th edn 2003), notes 72 et seq.; A. Beater (1995) 159 ZHR 217 (221); A. Beater, *Wettbewerbsrecht* (2002), § 30 note 126.

94 W. Nordemann et al., *Wettbewerbs- und Markenrecht* (9th edn 2003), note 74.

95 Recommendation 98/257/EC, reason for consideration 9 s. 2.

96 G. Jennes and P. Schotthöfer, *Germany*, in J. Maxeiner and P. Schotthöfer, p. 203.

97 See above A.II.2(e).

b) Complaint procedures

The proposal for regulation of marketing lays down in art. 6 para. 2 and 3 that the consumer has to institute complaint proceedings with provision for the consumer to receive a response to the complaint without cost within four weeks. Such a measure was not provided in the Misleading and Comparative Advertising Directive 84/450/EEC.

Such a procedure is helpful to the consumer because it is without cost. It will be preferable in doubtful cases to court proceedings. On the other hand, however, it must be checked whether there is a disproportionate burden on the opposite side, as the legal duty is directed not only at larger enterprises but also at any contractor, that is also small businesses. Nevertheless, the above experiences of various Member States have made clear regarding consumer rights of claim that no flood of claims need be expected. Thus such a complaints procedure without involvement of third parties is basically to be welcomed.

3. *Out-of-court dispute resolution through third parties (arbitration, mediation etc.)*

a) Significance

Germany knows out-of-court dispute resolution through third parties under § 15 UWG (ex-§27a UWG). However, it has only become accepted in the last few years.[98] In Austria there is no legal regulation for private mediation, although it exists in individual areas of voluntary dispute resolution which are of limited importance. Polish law knows only general regulations on dispute resolution. If such proceedings are instituted, however, the parties are bound by the decision.

In France, by contrast, there are no compulsory mediation procedures prescribed by general civil or procedural law in cases of torts. In competition matters it is more common for individual consumers or consumer associations to start professional mediation proceedings. In consumer law one can distinguish between the direct and indirect resolution of conflicts, either via a *mise en demeure*, sent directly to the infringer, or via mediation, arbitration or conciliation methods. There are no special rules for mediation in Spanish unfair competition law. Arbitration is only possible under agreement of the parties involved in the dispute (art. 1 Arbitration Act). It must be taken into account that in Spain the Asociación de Autocontrol de la Publicidad (Association for

[98] See Case 8 (Watch imitations II).

the Self-Regulation of Commercial Communication) works as an extra-judicial body to settle those disputes which arise from the application of the Codes of Conduct based on the ICC International Code of Advertising Practice. In Portugal, the proceedings of voluntary arbitration are completely optional, so they depend on the agreement of the parties. Arbitration still plays no significant role in the resolution of the competitors' conflicts, as there is a lack of confidence among competitors in the ability of arbitration procedures to resolve these kinds of problems. As a result arbitration is rare, as it always depends on the parties' agreement.

By contrast, in Sweden, besides the Consumer Agency and the Consumer Ombudsman there is also the *Allmänna Reklamationsnämnd* – ARN (Consumer Complaints Board) which resolves disputes by means of issuing recommendations. The ARN issues about 4,000 recommendations per year. It has therefore been established as an easy and effective form of arbitration in respect of disputes between consumers and commercial undertakings. The decisions of the ARN are not legally binding but to a great extent Swedish undertakings feel obliged to respect the tribunal's recommendations. In 75 per cent of all cases the recommendation is complied with. The Consumer Ombudsman may apply to the ARN if a group of consumers have similar claims on the same grounds, a so-called group action. In Finland, before taking the matter into the general court of first instance the competitor could ask for a non-binding opinion of the Consumer Complaints Board. The Consumer Ombudsman could demand that the entrepreneur should cease this kind of marketing and if the violator opposes take the matter before the Market Court. In addition, in Finland the Board on Business Practices is an important body, which is a part of the Finnish Chambers of Commerce. The Board issues statements on marketing disagreements between companies. In Denmark, there is no requirement for a preceding mediation and there is no Board on Business Practices at the Chamber of Commerce. There are some special tribunals such as the Radio and Television Advertising Board or the Medicinal Information Board which handle advertising issues between the parties. In Denmark, a special administrative complaints body, the Consumer Complaints Board, has been established.[99] According to § 1

[99] The Consumer Complaints Board was established in 1974 and is presently empowered by consolidated Act No. 282 of May 10, 1988; S. Kristoffersen and K.V. Gravesen, *Forbrugerretten* (2001), p. 459; B. Gomard, *Civilprocessen* (5th edn 2000), p. 763.

the Complaints Board can attend to complaints from private consumers concerning goods, work performances and service. If a decision from the Complaints Board is not complied with, the case must be brought before the regular courts. According to § 11 sec. 2 upon the request of and on behalf of a consumer – the complainant – the Board's secretariat shall in the event of non-compliance bring the case before the courts. Decisions from the Complaints Board are not binding on the courts. The courts will often reach the same result as the Complaints Board.[100]

But another means of achieving such a balance has been the creation of a special Consumer Complaints Board whose sole task is to attend to complaints concerning the consumers' minor purchases and accordingly the fees for bringing a complaint before the Board are low. In this respect it is noteworthy that the Board itself is responsible for seeking information in the individual case, and it can be added that a complaint is expected to be dealt with more expediently when compared with actions before the courts.

Evaluation

b) Reasons for the limited scope of actual application

The use of out-of-court procedures through third parties, though legally possible, is not particularly popular in Austria and Germany. This may be because they are difficult to classify. Disadvantages are that such procedures can normally only be instituted with the agreement of both parties. The sanction mechanisms are similarly weak. Settlement and publication of the decision on the other hand requires the agreement of both parties. However, it is more appropriate to immediately gain the declaration of a court than an out-of-court dispute resolution institution. In Germany the notice of violation costs already incurred also encourage a court decision.

The differences in legal cultures are revealed here. In Sweden acceptance is based on the fact that business parties are not of a litigious mentality.[101] By contrast in Germany mediation is not widespread perhaps because only a legal decision is accepted by many citizens. In other states, rather than out-of-court dispute settlement through third parties, the solution through self-regulation is of great importance. In

[100] S. Kristoffersen and K.V. Gravesen, *Forbrugerretten* (2001), p. 463.

[101] The former MFL mainly consisted of criminal offenses, with the result that a businessman would have had to report his competitor to the public prosecutor's office, see M. Treis, *Recht des unlauteren Wettbewerbs- und Marktvertriebsrecht in Schweden* (1991), p. 7.

favour of this is the factor of expertise in that the particular profession or business can best judge what is just.

c) Reform proposals

The original regulation proposal provided in art. 6 para. 4 for compulsory out-of-court dispute settlement or a code of conduct. This was criticized in that such dispute resolution would be of little sense as long as the consumer has no right of claim. It would be disproportionate as a complaints procedure in favour of the consumer would be sufficient and, finally, there was a lack of an overall concept.[102]

The criticism is justified insofar as in Germany the consumer has insufficient legal protection. To improve legal enforcement against infringements by the consumer is the declared intention of the Commission.[103] If, however, the civil law route is closed to the consumer, or if he is put off by the effort and expense, he should be provided with easier possibilities. These should include the chance to give notification to an authority or out-of-court dispute resolution through an independent third party or a self-regulating organization. Dispute resolution through a third party has the advantage over self-regulation in that it also applies if self-regulation is not available or where membership would be disproportionate. In Germany the extension of settlement proceedings has been called for because consumer protection associations could make use of it relatively easily.[104] An increase of fees has also been suggested in order to improve the professional standards of personnel.[105] Decisions should be published so that standards can be set and comparisons made.[106] Out-of-court dispute resolution should be promoted as the preferred mode of legal enforcement at the European level. The amended regulation proposal therefore correctly allows out-of-court dispute resolution according to the law of Member States.

4. Dispute resolution through self-regulation – ASA, CAP etc.

a) Scope of application

In Germany codes of conduct have been developed by the German Advertising Council (*Deutscher Werberat*),[107] a self-regulatory institution

102 See the criticism by the German Chamber of Industry and Commerce of November 30, 2001; see www.krefeld.ihk.de.

103 See the reasons for art. 6 of the proposal for regulation.

104 H. Köhler, in *Großkommentar zum UWG*, § 27a note 9; O. Teplitzky, *Wettbewerbsrechtliche Ansprüche und Verfahren* (8th edn 2002), chap. 42 note 7.

105 H. Köhler (1991) 37 WRP 617 (624).

106 See below B.I.3.

107 See www.interverband.com/dbview/owa/assmenu.homepage?tid=69392&fcatid.

created by the umbrella organization of the German advertising industry (*Zentralausschuss der Werbewirtschaft*). However, dispute resolution through voluntary procedures has remained undeveloped.[108] For example, in Germany the notice of violation with an associated expenses recovery claim is preferred.

In several states there are voluntary dispute resolution mechanisms, for example in the United Kingdom, France, Italy, Spain and Portugal, as well as the USA. The customary sanction is the publication and associated stigma of unfair competition measures and possibly exclusion from the association. In addition it is emphasized in England that the media, contractors and service providers may withhold their services or deny access to space. Adverse publicity, which acts as a deterrent, may result from rulings published in the ASA monthly report. Pre-vetting or trading sanctions may be imposed or recognition revoked by the media's, advertiser's, promoter's or agency's professional association or service provider and financial incentives provided by trade, professional or media organizations may be withdrawn or temporarily withheld.

In France, some of them even have the power to pronounce injunctions in case of non-conformity with the statements of these organisms and associations. This is the case, for instance, with the Committee for Advertising on Radio and Television whose injunctions and penalties are regulated by the *Conseil d'État* and the BVP who can summon its members to justify, or put an end to, any prohibited advertising under the threat of eventual exclusion from the association. Finally, the BVP is admitted as joint claimant. In 1989, for example, the BVP handled more than 6,000 cases. Since membership is often a criterion in selecting an advertising agency, expulsion from the BVP for unfair competition, including for non-observance of its recommendations, is the only sanction to be taken seriously. In Italy the panel can order cessation and publication. On the other hand, the panel has no power to award damages; an action for damages may be filed before the ordinary courts before or after the panel has issued its decision. Such a decision (as well as decisions by the *Autorità Garante*) may facilitate the plaintiff in proving that the advertisement is misleading. Self-disciplinary judgments

[108] E. von Hippel (1976) 40 RabelsZ 513 (521); K. Tonner (1987) 40 NJW 1917 (1921); the advertising council has only decided 135 cases on its own between 1993 and 2002, see the data in C. Käser, *Effizienz des Rechtsschutzes im deutschen und italienischen Wettbewerbsrecht* (2003), p. 259.

have a high degree of effectiveness, since most advertising media (including most of the important newspapers and magazine publishers, TV and radio broadcasters) will refuse further publication of an advertisement which has been banned by the panel. The significance is thus very high with 80 per cent of the features being concluded through self-regulation of advertisers and a success rate for filed complaints at over 75 per cent. In addition self-regulation is widespread in Spain and Portugal.[109]

Evaluation

b) Discussion

Self-regulation tends to be ineffective if it applies only to a few cases or, as in Germany, to cases which are given to associations for pursuing. In addition it is a very blunt instrument where only a small circle belongs to the association or where sanctions cannot be enforced.[110] In addition, it is frequently the case that no damages are awarded. Often the out-of-court proceeding is only a preliminary to court proceedings. Finally, conflicts of interest are feared.[111]

Numerous arguments, however, support dispute resolution through self-regulation. An amicable settlement facilitates cessation, the normal case under unfair competition law. Self-regulation does not exclusively make use of subsidiarity. Surprisingly, it seems that voluntary proceedings are often superior to out-of-court dispute resolution proceedings provided for by law. This is because these sanctions mechanisms, such as publication or exclusion from the association, are often more powerful than those proceedings suggested by law. A company has appropriate substantive expertise. In addition, it can react quickly, as for example in Italy or England. Procedural costs can therefore be reduced and procedural time periods shortened.[112] If as a result of overstretched state finances cost savings are looked for, one must also ask whether every trivial case must be dealt with before the courts.

[109] *Código de Ética na Publicidade* (Code of Fair Practices in Advertising).

[110] Regarding these two accusations of the Director General of Fair Trading, see Director's General Report for 1982, 1983 HCP, p. 11; also B. Harvey and D. Parry, *The Law of Consumer Protection and Fair Trading* (6th edn 2000), p. 361 et seq.; the last argument is also called upon by D. Oughton and J. and Lowry, *Textbook on consumer law* (2nd edn 2000), pp. 50 et seq.

[111] A. Beater, 2003 11 ZEuP 11 (49 et seq.).

[112] Recommendation 98/257/EC reason for consideration 5.

Finally, self-regulation is also known in other legal fields. In product safety law this route has been followed for twenty years since the Comitology decision.[113] Art. 16 E-Commerce Directive 2000/31/EC encourages trade, occupational, and consumer associations to create codes of conduct. In Germany this route has been followed in company law with the Corporate Governance Code.[114] On balance private circles can react more quickly than the legislature.[115] The consumer gains greater legal protection through enforcement by out-of-court proceedings or the consumer ombudsman, because on balance the legal infringement itself can be proceeded against. In addition these proceedings are often beneficial in terms of costs. If state expenditure is to be limited, the establishment of public authorities must be given up in favour of out-of-court dispute resolution through third parties or by way of self-regulation, to the greater benefit of the consumer.

c) Proposals

Self-regulatory bodies in advertising law have existed in many states already for decades, and naturally at the European level art. 5 Misleading and Comparative Advertising Directive 84/450/EEC designates these. In s. 2 the right is expressly conferred on member states to encourage such institutions of voluntary control. However these bodies, as s. 1 emphasizes, can only supplement the courts or administrative proceedings. At the European level the European Advertising Standards Alliance (EASA) has been founded.[116] In recent publications by the European Union self-regulation mechanisms are also repeatedly emphasized as helpful supplements.[117] The regulation proposal now provides for out-of-court dispute resolution under the law of Member States. However membership in a self-regulating body is not compulsory for every advertiser, as this would be disproportionate.

Self-regulation requires certain preconditions for success. Here the principles of independence, transparency and efficiency apply which

[113] T. Möllers, *Rechtsgüterschutz im Umwelt- und Haftungsrecht* (1996), § 6; discussing the law of unfair competition H.-W. Micklitz and J. Keßler (2002) 50 GRUR Int. 885 (897); opposing such a body on the European level A. Wiebe (2002) 48 WRP 283 (290), with the argument that standardization committees are probably not able to regulate market behaviour.

[114] See www.corporate-governance-code.de or www.corporate-governance-kodex.de.

[115] D. Oughton and J. Lowry, *Textbook on consumer law* (2nd edn 2000), p. 50.

[116] C. Beckmann (1991) 37 WRP 702 (706 et seq.); M. Kisseler, in *Festschrift Piper* (1996), p. 283 (297).

[117] *Grünbuch zum Verbraucherschutz*, COM (2001), 531 pp. 16 et seq.; BT-Drs. 851/01.

the Commission, among others, has mentioned in its Recommendations 98/257/EC and 01/310/EC for third parties in out-of-court proceedings.

(1) The recommendations mention the principle of independence. Thereby the post requires someone with expertise who has not been a member of an occupational association in the previous three years. It could instead be considered whether to involve various interest groups in the decision-making process or the selection of experts. Instead of independence, a balance of the commission would be necessary. In England for example consumer groups would be involved in the code[118] and in Italy through the *Guirì* und dem *Comitatio di Controllo,*[119] though not in the German Advertising Commission.[120] In terms of independence, out-of-court proceedings are superior to the notice of violation.

(2) The second principle is transparency. Here not only an annual report must be published, but also the sanctions and binding effect of the decision. The recommendations could also be extended. For example, publication of decisions would have a corresponding preventive effect, as for example in England with the Code.[121]

(3) Efficiency in decision making has been emphasized as a further principle. Here the commission intends a proceeding with no or only moderate costs and the possibility of participating in the proceedings without legal representation. Effectiveness also involves sanctions, which are not laid down in the recommendation. These would include not only the cessation order, but also publication, naming or exclusion from the association. Fines should also be considered. Effectiveness also includes, in the opinion of this writer, a greater participating circle involved in regulation. Only then is the threat of exclusion a true deterrent, and only then, for example, can the non-publication of advertising be threatened. The ASA in England, the BVP in France and the IAP in Italy owe their success to the fact that practically all representatives are members. Thus, the mandatory duties of the regulation proposal point in the correct direction.

(4) Finally the recommendation emphasises the principles of reasonableness and freedom of action.[122] The decisions have to give reasons and the consumer must retain the possibility of seeking legal

[118] D. Oughton and J. Lowry, *Textbook on consumer law* (2nd edn 2000), p. 51.

[119] Art. 29 et seq. CAP; on this issue C. Käser, *Effizienz des Rechtsschutzes im deutschen und italienischen Wettbewerbsrecht* (2003), p. 270.

[120] It exclusively consists of representatives of advertising businesses, advertising media and marketing professions, see *Jahrbuch Deutscher Werberat*, p. 24.

[121] Rule 61.4. Code. [122] Similar the recommendation 01/310/EC regarding fairness.

protection against decisions of an out-of-court proceeding. This is supported in England.

The out-of-court dispute settlement depends on its voluntary nature.[123] However, swift court proceedings should then follow. This is unfortunately not the case in England as the ASA often only refers the matter to the OFT. In contrast in France the BVP is admitted as joint claimant. Thus, the duty to encourage self-regulation under the already published Recommendation 98/257/EC should be accompanied by a directive.

5. *Action by the authorities*

a) Scope of application

There are public law institutes in the form of consumer ombudsmen in Sweden, Denmark and Finland. The public law authorities can take up the case and clarify the circumstances by means of the information right. In simple cases in Sweden, Finland and Denmark the Consumer Ombudsman may issue prohibition or information orders coupled with a default fine. In Finland in practice the commercial participant undertakes through an informal written cessation declaration to make no use in future of the marketing practice in question. Such an obligation is, however, not independently sanctioned under the law. If it is not approved, in Sweden the Consumer Ombudsman would have to take the case to court: sec. 22 MFL. The equivalent applies in Finland. In Denmark he has to conduct negotiations with the parties. It is, however, important here that the Consumer Ombudsman can decline to take a case if, in his opinion, it is only of minor importance. The Consumer Ombudsman is among others required to bring the case before the ordinary courts on the day after he has issued an injunction. Thus, an interlocutory injunction must be confirmed by the courts.

The Office of Fair Trading in England has had up until now the right to issue orders dealing with particular consumer trade practices that may raise concerns from time to time. In past years, however, only three such orders of minor importance have been issued. Also, the possibility of issuing orders under Part III of the Fair Trading Act against individual rogue traders in cases of persistent conduct which is unfair and detrimental to the consumer have been of limited success. In practice they are only used if a trader is unlawful under an existing provision of civil

[123] See Green Paper on EU Consumer Protection, COM (2002), 289, pp. 6, 13, 22.

or criminal law. As these regulations had so little practical relevance in the past, in 2003 they were supplemented by Part 8 of the Enterprise Act. The Director General was abolished and his competence transferred to the Office of Fair Trading. Experience under the FTA 1973 as well as in the field of unfair contract terms shows that the OFT has concentrated its activities on negotiation until now.[124] Court action is seen as a last resort.[125] The OFT can only sue for an injunction. In case of a breach of a court order, it would have to sue again.

In Italy, proceedings in front of the *Autorità Garante* are less expensive than any private law action, but the proceeding may take some months (the authority has the power to issue immediately an interlocutory cease and desist order, but it uses such power rarely). Public law authorities are also known in other states.[126]

On the other hand, in other states such as Austria and Germany supervision by state authorities is almost unknown. Numerous states thereby have preliminary or out-of-court procedures which are accompanied by public law authorities. Public settlement does not exist in Germany, Austria, Poland, France, Spain and Portugal.

Evaluation

Administrative authorities are comprehensively provided for in the Misleading and Comparative Advertising Directive 84/450/EEC. However, there is no detailed provision for the procedures preceding court action. The discussion of out-of-court legal protection can be supplemented by the arguments for or against authorities being involved in it. The more cost-intensive administrative apparatus must be weighed against the advantage of effective legal enforcement and the prevention thereby of gaps in the law.[127]

b) Discussion

The informal written cessation declaration, which is possible through the consumer ombudsman in Finnish law, may be compared with the violation notice in German law. However, it has the advantage of being agreed both with a competitor and with an independent authority. In

[124] See R. Ellger, *Die Bündelung gleichgerichteter Interessen im englischen Zivilprozeß*, in J. Basedow, K. Hopt, H. Kötz and D. Baetge, *Die Bündelung gleichgerichteter Interessen im Prozeß* (1999), p. 103 (125).

[125] See also C. Scott and J. Black, *Cranston's Consumer and the Law* (3rd edn 2000), p. 61, concerning misleading advertisement.

[126] See above B.II.4. [127] See above B.II.4.

addition, the Consumer Ombudsman in Sweden, Finland and Denmark, in contrast to German law, has an enforceable information claim. Decisions of the administrative authority are usually reached faster than a judgment.[128] In Sweden and Denmark the cessation order can be combined with an administrative fine. Thus the authority, in contrast to the trial with notice to the two parties, is not restricted to an adversarial procedure involving only the parties, but can additionally take into account the interests of the consumer and the general public.[129] This is clearly seen with the consumer ombudsman as he exists in the Nordic states. There he represents the interests of the general public and the consumer. An administrative procedure can take place if competitors or associations are either unable or do not wish to claim. The gaps in the German law pointed to above call for additions to public law mechanisms.[130] The *Autorità Garante* in Italy is subordinate to the self-regulatory procedure, but superior to court proceedings in terms of time.

It may be objected against the intervention of authorities that they are unwilling to intervene or only proceed according to opportunist factors. Ultimately, the constitutional state principle requires a rule by the courts, as clearly expressed in the Recommendation 98/257/EC. Also, administrative authorities customarily do not decide on compensation. Thus in the Nordic states (Sweden, Finland and Denmark) decisions of the Consumer Ombudsman can only then be made if the circumstances are straightforward or not in dispute. It has to be ensured that a court proceeding can be attached without problems. So far in England this has not been the case.

The advantages and disadvantages of the various legal routes are shown in Graphic 4.

[128] For Italian law see C. Käser, *Effizienz des Rechtsschutzes im deutschen und italienischen Wettbewerbsrecht* (2003), p. 275.

[129] Ibid., pp. 290 et seq.

[130] Ibid., p. 297 et seq.; contrary to the federal government, Referentenentwurf UWG, Begründung zu § 7, s. 42; Gesetzesentwurf, BT-Drs. 5/1487, Begründung zu § 8 UWG.

C. Results and conclusions for remedies in unfair competition law

I. Summary of theses

1. *Claim objectives*

a) Implementation deficits

All Member States have implemented the duty in domestic law to order cessation or prohibition for an advertising infringement.[1] However, in some countries there are deficits or ambiguities in the implementation.

(1) In Germany the easing of the burden of proof, called for in art. 6 lit. (a) Misleading and Comparative Advertising Directive 84/450/EEC, has only partly been implemented into national law. Because of the ambiguous wording of art. 6 it remains unclear what form of implementation is required.[2]

(2) In England interlocutory legal protection is subsidiary to the compensatory claim. The OFT also regards the injunction as a remedy of last resort. This low priority is not provided for in the Misleading and Comparative Advertising Directive 84/450/EEC.[3]

(3) The legal position in Sweden, Finland and England, which do not admit as a matter of principle the preventive cessation claim on the grounds of press freedom, is not in conformity with art. 4 para. 2 Misleading and Comparative Advertising Directive 84/450/EEC.[4]

b) Proposals for further harmonization

Art. 11–13 of the Directive on Unfair Commercial Practices largely adopts the legal harmonization which was already achieved in 1984.

[1] Art. 4 para. 2 Misleading and Comparative Advertising Directive 84/450/EEC.
[2] See above B.I.1(b). [3] See above B.I.1(d). [4] See above B.I.1(f).

Legal consequences which already exist in almost all Member States could lead without difficulties to further European legal harmonization.

(4) With the exception of the legal position in England all states provide for monetary fines in cases where orders of an authority or courts are infringed. This cessation or prohibition could be accompanied by the threat of a fine in cases where the advertiser repeats the unlawful advertising. The general enforcement requirement that in each Member State 'adequate and effective means exist to combat misleading advertising'[5] would in this way be clearly realized.[6]

(5) The claim for elimination is limited to the publication of a corrective declaration and in addition is made optional for the member states.[7] In almost all states the claim for elimination is either legally regulated or recognized in jurisprudence. Thus, the elimination of the consequences of unlawful advertisement could be introduced on the European level and could be made more general and not only limited to a corrective declaration.[8]

c) Further proposals for harmonization – limits to harmonization

(6) The Member States have the option to facilitate the right to publish decisions.[9] In legal practice the publication of decisions in the various Member States is therefore dealt with in different ways. In the weighing of the interests of the participants a middle path would seem to be appropriate. Under the circumstances a useful harmonization would be to make publication an appropriate measure for the elimination of persistent disturbance.[10]

(7) The introduction of a compensatory claim should also be considered. A number of Member States provide for treble damages calculated according to the loss suffered by the claimant, profits of the defendant or a licence fee, and this could be harmonized. However, gaps in the law remain because harm and profit are difficult to prove and the licence fee concept requires a legal right which is subject to protection. Finally,

[5] Art. 4 para. 1 Misleading and Comparative Advertising Directive 84/450/EEC.

[6] See above B.I.1(d).

[7] Art. 4 par. 2 subpara. 3 indent 2 Misleading and Comparative Advertising Directive 84/450/EEC.

[8] See above B.I.2.

[9] Art. 4 para. 2 subpara. 3 indent 1 Misleading and Comparative Advertising Directive 84/450/EEC.

[10] See above B.I.3.

civil law compensation is useless if, as in the Nordic countries, there are no corresponding claims.

(8) (a) Fines by contrast are noticeably more difficult to enforce on the European level, as here normally criminal law authorities must act. The monetary fine in European cartel law is not transferable to unfair competition law, because the severity of the injustice under unfair competition law is normally noticeably less. Even so two exceptions may be considered here.

(b) For example one exception is seen under art. 10bis Paris Convention, the offence of defamation of competitors.

(c) On the European level fines could be admitted optionally to treble damages, in order to secure effective legal protection under public law.

(9) The extension of the concept of harm could be made more effective under the civil law route. Here an optional clause could also be considered.[11]

(10) The establishment of public bodies would have the advantage that information claims could support the enforcement of rights against the advertiser.

(11) Information obligations to protect consumers are part of product safety or product liability law. Although in Nordic jurisdictions such duties exist already to some extent, this does not mean that information duties should be imposed under competition law regarding the protection of the consumer.[12]

The remedies of injunction, compensation and publication could therefore be further harmonized. Regarding the harm, however, only a first step in the direction of harmonization would be taken and the choice of methods left to the Member States.[13] At the European level the remedies could then be further formulated.[14]

2. *Parties*

a) Implementation deficits

(1) The Injunction Directive 98/27/EC designates consumer associations or independent public bodies in order to enforce the prohibition or cessation of misleading advertising. In some states (Sweden and Finland) both the consumer ombudsman and also the association can undertake proceedings.

[11] See above B.I.4(d), (e), (g). [12] See above B.I.5.
[13] See above Graphic 6. [14] See C.II.

(a) In other states (Germany and Austria) there is no public law control. Finally in England there is public law supervision alongside out-of-court proceedings. In states where only one legal route is provided for, a particular level of efficiency has to be guaranteed. In Germany the limited financial resources of consumer protection associations are complained of. They often pursue only certain claims.[15] It is beyond doubt that 20 per cent of relevant cases are not pursued.[16] In this way an implementation deficit arises because the Injunction Directive 98/27/EC requires that either the consumer association or public law authorities can proceed against the advertising infringement.[17] There is also an implementation deficit if in England the consumer associations can only claim, if at all, on a subsidiary level to the OFT and if they do not perform their supervisory functions adequately.[18]

(b) In order to reduce the liability risk of consumer associations a guarantee fund has therefore been proposed.[19] In order to ensure that harm to consumers is better compensated and at the same time the unlawful conduct of the infringer is effectively sanctioned, further proposals could be considered. Consumer associations should not only be able to enforce cessation claims but also to claim actual losses of consumers in the actions (Sweden and France). Alternatively, one could consider admitting an own immaterial loss claim for consumer associations, as is the case in France, Portugal and Greece.[20] The introduction of such remedies would have to be left to the member states.

b) Proposals for further harmonization

(2) The Misleading and Comparative Advertising Directive 84/450/EEC does not require that competitors can claim. Regulation by administrative authorities is sufficient. However, there is a right of claim by competitors in almost all Member States, as these are often the first to recognize the legal infringement. To increase the effectiveness therefore a right of claim by competitors for an infringement of the CMAR should be introduced in England for the offence of misleading advertising.[21]

(3) (a) The right of claim for consumer associations should be extended to Comparative Advertising Directive 97/55/EC and the Product Price

[15] K. Tonner (1987) 40, NJW 1917 (1922) referring to a study of R. von Falckenstein, *Die Bekämpfung unlauterer Geschäftspraktiken durch Verbraucherverbände* (1977), p. 506.
[16] See above A. notes 11 et seq. [17] See above B.II.2(a).
[18] See above B.II.2. [19] G. Schricker (1975) 139 ZHR 208 (243).
[20] See above B.II.2(c). [21] See above B.II.1(c).

Directive 98/6/EC. In its recent proposal on the Injunction Directive, Directive 97/55/EC appears in the annex but not the Product Price Directive 98/6/EC.[22]

(b) The surrender of profits claim is of doubtful value for consumer associations. Extensive information claims are necessary to determine the profits. Finally, it is unclear why the state in Germany should get the profits of the infringer.

(4) If it is true that the competitor knows best regarding the admission of advertising measures, then this is also true for advertising associations which can therefore react faster than authorities or perhaps have more financial resources than the single competitor or consumer association. If advertising associations are actively engaged in out-of-court dispute resolution, an associated right of claim is the logical consequence. Alongside consumer associations business agencies should have a right of claim, as such a right exists in all member states with the exception of England.[23]

(5) (a) In all Member States, with the exceptions of Germany, Austria, Luxembourg and the Netherlands, there is a public law supervision of advertising infringements. The Regulation (EC) No. 2006/2004 on Consumer Protection Cooperation demands the introduction of public authorities with the power to pursue cross-border infringements of unfair competition law. Therefore, it seems sensible to introduce a supplementary claim for the cartel authorities to the extent that advertising infringements are not enforceable by the competitor or the association. These could then claim, for example, before the commercial chamber of the regional court.[24]

(b) In England the OFT can only take legal proceedings to a limited extent by filing a claim. This requires a domestic infringement in terms of sec. 211 EA. The domestic infringement is an act or omission which is done by a person in the course of a business, harms the collective interests of consumers in the United Kingdom, and is of the description specified by the Secretary of State by order, in accordance with sec. 211 (2). Domestic infringements are now listed in The Enterprise Act 2002 (Part 8 Domestic Infringements) Order 2003. They do not include attracting consumers. In England therefore the right of claim is to be extended to the OFT.[25]

[22] Proposal for a Directive of the European Parliament and of the Council on injunctions for the protection of consumers' interests (codified version) of May 12, 2003, COM (2003) 241 final, annex I no. 1. Correctly the Follow-up Communication to the Green paper on Consumer Protection (p. 11) tries to relate the Injunction Directive 98/27/EC.

[23] B.II.3. [24] B.II.4(d). [25] B.II.4(d).

(6) In view of the fact that advertising agencies can be responsible for advertising infringements in all Member States, harmonization would seem to be sensible. This should be possible in the enforcement of the prohibition or cessation without having to prove fault on the part of the advertising agency. This corresponds to the provisions of the Misleading and Comparative Advertising Directive 84/450/EEC,[26] so that these requirements could be harmonized. By contrast the requirements for further responsibility should be left to the Member States.[27]

c) Further proposals for harmonization – limits to harmonization

(7) At the European level rights of claim for consumers could be harmonized.[28] The cessation claim offers little in substance to the claim for consumers, because the claim for compensation is often hardly provable as the consumer must show to the satisfaction of the court that the unlawful advertising was causal for a purchasing decision. For an extension of the claim of harm, as for example in the USA,[29] the claim would become interesting for the consumer.[30] If the consumer were to gain a right of claim it would in addition be consistent that he could enforce it through public authorities or through out-of-court dispute resolution.

(8) Supervision of unfair competition is found in practice only in France and Poland. Other states have suppressed criminal law. Unfair competition offences can only be described through general clauses. Punishment under criminal law can therefore often come up against the principle of *nulla poena sine lege scripta*. Thus, further harmonization should not be looked for.[31]

(9) The press is seldom considered responsible under the law of the member states because of press privilege. As infringements are rare, however, there is an argument for refraining from harmonization on grounds of subsidiarity.

3. *Out-of-court dispute resolution*

a) Proposals for further harmonization

(1) Dispute resolution through third parties has the advantage over dispute resolution through self-regulation because it also applies

[26] Art. 4 para. 2. [27] B.III.9. [28] See above B.II. [29] See above B.II.4.(g).

[30] For a claim for damages *de lege ferenda* already 30 years ago, see G. Schricker, *Soll der einzelne Verbraucher ein Recht zur Klage wegen unlauteren Wettbewerbs erhalten?* (1975) 7 ZRP 189 (194).

[31] See B.II.7.

where there is no self-regulation or where membership would be disproportionate. Decisions should be published so that corresponding standards are developed. Out-of-court dispute resolution should be encouraged as a means of legal enforcement of the European level. The amended regulation proposals therefore correctly allow out-of-court dispute resolution under the law of the member states.[32]

(2) The advertising law self-regulatory bodies in many states have existed for a number of years, so that it is not surprising that art. 5 Misleading and Comparative Advertising Directive 84/450/EEC designates them at the European level.

These include not only associations, such as the ASA in England, BVP in France, IAP in Italy, AAP in Spain and the *Instituto Civil da Autodisciplina da Publicidade* in Portugal, but also for example the consumer complaints board in Sweden, Finland and Denmark. The experience of these bodies shows that a cost-effective and swift proceeding is possible alongside the administrative or judicial legal route. Recommendations 98/257/EC and 01/310/EC, which were developed for the out-of-court dispute resolution through third parties, allow for further modification of self-regulating bodies. In addition these principles should be regulated in a directive rather than a non-binding recommendation.

The Recommendations uphold the principle of independence. For this the persons making decisions must have the necessary professional competence and may not have belonged to a professional body during the previous three years. An alternative possibility would instead be to involve the various interest groups in the decision making or in the selection of experts.

(3) Transparency is the second principle. This requires not only publication of an annual report but also sanctions and the binding nature of the decision. Here one could also go further than the Recommendations. For example, the publication of the decision has a corresponding preventive effect, as for example in England with the Code.[33]

(4) Recommendation 98/2577EC upholds efficiency as a further principle. Here the Commission understands no cost or low-cost proceedings and the possibility to take part in proceedings without legal representation. Effectiveness includes sanctions which are not designated in the recommendation, for example the ordering of cessation.

(5) Where decision making is undertaken through self-regulation, corresponding powers are necessary. This includes the need for a large

[32] B.III.3(c). [33] Rule 61.4. Code.

part of the circles involved to take part in self-regulation. Only then is the threat of exclusion an effective deterrent. Only then, for example, can non-publication of advertising be threatened. Accordingly effective sanctions are necessary such as publication, brand naming or exclusion from the association. Fines may also be considered.

(6) Finally, Recommendation 98/257/EC emphasizes the principle of reasonableness and the principle of freedom of action.[34] Decisions must be reasoned and the consumer must retain the possibility of seeking legal protection against the decision of an out-of-court proceeding. This has been supported in England. However, legal proceedings should then be fast. Unfortunately, this is not the case in England, as the ASA can only refer the case on to the OFT.

b) Further proposals for harmonization – limits to harmonization

(7) A complaints procedure for advertisers is helpful for the consumer because it is free of charge. The consumer will in some cases prefer court proceedings. The above-mentioned experiences of the various Member States on rights of claim for consumers make clear that no flood of claims need be expected. Such a complaints procedure without the involvement of third parties is acceptable for the applicant and therefore in principle can be welcomed.[35]

(8) The violation notice is provided for in a number of Member States without a corresponding expenses claim as found only in Germany. It is true that the notice of violation can end the legal infringement at an early stage. However, the checking of the legal infringement or correctness of the notice of violation is often not undertaken. Therefore, harmonization should not include a claim for expenses. The Member States are free under art. 5 Injunction Directive 98/27/EC to provide for further regulations between infringer and affected party before proceedings may be instituted.[36]

There follows a proposed draft of the legal provision.

[34] The recommendation 01/301/EC talks about fairness.
[35] B.III.2(b). [36] B.III.2(a).

II. Proposed draft

The remedies refer to the Misleading and Comparative Advertising Directive 84/450/EEC and the Product Price Directive 98/6/EC

Art. [ ] Aims of legal protection

The following claims can be raised against unfair advertising. Member States with administrative authorities may choose either administrative or civil remedies, or may choose both remedies:

1. Determination of the unfairness of the conduct when the conduct's negative effects persist after the claimed disturbance.
2. Cessation of the conduct or its prohibition to the extent not already undertaken.
3. Elimination of the consequences of the conduct. This can include, in particular, correction of misleading, unlawful or incorrect statements.
   A fine may be imposed to enforce cessation or elimination.
4. Compensation of harm and disadvantage incurred as a result of the conduct, provided intention or negligence is established.
   (a) The harm includes, alternatively, the losses of the injured party, the profits of the infringer or a licence fee, provided the conduct violates a legal right protected by a right of exclusivity or another right with comparable economic significance.
   (b) In addition immaterial loss may be recovered to the extent admissible under the law of the Member State.
5. Member States may make provision for administrative authorities to impose monetary fines in the case of unfair advertising instead of or alongside a compensatory claim.

Art. [ ] Standing

1. Proceedings may be brought by
   - competitors
   - consumer agencies and independent public bodies
   - business agencies
   - consumers according to the law of Member States.

   The Member States are free to regulate that public bodies only pursue legal proceedings where otherwise there is a likelihood of no such proceedings being taken.
2. Member States shall ensure that the persons, organizations or public bodies designated under para. 1 can effectively enforce their rights. This means in particular the right to bring proceedings before a court where out-of-court resolution has failed.

Art. [ ] Defendants

The competitor is responsible for its infringements. Alongside the competitor the advertising agency may be held responsible for the infringement. A prohibition or cessation order may be enforced without proof of fault on the part of the advertising agency. Further liability shall be in conformity with the law of the respective Member State. In view of the freedom of the press, the press may only be held liable for advertising infringements in exceptional circumstances under the law of the respective Member State.

Art. [ ] Out-of-court dispute resolution

1. The competitor shall provide an address under which any complaint may be brought without cost. The competitor shall respond to the complaint of the consumer within four weeks.
2. Member States may introduce or maintain in force provisions whereby a party can only commence proceedings after it has attempted to achieve cessation of the infringement in consultation with the defendant.
3. Member States shall maintain institutions for out-of-court dispute resolution under the law of the Member State.
4. Member States shall introduce or maintain self-regulatory bodies which monitor this directive. To this end it should be encouraged that all advertisers belong to a self-regulatory body.
5. To the extent that authorities regulate unfair competition, decisions shall be sufficiently reasoned.
6. Regulation by authorities, out-of-court dispute resolution or self-regulatory bodies must be conducted by independent experts who have effective powers of sanction. Decisions shall be published.
7. Affected parties shall have legal redress against decisions of out-of-court bodies, authorities or the self-regulatory body.

III. Instead of closing words - methods of harmonizing European law

1. *The complexity of unfair competition law*

This study was intended to investigate the extent of harmonization in the enforcement of unfair competition law. It must be stated that the legal enforcement of unfair competition law could hardly be more diverse. While almost all states have a combination of civil law, public law, criminal law and out-of-court dispute resolution,[1] the national systems differ markedly in their emphasis. Germany and Austria give priority to civil law, the Nordic states to public law, France and Portugal to criminal law, and England and Italy to out-of-court dispute resolution. The Member States in the Roman law jurisdictions often enforce competition infringements under civil and public law, thus they have twin-track enforcement. These states include alongside France, especially Italy, Spain and Portugal. In addition the USA can be counted a state with twin-track enforcement. Thus, it is possible to make provisional distinctions between the various Member States[2] in terms of groups distinguished by the primary means of sanction. However, there continue to be numerous hybrid forms.

Thus, it is not surprising that harmonization under the Misleading and Comparative Advertising Directive 84/450/EEC and the Injunction Directive 98/27/EC, while going further than regulation of legal remedies in other legal fields,[3] still allows broad areas of unregulated legal enforcement. This is to be regretted all the more because the harmonization of law is often criticized as law in the books.[4] For the further development of European law there are three possible routes - maintaining the status quo, complete harmonization, or further cautious harmonization of minimum standards by means of directives.[5]

2. *Correction of the status quo*

The investigation has shown that there are a number of deficits in implementation not only in England, but also in Member States such as Germany, Sweden and Finland. The comparative law cases have also made clear that the numerous options allowed by both directives have

[1] See above Graphic 1. [2] See already above A.I.2(b).
[3] See above A.III.4. [4] See above A.III.4.
[5] Regarding the different ways see T. Möllers, *Die Rolle des Rechts im Rahmen der europäischen Integration* (1999), translated as: *Role of Law in European Integration* (2003).

in many areas not led to a harmonization of law. Thus, if it is true that diverse legal consequences hinder an internal market,[6] the present status quo is unsatisfactory. In addition, legal enforcement is carried out in highly differing ways. Certain legal remedies are little used. The prevention of unfair practices through law is therefore to some extent meaningless. Thus, further harmonization is necessary in order to create the internal market and to expand the public benefit. In consequence it is unsatisfactory that neither the proposed directive nor the numerous scholarly investigations up until now have criticized the status quo.[7] Only the Regulation on Consumer Protection Corporation refers beyond the status quo.[8]

3. *Complete harmonization*

This study, however, does not attempt to suggest extremes by favouring the complete harmonization of legal enforcement. Complete harmonization would have the advantage of creating equal competition parameters. Such a path, has already been followed with various proposals for regulations.[9] However, a European and, perhaps more importantly, a comparative law component cast doubt on complete harmonization.

a) Reservations from the European viewpoint

Complete harmonization is to be supported as a legal ideal in certain areas where there is a corresponding competence of the European community.[10] Complete harmonization would have the result that stricter law of individual Member States would have to be qualified as restrictions of trade.[11] Thus, for example, the more extreme effects of criminal law would have to be blunted because such law acts as a deterrent or puts foreign undertakings off. The ECJ, however, in its *Keck* decision declared criminal law punishment of sale under the purchase price as admissible and not an infringement against freedom of trade in goods.[12] In the *Tobacco* decision the ECJ denied a corresponding

[6] See above A.III.1(b). [7] See above A.III.1(b).

[8] Regulation (EC) No. 2006/2004 on consumer protection cooperation of October 10, 2004, OJ L 364, 1.

[9] See above A.III.3(e) and (g).

[10] T. Möllers, *Die Rolle des Rechts im Rahmen der europäischen Integration* (1999), § 1.III, translated as *Role of Law in European Integration* (2003), § 1.III.

[11] H.-W. Micklitz and J. Keßler (2002) 50 GRUR Int. 885 (898). [12] See A.III.1(b).

power of the EC for a complete advertising ban.[13] On grounds of subsidiarity there are therefore justifiable doubts whether there is any power for such an extensive harmonization.[14] Ultimately favouring a single legal route would not be politically acceptable as there is no clear majority for legal remedies against unfair competition by the one route or the other.

b) Reservations from a comparative law perspective

In addition, law can only be implemented where it coincides at least in its aims with the legal culture of the respective country.[15] In the Member States however the application of civil law, public law, criminal law and out-of-court dispute resolution is far too diverse for one resolution form to be seen as the ideal and best route.[16] Rather, it must suffice to ensure that the various legal routes are similarly effective in sanctioning infringements, than that the various legal routes are similar in form. Therefore, this study strictly follows Schlesinger's approach of accepting cultural diversity[17] and of recognizing differing legal formats[18] as the structural basis for comparative law. Largely effective legal enforcement is performed in the German legal circle through the courts, in Nordic states by the consumer ombudsman and in England through self-regulation under the ASA. It would be unhelpful to compel a Member State to carry out its tasks through an ideal law.[19]

4. *A cautious middle path – minimal harmonization and mutual recognition*

Thus, this study seeks to pursue a middle path, that of further harmonization by means of minimal harmonization and cautious mutual recognition. This has a number of advantages.

[13] ECJ C-376/98 (2000), ECR I-8419, 53 NJW 3701 – 'Tobacco Advertisment Directive'.

[14] As well for material law, T. Stein (2001) 11 EWS 12, 16; A. Wiebe (2002) 48 WPR 283 (289). This does not apply if harmonization is restricted to cross-border circumstances only, see the Regulation (EC) No. 2006/2004 on Consumer Protection Cooperation of October 10, 2004, OJ L 364, 1.

[15] In general terms and without reference to full harmonization also E. Bastian, in G. Schricker and F. Henning-Bodewig, *Neuordnung des Wettbewerbsrecht* (1999), 199.

[16] For the argumentation, see above B.II.4.

[17] See M. Bussani and U. Mattei, 3 Colum.J.Eur.L. 339 (341) (1997/98).

[18] Ibid., (346) (1997/98); based on R. Sacco, *Legal Formants. A Dynamic Approach to Comparative Law*, 39 Am.J.Comp.L. 1 (1991).

[19] Regarding the whole purpose of comparative law, see above A.I.1(e).

a) Combination of different legal routes

If different legal routes are recognized as equivalent in legal enforcement rather than requiring complete harmonization, there is less interference with the legal culture of the Member States.[20] The starting point is the consideration that all forms of procedure (civil law, criminal law, administrative law, out-of-court resolution) have their own characteristic advantages and disadvantages.[21] The respective disadvantages can be ameliorated by combining procedural routes. The subsidiary power for authorities to proceed against infringements against unfair competition law is for, example, a feasible path.[22] This combination is recognized in theory by all Member States,[23] but is realized in practice by only a few. In particular mention should be made of France, Italy and the other states of Nordic and French legal circles as well as the USA. Here it is noticeable that administrative or criminal authorities are utilized above all to the benefit of the consumer.

b) The extension of objects of claims and persons with standing

The second approach is to balance the weaknesses of the respective procedural route by cautiously extending the objects of claim and the circle of persons with standing to bring legal proceedings. This applies for example to the extension of effective compensatory claims or the right to publish decisions which determine the unlawfulness of a competition act. In addition it is unsatisfactory to leave enforcement to the competitor alone.

With such development it will be necessary to require that member states are ultimately prepared to develop their respective laws. The reactions to the green paper on consumer protection by the Commission demonstrated that there is a significant majority for further harmonization of legal enforcement.[24] If the European Union requires a strengthening of legal enforcement by the consumer,[25] Germany will for example not be able to deny consumer claims for much longer.

[20] With a different opinion appearently E. Bastian, in G. Schricker and F. Henning-Bodewig, *Neuordnung des Wettbewerbsrecht* (1999), 199, (211), emphasizing that civil courts are the means for imposing sanctions in the classical individual law concept.

[21] See B.II.4 and Graphic 6.

[22] See above B.II.4.

[23] See A. Graphic 1.

[24] Follow-up Communication to the Green paper on Consumer Protection, COM (2002), 289 final, COM (2002), 289 final, p. 8 (25).

[25] See Green Paper of Consumer Access to justice, COM (93) 576 final.

Where however harmonization lies in the distant future the further development of compensatory claims will be a matter for the technical development of Member State law or left to an empowering clause. In conclusion, the investigation puts forward a combination of minimal harmonization and mutual recognition, because various legal routes are recognized here as of equal worth. Structurally, however, the proposal goes beyond the status quo[26] and will contribute to reducing the limitation to the internal market. In addition, considerations of subsidiarity are upheld.[27]

If the German legislature aims at being a reference model for a future unified European unfair competition law,[28] it will be contradicted in two respects in terms of legal remedies. On the one hand, with the pre-litigation notice of violation and related claim for expenses Germany pursues an individual path. On the other hand, the overwhelming majority of other Member States and the USA provide for public law supervision of competition law infringements. In the interests of closing legal gaps German law should be open to further development.

5. *Data*

If one gives up the idea of complete harmonization and on the other hand arranges the various legal remedies more effectively while recognizing different legal routes as of equal value, then future data on the relative effectiveness of such legal routes in the Member States must be created. It may be doubted whether a European agency with or without decision-making powers or a committee with legislative competence is necessary.[29] It would seem more helpful to create a database of all national and international court and administrative decisions on unfair competition law.[30]

Such a proposal, however, must be cautiously modified in that it at once offers too much and too little. The idea of completely recording all decisions and judgments is unrealistic. As long as Member States pass

[26] For a conclusion compare Graphics 2 and 7 as C.II.

[27] So e.g. H. Merkt, *Europäische Rechtsetzung und strengeres autonomes Recht. Zur Auslegung von Gemeinschaftsnormen als Mindeststandards*, 61 RabelsZ 647 (677 et seq.) (1997), generally pleading for minimum clauses.

[28] See E. Keller, in H. Harte-Bavenkamm and F. Henning-Bodewig, *UWG* (2004), Introd. A note. 11; for the wording of the BMJ see www.bmj.bund.de/enid/fad884-c433728e8a7d340bfd7b6efd49,0/al.html.

[29] See the discussion in: H.-W. Micklitz and J. Keßler (2002) 50 GRUR Int. 885 (896 et seq.).

[30] H.-W. Micklitz and J. Keßler (2002) 50 GRUR Int. 885 (897).

decisions on unfair competition law in different languages, the task of collecting those decisions becomes insurmountable.[31] The proposal offers too little in that it ignores significant judgments on unfair competition law from administratives bodies and out-of-court dispute resolution. It would therefore suffice if Member States were as a first step obliged to provide statistical data on the extent of litigation in unfair competition law, on the legal routes, whether out-of-court, administrative or court paths. In this way it could be attempted to translate the judgments into English and to create a database. Art. 15 Regulation (EC) No. 2006/2004 on Consumer Protection Cooperation provides that member states collect statistics on consumer complaints submitted to responsible authorities and communicate these to the European Commission.

[31] E.g. the data file of judgments regarding United Nations law on the sale of goods on www.cisg-online.ch or the database for misused clauses in consumer contracts on www.europa.eu.int/clab.

D. Graphics

Graphic 1: *Legal actions against unfair competition*

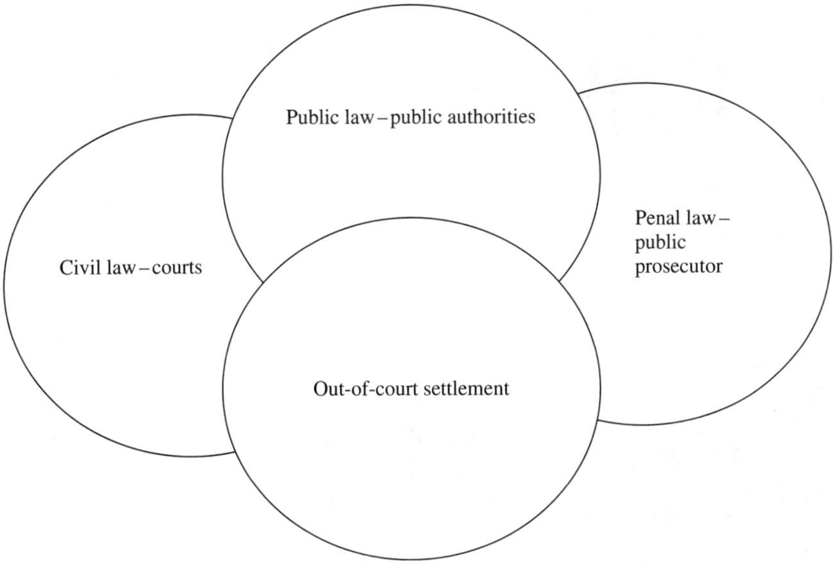

Graphic 2: *Remedies by harmonized European law*[1]

Objects of claims	Parties: Plaintiffs	Defendant	Sanctions by court/ administrative authorities	Self-regulated bodies
prohibition/injunction 84/450; 98/27	Persons with legitimate interests (MS) or 84/450	**(-)**	Court or 84/450; 98/27	
Pre-emptive legal protection 84/450	Organisations with legitimate interests (MS) 84/450		Administrative body 84/450; 98/27 - neutral - competent - reasons - judicial review 84/450, **not 98/27 (!)**	Consultation between parties (MS) 98/27 **out-of-court settlement (MS); amended proposal for a new regulation**
Accelerated proceedings 84/450, 98/27	Public authorities for the protection of consumers, cross-border, 98/27 or			**Complaints procedure, proposal for a regulation**
Burden of proof: - Injunction without fault or damage possible, 84/450 - Misleading advertisement and proof of truthfulness dependant on facts of the case, 84/450 **- Facts have to be proven by the violator according to proposal for a new directive**	Consumer associations, cross-border 98/27		Enforceable implementation of public authorities in cross bordering cases, Regulation (EC) No. 2006/ 2004	- Self-regulation besides courts or administrative bodies, 84/450 (o) **not in proposal for a new directive** **- Out-of-court recommendation 98/257/EC and 01/310/EC (o)**
Publication *84/450, 98/27 (o)*				

Elimination

84/450; 98/27 (o)

Fines (MS)

98/27

Damages are not regulated in 84/450 and 98/27

Optional clauses 'is allowed to' (o)

According to the law of a Member State (MS)

Not regulated (–)

[1] Directive 200/29/EC concerning unfair commercial practices adopts almost verbatim in Arts. 11–13 the remedies in Arts. 4–6 of the Misleading and Comparative Advertising Directive 84/450/EC, see part I.III.3(d).

Graphic 3: *Objects of claim (Case 1 – 3)*

	Injunction/ Prohibition	Administrative fine	Burden of proof	Interlocutary injunction	Preemptive legal protection	Rights of information
Austria	X	X	X	X	X	
Denmark	X	X		X		X
England	X	(-)		X	Pre-trial	X
Finland	X	X	X	(-)	(?)	X
France	X	X			X	
Germany	X	X	(?)	X	X	
Greece	X				X	
Hungary	X			X	X	
Ireland	X	(-)		X	Pre-trial	X
Italy	X	X		X / (-)		
Netherlands	X					
Poland	X				X	
Portugal	X	X				
Spain	X					
Sweden	X	X		X	(?)	X
USA	X	X	X	(-)	Pre-trial	X

X available
(-) rarely or not available
(?) deficits of implementation

Elimination	Publication	Civil law damages	Public law damages	Extension of damages	Information order
X	X	X		X	(-)
X	X	X			X
X	X	X		X	
X	X	(-) / X			X
X	X	X	Administrative fine	X Estimation of damages; damages for immaterial loss	
X	X	X			
X		X		X damages for immaterial loss	
X		X			
X	X	X		X	
X		X		Estimation of damages	
	X	X			
X		X		Estimation of damages	
X		X	Administrative fine	Estimation of damages	
X		X			
X		(-) / X	X Market violation fine		X
X	(-)	X		X Minimum damage; Treble damage	X

Graphic 4: *Legal routes*

Civil law (parties)	**Public law (public authorities)**	**Penal law (public prosecutor)**	**Out-of-court settlement**
A+ many claimants A+ decision by a court	A+ investigation *ex officio* A+ lack of legal protection	A+ investigation *ex officio* A+ effective joint proceedings	A+ fast and cheap A+ possibility of amicable agreement
A– risk of losing suit A– risk of being unable to clarify facts	A– principle of opportunity A– additional court proceedings A– no damages	A– *nulla poena sine lege scripta* A– disproportional	A– conflicts of interest A– hardly effective

↓

Increasing effectiveness ('potent, proportional and deterrent')

1. If necessary combination of legal actions (+)
2. Further possibilities, eliminate deficits of the individual legal actions, see below

⊕ ↓ ⊕

Civil law (parties)	**Public law (public authorities)**	**Penal law (public prosecutor)**	**Out of court settlement**
• Easing the burden of proof and duties of clarification • Extension of damages • Extension of standing	• Sanctions (fines) • Court proceedings for all parites concerned		• Ensure independance and expertise • Ensure effectiveness (Publication, exclusion etc.)

Graphic 5: *Plaintiffs, defendants and competent bodies to take sanctions (Cases 4 – 7)*

	Competitor	Consumer	Consumer associations	Business Ass.	Administrative procedure	Criminal procedure	Defendant: advertising agency	Defendant: Press
Austria	X	(–)	X	X	(–)	(–) / X	X	(–)
Denmark	X	X	X	X	X Consumer Ombudsman (!)	(–) / X	X	(–) / X
England	(–) / X	(–)	(–) / X but subsidiary in relation to OFT		X OFT X Local officer	(–) / X	X	(–) / X
Finland	X	(–)	X but subsidiary in relation to Ombudsman	X	X Consumer Ombudsman (!)	(–) / X	X	(–)
France	X in criminal cases	(–) code civil X but in criminal cases	(–) code civil X but in criminal case	X	(–)	X DGCCRF etc.- State prosecutor often	X	(–)/ X
Germany	X	(–)	X	X	(–)	(–) / X	X	(–) / X
Greece	X	X (!)	X		(–)	X	X	(–) / X
Hungary	X	(–)	X		X OEC	(–) / X	X	X
Ireland	X	X	(–)	(–)	X DCA	(–) / X	X / (–)	X
Italy	X	(–) / X under loi 281/98	X loi 281/98		(–) codice civile X Autorità Garante, but not self-active	(–) / X	X	(–) / X
Netherlands	X	(–)	X		(–)	(–)/X	X	X
Poland	X	(–)	X	X	X President of the u.o.k.k.; Consumer Ombudsman	(–) / X	X	(–) / X
Portugal	X	(–)	X	X	X Instituto Nacional da Defesa do Consumidor	(–) not any more(!)	X	X
Spain	X	X (!)	X		(–) / X Nacional del Consumo etc.	(–) / X	X	
Sweden	X	(–)	(–) / X also group of consumer		X Konsumentverket; Consumer Ombudsman (!)	(–)	X	(–) never injunction
USA	(–) not FTCA; X	(–) for the FTCA X in the States	(–)	X	X FTC X Attorney General	(–) / X	X	(–) / X

Enforcing the law

X available

(–) rarely or not available

Graphic 6: *Out-of-court settlements of disputes (Case 8)*

	Agreement between parties reprimand	Compensation for reprimand	Mediation or other competent authorities	Settlement by self-regulatory organizations	Settlement by public authorities – B2B	Settlement by public authorities – B2C
Austria	X		(–)	(–)	(–)	(–)
Denmark	X		X Consumer Complaint Board			X Consumer Ombudsman
England				X ASA, BACC, BCC, BSC etc.		X Local authorities; OFT
Finland			(–) / X Board of Business Practices; Consumer Complaints Board	X	X	X Consumer Ombudsman
France	X			X BVP, CNP, CSA, ICC, UDA etc.		(–)
Germany	X	**X**	(–)	(–) Werberat	(–)	(–)
Greece						
Hungary	(–)	(–)	(–)			
Ireland				Advertising Standards Authority for Ireland (ASAI)		X Office of the Director of Consumer Affairs (ODCA)
Italy	X			X Instituto di autodisciplina publicitaria(IAP)		X Autorità Garante (–)
Netherlands				X Reclame Code Commissie (RCC)		

Poland						X Consumer Ombudsman
Portugal			(–)	X Instituto Civil da Autodisciplina da Publicidade		(–)
Spain			(–)	X Associacion de Autocontrol de la Publicidad (AAP)		
Sweden	X		(–) / X Board on Business Practices; Consumer Complaint Board	X	X	X Consumer Ombudsman
USA	X			X NAD of the Better Business Bureaus (BBB)	X	X Attorney General, FTC

X available
(–) rarely or not available

Graphic 7: *Remedies in a further harmonized European law*

Objects of claims	Claimant/Defendant	Competent to take sanctions: court – administrative bodies	Out-of-court legal protection
prohibition/injunction 84/450; 98/27 easing the burden of proof (Germany) interlocutory legal protection (England)	**Competitor with legitimate interests**	Court 84/450; 98/27	Consultation (MS); 98/27 **Reprimand** (o)
pre-emptive legal protection 84/450 (Sweden, Finland, England)	*Consumer according to the law of the Member States*		**Complaint procedure**, proposal for a new regulation
Accelerated proceedings 84/450, 98/27	**Business organizations**		**Out-of-court settlement (MS)**; amended proposal for a new regulation
Publication obligatory, if necessary instead of publication 84/450, 98/27 (o)	Consumer associations (Germany; England) 84/450; cross-border 98/27		Self-regulatory bodies (o) 84/450/EEC; **high degree of organization (o)**
Claim for elimination Instead of only amendment 84/450; 98/27 (*o*)	Or public authorities for consumer protection, - 84/450; cross-border 98/27 *'and' instead of 'or'*	Or administrative authorities, 84/450; 98/27 Regulation (EC) No.2006/2004 *'and' instead of 'or'*	
Threat of fine obligatory Up to now only fine 98/27 (MS)	**Responsibility of advertising agency for injunction** **Besides according to the law of the Member States**	neutral; competent; reasoning – judicial review, 84/450, *not* 98/27	**Independent experts, effective sanctions, duty to publish** see recommendations 98/257, 01/310
Introduction of damages Not regulated in 84/450 and 98/27 **– (o) treble damages or (public**	**Restricted responsibility of the press because of the freedom of the press**		**Standing for advertisers, violated parties and self-regulatory bodies**

law fine)	**Responsibility according to the law of the Member States**		
– (MS) non-pecuniary damages			
NOT: INFORMATION ORDERS		NOT: PENAL LAW	NOT: COMPENSATION IN CASE OF REPRIMAND NOT: MEDIATION

Proposals for harmonization:	Enforcing harmonized law
NO HARMONIZATION	SMALL CAPITALS
Easily achievable further harmonization	**bold**
Optional clauses	(o)
According to the law of the Member States	(MS)
Further proposals for implementation	*ital.*

PART II. REMEDIES IN ANTITRUST LAW

ANDREAS HEINEMANN

A. Introduction

I. Methodological note

Antitrust law can be enforced in two ways. Antitrust authorities can pursue administrative proceedings to investigate, prohibit and sanction, for example, with a fine, anti-competitive behaviour. Alternatively, the party allegedly prejudiced by an antitrust infringement may bring proceedings against the unlawful behaviour under private law. The plaintiff may, for example, bring a cease and desist or compensatory claim. The defendant may raise the 'Euro-defence', that is defend contractual claims by pointing to the anti-competitive nature of the contract. In Europe the enforcement of antitrust law is almost entirely a matter of administrative law while private enforcement of antitrust law is of less significance. This phenomenon contrasts with the legal situation in the USA, where the number of private antitrust proceedings is many times greater. An important aim of this study is to learn more about private antitrust law in the reporting countries. A first step - in conformity with the basic approach of the Common Core Project - is to create a cartography of antitrust law remedies. The country reports will show that in fact there is extremely little case law on private enforcement in antitrust law, despite the fact that in theory private enforcement exists everywhere. A second step will consist in generating ideas on how to strengthen the position of private remedies. Here in particular European initiatives through Community institutions could play a significant role.

1. Basic goal

The main focus of the seven cases on antitrust law is on the private law consequences of infringements of national antitrust law. This implies the following limitations:

1. The legal consequences are more important than the conditions for an antitrust infringement. The examples have been so chosen that in most cases there is no question but that an antitrust infringement has occurred (hard-core cartels, boycott, resale price maintenance, etc). Had less clear scenarios been chosen, no antitrust infringement would have been apparent in certain jurisdictions, so that the central questions of this study would not have arisen. An exception is Case 15: this question of whether there can also be a duty of delivery below the threshold of market dominance is of great practical significance particularly in selective distribution, and receives varying answers across the different jurisdictions. But there were surprises also in the other cases (also originally conceived as 'universal' antitrust law infringements): the call for a boycott by a market dominant enterprise in Case 11, for example, was not classed as an antitrust infringement in certain countries. In this respect the study makes a contribution to substantive comparative antitrust law which extends beyond the question of remedies.
2. The main focus of the study is on private law remedies. In this regard Europe – unlike in administrative law controls – is lagging behind. However, classification difficulties arise from the fact that antitrust law is essentially both public and private law. This means that public law enforcement methods, particularly the activities of the antitrust authorities, are to be investigated to the extent that they are also significant for private claims.
3. The aim is to investigate private law remedies for infringements of domestic national antitrust law. In accordance with the Common Core method, the national regulation models are to be investigated and compared. Thus the central focus is not on the question of remedies for infringements against European antitrust law.[1] The results will nevertheless be significant in this regard: first community law with the exception of art. 81 para. 2 EC contains no statement on private law remedies. Secondly the ECJ laid down the 'principle of equivalence' in the *Courage* judgment, meaning that the modalities of claims under European antitrust law may not be constituted in a less favourable way than those for claims under national law. The regulations of private antitrust law are accordingly meaningful for claims against European antitrust law infringements.

2. *Main focus*

The structure of the cases on antitrust law parallels those on unfair competition law: Cases 9 to 11 concern objects of claim, while Cases 12

[1] See on this subject the six volumes edited by P. Behrens, *EC Competition Rules in National Courts* (1992–2001).

to 15 concentrate on plaintiff and defendant, particularly regarding the question of active legitimation. The objects of claim concern the cease-and-desist claim (Case 9), the claim for compensation (Case 10) as well as the pre-trial procedures and injunctive (interlocutory) legal protection (Case 11). With reference to the parties active legitimation (standing) of consumers is concerned (Case 12) and that of direct customers in the case of a cartel (Case 13), the claims of contracting partners in a vertical relationship (Case 14) as well as the claim to delivery in the event of withholding supply (Case 15). Given the limited space available we have necessarily restricted ourselves to the basic forms of claim and competitive relationships. Intriguing specific questions which were intensively discussed at the annual conferences in Trento had to be omitted here. For example, interest claims are of great practical significance. However, they are not dealt with here as they stray too far from the field of competion law and in many jurisdictions are anchored in general civil law. The same fate meets the question of whether company agents also incur personal liability, for example for damages claims. In the foreground there is the question of whether any antitrust law claims arise at all, and how broad the circle of potential claimants may be drawn. At the same time there was no room for the further problem of whether the managers of an enterprise can also themselves incur liability.

3. *Methodology: legal formants*

As already pointed out in the unfair competition law part (Part I A.I. 1(e)), the methodology of this study follows the concept of legal formants in the tradition of Rudolf B. Schlesinger and developed by Rodolfo Sacco. The country reports first analyse the operative rules, i.e. the solution that the legal order in question gives to the case. However, this is only the starting point. In a second and third step the descriptive formants as well as the metalegal formants are explored, i.e. the wider legal and metalegal context of the problems raised. In the comparative summaries, special weight is given to the legal and cultural diversity following from the country reports.

4. *Status of the discussion*

In most reporting countries the existence of private law claims based on antitrust infringements was not in question. Therefore, in general antitrust law literature, quite an amount of scholarly literature has always existed on this topic.[2] However, the practical significance of private claims was limited. Antitrust law was most frequently used as a means of defence, in that a contract could be vitiated under antitrust law. But given a general lack of court decisions, many questions remained uncertain resulting in turn in a lack of that security of application for which a considered combination of theory and practice is essential. A more intensive discussion developed in the second half of the 1990s. The European Commission, in its White Paper on modernization of the rules implementing articles 85 and 86 of the EC Treaty,[3] made proposals for a reform of European procedural antitrust law and advocated reform in part with the aim of strengthening the decentralized application of European antitrust law through the domestic courts in individual countries.[4] This led to the new Cartel Regulation 1/2003 and to an increased awareness of private law remedies.[5] In addition came the 2001 *Courage* ruling of the European Court of Justice,[6] which placed the subject at the centre of attention. The vitamin cartel, conducted until 1999, was also important. Alongside numerous administrative antitrust rulings,[7] the dimensions of the cartel gave rise to a flood of private compensatory claims in various countries. The theoretical treatment of these proceedings will give the topic of private remedies an additional boost. Parallel to this development a number of monographs have appeared on the subject. Of particular value is the broadly conceived investigation by Clifford Jones in 1999 relating the situation in the USA to developments in Europe.[8] Further

[2] For Germany see e.g.: R. Buxbaum, *Die private Klage als Mittel zur Durchsetzung wirtschaftspolitischer Rechtsnormen* (1972); G. Klein, *Individualschutz im Kartellrecht* (1977); L. Linder, *Privatklage und Schadensersatz im Kartellrecht* (1980); K. Mailänder, *Privatrechtliche Folgen unerlaubter Kartellpraxis* (1965); H.-M. Müller-Laube, *Der private Rechtsschutz gegen unzulässige Beschränkungen des Wettbewerbs und missbräuchliche Ausübung von Marktmacht im deutschen Kartellrecht* (1980); K. Schmidt, *Kartellverfahrensrecht – Kartellverwaltungsrecht – Bürgerliches Recht* (1977); B. Schmiedel, *Deliktsobligationen nach deutschem Kartellrecht* (1974); H. Ullrich, *Das Recht der Wettbewerbsbeschränkungen des Gemeinsamen Marktes und die einzelstaatliche Zivilgerichtsbarkeit* (1971).

[3] Available at: http://europa.eu.int/comm/competition/antitrust/wp_modern_en.pdf.

[4] Ibid., no. 99–100.

[5] See e.g. J. Bornkamm and M. Becker, *Die privatrechtliche Durchsetzung des Kartellverbots nach der Modernisierung des EG-Kartellrechts*, (2005) ZWeR 213.

[6] ECJ, 20.9.2001, C-453/99, *Courage v. Crehan* [2001] ECR I-6297.

[7] For Europe see *European Commission*, 21.11.2001, COMP/37.512 – *Vitamins*, ABl. 2003 L 6/1.

[8] C. Jones, *Private Enforcement of Antitrust Law in the EU, UK and USA* (1999). See also id., *Private Antitrust Enforcement in Europe: A Policy Analysis and Reality Check*, (2004) 27 World Competition 13–24.

monographs have been published[9] and more will follow. In 2001 the Annual Workshop on EU Competition Law and Policy at the European University Institute in Florence was devoted to the topic.[10] At this workshop van Gerven presented concrete proposals for an EC Regulation on private remedies. The European Commission investigated the topic further and a 'Study on the conditions of claims for damages in case of infringement of EC competition rules' was published on August 31, 2004.[11] The study is based on empirical investigation of unparalleled scope in twenty-five Member States of the EU and assisted the Commission in the preparation of further developments. The next step was the publication of a Green Paper on damages actions for breach of the EC antitrust rules of December 2005.[12] The purpose of this paper is to determine the main obstacles to private damages claims and to propose different options in favour of a stronger role of private antitrust remedies.

The general increase in activity in comparative antitrust law has also been of great importance. In 2004 two broadly conceived studies have appeared, which – similarly in this respect to the Common Core Project – arose out of national reports, the 'Utrecht/Bayreuth' Project[13] and the report on the proceedings of the FIDE Meeting 2004.[14] The Common Core Project in comparison focuses on private remedies and is not limited to antitrust law but rather by including unfair competition law seeks to deal with the entire field of competition law.

5. *Other projects on European Private Law*

The Common Core of European Private Law is part of the 'Network of Excellence' supported by the 6th EU Framework Programme for

[9] See e.g. C. Lang, *Die kartellzivilrechtlichen Ansprüche und ihre Durchsetzung nach dem schweizerischen Kartellgesetz* (2000); R. Hempel, *Privater Rechtsschutz im Kartellrecht* (2002); F. Bulst, *Schadensersatzansprüche der Marktgegenseite im Kartellrecht* (2006).

[10] See. C.-D. Ehlermann/I. Atanasiu (ed.), *European Competition Law Annual 2001: Effective Private Enforcement of EC Antitrust* (2003).

[11] Ashurst (prepared by Denis Waelbroeck, Donald Slater and Gil Even-Shoshan), *Study on the conditions of claims for damages in case of infringement of EC competition rules* (2004), available at: http://ec.europa.eu/comm/competition/antitrust/others/actions_for_damages/study.html.

[12] European Commission, *Green Paper on Damages Actions for Breach of the EC Antitrust Rules*, 19.12.2005, COM(2005) 672 final. See also European Commission, *Commission Staff Working Paper – Annex to the Green Paper on Damages Actions for Breach of the EC Antitrust Rules*, 19.12.2005, SEC(2005) 1732.

[13] G. Dannecker, O. Jansen (ed.), *Competition Law Sanctioning in the European Union – The EU-Law Influence on the National Law System of Sanctions in the European Area* (2004).

[14] D. Cahill, J. Cooke, W. Wils, (Ed.), *The Modernisation of EU Competition Law Enforcement in the European Union – FIDE 2004 National Reports* (2004).

Research and Technological Development. The mandate of the network is to elaborate a 'Common Frame of Reference' (CFR), i.e. a system of model rules, especially but not only in contract law. Later, the CFR could lead to an 'Optional Instrument' which the parties to a contract could choose as applicable law.[15]

The subject of this study is rather remote to the CFR project. Unfair competition and antitrust law are mainly governed by special rules which were developed in order to take into account the particular features of the competitive process. However, there is overlapping as far as general concepts of tort law are concerned: private remedies in competition law rely to a large extent on general liability rules. Therefore, it will be necessary to determine on the one hand the impact of general European tort law on remedies in competition law, and on the other hand the influence which special aspects of competition law remedies could exert on general tort law (see below A. III. 4).

6. *Overview of the study*

This introduction would be incomplete without a brief overview of antitrust legislation in the individual reporting nations (II.). There follows a presentation of the European law ramifications, necessary because antitrust law is even more influenced by European Community law than other legal fields, substantive antitrust law having even found its way into the EC Treaty (III.). No treatment of the topic would be complete without a look over the Atlantic. The editors are therefore extremely grateful to have gained David Gerber, the leading authority on comparative antitrust law, for a comparative essay on private enforcement of competition law. David Gerber analyses the differences between the USA and Europe, thereby opening an important perspective for the development of the subject in Europe (Part B.). Part C contains the seven cases on antitrust law, each with fifteen national reports and an interim assessment. In Part D conclusions are drawn with regard to the Europe-wide survey. Here it is less a matter of pointing out the specific differences between the individual countries. Rather it is intended to generate proposals aimed at strengthening a more decentralized application of antitrust law in Europe.

[15] European Commission, *European Contract Law and the Revision of the Acquis: the Way Forward*, COM (2004) 651 final of 11.10.2004.

II. National antitrust law - a survey

1. *The fundamentals of antitrust law in the various EU Member States*

a) Austria

Austrian antitrust law is based on the Austrian Cartel Law of October 19, 1988 (KartG), which has been amended a number of times. These amendments, which were largely in connection with Austria's accession to the European Union, have significantly increased the effectiveness of the national antitrust law through substantive and organisational measures. The regulations for the combating of cartels are now largely based on the prohibition principle (*Verbotsprinzip*). The misuse principle (*Missbrauchsprinzip*) applies only to the operation of constructive cartels (*Wirkungskartellen*) which result in an unintended restriction of competition, as well as to vertical restraints between enterprises. A notable peculiarity of Austrian antitrust law is the very regulation of these vertical restraints, which do not fall under the cartel definition and are subject to a special regime. They have to be notified, and may be operated as long they have not been prohibited by the cartel court. The Federal Justice Minister may permit certain groups of cartels and vertical restraints by decree (*Verordnung*). For the latter the regulatory powers offer the possibility of harmonizing the domestic rules with the relevant block exemption regulations of the EC, and this has frequently been resorted to. Austria introduced merger control in 1993; including more stringent provisions for media mergers so as to ensure media pluralism. Infringements of antitrust prohibitions are sanctioned through the imposition of fines. The previous penal antitrust law was largely abolished.

The Cartel Court rules on the permitting or prohibition of cartels, vertical restraints and mergers, as well as on the interdiction of market dominance abuse. The Court is staffed with professional judges and expert lay judges. The second and final instance is the Supreme Court. Austria recently established a Federal Competition Authority, whose task is to investigate distortions of competition and to ensure the functioning of competition through the implementation of the European competition rules in the country. In addition a Federal Antitrust Legal Officer (*Bundeskartellanwalt*) was appointed with responsibility for representing the public interest in competition law matters. Both institutions have broad standing before the Cartel Court; the influence of the chambers (social partners) was suppressed, although in important questions they have standing along with the concerned parties. Approved cartels and mergers are entered in the Cartel Register.

During the elaboration of the following case studies, it could not be foreseen that Austria would be going to enact a completely new cartel law of 1.1.2006. The case studies were based on the KartG 1988[1] described above. By enacting Antitrust Code 2005 (KartG 2005) Austria adopts the principle of legal exception following EC Regulation 1/2003. All restricting agreements are prohibited (§ 1 KartG 2005), except that there are legal exceptions (§ 2 KartG 2005) or block exemption regulations for certain groups of cartels (§ 3 KartG 2005). The distinct rules of Austrian cartel law on the prohibition of certain kinds of cartels until an administrative authorization or on the legality of certain agreements until an administrative prohibition (a mixture of 'prohibition principle' and 'misuse principle') were replaced by a general prohibition of restricting agreements inspired by art. 81 EC. A special treatment of vertical restraints (see Case 15) does not exist any longer. Individual exemptions were abolished, the cartel register (in which the exemptions were entered) will not be continued. Moreover, the rules protecting individual cartel participants against 'internal cartel pressure' were completely eliminated.

Changes made by KartG 2005 concerning merger control are of rather minor importance; rules on market domination and the abuse prohibition stay unchanged. As regards private remedies there is no change. Prohibited agreements and decisions are void (§ 1(3) KartG 2005). However, because of the general cartel interdiction the case studies may come to a different result.

Therefore, the answer of Austrian law to Cases 9–15 had to be reviewed. As all references (doctrine and case law) refer to the old law, it seemed appropriate, to cite in the case of identical rules both the old and the new paragraph number.

b) Denmark

Consolidating statute No. 539 of June 28, 2002 of the Competition Act (CA) governs the anti-competitive agreements of undertakings (§§ 6–10), their abuse of a dominant market position (§ 11) and mergers between undertakings (§§ 12 ff.). In 1997 the CA was amended with a view to adapting the Danish rules to the rules of the EC treaty's arts. 81 and 82. In 2000 rules were implemented in the CA on control with mergers. The

[1] BGBl 1988/600, the last time revised in BGBl 2003 I 33.

rules on merger control are similar to the rules in the EC merger regulation. In 2002 the CA has been amended, especially with a view to creating the basis for stricter sanctions (larger fines) for violations of § 6, sec. 1, of the CA concerning the prohibition of cartelization, and in order to strengthen the Competition Authority's powers when carrying out inspections of undertakings.

According to CA § 14 the enforcement of the Competition Act is placed under the Competition Council, which is an administrative body. According to CA § 23a the Competition Council is also empowered to ensure the observance of arts. 81 and 82 of the EC-Treaty. According to CA § 15 the Competition Council consists of a chairman and eighteen members. The members are selected due to their legal or financial expertise and some are representatives from trade and industry, professional bodies, etc. The Competition Authority is the bureau for the Competition Council, and the Competition Authority is in charge of the daily administration of the Competition Act. The Authority prepares the cases on which the Council is to decide, provides information, is in contact with the complainants, etc. According to CA § 19 the Competition Council's decisions may be brought before the Competition Appeals Tribunal, which is an administrative complaints body. The Competition Appeals Tribunal's decisions can be brought before the regular courts.

Violations of the Competition Act are sanctioned with a penalty. Based on the Competition Act only penalties in the form of fines may be imposed. According to CA § 23 penalties may be imposed on both firms (companies) as well as persons. The Competition Council is not authorized to impose fines on undertakings for violations of the Competition Act. The director of the Competition Authority is in charge of deciding whether or not in a specific case the public prosecutor should be requested to bring an action before the criminal courts with a view to imposing a penalty.[2] Furthermore, the director of the Authority suggests to the public prosecutor the level of fine to apply for.

Cases concerning violation of the Competition Act can be brought by persons with a proper legal interest directly before the regular courts based on the rules of the Administration of Justice Act. Anybody with a sufficient legal interest will also be entitled to approach the courts directly with an action for damages (compensation). It is not a prerequisite for bringing an action for damages that a previous hearing of the

[2] Executive order issued by the Ministry of Economic and Business Affairs No. 951 of December 2, 1997, § 6, sec. 1.

case before the Competition Council has taken place.[3] According to the Administration of Justice Act § 345 a court may defer the hearing of an action for damages if it is considered necessary to await a decision from the Competition Council or the Competition Appeals Tribunal. If a firm has chosen to approach the Competition Council first, the decision of the Competition Appeals Tribunal must be awaited before an action concerning the Competition Act can be brought before the courts.[4]

c) England[5]

With effect from March 2000, a new domestic competition law regime on anti-competitive agreements and abuse of dominant position came into force in the United Kingdom. This is in the Competition Act 1998. The 1998 Act is very closely modelled on arts. 81 and 82 of the EC Treaty. Unusually for a UK statute, it contains a clause (section 60) which expressly obliges the national courts (with some reservations) to interpret their own national law (not based on an EC directive) in a way that is consistent with the way that arts. 81 and 82 EC are interpreted by the European Courts.[6] The 1998 Act has been followed by the Enterprise Act 2002, which makes a number of additions and amendments to the 1998 Act.

Historically, in the UK competition law has been enforced mainly by public enforcement agencies. The two recent Acts have conferred greatly enhanced investigation and enforcement powers on the Office of Fair Trading (OFT), which is the principal public enforcement agency. They are thought to give the OFT some of the widest investigation and enforcement powers of any antitrust authority in Europe. The OFT, after a slow start, is now making an aggressive use of those powers.[7]

[3] M. Koktvedgaard, *Lærebog i Konkurrenceret*, (5th edn 2003), p. 170.

[4] Consolidated Statute nr. 539 of June 28, 2002, of the Competition Act, § 20, sec. 1.

[5] Concerning the problem that the UK is a single EU member state but with a number of separate internal jurisdictions see the clarification, Part I.A.I. 1 n. 24.

[6] See, inter alia, S. Goodman [1999] European Competition Law Review 73.

[7] See, for example, the OFT's leniency programme modelled on that applicable in the USA (description at www.oft.gov.uk/business/legal/competition/ca98+leniency.htm) and *Agreements between Hasbro UK Ltd., Argos Ltd. and Littlewoods Ltd. fixing the price of Hasbro toys and games* (decision of November 21, 2003, on the OFT website at http://www.oft.gov.uk/Business/Competition+Act/Decisions/Argos2.htm); appeal on liability dismissed in *Argos Ltd. and Littlewoods Ltd. v. OFT* [2004] CAT 24, penalties reduced on appeal in [2005] CAT 13; permission to appeal refused by the CAT [2005] CAT 16, and the replica football kit cases (fines totalling £16 m imposed, and in one case increased by the CAT on appeal: *Price-fixing of replica football kit*, OFT decision CA98/06/2003 of 1 August 2003, appeals on liability, *JJB plc v. OFT* and *Allsports Ltd. v. OFT*, judgment of October 1, 2004, [2004] CAT 17; appeals on penalty, judgment of 19 May 2005 [2005] CAT 22).

Although, unlike in the USA, private-party enforcement was not originally seen as central to the enforcement system, competition law has had a role in private party litigation for many years, and important developments are taking place at present.

In litigation between private parties, competition law issues can, of course, arise in one of two ways. Competition law issues can be raised by a *defendant*, as a defence to a claim for injunctive relief or damages or for the return of property etc. being made against him. This use of competition law arguments in the courts is (at least so far as EC competition law is concerned) well established in the courts of England and Wales and there is significant case law on it. In the light of the consistency requirement in sec. 60 of the (much more recent) Competition Act, it is considered that the principles for the use of UK competition law arguments in similar situations are identical. Where the litigation is a dispute between the parties to an agreement, the principles on which the courts will sever from the valid parts of the agreement the parts which are made void by the application of competition law[8] are well understood.[9] Where the defendant in litigation seeks to raise as a defence a breach of competition law by the claimant (perhaps acting in cooperation with someone else) but not arising specifically from an agreement between defendant and claimant, the going will be more difficult for the defendant. In such a case, the defendant will only succeed with his defence if he can prove that there is a genuine and close connection between the alleged breach of competition law by the claimant and the rights which the claimant is seeking to assert against him in the litigation.[10] Though things are starting to change, as a general proposition English judges have until now tended to be not very sympathetic to competition law arguments when used by way of defence.

Competition law issues can be raised by a *claimant* (a competitor, a customer or ex-customer, a supplier or ex-supplier, etc.), as the basis of a

[8] This being, in EC law terms, a question of national law: see ECJ 56/65 *Société Technique Minière v. Maschinenbau Ulm* [1966] ECR 235, confirmed in ECJ 319/82 *Société de Vente de Ciments et Bétons v. Kerpen & Kerpen*, [1983] ECR 4173.

[9] See the judgment of the Court of Appeal in *Chemidus Wavin v. TERI* [1978] 3 CMLR 514 and commentary in P. Freeman and R. Whish (eds.), *Butterworths Competition Law*, Section XI paras. 149–160.

[10] See *Chiron Corpn. v. Organon Teknika Ltd.* [1993] FSR 324 (para. 44 of the judgment), upheld on appeal [1993] FSR 567, and the discussion of earlier cases in P. Freeman and R. Whish (eds.), *Butterworths Competition Law*, paras. 163–168.

claim for injunctive relief or damages or of a restitutionary claim, for the return of money paid or property transferred. The use of competition law arguments as the basis for claims in the courts for injunctive relief in the courts is well established.[11] Similar principles apply to applications based on competition law (EC or UK) as apply to applications based on any other area of law. Because of the adversarial system of civil and commercial litigation in England and Wales (where it is left very largely to the parties to take the initiative in running the case, and the judge takes a relatively passive role), in some circumstances an application to a court for an injunction is seen by claimants as a more attractive (though more expensive) option than a complaint to the European Commission or the OFT, as the claimant will have much more control over the progress of the matter, and in particular can move quickly if desired.[12] Neither the European Commission nor the OFT, of course, has any power to order payment of damages.

The use of competition law as the basis for claims for damages and for restitutionary claims is, on the other hand, much less developed. There is more experience with EC law than under the Competition Act 1998, though given the 'cloning' of the latter from arts. 81 and 82 EC and the consistency principle in sec. 60, the principles are considered to be identical. For many years, lawyers in the UK have confidently assumed (without there being any court judgments definitively establishing the principle) that breach of arts. 81 and 82 EC gives rise to a right to damages for private parties.[13] Although the policy of the legislature in enacting the Competition Act 1998 included a desire to facilitate

[11] The leading case is the House of Lords judgment in *Garden Cottage Foods Ltd. v. Milk Marketing Board* [1984] AC 130.

[12] On the tactical choice between making a complaint to the OFT or the European Commission and commencing litigation, see T. Ward and K. Smith, *Competition Litigation in the UK*, pp. 17–21 and the more detailed discussion in P. Freeman and R. Whish (eds.), Butterworths Competition Law, Section X, paras. 413–417 (M. R. Smith).

[13] The basis of that assumption was *Garden Cottage Foods Ltd. v. Milk Marketing Board* (n. 11 above) (though the House of Lords in that case did not technically decide the damages point), taken together with the insistence of the ECJ that national courts must provide effective remedies to enable individuals to enforce their directly effective EC law rights (C-6 & 9/90 *Francovich* [1991] ECR I-5357 and C-213/89 *Factortame-I* [1990] ECR I-2433), and the statement by van Gerven AG that 'the national court is under an obligation to award damages' for loss suffered as a result of a breach of directly enforceable provisions of EC competition law (C-128/92 *H. J. Banks Ltd. v. British Coal Corporation* [1994] ECR I-1209). It is noteworthy that in both *Arkin v. Borchard Lines Ltd.* and *Crehan v. Inntrepreneur Pub Company* (see below), there was no dispute between the parties that a damages remedy was in principle available: in each case, both sides accepted that it was.

damages claims, no express right to damages was conferred by the Act,[14] though the matter has been made clearer by the Enterprise Act 2002.[15] For many years, though, damages claims for breach of competition law have been threatened or even begun in the English courts and then settled out of court before trial, sometimes for substantial sums, without any final judgment of the court. Even more than in other areas of commercial litigation, there are enormous commercial incentives for a defendant in a competition law-based damages claim to settle out-of-court, in private, rather than allowing the dispute to get to trial. A court judgment, in the public domain, awarding damages to the claimant may act as an invitation to (possibly numerous) other claimants (other competitors, customers, suppliers, etc.) to bring similar claims. It also risks attracting the attention of the OFT or the European Commission (if they have not already been involved), which could result in a subsequent investigation and the imposition of fines.

There is now a judgment of an English court for the first time awarding damages for breach of art. 81 EC. It is the judgment of the Court of Appeal of May 21, 2004 in *Crehan v. Inntrepreneur Pub Company*,[16] and follows from an ECJ preliminary ruling in the same case[17] where the ECJ made the clear statement that a damages remedy must in principle be available. It is currently the subject of a further appeal to the House of Lords.[18] The case concerns a dispute between customer (the operator of two bars, which he leased from a brewery) and supplier (the brewery) about a brewery tied house exclusive purchasing agreement between them. In obtaining the award of damages, the applicant customer has had to overcome, inter alia, the traditional refusal of the English courts to enforce by way of injunction or a damages claim, as between the parties to the relevant contract, a contract which is void for breach of competition law (or at least art. 81 EC and its national law 'clone'), which was based on the courts' long-standing treatment of such contracts as not just void, but also as illegal.[19] That approach has had to be changed in the light of the ECJ preliminary ruling in the case, where the ECJ held that such a rule of national law could not be maintained,

[14] See, inter alia, J. Turner [1999] ECLR 62.
[15] See the new sec. 47 A Competition Act 1998 inserted by sec. 18 Enterprise Act 2002.
[16] [2004] EWCA 637 (CA).
[17] Sub nom. *Courage Ltd. v. Crehan*, ECJ case C-453/99, [2001] ECR I-6297.
[18] The highest appeal court in the national judicial system
[19] Most recently confirmed, in a different context, by the House of Lords in *Tinsley v. Milligan* [1994] 1 AC 340.

but that it is permissible for national law to maintain a rule denying enforcement of the void contract to a party to the disputed contract where that party 'bears significant responsibility' for the breach of art. 81 EC.

On the other hand, there is still no judgment of an English court awarding damages to a third party who has not taken part in the breach of competition law. The claim in *Arkin v. Borchard Lines Ltd.*[20] (by the managing director of a competitor which, it was alleged, had been forced out of business by predatory pricing by the members of two liner conferences which together had a collective dominant position) failed for a number of reasons.[21] The damages claims brought in the English courts against cartel members by customers as a consequence of the European Commission decision in the international vitamins cartel case[22] have been settled out of court.[23] Particularly since the English courts have now (under instructions from the ECJ) overcome their hesitations about awarding damages to co-contractors,[24] there is absolutely no reason of principle why such third party damages claims should not succeed. There remain, however, many technical problems and uncertainties with damages claims, particularly in relation to causation, remoteness and quantifying the loss suffered by the claimant.

The UK now has, in the Competition Appeal Tribunal, a specialist competition court, originally set up as the tribunal to deal with appeals against OFT decisions under the Competition Act but which, since the Enterprise Act 2002, has had in addition a jurisdiction in respect of monetary claims in 'follow-on' cases (i.e. where a decision has already been taken by the OFT or the European Commission establishing breach

[20] [2003] 2 Lloyd's Reports 225, [2003] EWHC 687, QBD (Commercial Court), Colman J., judgment of April 10, 2003.

[21] Though the court found that the defendant members of the liner conference had a collective dominance position, their low prices were found to be normal price competition and not predatory. Furthermore, the court decided that the managing director's decision to carry on trading in very difficult market conditions was 'so irrational' as to break the chain of causation between the low prices charged by the members of the liner conferences and the failure of the claimant's business (on the basis that any reasonably prudent ship operator would, in the circumstances, have decided to leave the market and thus cut its losses rather than carrying on trading).

[22] Commission decision of November 21, 2001, COMP/E-1/37.512 *Vitamins*, OJ L6/1 of January 10, 2003.

[23] *BCL Old Co. Ltd. and others v. Aventis SA, Rhodia, Hoffman-LaRoche and Roche*; *Deans Foods Ltd. v. Roche, Hoffman-LaRoche and Aventis SA*: see the Competition Appeal Tribunal website, www.catribunal.org.uk.

[24] *Crehan v. Inntrepreneur Pub Company*, supra.

of arts. 81 or 82 by the defendant). The first of such cases, arising out of the international vitamins cartel, have been brought in the CAT and have settled. This is an alternative to, not a substitute for, action in the 'mainstream' courts. A practice direction of early 2004[25] now requires cases in the 'mainstream' courts of England and Wales which raise questions under arts. 81 and 82 EC or the Competition Act 1998 to be brought in the Chancery Division of the High Court in London, where the judges have had specific training in competition law. Cases such as *Arkin v. Borchard*, *Crehan v. Inntrepreneur Pub Company* and *Days v. Pihsiang*[26] show that the judges in the 'mainstream' courts are becoming much more confident than in the past in handling competition cases.

It appears that the English courts are minded to take a rather generous view of the territorial extent of their jurisdiction in competition-based damages cases, which seems likely to give rise to some forum shopping. *Provimi v. Aventis*[27] establishes that, provided there is an English and/or Welsh element to a cartel operating within the EC, the English courts are willing to handle damages claims by customers in respect of all their losses arising throughout the EC, instead of the claimant having to pursue a number of parallel damages claims in several EC countries at once.

d) Finland

Finnish antitrust law is governed by the Finnish Act on Competition Restrictions (480/1992). Undertakings in Finland rely mostly on the Finnish Competition Authority (FCA). Almost all processes are administrative ones (first an FCA decision or proposal to the Market Court and then the parties or FCA can complain to the Finnish Administrative Supreme Court). Civil law cases have been rare. An undertaking can ask – and many FCA cases begin this way – the FCA to investigate a supposed restriction of competition. If the FCA decides that there is no reason to investigate the matter further (e.g. it is not a restriction of competition in the opinion of FCA), then the undertakings have a right

25 Practice Direction – Competition Law – Claims relating to the application of Articles 81 and 82 of the EC Treaty and Chapters I and II of Part I of the Competition Act 1998, available at www.dca.gov.uk/civil/procrules_fin/contents/practice_directions/competitionlaw_pd.htm.

26 [2004] EWHC 44 (QBD Commercial Court), judgment of Langley J., January 29, 2004.

27 [2003] EWHC 961 (Queen's Bench Division, Commercial Court), a further case arising as a consequence of the European Commission decision in *Vitamins*: the judgment is on preliminary points only.

to complain about this decision. No undertaking has a right to make direct claims in the Market Court. Even if the Market Court would decide that there was indeed a restriction of competition, the Market Court only returns the case to the FCA for further investigation and new decision. To summarize: the Finnish antitrust and consumer protection systems in the case of unfair practices rely very much on administrative systems with the Market Court as the court of first instance. The Market Court is the only court in Finland that uses both administrative law and civil law proceedings when deciding on the one hand antitrust cases and on the other hand unfair trade practice cases.

e) France

The antitrust law (*droit de la concurrence*) was originally contained in Order No. 86–1243 of December 1, 1986. It has now been codified in Book IV of the commercial code (*code commercial*) under articles L 410–1 to L 470–8 (Act No 2001–420 of September 18, 2000) and since modified by Act No. 2001–420 of May 15, 2001 and more recently by Act No. 2003–660 of July 21, 2003.

Recent French antitrust law, as it was shaped in 1986, is based on the principle of free play of competition as stated by art. L 410–2 of the commercial code, whereas the former Order No. 1483 of June 30, 1945 used to proclaim price regulation to be the basis of competition law. Thus, from 1945 to the end of 1986 in France there were authoritarian price-fixing measures mainly by taxation and freezing techniques.[28] After 1970 modifications of the Order of June 30, 1945 introduced neo-liberal economic theories into French competition law and the focus went from price politics to enforcement of the fight against anticompetitive practices. The system itself, however, still remained a controlled economy, as shown by the fact that agreements and dominant market positions could only be prohibited by the French Board of Trade (*Ministère de l'Economie*).[29]

By the commitment to a price mechanism based on the free play of competition (art. 1 of the Order No. 86–1243 of December 1, 1986) the system of a state-controlled economy came to an end. This was underlined by the transfer of sanctioning powers in competition matters from the Board of Trade to a specially created national independent administrative institution, the Council on Competition (*Conseil de la Concurrence*).[30] The Council has autonomous powers when it comes to

[28] M. Malaurie-Vignal, *Droit de la concurrence*, p. 2. [29] Ibid., p. 3. [30] Ibid., p. 3.

giving favourable opinions on certain projects (such as exemptions of certain categories of agreements, art. L 420–4 II of the commercial code). The council may be or has to be consulted by several entities, administrative or jurisdictional, with regard to bills and any issues relating to competition (art. L 462–1 and following the commercial code). For other questions the Council on Competition has powers subject to judicial control, for example, in the field of administrative acts such as measures and orders concerning anticompetitive behaviour. The decisions of the Council on Competition are open to an appeal before the Paris Court of appeal (art. L 464–7 of the commercial code). Its decision can be subject to a final appeal to the commercial chamber of the *Cour de Cassation.*

Apart from this administrative supervision of competition, victims of anticompetitive behaviour can plead directly before the civil courts in order to obtain annulment of a contract or compensation for damages. As an anticompetitive behaviour often involves a criminal offence, criminal procedures can also be engaged.[31]

French antitrust law prohibits anticompetitive agreements (art. L 420–1 of the commercial code) and the abuse of dominant market positions (art. L 420–2 of the commercial code). In addition to these two categories that can also be found in European competition law (arts. 81, 82 of the European Treaty) French competition law prohibits price offers or sales prices being excessively low in relation to production, processing and marketing expenses in order to prevent access to the market by an undertaking (art. L 420–5 of the commercial code) and – inspired by German law – the abuse of a state of economic dependence such as in cases of linked sales or refusals to sell (L 420–2 II of the commercial code).

f) Germany

The relevant legal text for cartel law is the 'Law against Restraints of Competition' (*Gesetz gegen Wettbewerbsbeschränkungen* – GWB) from 1957 as amended by the 7th Cartel Reform from 2005 (entered into force July 1, 2005). The 7th Cartel Reform has adapted German law to the new procedural rules in European competition law brought about by regulation 1/2003. At the same time, the reform was used to align substantive law nearly completely on the European model. Essentially, only some stricter rules on unilateral conduct still differ from European competition law (which is allowed by Art. 3(2) regulation 1/2003).

[31] Ibid., p. 213.

Moreover, the prohibition test in merger control is still based on 'market dominance' and not on the significant impediment to effective competition as it is provided for in the European merger regulation.

Competition law plays a major role in German economic policy. During and after the Second World War the 'ordoliberal' thinkers of the Freiburg School developed ideas leading to the German Social Market Economy model in which a prominent place was reserved to competition law. Part of it is the strong and independent position of the Federal Cartel Office (*Bundeskartellamt* – BKartA) which is (together with the regional cartel authorities) in charge of public enforcement of the GWB and of the provisions of European competition law. The dominance of public enforcement has overshadowed private law remedies. The most frequent use of competition law in private actions is made on the defence side by invoking the nullity of a contract as the result of a competition law violation. Moreover, plaintiffs have become active on the basis of competition law violations in special situations. For example, in refusal to deal cases they have successfully invoked the interdiction of obstruction directed at enterprises in a strong or dominant position thus obtaining the contracts they wanted. On the other hand, there is no tradition in Germany for enterprises to sue their competitors based on competition law violations. The practical attractiveness of private suits seems to be low. As a result, there is no generally practised private enforcement of competition law.[32] This fact is not due to legal reasons: sec. 33 GWB makes fundamental provision for private claims in case of violations of antitrust provisions or cartel authority decisions. Prior to the 7th Cartel Reform, a condition for a private claim was that the provision (or decision) in question served 'to protect another'. Even if the protectionist character of the most important substantive GWB

[32] See the statistics in Wach/Epping/Zinsmeister/Bonacker, *'Germany'* (annex to: Ashurst (ed.), *Study on the Conditions of Claims for Damages in Case of Infringement of EC Competition Rules*, 2004), p. 30 et seq. The numbers are based on a comprehensive inquiry among all German district courts and higher regional courts competent for damage claims based on (national or European) competition law. Monetary damages were attributed only three times. In six cases, the general obligation to pay damages was stated in declaratory decisions. On the other hand, see the numbers advanced by the *Bundeskartellamt* in its working paper *Private Kartellrechtsdurchsetzung – Stand, Probleme, Perspektiven* (2005), p. 12 et seq. The *Bundeskartellamt*, receiving obligatory notifications from all German courts in competition law-related matters (§ 90 GWB), presents a more active picture of private competition law enforcement in Germany. Critical of the statistical data of the Ashurst Report also Th. Lübbig and M. le Bell, *Die Reform des Zivilprozesses in Kartellsachen* (2006) WRP 1209 (1211).

rules was recognized, the reform has facilitated private claims by abolishing this requirement. Now, anyone who is affected by a restriction of competition is entitled to take legal action. Apart from the reform of the legal prerequisites, a practical aspect could promote private enforcement in Germany. As a consequence of the international vitamin cartel, several private actions have been brought to the courts. As the lower instances have greatly differed, an intensive discussion on the subject of private claimes has emerged. This, together with the general goal of the 7th Cartel Reform to spur private enforcement as well as the awareness of the subject on the European level, could lead to much more practical significance of private remedies in the future.[33]

g) Greece

The regulatory framework of antitrust law is provided by L. 703/1977 on the control of monopolies and oligopolies and the protection of free competition.[34] The provisions of arts. 1 and 2 thereof reproduce almost identically arts. 81 and 82 of the EC Treaty. Arts. 4–4f refer to merger control. National antitrust law applies to all restrictions of competition that have or may have effects within the Greek territory.[35]

The same law established the Hellenic Competition Commission and provides for the functions and competence thereof and the procedures to be followed. The said Commission consists of a chairman and eleven members; some of them are selected from the judicial and academic sector due to their legal and economic specialization in the competition field, others are representatives of trade and industry bodies.[36] The Commission is an independent administrative body with quasi-jurisdictional functions; however, as recently held by the ECJ,[37] such an authority is not a court or tribunal within the meaning of art. 234 EC and therefore, is not entitled to refer a preliminary question to the

[33] On the private enforcement aspects of the German reform see e.g. G. Berrisch and M. Burianski (2005) WuW 878; R. Hempel (2004) WuW 362; (2005) WuW 137; J. Keßler (2005) BB 1125; W.-H. Roth, *Festschrift Ulrich Huber* (2006); M. Schütt (2004) WuW 1124. The Working Group on Competition Law (*Arbeitskreis Kartellrecht*), a forum hosted by the *Bundeskartellamt* and composed of scholars and judges specializing in competition law devoted its annual conference 2005 to the subject of private remedies, see the working paper note 32 above, and the report by C. Moch (2006) WuW 39.

[34] Government Gazette, issue A 278, 1977, as repeatedly amended by laws 1943/1991, 2000/1991, 2296/1995, 2741/1999, 2837/2000 and 2941/2001.

[35] Art. 32. [36] Art. 8(3) as amended.

[37] Judgment of the ECJ (Grand Chamber) of 31.5.2005, Case C-53/03, Reference for a preliminary ruling: Epitropi Antagonismou-Greece, 56 *EEmpD* (2005), 414.

Court of Justice regarding a case pending before it. The Commission is empowered to ensure the enforcement of the national antitrust law as well as of arts. 81 and 82 EC. For violations of L. 703/77, it may issue recommendations, order the cessation of the infringement, impose fines or impose other conduct and structural measures.[38] It is also exclusively competent to grant individual exemptions in accordance with art. 1(3) L. 703/77.[39] Its decisions are subject to appeal before the Athens Administrative Court of Appeal. A Secretariat (a fact-finding body) is set up and operates within the Commission, having as its function the preparation of cases and the drafting of proposals, on the basis of which the Commission adopts its decisions.

L. 703/77 has been amended several times, and more recently by L. 3373/2005. This last amendment aimed mainly at introducing into the Greek legal order the provisions of Council Regulation (EC) 1/2003 on the implementation of the rules on competition laid down in arts. 81 and 82 of the Treaty.[40] On this occasion, significant amendments to the substantive national law were also introduced or reintroduced, such as the abuse of state of economic dependence (art. 2a), the a posteriori notification of 'small' mergers,[41] for information and statistical purposes (art. 4a) as well as the possibility of the Competition Commission to proceed, by its own motion or upon request of the Minister of Development, to conduct all structural measures aiming at ensuring satisfactory competition conditions in specific economic sectors (art. 5). Although it was proposed to use the reform as an opportunity to align the national system to the European model, this idea was not finally followed. Thus, the obligation of notification remains for cartels falling within the scope of art. 1(1) L. 703/77; however, such notification no longer grants provisional immunity.[42] In practice, it seems also that the Competition Commission has diversified its focus of attention from the merger control to the control of anti-competitive practices.[43]

[38] Art. 9(1) as amended. See also Case 9.

[39] By contrast, group exemption to certain categories of agreements can only be granted by decision of the Minister of Development, upon concurrent opinion of the Competition Commission.

[40] OJ L 001, 4-1-2003, p. 0001–0025

[41] I.e. mergers covering a market share less than 10% or having a total turnover less than 15 million euros. For mergers exceeding the above total turnover, a preventive control is imposed by art. 4.

[42] Art. 23 as amended.

[43] See e.g. the recent decision 277/IV/2005 on the concerted practice regarding the resale prices of supermarket products, 11 *DEE* (2005), 571.

As will be developed in the following cases, private law claims for antitrust infringements may be brought only before the civil courts, independently of whether the Competition Commission has or has not declared the antitrust infringement. The civil courts are allowed to examine incidentally the validity of the agreement; in their evaluation, they are bound by the judgments of the Administrative Courts of Appeal or of the Council of State rendered upon appeal of the Commission's decisions as well as by the Commission's decisions which are no longer subject to an appeal. Still, private law enforcement, although it could constitute an important means of fighting against competition violations, is not very often used in practice.

h) Hungary

Act LVII of 1996 regarding the Prohibition on Unfair and Restrictive Market Practices (HCA) covers both unfair competition and cartel law. Therefore, to a large extent, reference can be made to the outline of Hungarian law in Part I of this book. The Office of Economic Competition (OEC) is in charge of the implementation of cartel law because situations that violate the cartel rules of the HCA are matters more of public than private interest. Proceedings of the OEC can be commenced as the result of a complaint against an infringement or a notification of an agreement or a planned merger. Furthermore, the OEC may also decide to open an investigation *ex officio* against unfair manipulations of consumer choice, infringements of the prohibition of restrictive agreements and abuse of dominant position, and infringements of the provisions laid down in arts. 81 and 82 EC. In its proceedings pursued under Community competition rules the OEC applies the procedural rules of the HCA together with those of Council Regulation (EC) No 1/2003 on the implementation of the rules on competition laid down in arts. 81 and 82 EC.

Lawsuits for damages are civil law disputes and on the basis of sec. 7 (1) of the HCC fall within the competence of the civil courts. That is true also for damages claims based on violation of cartel law. However, there is no significant case law regarding claims for damages based on breach of the competition rules on cartels and on abuse of dominant position. Moreover, the Hungarian Supreme Court decided on one occasion that the courts did not have power to assess the existence of an abuse of a dominant position.[44] It therefore stopped the procedure in this respect,

[44] Supreme Court Pf. IV. 24 909/2000/1. [2000], Éless, *Németh* (2004) pp. 2, 17.

but ruled that the courts did have power to proceed in respect of the claim for damages and therefore ordered the court of first instance to continue the proceedings in respect of the damage claim. Furthermore, the courts stopped or suspended proceedings until the decision of the OEC, because they did not consider themselves to have the power to decide on the question of the existence of cartels or abuse of dominant position. Moreover, on one occasion, the proceeding court ruled, that the decision of the OEC is a precondition for a ruling on the claim for damages.[45] Thus, before May 1, 2004, private actions for damages had to be based upon a pre-existing decision of the OEC.

This practice of the courts is criticized because no legal rules restrain courts assessing infringement of competition rules as one of the elements of liability in damages; they merely reserve the power of competition authority procedure to the OEC. The amendment of the HCA, which entered into force on May 1, 2004, could bring some changes. According to the new sec. 91/H. (1) of the HCA, in cases, where arts. 81 and 82 EC are to be applied, the provisions of Act III of 1952 on the Code of Civil Procedure will be applied along with the provisions in Regulation 1/2003 (EC). Under art. 6 of this Regulation, the courts have the power to apply arts. 81 and 82 EC. It would be desirable to adopt a similar view for violations of national competition law, otherwise the practice of the courts would remain unchanged.

According to the amendment of the HCA this exclusive competence is broken up and courts have the power to bring their judgments without the need to await for a decision of the OEC. This was already the case when claims are based on EC law. Under the new national regime the procedure of the courts would still be based on private interests and the public enforcement of competition law remains the competence of the GVH. Under the present (purely national) private enforcement system a statement or decision of the GVH or a competition authority from any EU Member State can be considered as evidence.

The legal basis for damages claims both for damages caused outside contractual relations and those caused in the context of contractual relations is sec. 318(1) HCC.[46] Sec. 339(1) HCC establishes the general

[45] Supreme Court, BH 2004/151. évi 4. szám 151. jogeset cited in Éless, *Németh* (2004) p. 2.

[46] 'In respect of the liability for breach of contract and of the level of the compensation for damages, the rules on the liability for damages caused outside contractual relations shall be applied, with the difference that the compensation for damages shall not be lowered, except provided otherwise by law.'

rule of liability for damages caused outside contractual relations.[47] Under the rules of the HCC there are no limitations to the standing of natural or legal persons bringing an action for damages. Although there are certain forms of actions available based on public interest,[48] collective or class actions are not available for claiming damages. As to the issues of passing on defence and indirect purchaser standing there is no case law.

The absence of relevant court practice may make actions for damages based on infringement of competition law more difficult. Absence of economic models for calculating damages may also cause difficulties in private enforcement. Under the current competition rules no punitive or treble damages are available. Administrative sanctions include fines of a maximum of 10 per cent of an undertaking's net turnover in the preceding business year (sec. 78 HCA).

The HCA was largely in compliance with the basic rules of EU competition law when it entered into force in 1997. Amendments to the act in December 2000 resulted in further harmonization. The next step in the harmonization process was Act X of 2002, based on sec. 62(3) of the Treaty on the Accession of Hungary to the European Union. Further to these harmonization measures, the Hungarian Parliament passed Act XXXI of May 26, 2003 amending the HCA. The amendments aim to bring the act fully into line with EU competition law. The new provisions entered into force on May 1, 2004, the date of Hungary's accession to the European Union.

The latest amendment of the HCA is Act LXVIII of 2005, which has implemented substantial changes. The amendments took effect on November 1, 2005. The most relevant changes with regard to cartel agreements and abuse of a dominant position concern the elimination of the notification system (individual exemptions, negative clearance), the introduction of private enforcement (sec. 88/A HCA) and the rules on complaints. Procedural rules have been also significantly changed: inspection of files by undertakings have been restricted, the OEC's powers of investigation have been extended, legal professional privilege has now been implemented.

[47] 'Who causes damage to another person by infringement of law shall compensate therefor. He is exempted from liability if he proves that he behaved as it is generally expected in the given situation.'

[48] On the basis of sec. 92(1) HCA the OEC, the chambers of commerce or consumer protection organizations may have standing.

Moreover, since September 1, 2005 the Hungarian Criminal Code criminalizes cartel activities such as price fixing, fixing contractual terms and conditions, other market restrictive agreements and concerted practices, as well as decisions by associations of undertakings if the aim of such cartel activity was to influence the result of a public procurement procedure or a concession tender. Sec. 93 HCA declares that the legal consequences flowing as a result of the violation of the provisions of the HCA and the enforced civil law claims shall not prejudice the possibilities of applying other civil law consequences defined in other legal norms or of initiating petty offence actions or criminal proceedings.

Sec. 14 of the Hungarian Criminal Code essentially makes bid-rigging a criminal offence. Anyone who tries to influence the result of a public procurement procedure or a public concession tender by agreeing to fix prices or other contractual conditions, or engages in other concerted practices, shall commit a criminal offence, punishable by a maximum of five years' imprisonment. The offence extends to decisions of associations of undertakings as well. If the value of the public procurement is less than HUF 2m (€8,100) then any bid-rigging is deemed to be a lesser offence, punishable with two years' imprisonment, public service or fine.

Sec. 14 also contains a 'criminal leniency programme': the offender will not be punished if he discloses the offence to the authorities (including the competition authority, the financial services supervisory body and the competent public procurement bodies) and submits the relevant circumstances of the offence to these authorities before they become aware of the offence.

i) Ireland

The principal Irish competition law statute is the Competition Act 2002, which repeals and replaces the Competition Act 1991 and the Competition (Amendment) Act 1996, as well as earlier Irish merger law statutes. Sec. 4 and 5 of the 2002 Act are modelled closely on articles 81 and 82 of the EC Treaty, as were the corresponding provisions in the 1991 and 1996 Acts. The 1991 Act was seen as flawed because it only allowed sec. 4 and 5 to be enforced by aggrieved persons, or by the Minister. This was remedied by the enactment of the 1996 Act, which introduced criminal penalties and gave the Competition Authority the power to impose fines.[49] The 2002 legislation was enacted to consolidate and modernize the competition and merger law system, and to

[49] The 1996 Act also took away the right of action of the Minister.

strengthen the advocacy and enforcement roles of the Competition Authority. In its abolition of the notification system, the 2002 Act took the bold step of modernizing Irish competition law in line with the modernization of EU competition law, although the latter was only at proposal stage when the Irish Act was adopted. This highlights an interesting element in Irish competition law, which is the tendency of both the Authority and the Irish Courts to look not only to EC law but also to US antitrust law for guidance and influence.[50]

Sec. 4 and 5 apply to undertakings. The term is defined differently than in EC law as 'an individual, a body corporate or an unincorporated body of persons engaged for gain in the production, supply or distribution of goods or the provision of a service'. Effectively however, the test is the same as under EC law.[51] The offence set out in sec. 4 more or less replicates that set out in art. 81(1) EC, and unlike its equivalent provision in the Netherlands, does contain a non-exhaustive list of examples of anti-competitive behaviour, which of course, does not prejudice the generality of the prohibition.[52] Neither the Act nor the Courts impose a *de minimis* rule. The offence set out in sec. 5 more or less replicates art. 82 EC. In 2004, the Competition Authority was successful for the first time in proving abuse of a dominant position before the High Court, under sec. 5 of the Competition Act 2002.[53]

The reliefs provided for by the 2002 Act include damages, injunctions, declarations and court orders requiring the discontinuance or adjustment of a dominant position. However, there are differences between the Irish and the EC antitrust rules. The Competition Authority does not have the power to fine, but has to enforce its decisions in the courts. Another difference is that, under sec. 4 of the Competition Act 2002, hard-core cartel offences such as price fixing are treated as per se offences. The exempting conditions of art. 81(3) are listed separately as possible defences in sec. 4(5) of the Act. Another important difference is that criminal sanctions (imprisonment in addition to fines) may be imposed for breach of the 2002 Act. Private enforcement of the

[50] See for example J. Keane in: *Masterfoods Ltd. v. HB Ice Cream Ltd.* [1993] ILRM 145. In 2004, two of the members of the Competition Authority were Americans who had formerly worked for the US Federal Trade Commission or the US Antitrust Department.

[51] *Deane v. Voluntary Health Insurance Board* [1992] 2 IR 319; *Carrigaline Community Television Broadcasting Co. Ltd. v. Minister for Transport and others* [1997] 1 ILRM. 241, and *Greally v. Minister for Education* [1995] 1 ILRM 481.

[52] *Chanelle Veterinary Ltd. v. Pfizer (Ireland) Ltd. (No. 2)* [1998] ILRM 161.

[53] *Competition Authority v. Irish League of Credit Unions*, High Court, Kearns J. October 22, 2004.

competition rules was originally the only method of enforcement envisaged by Irish competition legislation, as mentioned above. This proved to be most inadequate. The 2002 legislation, coupled with the modernization of EC competition rules and the Competition Authority's active and high-profile approach to enforcement, may lead to increased competition litigation in the Irish courts and more effective enforcement.

j) Italy

National antitrust law is regulated by the Law of October 10, 1990 n. 287, *Norme per la tutela della concorrenza e del mercato* (Law 287/90), which dictates the provisions aimed at protecting the state of competition and the market. In the drafting process, it was debated whether to take inspiration from the US or the EU system, with regard to the enforcement of antitrust law. On the one hand, in the US system private enforcement of antitrust law is much developed and characterized by remedies, which facilitate private claims (such as treble damages, contingency fees and class actions). On the other hand, the European model, favours independent authorities, without excluding intervention of courts. After a large debate, the legislator opted for the second solution. Therefore, next to the ordinary judges, an ad hoc authority operates.

The *Autorità Garante della Concorrenza e del Mercato* (the Authority), is a public enforcement agency. The Authority operates with complete autonomy and independently from the executive power and from other powers of the state. The Authority is entrusted to investigate undertakings, set deadlines to undertakings in order to eliminate infringements, prohibit mergers, inflict monetary fines, etc. The decisions of the Authority may be appealed before the *Tribunale Amministrativo* (TAR) of Lazio.

Besides public enforcement of antitrust law, private enforcement is available before (ordinary) courts: *Corte d'Appello* (Appellate Court) and low-level courts for breach of national and EC antitrust law, respectively. There are indeed no special courts, whose institution is prohibited under the Italian Constitution (art. 102). Nonetheless, the setting up of special divisions of ordinary courts having exclusive jurisdiction on damages claims for breach of competition law is currently under debate.

Appellate courts have sole competence to judge nullity and damages claims, and to grant interim relief in case of breach of national antitrust law. This constitutes an exception. First, the Court of Appeal normally acts as a second instance court. Second, no room remains for appeal on grounds of findings of fact. The legislature's choice seems to be based on the idea that higher courts 'are more equipped to deal with disputes involving complex economic assessments'.[54]

First instance ordinary courts, i.e. the *Giudice di pace* and the *Tribunale*, are competent for private enforcement of EC competition law, i.e. violation of arts. 81 and 82 EC. This follows from the fact that the Court of Appeal has an exceptional competence in the field of national antitrust law.[55] Their competence is determined by the value of the claim, and, furthermore, on the basis of territorial criteria (as follows from arts. 18 to 36 cpc). Decisions of the *Giudice di pace* and of the *Tribunale* may be appealed respectively before the *Tribunale* and the *Corte d'Appello*. The *Corte di Cassazione* is in principle competent only for law matters (*questioni di legittimità*) in relation to decisions of the *Tribunale*, when the latter operates as a court of second instance and the *Corte d'Appello*.

Private and public actions for the enforcement of antitrust law are not coordinated. Private parties have no access to the documents obtained via the Authority's investigations. Secondly, private parties are not entitled to claim damages in the course of the Authority's public proceedings since the Authority is an administrative body.[56]

Even if the search for private enforcement seems slowly to increase, public enforcement still prevails.[57] Scholarship has indicated several reasons for this phenomenon.[58] First, judges are not familiar with antitrust provisions, whose implementation normally requires complex economic evaluations. Second, contrary to the large public investigative

[54] G. Tesauro, *Private Enforcement of EC Antitrust Rules in Italy: The Procedural Issues, European Competition Law Annual 2001: A Community Perspective* (2003), pp. 267–281, at 269. The author observes that procedural issues undermine judicial enforcement of antitrust rules in Italy.

[55] M. Libertini, *Il ruolo del giudice nell'applicazione delle norme antitrust*, in Giur. Comm. I, 1998, 649–679, at 677.

[56] As regards the possibility of standing as a *parte civile* in such public proceedings, see J. Lever, *Effective Private Enforcement*, in: *European Competition Law Annual 2001: A Community Perspective* (2003), pp. 109–118, at 115.

[57] P. Giudici, *Private Antitrust Law Enforcement in Italy*, in (2004) 1 *The Competition Law Review*, pp. 61–85, at 69.

[58] M. Monti, *Effective Private Enforcement of EC Antitrust Law*, in *European Competition Law Annual: 2001, A Community Perspective* (2003), pp. 3–8, at 5; G. Faella, *Note to the Decision* Bluvacanze vs. I Viaggi del Ventaglio-Turisanda-Hotelplan Italia, *of the Corte d'Appello of Milano, 11 July 2003*, in (2004) *Il diritto industriale*, 170–177, at 177.

powers entrusted to the Authority, the judge has very limited ones.[59] This is due to the principle of allegation (*principio dispositivo*), which imposes a duty on the judge to decide on the basis of the evidence provided by the parties (art. 115 cpc). Furthermore, it is very difficult for parties to prove the infringement, the damage they have suffered as a consequence thereof and the causal link between the infringement and the damage.

k) Netherlands

The statutory basis for antitrust law in the Netherlands is laid down in the Dutch Competition Act (DCA) from 1998.[60] Pursuant to art. 6 (1) DCA agreements between undertakings, decisions by associations of undertakings and concerted practices of undertakings, which have as their object or effect the prevention, restriction or distortion of competition on the Dutch market, or a part thereof, are prohibited. Art. 24(1) DCA formulates a prohibition for undertakings to abuse a dominant position. The DCA has appointed the Netherlands Competition Authority (NCA) as the body responsible for enforcing compliance with the DCA. For the purpose of surveillance and investigation, the officials of the NCA have the powers assigned to them in the DCA and in the General Administrative Law Act. The Director General of the NCA can impose administrative fines for infringements of the DCA. Public antitrust law can have an important impact on private antitrust litigation because of the fact that an infringement of competition law establishes a wrongful act in the sense of art. 6: 162 of the Dutch Civil Code (BW). A decision of the NCA finding infringements of antitrust law will relieve the plaintiff of the burden of proving the infringement.[61]

An infringement of the DCA may give rise to civil claims and therefore to private antitrust litigation as such an infringement constitutes a wrongful act according to the regulation in the Dutch Civil Code.[62] Of particular importance to civil actions is the second paragraph of art. 6

[59] Among such limited investigative powers: appointment of experts (art. 61 cpc), free cross-examination of the parties (arts. 117 and 183 cpc), inspection and search (art. 118 cpc), request for information from the Public Administration (art. 213 cpc), interviewing of witnesses (arts. 253 cpc), supplemental oath (art. 240 cpc).

[60] History: Netherlands Government Gazette 1997, 242; 1999, 30; 1999, 470; 2000, 314; 2001, 461; 2001, 481; 2001, 584; 2001, 664; 2002, 71; 2004, 345.

[61] In that case the court can consider it likely that a wrongful act was committed as a result of which the infringer will need to prove the contrary.

[62] See the introduction to Dutch unfair competition law in Part I.

DCA which provides that agreements and decisions prohibited pursuant to art. 6(1) DCA are void by operation of law. Private antitrust litigation in the Netherlands is not very common. In most cases legal proceedings are not primarily founded on antitrust law but, for example, on contract law. There are, however, important incentives to start private antitrust proceedings as parties can obtain interim measures in a relatively short period of time. In the second place in civil proceedings parties can obtain compensation for damages. In the few cases where antitrust issues were brought up, the main objective of the proceedings was to obtain an (interim) injunction rather than compensation for damages. However, a series of recent decisions by the Netherlands Competition Authority, fining undertakings in the construction sector for bid-rigging practices, brought in its wake an important number of governmental agencies submitting claims for damages.[63] It is noted that these proceedings were initially started mainly to prevent the right to sue for damages from becoming barred by statutes of limitation, while an out-of-court settlement was being negotiated. However, recently the government has rejected the settlement offer of the construction companies so that the legal proceedings continue.[64]

l) Poland

Competition law *sensu largo* consists of norms protecting market participants from unfair competition as well as norms protecting competition – as a mechanism regulating economic processes.[65] In this respect, the Polish system is based on two statutes: the act on fighting unfair competition of 1993 (*Ustawa o zwalczaniu nieuczciwej konkurencji* – u.z.n.k.[66]), which covers the first of the aforementioned fields, and the act on competition and consumer protection of 2000 (*Ustawa o ochronie konkurencji i konsumentow* – u.o.k.k.[67]), which covers the latter one. The u.o.k.k. and u.z.n.k. differ therefore regarding the purpose of the regulation, the sphere of the protected interests and consequently the type of procedure. The u.o.k.k., as discussed below, protects the public interest, while the u.z.n.k. protects the private interests of undertakings and other

[63] See for example *Het Financieele Dagblad*, Februari 17, 2005, that refers to 1,100 claims of all public entities.

[64] *Het Financieele Dagblad*, March 5, 2005.

[65] E. Modzelewska-Wachal, *Ustawa o ochronie konkurencji i konsumentow – komentarz* (2002), p. 16.

[66] DzU z 2003 Nr 153 poz. 1503; zm. DzU z 2002 Nr 197, poz. 1661.

[67] DzU z 2003 Nr 86 poz. 804; zm. DzU 2003 Nr 60 poz. 535 oraz 2003 Nr 170 poz. 1652.

market participants. Accordingly, competition protection is executed through an administrative procedure, whereas fighting unfair competition practices is executed through a court procedure. The act on competition and consumer protection replaced the Antimonopoly Law of 1990. It is a complex piece of legislation and together with such acts as the Entrepreneurship Act (*Ustawa o dzialalnosci gospodarczej*) carries out the constitutional principle of freedom of economic activity (art. 22 of the Constitution).

In general, the u.o.k.k. defines the conditions for the development and protection of competition as well as the rules protecting interests of undertakings and consumers. The u.o.k.k. determines measures to counteract the practices restricting competition and anticompetitive concentrations of undertakings and associations thereof. Title II of the act deals with the prohibition of competition restricting practices and provides for a prohibition of competition restricting agreements and a prohibition of abuse of a dominant position. The following chapter deals with the concentration of entrepreneurs. Subsequently, in title IV entitled 'Organization of competition and consumer protection', u.o.k.k. defines the authorities competent in competition and consumer protection issues (the President of the Office of Competition and Consumer Protection – OCCP, and territorial self-governing and consumer organizations). One of the last chapters regulates the proceedings before the President of the OCCP.

As mentioned above, the u.o.k.k. belongs to the field of public law. Consequently, the infringement of a public interest constitutes a condition *sine qua non* for the actions taken before the President of the OCCP. In situations where private interests are being infringed, for example, interests of undertakings, consumers or other market participants, claims shall be brought on a different basis, for example, on the basis of the civil code.[68] However, the criterion differentiating the public interest from the private one is not always clear and the differentiation becomes even more difficult in cases concerning practices limiting competition. Therefore the Administrative Court developed a line of jurisprudence stating that the infringement of a public interest takes place if the consequences of an infringing action affect a broader circle of market participants or when an action has negative consequences on the market.[69]

[68] E. Modzelewska-Wachal, note 65 above.
[69] SA 24.01.1991, XV Amr 8/90, Wokanda 1992 nr. 2.

The President of the OCCP is appointed and supervised by the Prime Minister. The decision of the President is subject to appeal to the Antimonopoly Court. The provisions of the Code of Civil Proceedings (*Kodeks Postepowania Cywilnego* – k.p.c.) concerning proceedings in economic cases shall apply. If the President of the OCCP considers the appeal to be justified, he may – without forwarding files to the court – waive or change his decision. He shall inform the parties, without delay, by sending a new decision.

m) Portugal

The relevant text for antitrust law is Law no. 18/2003, 11 June. There are also rules from the European Union: arts. 85 and 86 Rome Treaty (current arts. 81 and 82). A general overview of Portuguese antitrust law concentrates on basic substantive areas of competition law such as: horizontal restraints of trade including price fixing, boycotts, bid rigging, allocations of customers and territories, and trade associations; vertical restraints including resale price maintenance, allocation of territories, exclusive distributorships and tying; abuses of market power, monopolization and attempts to monopolize and merger control policy and practice.

The Portuguese law is applied in the Portuguese territory (art. 1) to any companies. According to Portuguese law a company is an entity that develops an economic activity and offers goods and services in a market (art. 2). Horizontal restraints, independently of their form, are forbidden when they have the scope to hinder, to falsify or to restrict competition. In some cases these forbidden conducts are justified, if they improve the production and distribution of goods and services and contribute to economic and technical development.

According to arts. 6 and 7 of the Portuguese competition law the abuse of market power is also forbidden. There are two types of abuse: abuse of a dominant position in the market and abuse of economic dependence. The relevant cases of concentration must have been previously notified to the Competition Council, the agency which regulates and controls the market (arts. 8 and 9). Until there is a decision by the Council the concentration operation is suspended. Also state subsidies must not falsify competition (art. 13). Agreements that violate the law are void and of no legal effect (art. 41) and companies that violate the law are subject to fines (art. 43). The Competition Council's decisions can be appealed before the Commercial Court (art. 52).

Portuguese competition law involves a tension between fostering a competitive economy and protecting consumers from anti-competitive conduct such as monopolistic pricing and tying arrangements. With private remedies the Civil Code (*Código Civil* – CC) is normally applied: and for procedure aspects, the Code of Civil Procedure (*Código de Processo Civil* – CPC). For criminal aspects the relevant texts are the Criminal Code (*Código Penal* – CP) and the Code of Criminal Procedure (*Código de Processo Penal* – CPP).

n) Spain

Antitrust law is governed by Act 16/1989 for the protection of Competition (*Ley de Defensa de la Competencia* – LDC) of 17.7.1989. This act is inspired by European law and its main objectives are: (i) to prohibit all agreements that impede, restrict or distort competition in the domestic market; (ii) to repress abusive exploitation of dominant positions in the national market; (iii) to control concentrations between undertakings of national scope; and (iv) to supervise state aids granted to companies.

Antitrust law currently in force has been amended on several occasions, most recently on December 30, 2003. The most important amendment was introduced by Royal Law-Decree 6/1999 of 16 April which established an obligatory notification for those concentrations that meet or exceed the thresholds stated in art. 14 of Act 16/1989.

At present, there are two active competition authorities in Spain: the Competition Service (*Servicio de Defensa de la Competencia*), a department of the Ministry of Economy, which has investigative powers and is in charge of instructing the proceedings for conduct included in Act 16/1989; and the Competition Court (*Tribunal de Defensa de la Competencia*), configured as an autonomous body, which has decision-making powers.

In 2001, the Spanish Constitutional Court pronounced a decision of great importance as regards the distribution of powers between the state and the regions. According to this decision, the state must share powers in antitrust enforcement with regional governments. This important ruling led to the establishment of regional competition bodies and a Coordination Law (Act 1/2002 of February 21 regarding coordination of state and autonomous communities' powers in the protection of competition), which deals with the allocation of cases between national and regional competition authorities. This process has not yet been completed.

Spanish regulation on vertical restraints – which is identical to the European rules stated in Commission Regulation 2790/99 of December 22, 1999 – was recently introduced by the approval on March 28, 2003, of

Royal Decree 378/2003 related to block exemptions, individual exemptions and the Registry of the protection of Competition. This regulation also incorporates into Spanish law the new Commission Regulations on new motor vehicles, specialization agreements, research and development agreements, and the insurance sector.

o) Sweden

Antitrust law is regulated by the Act on Competition (*Konkurrenslagen* – KL). The *Konkurrensverket* is the competent competition authority, which is responsible for the maintenance of the state of competition in the Swedish Market under KL. As from 2001, the authority may also apply EC competition rules. KL is a blueprint of EC competition law, more or less. The Competition Authority has the same role in Sweden as the Commission traditionally has had under EC law, that is to supervise competition and to make decisions and confer fines where breaches are committed. The Competition Authority, though, cannot decide on fines itself, but has to make a claim before the specially designated courts (Stockholm District Court and the Market Court, the latter also being the court of last instance in cases involving the Marketing Act). Undertakings concerned may make appeals against decisions by the Competition Authority or the District Court.

Besides the administrative procedural structures laid down for the application of KL and the Marketing Act, the acts have private law consequences – triggering the question of private remedies – some of which may only be determined by ordinary courts. When studying solutions to the Cases considered below under Swedish law, one has to be aware of two things. First, under the Swedish constitution all governmental agencies are independent, insofar as the government may not interfere in a particular case (even indirectly) and tell the agency how to solve it. Second, preparatory documents are peculiarly important when interpreting statutes and acts.

2. *A first comparison*

The overview shows that in all reporting countries public enforcement of antitrust law by state authorities clearly prevails. Beside this one also finds everywhere the possibility of private enforcement. However, the lack of practical application contrasts with the legal possibility of private complaints. This is partly due to the absence of incentives. Another reason is the strong position of administrative enforcement. In some countries, private actions are practised only after a successful administrative proceeding. Now and then, this connection even is institutionalized, e.g. in Finland where the private law court first initiates an examination by the cartel authority. The impression is common that the weak position of private enforcement is deplorable. Even national legislatures have occasionally expressed the wish that the importance of private enforcement be strengthened (UK, Germany). Private enforcement might increase as a result of the actions of particularly ruthless cartels. The international vitamin cartel has triggered a large number of private actions, for example.[70] The success of private actions here is made easier by the existence of numerous cartel authority decisions, not only in Europe and the USA.[71] Thus, the vitamin case has virtually paradigmatic significance for private enforcement of competition law. It enables legal rules which have existed until now often only in theory to obtain practical importance.

[70] For private actions in Germany see F. W. Bulst, (2004) NJW 2201; for the English *Provimi* case see F. W. Bulst, *The Provimi Decision of the High Court: Beginnings of Private Antitrust Litigation in Europe*, (2003) 4 EBOR 623.

[71] Damages for developing countries have even been quantified, see S. Evenett, *Study on Issues Relating to a Possible Multilateral Framework on Competition Policy*, WTO-Document WT/WGTCP/W/228 of 19.5.2003 (available at: http://docsonline.wto.org/gen_search.asp), p. 92 et seq.

III. The European context of antitrust law

1. *Legal specifications in European community law*

Within the field of application of the EC treaty the relationship between national law and community law has usually developed as follows: at the beginning national law was untouched by European influences. Then primary legislation, notably the fundamental freedoms, and secondary legislation, particularly harmonization directives, have influenced or even created national law (see above concerning unfair competition law). This description does not apply to antitrust law though. From the beginning, the EEC treaty contained the basic rules of European competition law (arts. 85, 86 EEC treaty of 1957) which, however, apply only to cross-border and not purely domestic restrictions of competition. There have not to date been directives on the harmonization of *national* antitrust law. This leads to the following starting point: for purely domestic transactions the national legislator is free in the shaping of antitrust law. Since European antitrust law is not applicable here, the Member States could theoretically adopt or maintain completely independent rules. For cross-border transactions the primacy of Community law and especially art. 3, para. 2, of the European cartel regulation (Regulation 1/2003) merely provide that national antitrust law may not be applied with a result that contradicts European competition law. An exception applies – according to art. 3, para. 2 s. 2 of Regulation 1/2003 – to unilateral rules of national competition law on unilateral enterprise behaviour: the Member States have the possibility of applying stricter domestic regulations to such behaviour.

2. *Actual influence of community law*

Although there are no genuine harmonization obligations there is a strong actual influence of Community law on national competition law. Different rules for cross-border transactions on the one hand and for purely internal transactions on the other hand lead to unequal treatment, especially in the relationship between large and small and medium enterprises. Such differences are hardly communicable. Therefore there is a heavy pressure on the Member States to bring their national antitrust law into line with European competition law. Some legal orders even explicitly provide that national antitrust law has to be interpreted after the model of European competition law (UK, Italy). In the result, the national cartel codes move toward Community competition law. Only in the area of unilateral enterprise behaviour, stricter rules in national law may be upheld pursuant to art. 3, para. 2 s. 2 of Regulation 1/2003.

3. *Particularly: private remedies*

For private remedies the situation is different. In this area, the *Courage* decision of the ECJ has established the principle of equivalence.[1] Private law actions based on the violation of European competition law must not stay behind what would be awarded due to a violation of national competition law. Here, it is national law having an influence on Community law in so far as the consequences of a violation of Community law are partly guided by national law. The deeper reason for this is the fact that European competition law (with the exception of art. 81, para. 2 EC) stays silent about the private law consequences of a violation of European competition law. Nevertheless, national law is not free in the formulation of private remedies: the ECJ has – in the *Courage* decision – added the principle of 'effectiveness' to the principle of equivalence according to which national law must not render practically impossible or excessively difficult the exercise of rights conferred by Community law.[2] So, for example, the English courts had to change their practice according to which actions for damages based on a competition law violation are excluded from the start for a party which itself participated in the restricting agreement. Damages can be only refused now to participants who carry 'significant responsibility' for the violation of competition law. In legal doctrine the *Courage* decision has led to controversy on the nature of private remedies in the case of a violation of European competition law. Some authors draw a parallel to the liability of Member States according to the principles of the *Francovich* case[3] and classify the action for damages resulting from the violation of European competition law as a claim directly deriving from community law.[4] On the other hand, the predominant opinion holds the traditional

[1] See above note 6. Confirmed by ECJ, 13.7.2006, Joined Cases C-295/04 to C-298/04, Manfredi, n. 62.

[2] ECJ, *Courage* (note 6 above) n. 29. Confirmed by ECJ, 13.7.2006, Joined Cases C-295/04 to C-298/04, Manfredi, n. 62.

[3] ECJ, 19.11.1991, Joined Cases C-6/90 and C-9/90, Francovich/Italy, ECR 1991, I-5357.

[4] See e.g. C. Jones, *Private Enforcement* (note 8 above) p. 152; Keβler (2006) WRP 1061 n. 2.3.1; Komninos, (2002) CMLR 465 et seq.; G. Mäsch, (2003) EuR 825 (841 et seq.). In this sense already the Advocate General W. van Gerven, in ECJ, *Case C-128/92, Banks/British Coal Corporation*, ECR 1994, I-1209, differing W. van Gerven (2000) CMLR 501 (503).

view that such claims are rooted in national law which is simply modified by Community law via the principle of effectiveness.[5] No matter which opinion one shares: up to now the subject of private remedies has not yet been regulated in European secondary law. Uncertainties in the application of private remedies are the consequence. In our conclusions this problem will have to be dealt with (see below part D).

4. *European private law*

Several groups of scholars have been exploring common features of private law in the EU Member States. These groups have different starting points, different methodologies and different goals. The Commission on European Contract Law (Lando Commission) has elaborated the Principles of European Contract Law.[6] Its work was continued by the Study Group on a European Civil Code which has extended the field beyond contract law and tries to cover all substance matters which should be included into a European Civil Code.[7] The European Group on Tort Law (Tilburg Group) has published European Principles on Tort Law similar to the Lando Principles.[8] Contrary to these groups The European Research Group on Existing EC Private Law (Acquis Group) takes a starting point not from national private law but from existing EC law in the field of private law.[9] Many other groups or sub-groups exist. Some of them are, together with the Common Core of European Private Law, part of the 'Network of Excellence' supported by the 6th EU Framework Programme for Research and Technological Development (see A.I. 5 above).[10] It is important to analyse the impact which the results of the other groups on European private law have on the competition law project of the Common Core group. On this basis, it will be possible to determine which conclusions in return can be drawn from the special subject of competition law remedies into the general field of tort law. Thus, mutual inspiration of the different research projects will be tangible. To this end, the most pertinent elements of the other research

[5] T. Lettl (2003) 167 ZHR 476; Weyer (2003) ZEuP 318 (325 et seq.); W. Wurmnest (2003/04) GPR 129 (135). Equally in this sense European Commission, *Notice on the co-operation between the Commission and the courts of the EU Member States in the application of Articles 81 and 82 EC*, OJ 2004 C 101/54, n. 10.

[6] See Part I A. I. 2 above.

[7] See the homepage at http://www.sgecc.net. See also C. von Bar, *The Common European Law of Torts*, Vol. 1 1998, Vol. 2 2000.

[8] See the homepage at http://civil.udg.es/tort.

[9] See the homepage at http://www.acquis-group.org.

[10] See the homepage of the network of excellence at http://www.copecl.org.

projects are briefly highlighted before describing their effect on remedies in competition law.[11]

a) European Group on Tort Law

The principles of European tort law ('Tilburg' principles) contain – besides a basic norm – rules on the concept of damage, causation, fault, strict liability, liability for others, defences, contributory conduct, multiple tortfeasors and remedies.[12] Art. 3:201 provides that the scope of liability depends also on 'the protective purpose of the rule that has been violated'. Regarding the important question of evidence, Art. 2:105 admits that 'the court may estimate the extent of damage where proof of the exact amount would be too difficult or too costly'. According to Art. 10:103 benefits gained 'through the damaging event are to be taken into account unless this cannot be reconciled with the purpose of the benefit'. Normally, damages are a 'money payment to compensate the victim' (Art. 10:101). Restoration in kind can replace damages 'as far as it is possible and not too burdensome to the other party' (Art. 10:104). Normally, only pecuniary damages are compensated. However, depending on the scope of protection, the violation of a certain interest may trigger compensation of non-pecuniary damage (Art. 10:301). This concerns in the first place personal injuries and violations of personality rights. Punitive damages are not part of the Tilburg principles.

b) Acquis Group

The Acquis Group analyses European law having an impact on private law and strives to find common structures of European private law. In this respect there is a similarity to the Common Core of European Private Law project, which does the same for the national legal orders in the EU Member States. The work of the Acquis Group is supposed to lead to common principles of European private law, which aim at facilitating the existing law and to develop it further. Following the European Commission's Action Plan on a more coherent European Contract Law, the Acquis Group at present focuses on contract law. 'Principles of the Existing EC Contract Law' shall be published. The group is part of the Joint Network on European Private Law. It can therefore be expected that the principles elaborated by the Acquis Group will

[11] For a brief discussion of the Tilburg principles and the text of the Study Group see F. Bulst, *Schadensersatzansprüche der Marktgegenseite im Kartellrecht* (2006), p. 354 et seq.

[12] The text of the principles is available at: http://www.egtl.org/principles/pdf/PETL.pdf.

heavily influence the 'Common Principles of European Contract Law' which will be the basis of the 'Common Frame of Reference' (CFR). For the time being, results of the Acquis Group are not yet available.

c) Study Group

The European Civil Code as conceived by the Study Group will contain general rules as well as precise rules on contracts and other juridical acts, on contractual and non-contractual rights and obligations, specific contracts, benevolent intervention, non-contractual liability for damage, unjustified enrichment, transfer of movables, as well as on security rights in movables and trusts. Several parts are already completely drafted, e.g. the tort law of the Code.[13] In our context the following rules are of particular interest:

Any damage which 'is to be regarded as a consequence of that person's conduct' is considered as causal (Art. 4:101 (1)). Contrary to the Tilburg principles the Draft European Civil Code does not start from the idea that damages are in the first place a money payment, but that 'reparation is to reinstate the person suffering the legally relevant damage in the position that person would have been in had the legally relevant damage not occurred' (Art. 6:101(1)). 'Reparation may be in money (compensation) or otherwise, as is most appropriate, having regard to the kind and extent of damage suffered and all the other circumstances of the case' (Art. 6:101 (2)). As far as benefits gained through the damaging event are concerned, the Civil Code reverses the rule of the Tilburg principles: 'Benefits arising to the person suffering legally relevant damage as a result of the damaging event are to be disregarded unless it would be fair and reasonable to take them into account' (Art. 6:103). Non-economic loss may constitute legally relevant damage (Art. 2:101). However, punitive damages are not provided for in the draft code.

There is a special rule defining as legally relevant damage the 'loss caused to a consumer as a result of unfair competition . . . if Community or national law so provides' (Art. 2:208 (2)). This rule is restricted to the violation of unfair competition law. Antitrust law is not covered by this article.

[13] The rules on torts are available at: http://www.sgecc.net/pages/downloads/text_of_articles_final.doc.

d) Common Frame of Reference (CFR)

Up to now, the work undertaken in the CFR has focused on contract law. This corresponds to the history of the CFR resulting from the Commission's Communication on European Contract Law of 2001.[14] The next step was the Action Plan of 2003 proposing the CFR and triggering steps to its elaboration.[15] Of course, the most urgent task of all projects being a part of the Network of Excellence supported by the 6th EU Framework Programme for Research and Technological Development is to participate in the current work which has a priority on contract law, especially on consumer contract law.[16] However, the brief survey has shown that the scientific projects on European Private Law take a more general view. Hence, at the same time, they can participate in the current work, and conceive further steps. As shown in the first part of this book, the unfair competition part of this study has some points of reference to contract law as far as protection of consumers is concerned.[17] However, these points of reference do not exist for the antitrust law part of our study. The survey on national antitrust law has shown that in all reporting countries antitrust legislation is a separate field of law. However, as far as private remedies for violations of antitrust law are concerned, general concepts of tort law apply. Thus, the Common Core movement is preparing future work on a CFR on tort law. Competition law presents problems whose solution is sometimes surprising against the backdrop of general tort law. Some topics shall be mentioned here. They should be taken into account when further developing European tort law.

e) Impact of the Common Core of antitrust law remedies on European Tort Law

The following case studies will show that the existing groups working on European tort law could be more specific on the following

[14] European Commission, *Communication from the Commission to the Council and the European Parliament on European Contract Law*, 11.7.2001, COM(2001) 398 final.

[15] European Commission, *A More Coherent European Contract Law – An Action Plan*, COM(2003) 68 final; European Commission, *European Contract Law and the Revision of the Acquis: the Way Forward*, COM(2004) 651 final of 11.10.2004; European Commission, *First Annual Progress Report on European Contract Law and the Acquis Review*, COM(2005) 456 final of 23.9.2005.

[16] See European Commission, *First Annual Progress Report on European Contract Law and the Acquis Review*, COM(2005) 456 final of 23.9.2005, p. 4.

[17] See Part I A. I. 2 above.

questions: in case of breach of a statutory duty (e.g. of antitrust law, but also of any other legislation), according to which criteria shall the circle of those having standing be determined? Should indirect victims be compensated? Should consumer protection associations be given standing? If a public authority has prohibited certain behaviour as contrary to a particular statute, to what extent are private law courts bound by this administrative decision? Should it be possible to calculate damages on the basis of the violator's profit? Should punitive damages be introduced into European tort structures? Should the infringer be able to invoke the fact that the injured party passed the damage on to the downstream market? Should there be an alleviation of burden of proof in case of complex causal connection of economic factors?

The following studies and their analysis will give answers to these questions for the special field of antitrust law violations. The results obtained could serve as a test instrument for the general projects on tort law. Thus, the Common Core competition law study could be helpful for a future CFR on tort law by filling the gaps and by questioning if the general principles on torts are always appropriate for all fields of application.

5. *The reform of procedures in European competition law*

The procedural rules in European competition law were fundamentally altered with effect from May 1, 2004. Art. 81, para. 3 EC is directly applicable now, the notification and authorization system that was valid before being changed to a system of a legal exception. One of the reasons given in favour of the reform was the desire to promote the decentralized application in the field of competition law by the promotion of private actions.[18] In rendering art. 81, para. 3 EC directly applicable without a previous authority decision, the competence of national courts shall be strengthened. In this context, art. 2 Regulation 1/2003 regulates the burden of proof. Authorities and private plaintiffs have to prove the infringement of articles 81 para. 1 or art. 82 EC whereas the enterprise invoking art. 81 para. 3 EC has to prove the prerequisites of this rule. It is extremely questionable whether the new cartel regulation

[18] M. Monti, *Effective Private Enforcement of EC Antitrust Law*, 1.6.2001, SPEECH/01/258; id., *Private Litigation as a Key Complement to Public Enforcement of Competition Rules*, 17.9.2004, SPEECH/04/403.

really can make a contribution to the strengthening of private remedies, though.[19]

The danger exists that private actions based on art. 81 EC become even more unattractive. In future, the defendant can directly invoke art. 81, para. 3 EC. Even if he has to prove the prerequisites of this exception the risk for the plaintiff is increased.[20] The legislative goals of the new cartel regulation are not very ambitious anyway. As follows from recital 7 of Regulation 1/2003 private actions shall function as 'complement' to the administrative proceedings.[21] So private remedies have – in the view of the European institutions – merely a supplementary function. In contrast, there are voices in legal doctrine which demand the same or even primary importance for private remedies.[22] Before presenting the country reports on the status of private remedies in the Member States it is necessary to inquire why private complaints are so unattractive in Europe, and to develop a perspective. David Gerber does this in the following essay on a comparative basis including the US experience.

[19] Sceptical W. Wils, *The Modernization of the Enforcement of Articles 81 and 82 EC: a Legal and Economic Analysis of the Commission's Proposal for a New Council Regulation Replacing Regulation No.17*, 2000 Fordham Corp. L. Inst. (B. Hawk ed.), note 110.

[20] Under previous law the defendant normally could not invoke art. 81(3) EC. When the restrictive agreement had not been notified to the Commission, the application of art. 81, para. 3 EC was excluded from the outset.

[21] 'The role of the national courts here complements that of the competition authorities of the Member States.'

[22] W.-H. Roth, in: *Frankfurter Kommentar zum Kartellrecht* (2001), § 33 GWB notes 1 et seq.

B. Private enforcement of competition law: a comparative perspective

DAVID J. GERBER

Private enforcement has long been a central part of US antitrust law experience, while it has played minor roles or none at all in European competition law systems. This contrast is fundamental to understanding differences between European and US competition law and to assessing the potential consequences of increasing the role of private enforcement of competition law in Europe. It is also central to decisions about competition law development in much of the world, because in this respect most competition law systems in the world resemble European competition laws rather than US antitrust law.[1]

In this essay, I examine the private enforcement of competition law in the US and Europe against the backdrop of efforts in Europe to rely more heavily on private enforcement in the enforcement of its competition law.[2] As part of its so-called 'modernization' efforts, which went into effect on May 1, 2004, the European Commission seeks to reduce reliance on administrative authorities and to encourage those harmed by restraints on competition to bring private law suits in national courts.[3] There is, however, widespread uncertainty about the prospects

[1] I use the term 'competition law' here to refer to general legal regimes that impose sanctions on conduct because such conduct restrains competition. The term 'antitrust' is often also applied to this type of legal regime, particularly in reference to the competition law of the United States.

[2] Although the Commission's modernization plans call for increased reliance on private enforcement, some question this objective. See, e.g., W. Wils, *Should Private Antitrust Enforcement be Encouraged in Europe?* (2003) 26 World Competition 473.

[3] Council Regulation (EC) No. 1/2003 of December 16, 2002 on the implementation of the rules on competition laid down in articles 81 and 82 of the Treaty [2003] OJ L 1/l. For the early development of this project, see David J. Gerber, *Law and Competition in Twentieth Century Europe: Protecting Prometheus* (1998), p. 392–401.

for successfully incorporating private litigation into European competition law systems. There is also uncertainty about which, if any, measures should be taken to enhance acceptance of private enforcement.[4]

In assessing these issues, a comparative perspective can be of much value. It can provide a basis – perhaps the only sound basis – for making informed decisions. US experience with private enforcement is far more extensive than that of any other country, and thus our focus here will be on that experience and its potential relevance for decisions about private enforcement in Europe. In order for such a comparison to be of value, however, it must go beyond the juxtaposition of rules and institutions and ask what the operational differences between the systems are and how they are likely to affect the operation of private enforcement mechanisms.

While this type of comparative analysis can be of significant value in assessing the situation in Europe, we cannot expect to draw firm predictions or certain prescriptions from it; differences between US and European competition law institutions and experience are too great for that. We can, however, gain insight into both the likely consequences of particular implementation decisions and the kinds of measures, if any, that are likely to be useful in facilitating the development of private enforcement in Europe.

A central claim of this essay is that private enforcement of competition law is more than merely a specific way of enforcing competition law. It engenders, and is interwoven with, distinct patterns of thought, institutional relationships, styles of argumentation, distributions of power and social and economic structures. Understanding this imbeddedness is thus critical to assessing the potential impact of private enforcement on the development of competition law in Europe.[5]

The essay is part of the introductory material to a book on private enforcement issues in Europe that includes a series of national reports. As such, it is intended to provide a frame of reference for those reports –

[4] For extended discussion of these issues, see, e.g., C.D. Ehlermann and I. Atanasiu (eds.), *European Competition Law Annual 2001: Effective Private Enforcement of EC Antitrust Law* (2003); Clifford A. Jones, *Private Enforcement of Antitrust Law in the EU, UK and USA* (1999); W. Wils, *The Optimal Enforcement of EC Antitrust Law: Essays in Law and Economics* (2002).

[5] This essay focuses on issues relevant to the introduction of private enforcement into European competition law systems, but its potential relevance is far broader. As noted above, competition law systems around the world tend to be closer to the European 'model' in this regard than they are to the US system, and thus much of the analysis here is applicable also to those systems.

a means of relating them to each other and to competition law experience in the US.

The comparison has three components. The first focuses on US experience with private enforcement. I look at how private enforcement was introduced there, what roles it has played, and what factors have contributed to its continued prominence. I then turn to European competition law experience, highlighting the role and significance of administrative decision making in European competition law experience. The reliance on administrative direction of competition law has created a set of assumptions and institutional arrangements relating to competition law that differ significantly from those that have been generated in the US. The third part analyses the differences between these two experiences and assesses the relevance of European competition law systems and the lessons (or lack thereof) that US experience provides for pursuing the goal of increased private enforcement in Europe.

I. Private enforcement in US antitrust law

Private enforcement has been an integral part of US antitrust law experience since the enactment of the first antitrust law statute in 1890.[1] It has long been seen as a natural and even indispensable means of enforcing antitrust law. It has also shaped the operations of the system, the development of the substantive law, and the attitudes, capacities and roles of the individuals who participate in the system.

1. *From the beginning: neither choice, nor issue*

The decision to make private enforcement a key component of US antitrust law was not made in the context of a careful choice among alternatives. When the Sherman Act was enacted,[2] private enforcement was merely assumed to be a primary means of enforcing the statute. The legislation was understood as a tool for increasing the enforcement of existing common law principles by creating administrative support and by generating access to the federal courts for private litigants. It 'codified' existing case law and gave the federal government and the federal courts authority to apply those substantive principles.[3] The decision was not based on a careful study of alternatives, because no alternatives were apparent. There were no comparable systems in the world, and thus there was no foreign experience to evaluate. From the beginning, therefore, there has been little perceived need to justify or examine private law enforcement. Few have even called into question its predominant role in the system.[4]

2. *Private enforcement in the evolution of the US antitrust system*

The basic institutional structure of the US antitrust system has changed little since its inception.[5] The same vaguely worded statute (the

[1] This essay refers exclusively to enforcement of the federal antitrust laws. This is by far the most important area of experience with private enforcement, although there is occasional litigation involving enforcement of state antitrust laws.

[2] 15 U.S.C. §1 (2001).

[3] 'Codification' in US legal terminology refers to the act of legislation, and does not imply the creation or development of 'codes' as known in civil law systems.

[4] This does not mean, of course, that there have not been discussions on occasion about its value, but the issue of eliminating private enforcement has not been seriously considered.

[5] For leading discussions of the development of US antitrust laws, see H. Hovenkamp and G. Hosking, *Enterprise and American Law*, 1836–1937 (1991); W. Kovacic and C. Shapiro, *Antitrust Policy: A Century of Economic and Legal Thinking*, (2000) 14 J. Econ. Perspectives 43;

Sherman Act) is still its main text, and private enforcement has remained an important part of the system throughout its development. Private antitrust actions have not always been numerous, but they have generally been a serious option, and at times they have played more prominent roles than has public enforcement.

Specific elements, doctrines, and institutions of the system have evolved, however, and some of those changes are important for assessing the current role of private enforcement. We can identify three phases in this development. Private enforcement has played a role in each, but its roles and impact have varied over time.

During the first phase of development, which lasted until the Second World War, the role of antitrust law was often uncertain. At times there was significant debate about its effectiveness, and the courts often wrestled with the application of its vague statutory provisions. Both public and private forms of enforcement were episodic. There were periods during which the courts seemed hospitable to antitrust suits, and this usually led to increased litigation, but there were other periods during which there was little litigation, private or public. On several occasions there was increased political force behind public enforcement, leading administrative authorities to 'push' the courts and to encourage private litigation. Towards the end of the New Deal in the 1930s there were renewed efforts to reinvigorate antitrust law enforcement, but it was not until after the Second World War that the role and significance of the antitrust system expanded rapidly.

The second phase, which lasted for some three decades after the close of the Second World War, saw antitrust achieve exceptional levels of influence and importance. During this period, there was some new auxiliary legislation, but the primary factors in the expanded role of antitrust were the willingness of courts to expand interpretations of existing statutes and the willingness of law enforcement personnel to pursue such developments. These developments reflected shifting social and political values as well as an international situation which deterred investment in US market and encouraged US business firms to expand their activities internationally. With the domestic market largely protected from foreign economic pressures and international competition, antitrust laws were seen as a means of responding to the growing size and power of US domestic corporations.

W. Letwin, *Law and Economic Policy in America: the Evolution of the Sherman Antitrust Act* (1981); R. Peritz, *Competition Policy in America*, 1888–1992 (1996).

Increased judicial support for antitrust doctrines led to both increased public enforcement efforts and increased incentives for private litigation. The two were related: the likelihood of success in the courts encouraged greater public enforcement efforts, and increased public successes, in turn, combined with greater publicity and the perceived importance of antitrust law to induce more private litigation. As a result of these factors, antitrust law became a major factor in much business decision making. By the late 1960s, it seemed to some that plaintiffs seldom lost antitrust litigation.

In the 1970s, however, economic and political conditions in the US and in the world changed rapidly. As the US economy was exposed to increased international competition, judges and enforcement officials became more willing to assume that the competitive forces of the market would deter anti-competitive conduct and more reluctant to 'interfere' with the operation of US enterprises by imposing on them conduct obligations that many of their competitors did not face in other markets.

This change in perspective was associated with a radical reorientation of antitrust thinking that is often called the law and economics 'revolution'.[6] It was initially generated by a group of legal academics who sought to base antitrust doctrine on a particular form of economic analysis known as price theory.[7] They scrutinized the case law of the immediately preceding period and attacked it for its lack of rigour in economic analysis. This perspective quickly gained favour within US antitrust law. It was ideologically consistent with the laissez-faire ideology of Ronald Reagan, and, as a result, it became the framework for public enforcement. Moreover, it was congenial to many of the federal judges that President Reagan appointed.

As a result, the law and economics approach to antitrust law began to reshape the meaning of the antitrust laws, replacing the prevailing mixture of case law analysis and social and political values with analytical tools based on a specific set of economic principles. This set of ideas came to dominate antitrust thinking during the 1980s and remains a form of orthodoxy. For private enforcement, it has meant significantly

6 See R.A. Posner, *Economic Analysis of Law* (5th edn 1998). For discussion of this transition, see E.M. Fox and L.A. Sullivan, *Antitrust – Retrospective and Prospective: Where are we coming from? Where are we going?* (1987) 62 N.Y.U.L. Rev. 936.

7 For comparison of competition law thought and scholarship in the US and Europe, see D.J. Gerber, *Competition*, in *Oxford Handbook of Legal Studies* 510 (2003).

more obstacles to winning private antitrust suits and thus significantly less litigation.

3. *Operational features of the US antitrust systems*

In the US antitrust system, private enforcement has several features that are important for assessing its operation. Some are specific to antitrust law, while others are provided by the general procedural system that must be used in antitrust enforcement.

One is the concept of a 'private attorney general'. In general usage, the term 'attorney general' refers to the public prosecutor – i.e., the person who decides whether a criminal case should be submitted to the courts. Here, however, it refers to the use of private litigation as a means of bringing potential violations into courts and therefore assisting public authorities in their enforcement role. In this context, the private plaintiff plays a public role: she is cast as a surrogate for the government. In the US, public enforcement has long been assumed to be inadequate to achieve effective enforcement, and thus private litigation is used as a means of public enforcement. By giving private litigants incentives to bring civil suits, it is thought, government can more efficiently and effectively achieve compliance with the antitrust laws. The most important of these incentives is the availability of treble (i.e., triple) damages for violations of the antitrust laws. Where a plaintiff is successful in a law suit for compensation, the compensation awarded may be increased to three times the actual amount of harm caused by the antitrust law violation. This provision was part of the original Sherman Act and was specifically included as an incentive to private suits and an antidote to excessive reliance on public enforcement.

In addition to provisions such as this that are specifically aimed at encouraging private litigation, the general procedural rules of the US system contain other features that have the same effect. One is 'punitive damages' (or 'penalty' damages). In considering the amount of compensation to be awarded by a court for harm caused by a violation of the law, judges (and juries, where they are present) are often entitled to increase the compensation beyond the amount of harm caused in order to punish the offender and deter similar conduct in the future. Another potential incentive is provided by the US discovery system. Under that system, litigants in private litigation acquire extensive rights to request and, often, to compel the 'production' (or presentation) of information from other parties and sometimes even from others who are not parties to the litigation. Private litigation in the US federal courts requires litigants to make available to opposing litigants all information requested by them that can reasonably be expected to lead to evidence that is 'admissible' (i.e., that can be presented in court). This often enables litigants to acquire large amounts of information which they can use in the litigation itself, but which they can also use for other strategic purposes.

4. *Contexts of private enforcement*

The effectiveness of private enforcement depends on many factors other than the legal provisions relating to the private enforcement mechanism itself. It cannot be meaningfully assessed without taking into account its relationship to the rest of the system, because the context in which it operates shapes its operations and conditions its role.

Private enforcement is only one means of enforcement, and thus its relationship to other means of enforcement is central to its operation. In the US system, two agencies of the Federal government are authorized to enforce the competition laws. One is the United States Justice Department, which is part of the executive branch of government and subject, therefore, to political control. The Justice Department must operate through the courts. This means that it cannot issue enforce orders directly, but must bring a lawsuit in the regular courts to effectuate its enforcement objectives. Moreover, when it pursues litigation in court, it is basically subject to the general procedures of the courts. It may bring either civil or criminal actions, depending on the gravity of the conduct and other factors such as the intent of the defendants. The other enforcement agency is the Federal Trade Commission. It operates as an independent agency, but it depends for funding on Congress, and it is thus subject to political pressures. In some eras, it has played significant roles in antitrust enforcement; in others, its role has been marginal. It may issue orders directly to private decision makers, but its orders are reviewable by the regular courts.

Private enforcement operates parallel to these administrative enforcement mechanisms, applying the same substantive legal principles, using the same court system and, to a large extent, the same procedural rules and institutions. The private enforcement mechanism thus interacts with public enforcement at many points. Where public agencies decide not to pursue certain categories of cases, for example, this often tends to reduce the perceived importance of the claims. This often tends, in turn, to reduce judicial receptiveness to such claims and to deter potential private enforcement litigation.

The structure and characteristics of the legal profession are another important factor in the operation of the private enforcement mechanism. Private enforcement can be effective only if there are significant numbers of private legal professionals who are willing and able to pursue these claims aggressively. The organization, political position, and professional characteristics of private legal professionals – i.e. 'lawyers' – influence the opportunities for private litigation that are available within the system and the incentives for utilizing those opportunities. In the US, this group of legal professionals is large and politically powerful. It is organized in ways that encourage litigation generally and that also facilitate expensive private litigation. This includes, for example, common use of contingent fees in antitrust litigation,[8] employment of large numbers of 'associate' attorneys (junior lawyers) who can work in large teams and can be readily mobilized for large group efforts and 'paralegals' (employees who have minimal legal training, but who are permitted to perform certain kinds of data gathering and other tasks). Aggressive litigation techniques are also part of the culture of the profession.

Finally, the societal context plays a role. In the US, litigation is common and culturally approved, particularly among and between businesses, and high fees for litigation are generally accepted. Moreover, competition as a process is highly valued. It is a cultural symbol with significant political support and attraction. Not surprisingly, therefore, there is a long tradition of antitrust litigation.

5. *The impact of private enforcement on system operations*

Just as the systemic context influences the operation of private enforcement mechanisms, so private enforcement influences other elements of the system. Because private enforcement is deeply imbedded in the US system, there is no reliable way to specify cause-effect relationships here, but we can identify associations and interrelationships between private enforcement and other elements of the system.

Private enforcement has perhaps its most direct effect on public enforcement. Where private antitrust litigation is common, as in the

[8] Contingent fees (often known in civil law systems under the rubric *pacta de quota litis*) provide that attorneys for the plaintiff will receive a percentage of the amount, if any, recovered in the litigation. If the plaintiff loses, the lawyer receives no compensation.

US, the capacity of public officials to influence the development of the antitrust system is limited. Public institutions in the US can influence the direction of law in specific areas, but private litigation decisions are driven by private considerations and depend on private assessments of the potential value of litigation in relation to its costs. This may have little or nothing to do with the strategies of public enforcement officials, and thus efforts by public officials to develop particular types of arguments or focus on particular types of cases are less important than in systems where the only competition law enforcement efforts are those of an administrative body and, perhaps, a reviewing court.

This also means that the regular courts tend to a play a role in the development and operation of the system that is more central than it is in systems where courts merely review administrative decisions. In the US, the courts do not play the limited role of constraining competition authorities. They are instead the centre of the system – the arbiters of what the law is and the primary factors in determining the development of the law. Court decisions and the case law interactions among courts are the reference point for both public enforcers and private lawyers in making competition law decisions.

Not only are courts more important in the US system, but so are private attorneys. Their initiative and advice determine whether private litigation takes place, and thus they channel the flow of litigation. They also determine the strategies and arguments that are used in litigation, and thus they influence the terms of discussion and play a major role in influencing substantive law development. The potential for earning significant fees provides powerful incentives for private attorneys to learn about antitrust law and to pursue private grievances in the courts.

This structure of institutions and incentives means that the goals and concepts of competition law tend to be loosely defined. Since no competition authority directs the development of the law, and many courts may be involved, there are many voices involved in articulating goals and defining concepts. In the US system at least, this has led to frequent uncertainty about the goals of competition law and, often, little coherence and consistency in the definition and development of concepts.

The prominence of private enforcement also has a significant impact on awareness and perceptions of antitrust law and on attitudes toward it. It tends to heighten awareness of the antitrust laws not only among lawyers and business leaders, but also within the general public. Litigation in which business firms are pitted against each other also tends to make interesting reading and to be reported in the general press, especially where large sums of money or well-known businesses are involved. This awareness, in turn, increases the likelihood that potential private litigants will at least consider the possibility of private litigation. Depending on the content of the media exposure, however, it may lead to more or less confidence in predictions of the costs and benefits of private litigation.

6. *Private enforcement and the US antitrust system*

This brief overview of private enforcement in the US antitrust system reveals a component of the system that has been part of it from the beginning and that is accepted as a normal, effective, indeed almost indispensable part of that system. There is little need to justify it, and it is supported by many of the basic assumptions and institutions of the legal system and the society in which it operates.

II. Competition law in Europe: administrative centrality

Competition law is enforced very differently in Europe. There, competition law has developed primarily as an administrative, public law issue. Private enforcement has played only marginal roles, and only in a few systems. In this section we look at that very different experience and the competition law dynamics that it has created.[1]

1. *National experience*

In Europe, competition law was originally conceived as an administrative tool, a means for the state to intervene in market processes in order to achieve public goals. These ideas were first articulated in the 1890s in Vienna, where a group of administrators and scholars who were part of a small educational elite began to explore the idea of using law to protect the process of competition. Imbued with the values of classical liberalism and aware of the new theoretical developments in understanding the economic process that were emanating from the Austrian school of marginal utility economics, they began to investigate whether the two strands of classical liberalism (economic freedom as a value and law as a protector of rights) could be used together.[2]

The proposal that emanated from this project understood competition law as a means by which bureaucrats could intervene to reduce harms to competition (and perhaps enhance their own influence). This approach had two important advantages for the administrative elite: it gave them influence, and it could be implemented with minimal cost – either economic or political. Moreover, there was no obvious alternative to this approach. There was no pre-existing set of substantive principles that could be merely applied by courts, as was the case in the US.[3] The proposal almost became law in Austria, but in the end it was the victim of the political disruptions of the late 1890s.

The basic ideas were further developed, however, in Germany. They there attracted support from social democratic leaders and representatives of small and medium-sized enterprises, who saw competition law

[1] This section is based primarily on my detailed study of the development of competition law in Europe. See D. J. Gerber, *Law and Competition* (note 3 above).

[2] I recount this development in detail in D. J. Gerber, *The Origins of the European Competition Law Tradition in Fin-de-Siecle Austria* (1992) 36 Am. J. Leg. Hist. 405, and in D. J. Gerber, *Law and Competition* (note 3 above), at 43–68.

[3] There were Roman law provisions that formed part of the *jus commune*, but they were not considered relevant. See D. J. Gerber (note 3 above), at 34–7.

as a means of protecting their interests against the power of large industrial firms and cartels. Not until after the First World War, however, was a competition law enacted. In the midst of the battle against hyper-inflation in 1923, legislation was introduced that followed the administrative model. Although enforced with limited effect, it received attention in other parts of Europe. By the late 1920s this administrative model was being widely discussed in Europe, and additional statutes based on it were enacted.[4]

After the Great Depression and the Second World War, this model again began to spread. Throughout Europe, there was an effort to find new economic and political forms that would generate wealth and jobs and, at least as importantly, avoid the catastrophes of the first half of the century. Competition law ideas were sometimes included in those plans, but there was seldom strong political support for them, and the statutes that were enacted often remained without significant implementation.

In Germany, however, a new element was added that led to a temporary divergence between German developments and those in other European systems.[5] The German path was heavily influenced by what was originally an 'underground' intellectual movement during the Nazi period called ordoliberalism (or the 'Freiburg school' of law and economics). During the 1930s a group of lawyers and economists began to explore systematically the possibility of using law to protect the process of competition and thus prevent both the debacle of the Weimar period – too little control of economic power – and the calamity of Nazism – too much control of social life by the state. They sought a means of protecting economic liberty and competition from both the state and private accumulations of power. The result was a highly refined conception of how law could be used to accomplish those objectives, and competition law was at its centre.

The central idea was that a polity's choice of an economic order should be understood as an 'economic constitution'. They advocated an order based on competition and economic freedom and argued that legal processes should be used to protect this economic constitution in essentially the same ways that law is used to protect the political constitution. Accordingly, decisions relating to the economic constitution

[4] For discussion, see ibid. at 153–162.

[5] For discussion, see D. J. Gerber, *Constitutionalizing the Economy: German Neo-liberalism, Competition Law and the 'New Europe'* (1994) 41 Am. J. Comp. L. 25.

should be made according to judicial procedures! They should represent legal principles and be applied according to legal methods. Competition law was seen as the central tool for protecting this economic constitution, and thus it was to be implemented by the application of juridical principles rather than pursuant to administrative discretion.

In 1957, Germany enacted the first 'modern' competition law in Europe, the Law against Restraints of Competition (GWB).[6] Although modified several times since then, its basic principles remain in effect. While relying primarily on administrative mechanisms to enforce competition law principles, the German system is understood as an essentially 'juridical' system in the sense that decisions are generally to be made according to well-developed judicial methods and procedures. The Federal Cartel Office (FCO) is the central institution in the system, but the statute also provides for review by the regular courts of FCO decisions. As modified, it also allows for private enforcement in certain kinds of cases.

In the rest of Europe, competition law remained almost exclusively 'administrative' for several decades after the Second World War, with no private suits and minimal involvement by the regular courts. The decisions of administrators were typically subject to legal control only for violation of administrative law principles.

As these systems have developed in importance, however, they have often modified their reliance on administrative decision making. Governments have increasingly restructured competition law decision-making, moving from almost total reliance on administrative discretion and policy judgment to a more central role for the methodologically grounded application of legal principles. Accordingly, for example, administrative decision making has been subjected to increasingly extensive review by courts. At the same time, administrators have been given increasingly powerful tools for combating competitive restraints.

2. *Competition law in the European Union*

A key factor in this move toward a more 'juridical' conception of competition law has been the process of European unification and the development of a highly sophisticated competition law within the European Union. The Rome Treaty that created the European

[6] *Gesetz gegen Wettbewerbsbeschränkungen*, 1957 Bundesgesetzblatt [BGBl] I 1081 (July 27, 1957).

Economic Community in 1957 contained basic provisions concerning the protection of competition, and these were gradually developed into a system in which both administrative and judicial decision making play important roles.[7]

This development has frequently reflected significant German influence, particularly in its early years. Germany developed competition law earlier than other European systems, and German competition law has been consistently considered the best developed and most effectively enforced system in Europe. As a result, European Union developments have often drawn on German experience. Perhaps the most important element of that influence has been emphasis on a juridical conception of competition law rather than a merely administrative one.

From the early years of the evolution of the European Community, competition law has been a central component of its legal system. It has been used to break down barriers to trade and establish the conditions for positive economic development. The European Commission and the European Court of Justice have often used it to move the process of integration forward, especially during periods when the political impetus was weak. Although the Community competition law system contains strong administrative elements, it is imbedded in a juridical framework in which the two European Community courts play a central role.

EU competition law has been enforced almost exclusively by the European Commission. In interpreting and applying the European treaties and the secondary legislation of the European Union, the Commission can order the imposition of fines and prohibit cartels and other conduct such as mergers. The two European courts can review Commission actions to determine whether they are in conformity with the treaty and whether proper procedures have been followed.

Throughout this development private enforcement action has been non-existent or marginal. Originally, it was not even available under EU law. In the 1970s, legal barriers to private actions within European community law were removed, but such actions have remained rare. In the 1990s, the Commission took steps to encourage private enforcement, but they have had little effect. Those who consider themselves harmed by anti-competitive conduct continue to prefer to appeal to public enforcement authorities and to avoid filing private actions.

[7] For discussion, see Gerber, *Law and Competition in Twentieth Century Europe* (note 3 above), at 334–391.

The so-called 'modernization' of EU competition law will change this system in fundamental ways. According to plans adopted in December 2002, and in effect since May 2004, national competition authorities and national courts will become the primary mechanisms for enforcing EU competition law. These reforms were designed to respond to the enlargement of the EU from fifteen to twenty-five members by reducing reliance on the Commission and increasing the role of private enforcement actions in local courts. They are the primary impetus for the widespread interest in private enforcement in Europe today.

3. *Administrative centrality and its implications*

This brief sketch of competition law in Europe reveals a system that has relied almost exclusively on public initiative and public decision making throughout its development. At both the national and European levels, competition authorities apply competition laws and control the development of the law. Private initiative and private enforcement play minimal roles at best. It has been alien to European competition law experience – in both practice and theory.

This shapes the operation of European competition law systems in many ways. For example, it structures the roles of competition authorities and their relationships with courts, the public and private legal practitioners. It means that those authorities have extensive power to control the development of the law in the area, subject only to the often limited constraints that reviewing courts may impose. Because of the lack of private enforcement opportunities, the competition authorities can focus attention on particular types of conduct and particular lines of argument. In effect, they can set the agenda for competition law. Assuming adequate political support, this in itself ensures that those authorities are in a powerful position when dealing with business entities.

In this situation, relationships with the courts tend to be narrow – in both scope and substance.[8] They tend to be narrow in substance, because the courts can only approve or disapprove of the competition authority's decisions. They do not have a variety of opportunities and levels on which they can influence competition law outcomes and development. Its scope is narrow, because the relationship is typically

[8] For discussion of recent issues in this relationship, see D. J. Gerber, *Courts as Economic Experts in European Merger Law*, in 2003 Fordham Corporate Law Institute (2004), p. 475 et seq.

limited to one agency and one or two appellate courts. In practice, it is even narrower, because it usually involves only a few judges who sit in the competition law chambers of the reviewing courts. This means that there is little awareness of competition law issues among most judges. The narrowness of the relationship focuses the attention of administrators, business leaders and, often, politicians on those few judges. This can facilitate the development of sound knowledge of competition law among these few judges, but it also has other types of effects. In some systems, for example, it may encourage efforts by politicians to control the competition authority by influencing the reviewing judges. It can also create a competitive relationship between the few judges involved and the leaders of the competition authority that may lead to decisions that are influenced by personal considerations.

This means, in turn, that private competition lawyers in these systems are defence lawyers and advisors, not plaintiffs' lawyers, as they frequently are in the US. Where there is no tradition or practice of commencing litigation against other firms for competition law violations, the mentality of lawyers centres on defence, in general, and defence against the decisions of a small number of officials in the competition authority. It means that the focus of lawyers is on predicting what the competition authority will do and developing means of influencing its decisions. Lawyers tend to pay far less attention to courts than is the case in the US, because the courts typically play a far more peripheral role in enforcement. At an even more fundamental level, administrative centrality shapes images of competition law – not only among judges, lawyers and administrators, but also among business decision makers and the general public. Competition law tends to be seen as government regulation. It is usually taught in law faculties as part of administrative law and conceptualized and enforced as part of administrative law. It is not a tool in the hands of businesses, but part of the administrative apparatus. As such, it is sometimes met with the resistance and even hostility that in some countries is directed toward government regulation generally.

III. Incorporating private enforcement into European competition law: comparative perspectives

A comparison of US competition law and experience with European competition law and experience allows us to identify some of the effects that introducing and/or expanding private enforcement in Europe are likely to have. It also helps to identify factors that might influence the prospects for increased reliance on private enforcement in Europe.

The process of incorporating private enforcement into European competition law systems involves the introduction of an alien element into those systems. Many factors will determine the extent to which the newly created opportunities for private enforcement will actually be used and how rapidly any increase in usage will occur. For purposes of the following comments, I will assume that private enforcement of EU competition law will increase significantly as a result of the modernization reforms. Significant increases may, however, take several years – perhaps a decade or more.

1. *Public enforcement*

The most direct impact is likely to be on public enforcement. European competition law systems have relied primarily on administrative decision-making since their inceptions. Government officials have played the central role in those systems, and administrative decision making and initiative have shaped their operation and evolution. A significant role for private enforcement is likely to have profound effects on this administrative orientation. It will mean that administrators no longer control the operation and development of competition law. Private law suits will be filed in pursuit of private interests, and these will not necessarily coincide with the public (or private) interests of administrators. Private lawyers will decide what kinds of arguments to make in these cases – with little or no regard to the arguments that administrators would have made. And courts that make decisions in these cases will influence legal development and effectiveness as much or more than administrators.

This will diminish the status of administrators, at least in some ways and in some contexts. The centrality of administrative decision making gives status to those who make administrative decisions, and eliminating or reducing administrative centrality will diminish that status accordingly. Assuming all other factors remain constant, this is likely, in turn, to make it more difficult to attract and maintain top-level administrators. To the extent that administrators increasingly think of their roles as preparation for careers outside competition law agencies, this also affects their incentives, and it may influence their decisions.

Other factors will, of course, condition the impact of this reduction in status. Administrative law traditions and operations differ significantly between the United States and Europe as well as within Europe, and thus generalization is dangerous. For example, the status of administrators in many countries in Europe tends to be significantly higher than their status in the US, and this may tend to counteract the potential effects of increased privatization.

Finally, the reduced control of competition law by administrators may influence the roles that competition authorities play. For example, in Europe such authorities have often played constructive and educational roles rather than merely enforcement roles. They have viewed the construction of markets and the education of business decision makers and consumers as important tasks, whereas this type of activity has generally been comparatively secondary in the US. To the extent that a significant role for private enforcement reduces the status of administrators and diminishes their control over the competition law agenda, it may impede both the incentives for administrators to play these roles and their capacity to perform them effectively. Where the voice of administrators within a competition law system is not the single or at least dominant voice, businesses have less incentive to follow the 'advice' of administrators and to value cooperative efforts with those administrators.

2. *Judges*

Increased private enforcement may also alter the role of judges in competition law systems. As noted above, in an administrative model, few judges deal with competition law issues, and their roles are typically limited. In the context of widespread private enforcement, however, many judges will be required to deal with competition law issues, and their roles will be more complex. They will not only have to review the decisions of an administrative agency, but they will also have to resolve private conflicts in which large sums of money are often involved. This will increase public and political attention to those courts and heighten pressures on them.

Moreover, courts are likely to become more important relative to administrative authorities. They tend to become the common reference points for the operation of the system. All – administrators as well as private attorneys and business decision makers – will increasingly focus on court decisions rather than administrative decisions in assessing their legal positions. This may not always mean increased status for judges, however, because many judges may be inadequately trained to deal competently with competition law cases, and thus a greater role in the system may lead to conflict and controversy over the training of judges.

3. *Private practitioners*

The roles of private practitioners and company advisers are also likely to change. At the very least, the possibility of private litigation adds a new dimension to those roles. Assessment of antitrust risk becomes more complex. No longer is it solely or even principally a matter of predicting what a competition authority is likely to do. Instead it requires assessing the likelihood of suit by competitors, suppliers, purchasers and others, and it requires attention to new issues of jurisdiction, evidence production, and tactical planning. Moreover, private practitioners will become plaintiffs' attorneys as well as defence attorneys. They will have to consider whether to advise clients to pursue private claims and assess the implications that such litigation will have on current practices such as hiring new legal professionals and billing clients.

4. *Goals and concepts*

The goals and concepts of competition law are likely to become both less clear and less coherent. Private enforcement changes the 'voice' of competition law. Rather than having one administrative office and, perhaps, one or two courts using concepts and articulating and interpreting goals and norms, private enforcement is likely to mean that many voices will use concepts and participate in the process of defining the goals of the system. This is likely to lead to less consistency in conceptual usage and less clarity in the articulation of goals.

5. *Perceptions and attitudes*

Finally, perceptions and attitudes among businesses and consumers are also likely to change. The possibility that competition law can be useful to many businesses as well as to consumers and consumer groups creates incentives for them to learn more about it. This, in turn, also means that the potential sources of legal challenges increase, and the need to engage in compliance and other defensive strategies to reduce the risk of legal challenge grows. Clients need to be made aware of these expanded possibilities. In general, awareness of competition law norms and procedures is likely to increase accordingly. As private enforcement increases, competition law will increasingly be seen as a tool for private interests as well as a public legal regime. Private enforcement contributes to the perception that competition law is an accessible, useful part of the legal system. For better or worse, it will no longer just represent state 'regulation'.

IV. Concluding comments

As we have seen, private enforcement of competition law is largely alien to European competition law experience and to current European competition law systems. This has two important consequences for efforts to expand its role. First, it means that there is likely to be systemic resistance to such efforts. Institutional interests, patterns of thought, and the expectations of both public and private decision makers may, for example, create obstacles to the success of private enforcement efforts. Second, as with the introduction of any alien element into any system, it is likely to create new and unforeseen conflicts with existing ways of operating.

Where decision makers understand the relationship between private enforcement mechanisms and the current system and also recognize the potential obstacles that differences between them can create for private enforcement, they can take steps to deal with those obstacles. Moreover, the sooner they anticipate the kinds of consequences that private enforcement can have on the current system, the greater the likelihood that they can adjust the two enforcement mechanisms to function effectively together.

US experience can be of value in identifying the factors that are likely to influence the development of private enforcement mechanisms within Europe and the consequences those developments will have on the operation of European competition law systems. The value of US experience for these purposes depends, however, on effective comparison of US experience with its European analogues. As we have seen, effective comparison cannot be limited to discussion of rules and cases, but must view private enforcement as a specific mode of operation that involves institutions, power relationships and ways of thinking. Where this comparison is careful and informed, its value can be great. To the extent that it is superficial and haphazard, it will be at best valueless and at worse misleading and harmful.

Private enforcement of competition law in Europe is likely to develop along lines that are in some ways quite different from US experience. The institutions that have now acquired status within European competition law systems will continue to operate, and the ways of thinking, valuing and operating that have developed over the last half century will continue to have influence. The development of private enforcement is likely to depend in large part on careful adaptation to this European environment. Moreover, policy decisions relating to private enforcement are likely to be most effective if they take into account the relationship between the unique features of private enforcement and existing elements of competition law systems.

C. Case studies

I. Objects of claim

Case 9 Predatory price undercutting agreements – forbearance (cease-and-desist order)

A, B and C all operate gas stations in town X. D opens a new gas station in X in which petrol is cheaper than A, B and C sell it. To protect themselves against the new competition, A, B and C agree to regularly undercut D's price so as to make him close down his gas station. Thus, D is brought to the point of ruin.

1. Can D claim to compel A, B and C to refrain from price undercutting?
2. Does D's claim require that an (antitrust) authority be engaged against the conduct of A, B and C?
3. Can the claim for an injunction also be pursued by an association? If yes, which associations are entitled to take legal action?
4. Does the conduct of A, B and C constitute an administrative or criminal offence? If yes, who is competent to prosecute the offence, what powers of investigation are there, and what sanctions can be applied?

Austria (9)

(1) The case is one of predatory pricing by collectively dominant enterprises. On the basis of their agreement A, B and C exercise virtually total control over the local gas market in town X, or at any rate have a market share of at least 30 per cent (§ 34 para. 1 a n. 1 KartG 1988 = § 4 para. 2 n. 1 KartG 2005), so that market dominance is presumed under Austrian law.[1] Trade between Member States does not seem to be affected because the agreement has only an effect on a local market that has the size of a town. Anyway, the legal situation according to Austrian cartel law is the same as in European competition law. § 35 KartG 1988

[1] See OGH 9.10.2000, ÖBl 2001, 133 – subscription prices.

(= § 5 KartG 2005) and art. 82 EC Treaty prohibit a market dominant enterprise, or collective of several dominant enterprises, from intentionally suppressing a competitor and strengthening its position in that it employs methods other than those of competitive performance. The classic case of unfair competition is targeted predatory pricing (undercutting) with the aim of suppressing competitors. Abusive predatory pricing is given in principle if the market-dominant enterprise or, as here, enterprises which control the local market due to their agreement to offer their products at prices below their own average variable costs (costs which vary according to production levels). An abuse is also given if the prices are under average total costs (fixed plus variable costs) but above average variable costs. In this case, price fixing must be practised against the background of an overall strategy aimed ultimately at suppressing the competitor.[2]

If the abuse is not directed against enterprises on the other side of the market (suppliers, clients), but is directed against competitors, there may be in addition claims under § 1 UWG (possibly in connection with § 35 KartG 1988 = § 5 para. 1 KartG 2005). Predatory pricing can then be prosecuted under § 1 UWG together with § 35 KartG 1988 (now § 5 para. 1 KartG 2005) provided there is a competitive relationship[3] (as in the given scenario) between the market-abusing enterprise and the affected enterprise. Further, in the absence of market dominance, predatory pricing can be unconscionable (*sittenwidrig*) pursuant to § 1 UWG if it is thereby intended to harm competitors without regard to own losses incurred, or to expel them from the market so as to gain a free field for increased profits or to later dictate prices or, should that not be practicable, so that the level of competition is endangered through the suppression of competitors.[4]

Thus, D may require A, B and C to cease the unconscionable price fixing in contentious proceedings relying on § 1 UWG. He may file the action in the form of an injunction claim pursuant to § 24 UWG (see Case 1). If the defendants are at fault, which in the case of predatory pricing is most probable, D can as well claim damages pursuant to § 1 UWG because of 'immoral' breach of law – independently of the

[2] OGH as supreme cartel court 18.6.1998, SZ 71/103 – Power-Pack III; OGH 9.10.2000, ÖBl 2001, 135 – subscription prices; OGH 16.12.2002, 16 Ok 11/02 – Red Bull.

[3] OGH 9.9.1997, ÖBl 1998, 36 – 'Film hire'; OGH 17.3.1998, ÖBl 1998, 256 – 'Service voucher'.

[4] OGH 10.7.2001, ÖBl 2002, 127 – 'Best offer'.

existence of the abuse of market power - and pursuant to § 35 KartG (now § 5 para. 1 KartG 2005).

In the antitrust proceeding, which is a non-contentious proceeding in Austria (§ 43 KartG 1988 = § 38 KartG 2005), D may file an application under § 36 para. 4 n. 4 KartG 2005 to order the participating enterprises to cease the abuse of market dominance (§ 26 KartG 2005). The imposition of an injunction is possible in the proceeding (§ 52 para. 1 and 2 KartG 1988 = § 48 para. 1 and 2 KartG 2005). Damages cannot be claimed in a non-contentious cartel proceeding. If there is no competitive relationship between the parties (so that a claim based upon § 1 UWG is excluded), damages can be claimed in a contentious procedure pursuant to §§ 1295, 1311 ABGB.[5]

(2) D's claim does not require that a public authority intervene against the conduct of A, B and C. However in Austria the so-called 'official bodies' (*Amtsparteien*, § 44 KartG 1988 = § 40 KartG 2005) can participate in every antitrust proceedings even if they are not an applicant. Since the Competition Law 2002 official bodies are the federal competition authority which is equipped with comprehensive investigatory powers, exercises *ex officio* and is led by a general director - not subject to instructions - with wide powers and a subordinate federal antitrust attorney (in the federal justice ministry) to represent the public interest in competition affairs. The official bodies have standing to apply for the cessation of market abuses under § 37 n. 1 KartG 1988 (now § 36 para.4 n. 1 KartG 2005).

(3) Standing for an application to cease market abuses under § 36 para. 4 n. 4 KartG 2005 is conferred on any association of enterprises which has a legal or economic interest in the decision.[6] Qualifying associations also have the power to apply for injunctions (see above). In spite of the legislative change in § 36 para 4 n. 4 KartG 2005 associations in the sense of this article are also the so-called competition protection associations which are founded according to the rules on Austrian associations.

[5] Extensively T. Eilmansberger in H.-G. Koppensteiner, *Österreichisches und europäisches Wirtschaftsprivatrecht*, Teil VI/1 (1998) 121 et seq. and art. 81, 82 EGV (for § 35 KartG 1988 = § 5 KartG 2005 the same principles apply); H. Fitz/H. Gamerith, *Wettbewerbsrecht* (4th edn 2003), 123.

[6] The former rule, § 37 n. 2 KartG 1988, effective until 31.12.2005, was different: 'Associations representing economic interests of enterprises, if these interests are influenced by the behaviour subject to the interdiction'. The new wording seemingly does not restrict standing to the protection against a certain behaviour provided for in the statutes of the association.

Under § 14 UWG they have standing for cessation claims in the field of UWG, particularly in cases under § 1 UWG, to the extent that an association represents interests which are affected by the conduct. An association legitimated by its articles could therefore proceed under § 1 UWG in the present case.

(4) The conduct of A, B and C constitutes neither an administrative nor a penal offence. With the reformed antitrust law of 2002, penal antitrust law was abolished in Austria (with one exception not relevant here). However, pursuant to § 29 n. 1 lit. (a) KartG 2005 (similar until now § 142 n. 1 lit. (b) KartG 1988) the cartel court on application by an official body (§ 36 para. 1 and 2 KartG 2005) can impose a fine up to a maximum amount of 10 per cent of the turnover made worldwide in the previous year against an enterprise or an association of enterprises which acts wilfully or by negligence against the interdiction of abusive behaviour (§ 5 KartG 2005). Thus, strong sanctions are readily available which, however, cannot be classified either as administrative or as penal but which are imposed by a court.

Denmark (9)

(1) § 6, sec. 1, of the Competition Act (CA) prohibits the entering into of anti-competitive agreements. CA § 6 corresponds to art. 81, sec. 1 of the EC-Treaty. Joint pricing by competitors will be covered by the prohibition of CA § 6, sec. 1. Also price reductions will be covered by the prohibition of CA § 6, sec. 1, especially when they are agreed jointly by competitors and when the price reduction has the aim of eliminating a competitor. D may institute proceedings in the regular courts with the claim that A, B and C are acting in contravention of CA § 6 and that A, B and C must be ordered to end this behaviour. D can also apply before the enforcement court according to § 641 of the Administration of Justice Act to have an interlocutory injunction issued against A's, B's and C's behaviour.[7] According to § 643, sec. 2 of the Administration of Justice Act the enforcement court may refrain from issuing an interlocutory injunction if it will cause damage to A, B and C which are in a clear disproportion to D's interest in obtaining the injunction.[8]

(2) No – but it will be appropriate to attract the competition authorities' attention to A's, B's and C's behaviour. According to CA § 16 (see CA

[7] Ejler Bruun et al., *Fogedsager* (2nd edn 2000), pp. 635 et seq., B. von Eyben et. al., *Karnovs lovssamling* (2001), p. 3944.

[8] Ejler Bruun et al., *Fogedsager* (2nd edn 2000), p. 641.

§ 6, sec. 4), the Competition Council is authorized to issue orders to A, B and C with the aim of ending their anti-competitive behaviour. Based on a complaint from D or on its own initiative the Competition Council may take up the matter with a view to creating the basis for instituting criminal proceedings against A, B and C.

(3) In the Competition Act there are no special rules concerning organizations' competence to bring actions. It will follow from the general rules of § 255 of the Administration of Justice Act whether an organization has the necessary legal interest in bringing an action on A's, B's and C's violation of CA § 6, sec. 1, in relation to D. It will follow from § 641 of the Administration of Justice Act whether an organization has the necessary legal interest in having an injunction issued.

(4) A's, B's and C's agreement is a violation of CA § 6, sec. 1. Individuals' violation of this rule may lead to criminal liability being incurred. According to CA § 23, sec. 3 violations of CA § 6, sec. 1, are penalized by a fine. Also companies may, according to CA § 23, sec. 3, be subject to criminal liability. The subjective requirement is that the violation must have taken place deliberately (wilfully) or with gross negligence.

With a view to deciding whether a violation of the CA has taken place, the Competition Council has the power under CA § 17 to demand all information from the companies involved. According to CA § 18 the Competition Authority may carry out control investigations ('on-the-spot' investigations) on the premises of the companies involved. It is a prerequisite for carrying out a control investigation that the Competition Authority has obtained a court order in advance. Action on criminal liability and the incurring of penalties (fines) falls outside the Competition Council's authority. Action is brought before the regular courts by the public prosecutor based on an approach from the director of the Competition Authority who also suggests the level of fines which the prosecutor should try to obtain.[9] Under the criminal proceedings fines may be imposed by the courts for violations of CA § 6. Law No. 426 of June 6, 2002 intends a tightening of the level of fines, but it has at the same time been declared that the level of the fines must be below the EC level. The gravity and duration of a violation along with the size of the companies involved (turnover) will be taken into account when assessing a fine.[10]

[9] Executive order No. 951/1997, § 6, sec. 1; K. Levinsen, *Konkurrenceloven med kommentarer* (2001), p. 577 et seq.

[10] Ibid., p. 575 et seq.

England (9)

(1) On the basis that the price undercutting is the implementation of an agreement between A, B and C, yes. This is an obvious 'hard-core' horizontal price cartel operating in a part of the UK and is thus caught by the Chapter I prohibition in the Competition Act 1998 (which is 'cloned' from art. 81 EC). The object of the agreement is manifestly anti-competitive; plainly it has also had an anti-competitive effect; and there is no prospect of the exemption criteria in sec. 9 of the 1998 Act (which reproduce those of art. 81(3) EC) being satisfied. It does not matter that the prices A, B and C are charging are not identical. There may also be the abuse by A, B and C of a collective dominant position, illegal under the Chapter II prohibition in the 1998 Act (which is 'cloned' from art. 82 EC), if A, B and C taken together are collectively dominant and, if so, if the conduct of A, B and C amounts to predatory pricing.

(2) Procedurally, D has the choice of (i) making a complaint to the Office of Fair Trading (OFT), requesting that the OFT investigate with a view to making an order that A, B and C end their breaches of the act and the possible imposition of fines. In view of the serious and immediate threat to D's continued existence, D should ask the OFT, in addition, to order urgent interim measures under sec. 35 CA 1998, requiring A, B and C to cease their conduct immediately pending the final outcome of the full investigation; or (ii) applying immediately to the court[11] for an interim injunction to restrain breach by A, B and C of the Chapter I prohibition in the Competition Act 1998.[12] There is no need whatsoever to have applied to the OFT before doing this.

Although the application to the court would be for an interim (temporary) order to seek to maintain the status quo until a full trial could be heard, in practice a case like this one would almost certainly be finally resolved at the stage of the interim order, i.e. it would never need to proceed to full trial, as the parties would be likely to accept the outcome at this preliminary stage as a fair indicator of the likely outcome if the case were to go to full trial.

[11] Which, since January 2004, will have to be the Chancery Division of the High Court in London; not any other court, and (curiously, perhaps) not the Competition Appeal Tribunal, the specialist competition court in the system.

[12] On interim injunctions generally, see J. O'Hare and K. Browne, *Civil Litigation* (11th edn 2003) ch. 27 and C. Plant (ed.), *Blackstone's Civil Procedure 2005* (6th edn 2005), ch.37.

An application for an interim injunction may be made, and the court may, if it thinks appropriate, award the interim injunction on D's application but without the need for A, B or C to have been given notice of the application or to have had the chance to argue against it. In such a case, the court order will only be made for a *very* short time (generally no more than seven days, and often less) and on terms that the applicant must immediately inform the defendants, so that they can attend a hearing and state a case very shortly afterwards. (By contrast, the OFT can only make an interim measures order under sec. 35 CA 1998 if it has first given written notice of its intention to do so to the intended recipient of the order and has given that undertaking a chance to make representations to it.)

In an application to the court for an interim injunction, the applicant is required to give a 'cross-undertaking as to damages', i.e. a promise to pay compensation to the defendant if the applicant later fails to establish that he was entitled to the interim injunction. There is no similar requirement in relation to an OFT interim measures order.

D is also at risk of having to reimburse A, B and C for their legal fees in defending an interim injunction application if, when A, B and C are heard (the court having granted an urgent interim injunction), the court is persuaded that the interim injunction was not justified. By contrast, the OFT has no power to order D to reimburse A, B and C for anything (see further the answer to Case 11, Question 3 on interim relief).

Commencing litigation and lodging a complaint with the OFT simultaneously, in the UK at least, is not a good idea (though people used to do this in the past). The OFT is likely to take the view that the complainant is well capable of fighting its own battle in court, and so is likely not to prioritize the complaint. The court, for its part, will almost certainly tend to the view that it is unfair that a defendant should have to defend itself in two fora in respect of the same thing, and will normally suspend ('stay') the case, awaiting the outcome of the complaint.[13] On the other hand, making a complaint first, with a view to the OFT (or the European Commission) taking a decision and then of using such decision (with the benefit of the investigatory powers of the regulators, 'dawn raids' etc. – especially helpful if defendants are a multinational cartel with relevant business bases spread across several jurisdictions) as the basis of a damages claim, is generally a very good idea (see comments on such 'follow-on' damages claims below).

[13] *MTV Europe v. BMG Records* [1995] 1 CMLRep 437; [1997] 1 CMLRep 867.

It seems that D has a clear need for very urgent interim relief if its business is not to be destroyed. D should bear in mind that the OFT seems reluctant to make interim measures orders[14] and that, even if it is willing, the process is likely to take much longer than an application to the court would take. Subject to the concerns about legal fees and the cross-undertaking in damages, an application to the court for an injunction would seem the better way forward.

(3) Sec. 11 Enterprise Act 2002 introduces a new class of 'super-complaint' which can only be made by 'designated consumer bodies' (such as the Consumers' Association, to be designated by the Secretary of State for Trade and Industry). The difference between a 'super-complaint' under sec. 11 and an 'ordinary' complaint (made by anyone else) is that the OFT is obliged to investigate the former and within 90 days of receiving the 'super-complaint' to publish a response saying whether or not it proposes to take action and, if so, what action it proposes to take. 'Designated consumer bodies' may make super-complaints to the OFT about 'any feature or combination of features of a market [which] is or appears to be significantly harming the interests of consumers'. Although the conduct of an individual firm or small group of firms is within the definition of 'a feature of a market' in sec. 131(2) of the act, the super-complaint procedure is not primarily intended for dealing with the conduct of the likes of that of A, B and C. Action under the Competition Act 1998 would seem far more appropriate. In any event, if D is close to ruin, it may not survive long enough for a super-complaint to be of any practical help to it.

Beyond sec. 11 EA 2002, UK competition law nowhere makes any clear statement of who has a legitimate interest to bring a complaint, and is virtually silent on the rights of complainants. Given the OFT's publicly stated keenness to encourage complaints,[15] we believe that it would not be difficult for an association of consumers or road hauliers (say) to satisfy the OFT that it had a legitimate interest in bringing a

[14] Despite the OFT having had the power to do so since March 2000 and repeatedly stating that it is keen to encourage complaints, we are only aware of one published case where the OFT has indicated that it was minded to make an interim measures order. The temporary situation there was resolved by the business under investigation (it was an alleged abuse of dominant position case) giving voluntary undertakings as to its conduct pending the outcome of the full investigation (*Robert Wiseman Dairies PLC*, OFT press release PN 39/01, September 14, 2001).

[15] See in this respect the comments of the CAT in *Pernod-Ricard v. OFT*, [2004] CAT 10, para. 197.

complaint. An analogy would probably be drawn with the European Commission Notice on the handling of complaints.[16]

Under the new sec. 47B CA 1998 (inserted by the EA2002) 'specified bodies' (to be specified by the Department of Trade and Industry) are permitted to bring 'follow-on' damages claims on behalf of consumers in the Competition Appeal Tribunal (i.e. subsequent to a decision by the OFT or European Commission establishing a breach of UK or EC competition law), but this power does not extend to applications for injunctive relief. There is no other possibility for a public body to bring a claim for damages.

Beyond this, the normal rules of civil litigation apply.[17]

(4) In the case of 'normal' breaches of the Competition Act 1998, the OFT has powers of investigation and enforcement (including fining undertakings) under secs. 25–44 CA 1998,[18] which, in general terms, are not dissimilar to those enjoyed by the European Commission under Reg. 1/2003. The sanctions which can be imposed on undertakings by the OFT and the procedures which lead up to them are not, in national law, classified as criminal (contrast the treatment of such legislation under Article 6 of the ECHR, for which purposes they would almost certainly be treated as penal in nature[19]).

In the case of 'normal' breaches, the OFT has no power to impose sanctions on individuals (directors, employees etc.). The OFT can, however, apply in the High Court for an order that an individual who is a director of a company which has breached competition law (but not someone who was an ordinary employee) should be disqualified from acting as a company director for a period of up to fifteen years.[20]

Traditionally, cartels have not been treated as criminal in English law. If, however, such an agreement involves *dishonestly* doing something

[16] OJ C 101/65 of April 27, 2004, paras. 33–40. See further C.S. Kerse and N. Khan, *EC antitrust procedure* (5th edn 2005), pp. 74–78; T. Ward and K. Smith, *Competition Litigation in the UK* (2005), pp. 59–61.

[17] See Civil Procedure Rules r. 19.6 and O'Hare and Browne, n. 12 above, n. 2, paras. 7–021ff (representative proceedings) and Civil Procedure Rules r. 19.11 (group litigation orders). There are no reported instances of these being used in a competition case.

[18] As to which, see R.Whish, *Competition Law*, ch.10; P. Freeman and R. Whish, *Butterworths Competition Law*, Section X ch.17; T. Ward and K. Smith, n. 16 above, ch. 3.

[19] See *Société Stenuit v. France*, (1992) 14 EHRR 509 etc. and generally A. Riley (2000) 25 European Law Review 264.

[20] See the Company Directors Disqualification Act 1986 as amended by the Enterprise Act 2002 and the OFT published guidance note Competition disqualification orders, OFT5 May 10, 2003.

that is prejudicial to another, then the agreement will generally amount to a conspiracy to defraud, a criminal offence at common law, and businesses and directors and employees could be (and could, subject perhaps to the idea of what is dishonest changing over a period, at any time in the past have been) prosecuted as such (though until now they have not been).[21] A major criminal fraud investigation is being conducted at present by the Serious Fraud Office[22] into alleged price fixing by pharmaceutical companies going back over many years. With effect from June 20, 2003, however, the Enterprise Act has, in addition, made it a specific criminal offence (punishable by fining or by up to five years' imprisonment or both) for directors and employees 'dishonestly' to participate in certain kinds of 'hard core' horizontal cartel.[23] There have so far been no prosecutions for the 'cartel offence'.

Finland (9)

(1) A, B and C are operating on the same production level. A, B and C have formed a price cartel in order to force D out of the market. According to sec. 4, para. 1 of the Finnish Act on Competition Restrictions (318/2004), all agreements between business undertakings, decisions by associations of business undertakings and concerted practices by business undertakings which have as their object the significant prevention, restriction or distortion of competition or which result in the prevention, restriction or distortion of competition shall be prohibited.[24] In particular, agreements, decisions or practices which directly or indirectly fix purchase or selling prices or any other trading conditions shall be prohibited. According to sec. 1 para. 2 of the Act, when the Act is applied, special attention must be paid to the interests of consumers and the protection of the freedom of business undertakings to operate without unjustified barriers and restrictions. The central purpose of sec. 4 para. 1, is to ensure that the market mechanism functions properly.[25]

[21] See further in this vein Sir Jeremy Lever and J. Pike (2005) 26 ECLR 90 and 164.

[22] The independent department of central government which investigates and prosecutes serious or complex fraud.

[23] EA2002 ss. 188–202; and see M. Jephcott and T. Lübbig, *Law of Cartels* (2003), ch. 6; T. Ward and K. Smith, n. 16 above, ch. 5.

[24] The term 'business undertaking' is here defined according to sec. 3 para. 1 of the Finnish Act on Competition Restrictions: 'In the context of this Act, a business undertaking shall mean a natural person, or a private or public legal person, who professionally offers for sale, buys, sells, or otherwise obtains or delivers goods or services (product) in return for compensation.'

[25] HE 11/2004 vp, pp. 32–33.

It is therefore important to protect consumers from the harmful effects of price-fixing agreements. Sec. 4 para. 1 can also be applied to situations where business undertakings operating on the same production level fix prices with the intention of forcing out a competitor.

Sec. 4 of the Finnish Act on Competition Restrictions is based on the principle of prohibition. Sec. 4 can be applied in civil courts. Under sec. 18 of the Act, a condition included in an agreement, statute, decision or other legal act or arrangement which violates sec. 4 or 6, or an injunction, prohibition or an obligation issued by the Market Court, or an interlocutory injunction or an obligation issued by the Finnish Competition Authority, must not be applied or implemented.[26] An actor whose rights have been violated by an illegal act can ask a civil court to prohibit the defendant from continuing the illegal act.[27] The price cartel of A, B and C violates sec. 4 para. 1 and it is directed against D. D can demand that A, B and C refrain from price undercutting.

There have been only a few cases in which the Finnish Act on Competition Restrictions has been applied in civil courts. The act has been mainly applied by the Finnish Competition Authority and the Market Court. One of the main reasons for this situation is that there has not been sufficient incentive for firms to bring private suits in civil courts.

(2) Sec. 4 of the Finnish Act on Competition Restrictions is based on the principle of prohibition. Sec. 4 can be applied in civil courts without any prior decisions of the Finnish Competition Authority or the Market Court. A decision of the Finnish Competition Authority or the Market Court is not therefore a precondition for a civil court decision concerning D's private law claims. It should be remembered that sec. 18 of the Finnish Act on Competition Restrictions provides that there is an obligation for a civil court to take into consideration an injunction, prohibition or an obligation issued by the Market Court, or an interlocutory injunction or an obligation issued by the Finnish Competition Authority in the same case.[28]

(3) The application for an injunction has to be made by the business undertaking whose rights have been infringed by the restrictive act. There is no special provision in the Finnish Act on Competition

26 See generally A. Aine (1999a), pp. 60–78.

27 T. Tirkkonen, p. 388 and J. Lappalainen 1995, p. 363.

28 Säveltäjäin Tekijänoikeustoimisto Teosto ry, case 22/359/96, Decision of the Competition Council of June 1, 1998, pp. 27–28.

Restrictions, which would allow the application for an injunction to be made by an association.

(4) The conduct of A, B and C does not constitute a criminal offence. According to sec. 7 of the Finnish Act on Competition Restrictions, a business undertaking or an association of business undertakings which violate the provisions under sec. 4 must pay a competition infringement fine, unless the practice is considered to be minor or the imposition of a fine is otherwise unjustified with respect to protecting competition. The fine is imposed by the Market Court upon the proposal of the Finnish Competition Authority. When the amount of the fine is set, attention must be paid to the nature, extent and duration of the competition restriction. The amount may be as much as 10 per cent of each undertaking's previous year's turnover.

According to sec. 12 of the Finnish Act on Competition Restrictions, the Finnish Competition Authority must investigate competition restrictions and their effects. The authorised officials of the Finnish Competition Authority and of the State Provincial Office have the right to carry out inspections in order to supervise compliance with the Finnish Act on Competition Restrictions and any subsequent rules and orders issued under it. A business undertaking or an association of business undertakings must, for the purpose of an inspection or an investigation, allow an official to enter any business premises, storage areas, as well as land and vehicles in their possession. The official performing an inspection or an investigation has the right to examine the business correspondence, financial accounts, computer files and other documents of a business undertaking or an association of business undertakings which may be relevant to ensuring compliance with the Finnish Act on Competition Restrictions and with any subsequent rules and orders issued under it.

There were criminal sanctions in the Finnish Act on Competition Restrictions of 1987. Infringing the prohibitions on resale price maintenance and tender cartels was punished by a fine or imprisonment for a maximum period of one year. These criminal sanctions were abolished in 1992.[29]

France (9)

(1) According to art. L 420-1 number 1 of the Commercial Code are considered being anti-competitive practices common actions, agreements,

[29] See also HE 162/1991 vp, p. 6.

express or tacit undertakings or coalitions, particularly when they are intended to limit access to the market or the free exercise of competition by other undertakings or to prevent price fixing by the free play of the market, by artificially encouraging the reduction of prices, art. L 420-1 no. 2 of the commercial code. But apart from just being a prohibited agreement (*entente*) between the petrol stations, price undercutting is also penalized by art. L 420-5 of the Commercial Code introduced by the Act of July 1, 1996. It says that price offers or sale prices offered to consumers which are excessively low in relation to the production, processing and marketing expenses, where these offers or prices have the aim or may have the effect of eliminating from the market by preventing access to the market by any undertaking or one of its products are prohibited. Art. L 420-5 of the Commercial Code only applies where there is no sale with loss (*revente à perte*) incriminated by art. L 442-2 of the Commercial Code nor a predatory price existing in a stricter sense only on the hypothesis of an abusive dominant position.[30] Art. L 420-5 of the Commercial Code supposes that the sale goes from a professional to a consumer. Secondly, the price policy has to translate the aim of evicting the newcomer from the market.[31] In terms of evidence the simple application of predatory prices suffices in case of a dominant position; in all other cases the application would just constitute a simple presumption that has to be completed by proving other indices showing a voluntary eviction.[32] Against these practices D can act in different ways. As an undertaking, he can either refer to the Council on Competition (*Conseil de la concurrence*): art. L 462-5 of the Commercial Code. The dispute between D and A, B and C can also be assigned to the *tribunaux de grande instance* or *tribunaux de commerce*, that is to say to the common jurisdiction (art. L 420-7 of the commercial code). In both cases there are possibilities to obtain provisory measures against the infringement.

The Council on Competition has a dual function: first it has an administrative function of information and declaration in competition matters, secondly it has jurisdictional powers.[33] Art. L 420-5 of the Commercial Code introduced by the Galland Act in 1996 now also contains the sale with loss of transformed products. Thereby, the

[30] M. Malaurie-Vignal, *Droit de la concurrence*, p. 199. [31] Ibid., p. 200.
[32] Decision of the Council on competition n° 02-D-66, November 6, 2002 in Contrats, concurrence, consummation (May 2003), n° 74.
[33] M. Malaurie-Vignal, *Droit de la concurrence*, p. 151/152.

legislature wanted to act against major retailers who, by effecting a small transformation (packaging), offered products at very low prices, for instance the *baguette* at one franc.[34] The provisions of art. L 442-2 of the Commercial Code prohibiting any trader from reselling or advertising to resell a product in an unaltered state at a price lower than its actual purchase price with a fine of €75,000 aim to protect small traders against the hypermarkets.[35] According to the text of the law it makes no difference whether the sale is to other consumers or only to businesses. Finally, a French specificity consists in the fact that in case of a cartel agreement, a company may be exempted from all or a part of the fines when it helps to prove the existence of a prohibited practice and to identify those responsible (art. L 464-2.3 of the Commercial Code). This constitutes a regulation on leniency.

(2) In French law there is no obligation for the undertaking first to refer to the antitrust authority that is to say to the Council on Competition. It is possible to refer to the Council on Competition and the civil or commercial tribunals either simultaneously, successively or alternatively.[36] It is also possible to refer to an arbitrator even if the anticompetitive provisions are a part of the economic *ordre public*. This means that the arbitrator has no power to apply fines or injunctions, but he can make a declaration concerning the civil law consequences (damages and interest for example).[37]

It is better to initiate a damage claim after the Council on Competition has established the prohibited behaviour, because this almost necessarily implies that there was fault involving civil responsibility according to art. L 1382 and 1383 of the Civil Code.[38] On the other hand, concerning provisional measures civil tribunals are often more rapid and efficient on this.[39]

(3) According to art. L 462-1 of the Commercial Code a number of bodies such as the territorial authorities, professional associations, consumers' associations, trade unions, chambers of agriculture, chambers of trade and industry, may refer to the Council on Competition with regard to the interests for which they are responsible.

[34] Ibid., p. 200. [35] Ibid., p. 118.

[36] V. Selinsky in Juris-Classeur, *Concurrence, Consommation* (1993), Fasc. 380, 'Procédures de contrôle des pratiques anticoncurrentielles', n° 165 and 170.

[37] Ibid., n° 163; Cour d'Appel de Paris of March 19, 1993.

[38] V. Selinsky in Juris-Classeur, *Concurrence, Consommation* (1993), Fasc. 380, 'Procédures de contrôle des pratiques anticoncurrentielles', n° 170.

[39] Ibid., n° 156.

In spite of the possibility given to associations to act against anticompetitive practices they do not play an important part. For example, in 2002 consumer associations referred to the Council in only 4 out of 58 of cases in 2002, whereas undertakings have referred to the Council on Competition in 34 out of 58 cases.[40]

(4) The agreement prohibited by art. L 420-1 of the Commercial Code does also constitute a criminal offence (art. L 420-6 of the Commercial Code). It provides that any natural person who fraudulently takes a personal or decisive part in the conception, organization or implementation of this practice shall be punished by a prison sentence of four years and a fine of €75,000. Nevertheless, there have been few convictions to date, mainly referring to trusts in the field of private and public markets; still, it seems that their number is remarkable in comparison to other European countries.[41] Concerning the procedure, if a criminal offence is suspected, the file is transmitted to the *Procureur de la République*. This notification interrupts the period of prescription of the public action: art. 420-6 of the commercial code. It is a specificity of French criminal law to have a double sanction of prison and fine, cumulatively. Another French specificity consists in the criminal responsibility of corporate bodies (*personnes morales*). The question is how to determine the frontier between the administrative and the criminal responsibilities.[42]

Germany (9)

(1) A, B and C have formed a price cartel with the intention of forcing D out of the market. D has a cease-and-desist claim against A, B and C under § 33 para. 1 GWB together with § 1 GWB. § 1 GWB is the norm of German antitrust law (corresponding to art. 81 (1) EC) which prohibits restricting agreements. § 33 GWB provides for cease-and-desist and compensatory claims where there is an infringement of the GWB or of European competition law or of an injunction issued by the antitrust authority. Until 2005, § 33 GWB demanded that the infringed law or injunction were intended to protect the claimant.[43] After the 7th GWB

[40] Report of the Council on Competition, 2002, n° 20, table 5 on www.conseil-concurrence.fr/doc/ra2002-p1.pdf.

[41] M. Malaurie-Vignal, *Droit de la concurrence*, p. 213.

[42] V. Selinsky in Juris-Classeur, *Concurrence, Consommation* (1993), Fasc. 380, 'Procédures de contrôle des pratiques anticoncurrentielles', n° 183.

[43] *Schutzgesetz* as in § 823 sec. 2 BGB. See K. Schmidt, *Wirtschaftsrecht: Nagelprobe des Zivilrechts – Das Kartellrecht als Beispiel* (2006) 206 AcP 169 (194).

reform (effective as from July 1, 2005) it is sufficient that the claimant is affected (*betroffen*) by the infringement.

In the present case, there is a clear infringement of the prohibition in § 1 GWB, and D obviously is affected by the cartel. The answer under old law would not have been different. § 1 GWB was considered as a protective law pursuant to § 33 GWB. The details were contested. But if the cartel was directed, as in the instant case, directly against competitors, then it was generally recognized that the competitor fell within the protective scope of § 1 GWB and could claim in its own right.[44] Therefore, according to old and new law, D has a cease-and-desist claim under § 33 para. 1 GWB. Thus, D can demand that A, B and C refrain from coordinated price undercutting. The price undercutting with the aim of forcing out of the market is also contrary to proper business practice under § 3 UWG, so that a cease-and-desist claim is also based on this provision. Equally, there is a claim under § 826 BGB.

The case is similar to the 'Benrath Gas Station' case decided by the German Reichsgericht in 1931.[45] As the German cartel regulation of 1923 had a very restricted area of application the case was decided (against the established gas stations) on the basis of unfair competition law (and § 826 BGB). The case has a fundamental importance for German competition law. Although the German Reichsgericht followed a cartel-friendly line,[46] it concluded that predatory cooperation against competitors is illegal. Thus, the case shaped competition law thinking and was very helpful on the way to an effective German antitrust law.

(2) A cartel authority injunction would not be constitutive, but purely declaratory. D's private law claims thus arise independently of whether a cartel authority has taken measures against A, B and C. This result has not been obvious in the history of German competition law. In fact, German doctrine draws a borderline between the 'misuse principle' (*Missbrauchsprinzip*) and the 'interdiction principle' (*Verbotsprinzip*): competition rules following the interdiction principle are directly applicable whereas rules following the misuse principle presuppose imperatively a prior decision of the competition authority. In Germany, the opinion is widespread that an effective competition law must provide for rules following the interdiction principle – at least for the most

[44] V. Emmerich, in Immenga/Mestmäcker (3rd edn 2001), § 33 GWB notes 12 et seq.

[45] RG, 18.12.1931, RGZ 134, 342.

[46] See the 'Saxon Wood Pulp' case of 1897, RGZ 38, 155, where cartels were in principle allowed.

important antitrust violations. However, direct applicability of competition rules in national courts must not exclude public enforcement. Very often, the evidence found by the antitrust authority will be indispensable to substantiate a private claim. In this context, the reform of 2005 has introduced a new advantage for plaintiffs. According to § 33 para. 4 GWB a court dealing with a damages suit is bound by the decision of a competition authority (or of a court having confirmed the decision of the competition authority) in so far as the authority has established a competition law violation. This strengthens private law follow-on actions although in the past courts would probably not have differed from non-appealable decisions of a competition authority. It has to be emphasized that the binding effect is not reserved to decisions of the German competition authority or of the European Commission but extends to the decisions of competition authorities in all EU Member States.

(3) Pursuant to § 33 para. 2 GWB the cease and desist claim can also be brought by registered associations for the promotion of commercial interests. It is a claim for own rights and therefore, it does not matter, for example, whether the interests of the association members are affected.[47] Associations pursuant to § 33 para. 2 GWB include, for example, competition associations, commercial associations or public corporations such as pharmacists or lawyers' professional associations.[48] In practice, the right of associations to claim has played almost no role.[49] Perhaps, the fact that very often both the plaintiff and the defendant are members of the same commercial association may have prevented such activity. Or, there are simply no incentives strong enough to trigger such a claim. A solution could be to extend standing to consumer associations. This question will be treated in Case 12 where the question of consumer protection is more relevant.

(4) The behaviour of A, B und C does not constitute a criminal offence but is a breach of administrative regulation pursuant to § 81 para. 2 n. 1 GWB. The antitrust authorities are charged with the prosecution of antitrust infringements. Where the effect of the cartel does not extend outside the region (*Bundesland*) in which town X is situated, the regional antitrust authority is competent. Otherwise, the federal antitrust

[47] R. Bechtold, *Kartellgesetz* (3rd edn 2002), § 33 GWB note 10.

[48] J. Bornkamm, in Langen/Bunte, *Kommentar zum deutschen und europäischen Kartellrecht* (9th edn 2001), § 33 GWB note 38.

[49] W.-H. Roth, in *Frankfurter Kommentar zum Kartellrecht* (2001), § 33 GWB note 26.

authority (*Bundeskartellamt*) is charged with the prosecution of cartels (§ 48 para. 2 GWB). The antitrust authority can carry out investigations and gather any necessary evidence, for example eye-witness evidence, call witnesses and take expert depositions (§ 57 GWB). It can seize material evidence (§ 58 GWB) and subpoena involved parties as well as inspect business records (§ 59 GWB). Judges can also authorize searches for these purposes (§ 59 para. 4 GWB). Sanctions include fines up to 1 million euros, or up to 10 per cent of the total turnover made in the preceding business year (§ 81 para. 4 GWB). As antitrust violations are not criminal offences under German law, imprisonment is not possible. Only in particular circumstances, i.e. a tender cartel pursuant to § 298 of the German Penal Code (*Strafgesetzbuch*, StGB) or fraud pursuant to § 263 StGB, is there a criminal offence punishable with imprisonment or pecuniary penalty.

German antitrust law does not provide for criminal sanctions, but only fines based on administrative offences. When adopting the GWB in 1957 the general opinion did not regard antitrust violations as a criminal offence. The adoption of an antitrust code as such was highly controversial. Therefore, it is not surprising that sanctions did not constitute criminal punishment.[50] However, the insertion of § 298 StGB for tender cartels in 1997 and the extension of the general fraud provision (§ 263 StGB) to cartels by the courts have introduced criminal elements into antitrust law. Moreover, the uncovering of particularly ruthless phenomena like the vitamins cartel, and the perception of US-American law which provides for custodial sentences for managers, makes a considerable part of the body of legal opinion believe that there should be criminal sanctions at least for hard-core cartels.[51]

Greece (9)

According to art. 1(1) of the antitrust law (L. 703/1977), all agreements between undertakings, decisions by associations of undertakings and concerted practices which have as their object or effect the prevention, restriction or distortion of competition within the Greek market are prohibited. One group of prohibited agreements that is specifically stipulated in the law refers to agreements that directly or indirectly fix purchase or selling prices or any other trading conditions.[52] The gas vendors in the present case have formed a prohibited hard core (price

[50] See G. Dannecker/Biermann, in Immenga/Mestmäcker, Vor § 81 GWB notes 1 et seq.
[51] Ibid., notes 9 et seq. [52] Art. 1(1)(a) of L. 703/1977.

fixing) cartel according to the above-mentioned analysis, since they mutually decided to undercut D's price. Such conduct aims at and succeeds in limiting their competitor's activity and therefore obstructs competition in the gas stations market of city X. Moreover, if we presume that A, B and C dispose of a collective dominant position in the relevant market, their conduct would constitute an *abusive* predatory pricing, prohibited by art. 2(1) of L. 703/77.

At the same time, A, B and C are also violating art. 1 of L. 146/1914, since their conduct constitutes unfair price undercutting with the intent to eliminate their competitor. In general, the fixing of extremely low prices in goods sold or services provided, even below cost, does not, in itself, render the act unfair, as the freedom of price-setting is focal for competition. In any case, underpricing aiming at eliminating a specific competitor or business branch from the market or the imperilment of the financial status of a competitor or a related sector is contrary to good morals and thus prohibited.[53]

(1) In accordance with the provisions of L. 703/1977, the gas vendor thus offended may lodge a complaint before the Competition Commission; the latter, if it finds that there has been an infringement of arts. 1(1) and 2, it has, inter alia, the power to require the undertakings concerned to put an end to such infringement and to refrain from committing it in the future as well as to impose fines.[54] Moreover, the law on unfair competition (L. 146/1914) provides D with the right to request the cessation of the violation and reparation.[55]

(2) There is no obligation for the offended undertaking first to lodge a complaint before the Competition Commission, since it is clearly provided by art. 3 of L. 703/77 that: 'without prejudice to Article 1(3), the agreements, decisions and concerted practices referred to in Article 1(1), the abuse of dominant position referred to in Article 2, shall be prohibited without any prior decision to that effect by any authority being required'. That means that D may exercise his private law claims before the civil courts independently of whether the Competition Commission has declared the antitrust infringement. The civil courts, even though they do not have jurisdiction to declare the non-compliance of an agreement or concerted practice with art. 1 of L. 703/1977

53 Areios Pagos, decision 15/1972, 20 *NoV* (1972) 490 [in Greek]; *Patra single member CFI*, decision 1397/2003, 9 DEE (2003) 1050 [in Greek].

54 Art. 9 (1) L. 703/77 as amended.

55 Triantafyllakis, 'Article 1' in N.K. Rokas (ed.), *Unfair Competition* (1996), p. 205.

may, according to art. 18(2) of the same law, decide on the incidental issue of the violation of the antitrust law when adjudicating on a dispute raised by an action for payment of reparations.[56] However, while incidentally examining the validity of the agreement, civil courts are bound by decisions of the Competition Commission which are *res judicata*.[57]

(3) According to art. 24(1) of L. 703/1977, any natural or legal person has the right to lodge a complaint on the violation of the provisions of articles 1(1) and 2 of the same law as well as of arts. 81 and 82 EC. Therefore, any association has the right to initiate procedures before the Competition Commission, since the legal interest in cases involving violations of antitrust law is also a public interest. Before the amendment of the antitrust law by L. 3373/2005, art. 9(4) provided that any person who had lodged a complaint was also entitled to request the Commission to award provisional remedies. The new art. 9(5) of L. 703/77[58] has considerably and unjustifiably restricted this possibility; the Competition Commission has the exclusive competence to take provisional measures, *only* upon its own initiative or upon request of the Minister of Development, provided that there is: (a) a *prima facie* proof of violation of arts. 1, 2, 2a and 5 of L. 703/77 or of arts. 81 and 82 EC and (b) a state of urgency necessitating the avoidance of imminent danger of irreparable damage to the public interest.[59]

Moreover, in accordance with art. 10 of L. 146/1914, the cessation of the unfair practice may be requested before the civil courts, among others, by commercial chambers and commercial associations. In the present case, this possibility is given to the association of gas vendors of city X or the wider district of city X and to the commercial and industrial chamber of the area.

(4) The Competition Commission will prosecute the case *ex officio* or following the lodging of a complaint. If a violation of arts. 1(1) and 2[60] is ascertained, the Commission may issue a decision and: (a) require the undertakings concerned to put an end to such infringement and to refrain from committing it in the future; (b) accept commitments voluntarily assumed by the undertakings or associations of undertakings and render them mandatory; (c) impose the conduct or structural measures which are necessary in order to have such infringement

[56] Patra court of appeals, decision 18/2002, 9 *DEE* (2003) 524 [in Greek].

[57] Art. 18(1), (2) of L. 703/1977.

[58] As amended by art. 16 par. 4 of L. 3373/2005.

[59] About the conditions under the previous regime, see Athens administrative court of appeals 2846/1999, 6 *DEE* (2000) 273.

[60] Referring to the abuse of dominant position.

terminated; (d) address recommendations in case of violation of art. 1, 2 and 2a of L. 703/77 or threaten a fine or penalty payment or both in the case of continuing or repeating the offence; (e) consider that the fine or penalty payment or both are due, where it confirms by decision that the infringement has been continued or repeated, and (f) impose a fine on the undertakings or associations of undertakings that have committed the offence.[61] Additionally, as explained above, the Commission is competent to take provisional remedies.

Even though the Competition Commission mainly imposes fines of administrative character (because the conduct of A, B and C is primarily considered as an administrative offence), art. 29(1) of L. 703/1977, as amended, provides for criminal sanctions in the form of pecuniary penalties. Thus, whoever concludes agreements, decides or implements a concerted practice that is prohibited by art. 1(1), either in his own capacity or as representative of a legal person, is punished with a penalty of €3,000 to €30,000. In case of relapse, the aforementioned limits shall be doubled. According to the provision of para. 2 of the same article, any person who in any way obstructs the control exercised by the Competition Commission can be punished by imprisonment of at least three months and pecuniary penalties. Such sanctions are not often imposed.

As to the investigating powers of the Commission, arts. 25–28 of L. 703/1977, as amended, provide that the President of the Commission or his authorized representative or secretary may request in writing any information from enterprises, enterprise unions or other natural or legal persons or public or other authorities.[62] According to art. 26 of the said law, the authorized personnel of the secretariat, having the powers of a tax inspector, may: (a) examine all books, records and documents held by undertakings or associations of undertakings and take copies of or extracts from them, independently of the place of their storage; (b) carry out investigations in the offices, other premises and transport means occupied or used by the undertakings or the associations of undertakings; (c) seal any professional premises, books or documents during the period of the investigation; (d) make house searches and (e) take sworn or unsworn evidence, where they find it appropriate, subject to the provisions of Rule 212 of the Code of Criminal Procedure. In any case, the data selected are covered by the obligation of secrecy

[61] Art. 9(1) of L. 703/1977 as amended. [62] Ibid., art. 25(1).

and may be used solely for the purposes, for which they have been selected, i.e. the application of L. 703/1977.[63]

Hungary (9)

(1) Sec. 11 HCA (Hungarian Competition Act) contains the general prohibition of cartels. According to sec. 11(2)(f), HCA, this general prohibition applies when a cartel agreement has the object or the effect of hindering market entry. In this case A, B and C form a price cartel within the meaning of sec. 11 with the object of driving D out of the market. On the basis of sec. 43/G HCA D can make a complaint or an informal complaint to the OEC (Office of Economic Competition). The procedure relating to complaints or informal complaints is not part of the competition supervision proceedings.

Sec. 43/H declares that complaints can be made by the submission to the OEC of a properly completed form issued by the OEC. The form shall contain the important facts required for the assessment of the complaint. Within sixty days of receipt of the complaint, the investigator shall issue an order:

(a) opening an investigation pursuant to sec. 70(1), or
(b) stating, based on the data supplied by, or obtained in the procedure conducted on the basis of, the complaint that the conditions for the opening of an investigation set out in art. 70(1) are not fulfilled.

Furthermore, complainants shall be informed of the order made pursuant to (b), above and they may seek legal remedy against such an order within eight days of the service of the order (sec. 43/H 10 and 11).

Documents other than complaining documents are treated as informal complaints pursuant to sec. 43/I HCA. This is the case when a submission does not include all the necessary information. The rights of the informal complainant are more narrowly defined. In particular, an informal complainant has no right of access to the file, and no right to appeal if the complaint is rejected. A formal complaint must be dealt with by the OEC within sixty days (extendable by sixty days), whereas the deadline in the case of an informal complaint is thirty days (also extendable).

(2) According to case law of the Hungarian Supreme Court[64] a decision of the administrative authority, such as the OEC, is constitutive when it

[63] Ibid., art. 27.

[64] Supreme Court. Nr. Pf. V. 28.355/1997 cited in Boytha Györgyné (2001) p. 314.

decides on the merits of the case, passes a judgment on a legal relation, ascertains rights or obligations or exhibits facts and data. The revision of such decision may be requested from the court through submission of a claim within thirty days of the serving of such a decision. The claim has no suspensive effect on the implementation of the decision against which appeal can be made to the courts (sec. 83 (1) HCA).

However, on the basis of sec. 88/A D can enforce his claims directly before a national court. On the basis of sec 88/B the court shall notify, without delay, the Hungarian Competition Authority of lawsuits before it. The OEC may submit written observations on issues relating to the application of the provisions laid down in and oral observations at the trial. If the OEC intends to exercise its right to make oral observations, this must be notified to the court. The information provided by the observation of the OEC may be used in evidence in the lawsuit.[65]

(3) The complaint D can make, as explained at (1) above, can also be pursued by associations, which are able to prove that the interest they represent is directly affected by the conduct.[66] The organization protecting consumer interests, the OEC, or a chamber of commerce, on behalf of its members, may file a lawsuit against any party who is allegedly committing illegal acts if the identity of the aggrieved consumers cannot be established (sec. 92 HCA). This means according to sec. 92 (1) HCA that only in cases that fall within the competence of the OEC and if the OEC have established an infringement by its decision, chambers of commerce in respect of their members or consumer protection organizations may file an action against persons who have put consumers at a substantial disadvantage or have disadvantaged a wide range of consumers by their activities infringing the act even if the identity of the consumers suffering damage cannot be established.

(4) The conduct of A, B and C constitutes an administrative offence. According to sec. 44 HCA the economic competition supervision proceedings of the OEC shall be governed by the provisions of Act CXL of

[65] Furthermore, where at any phase of the lawsuit, the Hungarian Competition Authority notifies the court hearing the lawsuit of competition supervision proceedings it has initiated in the case concerned, the court shall stay its proceedings until the expiry of the time limit for filing an action in the court against the decision reached in the competition supervision proceedings or, in cases where an action is filed against that decision, until the date on which the decision of the review court becomes final. The statement on the existence or absence of an infringement, made in the decision of the OEC against which no action has been filed or in the decision of the review court, shall be binding on the court hearing the lawsuit.

[66] Boytha Györgyné (2001) p. 302.

2004 on the General Rules of Public Administrative Procedures and Services. According to sec. 45 HCA, the OEC's competence covers the whole territory of the country in all cases relating to competition supervision which do not belong to the competence of the courts.

On the basis of sec. 65 HCA in proceedings started *ex officio* the investigator or the OEC bringing proceedings in the case can request the parties to supply the data which are necessary to decide on the substance of the case, including personal data. In proceedings started *ex officio* investigative measures may be carried out on any sites where evidence necessary to clarify the facts of the case is kept. For the purposes of the clarification of the facts of the case, any persons or organizations are obliged to provide the necessary information in writing and send any documents relating to the subject of the investigation to the OEC. Parties or other persons possessing documents are obliged, at the request of the investigator, to display, in a readable form or a form which is suitable to be copied, information recorded on data carriers. The investigator and the OEC bringing proceedings in the case shall be entitled to make copies of documents. In proceedings started *ex officio* the investigator shall be entitled to make physical back-up copies of data carriers and to scrutinize, by means of the back-up copies, the data stored on those data carriers where the data carriers are likely to store data relating to the infringement of the law.

When the subject matter of the investigation is an infringement of the prohibition of cartels or the prohibition of the abuse of a dominant position and the investigation is started *ex officio*, the investigator may on the basis of sec. 65/A search, and enter on his own, against the will of the owner, any site or open to this end any land, buildings and premises that are closed. It may oblige the party or its agent or former agent, employee or former employee to provide information and explanation orally or in writing, or collect information on the spot in any other manner. Investigation can be carried out in premises used for private purposes or privately used, including vehicles and other land if they are in the use of any executive official or former executive official, employee or former employee, agent or former agent of the party or of any other person who exercises or exercised control as a matter of fact.

These investigative measures can be carried out subject to obtaining prior judicial authorization. The application by the OEC for such an authorization shall be considered by the Municipal Court of Budapest, within seventy-two hours of receipt of the application. There is no appeal against the order of the court and no review is possible.

Investigative measures may be carried out, based on the decision of the court, within ninety days of the issuance. In carrying out their investigations the OEC may seek the assistance of the police. The police may use coercive measures and methods as set out in the relevant rules.

In the course of an investigation the investigator shall be entitled to make copies of, or seize, pieces of evidence, which are not related to the subject of the investigation and are not covered by the authorization of the court, but which are indicative of an infringement of art. 11 or 21 HCA or of art. 81 or 82 of the EC Treaty. In respect of such pieces of evidence, the authorization of the court shall be obtained subsequently. The application for authorization must be submitted within thirty days, at the latest, of the measure taken. Sanctions include administrative fines of a maximum of 10 per cent of the undertaking's net turnover in the preceding business year (sec. 78 HCA). The OEC may impose a fine on persons violating the provisions of this act. The maximum fine shall not exceed 10 per cent of the net turnover, achieved in the business year preceding that in which the decision establishing the violation is reached, of the undertaking or, where the undertaking is member of a group of undertakings which is identified in the decision, of that group of undertakings. The maximum fine imposed on social organizations of undertakings, public corporations, associations or other similar organizations shall not exceed 10 per cent of the total of the net turnover in the preceding business year of undertakings which are members of them. The amount of the fine shall be established with all the relevant facts of the case taken into account, in particular the gravity of the violation, the duration of the unlawful situation, the benefit gained by the infringement, the market positions of the parties violating the law, the imputability of the conduct, the effective cooperation by the undertaking during the proceedings and the repeated display of unlawful conduct. The gravity of the violation shall be established, in particular, on the basis of the threat to economic competition and the range and extent of harm to the interests of consumers. In order effectively to detect secret agreements infringing art. 11, the OEC may frame a leniency policy, in which it may lay down, on the one side, the principles governing its approach when it takes into account, in determining the amount of the fine it intends to impose, the effective collaboration of an infringing undertaking in the detection of the infringement and, on the other side, the extent to which it can take into account this collaboration.

Ireland (9)

(1) Pursuant to sec. 14 of the Competition Act 2002, D can take action against A, B, and C in the Circuit Court or the High Court for breach of sec. 4 of the Competition Act 2002. He may accuse A, and/or B and/or C of being parties to an agreement between undertakings having as its object or effect the prevention, restriction or distortion of trade in the relevant market. Sec. 14 of the Competition Act 2002 grants the right to take such an action to 'any person who is aggrieved in consequence of any agreement, decision, concerted practice or abuse which is prohibited by the Act'. The right of action exists against either or all of the undertakings which is party to the agreement, decision or concerted practice or which has done any act which constitutes an abuse. Action may also be taken against any director, manager or other officer of that undertaking.

The Court may grant D relief by way of an injunction ordering A, B and C to refrain from this price-undercutting agreement, which may effectively amount to a collective boycott. The Court may also grant relief by way of a declaration that A, B and C are in breach of sec. 4 of the Competition Act 2002. In addition D may be entitled to damages, including exemplary damages. Depending on the circumstances of the case and the market shares of the parties, it may be possible for D to claim that A, B and C have abused a position of joint dominance in the relevant market.

Prior to the Competition Act 2002, private antitrust actions were brought under the Competition Acts 1991–1996. Initially the chief remedy in the Competition Act 1991 was that civil actions could be brought by competitors against undertakings engaged in anti-competitive behaviour. On paper the 1991 legislation also allowed a government minister to seek court orders to enforce competition law, but this power was never used. This led to a difficulty in enforcing competition law and the legislation was reformed in 1996 to grant the Competition Authority the power to pursue civil and criminal actions against undertakings in breach of the provisions of the Competition Act. Finally, the Competition Act 2002 as well as amending Irish merger law, granted the Competition Authority even more powers of investigation to assist the prosecution of offenders under the Act, and criminalized breaches of Irish and EC Competition rules. Under sec. 14(3) of the Competition Act 2002, an individual may take a sec. 4 or sec. 5 action in either the Circuit Court or in the High Court. The Circuit Court is a lower court and as such has only a limited jurisdiction to award damages, but a Circuit Court action is likely to be less expensive for the plaintiff.

(2) There is no requirement that the Competition Authority be engaged in action against the conduct of A, B or C for D's claim to be valid. However, if D does not wish to take the claim himself, he may complain to the Competition Authority in the hope that it will take an action against A, B and C, which it is entitled to do under sec. 14(2) of the Competition Act 2002. However, while the Competition Authority is empowered to take such action, like the European Commission, it cannot be obliged to do so.

(3) Consumer associations or trade unions are not permitted to take the action on D's behalf, unless the association could show some special interest and sue on its own behalf, which seems unlikely under the circumstances. (See Case 5 above.)

(4) Under the Competition Act 2002, the Competition Authority has the power to take action against parties in breach of sec. 4, and may choose to take a civil action in which case the Court may grant to the Authority relief by way of an injunction or a declaration. The Competition Authority may not sue for damages. If the breach is considered serious enough, the Competition Authority may institute criminal proceedings against A, B and/or C under sec. 6 of the Competition Act 2002. The Competition Authority is the prosecuting authority for summary offences. Such less serious offences may be prosecuted by the Competition Authority in the District Court (the lowest court). More serious indictable offences may be prosecuted by the Director of Public Prosecutions.[67] The sanction is imposed by the court. Undertakings found guilty of the hard-core offences, of market sharing, output limitations or price fixing listed in sec. 6(2) of the Competition Act may be fined up to €4 million or 10 per cent of annual turnover, whichever is higher. Further periodic fines may be payable if the breach does not cease. If a criminal action is taken against the company, a finding of such hard-core offences could result in a maximum sentence of five years imprisonment for the director concerned. The agreements between A, B and C amount to a collective boycott. This would likely be seen as a hard-core infringement of Irish Competition law.

The Competition Authority has extensive powers of investigation along the lines of those granted to the European Commission under

[67] Prosecution of Offences Act 1974.

the EC Competition rules. It can carry out investigations and summon witnesses. Having obtained a warrant from the court, the Authority can conduct dawn raids and seize documents. Under sec. 45 of the Competition Act 2002 the search powers of the Competition Authority are extended, with powers to enter premises if necessary by force, to search private dwellings and to take original documents, rather than copies, and keep them for up to six months (or longer if a court order is obtained). If D is taking the action, then it will be a civil action for damages, and his only powers of investigation are that he may ask the court to order the discovery of certain documents. (See Case 10.)

The Competition Act 2002 introduces a new distinction between those offences, which are regarded as being unequivocally harmful to consumers and others (particularly offences relating to vertical agreements) that are less seriously restrictive of competition. The term hard core does not appear in the legislation but is used to describe the offences listed in sec. 6(2) of the Act. In US antitrust law, the parallel with these hard-core offences are the per se offences, where the entering into the agreement is itself the offence, and it is not necessary to prove in every case that the object or effect is to prevent, restrict or distort competition. The fines applicable under sec. 6 of the Competition Act 2002 are the same for hard-core breaches as for less serious breaches of sec. 4, but there is no imprisonment term for non hard-core sec. 4 infringements. The provision in the Competition Act for a maximum five-year penalty of imprisonment makes it an 'arrestable offence' under sec. 2 of the Criminal Law Act 1997. Suspected offenders may be arrested by the Irish police, and members of the police force work within the Authority. Since 1991, there have only been two criminal convictions for competition offences.[68] Should greater numbers of convictions materialize, private actions may increase against those found guilty of criminal offences under the Competition Act 2002. Under sec. 8 of the Act, a director or one acting in such capacity who consents to or authorizes the breach of the Competition Act is also

[68] *Competition Authority v. Estuary Fuel Ltd.* Competition Authority Press Release October 4, 2000. A fine of I£1,000 (€1,250) was imposed on Estuary. On March 16, 2004, the Competition Authority was successful in a summary conviction against six farmers attempting to block the unloading of a ship of its cargo of grain in Drogheda port. A fine of €14,000 was initially imposed, but the Circuit Court judge lifted the fine on appeal, on October 8, 2004.

guilty of an offence. There is a presumption that the director has consented to the breach, unless he or she can prove the contrary.

Italy (9)

(1) In the case at hand, A, B and C have reached an agreement between themselves which is prohibited under art. 2(a) of Law 287/90. This article, as with art. 81 of the EC Treaty, prohibits agreements whose object or effect is that of eliminating, distorting, or restricting the state of competition in the market. Both provisions present illustrations of agreements, which are deemed intrinsically restrictive of the state of competition (e.g. the fixing of prices or other contractual conditions). In addition, the Italian law requires the agreement to 'considerably' (*in maniera consistente*) affect the state of competition within the national market or a substantial part of it. In assessing this 'consistency' requirement, the Authority (the *Autorità Garante*) has mostly applied a market share test. Should the requirement not be met, then the agreement, even though restrictive, would not fall under the scope of application of Law 287/90. The case-by-case analysis and a larger employ of economic analysis by the Italian Authority have brought results, which are partially different from the ones achieved on a EU level. However, the difference quasi-exclusively occurs in relation to agreements, which are not intrinsically anti-competitive, i.e. the ones listed in the antitrust laws. In fact, for the most detrimental agreements a quasi-automatic ban operates.

On such grounds, D could seek a restraining order from the Authority, compelling A, B and C to refrain from price undercutting. Any interested party can refer to the Authority, which, after having assessed the elements of the alleged infringement brought to its attention, shall conduct an investigation. From the elements of the case, the cartel between A, B and C seems to considerably affect the state of competition within the gas market in town X. There are not enough elements though to evaluate whether the town X is a substantial part of the national market. Should the investigation reveal that the agreement between A, B and C indeed considerably affects the state of competition and concerns a relevant part of the national market, the Authority would then prevent A, B and C from price undercutting, via a cease-and-desist order. Permanent preventive orders are explicitly entrusted to the Authority by art. 15 of the Law 287/90. The same does not hold true for the Court of Appeal. Art. 33 of Law 287/90 only refers to (temporary) interim relief. Thus, D could also opt for quicker, but temporary, relief by referring to the Court of Appeal. There is no consensus on the issue of whether D could also claim a permanent restraint order before the Court of Appeal, which is not expressly foreseen.[69]

(2) Public and private enforcement lanes are independent from each other. Consequently, D is entitled to seek judicial enforcement, notwithstanding the fact that an antitrust authority is engaged against the conduct of A, B and C. Prohibited agreements are indeed null and void, independently from any intervention of the Authority. D can thus choose whether to seek public enforcement from the Authority or to bring a claim before the Court of Appeal.

(3) Pursuant to art. 12 of the Law 287/90, the Authority, in performing its investigations (aimed at ascertaining violations of art. 2 and 3 of the Law 287/90), evaluates the elements it possesses and those brought to its knowledge by public organizations or by anybody who has an interest in the matter in issue. Within the last category associations are also included. As far as private enforcement is concerned, claims brought in the form of a class action have an exceptional character.[70] In the field of antitrust law there is no specific provision, which explicitly grants such a legal action.

(4) The conduct of A, B and C constitutes an administrative offence. The Authority is competent to prosecute the offence. Once it has verified the violation of art. 2 of the Law 287/90, the Authority shall fix a deadline for its elimination. In the case of grave infringements, the Authority can inflict administrative fines (depending upon the gravity and the duration of the infringement). In this respect, the Italian system takes a different approach from European antitrust law. Pursuant to art. 15 violation of the substantial provisions is not in itself sufficient for the imposition of administrative fines. In addition the breach must be in the 'most serious' category. During the first years of application of Law 287/90, the intervention of the Authority was mainly aimed at inducing the enterprises to spontaneously observe the antitrust discipline while sanctioning was an extreme remedy. Over time the approach has changed and the Authority has started applying sanctions in a more incisive way. Nowadays, sanctioning seems to be the key element in competition policy.

[69] On this issue, see M. Libertini, *Il ruolo del giudice nell'applicazione delle norme antitrust*, in Giur. Comm. I (1998), 649–679, at 664.

[70] Ibid., at 666.

Netherlands (9)

(1) There are two types of injunction proceedings, namely civil proceedings and public proceedings. D can start a civil action against A, B and C based on art. 6:162 of the Dutch Civil Code. This could be a very difficult route for D to choose because of the fact that the burden of proof lies with him. In the first place D has to prove that A, B and C are party to an anti-competitive agreement. If he cannot prove the existence of such an agreement the court probably will reject the claim. After all it is possible that parties have acted individually in which case there is no infringement of the cartel provisions and therefore no wrongful act. Furthermore, public proceedings can be started. D can file a complaint with the Netherlands Competition Authority (NCA) and request the NCA to take action against this anti-competitive behaviour of A, B and C. The NCA may start an investigation if there are sufficient indications for an infringement.[71] In case the NCA finds A, B and C to infringe the cartel provisions it can take injunctive measures. The Director General can in accordance with art. 58 Dutch Competition Act (DCA) impose an order subject to a penalty. Such an order serves to reverse the infringement or to prevent its recurrence. Conditions relating to the provision of information to the Director General may be attached to an order subject to a penalty. According to art. 83 DCA the Director General may also impose a provisional order subject to a penalty if, in his provisional opinion, it is probable that art. 6(1) or art. 24(1) have been infringed and immediate action is required, in view of the interests of the undertakings affected by the infringement or in the interest of preserving actual competition.[72] However, the NCA has used a provisional order only twice.

(2) For a civil action it is not required that an antitrust authority is engaged on the facts of the case. However, in the Netherlands it is common that parties engage the antitrust authority to 'help' them in their difficult position in civil proceedings concerning the burden of proof with respect to the existence of an infringement. The NCA can start an investigation against A, B and C, and can use its powers to collect further information on the existence of the alleged infringement

[71] For a case based on similar facts see the decision of the Director General Netherlands Competition Authority in the case 1893/Texaco, July 6, 2001.

[72] According to art. 84 DCA the Director General shall notify interested parties in writing of his intention to impose a provisional order, stating his reasons for this.

of the DCA. Of course the NCA will only start an investigation if there are sufficient indications for such an infringement.

(3) The two types of injunction proceedings mentioned above can be pursued by an association as well. There are no conditions as to the identity of a person filing a complaint with the NCA. According to art. 3:305a DCC associations or foundations with full legal capacity can institute a civil action to protect similar interests of other persons to the extent that its articles promote such interests. Such an association or foundation shall have no *locus standi* if, in the given circumstances, it has not made a sufficient attempt to achieve the objective of the action through consultations with the defendant. A two-week period from receipt by the defendant of a request for consultations giving particulars of the claim shall in any event suffice for such purpose.

(4) As the agreement can be characterized as an infringement of the rules of the DCA the conduct constitutes an administrative offence. The conduct does not constitute a criminal offence. The DCA attributes the powers of surveillance and investigation to the NCA officials. The character of and the limits to the powers of surveillance and investigation are defined in art. 5:15, 5:16, 5:17 and 5:20 Dutch General Administrative Law Act. The distinction between surveillance and investigation is relevant in practice in that from the moment an investigation starts there is a right to remain silent (i.e. a right not to answer questions if this could lead to incriminating answers). The officials are authorized to enter all premises, no prior judicial authorization being required. Private homes are an exception in which case the officials are not allowed to enter without the consent of the occupant.[73] The officials are also authorized to request information. Furthermore, the officials have the power to examine books and other business records,[74] to make copies of the relevant information[75] and they may, if necessary, exercise these powers with the assistance of the police. Art. 54 DCA states that the officials of the NCA are authorized to place business premises and objects under seal between the hours of 18.00 and 8.00, in so far as this may be deemed necessary, within reason, for exercising the powers regarding the examination of books and other business records. If the undertakings infringe the obligation to cooperate, the Director General

[73] However, the Dutch cabinet has proposed changes, in line with European Commission powers, to allow searches of private homes with the prior authorization of the courts.

[74] There is a legal privilege for attorney-client correspondence.

[75] The investigations are more and more focused on computer records. In this respect the officials may make a so-called 'forensic image' of the hard disk of computers.

may impose on a party that acts in contravention of sec. 5:20(1) of the General Administrative Law Act a fine not exceeding €450,000 or, if this relates to an undertaking or an association of undertakings, and if this amount is greater, a fine not exceeding 1 per cent of the turnover of the undertaking or, respectively, the joint turnover of the undertaking comprising the association of undertakings, in the financial year preceding the decision.[76] If the infringement involves a refusal to cooperate in the application of art. 5:17(1) of the General Administrative Law Act, the Director General may impose an order subject to a penalty, ordering the business information and documents specified in the order to be made available for inspection. A fine and an order, as referred to, may be imposed together.

As part of the enforcement of the DCA, the Director General may in the event of an infringement of art 6(1) or art 24(1) DCA: (a) impose a fine; (b) impose an order subject to a penalty on the natural person to whom or the legal entity to which the infringement can be attributed.[77] A fine and an order subject to a penalty may be imposed together. The maximum fine shall amount to €450,000 or, if this is greater, to 10 per cent of the turnover[78] of the undertaking, or, if the infringement is committed by an association of undertakings, to the combined turnover of the undertakings, which are members of the association. In determining the level of the fine, the Director General shall take into account the seriousness and duration of the infringement. The Director General shall not impose a fine if the natural person to whom or the legal entity to which the infringement can be attributed can show, within reason, that the person or entity in question cannot be held responsible for the infringement.

Poland (9)

(1) Practices restricting competition can take the form of agreements restricting competition (art 5 u.o.k.k.) or individual practices that abuse a dominant market position (art 8 u.o.k.k.). Agreements whose object or effect is the elimination, restriction or any other infringement of competition in the relevant market are prohibited. In particular,

[76] The Director General shall not impose a fine if the interested party can show, within reason, that the person or entity in question cannot be held responsible for the infringement.

[77] A manager of a legal entity shall not be regarded as a natural person as referred to.

[78] The turnover must be calculated in accordance with the provisions of art. 2: 377(6) DCC in respect of net turnover in the financial year preceding the decision.

agreements directly or indirectly fixing prices and other conditions of purchase or sales of products are prohibited (art 5.1 (1) u.o.k.k.), as well as agreements limiting access to the market or eliminating from the market undertakings which are not party to the agreement (art 5.1 (6) u.o.k.k.). Such agreements are deemed void, entirely or in part. Moreover, the particular act of limiting access to the market (according to the open, exemplifying catalogue in art 15 u.z.n.k) by selling goods and services below the costs of production[79] constitutes an act of unfair competition (art 15. 1 (1) u.z.n.k). A, B and C have entered into the agreement to undercut D's price of gas. This way they have committed an act of unfair competition and restricted competition in the market. D can claim that A, B and C refrain from price undercutting.

(2) It is possible to undertake independent/separate (parallel) proceedings on the basis of both the u.z.n.k. and u.o.k.k. Although the interests protected by both acts are similar (public interest, businesses' and consumers' interests), their subject matters differ. The u.z.n.k. protects fair competition while the u.o.k.k. protects freedom.[80] Proceedings under one will not prejudice proceedings under the other (no preconditions exist), although a final decision in one can be helpful in issuing the decision in the other.[81] Even though the results and sanctions of both proceedings may differ, in essence, the result is similar: the defendant must refrain from his illegal activity.[82] In case of the President of the office for Competition and Consumer Protection (OCCP) bringing a claim on the basis of art. 19.1 u.z.n.k he does not have a privileged position in the proceedings. In particular, no confidential information or trade secrets acquired during the operational procedures of the OCCP can be used as evidence in the civil procedure.[83]

(3) The antimonopoly investigation before the President of the OCCP in the case of competition restricting practices and control of concentrations shall be instituted upon a motion or *ex officio* (art 44.1 u.o.k.k.). The entities, which are authorised to bring a motion for instituting the antimonopoly investigation related to competition restricting

[79] Proving that goods and services are being sold below the costs of production is difficult since it is easy to manipulate the costs, V. Emmerich, *Prawo antymonopolowe*, w: Prawo gospodarcze Unii Europejskiej; R. Skubisz (red wydania polskiego) (1999), p. 768.

[80] E. Nowinska, M. Du Vall, *Komentarz*, p. 123.

[81] J. Szwaja (red), *Ustawa*, p. 385.

[82] E. Nowinska, M. Du Vall, *Komentarz*, p. 124.

[83] E. Nowinska, M. Du Vall, *Komentarz*, p. 124.

practices, are listed in art. 84 u.o.k.k.[84] As mentioned above, in the situation when private interest e.g. interests of entrepreneurs, consumers or other market participants are being infringed the claims shall be brought on a different basis, for example on the basis of the civil code, and consequently the rules of civil procedure will be applicable.

(4) The President of the OCCP shall issue a decision assessing the practice as restricting the competition and ordering cessation of this practice where he finds an infringement of the prohibition defined in art. 5 u.o.k.k. (art 9 u.o.k.k). The decision assessing the practice as restricting competition will be taken into account by the civil court deciding on the damages under u.o.k.k.[85] The undertaking can also be subject to a fine which can be imposed both on a natural and a legal person. Fines are regulated in Title VI u.o.k.k.: some of them are obligatory (failure to notify the intention of concentration), some of them have a discretionary character (competition restricting agreements, or abuse of a dominant position). A fine should be appropriate to the circumstances i.e. related to the economic power of the entrepreneur and the benefits he was aiming to achieve.[86] The financial sanction can be imposed independently or as complementary to the administrative sanction, e.g. together with the decision ordering the infringing practices to cease. Some authors are of the opinion that the discretionary fines should be imposed in particular if the entrepreneur benefited from such practices and the potential plaintiff is unlikely to bring a claim for damages in the court/civil proceedings.[87] The jurisprudence of the Administrative Court seems to support this statement.[88] In the instant case, the President of the OCCP may impose a fine[89] upon A, B and C, as infringing the provisions forbidding competition restricting agreements (art. 101.2.1 u.o.k.k.).

During the proceedings the President of the OCCP can request all necessary information and documents. The President, upon request of one party or *ex officio*, may restrict the other party's right to inquiry

[84] Entrepreneur or association of entrepreneurs, which prove their legal interest; territorial self-government body; organ of state inspection; consumer advocate; consumer organization.

[85] High Court Decision (SN 27.10.1995, III CZP 135/95; OSP 1996, z. 6, poz 112).

[86] E. Modzelewska-Wachal, *Ustawa*, p. 330.

[87] S. Gronowski, *Ustawa antymonolpolowa, Komentarz* (1999), pp. 402–403.

[88] SA 20.09.1995, XVII Amr 15/95; SA 8.10.1997., XVII Ama 22/97.

[89] In the amount equivalent to €1,000 up to €5 million, but not exceeding 10% of the annual income attained in the year of account preceding the year of imposing the fine.

into the evidence (documents), where rendering this material accessible would threaten the business secrecy as well as other secrets protected by separate provisions (art. 62 u.o.k.k.)

For the violation of unfair competition law, the OCCP does not itself decide. A prohibitory injunction (art 21.2 u.z.n.k) may be granted by the court within whose jurisdiction the defendant has got assets or within whose jurisdiction the act of unfair competition took place. With the injunction the court may prohibit the sale, sale at a certain price or bringing into trade of certain goods and services as well as prohibit certain kinds of advertisement.

Portugal (9)

(1) D can claim against A, B and C under art. 4/1/a) Law no. 18/2003, 11 June, which prohibits cartels or any kind of horizontal agreements restricting competition. This price cartel, according to Portuguese antitrust law, is null and void, and is of no legal effect. D has a cease-and-desist claim against A, B and C under art. 2 CPC.

Normally, competitors do not claim in civil courts against antitrust practices. Instead, they rather complain to the antitrust authorities that investigate the restrictive behaviour in competition and apply administrative fines. There are normally considerable difficulties concerning the burden of proof in distinguishing agreements from simple parallel behaviours.[90]

(2) The claim against A, B and C does not require that an antitrust authority be involved against the price cartels. In fact, D claims under civil law and the civil procedure code. The administrative procedures are derived from the powers of public bodies. Under Portuguese law these are the Directorate General for Trade and Competition and the Competition Council. The administrative procedures against antitrust behaviour end normally with the application of an administrative fine. An antitrust authority injunction is purely declaratory because the cartel is completely invalid. The civil claims are independent from the administrative procedures.

(3) In Portuguese antitrust law there is no reference to professional associations; therefore, under the law against restrictive practices they do not have standing. However, in the case at issue there is a specific intention to destroy a competitor which may also constitute unfair competition under art. 260 CPI. According to art. 273 CPI professional

[90] E. Paz Ferreira, *Lições de Direito da Economia* (2001), 497.

associations have the right to take legal action.[91] But in this case criminal sanctions against the conduct in question are not foreseen.

(4) The conduct of A, B and C constitutes an administrative tort. The competence to prosecute the offence is attributed to the antitrust authority charged with the prosecution of antitrust infringements. This is the Competition Council (art. 14 Law no. 18/2003, 11 June). The Competition Authority has competence to carry out investigations and to search for any material evidence and decides according to the evidence on the application of administrative fines. The administrative fines can achieve 10 per cent of an undertaking's annual turnover.

Spain (9)

(1) Yes, A, B and C have entered into an anti-competitive agreement (a price-fixing cartel) forbidden by art. 1 LDC. This article follows art. 81 EC principles. D would be legally able by art. 36 LDC to bring a claim before the Spanish Competition Service (*Servicio de Defensa de la Competencia* – SDC), an administrative body that belongs to the Ministry of Economy.

(2) Yes, because infringements of LDC are subject to the exclusive competence of the Spanish competition authorities, which must declare that this infringement has been committed. So the competence of the administrative authorities are exclusive in declaring the existence of a cartel when this is the central or exclusive objective of the claim. Courts can declare the existence of a cartel incidentally, i.e. when they need to do so in order to resolve a conflict between private parties (e.g. the customer and the supplier where the latter asks for performance of a contract that the former considers to be prohibited by antitrust law).

(3) Claims alleging an infringement of LDC are public, therefore any person, having a direct interest or not, is legally entitled to bring a claim before the SDC (art. 36 para. 1 LDC).

(4) The conduct of A, B and C constitutes an administrative offence, an anti-competitive agreement forbidden by art. 1 LDC. The Spanish competition authorities are therefore charged with the prosecution of this kind of infringement. Once the SDC initiates a procedure, it has the investigative powers that are deemed necessary to clarify the facts and determine any liability (art. 37 LDC). The SDC may require information from any individual or corporation and, in carrying out the duties assigned by art. 37, it may undertake all necessary investigations into

[91] Oliveira Ascensão, *Concorrência Desleal*, 623 argues that this kind of antitrust conduct cannot be qualified as unfair competition.

companies or associations of companies and civil servants are empowered to examine the books, take copies and ask for oral explanations (arts. 33 and 34 LDC). Once the investigative phase of the procedure finishes, the SDC presents its Report to the Spanish Competition Court (*Tribunal de Defensa de la Competencia* – TDC), an autonomous administrative body that is charged with the final, decisive and punitive powers concerning infringements of the LDC (art. 20 LDC).

Art. 9 LDC establishes that the TDC may order those participating in the infringement to cease the anti-competitive conduct and to remove the effects this conduct may have caused. Moreover art. 10 LDC allows the TDC to impose fines of from €901,518.15, or a sum which does not exceed 10 per cent of the turnover in the preceding business year of those economic agents, undertakings, groups, unions or associations of undertakings where, intentionally or negligently, they infringe art. 1 LDC. An additional fine of €30,050.60 may be imposed on the undertakings' legal representatives or on persons belonging to their boards of management.

The conduct of A, B and C would only be considered as a criminal offence if it had fulfilled the requirements set out in art. 284 of the Spanish Criminal Code (*Código Penal* – CP), namely altering prices resulting from free competition by spreading false news, exercising violence, menace or using privileged information. As these requirements are not met, art. 284 CP is not applicable.

Sweden (9)

(1) A, B and C have formed a price cartel with the intention of forcing D out of the market. In the same way as art. 81 of the EC Treaty, sec. 6 of the Swedish Competition Act (KL) prohibits agreements between undertakings, which have as their object or effect to distort competition. According to case law, agreements concerning prices are normally prohibited *per se*. Thus, there should be no doubt as to whether the relevant agreement is in breach of sec. 6 KL. Under sec. 23 KL (para. 2) an undertaking concerned by an infringement may make an application to the Swedish Market Court that an injunction should be ordered due to a breach of sec. 6 KL. But this is only in situations where the Competition Authority decides not to apply for an injunction. Thus, D's right to apply for an injunction order is dependant upon the Competition Authority's not taking action.

However, it seems at least theoretically possible for D to bring an action for an injunction before the ordinary courts under the general rules in the Code of Civil and Criminal Procedure (Ch. 13 sec. 1). As far as we know, this has never been tried. But unlike the Marketing Act in some respects at least (see Cases 1–7), the Competition Act is built on the assumption that the act creates effects in private law which the ordinary courts have jurisdiction to deal with. Thus, it may be said that an undertaking concerned by the activities of a price cartel should be entitled to bring an end to an ongoing infringement of his individual right, i.e. his right to compete in the petrol market on the terms provided for by law. It should be observed though, that when choosing this path D will have to bear the burden of proof in respect of whether or not there is an illegal price cartel etc.

Alternatively, it seems possible that D may bring an action for a declaratory judgment under general private law and civil procedural rules, claiming a declaration[92] that the activities of A, B and C are unlawful as regards D. A declaratory judgment is a weaker weapon in comparison to an injunction, since the former may not be combined with periodic penalty payment and cannot be executed in any way in the absence of a judgment requiring some sort of performance on the sides of A, B and C.

(2) According to sec. 23 KL an undertaking can only bring its case before the Market Court if the Competition Authority has decided not to investigate the matter and/or not to apply for an injunction against the parties. In practice this means that D has to file a complaint to the Swedish Competition Authority first, submitting that the Authority either investigate the matter further or make a decision not to pursue the matter further. If the latter is decided D must file a copy of this decision with his submission to the Market Court. Usually the Authority decides whether or not to pursue the matter further within 30 days. But this does not guarantee that the Authority will order an injunction against the parties. It only means that the Authority preserves the right to investigate the matter further, when the Authority is ready to adopt a final position on the question.

But as was said above, the activities of the Competition Authority are not an obstacle to D bringing proceedings under general private law and civil procedural rules. Still, this path is not attractive since it may cause D considerable costs and the immediate effect of applying for a court order would probably be that the court orders a stay of proceedings

[92] Under chap. 13 sec. 2, Code of Civil and Criminal Procedure.

awaiting the outcome of the pending matter/case before the Competition Authority/Market Court.

(3) In accordance with sec. 23 KL any undertaking concerned by the breach of KL has the right to claim an injunction against the practice. In the preparatory documents it is explained that undertakings concerned by the infringement are primarily competitors, customers and suppliers to the undertaking, which have violated the prohibitions in the Competition Act.[93] As to the right of appeal against decisions by the Competition Authority, undertakings concerned by the decision, but not necessarily subject to it, have standing.[94] Among these the legislation suggests that 'undertakings later or earlier in the line of trade are directly concerned by the decision'. It is quite clear, though, that undefined groups of *consumers* with no contractual relation to A, B and C have no rights to action under KL. As a matter of a fact there is no reference, either in the wording of the law or in the preamble, suggesting this right to anyone but the 'undertakings' 'concerned' or to parties to a dubious agreement.

As in EC competition law an association has the same rights and obligations following KL as any single undertaking. This being the practice, many cases before the Market Court have been pursued or defended directly by trade associations. Even in cases where the members of an association in general are concerned by a certain practice, the association would be considered to have the right to pursue the matter in court.[95] Obviously a trade association or any other association would have the opportunity to pursue the matter on behalf of the concerned undertaking as legal counsel, but only as far as the association thereby protects the rights of the individual undertaking concerned.

It is interesting to note that the Swedish Competition Authority in a decision held a clause of a collective agreement between the Transport Workers' Union and an organization of employers to be in breach of sec. 6 KL and thus void. In that case the union had no standing to appeal the decision by the authority, the reason being that the Competition Authority found that the anti-competitive agreement was concluded between the undertakings in the organization of employers, when deciding collectively to enter into an agreement which included

[93] Governmental bill 1992/93:56 at p. 144 and governmental bill 1998/99:144 at p. 130.

[94] Sec. 60 KL.

[95] See e.g. MD 1996:24 Telia/Svenska Teleinformations Föreningen; MD 2002:5 Svenska bokhandlarföreningen/Månadens bok; MD 1999:13 Svenska Konstnärsförbundet och Föreningen Förlagsutgiven Gackpress/BONUS Presskopia: MD 1999:18 STIM/TV3.

the anti-competitive clause, and not between organization and the union. Accordingly, the union did not have a right to appeal as a party to the anti-competitive agreement, since it was not considered an undertaking within the meaning of the Competition Act. The practical result, though, was that a clause in the collective agreement between the union and the organization was to be treated as void without the union being able to have the decision reviewed by a court.[96]

(4) The conduct of A, B and C constitutes an administrative offence and cannot be prosecuted with criminal charges. The current competition act, KL, came into force in 1993. According to the previous act criminal charges could be brought against price cartels, among other competitive restrictions. When the new act was considered there was a general conception that the administrative fine, in line with EC competition law, should be sufficient to deter companies and their representatives from violating the prohibitions of the Act. This was, however, not elaborated further but examined rather summarily. Since the new competition act was adopted there have been suggestions that the remedies should be supplemented by criminal sanctions. These suggestions, mainly from the Competition Authority, did result in inquiries and considerations from the government. However, the most recent studies in the field seem to take the position that the existing remedy of administrative fines has not yet been fully explored in the Swedish courts. Accordingly, the government has held that further consideration on criminal law sanctions in the area of competition law ought to wait until there is better knowledge about how deterrent the existing fines are.

Summary (9)

1. Aim of the case

Case 9 is intended to deal with the basic characteristics of the respective jurisdictions in the treatment of antitrust violations. The case is conceived as a hard-core cartel, that is collective predatory pricing (price fixing) with the intention to eliminate competition. It was expected that such a scenario would be classified as a cartel violation in all jurisdictions. This expectation was confirmed by the country reports. Therefore, the emphasis of the reports – as intended – has been on the available

96 This may be in breach of the European Convention on Human Rights etc, art. 6.

remedies. Case 9 does not concern the difficulties of calculating compensatory claims (quantum). It should rather be clarified whether and how the injured third party can achieve the cessation of the cartel violation (anti-competitive conduct). Even if the focus of the project is on the private law remedies, antitrust law approached from the perspective of comparative law cannot ignore the involvement of public law enforcement mechanisms. Questions 1 and 2 are therefore aimed at the cessation claim and the involvement of the antitrust authorities. In some scenarios the existence of standing for associations is of decisive importance (Question 3). Ultimately, there is the question of whether, apart from private and administrative law methods, a penal law route is also feasible (Question 4).

2. *Status of private claims*

The overwhelming majority of reporting countries know private law claims against antitrust violations. Private law claims are distinguished from administrative enforcement mechanisms. Thus, in the majority of countries it may well be the case that a civil proceeding runs parallel to administrative proceedings, at least in theory. However, the practical significance of civil proceedings is limited. There is a general lack of empirical material. The reports show that the incentives to pursue a civil claim are limited in view of the uncertainty regarding legal costs awards and the distribution of the burden of proof. The antitrust administrative proceeding on the other hand is not only without cost to the applicant but in addition gives access to an entire public apparatus for the clarification of evidence and the imposition of sanctions. As antitrust authorities are everywhere to be found, it is a matter of convenience to resort to them. In individual cases on the other hand civil proceedings have advantages; with injunctive claims in particular civil courts can be faster and more efficient (France, Netherlands). In addition administrative law is characterized by the 'opportunity principle': the applicant does not know in advance whether the antitrust authority will decide to take action (England). Consequently, it is often advisable (from the claimant perspective) to adopt a dual approach; the results of administrative proceedings should first be awaited and civil law proceedings pursued on that basis.

Such a dual approach, that is a combination of first administrative followed by civil proceedings, may be dubbed the mainstream European solution. Parallel administrative and civil proceedings are possible in most countries. The initial commencement of administrative proceedings is recommended on pragmatic grounds alone. In contrast there is the system where parallel proceedings are excluded (Spain). Here, the administrative proceedings take priority. The injured party has first to apply to the administrative authority. Only after a successful administrative proceeding can he seek redress through a claim in the civil courts. Between these two extremes of parallel administrative and civil proceedings or of the primacy of administrative proceedings there are hybrid forms. Thus, in Sweden a private claim before the Market Court is only admissible if the administrative authority has refrained from a claim on its own behalf. Private claims before the general civil courts are possible at any time. But to avoid a setting aside proceeding, it is also here advisable for plaintiffs to present a certificate by the administrative authority confirming that there are no plans for official intervention. The plaintiff will therefore generally turn to the antitrust authority as a matter of course because he needs such a certificate. The situation is different again in Greece where the administrative antitrust proceeding has priority as a matter of fundamental principle. A cessation claim can therefore not be pursued before a civil court. The position is different for a compensatory claim, in that here the antitrust authority has no competence and claims for damages are possible before the civil courts. Only very rarely are the civil courts formally bound by rulings of the antitrust authority (as is the case in Greece, Hungary, England with respect to fact finding, and in Germany since 2005), although in fact the civil courts normally do not deviate from the findings of the antitrust authorities.

In summary it may be said that while in Europe the administrative law enforcement of antitrust law is of prime importance, the possibility for private enforcement is recognized in all the reporting countries. Only in certain countries is it subordinate to administrative proceedings. It is evidently more the lack of incentives than of legal structures which is responsible for the relative insignificance of private enforcement in Europe as a whole.

3. *Claims by associations*

A general tendency may be seen regarding the standing of associations in that standing is more likely to be granted in antitrust authority proceedings than in civil proceedings. For claims to the antitrust authority the claimant is frequently not even required to be directly affected. Regarding civil proceedings an association can be party to the proceedings if it is itself the perpetrator or victim of an antitrust infringement.[97] Beyond this in numerous countries there are no special rules. Thus, it is often only general rules of civil proceedings which are applicable, which may be appropriate to the association claim to a greater or lesser extent. In certain countries there are special rules for the association antitrust claim. In Germany and Austria cessation claims can also be pursued by associations for the promotion of trade interests. Standing for consumer protection associations on the other hand is the exception (e.g. a general standing for associations exists in the Netherlands), aside from the involvement of consumer associations in antitrust administrative proceedings. Here there seems to be a gap throughout Europe in the enforcement of antitrust law. Despite this, in cases of widely dispersed loss sustained by large numbers of consumers, standing for consumer protection associations represents the only feasible possibility for finding a suitable claimant (another possibility would be group litigation as provided for in the English Civil Procedure Rules). Here the rights accorded to consumer protection associations in the field of unfair competition law could be taken as a model.

4. *Administrative law and penal law sanctions*

In all the reporting countries there are antitrust authorities conferred with strong investigatory powers, e.g. requests for information, power to take statements, powers of inspection, which extend to the carrying out of 'dawn raids'. Everywhere there is the power to impose fines, which, however, in accordance with art. 23 para. 5 Regulation 1/2003 cannot be characterized as penal. Thus, we are dealing with tortious administrative law infringements. The fines are in the main imposed by the antitrust authority. In some countries, however, the antitrust authority does not have this power. Here the antitrust authority has to file claims with a court (often a specialized competition law court), which then decides on the imposition of a fine (Austria, Denmark, Finland, Ireland, Spain, Sweden).

In the Competition Act 2002 Ireland introduced comprehensive penal law sanctions (fines and custodial sentences) for antitrust infringements, as did the UK in the Enterprise Act 2002 concerning the 'dishonest' participation of directors and employees in certain hard-core horizontal cartels. France has similar rules. In this respect the three countries provide an exception in Europe: only in individual cases and

[97] See the restrictive treatment of even this starting point under Swedish law – above Question 3.

under narrowly specified circumstances are there penal rules in the reporting countries. There is even a contrary trend to be recognized. Countries which originally had penal antitrust rules abolished them on accession to the EC (Finland, Sweden). However, an intensification of the discussion is apparent[98] under the influence of Anglo-American legal development, which gives high importance to penal law sanctions. A parallel to the private law sanctions may be seen in that both penal law and private law occupy a subordinate position in antitrust law. While private law could already be further developed within the existing law, it would require legislative measures for the introduction or strengthening of penal law sanctions. There is no Europe-wide consensus in this question. As the question lies within the competence of the Member States, countries with extensive antitrust law experience could lead the way.

5. *Conclusions*

The overall results are surprising. Case 9 was actually intended to raise the issue of private enforcement of competition infringements. The case should be simply conceived, that is to investigate whether the party injured by a hard-core cartel can demand cessation of further infringements before the civil courts. As the civil law cessation claim leads de facto to the same result as an antitrust authority cessation injunction, tensions arise in the relationship between private law and public law. In some jurisdictions what is achievable by the administrative law route cannot be 'duplicated' by private law. For this reason the cessation claim raises greater problems than the compensatory claim. In none of the reporting countries are antitrust authorities competent to grant compensatory claims. Thus, with compensatory claims there is more scope for private law claims than with cessation claims.

The association claim represents a singular phenomenon. Although the public interest in a system of free competition is also protected under antitrust law, only in limited cases does this lead to standing for associations not themselves directly harmed. The dominant impression is evidently that the public interest in free competition is already sufficiently well served by the involvement of antitrust authorities. However, if it is required to strengthen the status of private enforcement, then a

[98] See in particular G. Dannecker, O. Jansen (eds.), *Competition Law Sanctioning in the European Union – The EU-Law Influence on the National Law System of Sanctions in the European Area* (2004).

stronger involvement of associations is indispensable. The difficulties and costs associated with claims are often so great for the individual injured party that private antitrust proceedings are not pursued. The introduction of standing for associations would offer a private alternative. Another surprising finding is that although consumer protection is a significant aim of antitrust law, reporting countries generally do not provide for standing for consumer protection associations. This contrasts with the legal position under unfair competition rules. In antitrust law in particular the strengthening of consumer protection organizations would be highly significant. Often the loss sustained by the individual consumer is lower than the costs of bringing a claim. Only by combining individual interests will the enforcement of private rights be possible. More attention should be paid to the topic of standing for associations and in particular for consumer protection associations.

Case 10 Abuse of a dominant market position against a competitor – damages

Airline F has a dominant market position for all inland flight routes. F sells the flight tickets through travel agencies. F agrees on loyalty discounts with the travel agencies. Where the turnover of the respective travel agent on tickets for flights with airline F reaches a certain threshold level, the travel agency receives a 5 per cent discount from F for the entire sales volume. L is an airline competing with F, which has a relatively limited market share. F's discount policy is making it difficult for L to get travel agencies to increase the turnover on L's tickets. L suffers significant losses of turnover and profit.

1. Can L claim damages from F? What is the basis for calculation of the damages claim? Does the loss include loss of profit (*lucrum cessans*)? Can L also claim punitive damages, e.g. treble damages?
2. Is L's claim subject to the precondition that an (antitrust) authority is involved in the claim?
3. How is the burden of proof distributed? How is the level of profit loss to be established? Are the infringer's profits part of the damages ('restitutionary damages')?
4. Does L have claims to remedies in the enforcement of his compensatory claim, such as claims to discovery or rendering of accounts?

Austria (10)

A 5 per cent discount allowed by a market dominant enterprise *may* be an abuse of a dominant position if it disadvantages a contracting party by applying dissimilar conditions to equivalent transactions in the sense of § 35 para. 1 n. 3 KartG 1988 (= § 5 para. 1 n. 3 KartG 2005). This rule is a copy of Art. 81(1) lit. (d), respectively Art. 82 lit. (c) EC. Even without market power such a behaviour may be prohibited in Austria under § 2 para. 1 *Nahversorgungsgesetz* (local supply law).[1] The ECJ has found, that a market-dominant enterprise is also allowed to grant bulk discounts to its clients if they are exclusively dependent on the sales made with it.[2] In a graded turnover rebate system all clients are treated equally to the extent that everyone receives the same bonus for a certain turnover in a determined period. However, such an individual turnover rebate scheme may cause attraction to the prejudice of third parties whose commercial strength

[1] 'Whoever as a supplier grants or offers different conditions in equivalent situations without objective justification to legitimate resalers, may be sued for an injunction.'

[2] ECJ, C-163/99, ECR 2001, I-2613 – Portuguese Republic.

depends above all on the market share of the supplier, on the length of the relevant period and on the amount and sort of the discount granted. One could have a case where the attractiveness of the bonus scheme impedes third parties' room to move to such an extent, that the impediment has to be considered inequitable unless there are exceptional justifying circumstances.[3] Even if the rebate does not depend on the commitment of the client to buy his entire supply or at least a considerable part of it exclusively with the market-dominant enterprise,[4] an impediment may be caused by the fact that the client has to strive for reaching the agreed threshold in order not to lose the rebate linked to the complete turnover, and that therefore he will often not be in a position to take into account more advantageous proposals by competitors.

(1) F has infringed § 35 KartG 1988 (= § 5 KartG 2005), the prohibition against the abuse of a market dominant position. L may claim damages from F, as § 35 KartG (= § 5 KartG 2005) is a protective law in the sense of § 1311 Austrian Civil Code. The injured party may therefore claim damages under the remaining preconditions of the general rules. The damages claimed comprise the loss of profit, provided F has acted intentionally or with gross negligence (§§ 1323, 1324 Austrian Civil Code). If there is not only a relationship of exchange but also a competitive relationship between F and L, then the compensatory claim may also be based on § 1 UWG together with § 35 KartG 1988 (= § 5 KartG 2005; unconscionable legal infringement). Under these conditions, there have been several claims for infringement of antitrust law regulations (particularly § 35 KartG 1988) based on § 1 UWG.[5] Every compensatory claim based on § 1 UWG also comprises the loss of profit (§ 16 para. 1 UWG). The basis for the calculation of compensation (quantum) is the turnover that L would have achieved in the normal course of events (without the antitrust infringing conduct of F), although turnover cannot be equivalent to harm.[6] In practice in such cases the Austrian court determines the compensation – providing it finds actual harm – pursuant to § 273 Austrian Procedural Code (ZPO) (judicial discretion). L may not claim penal damages; such rules in Austria only apply to intellectual property law, but not antitrust law and the UWG.

[3] OGH 3.4.2001 ÖBl 2001, 229 – Key account-rebates.

[4] OGH 22.6.1999 ÖBl 2000, 82 – Annual bonus.

[5] OGH, 9.9.1997, SZ 70/173 = ÖBl 1998, 36 – 'Film hire'; OGH 30.6.1998, WBl 1998, 503 = ÖBl 1999, 50 – 'repair of leased cars'; the application of the identical § 5 KartG 2005 will not change this practice of the courts.

[6] See OGH 21.1.2003, ÖBl 2003, 188 – 'key account refund II'.

(2) The involvement of a public authority is not a precondition for a compensatory claim by L. However, the civil court (commercial court) would in practice be bound by an interdiction order of the antitrust court (now § 26 KartG 2005).

(3) The claimant has to assert the market power of the respondent, the abuse of market power and basically also the level of loss of profit; here however he is aided by § 273 ZPO. The profits of the infringer are no part of the compensatory claim. Such provisions however are found under intellectual property law. If antitrust proceedings for cessation of abuse result in the imposition of a fine (§ 142 Z 1 lit. (b) KartG 1988; now § 29 n. 1 lit. (a) KartG 2005) then the level of fine will be determined in terms of the enrichment resulting from the infringement (§ 143 KartG 1988 = § 30 KartG 2005). Actions for surrendering profits (formerly §§ 21 and 40 KartG) have already been abolished by the competition law reform of 2002.

(4) KartG and UWG know no claims for the rendering of accounts in such cases.[7]

Denmark (10)

(1) A violation of the Competition Act (CA) § 11 exists, corresponding to art. 82 of the EC Treaty. Such violation may be part of the necessary basis of liability in an action for damages. L has the burden of proof for having suffered a loss. CA contains no rules on liability for damages. The general rules of Danish law concerning liability for damages must be applied when assessing the liability for damages for violations of the CA. Under the Danish law of torts the tortfeasor has to pay full compensation for a financial loss caused by damages for which the tortfeasor is responsible.[8] L's financial loss is the base for the assessment of the compensation. If F's profit in connection with the violation is calculable, this will also be relevant. In principle there will be a basis for recovery of damages for lost profits. Due to problems with the assessment of damage and lack of documentation for causality, losses of this kind will normally result in an estimated compensation. As the basis for the assessment of the compensation one will require a certain degree of probability for the losses sustained. Furthermore, part of the assessment will be as to how evident and grave a violation of the rules is present. There is no legal basis in Danish law to award 'treble damages'.

[7] § 9 Abs 4 UWG applies only to trademark infringements.

[8] A. Vinding Kruse, *Erstatningsret (Law of Torts)* (5th edn 1989), p. 339.

(2) No – but it will be appropriate with the aim of establishing a violation and thus for providing a basis of liability to pay damages. According to CA § 18 the Competition Authority is authorized to carry out investigations at the premises of the suspected companies. Material produced by such investigations may provide an important basis for establishing whether a violation of the CA has taken place and therefore also whether or not there is liability in any later action on compensation.

(3) The burden of proof rests with the plaintiff. Lost profits may be established through the decline of L's business volume, historical data for L's business, or F's improvement of business volume. Furthermore, there is a tendency in case law towards the fact that the more grave the behaviour from F's – the tortfeasor's – side is, the less heavy are the demands for proving or substantiating the economic loss and for causality between the liability incurred and the loss.

(4) No – according to § 339 sec. 3, of the Administration of Justice Act the court may request a party to provide documents and other types of information. If the necessary documentation is not provided, the lack of production may, according to § 344 sec. 3, of the act, at the evaluation of evidence be construed in favour of the opponent. As mentioned above under Question 2 the parallel investigations of the competition authorities may be vital for obtaining the necessary basis for carrying through an action for damages.

The assessment of the economic loss suffered will be difficult. A comparison between two courses of events must be carried out: the factual and the hypothetical.[9] One must try to establish how L's market position would have been without the violation of CA § 11. In this assessment may be included whether there is a preceding relevant period in which there has been no violation. Especially a causality between F's behaviour and a loss will be less certain. Many factors may influence both the factual and the hypothetical course of events: incompetence, lack of resources, incidental occurrences and luck. Only a few judgments have been given on liability for damages concerning violations of the CA. An important factor concerning the modest number of actions before the courts must be that the documentation of causality between a loss of sales and behaviour contrary to CA is difficult. The clarity and gravity of the violation will be included in the courts' assessment of which requirements must be demanded for the

[9] B. von Eyben et al., *Erstatningsret (Law of Torts)* (4th edn 1999), p. 208.

proof that a loss has been suffered.[10] It may be particularly relevant in cases on damages for injuries in contravention of the Competition Act to ease the demand for proof as the damages in these cases typically consist of loss of sales, costs paid in vain, lack of possibility to exploit scale economies etc., which will be difficult to assess. Promulgation of new legislation will be necessary for awarding 'treble damages' as the actual economic loss of the claimant constitutes the maximum amount that can be recovered for damages under Danish tort law.[11]

England (10)[12]

(1) It has been assumed for many years in the UK that English law provides a right to damages for breach of directly effective provisions of EC competition law.[13] Although the Competition Act 1998 as originally drafted was silent on a right to damages for breach of that act,[14] the existence of a right to damages for breach of art. 81 EC (and, because of the 'consistency' principle, for breach of the Competition Act too) is now confirmed beyond any doubt by the judgment of the Court of Appeal of May 21, 2004, in *Crehan v. Inntrepreneur Pub Company*,[15] following on from the ECJ preliminary ruling in the same case.[16] It is inconceivable that the outcome of the currently pending appeal to the House of Lords, the highest appeal court in the country, will reverse this position.

In relation to breach of both EC competition law and UK competition law, English law classifies the cause of action as breach of statutory duty

[10] An example of this can be seen in the Danish Supreme Court judgment referred in UfR 2000.521 HD.

[11] B von Eyben et al., *Lærebog i Erstatningsret* (4th edn 1999), pp. 207 and 24; A. Vinding Kruse, *Erstatningsretten* (5th edn 1989), pp. 338 et seq.

[12] See particularly in relation to this, and the other Cases, the UK section of the exceptionally useful Ashurst Report for the European Commission (see General Bibliography).

[13] See the general overview on the UK, supra.

[14] A very strong hint that a damages remedy was intended was provided by sec. 58 (which provides, in summary, that in court proceedings concerning alleged infringement of the 1998 Act where the claimant is someone other than the OFT, a finding of fact by the OFT made in a decision under the 1998 Act (notification or investigation) is to be binding on the parties to the litigation, at least if that decision has not been the subject of an appeal to the CAT or the finding of fact has been confirmed by the CAT on appeal) and was further supported by amendments introduced by the EA 2002, sec. 47A (the new 'follow-on' damages jurisdiction for the CAT).

[15] [2004] EWCA Civ 637, which is presently subject to an appeal to the House of Lords (the highest appeal court for the UK). See further the overview on the UK, supra.

[16] Sub nom. C-453/99 *Courage Ltd. v. Crehan*, [2001] ECR I-6297.

(sec. 2 of the European Communities Act 1972 in the case of arts. 81/82, and the Competition Act 1998 in the purely domestic context). Breach of statutory duty is an established sub-set of the law of tort (*delict*).

It is necessary to prove that:

(i) the statute in question was intended to provide a private law tort remedy to individuals who suffer loss as a result of the breach of the duty in question (in the case of art. 81 EC this is established by the ECJ preliminary ruling in the *Crehan* case; there is no reason why art. 82 EC should be any different);

(ii) the claimant is within the class of people to whom the duty is owed (post the ECJ preliminary ruling in *Crehan*, this is taken as meaning anyone, including (as in *Crehan*) a party to an allegedly anti-competitive agreement);

(iii) the type of loss the claimant suffered was of the type of damage the statute was intended to prevent (in *Crehan*, one problem for the claimant was that the restriction of competition had taken place at the level of supply manufacturer-to-wholesaler but the claimant had suffered his loss at the downstream level of retail sales (Mr Crehan's public houses had failed because the high prices he had to pay for beer to the brewery under the exclusive purchasing agreement made him uncompetitive against other bars in the area). The Court of Appeal in *Crehan* in effect disapplies the normal requirement and takes a more generous view, reasoning that to insist on the normal principles on this aspect would mean that UK law would not meet its obligation under EC law to provide an effective remedy);

(iv) the breach of statutory duty was the cause of the claimant's loss (normally it suffices to show that the breach materially contributed to the harm; the claimant must show that it is more likely than not that the damage would not have occurred but for the breach of duty). In *Crehan*, the judge at first instance[17] found on the facts that, if Mr Crehan had been free to buy (cheaper) beer on the open market instead of being forced to buy more expensive beer under the exclusive purchasing agreement, his business would (just) have survived, so the causal link was satisfied (and the Court of Appeal did not interfere with this finding[18]);[19] and

(v) the damage must not be too remote: English law will not award damages in respect of losses which it considers are too uncertain or speculative to have been provably caused by the breach of duty. This overlaps with (iv). In *Crehan*, the Court of Appeal takes a very much

[17] *Crehan v. Inntrepreneur Pub Company* [2003] EWHC 1510, judgment of Park J of June 26, 2003, para. 263.

[18] *Crehan v. Inntrepreneur Pub Company* [2004] EWCA 637, paras. 169–171.

[19] Contrast *Arkin v. Borchard Lines Ltd.* (see the general overview, supra).

more conservative view than the trial judge as to Mr Crehan's losses of future profit as a result of his business failing (though at first instance Mr Crehan had lost on another point,[20] so the trial judge's views on quantum were hypothetical only). The trial judge clearly felt that the EC law requirement that national law provide effective remedies obliged him to take a very generous approach on future losses and (hypothetically) would have awarded £1.3m. The Court of Appeal, taking much more the conventional approach in breach of statutory duty cases, considered that the trial judge had allowed for losses that were far too speculative and uncertain, and awarded actual damages of about £130,000.[21]

Loss of profit: whilst loss of profit is, in principle, then, recoverable (as it is for 'ordinary' economic torts in English law, though in tort law generally it is seen as too remote and uncertain), there is still considerable uncertainty as to the right approach to remoteness and calculation (which may be resolved by the current appeal to the House of Lords in the *Crehan* case).

Punitive damages: there is no reported competition case on these (which in English law are called 'exemplary damages'). They are a quasi-criminal sanction added on to civil litigation. The classes of tort where they can be awarded were until recently limited by case law,[22] but that limitation has now been removed by a recent House of Lords judgment, *Kuddus v. Chief Constable of Leicestershire*.[23] With relevance to the issues raised here, the English courts have held, as a general proposition, that the fact that national law sanctions for breach of EC law must (per the ECJ) provide effective remedies only requires them to award compensatory damages (albeit full compensatory damages) and not exemplary damages.[24] Those decisions predate, however, the

[20] Park J considered on the facts that the entirety of brewery tied house exclusive purchasing agreements in the UK did not lead to foreclosure to new entrants of the market for the supply of beer for consumption in licensed premises, so that, on the first principle in *Delimitis v. Henninger Bräu* there was no breach of art. 81. He nevertheless proceeded to deal hypothetically with all the other issues raised in the case, as he was confident that his judgment (whatever he decided) would be appealed. The Court of Appeal was highly critical of him for forming his own view on foreclosure of the market rather than regarding himself as being bound by contemporaneous European Commission decisions in the sector made in relation to other breweries.

[21] *Crehan v. Inntrepreneur Pub Company* [2004] EWCA 637 (CA), paras. 172–183.

[22] See, inter alia, *Halsbury's Laws of England*, Vol. 12, para. 1116 ff.

[23] *Kuddus v. Chief Constable of Leicestershire*, [2001] UKHL 29.

[24] *Marshall v. Southampton and S. W. Hampshire Area Health Authority* [1994] QB 126; *Ministry of Defence v. Meredith* [1995] IRLR 539 (Employment Appeal Tribunal); *MoD v. Cannock* [1995] 2 All ER 449 (EAT).

judgment of the House of Lords in *Kuddus*[25] which removed the 'class of tort' limitation. It is accordingly possible that the decisions in *Marshall*, *Meredith* and *Cannock* might not now be followed (and in any event, none of them is a competition case). In any event, even if exemplary damages are in principle available for breach of statutory duty in competition cases, they will only be ordered in very rare circumstances (e.g., for present purposes, where the defendant has done a cost-benefit evaluation and worked out that by breaching the contract or other legal rule he can make a profit for himself which may well exceed any compensation he has to pay out to a claimant). The fact that a defendant may have been or could be fined by the European Commission or the OFT for breach of competition law may well be a factor that would point a court away from awarding exemplary damages, on the basis that it thought the defendant had been or could be penalized sufficiently in that way. An award of exemplary damages would be highly unlikely on these facts.

(2) There is absolutely no need for L to involve a competition authority prior to bringing its damages claim. If it wishes to run all stages of the case itself (including proving breach), it must sue in the Chancery Division of the High Court and cannot proceed in the CAT.

On the other hand, if F's behaviour has already been the subject of a decision of the European Commission or OFT establishing a breach of competition law, L can use that decision as the basis of a damages claim in the courts (either the Chancery Division of the High Court or the CAT). Provided the decision is not under appeal and that the time limit for lodging an appeal against it has passed, the court (be it the CAT or the Chancery Division of the High Court) is bound to accept without question the findings of fact made by the relevant competition enforcement agency.[26] That will make L's litigation much easier (though the difficult issues referred to in Question 1 will of course remain to be resolved).

[25] See supra.

[26] On the basis of sec. 47 A CA 1998 as to both OFT decisions and European Commission decisions in the case of the CAT; on the basis of sec. 58 A CA 1998 as to OFT and CAT decisions in the case of the 'ordinary' courts; and on the basis of the ECJ judgment in C-344/98 *Masterfoods* [2000] ECR I-11369 as to European Commission decisions in the case of the 'ordinary courts (and n.b. the Court of Appeal's strong criticisms of the trial judge in *Crehan* for failing to comply with the duty of sincere cooperation, ignoring the Commission's findings (made in decisions involving other parties) and forming his own view on the question of foreclosure in the brewery tied house sector (*Crehan* [2004] EWCA Civ 637, paras. 59–112)).

(3) The burden of proof that conduct constitutes a breach of the competition rules lies on the party who claims it is such.[27] The standard of proof is the normal English civil law 'balance of probabilities' standard,[28] i.e. 'the court is satisfied an event occurred if the court considers that, on the evidence, the occurrence of the event was more likely than not'.[29]

See earlier comments (Question 1) about the difficulties with establishing the level of loss of profit.

Restitution and/or a court order that the defendant pay over to the claimant the profits he has made from his breach (an 'account of profits') may be available remedies, but there is no reported English case law in this area.[30]

(4) Ordinary procedural rules in civil and commercial litigation apply. As regards disclosure, a peculiarity of UK litigation procedure is that each party is obliged (with some exceptions) to disclose to the other side those documents he has or has had under his control that he intends to rely on as evidence, as well as those documents which adversely affect his case. He must specifically describe them in a list, and must allow the other party to inspect the contents and/or to take copies of them. If a party to litigation does not do this voluntarily, the court will order him to do it. The aim of disclosure is to enable the parties to better evaluate the strength of their respective cases in advance of trial, and so to encourage the settlement of disputes out of court and the saving of expense. Exceptions to the obligation of disclosure are: documents where the court orders that disclosure would be damaging to the public interest; documents the disclosure of which would be disproportionate to the issues in the case; and documents privileged from disclosure (legal professional privilege; privilege against self-incrimination; etc.).[31]

Finland (10)

(1) Sec. 6 of the Finnish Act on Competition Restrictions prohibits the abuse of a dominant market position. It focuses on the acts of a business undertaking in a dominant market position, which has as its principal objective the elimination, or serious weakening of a competitor. The turnover thresholds and bonus systems imposed by F can be seen as

[27] *Potato Marketing Board v. Robertsons* [1983] 1 CMLR 93, 98.

[28] *Panayiotou v. Sony Music Entertainment Ltd.* [1994] 1 All ER 755.

[29] *Re H (minors)* [1996] 1 All ER 1, 16 (HL).

[30] See further A. Jones, *Restitution and European Community Law* (2000), ch.6.

[31] See further J. O'Hare and K. Browne, *Civil Litigation*, Case 9 note 12 above, ch.30.

infringing sec. 6 because their object is to bind customers.[32] There has been a failure to show any objective grounds for the discount system (e.g. savings based on economies of scale). According to sec. 18(a) of the Finnish Act on Competition Restrictions, a business undertaking, which, either intentionally or negligently, violates the prohibitions prescribed in sections 4 or 6, or art. 81 or 82 of the EC Treaty, is obliged to pay compensation for the damage caused to another business undertaking.[33] L has a claim for damages pursuant to sec. 18(a). The compensation for damage entails compensation for the expenses, price difference, lost profits and other direct or indirect economic damage resulting from the competition restriction. There is no provision under Finnish law for punitive damages.

No cases have been reported in judgment collections where sec. 18(a) has been applied. There is, at least, one case pending. One of the reasons for this situation is that the incentive to bring private suits to civil courts has been very insufficient. There are often high economic risks involved in these cases.

(2) Sec. 6 of the Finnish Act on Competition Restrictions, can be applied directly in civil courts. Private claims based on sec. 6 do not require a previous decision of the Finnish Competition Authority or the Market Court. If the Market Court has issued a decision stating that the business undertaking in question has breached sec. 6, the civil court has to take this decision into consideration.[34]

(3) Sec. 18(a) of the Finnish Act on Competition Restrictions concerns compensation for damage which a business undertaking has caused to another business undertaking by competition restrictions irrespective of whether the business undertakings in question are based on a contractual relationship or not. The division of the burden of proof depends on whether there is a contractual relationship or not.[35] When a contractual relationship exists between business undertakings and when violation of the Finnish Act on Competition Restrictions also means a breach of a contract, the defendant has to prove that he has not negligently violated the prohibitions prescribed in secs. 4 or 6, in order to be released from the obligation to pay damages. When a contractual

[32] See Ajasto Oy, case 34/359/97, Decision of the Competition Council of September 13, 1999. Ajasto Oy appealed the decision as to the infringement fine, the Supreme Administrative Court dismissing the appeal on August 22, 2001 (3590/1/99). See also P. Kuoppamäki (2000), pp. 175–176, and P. Kuoppamäki (2003), pp. 874–875.

[33] See generally A. Aine (1999b), pp. 799–805.

[34] A. Aine (2000), p. 185.

[35] HE 243/1997 vp, p. 32.

relationship does not exist between business undertakings, the claimant has to prove the existence of negligence. Because there is no contractual relationship between F and L, L has to prove that F has either intentionally or negligently breached sec. 6.

L has to prove actual loss. It is very often difficult to estimate the extent of damage caused by competition restrictions. According to chap. 17, sec. 6 of the Finnish Procedural Code, a civil court may estimate the amount of damages according to the principle of fairness if evidence of the amount of damages is not available, or it is not possible to provide evidence of the amount of damages without considerable difficulty. Sec. 18(a) does not provide for claims for the surrender of infringement profits.

(4) Neither the Finnish Act on Competition Restrictions nor the Finnish Procedural Code provides for a general discovery claim. The basic principle is that the claimant is responsible for providing evidence to support his claim. According to chap. 17, sec. 6 of the Finnish Procedural Code, a civil court may, however, order a party to produce a specified document to the court on the presumption that this document contains information, which can be used as evidence in the ongoing case.[36] If the specified document contains business secrets, the order may only be given in exceptional circumstances. In the present case it would be possible for L to require F to produce a specified document containing evidentiary information.

France (10)

(1) The violation of art. 420–2 of the Commercial Code is a fault engaging the civil responsibility of the infringer according to art. 1382 and 1383 of the civil code.[37] Thus fault, detriment and the causality between both has to be demonstrated. Nevertheless, even if the demonstration of the detriment might be easy, the estimation of the quantum of the damage as well as the proof of causality stays delicate.[38] The classic detriment in unfair competition law is the loss of clients, but difficult to prove and to

[36] J. Lappalainen (2001), pp. 189–199.

[37] CA Paris June 28, 2002, RTD com 2003. 78 ; M. Malaurie-Vignal, *Droit de la concurrence*, p. 212.

[38] V. Selinsky in Juris-Classeur, *Concurrence, Consommation* (1993), Fasc. 380, 'Procédures de contrôle des pratiques anticoncurrentielles', no. 171; D. Fasquelle, 'Les dommages-intérêts en matière concurentielle'; Rév. Concurrence consommation, mai-juin 2000, no. 115, p. 14 ; Fourgoux, 'La reparation du préjudice des entreprises victimes de pratiques anticoncurrentielles', JCP éd. E 1999, 2005.

evaluate. Apart from this material damage, the existence of 'moral' damage is also admitted. This is the *trouble commercial.*[39] The actual amount of the damage is fixed at the entire discretion of the judge.[40]

The exact method of evaluating the classic damage of loss of clients or moral damage remains unclear in reality as the decisions only present a figure. As has been pointed out earlier even a statistical study of the Business Law Research Centre of the Paris Chamber of Commerce and Industry (CREDA) of about 200 decisions from 01/1997 to 06/1998 in the field of competition did not reveal any further details. On the contrary, it stated that in most decisions there was no allusion to the calculation method at all.[41] In French civil law, there are no punitive damages or treble damages even if in legal writing an interest in their institution can be seen.[42]

(2) Civil and commercial court jurisdictions are competent independently of proceedings brought before the Council on Competition (*Conseil de la Concurrence*).[43] A parallel use of proceedings is also possible, but there is no suspension of one set of proceedings. Thus, there is a serious risk of diverging decisions.[44] This is the main reason why in the case of simple damage claims (not claims for specific performance and the like) civil proceedings for reparation are better after the *Conseil de la concurrence* has established the prohibited behaviour because this almost necessarily implies that there was fault involving civil liability.[45]

(3) The burden of proof follows general guidelines for civil actions. The plaintiff has to prove that there has been fault, prejudice and causality.[46]

(4) Personally L has no means to get information from the infringer. But the *Conseil de la Concurrence* has special powers to obtain disclosure of documents with the exception of those containing trade secrets.[47]

[39] Cass. Com. February 9, 1993, in: Bulletin civil IV no. 53.

[40] Cass. civ. May 23, 1911, in: DP 1912.1 421.

[41] Report of the Colloquium organized on December 6, 2000 at the CREDA – the business law research centre of the Paris Chamber of Commerce and Industry – in Paris, Round table on '*Concurrence déloyale: Amendes civiles ou dommages punitifs*', p. 10 intervention of A. Ronzano, http://www.ccip.fr/creda.

[42] Ibid.

[43] V. Selinsky in: Juris-Classeur, *Concurrence, Consommation* (1993), Fasc. 380, Procédures de contrôle des pratiques anticoncurrentielles, no. 159.

[44] Ibid., no. 169. [45] Ibid., no. 170. [46] Ibid., no. 171. [47] Ibid., no. 84.

Germany (10)

(1) L has a compensatory claim for damages pursuant to § 33 para. 1 together with § 19 GWB. F is deemed to be in a dominant market position. There is also an abuse of this dominant position: turnover threshold discounts and comparable bonus systems are an abuse to the extent they are intended to bind customers. This would be different if there were objective grounds for the discount such as cost savings on the basis of economies of scale.[48] There is no indication of such a ground in the facts given. Thus, there is a violation of § 19 GWB, and L is affected by it.[49] L can thus on the one hand claim cease and desist of F's discount scheme, on the other hand compensatory damages.

In this case the usual difficulties of calculating damages are seen. There are no antitrust-specific rules, but rather this is subject to general civil law. Pursuant to § 252 s. 1 BGB the loss to be compensated comprises the lost profit. As the determination of the lost profits requires a difficult calculation of hypothetical business dealings, § 252 s. 2 BGB contains an easing of the evidence requirement. According to this norm, lost profit is that 'which could have been expected as likely given the normal course of event or according to particular circumstances, especially the institutions and arrangements concerned'. Thus, an abstract calculation of damages is possible, permitting an average figure for quantum.[50] In addition, § 287 Code of Civil Procedure (ZPO) permits the competent court to estimate the amount as necessary. There is no provision under German law for penal damages or three-fold compensation. Only the actual losses will be compensated.

The determination of the exact amount of damages in competition law is extremely difficult because economic effects are very complex. Nevertheless, German law has no specific rules in this area. On the other hand, the general rules provide for sufficient flexibility in determining the quantum. German courts have made sufficient use of this flexibility, so that the relative scarcity of private antitrust suits is not due to the difficulty of determining the damage. Certainly, treble or penal damages would increase the incentive to bring private suits to the courts.

48 R. Bechtold (3rd edn 2002), § 19 GWB note 64.

49 The result would not have been different before the reform of 2005: § 19 GWB was considered as a protective provision pursuant to § 33 GWB. Where the abuse was directed at a competitor, he fell under the protective scope of the abuse prohibition in § 19 GWB. See R. Bechtold (3rd edn 2002), § 33 GWB note 4.

50 W.-H. Roth, in: *Frankfurter Kommentar zum Kartellrecht* (2001), § 33 GWB note 155.

However, treble damages would not fit into the German system of damages which declines an overcompensation of the injured party. Therefore, most German competition law commentators are not in favour of introducing treble or penal damages.

(2) Until January 1, 1999, abuse of a dominant market position was not subject to a legal prohibition.[51] Under previous law, the injunction of the antitrust authority was accordingly indispensable before taking a private action. Since January 1, 1999, § 19 GWB follows the prohibition principle: private claims including compensatory claims no longer require the previous decision of an antitrust authority.[52]

The rule on abuse of dominant positions in § 19 GWB was tightened with the express intention to strengthen private claims.[53] This shows the high importance which is given to the subject of private competition claims not only by legal commentators but also by the legislature. Before 1999, in the field of unilateral restraints of competition, there were only specific rules prohibiting unfair hindrance of competitors or discrimination of suppliers and customers which were directly applicable.[54] After 1999, only the provision on exclusive dealing in § 16 GWB still followed the misuse principle and therefore was not directly applicable. Since the reform of 2005, there are no more rules following the misuse principle. Finally, forty-seven years after the enactment of the GWB, the interdiction principle has achieved a complete success.

(3) L has to prove that F has behaved in such a way as to infringe the prohibition against the abuse of a dominant market position. L has to establish actual loss. This is difficult as he is dependent on a hypothetical market development: what profit would he have made if F had not abused his dominant market position? § 287 ZPO therefore allows the competent court considerable scope in the calculation of quantum. If necessary, a minimum amount of damages may be awarded.[55] In principle, German law does not provide for claims for the surrender of infringement profit (*Verletzergewinn*), i.e. the profit which the defendant has gained through the antitrust infringement. Until 2005, this was also true for antitrust law.[56] Restitutionary damages only existed in

[51] Concerning the difference between 'prohibition principle' and 'misuse principle' see supra Case 9 question 2.

[52] Accordingly, the answer to this question is now identical with supra Case 9 question 2.

[53] Bundestagsdrucksache 13/9720 of 29.1.1998, p. 35.

[54] See infra Case 15.

[55] W.-H. Roth, in *Frankfurter Kommentar zum Kartellrecht* (2001), § 33 GWB note 151.

[56] Ibid., note 149.

intellectual property law and in unfair competition law as far as intellectual property rights are concerned.[57] This has changed since the reform of 2005. Pursuant to the new § 33 para. 3 s. 2 GWB, the profit of the infringing enterprise can be taken into consideration when estimating the quantum.[58] Although this wording is not at all clear, it can be deduced from it that the way is now open to include the infringer's profit when calculating damages on the basis of § 287 ZPO.

(4) German antitrust and civil law provides for no general discovery claim.[59] Under customary law, however, an auxiliary claim to discovery is a component of tortious claims.[60] If all claim prerequisites can be established apart from the existence of loss, then the injured party has a discovery claim provided he cannot obtain the necessary information himself and this information lies within the sphere of knowledge of the infringing party.[61] In the individual case a duty to render an account can arise from this.[62] On the other hand so-called preliminary discovery (*Ausforschungsbeweis*), under which the claimant attempts to gain information on which to first base a claim, is inadmissible.[63] In the instant case L has a claim against F for communication of how long and with how many travel agents the infringing loyalty discount has operated.

German law is reluctant to allow general information claims. It is the responsibility of the claimant to procure evidence in favour of his claim. The US-American pre-trial discovery appears excessive. A more focused approach is preferred.

Greece (10)

(1) In the present case, airline F is abusing its dominant position in the relevant market by providing discounts to travel agencies that promote its tickets. By doing so, it is acting unfavourably towards its competitors and is also violating art. 2 of L. 703/1977. Based on the above, L may request reparations in accordance with the general provisions on tortious

[57] *Ergänzender wettbewerbsrechtlicher Leistungsschutz*, See H. Köhler/H. Piper, § 1 UWG notes 482 et seq.

[58] See BT-Drs. 15/3640 of 7.6.2004, p. 54.

[59] See more in detail Th. Lübbig and M. le Bell (2006) WRP 1209 (1213 et seq.).

[60] H. Köhler, *Der Schadensersatz-, Bereicherungs- und Auskunftsanspruch im Wettbewerbsrecht* (1992) 45 NJW 1477 (1480).

[61] BGHZ 81, 24, established practice of the courts.

[62] W.-H. Roth, in *Frankfurter Kommentar zum Kartellrecht* (2001), § 33 GWB note 206.

[63] Köhler (supra note 60), 1481.

liability of art. 914 CC. The conditions for such liability are: (a) the unlawful character of the act committed by the author of the damage, which in the present case consists of the violation of art. 2 of L. 703/1977, (b) fault thereof, and (c) the existence of damage resulting from the unlawful and culpable act.

The reparation will be calculated on the basis of what the plaintiff would have had, if the damaging incident had not taken place, i.e. the damage is restituted.[64] Therefore, lost profit (the damage that resulted from the absence of increase in the damaged person's resources) may also be requested.[65]

By contrast, punitive damages are not provided by the antitrust law, although such provisions exist in intellectual property law[66] and consumer protection law.[67] It is noted that awarding and collecting punitive damages ordered by foreign judgments is not contrary to the rules of the Greek public order.[68] Thus, foreign judgments awarding punitive damages may be declared enforceable in Greece.

(2) L is not under an obligation to apply to the Hellenic Competition Commission before seeking reparations before the civil courts. The courts, even though they do not have jurisdiction to declare the non-compliance of an agreement or concerted practice with art. 1 of L. 703/1977 or the non-compliance of a behaviour with art. 2 of the same law, may, according to art. 18(2) thereof, decide on the incidental issue of violation of the antitrust law when adjudicating on a compensatory claim.[69] As already mentioned in Case 9, civil courts are bound by decisions of the Competition Commission declaring that an infringement of the antitrust law has taken place.

(3) The plaintiff must prove both that the conditions for the existence of a liability in tort have been met and also the scale of the damage incurred. Only in cases when the fact to be proven is exclusively related to the activity of the defendant will the burden of proof be reversed. Therefore, L is burdened with proving the existence and scale of the

[64] M. Stathopoulos, in Georgiades-Stathopoulos (ed.), *The Civil Code, Articles 297–298* (1979), p. 60.

[65] Art. 298 CC. [66] Art. 65 (2) L. 2121/93. [67] Art. 10 (9) (b) L. 2251/1994.

[68] *Areios Pagos* (full bench), decision 17/1999, 6 *DEE* (2000) 181 [in Greek]: 'A decision by a court of an American state awarding to the creditor punitive damages for contractual liability based on a legal provision of the state law allowing for the imposition of such damages to the debtor, because the latter intentionally violated the contractual provisions, is not contrary to domestic public order and may be declared enforceable.'

[69] Patra court of appeals 18/2002, (2003) 9 *DEE* 524.

damage incurred. However, the volume of the *lucrum cessans* may only be determined through speculation. Indeed, art. 298 CC stipulates: 'Reparation includes the decrease of the existing property of the creditor (positive damage), as well as the loss of profit. Such profit is presumed to be that, which may be anticipated according to the natural course of affairs or the special circumstances and especially the preparatory measures that have been taken.' Thus, speculation should be effectuated on the basis of objective criteria and the circumstances applicable at the time at which the lost profit would be expected,[70] taking into account the perceptions of the average reasonable person.[71] Additionally, art. 938 CC stipulates that the profit made by the tortfeasor may be claimed even after the compensation claim based on art. 914 CC has been prescribed. Thus, the said article provides for a specialized form of unjust enrichment to be activated in case of prescription of the tort claim. However, any revenue made by the tortfeasor as a result of the tort does not constitute grounds for additional reparation for the damaged party; it will be rendered thereto according to the provisions on cumulative claims: the satisfaction of a claim for reparations extinguishes a claim for unjust enrichment, to the extent the two claims coincide.[72]

(4) Neither the antitrust law nor the civil and procedural law provide for a general discovery claim. However, one should mention art. 902 CC providing for the right to request the production of a document in the possession of another person, if the said document has been executed in the interest of the claimant, or it certifies a legal relationship involving him or refers to negotiations made by the claimant. It seems that the above provision is of a little help, as the claimant has to specify the actual document production of which is requested; a fishing expedition is not allowed.

Hungary (10)

(1) On the basis of sec. 21(i), (j), HCA an abuse of a dominant position can be established when the conduct hinders without justification or in any other manner market entry, or it creates, without justification, disadvantageous market conditions for competitors, or influences their

[70] A. Liakopoulos, *The Economic Freedom as Subject of Protection in Antitrust Law* (1981), p. 309–310.

[71] M. Stathopoulos, in Georgiades-Stathopoulos (ed.), *The Civil Code, Articles 297–298* (1979), p. 65.

[72] A. Georgiades, ibid., *Article 938*, p. 844.

business decisions in order to obtain unjustified advantages. The Competition Council can on the basis of sec. 77 (d), (f), HCA establish that the conduct of F is unlawful and can prohibit the continuation of the conduct. Furthermore, on the basis of sec. 77(g), HCA the Competition Council, where it finds an infringement of the law, may impose obligations, including in particular the obligation to conclude a contract where an unjustified refusal to create or maintain business relations appropriate for the type of the transaction (point (c) of sec. 21) has been found.

As L is not in a contractual relationship of any kind with F, it seems unlikely that he can claim damages. The basis for calculating damages can be found in case law, but no general rules are followed and no special rules have been provided for competition law cases. According to sec. 355(4) HCC damages include loss of profit. On the other hand, L cannot claim punitive or treble damages.

(2) Since 1 November 2005 L can bring private damage claims directly before a civil court. There is no precondition that the OEC has to be involved in the case: see sec. 88/A HCA and Hungary (9) above.

(3) L has to prove the unlawful conduct of F as sec. 164 HCP says that evidence has to be provided usually by the person with a legal interest in the recognition of these facts as positive by the court. In case of a claim for compensation the person who suffered the damages shall prove the following: (i) the amount of his/her damages suffered as a consequence of the activity of the other party, and (ii) the causality link between the activity of the defendant and the damage suffered. The responsibility of the defendant is directly linked to the culpability (contrary to the claim aiming at a prohibition – when the liability of the defendant is strict liability). In the course of litigation and the fact-finding procedure, difficulties may arise in proving the reduced turnover of the plaintiff and the amount of the resulting damages (lost profits) or the damage arising from the infringement. Therefore, in the course of the litigation, first of all, it is reasonable to request the establishment of the violation of the law and the prohibition of the defendant from the violation of law. Any other claim (claim for compensation) shall subsequently be requested in order to avoid the continuance of the claim. There is no general rule on the calculation of level of profit loss. Loss of savings, loss of fruits and loss of rebates are also taken into account. Restitutionary damages are not calculated as part of the damages.

(4) There are no claims for discovery or rendering of accounts.

Ireland (10)

(1) Under sec. 14 of the Competition Act 2002, L has a right of action against F in respect of its abuse of a dominant position in breach of sec. 5 of the act. L would have to show that F is dominant and that the loyalty discount scheme amounts to an abuse because, for example, the threshold is not based on a quantitative standard. The damages that L claims can include loss of profit, if he has solid evidence of such loss. Under sec. 14 of the Competition Act 2002 a plaintiff may, where the court deems it appropriate, be awarded exemplary damages, the purpose of which is to punish the defendant and deter future breach.

The principle underlying the award of damages is *restitutio in integrum*. The injured party is entitled to be restored to the situation he was in before the abuse of dominance occurred, insofar as financial compensation allows. Generally, two types of damages are available, general damages and special damages. General damages are assessed by the court to compensate the plaintiff for the inconvenience, annoyance and frustration caused by the defendant's actions. Special damages are awarded to compensate for specific items of expense, which the plaintiff can prove have been incurred up the date of trial and continuing losses into the future (usually based on actuarial calculations). The plaintiff will have to provide evidence that such specific expenses have been or will be incurred.

Exemplary (punitive) damages are awarded in exceptional circumstances. An example would be where there has been a deliberate and conscious violation of rights. In Ireland, awards of punitive damages tend to be in fractions of the general damages award, rather than multiples thereof (in contrast to the treble damages rule in the USA). Under the Courts Act 1981, any award for damages attracts interest from the date of judgment.

(2) Under sec. 8(10), there is no requirement for an antitrust authority to be involved in the claim. Having established a breach of sec. 5 of the Competition Act 2002 by an undertaking abusing its dominant position, the court may, under sec. 14(7) of the act, either at its own instance or on the application of the Authority, order the dominant position to be discontinued unless the court's specifications are complied with. Alternatively, the court may require that the dominant position be adjusted in a manner and within a period specified in the order, by a sale of assets or otherwise as the court may specify. It seems likely that the Irish courts would be cautious of taking the radical step of

dismantling a dominant position. In *Competition Authority v. Irish League of Credit Unions*, Judge Kearns made it clear he was unwilling to go so far.[73] Breach of sec. 5 of the Competition Act 2002 may also be prosecuted by the Competition Authority as a criminal offence. The fines are the same as for a breach of sec. 4 of the act, see Case 9 above. There is no possibility of imprisonment for a sec. 5 offence.

(3) The burden of proof is on the applicant L to prove 'on the balance of probabilities' that F is in breach of sec. 5 and that he has suffered damages as a result. If it is proved that an action was done by F there is a rebuttable presumption that directors or other decision makers consented to it, which gives L an additional right of action against those persons. The level of profit loss could be established by showing sales figures prior to the introduction by F of its discount scheme, by showing expected sales figures, or equivalent sales figures in an adjacent market, and by showing that such loss was not accountable to external factors. The infringer's profits are not automatically part of the damages, although they may assist in the calculation of damages.

In a criminal case the standard of proof is normally for the prosecution to prove the case 'beyond reasonable doubt'. For the hard-core offences listed in sec. 6(2) of the Competition Act 2002 (including price fixing and market sharing agreements), there is effectively a reversal of this burden of proof: the court is obliged to presume that the object of the agreement is to prevent, restrict or distort competition, unless the defendant can prove otherwise. The standard of proof for the defendant to overturn this presumption is the balance of probabilities, as per sec. 3(3)(a) of the Competition Act 2002. This reversal of the burden of proof does not apply to abuse of dominance cases.

(4) In the enforcement of his compensatory claim, L could request the court to order the discovery of F's accounts. Discovery prior to the institution of proceedings is only granted in very exceptional circumstances. Generally, discovery of documentary evidence may only be sought once pleadings have closed and a defence has been delivered by the defendant. Discovery should be sought first on a voluntary basis and, if voluntary discovery is refused, it can then be sought by way of an application to court. Discovery relates to all documentation in the power, possession or procurement of the party to the proceedings (or non-party) which, subject to relevance and necessity, relates to matters at issue in the proceedings. In relation to discovery, the Irish

[73] *Competition Authority v. Irish League of Credit Unions*, High Court, Kearns J, October 22, 2004.

courts recognize that documents containing legal advice and prepared in contemplation, or for the purposes, of the proceedings are covered by legal professional privilege and does not require these to be produced on discovery. It is unlikely that an Irish court would distinguish between in-house legal counsel and external lawyers for the purposes of recognising legal professional privilege.

Italy (10)

(1) The case at hand seems to fall somehow half way between 'pure' quantitative discounts and loyalty discounts. Simple quantitative discounts, set at a particular level in order to allow retailers to buy large quantities by awarding a premium for the realization of a determinate volume of sales appear possible, while this is not the case for loyalty discounts. When sales targets are not predetermined, retailers may be induced to obtain supplies from the producer, for fear of losing the loyalty premium, i.e. for not having achieved the volume of sales by just a few units. In the present case, discounts are qualified as loyalty ones, although a specific threshold level is mentioned. Should discounts indeed be loyalty ones, L would then be entitled to claim damages for F's abuses of his dominant position (art. 3 of the Law 287/90) by offering them to the travel agency for all inland flight routes.

Art. 33(2) of the Law 287/90 entitles the victim of anti-competitive behaviour to claim damages in the Court of Appeal. However, it does not specify who is entitled to damages or how to qualify and calculate them. Therefore, one has to combine this article with the general provisions of the Civil Code (cc) on tort liability and of the Code of Civil Procedure (cpc). The main provision is art. 2043 cc. Under this article, whoever commits an act either with intent or with fault, which causes others an unjustified injury, has to compensate them in damages. Pursuant to art. 1223 cc monetary compensation embraces both the loss borne by the aggrieved party (*danno emergente*) and the lost profit (*lucro cessante*), as long as they are an immediate and direct consequence of the banned behaviour. When it is impossible to determine the precise amount of damages (and this often occurs in the field of antitrust law when it comes to the calculation of the profit loss), art. 1226 cc provides that the judge has to decide on the basis of an equitable evaluation.

Case law offers two key examples in which courts awarded damages as a consequence of violation of antitrust law. In both cases (SIP) Telecom was the defendant. In the one case, Telsystem, a company offering telecommunication systems to business clients requested to be connected to Telecom's network.[74] Telecom denied access to it. In the other case Albacom asked to be connected to the network of Telecom, obtaining only a delayed access, which caused obstacles to the starting up of its business.[75]

(2) L's right to claim damages is not conditional upon prior involvement of the Authority (*Autorità Garante*) in the case. As already pointed out, private and public enforcement of antitrust law follow two independent paths. Nonetheless, there is no uniform view as to the issue of whether courts are completely free to judge, to the extent of ignoring the decisions of the Authority.[76] It is interesting to observe that in the Telsystem/Telecom case, the Court of Milan initially rejected the claim of Telsystem for interim measures. Only after the Authority had verified Telecom's abuse of its dominant position,[77] did the court award damages to Telsystem.

(3) Art. 2697 cc provides that whoever wants to assert a right before a court has to bring evidence of the facts upon which the right is grounded. L has to prove the damage (i.e. significant losses of turnover and profit), the existence of a causal link between F's discount policy and his damage, F's fault, and indicate the amount of the damage he suffered as a result.

Proof of the causal link between the damage and the alleged infringement of antitrust law is a difficult task. The reason is that a variety of elements can affect a company's capacity to generate profits. Among other factors, there are changes in consumer preferences, poor commercial strategy, economy slowdown, etc. The other *punctum dolens* is the quantification of the profit loss. Its difficult calculation deters parties from seeking private enforcement.

In the Telsystem/Telecom case, the court appointed a group of experts who had to calculate damages.[78] First of all, the team of experts assessed whether the victim was indeed ready to enter the market and if the only impeding reason was Telecom's denial of access. This became

[74] Corte d'Appello of Milano, July 18, 1995, *Telsystem S.p.A. vs. SIP S.p.A.* in *Foro It.*, 1996, I, 276, with note of A. Barone. This decision constitutes a fundamental step in Italian case law as regards determination of 'competition' damages.

[75] Corte d'Appello of Roma, January 20, 2003, *Albacom vs. Telecom Italia*, in *Foro It.*, 2003, 2474, with note of E. Scoditti.

[76] For an overview on this issue, see M. Libertini, *Il ruolo del giudice nell'applicazione delle norme antitrust*, in Giur. Comm. I (1998) 649–679, at 659.

[77] AGCM January 10, 1995, n. 2622, Bollettino n. 1-2/1995.

[78] Corte d'Appello of Milano of December 24, 1996, *Telsystem S.p.A. vs. Telecom Italia*, in *Danno e Responsabilità* (1997) 602, with note of S. Bastianon.

immediately clear. Telsystem had already created the network infrastructures and undertaken commitments towards some clients, eager to benefit from the new telecommunication system. For determining the pure economic loss the experts analysed Telsystem's accounting books. As for the calculation of the profit loss, the experts focused first on the profits that Telsystem could have obtained in a scenario with no obstacles created by Telecom. Second they analysed the loss due to the delayed access to the market as the first enterprise operating on the Italian market in vocal telephony for closed groups of subscribers. The experts verified, on the basis of economic arguments, that Telsystem's initial part of the curve, which expresses probable economic results, had been altered (e.g. a more limited portfolio of clients). Another interesting decision offering an example of how profit loss has been assessed, is *Bluvacanze/Viaggi del Ventaglio-Turisanda-Hotelplan Italia.*[79] The case concerned a collective boycotting performed by way of refusals to deal with Bluvacanze. The court estimated the volume of sales that the agent could have obtained during the time suppliers refused to deal, i.e. April, May and June. The court added to the medium volume of sales of the previous three months (January–March), multiplied by three, a percentage of increase in sales based on what had been registered the previous year (since the period between April and June is especially fruitful for travel agencies). Once it had calculated the volume of non-realized sales, the court added the commission agreed upon by the commercial parties, minus the 10 per cent discount that Bluvacanze was offering to its clientele.

(4) L has no specific claims for discovery or rendering of accounts. There is no specific provision giving the Court of Appeal the power to impose additional positive injunctions. The Court of Appeal is entitled to adopt emergency measures, but has no specific power to issue additional orders at the time of the decision (on nullity or damages). This follows from the wording of art. 33(2). Nonetheless, some scholars believe that the Court of Appeal should also be capable of adopting additional remedies, i.e. permanent inhibiting orders (*inibitoria finale*).[80] The

[79] Corte d'Appello of Milan, July 11, 2003, *Bluvacanze vs. I Viaggi del Ventaglio-Turisanda-Hotelplan Italia*, in Il diritto industriale, n. 2/2004, 157, with note of G. Faella, 170–177.

[80] M. Libertini, *Il ruolo del giudice nell'applicazione delle norme antitrust*, in Giur. Comm. I (1998), 649–679, at 662. The author considers the list of remedies stated in art. 33(2) as a non-exhaustive list. Following his interpretation, this provision only affirms the sole competence of the Court of Appeal in the field of antitrust law. As to the (content of) the remedies, general provisions of the cpc apply.

reason is that monetary compensation is not sufficient to re-establish the *status quo ante*. Case law, on the other hand, follows a strict interpretation of art. 33(2) of the Law 287/90 and denies any possibility of issuing additional positive injunctions.[81] This stream has been confirmed by a recent decision of the Appellate Court of Torino, which has underlined that any additional injunction is reserved to the (discretion of the) Authority.[82] Nonetheless, the *Bluvacanze/Ventaglio-Turisanda-Hotelplan* decision[83] shows a slight opening towards the view prompted by scholars. The court did not reject the request for an inhibiting measure because it is in principle impossible to obtain it from the court, but simply because the commercial relationship between the parties was not ongoing at the time the decision was issued.

The only judicial remedy L could count upon, in addition to his monetary compensation, is offered by art. 102 cpc. Any interested party can ask the judge to order the publication of the decision in one or more newspapers, costs to be sustained by the loser, whenever this publication may contribute to compensate the damage. The judge has complete discretion in this evaluation.

Netherlands (10)

(1) If the conduct infringes art. 24 DCA the conduct can be regarded as a wrongful act according to art. 6:162 DCC. L can start an action before the civil courts as they have the ability to award damages to individuals for losses suffered as a result of an infringement of competition law. The NCA does not have the power to award civil damages. According to the general rule of art 6:95 DCC the amount of damages 'consists of patrimonial loss (loss to property, rights and interests) and any other prejudice, to the extent that the law confers a right to damages therefor'. In principle, damages consist of full compensation for actual damage.[84] According to art. 6:96 DCC damages consist of loss incurred (*damnum emergens*) and profit deprived (*lucrum cessans*). Furthermore, in accordance with art. 96(2) DCC the following costs may be claimed as loss: (a) reasonable costs to prevent or mitigate damages which could be

[81] On the evolution of case law on this issue, see M. Scuffi, *Orientamenti Consolidati e Nuove Prospettive nella Giurisprudenza Italiana Antitrust*, in (2003) Riv.Dir.Ind., I, 95.

[82] Corte d'Appello of Turin, August 7, 2001, in Rep. Foro It. (2002), under *Concorrenza (disciplina)*, 172.

[83] Corte d'Appello of Milan, July 11, 2003, *Bluvacanze vs. Ventaglio-Turisanda-Hotelplan*, in (2004) Il diritto industriale, n. 2, 157, with note of G. Faella, 170–177.

[84] See Supreme Court, February 1, 2002, NJ 2002, 122.

expected as a result of the event giving rise to liability, (b) reasonable costs incurred in assessing damage and liability, (c) reasonable costs incurred in obtaining extra-judicial payment. As the basis of the calculation is the full compensation of actual damage, D cannot claim punitive damages.

(2) No, L can start proceedings autonomously. However, if a public entity finds a conduct to infringe antitrust regulation, this might be a fact to which the court may give importance. The evaluation of the evidence is left to the discretion of the courts.[85] If for example the competition authority has found the defendant to have infringed the DCA, the court may consider it likely that the defendant has committed a wrongful act and may allow the defendant to prove evidence to the contrary.

(3) Reparation of damages can only be claimed for damages related to the event giving rise to the liability of the obligor, which, also having regard to the nature of the liability and the nature of the damage, can be attributed to him as a result of such event. It is to be noted that a more direct link between a risk of damages and the damage actually incurred may result in a reduction of the burden of proof on the plaintiff on the question whether the damage incurred was caused by the wrongful act. The court may even reverse the burden of proof where a causal link between the wrongful act and the damages incurred is considered likely.[86] There is no case law on this issue. The amount of damages should, as far as possible, put the plaintiff in the same (financial) position it would have been in, absent the infringement. The court shall assess the damage in a manner most appropriate to its nature. The valuation may be done by making a comparison between the actual position of the plaintiff (at the time of the trial, therefore: ex-post) and the position it would probably have been in without the infringement. In many cases it is not possible to calculate the damages very precisely. Where the extent of the damage cannot be determined precisely, it shall, in accordance with art. 6: 97 DCC, be estimated. It is left to the discretion of the court to assess whether and, if so, to what extent, the amount of the damage can be determined and which criteria should be applied determining the amount of the damage. In certain cases, the Supreme Court accepted a calculation of damages not based on the actual losses but on objective criteria, the so-called 'abstract

[85] Art. 152 (2) BRv.

[86] See Supreme Court November 29, 2002, NJ 2004, 305, April 18, 2003, NJ 2004, 306 and May 7, 2004, NJ 2004, 422.

method' for calculation of damages.[87] In the abstract method, damages are calculated irrespective of the actual damage suffered.[88] It has been suggested to use this method in antitrust litigation as well. At present there is no case law on this issue.

(4) The Dutch legal system does not provide for discovery as such. However, it does have limited forms of discovery. Before main proceedings are initiated, it is possible to have a provisional hearing of parties and witnesses at the request of an interested party in order to find out if sufficient evidence can be produced to substantiate a possible claim.[89] Such request must state the identity of the witnesses, the identity of the opposite party, the nature and amount of the claim and the facts he aims to prove.[90] The court will enable both parties to be heard prior to deciding on the request.[91] If the requesting party finds the results of the pre-trial hearing not satisfactory, it can decide not to pursue the case. Furthermore, the court may, upon request or *ex officio*, order a party to make its administration available for inspection or to submit documents relevant for the case.[92] However, parties are not obliged to do so.[93] In addition, any person with a legitimate interest may request the court to order a third party to allow to be inspected or copied records that relate to legal relationships to which the person making the request is a party.[94]

Poland (10)

(1) and (2) The behaviour of F constitutes an abuse of a dominant position under art. 8 u.o.k.k., especially art 8.2(1) (direct or indirect imposition of unfair prices, including predatory prices or prices evidently low) and art 8.2(5) (preventing formation of conditions necessary for the emergence or development of competition). Such actions shall entirely or partly be held null and void. At the same time, there is a violation of unfair competition law, i.e. causing clients to purchase goods and services from a particular undertaking or making them do

[87] See Asser-Hartkamp 4-I (12th edn 2004), no. 417.

[88] Cases in which the abstract method is used concern non-delivery of certain goods at a certain price. The abstract amount of damages is the difference between the agreed price and the market price at the moment of default, irrespective whether the plaintiff actually bought replacing goods.

[89] Art. 186 BRv. [90] Art. 187(3) BRv. [91] Art. 187(4) BRv. [92] Art. 162(1) BRv.

[93] In accordance with art. 162(2) BRv it is in the court's discretion to decide on the consequences of such a refusal.

[94] Art. 843a DCCP. The party in principle must comply with the order, unless it has a legal privilege, if there are compelling reasons not to do so or in case it is likely that justice can be done without the inspection or copy of the documents concerned.

so (art. 15.1(5) u.z.n.k). For the antitrust violation, the President of the OCCP is competent. He issues the 'decision to refrain from competition restricting practices' if such practices take place. For the violation of unfair competition law, the ordinary courts are competent. As regards the relation between these two actions, some authors assume that each act recognized by the President of the OCCP as an act restricting or infringing competition will at the same time constitute an act of unfair competition on the basis of the u.z.n.k. Consequently, after the President of the OCCP has issued a decision recognizing an act restricting or infringing competition, the undertaking can with considerable confidence bring a civil claim on the basis of art 15 u.z.n.k. This view, however, remains controversial in Polish legal doctrine.[95] In any event, it is possible to undertake separate proceedings on the grounds of the u.z.n.k. and u.o.k.k. None of the proceedings prejudices the other. There is no precondition that the President of the OCCP must be involved in the proceedings on the basis of u.z.n.k.

As far as damages are concerned, they can be claimed only on the basis of unfair competition law, i.e. art 15 u.z.n.k. and art. 19 u.z.n.k., but not (directly) on the basis of a violation of u.o.k.k.[96] No punitive damages *sensu stricto* can be claimed. However, the undertaking (L) can demand F that pay a certain amount of money for a social goal preserving Polish culture or national heritage (art 18. 1(6) u.z.n.k.).

(3) Art. 18a u.z.n.k introduces a reversed burden of proof in cases regarding misleading branding and advertisement. However, art. 18 should be interpreted narrowly. In cases other than misleading branding and advertisement the standard rules should apply.[97]

(4) According to art. 232 k.p.c., parties are obliged to point out the evidence necessary to prove the claimed facts. In the instant case, L would have the right to ask F to disclose documents. However, his right to inquiry into the evidence may be restricted (however the facts of the case make it rather unlikely).

Portugal (10)

(1) According to art. 6 Law no. 18/2003, June 11, F is in a dominant market position and is abusing his dominant position.[98] The turnover

[95] E. Nowinska, M. Du Vall, *Komentarz*, p. 125.
[96] See above Cases 6 (Child labour, 1 (Risky bread), and 3 (Whisky).
[97] E. Nowinska, M. Du Vall, *Komentarz*, p. 197.
[98] See C. Alberto Caboz Santana, *O Abuso de posição dominante no direito da concorrência* (1995).

threshold discounts and comparable bonus systems are an abuse to the extent they are intended to bind customers. L suffers damage due to the behaviour of F. Those damages are pure economic loss. If we consider that art. 6 Law no. 18/2003, June 11 is a protective norm for the individual competitors, L could ask for compensation. Our opinion is that art. 6 Law no. 18/2003, June 11 directly protects the public interest and competition as a whole and indirectly protects individual competitors. That is the reason why L can bring a civil liability action to obtain compensation. However, there are great difficulties in calculating the loss L suffers. Art. 564/1, 2 CC determines that 'the duty of compensation not only comprehends the damage caused, but also the benefits that the injured party has lost as a result of the injury' and 'when setting the compensation the court can consider future damages, since they are foreseeable; if they cannot be determined, the assessment of appropriate compensation will be referred to a later court decision'.

Portuguese law does not allow punitive damages. But there is some flexibility due to art. 494 CC ('When the liability is to be established only based on negligence, the compensation can be fixed in equity, at less than the actual amount of damages, since the degree of culpability of the agent, the economic situation of the injured and the circumstances of the case justify it'). However, the compensation is always limited to the damage suffered, therefore punitive damages cannot be claimed.

(2) Civil actions including compensatory claims do not require any previous decision of the antitrust authority. There are still few private actions concerning abuse of dominant position. Normally, the fight against conduct in restraint of free competition is pursued by the antitrust authorities.

(3) In a civil liability action, L has to prove the illegal conduct of F, the abuse of a dominant position, the damage he has suffered, the connection between the illegal conduct and the damage and also L's fault. If L cannot determine and prove his damages, he can, according to articles 565 and 569 Civil Code, bring a generic demand, which the court will later determine. Portuguese civil liability law does not provide for restitutionary damages, only for the victim's actual damages.

(4) There is no general discovery claim. In civil procedure, the parties have information duties and the duty to contribute to the discovery of truth. As a palliative solution for the difficulties of *onus probandi* claims where the assessment of damages is straightforward can be made to support claims of civil liability.

Spain (10)

(1) F's conduct may constitute an infringement of art. 6 LDC. This article contains the same principle as art. 82 EC. Loyalty discounts are considered as abuse if practised by a dominant undertaking and L, like any other person, could initiate a claim before the Service for the Defence of Competition (SDC). As far as damages are concerned, art. 13 LDC declares that a claim for damages based on the grounds of an illegal infringement of the LDC may be brought by any person who is considered harmed by such infringement before the ordinary civil jurisdiction once there is a final administrative or judicial decision on the question. The substantive and procedural regime that applies to the damages claim is provided by general civil law (Spanish Civil Code – CC, and the Spanish Code of Civil Procedure – LEC), which considers as a part of the damages suffered the *lucrum cessans* (art. 1106 CC) and covers *all the damages* that can be connected to the abusive behaviour, but not any other punitive damages.

(2) Yes. The SDC and the TDC have exclusive competence over the application of the LDC, therefore a final decision by the TDC declaring that F has entered into a conduct forbidden by art. 6 LDC is indispensable in order to claim for damages as foreseen in art. 13 LDC.

(3) As in any other declaratory procedure before a civil judge, the burden of proof relies on the plaintiff, who must prove that he has suffered the said damages because of the infringement committed by the defendant. The infringer's profits are only part of the damages if the plaintiff can show that he had a 'property right' that was unduly exploited by the defendant (unjust enrichment).

(4) The Spanish Competition Authorities are charged with the prosecution of LDC infringements. Once the SDC initiates a procedure, it has all the instruction powers that are deemed necessary to clarify the facts and determine any liability, including requiring information from any individual or corporation and undertaking all necessary investigations into companies or associations of companies, as well as examining the books, taking copies and asking for oral explanations. In order to calculate the amount of fines, the SDC will use accounts of the defendant. LEC provides the plaintiff, in the subsequent claim before the civil court for damages with the right to ask the defendant to render accounts.

Sweden (10)

(1) F's behaviour constitutes a breach of sec. 19 of the Swedish Competition Act and L has, according to art. 33 in the Act, a right to

compensation for damages caused by the infringement provided that the breach was intentional or negligent. The right to compensation is subject to a ten-year limitation from the time when the damage occurred. The preparatory documents stipulate that compensation will only be afforded for pure economic loss, i.e. not damage to person or object. The purpose of sec. 33 is, according to the preparatory documents, to compensate for loss of income and encroachment in business activity. Accordingly, L has no right to punitive damages.

Cases concerning compensation for damages will be brought before the ordinary courts. According to the Swedish general rules on compensation, the basis for calculation of damages is normally that the compensation should put the injured party in the same economic situation as if the damage had not occurred. That is, loss of profit should be included in the compensation. However, neither KL nor the preparatory documents state whether compensation for infringements of the prohibitions in KL shall include loss of profit or simply put the injured party in the position he would have had if the agreement had not been entered into. It is possible to find some guidance from general contract law where the general rules provide that when there is an agreement between two parties the compensation shall include loss of profit, but when there is no agreement between the parties the situation is more uncertain. The obligation to compensate damages in *culpa in contrahendo* is not considered to include loss of profit under Swedish contract, or quasi-contract, law. One could argue that when applying art. 33 of the Swedish Competition Act one should not make a distinction as to whether there has in fact been an agreement between the parties or whether the damage occurred is due to something else. Since loss of income is something that the injured party is entitled to it seems only reasonable to assume that art. 33 of the act includes compensation for loss of profit as well.[99]

(2) Compensation for damages does not require that the antitrust authority get involved.[100] On the contrary, these types of cases are to be brought by the injured party, in this case L, directly against the company in breach, in this case F.

[99] C. Wetter, et al., *Konkurrenslagen – en handbok* (2nd edn 2002), p. 823.

[100] Thus, the situation is slightly different in comparison to the possibility to make a claim for damages for breach of the Marketing Act, at least some of its prohibitions, see Cases 1–8 supra.

(3) In cases concerning damages, there are usually three sets of substantive facts which have to be established by one of the parties: an intentional or negligent breach of law, the damage (including the size of the damage) and a causal link between the breach of law and the damage. Although, the plaintiff generally has the burden of proof for all three sets of facts, the theoretical starting point is that the burden of proof should be placed upon the party who is in control of the relevant evidence so that the purpose of the rules are best fulfilled. As to cases concerning damages, these considerations generally lead to the result that the plaintiff has the burden of proof, but often the level of probability required is lowered in comparison to other areas of private law. This is particularly so, when complex causal relations are involved and where the plaintiff can only with difficulty investigate the presumably negligent activities of the defendant.

But in principle, in order to get compensation for damage L has to prove that there has been an infringement by F, that he has suffered loss and that the loss is due to F's actions. Of course, it will be quite difficult to prove exactly how much a certain conduct has affected your business and thereby how big the compensation should be. It is possible, though, under Swedish law for the court to estimate the damage in a reasonable amount, where it is difficult to prove how big the damage is.[101] It has been suggested that the level of profit made by the infringing party may in some cases serve as a guide when it comes to calculating the level of the compensation.[102]

(4) Claims for compensation for damages, unlike cases solely concerning suspected breaches of KL, belong before the ordinary courts. In these kinds of cases the question of costs is subject to the general rules, under which the losing party must compensate the winning party for all his costs, incurred prior as well as during proceedings, as long as they may be considered to be reasonable in order to ensure ones rights. It is not possible to make a claim for discovery or rendering of accounts alone. But within the ambit of a dispute over liability a party has to produce whatever evidence the opposite party applies for.[103] Thus, in principle it should be possible to require access to accounts. So far there are no judgments by the Swedish courts dealing with the question of

[101] Chap. 35 sec. 5 Code of Civil and Criminal Procedure. [102] Bill 1992/93:56 p. 97.
[103] See Code of Civil and Criminal Procedure chap. 42 sec. 7 and chap. 38 sec. 2.

compensation for damages. The cases that have been filed have been withdrawn after out-of-court settlements.

Summary (10)

1. *Damages claim*

The underlying factual scenario was classified in all reporting countries as abuse of a market dominant position (and sometimes as an infringement of unfair competition law). Bonus systems by a market dominant party constitute an abuse if they are not justified on objective grounds. The intention of the case is to clarify the question of whether the infringement of the abuse interdiction brings with it a compensatory claim, and if so, which modalities are involved in this claim. The majority of reporting countries provide for such a claim. Sometimes there is a special legal basis for the claim in antitrust law, in others grounds drawn from general civil tort law are relied upon to justify claims. These differences are simply of constructive nature and have no influence on the result. Also in those countries which have their own antitrust law basis for claims, general civil law is relied upon to clarify matters not expressly provided for. UK law takes an individual route. Here, in the Competition Act 1988, the question of private compensatory claims was left open. From the preparatory materials it can be inferred that the legal position in a case of infringement of national antitrust law should be in line with European antitrust law with regard to the available remedies. And here English courts in accordance with the decisions in *Banks*[104] and *Courage*[105] have awarded damages claims. According to this private compensatory claims are also available for infringements of national antitrust law. This is also the position under Polish law. True, there are no specific compensatory claims for antitrust infringements. Since in Polish practice, however, there is a strong tendency to classify antitrust infringements as parallel to unfair competition violations, private compensatory claims are available through this route. The only country which departs from the basic principle of compensatory claims is Hungary. Here compensatory claims fail for lack of a contractual relationship between infringer and aggrieved party, even though the abuse of a market-dominant position is present here. Nevertheless, this general finding has to be qualified in that there

[104] ECJ, 13.4.1994, C-128/92, *Banks v. British Coal Corporation* [1994] ECR I-1209.
[105] ECJ, 20.9.2001, C-453/99, *Courage Ltd v. Crehan* [2001] ECR I-6297.

are no relevant court decisions to date. In general it can be said that court decisions on compensatory claims for antitrust law infringements are 'thin on the ground'.

2. *Determining of damages and punitive damages*

In the calculation of damages (quantum) there are many points in common between the reporting countries. Generally speaking, loss of profit (*lucrum cessans*) is to be compensated as part of economic loss. In some countries future loss of profits may also be compensated provided they are foreseeable (Italy, Portugal). Throughout the basic principles of compensation under civil law apply.

There is also broad consensus on the topic of punitive damages. With three exceptions no punitive damages will be awarded. The first exception is under English law, which provides for exemplary damages, albeit not specifically for antitrust law but rather as a general principle of law. Where the infringer intentionally aims to make profits which are higher than the damages he would normally be obliged to pay, then he may be liable for exemplary damages. The English courts have until now declined to apply the principle in cases on antitrust law. The House of Lords has, however, disapproved such a limitation on the doctrine of exemplary damages, thereby opening the way to punitive damages under English law although there is no reported case concerning competition law yet. The second exception arises under sec. 14 of the Irish Competition Act 2002 according to which a plaintiff may, where the court deems it appropriate, be awarded exemplary damages, the purpose of which is to punish the defendant and deter future breach. And, finally, there is a peculiarity under Polish law. Here the infringer can be required to make payment to a non-profit organization.[106] This is not punitive damages in the narrow sense as the money does not accrue to the aggrieved party. However, the deterrent effect on the violator is the same, as he is subject to a duty to pay which exceeds the mere compensation of the actual loss incurred.

Even if in the other countries there are in principle no punitive damages, there are occasionally rules which move in this direction from a functional viewpoint. Under French law damages for *trouble commercial* can be awarded. This is not limited to economic loss but may be determined by the court. By reason of the wide judicial

[106] The rule under which the payment is to accrue to an institution which protects Polish culture or the national heritage seems to be non-conform with Community law.

discretion and the paucity of French court decisions, it is, however, not possible to make generalizations, e.g. on the factors determining such compensation awards or on particularities in the field of antitrust law.

3. *Damages only after the decision of an antitrust authority?*

In the large majority of countries the compensatory claim is not dependant on whether the abuse of a dominant market position has previously been ascertained by an antitrust authority. In these countries administrative and private law proceedings are entirely independent of each other. Corresponding to the result in Case 9, however, there is one exception. Since in Spain the antitrust authority and cartel court have exclusive jurisdiction in the application of antitrust law, a compensatory claim is only possible once the antitrust authority has intervened. Even if in other countries the enforcement of a compensatory claim is not dependant on an administrative decision, it is often advisable to call upon the antitrust authority to act first. As the authority has comprehensive investigatory powers, this will bring benefits in terms of collating evidence.

4. *Burden of proof*

This leads to the question of distribution of the burden of proof. In no reporting country were peculiarities in the question of the distribution of proof raised. Hence the aggrieved party in general has to establish the antitrust law infringement, its losses, causation, and fault of the other party. An easing of the burden is only found in certain countries, e.g. in Sweden in relation to causation where, as so often in antitrust law, it is highly complex. Here it must also be emphasized that there is no easing of the burden of proof specific to antitrust law but rather in the application of general rules of evidence. This statement also applies regarding the calculation of quantum. Here numerous jurisdictions provide for an easing of the burden. If through no responsibility of the aggrieved party the precise calculation presents difficulties, then the courts often have the discretion to estimate the extent of losses incurred. In all countries only losses actually incurred can be claimed, but not the profits gained by the infringer. In certain countries, however, infringer profits can be cited as the starting point for the calculation of losses (Germany since 2005, Sweden). In Denmark the extent of fault can be referred to as a basis of calculation.

5. *Discovery and rendering of accounts*

In no reporting country is there a specifically antitrust law right to discovery or claim for rendering of accounts. General legal rules are applied. In the majority of countries there is a reluctance to recognize such rights. England (and to a lesser extent Ireland) provides the exception, where wide powers of discovery exist in accordance with general civil procedural law. Discovery rights also exist in Denmark, Finland and Sweden where the courts can order the disclosure of particular documents. In the other countries there are rights of discovery under limited conditions. In principle it is the task of the claimant to collate all material evidence.

6. *Conclusion*

Almost everywhere the aggrieved party in an antitrust infringement has a compensatory claim. However, in practice very little avail is made of this and only in certain countries are there relevant court decisions. Case 10 illustrates the influence of the burden of proof in this finding. The problems begin with the various elements of the compensatory obligation. First it must be established that an antitrust infringement is present at all. The almost universal absence of discovery rights is responsible for the fact that the claimant may be confronted with an insurmountable obstacle at this stage. Antitrust infringements are often practised secretly. Without special investigatory mechanisms it is often impossible to reveal the factual basis. This explains the high practical importance of antitrust administrative proceedings. As the factual investigation is not feasible for the claimant, only the antitrust authority with its comprehensive investigatory powers can achieve the necessary discovery of facts. Although only in Spain is an antitrust authority decision a mandatory precondition for the enforcement of a compensatory claim, the administrative proceeding occupies a central role in all remaining countries. In comparison the evidentiary problems regarding losses, causation and fault seem of lesser importance. The difficulties here are not specific to antitrust law. Similar to the substantive rules on damages, the procedural rules on burden of proof are sufficiently flexible to allow the victim of an antitrust infringement the assertion of its claims. To a large extent the amount of damages may be estimated.

As a further reason for the limited significance of private enforcement, the limited financial incentives for the claimant are cited. In fact the victim of an antitrust infringement can nowhere (with the exception of England and Ireland, at least theoretically) claim punitive damages. This finding is not specific to antitrust law, but derives from the fact that punitive damages are generally rejected in continental Europe. It is hardly realistic that an exception for antitrust law will be made here. Another measure to increase the incentives for private claims is to target infringer profits. In intellectual property law there is in many jurisdictions the possibility to claim surrender of profits made by an infringer. Van Gerven has proposed extending this also to violations of antitrust law.[107] This proposal would strengthen the incentives for private claims and at the same time the infringer will be deprived of the unjust gains from the antitrust infringement (independent of administrative fines or surrendering profits). On the other hand it is not possible simply to transfer the rights to surrender of profits from intellectual property law to antitrust law. Intellectual property law confers absolute rights whereas competition law only constitutes relative rights. Therefore, it has to be determined, where there are multiple victims, to which victims the infringer's profit should be attributed. However, the problem is not insoluble if the aggrieved party is accorded a proportionate claim to the gains. Targeting infringer profits seems to be a workable compromise, avoiding the introduction of punitive damages on the one side, and enhancing the attractiveness of private enforcement on the other.

[107] W. van Gerven, *Substantive Remedies for the Private Enforcement of EC Antitrust Rules Before National Courts*, in Ehlermann/Atanasiu (eds.), *European Competition Law Annual 2001: Effective Private Enforcement of EC Antitrust Law* (2003).

Case 11 Boycott - pre-trial measures and temporary relief

A has a dominant position in the textile retailing market in town R. When the clothing concern T wishes to open a branch in R, A publicly calls upon the citizens, companies and public institutions to have nothing to do with T so as to preserve the traditional structure of local retailing.

1. What claims does T have against A?
2. How must T actually proceed when bringing a claim? Is he required to give A notice of the claim? Will T have to bear his own pre-trial or trial costs, or can he (if successful) pass his costs on to A?
3. Can T pursue his claim by means of a temporary injunction? What are the preconditions for this?
4. Can the parties reach an out-of-court settlement? What requirements are to be observed in this?

Austria (11)

(1) Legal action against a boycott can be brought under both the UWG and the KartG. The OGH defines a boycott as the systematic exclusion of a competitor from trade by the non-acceptance or interruption of business connections by third parties initiated by one or more persons.[1] The third party within this definition may of course be a consumer or, as here, the general public (the town). The boycott is not expressly regulated in either the UWG or the KartG. In the context of UWG it is assessed under the general clause; in the KartG it is seen as a case of abuse of market power. Accordingly T has two remedies against A. As an enterprise whose legal or economic interests are affected by the conduct in question, T, as an enterprise which has a legal or economic interest into the decision,[2] may, pursuant to § 37 n. 3 KartG 1988 (= § 36 para. 4 n. 4 KartG 2005), file a claim with the cartel court to require A to cease the abuse. But T may also bring a cessation claim before the commercial court pursuant to § 1 UWG for unconscionable legal breach, if necessary also a claim for removal (e.g. against a poster campaign by A), since there is a competitive relationship between T and A.

(2) T does not need to notify A before filing a claim. § 45 ZPO will not assist the respondent.[3] Through the acknowledgment of an unfair trade law cessation claim the respondent has also admitted the existence of a

[1] OGH 8.7.1980, SZ 53/102 = JBl 1981, 380 = ÖBl 1981, 13 – 'travel agent boycott'.

[2] For the text difference between old and new law see above note 6.

[3] 'Where the respondent has not given cause by its conduct for the withdrawal of the claim and acknowledged the claim promptly then the judicial costs are borne by the

risk of repetition or perpetration and has thereby given cause for the proceedings. If the respondent resists the claim, the award of costs will be based on success in the proceedings. Pursuant to § 41 ZPO the wholly unsuccessful party in the proceedings has to reimburse its opponent for all costs necessarily incurred and reasonable in connection with the claim. These costs include pre-trial costs. Which costs are deemed necessary will be determined by the court at its discretion on careful assessment of the surrounding circumstances without a hearing.

In the cease-and-desist proceeding, the ZPO rules on reimbursement of costs have to be applied in the same way, taking into account that the losing party has to bear the costs to the extent that the proceeding or the defence was wanton. § 273 ZPO applies to the decision about costs (see Case 10 question 1).

(3) The claimant can bring an injunction claim before the cartel court (§ 52 para. 2 KartG 1988; now § 48 para. 1 KartG 2005) to secure cessation and removal of the infringement, or in contentious proceedings before the commercial court. According to § 24 UWG an injunction may be granted to secure a cessation claim under UWG, even where the preconditions under § 381 EO (need to preserve the status quo where the subject matter of the claim is endangered) are not fulfilled. The injunction does not require 'urgency' or 'necessity to expedite' (§§ 935, 940 German ZPO).[4] According to § 48 para. 1 KartG 2005 it is sufficient for the grant of an injunction that the conditions for a cease-and-desist order are certified. On the request of a party the cartel court has to give the necessary orders.[5]

(4) The reaching of an out-of-court settlement is at the discretion of the parties. If the claim has already been filed, then the parties may agree to stay the main proceedings and conclude their settlement out of court. The claimant has to withdraw the injunction claim. The aggrieved party also has to withdraw the claim under § 37 KartG 1988 (now § 36 para. 4 n. 4 KartG 2005) in the event of an out-of-court settlement. However, in this case the procedure is only terminated if the official bodies (Case 9 question 2) do not request the continuation of

claimant. Claimant also has to meet the respondent's extrajudicial costs incurred in the case.'

[4] OGH 11.9.1984, ÖBl 1984, 161 = JBl 1985, 430; OGH 25.5.2004, 4 Ob 116/04v, ÖBl-LS 2004/190 = ÖBl-LS 2004/182; OGH 30.11.2004, 4 Ob 249/04b, ÖBl-LS 2005/69.

[5] R. Hoffer/J. Barbist, *Das neue Kartellrecht* (2005), p. 70, deduce from this wording that – different to the situation under KartG 1988 – measures may be imposed which are different from the requested ones.

the proceeding within fourteen days after service of the withdrawal (§ 36 para. 5 KartG 2005).[6]

Denmark (11)

(1) The unlawfulness of A's behaviour is doubtful according to Danish law. The matter may concern an advertising message: go on conducting business with me instead of with my competitor. According to the rules of the Competition Act (CA) there will normally be a violation of CA § 11 concerning the prohibition on abusing a dominant position at a market if A directly or indirectly threatens to refuse delivery or states that he will deliver on inferior terms to customers who are also dealing with the competitor T. It will be a violation of § 2, sec. 1 and 2, of the Marketing Practices Act if A makes derogatory remarks of T or disparaging statements of T's products. According to the Administration of Justice Act, T can bring an action before the regular courts with a view to having it established that A's remarks are contrary to CA § 11. An action for an interlocutory injunction based on the remarks may be brought on the basis of §§ 641 ff. of the Administration of Justice Act. If T suffered a financial loss by reason of A's remarks, T may bring action for damages before the regular courts.

(2) The costs of actions are decided by the courts according to the rules of §§ 311 ff. of the Administration of Justice Act.[7] The losing party will according to § 312 be ordered to pay the costs of the winning party (lawyers, fees etc). The costs are estimated on the basis of the value of the case decided and not on the basis of the expenses, which the winning party actually incurred. The costs of out-of-court negotiations are borne by each of the parties or divided between them according to agreement.

(3) T may try to have A's behaviour hindered by an interlocutory injunction. The conditions are – as in case No. 2 and Case No. 8 above – that it must be very probable that a violation of the Competition Act or the Marketing Practices Act exists, that A may be expected to make the statements again, that it is necessary to issue an interlocutory injunction as T's interests cannot await a regular action before the courts, and that a ban will not be a disproportionate measure towards A. Security must normally be provided for A's possible losses incurred as a

[6] Similar already OGH als KOG 20.12.2004, 16 Ok 6/04 – Bankomat contract = ÖBl-LS 2005/87.

[7] B. von Eyben et al., *Karnovs lovssamling* (2001), p. 3844.

consequence of an interlocutory injunction, if the later action before the court proves that the conditions of the Administration of Justice Act § 642 and § 643 for issuing an injunction were not fulfilled.

(4) Settlements may be entered into at any time. There are no formal requirements concerning settlements. According to § 270, sec. 1 of the Administration of Justice Act settlements can be entered into as part of the court proceedings. It must be documented explicitly in court under the presence of both parties that the case has now been settled. Settlements may also be entered into as a contract between the parties and the court will have to be notified.[8]

England (11)

(1) On the assumption that the facts are as stated and nothing more, i.e. that (i) no disparaging comments have been made about the quality or provenance of T's products or the nature of T's business (such as would give rise to remedies of a defamation nature) and that (ii) no efforts by A have been made to encourage local businesses to break off any existing contractual relations with T (which would give rise to a possible liability in tort for inducing breach of contract or interference in contractual relations), a unilateral statement of this type would not, if A was non-dominant, give any cause of action known to English law. It is very doubtful whether the fact of A being dominant makes any difference to this. The answers to the following questions under Case 11 assume, nevertheless, that some abuse of dominant position *is* taking place here.

(2) Urgent interim relief can be applied for by T to restrain A from making further statements. See the explanation in answer to Case 9, question 2 above. On costs, the court has considerable discretion as to costs orders, the general principle being that the loser has to pay a substantial proportion of the winner's costs.

(3) Certainly, it would be possible to seek an interim (temporary) injunction here. The principles would be no different in a competition case from any other case. An interim injunction is, in English law, like any other injunction (a court order to do something other than pay money) an *equitable* remedy (being one developed by the separate courts of equity in the pre-1875 court system). This means, inter alia, that even if the facts and law showing a breach of the relevant law are proven to the court's satisfaction, the court nevertheless has a *discretion* whether

[8] Bernard Gomard, *Civilprocessen* (5th edn 2000), pp. 475 et seq. and p. 671; B. von Eyben et al., *Karnovs lovssamling* (2001), p. 3841.

to grant the injunction or not. There is, nevertheless, detailed case law which has been developed over many years as to the criteria which judges should consider in exercising their discretion to grant or not to grant an interim injunction. The leading case is the House of Lords judgment in *American Cyanamid Corp. v. Ethicon*,[9] where the House of Lords said that as long as a claim is not frivolous or vexatious and has some prospect of succeeding, the only factor the court should take into account is 'the balance of convenience'. In other words, it should simply ask itself the question: 'Would it hurt the claimant more not to have the temporary injunction pending trial than it would hurt the defendant to be subject to it?' A slightly different way of putting it would be 'the balance of the risk of doing an injustice' to one party as against another.[10]

(4) The parties can always reach an out-of-court settlement. Assuming proceedings have already been commenced, the settlement will need to be approved by the court in the form of a consent order (that by the agreement of the parties, it is ordered that [whatever the agreed terms of settlement are] and that the action be discontinued). In the adversarial English litigation system, as long as the parties are agreed on the settlement terms, the court will in principle approve whatever has been agreed between them.

Finland (11)

(1) Sec. 6 of the Finnish Act on Competition Restriction prohibits abuse of a dominant market position. A's intention is to prevent a new competitor from entering the market by inciting citizens, companies and public institutions to boycott T. A's behaviour constitutes a breach of sec. 6. A's conduct is clearly directed against T. According to sec. 1 para. 2 of the Finnish Act on Competition Restrictions, when the Act is applied, special attention must be paid to the interests of consumers and the protection of the freedom of business undertakings to operate without unjustified barriers and restrictions. An actor whose rights have been violated by an illegal act may apply to a civil court for an order compelling the defendant to refrain from the illegal act. Under secs. 6 and 18, T can demand that A refrain from boycott measures. T may also make a claim for compensation based on sec. 18(a).

9 [1975] AC 396.

10 May LJ in *Cayne v. Global Natural Resources* [1984] 1 All ER 225. See further J. O'Hare and K. Browne, Case 9 note 12 above, ch.27.

(2) A civil case is initiated when a written application for summons is sent to the office of a lower civil court. It is the duty of the civil court to attend *ex officio* to the service of the summons. It is not necessary for A to have been warned in advance. According to the main rule (the Procedural Code 21:1), the losing party has to provide compensation for all the necessary and reasonable litigation costs of the opposing party. Therefore, if T wins his case, A has to bear all the necessary and reasonable litigation costs of T.

(3) According to sec. 14 of the Finnish Act on Competition Restrictions, the Finnish Competition Authority may issue an interlocutory injunction if the application or implementation of a competition restriction has to be prevented immediately. There is no special provision in the Finnish Act on Competition Restrictions concerning temporary injunctions in civil court procedures. T can base his application for a temporary injunction on the Finnish Procedural Code (7:3). A temporary injunction may be granted if it appears that exercise of T's rights would be infringed by A's actions.

(4) T and A can reach an out-of-court settlement. T can cancel his claim or T and A can inform the civil court that the case has been settled. The settlement between A and B must not itself constitute a restraint of competition.

Private settlements do not affect administrative procedures. The powers of the Finnish Competition Authority are directly based on the Finnish Act on Competition Restrictions. According to sec. 12 of the Act, the Finnish Competition Authority must initiate the necessary proceedings to eliminate a competition restriction if it finds that a business undertaking or an association of business undertakings restrains competition in a manner referred to in sec. 4 or 6 or art. 81 or 82 of the EC Treaty.

France (11)

(1) The boycott is constituted by a deliberate action directed against another undertaking in order to evict it from the market.[11] Boycott is subject to no specific regulation in French antitrust law. It is actually a case of a prohibited agreement: art. L 420-1 of the commercial code.[12] Otherwise, it is only a unilateral intention that might have no effect on

[11] Cass. Com October 22, 2002 *SA Vidal v. Fédération française des sociétés d'assurances* in *Contrats, concurrence, consommation* (02/2002), p. 17.

[12] M. Malaurie-Vignal, *Droit de la concurrence*, p. 179.

the market.[13] In jurisprudence a boycott was always considered to be an anti-competitive practice in itself.[14] Since the case of *SA Vidal v. Fédération française des sociétés d'assurances*[15] it seems, however, that now there is a threshold (*théorie du seuil sensible*) that has to be passed in order to consider a practice being a prohibited agreement. This means that assessment of the effect of the agreement is no longer deduced from the gravity of the practice; the judge now has to verify first if there has actually been a significant effect on the market.[16] Furthermore, a prohibited agreement in order to be qualified as a boycott has either to produce an effect, or in case of simple agreement without effect, the anti-competitive intention has to be proved.[17] Nevertheless, a boycott might be tolerated when constituting a defence measure by the victim of an abuse of a dominant market position or other illegal practices directed against the boycotting undertaking.[18]

In the present case A's behaviour in French law does not constitute a boycott or an abuse of a dominant position. Concerning the boycott the proof of an agreement is impossible. Concerning the dominant position that A certainly has on this market, there is no abuse in his calling for boycott. As a matter of fact, in French antitrust law, art. 420-2 of the commercial code prohibits two types of abuse (dualistic approach): structural abuse (*abus de structure*) and abusive behaviour (*abus de comportement*), whereas the European law tends to consider only structural abuses.[19] Art. L 420-2 of the commercial code cites as particular examples of such abuses refusals to sell, linked sales or discriminatory conditions of sale and the severance of established commercial relations solely because the partner refuses to submit to unjustified commercial conditions. An instigation to boycott does not come within any of these categories.

(2) Supposing that there had been a boycott, the Council on Competition may be referred to by the Minister for Economic Affairs. It may assume jurisdiction of its own motion or be referred to by undertakings, or for matters relating to the interests for which they are responsible, by the bodies indicated in art. 462-1 of the commercial

[13] Cour d'appel de Paris, April 9, 2002: BOCC June 24, 2002, p. 392.

[14] Cour d'Appel de Paris, March 10, 1998, Dalloz 1998. IR 106.

[15] Cass. Com October 22, 2002 in: *Contrats, concurrence, consommation* (02/2002), p. 17.

[16] Note to Cass. Com October 22, 2002 in: *Contrats, concurrence, consommation* (02/2002), p. 19.

[17] Ibid. [18] Cour d'Appel de Paris, July 4, 1996, (1996) *Dalloz Affaires*, 1054.

[19] M. Malaurie-Vignal, *Droit de la concurrence*, p. 190.

code, that is to say the territorial authorities, professional associations, trade unions, approved consumer organisations, chambers of agriculture, chambers of trade and industry, with regard to the interests for which these are responsible. The Council on Competition may impose financial penalties applicable either immediately or in the event of non-fulfilment of the orders, art. L 464-2 I of the commercial code. These penalties are collected as claims of the state: L 464-4 of the commercial code. Measures ordering the publication, circulation or posting on a notice-board of the decision or a summary thereof or the insertion of the decision in the report prepared on the operations for the financial year by the managers, board of directors or the management of the undertaking are expenses to be borne by the concerned person: art. L 464-2-I of the commercial code.

Before the civil or commercial tribunals the expenses of the trial are to be borne by the party specified by the judge: art. 700 of the new code of civil procedure. Usually, this is the losing party: art. 696 of the new code of civil procedure, unless the judge makes a different decision for which there will need to be particular reasons. In both cases a pre-trial summoning is not usual or necessary.

(3) According to these two possible procedures, that is to say referring to the Council on Competition or the civil or commercial tribunals, there are two ways to obtain temporary measures that can also be combined.[20] In the procedure before the Council on Competition the possibility to obtain temporary measures is provided for in art. L 464-1 of the commercial code. The other possibility consists in using a summary interlocutory procedure (*référé*) referring the matter to civil or commercial tribunals giving the victim in certain antitrust matters of an anti-competitive practice the choice between two procedures: on the one hand, the normal summary interlocutory procedure of art. 808, 809, 872 or 873 of the new code of civil procedure that has to respond to the classic conditions of imminent damage or an obviously illegal act, or, on the other hand, the so-called competition summary interlocutory procedure (*référé concurrence*) of art. L. 442-6 IV of the commercial code.[21] According to this provision the judge ruling on urgent applications may order the cessation of discriminatory or abusive practices or any other provisional measure. Nevertheless, the special procedure of art. 442-6 IV

[20] Cour d'Appel de Paris, June 27, 1990, in Dalloz 1991 Somm. 251.

[21] V. Selinsky in: Juris-Classeur, *Concurrence, Consommation* (1993), Fasc. 380, 'Procédures de contrôle des pratiques anticoncurrentielles', no. 156.

of the commercial code is not very common, due to a decision of the *Cour de Cassation*, ruling that even in this case the conditions of the normal summary interlocutory procedure of art. 808, 809, 872 or 873 of the new code of civil procedure that there is an imminent damage or an obviously illegal act have to be proved.[22]

Temporary measures are applied rather seldom by the Council on Competition as it is very strict with regard to the notion of urgency and gravity of the damage.[23] Thus the *référé* procedures in front of the civil and commercial tribunals are far more efficient and rapid.[24]

(4) An out-of-court settlement is always possible between the opposed parties, but this does not affect the provisions of antitrust law by which the Council on Competition exercises its own jurisdiction in order to impose fines. This means that the arbitrator is not competent to impose fines or injunctions; nevertheless, he can make a declaration concerning the civil law consequences (damages and interest for example).[25]

Germany (11)

(1) A's behaviour constitutes a prohibited incitement to boycott pursuant to § 21 para. 1 GWB as well as the abuse of a dominant position according to § 19 GWB. T is affected by the prohibited conduct.[26] The factual requirement of § 21 para. 1 GWB is, however, only fulfilled if the addressees of the boycott incitement are enterprises. This is only partly so here, as consumers and the authorities are also called upon to boycott. There are no lacunae in the protective provision, however, as §§ 1 UWG and 826 BGB are applicable to this behaviour; these provisions are applicable together with §§ 33, 21 para. 1, 19 GWB. Thus, T has a claim against A for a cessation of his behaviour and possibly a compensatory claim if losses have been incurred.

In German law, a boycott is regarded as a hardcore restriction. Therefore, § 21 para. 1 GWB would be applicable even if A did not have a dominant position. Exceptions from the boycott interdiction can be based on fundamental rights, e.g. freedom of speech. In the present case however, purely economic interests are pursued so that no exception is awarded.

[22] Cass com July 17, 1990, in JCP 1991 éd E I no. 30.

[23] V. Selinsky in Juris-Classeur, *Concurrence, Consommation* (1993), Fasc. 380, 'Procédures de contrôle des pratiques anticoncurrentielles', no. 105.

[24] Ibid., no. 156. [25] Ibid., no. 163; Cour d'appel de Paris of May 19, 1993.

[26] And both prohibitions were considered as protective laws pursuant to § 33 GWB, a condition of liability until the reform of 2005.

(2) The claim will be filed with a court and served on the defendant by the court. It is not necessary that A be warned in advance or the claim be served on him. Such advance notice only influences the distribution of the costs of proceedings. Where no notice is given and if A acknowledges T's claims immediately, then T has to bear the procedural costs (§ 93 ZPO). Otherwise, that is if T has initially given a warning outside proceedings or if A fails to acknowledge the claim immediately, then the losing party, that is A, has to bear the costs of proceedings (§ 91 ZPO). T can also claim his costs of legal representation from A.

(3) Antitrust law contains no special provisions for temporary injunctions, so that the general provisions, that is §§ 935 et seq. ZPO, will be applicable. Accordingly, T has the possibility of pursuing his claims by means of a temporary injunction. There must be a threat that the exercise of T's rights can be lost or made significantly more difficult by a change in the existing situation (§ 935 ZPO). If there is such an urgent need, T can effect a temporary injunction.

(4) Of course the parties are able at any time to reach an out-of-court settlement. There are no particular requirements for concluding such a settlement contract. The out-of-court settlement has no direct influence on the running trial.[27] Therefore, in the court both parties in concert have to declare the trial as settled (§ 91a ZPO).

Private settlements do not influence administrative procedures. Therefore, measures of the cartel authority would not be affected. Moreover, private settlements must not constitute themselves a restraint of competition. German legal doctrine focuses on the question whether conditions in restraint of competition are disguised in a settlement agreement.[28]

Greece (11)

(1) The facts described in the above case are an example of prohibited *tripartite* boycott. This term defines the organized action by natural or legal persons motivating third parties not to conclude or to interrupt financial or legal relations with an enterprise, aiming at the exclusion of the enterprise from business dealings and, naturally, its exclusion from the market.[29] The essential element of such a boycott is the

[27] BGH, March 7, 2002, (2002) 55 NJW 1503 (1504).

[28] D. Zimmer, *Zulässigkeit und Grenzen schiedsgerichtlicher Entscheidung von Kartellrechtsstreitigkeiten* (1991).

[29] *Athens single member CFI* 5706/1998, (1998) 4 *DEE* 846 [in Greek].

involvement of at least three persons: (a) the motivating person, (b) the person carrying out the exclusion or the abstention from business dealings, and (c) the enterprise targeted through boycott. In the present case, A is abusing his dominant position and at the same time violates art. 1 of L. 146/1914, since he is a competitor of T.[30] Therefore, T has a claim for cessation and compensation based, on one hand, on antitrust law (art. 2 of L. 703/77) combined with the general provisions on liability from tort,[31] and on the other hand, on unfair competition law.

(2) Unfair competition claims as well as compensation claims resulting from antitrust law infringements will be filed with the civil courts; a copy of the action filed must be served on the defendant in order for the action to be considered as being brought and for the litigation to be regarded as pending.[32] In accordance with art. 19 of L. 146/1914, the statute of limitations for claims on unfair competition is six months, while the statute of limitations for a compensation claim based on tortious liability is five years. The action filed with the civil courts may contain a request for the payment of judicial costs and of the lawyer's fee. Usually, the losing party pays the judicial costs of the winning party.[33] Such costs may, however, be set off between the parties, as in cases involving a reasonable doubt as to the outcome of the dispute.[34]

Moreover, T may lodge a complaint before the Competition Commission; such a complaint is not served by the applicant. The Commission itself is under obligation to send documents to the enterprises involved, by which it will request information, provided that it finds that the case needs to be examined. The right to lodge a complaint before the Competition Commission against a practice limiting competition falling under the scope of application of L.703/1977 is indefinite and unlimited, since agreements and/or practices violating art. 1 par.1 and art. 2 of the said law are in all cases prohibited, regardless of whether the relevant Commission decision has or has not been issued.[35]

(3) Under the previous antitrust regime, if T had elected to complain about A's conduct before the Competition Commission, he was also given the right simultaneously to request provisional remedies.[36] As already mentioned in Case 9, the new article 9 para 5 of L. 703/77[37] has considerably and unjustifiably restricted this possibility; the

[30] See also *Larissa single member CFI*, decision 557/1987, (1988) 29 *EllDni* 388 [in Greek].
[31] Articles 914 et seq. CC. [32] Art. 215 par.1 CCP. [33] Art. 176 CCP.
[34] Art. 179 CCP. [35] Art. 3 of L. 703/1977.
[36] Art. 9 par. 4 [in its previous version]. [37] As amended by art. 16 par. 4 of L. 3373/2005.

Competition Commission has the exclusive competence to take provisional measures, only upon its own initiative or upon request of the Minister of Development, provided that there is: (a) prima facie proof of violation of articles 1, 2, 2a and 5 of L. 703/77 or of arts. 81 and 82 EC, and (b) a state of urgency necessitating the avoidance of imminent danger of irreparable damage to the public interest. One should deduce that, under the current antitrust regime, T may only seek provisional measures before the civil courts,[38] on the basis of the general procedural law. He may also seek provisional measures according to art. 20 of L.146/1914 and request the termination of the boycott.

Art. 682 CCP stipulates that provisional measures may be granted if the case refers to urgent matters or the avoidance of imminent danger. If the court finds that urgency indeed exists, it may issue a provisional order immediately after the action has been filed, which will remain in force until the decision on the provisional remedies requested is issued.[39] However, T may not request a provisional award of the whole or part of the reparation he is entitled to: art. 728 CCP contains an exclusive list of instances for which the court is allowed to make a provisional award on the claim. These instances are mainly claims for alimony, labour claims and claims for reparation due to injury or death.[40]

(4) A and T have the right to arrive at an out-of-court settlement of their dispute, before or subsequent to the filing of the relevant action. Their settlement may be entered into by contract, in accordance with arts. 871 and 872 CC. Prior to the filing of the action, the person interested in filing it may submit a request for conciliation before the competent justice of the peace in accordance with arts. 209–214 CCP.[41] As shown above (Case 9), an attempt to settle out of court is required as a condition of admissibility for all actions falling within the jurisdiction of the multi-member civil courts. The settlement may also be requested at any stage of the trial and may be incorporated in the court records, thus creating an enforceable entitlement.[42] In such cases, the trial is discontinued.[43]

[38] See *Athens single member CFI* 6009/1985, (1985) 36 *EEmpD* 725 with comments by E. Perakis, Rocas/Perakis, *World Law of Competition (Greece)*, (1983), § 5.02(2) D.

[39] Art. 691(2) of the Code of Civil Procedure.

[40] *'Article 728'*, in K.D. Kerameus/D.G. Kondilis/N.T. Nikas (D. Kranis), *Code of Civil Procedure. Article-by-Article Commentary*, vol. 2 (2000), 1422 et seq. [in Greek].

[41] In practice, these provisions remain inapplicable.

[42] Art. 904(2)(c) CCP. [43] Ibid., art. 293.

By contrast, settlement is not provided for procedures followed before the Competition Commission. This is because disputes arising from the violation of arts. 1 and 2 of L. 703/1977, although of a private character, nevertheless bear a high interest for the public order. Thus, the parties do not enjoy the right freely to dispose of them[44] and therefore they do not have the right to discontinue the trial with an out-of-court settlement or submit their dispute to arbitration, as the state has awarded the competence of resolution to the Competition Commission.[45]

Hungary (11)

(1) Boycott can be assessed under sec. 5 HCA. However, a conduct violates this section only if it is an unfair appeal to boycott. This seems to be the case here, as the boycott is not based on justifiable grounds like lower prices, better service or better quality of A's goods or services. T can bring a private law claim before the courts, as the unfair competition rules of the HCA fall within the competence of the civil courts (sec. 86(1) HCA). According to sec. 86(2) HCA T can claim a ruling that A's conduct violates the law, the termination of the violation and the prohibition of continued violation by A, that A make amends – through making an announcement or in some other appropriate manner – and, if necessary, that sufficient publicity is given to such an announcement by the offender and at his cost. T can claim the termination of the infringing state of affairs, restoration of the situation preceding the infringement, and removal of the infringing features from the goods produced or distributed or, where this is not possible, destruction of such goods, as well as the destruction of any special facilities used for the production of such goods. On the basis of sec. 21(c) HCA, if A himself refuses without justification, to create or maintain business relations with T, T can further claim damages subject to the provisions of civil law, and that A supply information about the persons who participated in the production and distribution of the goods concerned by the infringement and about the business relations created for the dissemination of such goods.

[44] See Stelios Koussoulis, *Procedural Issues before the Competition Commission and Consumer Protection*, in Ioannis G. Schinas (ed.), *Antitrust Law* (1992), p. 298.
[45] Ibid. at p. 299.

(2) According to sec. 88(1) HCA action in court may be started with reference to practices defined in secs. 2–7 HCA within six months of acquiring knowledge thereof. No action may be started more than five years after the display of such conduct. T does not have to inform A of his claim. It is not required by law to send a preliminary notice to the violating party. It depends on the plaintiff whether he deems it practical or reasonable to send such a preliminary notice. The consequence of failing to send such a preliminary notice shall be to cover the costs of a lawsuit if the defendant acknowledges the claim on the first trial and terminates the infringement. On the basis of sec. 76 HCP T bears the pre-trial costs related to the evidence, such as witness, expert and interpreter's fees or the costs of local inspection and hearing. If it is reasonable the court may exceptionally oblige A to pay these pre-trial costs or part of it. According to sec. 78 HCP the trial costs of the successful party are paid by the losing party. In case of winning the suit, the plaintiff will generally be awarded the costs of the procedure – i.e. the defendant loses the suit and covers the costs. Therefore, if T succeeds in his claim he can pass on the costs to A.

(3) According to sec. 156(1) HCP a court may, upon application, issue a preliminary injunction in order to prevent imminent damage to a party, to maintain the status quo during a legal dispute, or to protect the claimant's rights should they require special recognition, as long as the burdens imposed by such a measure do not exceed the benefits that may be gained by it. The court will decide immediately whether to grant a request for a preliminary injunction. The parties must be heard personally, unless the urgency of the situation makes a hearing impossible. The order for a preliminary injunction is enforceable in advance of a final decision. Therefore, T could pursue his claim by means of a temporary injunction.

(4) No, they cannot. There are no provisions for out-of-court settlements. There are no out-of-court settlements possible for private law disputes under Hungarian law. The parties can, however, always amend a contract or settle matters in dispute under a contract without going to court (sec. 240 HCC).

Ireland (11)

(1) T could sue for an injunction against A under sec. 4 of the Competition Act 2002 if it can be established that A has engaged in agreements with undertakings to restrict competition. Alternatively, T could sue A under sec. 5 of the Competition Act 2002 if T can show that

A has abused its dominant position by, for example, putting pressure on its customers or suppliers not to deal with T.[46] A has no action in competition law against citizens and public institutions except in so far as they are acting as undertakings. T could also sue A under the Defamation Act 1961 and claim an injunction to prevent A from defaming him by innuendo, in implying that T will be disrespectful of the town's traditions and customs, and will engage in unfair business practices. T is not required to show special damages provided he can show that A intended to cause him pecuniary loss. See Case 1 above.

(2) T must lodge his competition claim in the Circuit Court. He is required to give A notice of the claim. T will not have to bear his own pre-trial costs if he is successful in the action, as these will be passed on to A.

(3) T can pursue his claim by means of an interim injunction. The preconditions are those that generally apply to interim injunctions.[47] T would have to show that in all the circumstances immediate protection should be afforded to him against A's actions. T would have to demonstrate a reasonable prospect of succeeding in the case when it is eventually heard. The other major consideration is that the balance of convenience must favour granting the injunction. In assessing the balance of convenience, the court considers the nature of the potential injury to T and weighs the detriment that T would suffer if no injunction were granted against the loss or damage A would suffer if the injunction were granted. If an injunction is granted, T will be required to give an undertaking as to damages, which means that any loss A will suffer as a result of the injunction being awarded will be compensated in the event of T's losing the case. Often the application for the injunction will be made ex parte and on affidavit only. A will not have been notified. Within a few days, T will apply for an interlocutory injunction which if granted, will last until the trial takes place.

[46] When Tesco, the UK supermarket chain, took over Quinnsworth, an Irish supermarket chain in the 1990s, small producers successfully won over the media and the general public in what was effectively a semi-boycott of the new undertaking, which was perceived as being insufficiently 'Irish', and was accused of neglecting local producers. The campaign was widely seen as being successful. Tesco became known as Tesco (Ireland) and made a concerted effort to source produce locally. It also labelled goods to inform customers of their source and engaged in a sensitive advertising campaign, for example, advertising goods in the Irish language, rather than in English. No action was taken in court.

[47] *Campus Oil v. Minister for Industry and Energy (No. 2)* [1983] IR 88.

(4) The parties may reach an out-of-court settlement. No particular conditions apply, but if A is really in breach of secs. 4 and 5 of the Competition Act 2002, the Competition Authority may decide to proceed in an action against A regardless of any out-of-court settlement. Under sec. 11 of the Competition Act 2002, an action against an attempt or a conspiracy to breach secs. 4 or 5 is taken in the Central Criminal Court.

Italy (11)

(1) By calling upon citizens, companies and public institutions to have nothing to do with T, A boycotts T's products. In principle, T could count upon remedies offered by antitrust law and by unfair competition law. Both sets of provisions are grounded on homogeneous principles and could apply cumulatively. The plaintiff would be able to choose among different judges and a one-instance process or a double-instance one. Some scholars have pointed out that this solution is not adequate.[48] On the basis of the speciality criterion, should an anti-competitive behaviour fall under the scope of application of the Law 287/90, the only applicable provision as regards remedies would be art. 33.

Nonetheless, boycotting in the field of antitrust law is rather unexplored when compared to boycotting as an act of unfair competition.[49] In fact, case law has often sanctioned boycotting behaviours, by using the specific provisions on unfair competition (2598–2601 cc). Under art. 2598 cc, anyone performs an act of unfair competition when (directly or indirectly) using means which violate professional correctness, causing damages to others' business activity.

As far as antitrust law remedies are concerned, T could simply claim a cease-and-desist order from the *Autorità Garante*. However, the Authority would first assess whether there is indeed a ground for starting an investigation (generally over a year), subsequently investigate, and eventually issue a cease-and-desist order. T could find a quicker (temporary) relief by bringing a petition for an emergency measure (under 700 cpc) in front of the ordinary courts, and in addition to this, claim damages.

[48] M. Libertini, *Il ruolo del giudice nell'applicazione delle norme antitrust*, in Giur. Comm., I (1998), 649–679, at 679.

[49] G. Faella, *Note the decision Bluvacanze v. I Viaggi del Ventaglio-Turisanda-Hotelplan Italia, of the Corte d'Appello of Milano, 11 July 2003*, in Il diritto industriale, n. 2/2004, 170–177, at 170.

(2) T will bring his damage claim by means of an *atto di citazione a giudizio* (writ). This is addressed to the judge and to the defendant. As a consequence, it has to contain both the *vocatio in ius* (in order to inform the other party of the day of the hearing) and the *editio actionis* (the objective elements which identify the claim of the plaintiff, i.e. *petitum* and *causa petendi*). The writ will have to be notified to the defendant as provided by arts. 137 ff. cp.

As far as trial costs are concerned, each party shall make provision for his own costs. However, should T succeed in his claim, he would be able to pass his costs on to A. Art. 91 cpc provides that the judge, with the decision that closes the trial, condemn the losing party to pay the costs in favour of the other party. This prevents a loss of his capital by the party that had to bear costs for obtaining recognition of his own right. Art. 82 cpc renders this regime slightly milder by giving the judge room for a discretional assessment of what costs he deems 'excessive' or 'superfluous', and to exclude repetitious expense.

(3) T can bring a claim for a temporary injunction before the Court of Appeal. Parties might pursue interim relief in order to prevent infringements, or aggravation of infringements already perpetrated, or to obtain measures which serve the purpose of the final judgment. In the present case, T could seek an injunction which freezes A's boycotting practice and confines the damage. Art. 33(2) of the Law 287/90 explicitly recognizes the competence of the Court of Appeal to issue urgent measures granting a temporary relief in cases of breach of national antitrust law.[50]

Under Italian law, there are typical and atypical interim measures. In practice though, parties, in the field of antitrust law, mostly claim atypical measures such as restraining injunctions under art. 700 cpc. The content of an injunction under 700 cpc is not predetermined by the law. Depending on the circumstances of the case, the judge will adopt the measure he deems most appropriate to ensure temporary relief. Art. 700 cpc offers urgent and temporary relief. Preconditions are: (a) the existence of a right that the party desires to protect (*fumus boni iuris*) and (b) the fact that a delay due to ordinary (long) terms for

[50] The majority of case law considers that interim relief measures by the Court of Appeal, both before and during the proceedings, have to be instrumental to nullity and damage claims. For an overview on this issue, see M. Tavassi/M. Scuffi, *Diritto Processuale Antitrust, Tutela Giurisdizionale della Concorrenza* (1998), at 228.

reaching a decision on the merits, would expose the right to a danger (*periculum in mora*).

Case law shows that courts have often awarded interim relief.[51] An interesting case, dealing with boycotting practices in the field of antitrust law, is the *Bluvacanze v. I Viaggi del Ventaglio-Turisanda-Hotelplan Italia* decision.[52] The case regarded a collective boycotting behaviour, consisting in the concerted refusal to supply the agent, i.e. Bluvacanze, in order to stop his discount policy. The Appellate Court of Milan, within a few months from the bringing of the claim, prohibited the boycotting practice.

(4) There is still uncertainty as to whether antitrust claims can be brought before arbitrators (*arbitri*).[53] Art. 806 cpc in recognizing the possibility of out-of-court settlements foresees a series of exceptions. First of all, this is not possible for those controversies, which cannot be the object of transactions (*transazioni*). In view of this, parties need to be entitled to enforce the right in question or it has to be allowed by the law. Should the parties opt for an out-of-court settlement, the Court of Appeal would still be competent as regards interim measures (art. 669 *quinquies* cpc). Case law has rarely faced the problem of out-of-court settlements in the field of competition law.[54]

Netherlands (11)

(1) The action can be characterized as an infringement of art. 24 DCA and therefore as a wrongful act in the sense of art. 6:162 BW. T can start (interlocutory) civil proceedings claiming an (interim) injunction and damages. T can also file a complaint with the NCA requesting a (provisional) order subject to a penalty.

(2) Strictly speaking it is not necessary to give notice of a claim to the defendant before bringing a claim to court. Therefore, it is possible that the first communication between T and A is by writ of summons.

[51] For an overview of case law applying art. 700 cpc in this field, see M. Tavassi, *Substantive Remedies for the Enforcement of National and EC Antitrust Rules before Italian Courts*, in: *European Competition Law Annual 2001: A Community Perspective* (2003), 147–154, at 149.

[52] Corte d'Appello of Milano, July 11, 2003, Bluvacanze vs. I Viaggi del Ventaglio-Turisanda-Hotelplan Italia, in Il diritto industriale, n. 2/2004, 157–169, with note of G. Faella.

[53] M. Tavassi/M. Scuffi, *Diritto Processuale Antitrust, Tutela Giurisdizionale della Concorrenza* (1998), at 225.

[54] M. Tavassi/M. Scuffi, *Diritto Processuale Antitrust, Tutela Giurisdizionale della Concorrenza* (1998), at 227. The Court of Appeal of Bologna considered valid a clause (*clausola compromissoria*) inserted in a contract having as an object a non-competition clause.

However, according to the Code of Conduct of the Dutch Bar Association, the lawyer of the claimant is obliged to first refer to the opponent, in this case A. Therefore, in practice notice shall almost always be given to the opponent before bringing a claim to court. T is not required to give notice to A before filing a complaint with the NCA. The NCA shall, however, hear the defendant before imposing any measures.

In general, the losing party will be ordered by the court to pay the winning party's costs incurred in respect of the proceedings.[55] These costs include an amount for legal fees, the bailiff's fee and the court fees paid up front.[56] The amount for legal fees is fixed using the so-called 'liquidation tariff' (*liquidatietarief*). According to this system the legal fees are calculated based on the number of acts of procedure and the financial weight of the case. Acts of procedure are standardized and are valued in points.[57] The financial weight of the case is classified in eight Tariff-groups.[58] The court fixes the amount for the legal fees irrespective of the fees that the winning party actually paid to its attorney. This fixed amount is in general substantially lower than the legal fees actually paid. The court may also order the losing party to pay, to the extent claimed, the reasonable costs that the winning party incurred in order to prevent or mitigate damage, reasonable costs incurred in assessing damage and liability as well as reasonable costs incurred in obtaining extra-judicial payment.[59]

(3) Yes, he can. The important precondition is that T has an urgent interest in his claim. In this case the urgent interest of T seems to be obvious.

(4) There are no special requirements but it is possible if parties reach an agreement pending a procedure to ask the court to lay down the settlement in the record of the proceeding.[60] The plaintiff must be aware that, in case the settlement recognizes the claim, the record constitutes an entitlement to enforcement including a settlement on interest and costs.

[55] Art. 237 BRv. [56] Articles 239–241 BRv.

[57] Points for the acts vary from 0.5 point for minor acts, to 1 point for a statement and 2 points to argue the case.

[58] For each group points have a certain tariff-value between €384 for Tariff I and €3,211 for Tariff VIII as from November 1, 2004.

[59] Art. 96 (2) BW. [60] Art. 87 (3) DCCP.

Poland (11)

(1) Calling upon third persons to refuse to sell to certain undertakings or purchase from certain undertakings constitutes an act of unfair competition (art. 15. 1 (2) u.z.n.k). At the same time there is an illegal abuse of a dominant position.

(2) The provisions of the Polish Code of Civil Procedure (k.p.c.) apply. The plaintiff must bring a claim in a required written form. He/she must precisely describe the subject and value of the claim as well as all the facts and the circumstances essential for the claim (art 187 k.p.c). The first phase of the proceedings is dealt with in writing. The plaintiff submits the claim in a written form along with the necessary documents (preparatory document). The copy of the claim and the documents will be delivered to each person participating in the proceedings. The general rule imposes an obligation to pay the necessary cost of the proceedings to the winning party on his/her demand (art 98 k.p.c). However, there are numerous exceptions to this rule.

(3) The u.o.k.k. is silent on the issue of injunctions. The president of OCCP can however issue an immediately enforceable decision if it is necessary for the protection of competition or important interests of consumers.

(4) See Case 2 *(2)*.

Portugal (11)

(1) The boycott and its incitement are not expressly covered in Portuguese statutes. However, the behaviour of A, in this case, would be considered as abuse of a dominant position. Therefore, according to art. 6 (Law no. 18/2003, June 11) this behaviour is illicit. The antitrust law only foresees administrative fines. Besides that, this behaviour can also be considered unfair competition under art. 317 CPI.[61] T, under art. 6 Law no. 18/2003, June 11 and art. 317 CPI, has a claim against A for termination of his conduct and if losses occurred can also claim compensation, because art. 317 CPI can be qualified as a protective norm. It is rare that individual competitors claim against other competitors in civil courts. Normally, competitors just complain to the antitrust authorities which are responsible for administrative proceedings.

(2) There is no special procedure for bringing a claim. In fact, it is not necessary that A be warned in advance, but, according to the principle

[61] Oliveira Ascensão, *Concorrência Desleal*, p. 579.

of fairness that governs all civil procedure, A has the right to defend himself. The costs of the proceedings are wholly borne by the losing party.

(3) Under the Civil Procedure Code, T can claim a temporary injunction if the two conditions required for a provisional claim are fulfilled. They are *periculum in mora* and *fumus boni iuris* (art. 381 CPC). In fact, to bring a temporary injunction the fear of an important violation (right injury) and the difficulty of its repair after the injury of the 'right' are required (*in casu*, the probability of the violation of the protected interest). The preventive claim is urgent (art. 382 CPC) and it is possible for the court to impose a compulsory monetary sanction (art. 384/2 CPC). Sometimes the defendant is not heard, casting a doubt on the principle of *audi alteram partem*. Under art. 27 Law no. 18/2003, June 11 the antitrust authority can also order the immediate termination of the conduct for a period of ninety days.

(4) Until the court decision the parties can come to an out-of-court settlement. The only requirement for that is the agreement of both parties. There are no special requirements for concluding such a settlement contract. Private settlements do not interfere with the administrative procedures.

Spain (11)

(1) A is a dominant undertaking in the geographic market comprised by town R; his conduct could be deemed as an abusive exploitation of his dominant position even though this call for a boycott is not expressly provided for in the examples described by art. 6 LDC. Under art. 36 para. 1 LDC T is legally entitled to report A before the SDC.

(2) Once the claim is brought before the SDC, T is not obliged to serve any notice on A. The SDC will inform A of the claim and require him to present his arguments. T will bear his own costs, as the LDC does not provide for the plaintiff to pass his costs onto the defendant if he is successful.

(3) Art. 45 LDC allows the plaintiff to ask the TDC for interim measures necessary to ensure the effectiveness of the final decision such as: to stop the conduct or to impose conditions in order to avoid harmful effects or to pay a security in order to cover the damages the defendant may cause. These measures are of a limited duration of six months.

(4) Antitrust law is of a public nature; therefore even if the claimant desists from the procedure, the authorities are entitled to continue. Nevertheless, art. 36-bis LDC foresees a procedure of conventional

settlement. This settlement must not affect third parties and be convened before the publication of the list of charges.

Sweden (11)

(1) The Swedish Competition Act is a blueprint of EC competition law and Swedish competition law shall be interpreted in the light of community law and EC case law although the legislature also opened the window for some differences.[62] This is not the place to elaborate further on the question on whether the practice in Case 11 is in fact contrary to EC law. Still, in our view, it is most unlikely that a general statement or an act of lobbying alone would be sufficient to constitute a violation of the prohibitions in arts. 81 and 82. And it is unlikely that the activities of A in Case 11 would constitute an abuse of a dominant position under Swedish law. In any event, we will suggest that there may be reason to believe that it is not completely ruled out that the Swedish Market Court could find the exemplified practice as an abuse of a dominant position under sec. 19 of KL. The activities could also constitute an infringement of sec. 6 KL (art. 81 EC) if any citizen, company or public institution involved in the case were to engage in, for example, blocking T from entering the market as part of their business relations with A.

As the position of the undertaking in question has been presumed to be dominant in the case, the relevant question is whether or not the conduct would in fact constitute an abuse or not in the legal sense of sec. 19 KL (or art. 82 EC). In the same way as in community law the concept of abuse under Swedish law should be evaluated objectively on an ad hoc basis. Even though it is clear that neither sec. 19 KL nor art. 82 EC Treaty require an anti-competitive objective or effect, these two prerequisites will have significant importance in deciding this case on a national level. When considering the question of abuse, the Swedish courts will make an actual assessment of the degree of negative effects that the practice has on competition, not unlike the 'rule of reason' in American antitrust law. Consequently, the actual effect of the conduct is important as well as the question of whether or not the reaction to meet competition should be considered to be a fairly normal business behaviour or not. Even though there is no need for causality between dominance and the abuse, we are fairly certain that the Swedish Market Court would elaborate further on this matter. Since the Market Court

[62] Governmental bill 1992/93:56.

has proved to be quite lenient when it comes to 'normal business behaviour' it is not unreasonable to assume that the court would conclude that the exemplified practice is in fact not unusual or disproportionate, neither dependant on, nor exclusive to, the dominant firm and therefore not in violation of sec. 19 KL. It would obviously be a completely different matter if A had extended his conduct to direct or implied threats.

When it comes to the application of sec. 19 KL (art. 82 EC) the general rule is that the Swedish prohibitions should be applied in accordance with community law. There might, however, be reason to assume that the Swedish courts have in fact been somewhat more restrictive than their community counterparts when deciding on abuse. It is worth mentioning the case before the Market Court (the highest instance in deciding the KL) between the Swedish postal service (Posten) and its newly established competitor.[63] Citing community law, the court made it quite clear that even a dominant firm is entitled to take measures to meet competition from a new undertaking. According to the court the important question, among others, was whether the activities of Posten constituted normal business behaviour and/or whether or not it had the purpose of excluding the new competitor from the relevant market. When establishing the purpose the Market Court took into account a number of facts, including several selective price-cuttings, to establish an anti-competitive intent. The explicit fact that Posten could not show that the selective prices were motivated by differences in costs constituted grounds for suspicion that such variations in cost could in fact exclude an abuse. In a subsequent case the Market Court established that it will consider the 'direct and indirect effects' on competition of the dominant firm's actions as well as the character of its conduct in comparison to normal business behaviour.[64] This suggests that the Swedish courts would not consider something that had no actual effects on competition an abuse. Simply informing the community about the prospect of change would probably not be considered an infringement, in the absence of other measures ensuring the customers' loyalty.

(2) T has the right according to sec. 23 para. 2 KL to claim before the Market Court an injunction to have A cease and desist his actions. For damages T must according to sec. 33 KL make a claim before an ordinary court. As submitted above, T may make a claim for an administrative

[63] MD 1998:15 Posten/CityMail. [64] MD 2001:4 Scandinavian Airlines (SAS).

fine before the Market Court only when there is a decision by the Competition Authority, not to investigate the subject matter further. T does not have an obligation to inform A in advance and neither does the Competition Authority.

Cases under sec. 33 concern damages and are accordingly considered private law. As submitted in sec. 64 KL cases involving application of sec. 33 KL should be subject to general Swedish provisions on procedure, i.e. the Code on Civil and Criminal Procedure (*Rättegångsbalken*). This includes questions such as who will bear the costs for the procedure as well as the pre-procedural phase. Under Ch. 18 secs. 1–15 the losing party will as a general rule bear all the costs for both parties. This obviously encompasses only reasonable and appropriate costs and not costs as a result of obstruction or unnecessary court procedures where the winning party must carry his own costs.

(3) It stems from sec. 25 KL that the court on the submission of an undertaking following sec. 23 KL may issue an interim injunction concerning an infringement of the competition rules. According to case law[65] the court should, when considering an interim injunction, weigh the interests of the plaintiff against the possible irreparable loss and inconvenience suffered by the defendant. Since this ruling of the court the prerequisite in the law for issuing an interim injunction has been made less restrictive.[66]

(4) The procedure as to private remedies under the Swedish Competition Act follows two different sets of rules. Sanctions under sec. 23 KL belong to public law and are pursued before special courts (Stockholm District Court and the Market Court). Matters concerning claims for injunctions as well as for interim injunctions under that section are therefore not open for settlements. As to civil law consequences of competition law, KL only regulates claims for damages. Such claims are considered part of private law, must be pursued before ordinary courts and they are open both for settlements and arbitration.[67] That is, as long as a settlement as such does not infringe the prohibition on anti-competitive agreements. Both ordinary courts and special courts have the competence to declare an agreement void. Neither the Competition Authority, nor the special courts are bound by the *res judicata* of decisions by the ordinary courts, including decisions by the Supreme Court.

[65] T-8-768-96 & MD 1998:5; TV3/STIM. [66] See amendment of KL by Act 1998:648.
[67] See Case 2 (Watch imitations I) above.

Summary (11)

1. *Boycott as substantive antitrust law infringement*

In accordance with the focus of the project on legal remedies, Case 11 was also originally conceived in terms of a clear antitrust law infringement so that emphasis could be laid on the pre-trial and procedural possibilities of the injured party. This expectation was not fulfilled. An incitement to boycott is by no means in all jurisdictions seen as anticompetitive. In England, the incitement to boycott is not prohibited, even when the initiator is in a dominant market position. The same applies to France, where the boycott is not classed as an abuse. Doubts on the antitrust infringing nature of the boycott are also expressed in Sweden. The simple incitement to boycott is here classed as a legitimate lobbying measure. The area of legality is first departed from if the incitement to boycott is accompanied by actual threats. The legal position is similar in Denmark, where particular accompanying circumstances are required (actual threats, discriminatory statements), to trigger the application of antitrust law. In the majority of reporting countries by contrast there is a legal infringement. In some countries there is even a specific rule for boycott, e.g. a special rule in German antitrust law or an unfair competition rule in Hungary. But also in countries with no specific regulation, the incitement to boycott by an enterprise with market dominance qualifies as an antitrust infringement, often together with an unfair competition violation. In this way Case 11 impressively reveals the limits of European convergence. Even with forms of conduct like the boycott, which has a long tradition in legal debate,[68] there is no unity in Europe between national antitrust and competition laws. This has no influence on the investigation of legal remedies. The reporters on the countries in which no legal infringement is presumed helpfully assumed for further questions that an infringement had occurred.

2. *Injured party claims*

In all countries the injured party has the possibility to ban the infringer from continuing the infringement and – in case of fault – to claim

[68] The concept derives from *Charles Cunningham Boycott* (1832–1897), a retired English army officer who worked as land agent in Ireland. The Irish Land League called for a non-violent shunning of contacts with him because of his intransigence towards Irish tenants.

compensation. In conformity with the results of Cases 9 and 10, this finding is, however, complicated by the interplay between public and private law. Under Swedish law cessation claims are primarily asserted through the Market Court, that is under public law. This requires that the antitrust authority has first decided not to pursue the particular matter itself. Compensatory claims by contrast are asserted in the ordinary courts. In the large majority of countries the injured party can by contrast freely elect whether to engage the antitrust authorities for its cessation claim or whether to follow the civil law route. Spain is an exception, where private law claims may only be filed once the antitrust authority has reached a decision. There are also peculiarities in those countries where a boycott at the same time constitutes both an antitrust and an unfair competition infringement. Thus, in Austria different courts are responsible for both forms of infringement. The limitation periods for both forms of claim may also vary. Regarding remedies, the injured party generally has a greater number of remedies at its disposal in the case of unfair competition violations than under antitrust law. Under antitrust law only claims for cessation and damages are available, whereas the law of unfair competition knows a highly differentiated range of remedial instruments.

3. *Pre-trial measures*

There are no special requirements for the commencement of judicial proceedings. A pre-trial caution is generally not necessary, although it can in practice follow from professional rules for lawyers (Netherlands). In some countries the prior caution is simply relevant for the allocation of costs. If the respondent acknowledges the claim immediately on filing of the complaint, it avoids the risk of costs (Austria, Germany, Hungary). This is different only if its conduct has given rise to the claim, which for example is presumed under Austrian law in the case of an incitement to boycott.

4. *Interlocutory relief*

The intertwining of public and private law also affects the availability of injunctive relief. Interlocutory relief can be awarded by both administrative and civil courts but the preconditions vary according to the route chosen. The injunction award by an antitrust authority is the more significant route as antitrust administrative proceedings are more numerous in practice. In Spain, where the antitrust authority proceeding is a compulsory preliminary, the expedited ruling of the antitrust authority is even the only means of achieving interlocutory relief. In the other countries by contrast there is – *cum grano salis* – a free election between relief under administrative law or private law. The preconditions for an interlocutory order differ in the individual case. The criteria described in the country reports can, however, be summarized under those given in the Italian and Portuguese national reports of *periculum in mora* and *fumus boni iuris*. Thus, there must be a particular need for urgency, which can only be determined through a comprehensive weighing of the interests. In addition the claim must be prima facie valid and have prospects of succeeding. In comparison with interlocutory relief under administrative and private law, the impression is that interlocutory relief is achieved markedly faster under private law. Here also interlocutory relief applies to the cessation claim but not to the compensatory claim. There is no particular need for urgency in the assessment of incurred loss.

The proceeding often ends with the expedited ruling as the parties declare themselves satisfied with this and do not proceed to full trial. If full trial proceedings are commenced, the risk of loss incurred through the interlocutory relief lies with the applicant: he has to bear the risk of losing the main proceedings after having gained interlocutory relief in the beginning. Therefore, a guarantee has sometimes to be made before the obtaining of interlocutory relief (Denmark).

5. *Responsibility for costs*

In the large majority of reporting countries the costs of proceedings are borne by the party who loses the legal dispute. In most countries the claim for costs comprises the extra-judicial as well as litigation costs.[69] This applies to costs generated in civil proceedings while costs incurred through applications to the antitrust authority are generally not recoverable. This is a disadvantage of the administrative route, or correspondingly an advantage of private law proceedings: success in civil proceedings enables a claim for recovery of costs from the opponent. This statement must be qualified, however: the duty to refund costs in civil proceedings generally refers only to 'appropriate costs'. Antitrust disputes are often complicated and require highly qualified and expensive legal representation. As a result such costs are often only partly recoverable.

69 Denmark and Hungary are exceptions, where each party bears their own extra-judicial costs absent agreement to the contrary.

6. *Settlement*

The contrast between private and administrative law disputes is also significant for the modalities of amicable settlement of the legal dispute. While under private law with the influence of the disposition maxim settlements are always possible,[70] under administrative law in many countries the ending of a dispute by means of settlement is excluded. There are certain exceptions to this, for example, under Spanish law, for situations where no third party is affected by the settlement. At times, too, in civil proceedings judicial approval in the form of a consent order is required, which is then generally granted (England). The settlement of a civil proceeding has no influence on the antitrust administrative proceeding. The antitrust authority is naturally not restricted by the fact that enterprises have settled their private law disputes out of court. On the other hand antitrust standards apply to the settlement itself: the settlement may not itself constitute a restriction of competition. For example, competitors may not fake an antitrust conflict in order to agree in a settlement on prohibited restrictions on prices or market territories.

7. *Conclusions*

Case 11 is directed at the practical pursuit of remedies. What must the victim of an antitrust infringement do in order to bring legal proceedings? Who will bear the costs of the proceedings? What possibilities are there to uphold one's rights at least provisionally and with the minimum of delay? These questions are highly significant for the enforcement of law in general, and the election between an administrative and private law remedies in particular. Interlocutory relief is available in both forms of proceeding, although in this respect it would seem that the civil courts are more attractive since here interlocutory relief may be obtained more rapidly. In addition interlocutory relief often has such authority that it renders the main proceeding unnecessary. On the other hand interlocutory relief in civil proceedings poses a high risk for the applicant in that he is liable for damages if he loses the main proceedings.

Another point of relevance for the legal strategy of an aggrieved party is that of costs. In all reporting countries the aggrieved party in the civil proceeding has a claim to recover its costs against the infringing party if

[70] Hungary is the sole exception where settlement agreements are not allowed under antitrust law.

it is successful. This claim also includes in most countries the extra-judicial costs of pursuing the case. As the winner has a claim for pre-trial and trial costs there is perhaps less need for the introduction of three-fold or punitive damages, which often tend to cover these costs. In the procedure before the antitrust authority the aggrieved party by contrast has no such claim; that is, it has to meet its own costs, for example for legal advice. This circumstance, however, should not be overestimated. The claim for costs in the reporting countries is limited to an 'appropriate' or 'necessary' level. If the costs of legal advice, for example, are high because a specialist law firm with high hourly rates has been engaged, the claimant will have to meet a high proportion of these costs itself.

Thus, Case 11 demonstrates that the attractiveness of private claims is only to a limited extent strengthened by the better possibilities of interlocutory relief and of costs recovery.

II. Plaintiffs and defendants

Case 12 Horizontal restraints of competition – consumer claims against general cartel effects

A, B and C are competitors in the production and marketing of certain vitamin products. They each have a one-third market share. The vitamin products are disseminated to the ultimate consumer over various commercial levels. In a secret agreement A, B and C agree upon a 20 per cent price increase. The consumer V pays a higher price than the otherwise competitive price because of the price cartel.

What claims does V have against A, B and C?

Austria (12)

Austrian antitrust law does not provide for compensatory claims by consumers (neither in the antitrust law nor the Local Supply Law). Compensatory claims by enterprises are possible under § 1 UWG, if they are not only market counterparts, but at the same time competitors of the cartel members (see Case 10). In the area of § 1 UWG the OGH has on one occasion affirmed the compensatory claim of a consumer with respect to the protective aim of the UWG (including protection for consumers) and relied on a thorough investigation of this question by Sack.[1] In this decision the OGH relied above all on the fact that by awarding standing to the associations named in § 14 UWG consumer interests would be considered alongside the interests of competitors. Evidently, the OGH derived the compensatory claim directly from the applicable norm of the UWG, in the case in question from § 2 UWG. The court left the question open[2] of whether the norms of UWG are protective laws in the sense of § 1311 Austrian Civil Code.[3] Fitz and Gamerith[4] derive, if necessary, compensatory claims from the infringement of protective laws (§§ 1295, 1311 Austrian Civil Code). The individual consumer has no cessation claim under the UWG or the antitrust rules, but he can turn to the official bodies and other parties entitled to claim

[1] E.A. Kramer/H. Mayrhofer, *Konsumentenschutz im Privat- und Wirtschaftsrecht*, pp. 99 et seq.

[2] OGH, 24.2.1998 = SZ 71/36 = ecolex 1998, 497 = EvBl 1998/124 = MR 1998, 77 = ÖBl 1998, 193 – '1. Main price (Langer)' = RdW 1998, 394 = WBl 1998, 228 = WRP 1998, 789 = GRUR Int 1999, 181.

[3] Negated by R. Sack, *Schadenersatzansprüche wettbewerbsgeschützter Verbraucher nach deutschem und österreichischem Wettbewerbs- und Deliktsrecht*, in M. Kramer and H. Mayrhofer, *Konsumentenschutz im Privat- und Wirtschaftsrecht* (1997), pp. 99 et seq.

[4] *Wettbewerbsrecht* (4th edn 2003), p. 92.

under the cartel law requesting the filing of an application for imposition of an antitrust law prohibition.[5] Directive 2005/29/EC of the EP and of the Council on unfair commercial practices does not concern individual actions of single persons which have been harmed by an unfair commercial practice[6] and leaves the enforcement of collective legal protection to the Member States.[7] Consequently, these are not subject to new obligations with respect to the modalities of enforcement.

It is not to be expected that Austria on the basis of the directive on unfair commercial practices will introduce such individual standing.[8] UWG and antitrust law also provide no special reasons for challenging a contract. V could only rely on the general grounds for challenging a contract (e.g. material misrepresentation, *laesio enormis*[9]).

Denmark (12)

There is no authority for the Competition Council to bring actions before the court with the aim of obtaining damages on behalf of a group of consumers. In this respect the Competition Act is contrary to the Marketing Practices Act where the Consumer Ombudsman according to § 20 of the Marketing Practices Act can bring actions for damages on behalf of a group of consumers with homogeneous demands.[10]

The individual consumer may in principle - like any other person with a legal interest - bring an action before the regular courts against A, B and C.[11] In the action, the consumer may claim that A, B and C have violated CA § 6, sec. 1, which provides a prohibition on anti-competitive agreements, and that A, B and C must cease this behaviour. A consumer who is a direct customer of A, B and C may be expected to have a legal

[5] Concerning standing of the directly injured person in the context of the reform of German unfair competition law (which then was upcoming and has now been adopted) see R. Sack, *Regierungsentwurf einer UWG-Novelle - Ausgewählte Probleme*, (2003) BB 1073 (1077).

[6] Consideration 9 of Directive 2005/29/EC.

[7] Art. 4(1) of the Directive on misleading advertising is amended by art. 14 n. 4 of the Directive on unfair commercial practices.

[8] Extensively on this subject H. Gamerith, *Der Richtlinienvorschlag über unlautere Geschäftspraktiken - Möglichkeiten einer harmonischen Umsetzung*, (2005) 51 WRP 391 et seq.

[9] The party to a bilateral contract who receives a counter-performance worth less than 50% of the value of its own performance may bring an action for rescission of the contract and restoration of the status quo; see H. Hausmaninger, *The Austrian Legal System* (3rd edn 2003), p. 265.

[10] See concerning the background for § 20 of the Marketing Practices Act, S. Kristoffersen og K.V. Gravesen, *Forbrugerretten* (2001), pp. 163 et seq.

[11] Bernard Gomard, *Civilprocessen* (5th edn 2000), pp. 327et seq. and 336 et seq.

interest in such legal proceedings. An indirect customer of A, B and C cannot be expected to have the necessary legal interest in a lawsuit. The consumer may also bring an action before the court with the claim that A, B and C must compensate for the financial losses which V has suffered in consequence of the agreement. A direct customer will have to document a financial loss being a consequence of the raised price. The elements of a suit for damages are mentioned in the connection with Case 3 above in relation to question No. 1, part 1. An indirect customer may be expected to face big difficulties in producing this proof.

The costs for the individual consumer of bringing such an action before the courts will normally exclude a financial interest in bringing an action. As agents for one or more parties individual consumer organizations may bring actions for compensation. A number of lawsuits are pending in Denmark, where local authorities/municipalities have brought actions to obtain damages against members of a price cartel within the electronics industry. These actions for damages are brought following a decision of the Competition Council that a number of firms within the electronics industry have violated the prohibition in of CA § 6 against entering into anti-competitive agreements.

England (12)

This case raises the question of the *locus standi* to sue of the indirect purchaser. The issue is, of course, closely related to that of whether defendants should be allowed a defence of 'passing on', i.e. to say that, even if they have acted in breach of the competition rules, the claimant customer from the cartelist has suffered no loss because he has simply passed on, in turn, the cartel-inflated supra-competitive price by way of higher prices to his own customers, so that to award damages to him would unjustly enrich him. There is no decided law on this in the UK at present.

The language used by the ECJ in the preliminary ruling in C-453/99 *Courage Ltd. v. Crehan*, taken at face value, says that national law will be failing in its obligation to provide effective remedies for breach of the competition rules if 'any individual' who suffers loss as a result of a breach of the rules is in principle denied the right to claim damages.[12] On the face of it, that suggests that national law must in principle make it possible for indirect purchasers to obtain damages.

[12] See in particular paras. 22, 25–26 of the judgment.

On the other hand, there are very serious practical problems in allowing indirect purchasers to sue, particularly (1) showing that the illicit actions of A, B and C were the *cause* of the claimant's loss when other events and influences in the supply chain will often intervene, (2) the question of through how many links along the supply chain one should allow indirect purchasers to sue (the remoteness of damage issue), and (3) proving to the court's satisfaction the *amount* of the indirect purchaser's loss.

Whilst it is impossible to predict how this will be resolved in the UK, the treatment of this issue under the Sherman Act is likely to be influential. The US Supreme Court in *Illinois Brick Co. v. Illinois*[13] has in principle denied indirect purchasers a right to sue for damages under sec. 1 of the act, expressing great concerns about the risk of manufacturers facing multiple litigation and the difficulties of proof of tracing overcharging the further one goes down the supply chain. The *Illinois Brick* rule appears, however, not to be very popular. There seem to be a number of exceptions to it, where the indirect purchaser will be allowed to sue for damages, viz. (1) where the 'first-line' direct purchaser can, under its arrangements with its customers, force its customers to take fixed quantities of product from it at whatever price it likes (i.e. can directly pass on the supra-competitive input prices in full),[14] (2) if the downstream distributor has taken part in the price-fixing by the manufacturer (so that he is then a co-participant in the cartel),[15] and (3) if there is no realistic possibility that the 'first-line' direct purchaser from the cartel members will ever sue,[16] etc.[17]

The practical financial incentives for individual consumers to sue are likely to be very small, so this is an area where super-complaints, group litigation orders etc.[18] could well have a role to play.

Finland (12)

Sec. 4 para. 1 of the Finnish Act on Competition Restrictions prohibits horizontal agreements, recommendations and other equivalent arrangements concerning prices or charges. V has suffered damage

[13] (1977) 431 US 720, at 728 and 730–737. [14] *Illinois Brick Co. v. Illinois*, at p. 736.

[15] *In re. Brand Name Prescription Drugs Antitrust Litigation*, 123 Fed.3d. 599, 614–615 (7th Circuit, 1997).

[16] *Freeman v. San Diego Association of Realtors*, 322 Fed.3d. 1133 (9th Circuit, 2003).

[17] For more detail, see H. Hovenkamp, *Federal Antitrust Policy* (2nd edn 1999), ch. 16.6; D. Broder, *A Guide to US Antitrust Law* (2005), pp. 76–81.

[18] See answer to Case 9, question 3.

resulting from the price cartel of A, B and C. Under sec. 18(a) of the Act, a business undertaking, which, either intentionally or negligently, violates the prohibitions prescribed in sects. 4 or 6 or art. 81 or 82 of the EC Treaty, is obliged to pay compensation for the damage caused to another business undertaking. Sec. 18(a) thus only applies to situations where one business undertaking causes damage to another business undertaking.[19] It is not possible for V to base his claim on sec. 18(a).

Consumers are primarily protected in the Finnish Act on Competition Restrictions by the Finnish Competition Authority. It is clear from the wording of sec. 18(a) that claims for compensation made by consumers cannot be based on sec. 18(a). It might be argued that consumers could base their claims for compensation on the Finnish Damages Act.

France (12)

According to art. L 462-5 of the Commercial Code the Council on Competition may be referred to by the bodies indicated in art. L 462-1 of the Commercial Code, that are also approved consumer organizations with regard to the interests for which they are responsible. Thus V can apply to one of them. In this way he can influence the administrative procedure against A, B or C. However, a procedure before the Council on Competition will not lead to damages and interest but only to a fine that goes to the state. Nevertheless, it is an appropriate means to end the illegal behaviour. Apart from a representative action that may be taken by consumer associations, V as a person has no damages claim against A, B or C.

Although consumer associations can refer to the Council on Competition and despite the comparative versatility that the Council shows in accepting their demands, consumer associations often lack sufficient proof of the anti-competitive practice.[20] The Council itself has proposed seeking the reasons and possible remedies in order to render consumer protection more efficient.[21] Nevertheless, consumers associations do not represent an important part of the cases – only 4 out of 58 in 2002 – whereas referrals to the Council on Competition number 34 out of 58 cases.[22]

[19] HE 243/1997 vp, p. 32.

[20] V. Selinsky in: Juris-Classeur, *Concurrence, Consommation* (1993), Fasc. 380, 'Procédures de contrôle des pratiques anticoncurrentielles', no. 52.

[21] Report of the Council on Competition, 1991, p. VII.

[22] Report of the Council on Competition, 2002, no. 20, table 5 on www.conseil-concurrence.fr/doc/ra2002-p1.pdf.

Germany (12)

V could have a cease-and-desist claim against A, B and C pursuant to § 33 para. 1 together with § 1 GWB, that is the general prohibition of restrictive agreements. Until the reform of German competition law in 2005 the question of whether consumers not directly affected by a cartel could take action against it was much debated. As already explained (Case 9, question 1), the protective nature of § 1 GWB was affirmed but its scope was subject to disagreement. The inclusion of the market counterpart, for example the customer, was in principle recognized, but the details were subject to controversy. According to the traditional view of German courts, customers were only protected under § 1 GWB if the cartel was directed specifically against them, to worsen their conditions, for example, or to prevent entry to the market altogether.[23] In the legal doctrine, on the other hand, the criterion of targeting was largely rejected.[24] The same was true for the Federal Cartel Office (FCO).[25] Recently, lower courts have followed this line; for the first time, damages were attributed to a general victim of the vitamin cartel.[26] Even if the circle of protected subjects was drawn widely in this sense, a limitation to direct market counterparts was often made. Commercial levels which are more remote were not considered to lie within the protective scope of § 1 GWB. Mere popular involvement was not sufficient.[27] Therefore, according to the law before 2005, consumers, who like V are several market levels removed from the cartel, were not included in the protective scope of § 1 GWB, neither according to the

[23] BGH, 25.1.1983, BGHZ 86, 324 – *Familienzeitschrift;* LG Mannheim, 11.7.2003, *Vitamins*, (2004) GRUR 182; LG Mainz, January 15, 2004, *Vitamins*, (2004) NJW-RR 478; LG Berlin, *Philipp Holzmann/Readymix*, 102 O 134/02 Kart – *Transportbeton.* Undecided OLG Karlsruhe (2004) 57 NJW 2243 with critique by J. Beninca (2004) WuW 604; F. Bulst (2004) 57 NJW 2201.

[24] J. Topel, in: Wiedemann, *Handbuch des Kartellrechts* (1999), § 50 note 61; V. Emmerich, in Immenga/Mestmäcker (3rd edn 2001), § 33 GWB note 16; W.-H. Roth, in *Frankfurter Kommentar zum Kartellrecht* (2001), § 33 GWB note 53; F. W. Bulst (2004) 57 NJW 2201; T. Lettl (2003) 167 ZHR 476 at 481 et seq.; H. Köhler (2004) GRUR 99; W. Wurmnest (2003/04) GPR 129 (135).

[25] See the *amicus curiae* brief of the FCO of August 27, 2004 in the case *Philipp Holzmann/Readymix* no. 2 U 16/03 Kart before the Kammergericht, Berlin.

[26] LG Dortmund, Az. 13 O 55/02 Kart (available e.g. at (2004) EWS 434), annotated by F. Bulst (2004) EWS 403. See generally T. Lübbig (2004) WRP 1254.

[27] H. Köhler (2004) GRUR 99 (100 et seq.); W.-H. Roth, in *Frankfurter Kommentar zum Kartellrecht* (2001), § 33 GWB note 50. In favour of the inclusion of indirect purchasers W. Fikentscher, *Wirtschaftsrecht*, vol. 2 (1983), p. 270.

courts nor according to the majority of legal scholars. Thus, V would not have had claims against A, B and C.[28]

It is probable, albeit not absolutely clear, that the reform of German competition law in 2005 has changed this situation. The requirement of defining the protective scope of § 1 GWB has been abolished. Anyone affected by a restrictive agreement can take legal action now. This should be interpreted in the sense that consumers as indirect purchasers are also entitled to claim damages or to use other remedies.[29] However, there is no case law in this sense, and legal doctrine has not yet reached consensus.[30] With this reservation, it should now be answered in the affirmative that V can claim damages against A, B and C.

In Germany, there have been legislative proposals to introduce standing for consumer associations into cartel law. For a very long time, however, these plans have remained unrealized.[31] This result is in contradiction to unfair competition law, where standing for consumer associations is recognized.[32] In some constellations, as in the present case where all competitors are part of the cartel, a consumer association would be a highly motivated plaintiff having an interest in pursuing the cartel. In an early draft of the 7th Cartel Reform standing for consumer associations was proposed. They would have been able to proceed against restrictive behaviour.[33] However, in the final version, this proposal did not succeed. Thus, the most important gap in German competition law could not be filled.

Greece (12)

The present case describes an agreement prohibited by art. 1 of L. 703/1977. In particular, it refers to prohibited price fixing above the

[28] This result corresponds to the 'Indirect Purchaser Rule' of US-American law according to which only the direct, but not the indirect purchaser may claim damages (even if the direct purchaser passed most of the overcharge on to its customers), see H. Hovenkamp, *Federal Antitrust Policy* (1994), pp. 564 et seq.

[29] See BT-Drs. 15/3640 of 7.6.2004, p. 53. In this sense e.g. J. Basedow, *Perspektiven des Kartelldeliktsrechts* (2006) ZWeR 294 (302); F. Bulst, *Schadensersatzansprüche der Marktgegenseite im Kartellrecht* (2006), p. 132; J. Kessler, *Private Enforcement – Zur deliktsrechtlichen Aktualisierung des deutschen und europäischen Kartellrechts im Lichte des Verbraucherschutzes* (2006) WRP 1061, n.3.2.2; Mestmäcker/Schweitzer, *Europäisches Wettbewerbsrecht* (2nd edn 2004), § 22 no. 35.

[30] See Bundeskartellamt, *Private Kartellrechtsdurchsetzung – Stand, Probleme, Perspektiven* (2005), p. 7 et seq.; F. Al-Deb'i/B. Krause (2006) ZGS 20; J. Koch (2005) WuW 1210.

[31] W.-H. Roth, in: *Frankfurter Kommentar zum Kartellrecht* (2001), § 33 GWB note 27. In favour of consumer claims see W. van Gerven (Case 10 above, note 107), p. 7 note 30, p. 27.

[32] § 8 para. 3 n. 3 UWG. [33] See BT-Drs. 15/3640 of June 7, 2004, p. 53.

competitive price. V has the right to lodge a complaint with the Competition Commission, which in its turn shall impose sanctions.[34] However, the procedure before the Competition Commission cannot lead to civil law remedies, such as damages or nullity of the contract.

Regarding the civil law remedies, the following should be noted:

a) The validity of the sale contract by virtue of which consumer V purchased products bearing the unlawfully increased price, may not be contested, as will be analysed in the next case. This is even truer in the present case, given the fact that V acquires the product, as an ultimate consumer, over various commercial levels.
b) The next question to arise is whether V has a compensation claim against the members of the price cartel. It should be accepted that, in accordance with art. 914 CC, the consumer may request compensation for the damage caused by the artificially raised prices. The conditions of tortious liability based on art. 914 CC are: (a) unlawful act committed by the tortfeasor, (b) fault, (c) damages suffered by V, and (d) a causal link between the damages and the unlawful and culpable act. The unlawful act consists in the violation by A, B and C of art. 1(1) of L. 703/77. According to the view prevailing in legal doctrine, the prohibitions contained in antitrust law aim at protecting not only the general interest (i.e. the institution of competition as such) but also the private interests of third parties wishing to participate in the economic process.[35] This approach is wide enough to include not only competitors but also consumers who have suffered damages by reason of the prohibited agreement. The difficult burden of proof that all conditions of tortious liability have to face lies with the claimant. To our knowledge, no jurisprudence exists on this issue.

Hungary (12)

This agreement would fall under sec. 11 HCA, i.e. the general prohibition of cartels. An individual consumer can only take action against A, B and C in accordance with the provisions of civil law. This means that V can demand damages against A, B and C because he paid too much for the vitamins. According to sec. 92(1) HCA consumer protection organizations may file an action against persons who have put consumers at a substantial disadvantage or have disadvantaged a wide range of consumers by their activities infringing the act even if the identity of the

[34] See supra Case 9(3).

[35] A. Liakopoulos, *The Economic Freedom as Subject of Protection in Antitrust Law* (1981), p. 298 et seq.; A. Liakopoulos, (2000) 5 *Industrial Property* 498–499; L. Kotsiris, *Unfair Competition and Antitrust Law* (2001), p. 482.

consumers suffering damage cannot be established. According to sec. 92 (3) HCA the court may oblige the offender to implement a price cut, repair or replace the goods, or refund the purchase price. In its judgment the court may authorize the party taking the action to publish the judgment in a national daily at the expense of the offender. Furthermore, under sec. 92(4) HCA the offender must satisfy the claim of the consumer suffering damage in accordance with the judgment. This does not prejudice the right of the consumer to take further action against the offender in accordance with the provisions of civil law. The consumer association is, however, not entitled to claim damages.

Ireland (12)

V can take action against A, B and C under sec. 14 of the Competition Act 2002 for conducting a naked cartel in breach of sec. 4 of the Act, and claim damages. Given that V is a consumer, V may have difficulty gathering the necessary evidence to be successful in such a claim, and, for this reason, may request the Irish Competition Authority to take action against A, B and C. The Competition Authority has extensive investigatory powers to enable it to gather evidence of the cartel. However, the Competition Authority is not obliged to prioritize or pursue V's request. If the Competition Authority does take a successful claim, V can proceed more easily with a damages claim against A, B and C, as the illegality of their activity will, at that point, have been proven.

The findings of a court following criminal proceedings can be referred to by a plaintiff in a civil action and could form part of the evidence put forward by the plaintiff in advancing his/her claim. The position in relation to admissibility of evidence is more complex. As a rule, a private litigant will be required to prove his/her case afresh. The general principle is that hearsay evidence is not admissible.

Italy (12)

Article 2(2)(a) of the Law 287/90 prohibits agreements between business actors, which directly or indirectly fix purchase or selling prices. The Competition Authority (*Autorità Garante*) is entrusted to assess whether the agreement affects a relevant part of the internal market and whether competition is altered in a substantial way. In the case at hand, A, B and C have reached an agreement which does apparently affect competition in a relevant part of the market (since they each have a third market share) and in a substantial way (because as a result of their price agreement, the final consumer has to pay 20 per cent more than what he would have paid in a state of normal competition). The question of whether the final consumer is entitled to any claims against general cartel effects (i.e. the nullity of the agreement and damages) has been the subject of much debate.[36] In fact, one of the main problems in the private enforcement of antitrust law is identification of those who are entitled to bring a claim, since anti-competitive behaviours have an intrinsic multi-offensive nature.

A key case related to insurance companies has to be mentioned in this context. In Summer 2000 the Authority sanctioned several insurance companies for an agreement causing restraint of competition in the market.[37] The *Cassazione* (Supreme Court of Cassation) denied the standing of consumers to bring actions before the Court of Appeal against the concerted practice.[38] The reason is that final consumers (in principle) have no (direct) interest since they do not operate on the same level as the companies that have reached the agreement. The *Cassazione* pointed out that art. 2 and 33 of the Law 287/90 primarily address companies. And, the mere existence of a prohibited practice is not sufficient for the consumer to claim damages since the damage is not *in re ipsa*. As a result, the consumer will have to bring evidence of the unjust damage he incurred, the unjust infringement of a specific subjective right, and the causal link between the infringement and the prejudice suffered. The competent judge will be the one identified on the basis of ordinary criteria of competence given that there is no competence *rationae materiae* of the Court of Appeal. On such grounds, the consumer V could claim damages in front of ordinary (lower) courts, in compliance with general rules on damages. Yet, the issue of the standing of consumers is still open because in September 2003 the *Cassazione* approached the matter differently.[39] The Court affirmed that the identification of the subjects entitled to bring nullity and damage claims has to be carried out on a case-by-case

[36] On this issue, see C. Castronovo, *Antitrust e Abuso di Responsabilità Civile*, in *Danno e Responsabilità*, 5/2004, 469–474 and M. Granieri, *A Proposito di Intese Restrittive della Concorrenza*, in *Foro It.* (2004), 2, 466/469, pt. I.

[37] AGCM, July 28, 2000, n. 8546, in *Bollettino* n. 30/2000, confirmed by TAR Lazio, sez. I, July 5, 2001, n. 6139, and from the *Consiglio di Stato*, sez. VI, April 23, 2002, n. 2199, in *Foro It.* (2002), III, 382.

[38] Cass. Sez. I Civ., December 9, 2002, *Soc. Axa Assicurazioni v. Isvap-Larato*, n. 17475, in *Danno e Responsabilità*, n. 4/2003, *Antitrust e Tutela Civilistica: Anno Zero*, 390–393 with note S. Bastianon.

[39] Cass. Civ. Sez. III, October 17, 2003, n. 15538 (ord.), *Unipol Compagnia Assicuratrice v. Ricciarelli*, in *Danno e Responsabilità*, n. 12/2003, 1181, *Intese Restrittive della Concorrenza e Legittimazione ad Agire del Consumatore*, with note by G. Colangelo.

basis. And, because of the relevance of the issue, the Court forwarded the case to the first president of the *Cassazione* that will have to consider whether a definitive decision by the *Sezioni Unite* is needed.

Netherlands (12)

V can file a complaint with the Netherlands Competition Authority. The NCA can investigate the alleged practices. If it finds A, B and C to have infringed art. 6(1) DCA and/or art. 81(1) EC, the Director General may impose a fine or an order subject to a penalty. V can start private antitrust litigation and claim damages before the civil courts. This claim should be based on the general norm of art. 6:162 DCC. Therefore, V has serious problems regarding the burden of proof: Concerning the existence of an infringement of the DCA and therefore of a wrongful act, V has the burden of proof on the existence of a wrongful act. If the Competition Authority has not (yet) established an infringement of art. 6 DCA and/or art. 81 EC the court will probably not consider it likely that A, B and C have committed a wrongful act. Regarding the amount of the damage and proving causation it has to be established what the claimants' actual damages are, and to what extent A, B and C must be held responsible for these damages. V could state that he overpaid by 20 per cent. But, that implies that the intermediaries (wholesaler and retailer) have passed on the price increase and have passed it on for 20 per cent. There appear to be serious problems showing a causal link. In this case, it is even more complicated due to the intervention of different commercial levels. If the court finds it reasonable in a given case to do so, the court may assume it likely that the damage is caused by the infringement and allow the defendants to prove the contrary. Whether the court will do so depends on the facts of the case and the court's consideration of the facts. It may occur in a situation where the norm infringed has as its objective prevention of the damage that actually occurred. In the Netherlands, however, there is no case law in antitrust damage cases regarding this issue.

Poland (12)

The abuse of a dominant position in the relevant market by one or more undertakings is prohibited. The abuse of a dominant position may, in particular consist of: direct or indirect imposition of unfair prices or other conditions of purchase or sale of products (art 8.2(1) u.o.k.k), or imposition by the entrepreneur of onerous contract conditions giving him unjustified profits (art 8.2(6) u.o.k.k). Legal actions, which constitute abuse of a dominant position, shall be entirely or partly null and void. The u.o.k.k. does not provide any criteria according to which 'unfairness' of the price or other conditions of the purchase could be determined. In practice, the interests of the parties should be balanced and their contributions should be equal.[40] To calculate whether the prices are extensively high such factors as costs of production, profit margins, competitors' prices or prices used by the undertaking in other markets can be taken into account.[41] Since V pays a higher price as a consequence of the price cartel and such a significant increase cannot be justified by (for example) the increase of costs of production, he can claim abuse of the dominant position by A, B and C.

Together with the abuse of a dominant position there is a restrictive agreement prohibited by art 5 u.o.k.k. As a result of the agreement, A, B and C eliminate competition between themselves and at the same time on the entire market. Due to the price increase, the consumer V has to pay more than the otherwise competitive price.

The President of the OCCP is the organ of central administration competent in the protection of competition and consumers.[42] Local authorities, consumer organizations and other institutions (such as the consumers' ombudsman), whose statutory tasks include the protection of consumer interests, also perform tasks in the field of consumer protection. In particular the consumers' ombudsman shall address undertakings in cases regarding protection of consumer rights and interests. The aforementioned organizations can bring a claim in accordance with the provisions of art. 100a et seq. u.o.k.k regarding cases of infringement of collective consumer interests.

The President of the OCCP is not competent to decide on the nullity of an agreement. He is competent to decide that a practice restricts competition and can order its cessation. The civil court hearing the case on the basis of art 189 k.p.c. has authority to determine questions of nullity.[43]

[40] E. Modzelewska-Wachal, *Ustawa o ochronie konkurencji i konsumentow. Komentarz* (2002), p. 101.

[41] Ibid.

[42] The President of the OCCP controls, inter alia, the observance by entrepreneurs of the provisions of the u.o.k.k. and addresses entrepreneurs and associations in order to protect the rights and interests of consumers. The President cooperates with the local authorities and with organizations whose statutory tasks include the protection of consumer interests (art 26 u.o.k.k. – competences of the President of the OCCP).

[43] SA 29.12.1993, XVII Amr 44/93, 'Wokanda' 1994, 6.

Portugal (12)

Under Portuguese law, V has no claim against A, B and C. Actually, the agreement between A, B and C is illicit according to art. 4/1/a) Competition Defence Law. But the purpose of this law is the protection of competition and, ultimately, the individual competitors and not the protection of consumers.[44] Therefore, consumers cannot make claims under this legislation for compensation (art. 483/1 CC). However, the consumer can claim for an injunction against any commercial practice that is illegal if he is directly harmed. Art. 46.° Law no. 18/2003, June 11 also determines that a compulsory sanction can be applied.

The antitrust legislation is grounded on the public interest in free competition and is not created to protect individual interests, so consumers cannot normally react against these kinds of cartels. In this case, there are collective and diffuse consumers' interests and the bodies with legal competence to act in defence of consumers are the Public Prosecution Service and the National Consumer Protection Institution.

Spain (12)

V is entitled to bring a cease-and-desist claim against A, B and C before the SDC on the grounds that they have entered into an agreement forbidden by art. 1 LDC (see Case 9). He could also ask the SDC to order A, B and C to remove the effects provoked by their agreement (art. 36 LDC). After the administrative decision, consumer V could claim damages (arising from payment of the higher price) before a civil court (art. 13 LDC).

Sweden (12)

Under KL (Swedish Competition Act) the only private remedy available is the possibility of compensation for damages. Other private remedies, like declaratory judgments, injunctions and interim relief, are not regulated by KL. The entities entitled to sue for such a remedy are those that the act may be said to protect, i.e. competitors and undertakings operating in upstream downstream markets. Before August 1, 2005 only competitors and other undertakings were assumed to be directly affected by the activities of a cartel. Besides, persons not considered undertakings within the act but who entered into agreements with the

[44] With the same opinion, A. dos Santos/M.E. Gonçalves/M.M. Leitão Marques, *Direito Económico* (4th edn 2001), p. 349.

member of a cartel were entitled to compensation for the damage they suffered as a result of the prohibited agreement. Sec. 33 opened up the possibility of an indirect right for others, such as consumers or other private entities, when they had been party to an illegal agreement. Nonetheless, when it came to unidentifiable groups of consumers, as would include V, who were affected indirectly by a prohibited agreement, they had, according to the preparatory documents,[45] no right to compensation. Accordingly, V had according to the Swedish Competition Act no private claim against A, B and C.

As from August 1, 2005, KL sec. 33 has been altered, now explicitly dropping the bar to consumers making claims for damages where they are not in a contractual relation with the undertaking in breach of the prohibitions in KL. The alteration has two objectives. First, it is submitted that it is desirable to make clear that public bodies may also claim damages under KL. Under the old wording only public bodies with a contractual relation to an infringing undertaking could claim damages.[46] Second, the legislator has changed its mind about how to view consumers. Now it is said that the purpose of the act is to safeguard the general interest of consumers, at least to the same extent as the act is there to protect the general interest of undertakings. It is explicitly said that it is not one of the act's purposes to protect individual undertakings. In the light of this, the legislature finds it difficult to accept that a consumer, the victim of a cartel, could only make a claim in damages against the cartel member with whom he or she has entered into contract, whereas an undertaking in a similar situation could make a claim in damages against any of the cartel members.[47]

It is worth mentioning that the alteration of sec. 33 also contains an extension of the prescription time from five to ten years from when the damage occurred.

The alterations of sec. 33 are obviously and explicitly an expression of a shift in attitude in favour of individual consumers. Still, it must be remembered that the preconditions for damages have not been altered; the individual consumer or a group of consumers has to prove an infringement, damage and the casual link between infringement and damage. It remains to be seen whether the alterations will have a practical effect.

[45] Bill. 1992/93:56 op cit. [46] SOU (Public Enquiries by the State) 2004:10 at p. 84.
[47] SOU 2004:10 at p. 85.

Summary (12)

1. *Outline*

The question of consumer claims touches the foundations of consumer law. If the aim of undistorted competition is to guarantee production at the cheapest price and the highest quality possible to the benefit of consumers, why not give consumers their own claims with which to enforce respect for competition law? Case 12 therefore takes on a key significance: what is the position in the reporting countries regarding the standing of consumers who are not directly affected by anti-competitive conduct, but, as frequently occurs in commercial reality, merely indirectly? Do national jurisdictions afford the consumer the legal power to proceed independently against such conduct? In order to concentrate attention in the case on this central issue the example was chosen of a horizontal price agreement, that is the clearest form of hard-core cartel. Accordingly, the starting point in all the countries is the same: the pricing agreement constitutes a prohibited horizontal restriction of competition. The sales agreements with consumers are valid as so-called 'subsequent contracts' (see Case 13 on this). The focus of this case therefore is on the claims of the consumer against the cartel members.

2. *The legal position in reporting countries*

The precise legal analysis of the case raises difficulties everywhere. There are only few and isolated court rulings (Denmark, Germany, Italy, regarding unfair competition also Austria). Thus one is often forced to resort to the interpretation of the relevant laws in the scholarly literature. However, even a majority view in the scholarly literature does not offer a sufficient guarantee that legal practice will choose this route. Even if the following presentation therefore cannot be taken as absolutely definitive, the following picture emerges: in the majority of reporting countries the consumer has no claims against the cartel members, and in particular no compensatory claim. The reason for this is largely that only enterprises, but not consumers, will be seen as falling within the protection of antitrust law (Finland, France, Poland, Portugal). In these countries it is assumed that the interests of the consumer are already protected by the intervention of the antitrust authority on the public law level. Even in countries where an independent claim by consumers is not excluded from the beginning, there is a requirement that the claimant be directly affected (Denmark, Germany until July 1, 2005, Sweden until August 1, 2005). Consumers who are merely indirectly affected fail to meet this requirement. Only in few countries are compensatory claims by indirectly affected consumers upheld (Germany since July 1, 2005, Italy, Spain,[48] Sweden since August 1, 2005) or at least held to be possible (England, Greece, Hungary, Ireland, Netherlands). In this context, the recent reforms of German and Swedish law have to be mentioned: direct targeting or the existence of a contractual relationship to a cartel member is no longer a prerequisite for damage suits. The development in Germany and in Sweden may be interpreted as a tendency to strengthen the rights of consumers in antitrust law.

3. *Evidence issues*

However, even where compensatory consumer claims are possible, there is a high evidentiary threshold which, while not excluding such claims, makes them significantly more difficult. The violation of the cartel prohibition, the resulting loss and the causal connection between the violation and the loss must be proved by the plaintiff. In the absence of discovery, the consumer has very few prospects of proving the existence of a cartel operating a secret price agreement. At this point the importance of intervention by the antitrust authority is again underlined in order to solve the problems of furnishing sufficient evidence. However, the antitrust authority cannot help with the next step in that the claimant has to prove the level of his losses and causation of this loss by the antitrust violation. As very aptly expressed in the Italian report: 'The damage is not *in re ipsa*', that is the antitrust law violation does not in itself indicate the sustaining of loss. Even where as in Case 12 it is established that the agreement has led to a 20 per cent increase in the sales price at the manufacturing stage, this does not automatically determine whether or to what extent this price increase will be passed on to the consumer. It still has to be asked whether, as a result of the 20 per cent increase of the purchase price, subsequent processors or retailers have themselves increased their sales prices, and if so, to what extent. Could they pass the price increase on fully or perhaps even disproportionately, or only in part to the next economic level? Nor is it certain what influence this has on the price paid by the ultimate

[48] Spain requires a prior decision by the antitrust authority. However, once this decision has been made the consumer can file an independent claim for damages.

consumer. This last question requires us to remember that the product concerned, that is vitamins, is generally an intermediate product which only to a limited extent influences the sales price of the final product. The difficulties which arise in determining loss in countries where claims are possible can therefore be so severe as to prevent a judge being able to assess quantum (see also Case 10).

4. *The 'passing on' defence*

The question of consumer claims is closely linked to the 'passing on' problem. If consumer claims are admitted, in what relationship do they stand to other private claims, for example by direct purchasers? Is it fair to expose defendants to a multiplicity of possible plaintiffs? This depends on the question whether direct purchasers (who have become victims of a cartel) should be allowed to claim damages even if they have passed the higher prices on to the next commercial level. In US-American law, the 'passing on' objection is not recognized in principle.[49] Thus, the victim of a cartel can claim damages even if the higher prices were passed on to their own customers. In return, according to the 'indirect purchaser rule' the next commercial levels do not have own claims against the cartel members.[50] Within the bounds of this study it was not possible to include the problem of 'passing on'. In our view, the problem can only be solved in two ways: either the passing on defence is rejected – then it would not be fair to give standing to remote commercial levels; or the passing on defence is recognized – then the next commercial levels down to consumers should have the right to take legal action themselves.[51] The answer to this question depends on how much autonomy one is prepared to give to consumers in antitrust law.[52]

[49] See US Supreme Court, *Hanover Shoe, Inc. v. United Shoe Machinery Corp.*, 392 U.S. 481 (1968).

[50] See US Supreme Court, *Illinois Brick Co. v. Illinois*, 431 U.S. 720 (1977).

[51] In this sense G. Wagner, *Prävention und Verhaltenssteuerung durch Privatrecht – Anmaßung oder legitime Aufgabe?* (2006) 206 AcP 352 (407).

[52] See more in detail, Conclusions II 2 (b) below. For a survey on the 'passing on' defence in Europe see Ashurst (prepared by D. Waelbroeck, D. Slater and G. Even-Shoshan), *Study on the Conditions of Claims for Damages in Case of Infringement of EC Competition Rules* (2004), p. 77 et seq.; and the fundamental monograph by F. Bulst, *Schadensersatzansprüche der Marktgegenseite im Kartellrecht – Zur Schadensabwälzung nach deutschem, europäischem und US-amerikanischem Recht* (2006).

5. *Variations*

Even where the above difficulties can be overcome, the consumer has only limited incentives to bring a claim. His loss will be so marginal that the trouble and costs of legal proceedings will be disproportionately high compared to the compensation sought.[53] It is better therefore to seek a solution in which the scattered losses sustained by individual consumers can be combined and pursued by a special central institution. In the country reports in this connection two regulatory models are pointed to, the Ombudsman of Scandinavian origins (also found in Poland) and the consumer protection association. The Ombudsman however has no competence in the field of antitrust law. He is therefore only involved if there is conduct which is not only an antitrust violation but also infringes the law of unfair competition. Here the Ombudsman can even pursue compensatory claims on behalf of aggrieved consumers (Denmark). Unlike the Ombudsman, consumer protection associations are to be found in all reporting countries. Their powers in antitrust law are, however, severely curtailed. Generally, the consumer protection associations can only recommend or apply for commencement of an antitrust authority proceeding (see Case 9 (3)).[54] They have no standing in civil proceedings, neither for a cessation claim nor for a compensatory claim. The introduction of rights of action for consumer protection associations has been discussed in some countries (e.g. in Germany), but to date no such rights have actually been created in practice. Finally, mention should be made of the possibility of group litigation in English law. However, to date there has been no case with reference to competition law.

6. *Conclusions*

The results are paradoxical: antitrust law is intended to secure freedom of competition, so that the consumer can obtain the best results in the market. If enterprises violate the regulations, however, the consumer has no rights of his own. Rather he must rely on the activities of others, in particular the antitrust authorities. Here as always, under administrative law he can only call for action on the part of the authorities. As,

[53] An improvement in terms of awarding punitive damages is generally rejected in continental Europe, see above Case 10(1).

[54] The figures available for France (see above in French report) indicate that the practical significance of the consumer protection association is limited even in the administrative proceeding.

however, in the field of cartel regulations the opportunity principle is dominant and widespread, the consumer has in effect no right to the intervention of the antitrust authority. The 'consumer sovereignty' familiar from economic theory is not matched by a corresponding 'sovereign' right of claim for consumers under antitrust law. This goes so far that even consumer protection associations have no standing in civil proceedings. This situation fails to convince. From the systematic point of view it is necessary to grant standing to the consumer, the party who ultimately has to bear the consequences of competition restrictions. Admittedly, the consumer will seldom exercise such a right as individual claims will seldom be worthwhile. Therefore, a second step is necessary to extend standing to consumer associations. This right should not only be for cessation, but also for compensatory claims. The consolidation of fragmented compensatory claims into one action would mean the judicial value of claims would make legal proceedings commercially viable. It is not enough to point the consumer in the direction of the antitrust authorities. Fines or surrender of profits (elimination of additional revenues) only serve to deprive the infringer of its unlawful profits. This, however, does not compensate for the harm to the consumer. This requires an own right of claim, which the consumer can either exercise on his own behalf or, on grounds of practicability, through the agency of a consumer protection association.

Case 13 Horizontal restraints of competition – validity of subsequent contracts

A, B and C produce high-tension cable. They each have a one-third market share. The cable is sold direct to energy-producing companies with no intermediaries. A, B and C agree together to raise their prices by 10 per cent. The energy producer E concludes a sales contract with A for 10,000 metres of cable at the new, increased price. Before delivery and payment E learns of the price agreement between A, B and C. He refuses to accept the 10,000 metres of power cable.

Does he have a right to do this? What other claims does E have?

Austria (13)

The agreement entered into by A, B and C to increase their prices by 10 per cent constitutes a cartel agreement pursuant to § 10 para. 1 KartG 1988, which is intended to create a restriction of competition in particular through prices (intentional cartel), now governed by § 1 para. 1 KartG 2005 which as a matter of principle prohibits all agreements no matter whether restriction of competition is their object or only their effect. § 1 para. 2 KartG 2005 mentions especially the direct or indirect fixing of purchase or selling prices. The legal prohibition of practising such agreements does not depend any longer on a certain cartel form (as under § 18 para. 1 KartG 1988), and the nullity in civil law does not depend any longer (as was the case under § 22 KartG 1988) on the prohibition against practising the agreement. Agreements and decisions prohibited under § 1 para.1 KartG 2005 are void (§ 1 para. 3 KartG 2005).[1] This legal consequence applies, however, only to the clauses in restriction of competition but not to the agreement as a whole. In the present case the clause restricting competition is indeed invalid and prohibited.

Under Austrian law, in contrast to mere voidability, any person, including a third party, can rely on invalidity (rescission). Ultimately, this depends on the prohibitory purpose of the norm in question. The stringent legal consequences of absolute invalidity apply above all to violations of those regulations which serve to protect the general interest, public order and security. It has, however, already been said that invalidity or unconscionability of the contract can only be relied on by

[1] Nullity arises without decision of a cartel authority; the nullity is absolute (R. Hoffer/ J. Barbist, p. 17).

someone affected by the void transaction in his legal interests, but not by a third party external to the contract.[2] A beneficiary of the contract or party under its protection is not an 'external third party'. Accordingly, to this extent it is not inconceivable that third parties may also seek termination (rescission) of the contract. As the prohibition on the operation of cartels serves to protect general interests, in the present case a third-party effect of the invalid cartel agreement on the purchaser of the goods may be presumed. However, no relevant court decisions on this point have been found.[3] In the view of the present writer, the buyer may thus refuse to accept the goods and if payment for the goods is claimed (concurrently with delivery) the invalidity of the price agreement may be relied on.

Denmark (13)

According to CA § 6, sec. 5, an agreement is invalid if the agreement is contrary to the ban of CA § 6, sec. 1. The invalidity is, however, limited to the relation between the parties to the agreement. The invalidity will not influence a supply contract agreed between A and E. The specific violation of CA § 6, sec. 1, may according to CA § 23 be subject to a penalty in the form of a fine. A violation may also be the basis for a liability for damages in a civil lawsuit, which E will bring before the regular courts. Please compare Case 9 above.

The contract between A and E is based on the fact that A is participating in an agreement, which is in contravention of CA § 6, sec. 1, and which may be the basis for a penalty under CA § 23. From a civil law point of view it will – based on this fact – presumably be possible to claim that the contract is invalid and/or that there is a basis for cancelling the contract without incurring a liability for damages. There is no case law on this issue.

England (13)

The theoretical alternatives for E would seem to be (1) to repudiate the contract and reject the goods or (2) to accept the goods at the contract price and then sue for damages for breach of art. 81(1) EC, the measure of damages in principle being the difference between the

[2] OGH 29.9.1965, JBl 1966, 254.

[3] Also H.-G. Koppensteiner (p. 168) points out, that there is on this subject no sufficiently thorough study; H. Koziol (II, p. 105) thinks that the cartel law protects competitors, but not the illegally harmed clients; F. Gschnitzer (p. 217) however holds that the protected third parties (public, suppliers) may also invoke the nullity.

(supra-competitive) contract price and the lower price at which E could have bought the goods in a market that was not affected by the cartel.

A damages remedy would in principle be available to a claimant who had been a party to an illegal supply agreement, provided at least that he did not bear 'significant responsibility' for the breach of competition law.[4] A fortiori, it will not be a problem for a claimant such as E who is not a party to the illegality.

A right for E to repudiate the contract and reject the goods is much more difficult. Taking a normal English contract law analysis, for E to have a right to repudiate the sale of goods contract there must have been a breach by A of a term of E's contract with A (a separate contract from the cartel agreement). Furthermore, not every breach of contract gives rise to a right for the other party to repudiate the contract (rather than simply seeking damages, but leaving the contract in place): only breach of a condition (a major term) or a fundamental breach of an innominate term (in the condition/innominate term/warranty trilogy) will suffice.[5] Giving E a right to repudiate would seem to involve having to (1) imply a term into the contract between A and E that A has not been in breach of competition law in relation to anything to do with this contract, and (2) if there is such an implied term, establish that its status is either a condition or an innominate term (the latter having to have been breached in a fundamental way before there can be a right to repudiate). The English courts are generally reluctant to imply terms into contracts, certainly where commercial contracts are concerned.

The ECJ in the preliminary ruling in C-453/99 *Courage Ltd. v. Crehan* appears to be of the view[6] that effective remedies for individuals for breach of EC competition law are provided by rights to sue for damages (albeit full compensatory damages), implying that it is not necessary for national law to go so far as to enable purchasers from the cartel members to repudiate resulting contracts for the sale of goods. Always assuming that a defendant was financially able to meet a damages claim, that would make sense. To give E a right to repudiate his purchase agreement here would require some major changes in some fundamental principles of English contract law, with some far-reaching

[4] This, of course, was the position of Mr Crehan (see *Courage Ltd. v. Crehan* [2001] ECR I-6297).

[5] For more detail, see R. Bradgate, *Commercial Law* (3rd edn 2000), chs. 2, 9 and 12.

[6] Para. 26.

implications. The view of this writer is that a damages claim is the most that could be contemplated here.

Finland (13)

According to sec. 4 para. 1 of the Finnish Act on Competition Restrictions, all agreements between business undertakings, decisions by associations of business undertakings and concerted practices by business undertakings which have as their object the significant prevention, restriction or distortion of competition or which result in the prevention, restriction or distortion of competition shall be prohibited. In particular, agreements, decisions or practices which directly or indirectly fix purchase or selling prices or any other trading conditions shall be prohibited. Under sec. 18 of the Act, a condition included in an agreement, statute, decision or other legal act or arrangement which violates sec. 4 or 6, or an injunction, prohibition or an obligation issued by the Market Court, or an interlocutory injunction or an obligation issued by the Finnish Competition Authority may not be applied or implemented. It is clear that the prohibited price-fixing agreement between A, B and C is void pursuant to sec. 18. The question remains as to whether sec. 18 affects the validity of the contract between A and E. The rationale behind sec. 18 is to prevent the enforcement of competition restrictions. Legal certainty concerning contractual relationships should also be taken into consideration. These aspects lead to the conclusion that the contract between A and E which is based on the cartel price is valid. On the other hand, according to sec. 1 para. 2 of the Finnish Act on Competition Restrictions, when the act is applied, special attention must be paid to the protection of the freedom of business undertakings to operate without unjustified barriers and restrictions. From this point of view it could be argued that E should not only be protected by damages based on sec. 18 but also by a nullity sanction.

E has suffered damage based on the price-fixing agreement between A, B and C. E may have a claim for compensation against A pursuant to sec. 18a. The compensation for damage covers among other things compensation for price difference.

France (13)

Art. L 420-3 of the Commercial Code provides that any undertaking, agreement or contractual clause referring to a prohibited practice such as cartels (L 420-1) and the abuse of dominant positions (L 420-2) shall be invalid. This can even occur when not all of the contracting parties were aware of the illegal practice or even if they did not participate because it is an absolute annulment and not a relative one.[7] However, this only concerns the agreement between A, B and C, not the subsequent contract between A and E. Here the general principle in French civil law applies that says that contracts are binding (*pacta sunt servanda*) as provided by art. 1134 para. 1 of the Civil Code.[8] In order to be released from the contract or to revoke it, the contractor has to prove that his will has been affected by error, fraud or violence, art. 1109 of the Civil Code. Otherwise, a contract can only be revoked by mutual consent of the parties to the contract or for reasons prescribed by law art. 1134 para. 2 of the Civil Code. None of this is the case here. Thus, E has to execute the contract.

Nevertheless, E can use an administrative procedure against the agreement before the Council on Competition as undertakings are enabled to refer directly to the Council on Competition.[9] The condition for referring successfully to the Council on Competition is the existence of damage.[10] For undertakings the damage has to be personal and direct, as it also has to be according to art. 2 of the Code of Criminal Procedure.[11] Furthermore, a criminal procedure can be used directly by referring to the *Procureur de la République*. In cases where the Council on Competition suspects criminal behaviour it can also submit a dossier to the *Procureur* on its own initiative.[12]

The violation of art. L 420-1 and 420-2 of the Commercial Code constitutes a fault engaging the responsibility of the infringer under the general tort principles in arts. 1382 and 1383 of the Civil Code.[13] But it supposes that there has been competition damage (*préjudice concurrentiel*).[14] This concerns above all victims of abuses of dominant market positions.

[7] M. Malaurie-Vignal, *Droit de la concurrence*, p. 212; Cour de cassation, chambre commerciale of October 24, 2000, in: Bulletin civil IV.

[8] Art. 1134 Code civil: '*Les conventions légalement formées tiennent lieu de loi à ceux qui les ont faites …*'.

[9] V. Selinsky in: Juris-Classeurs, *Concurrence, consommation* (1993), Fasc no. 380, «Procédures de contrôle des pratiques anticoncurrentielles», no. 53.

[10] Ibid., no. 59. [11] Ibid., no. 59. [12] Ibid., no. 177.

[13] M. Malaurie-Vignal, *Droit de la concurrence*, p. 212; Cour d'appel de Paris, June 28, 2002, in RTDcom 2003, 78.

[14] M. Malaurie-Vignal, *Droit de la concurrence*, p. 212; 'Les dommages-intérêts en matière concurrentielle', D. Fasquelle in: Rev. Conc. consom. 2000 no. 115, p. 14.

Germany (13)

E correctly refuses to accept the cable if the sales contract with A is void (or voidable). The prohibited price-fixing agreement between A, B and C is certainly void pursuant to §§ 134 BGB, 1 GWB. However, the question is whether this invalidity extends to the subsequent contract (*Folgevertrag*) between A and E which is based on the cartel price. In the interests of legal certainty the majority opinion assumes that such subsequent contracts with parties which are not cartel members are not affected by the nullity.[15] Therefore, in the present case the contract between A and E is valid, so that E is not entitled to refuse the cable.

However, E could have a compensatory claim against A pursuant to § 33 para. 3 together with § 1 GWB. Until the reform in 2005, E had a claim only if he fell within the protective scope of § 1 GWB. As shown for Case 12 the courts made this dependant on whether the price cartel was directed at E.[16] The majority opinion in the literature (and a minority of the courts[17]) saw it as sufficient if the freedom of choice of the market counterpart was perceptibly limited.[18] This opinion seemed convincing because otherwise global cartels which are not specifically directed at specific market participants would have been privileged. Since 2005 anyone affected by a restrictive agreement has private law claims. E is directly affected by the price increase and therefore has a compensatory claim against A pursuant to § 33 para. 3 GWB. The harm consists in the additional amount that E must pay because of the cartel.[19] Thus, E has a claim for reduction of the sales price to the original level.

The validity of subsequent contracts aims at legal certainty. Contracting partners shall rely on the validity. However, this result seems convincing only if, at the same time, a compensatory claim is awarded which reduces the price to its normal market level. Otherwise, a contract would be upheld which obliges a contracting party to pay a price which was effected by anti-competitive behaviour. Therefore, the

[15] H.-J. Bunte, in Langen/Bunte, *Kommentar zum deutschen und europäischen Kartellrecht* (9th edn 2001), § 1 GWB note 239; J. Topel, in Wiedemann, *Handbuch des Kartellrechts* (1999), § 50 note 22.

[16] See e.g. BGH, January 25, 1985, WuW/E BGH 1985 (1987) – '*Familienzeitschrift*'.

[17] OLG Stuttgart, May 22, 1998, WuW/E DE-R 161 – '*Carpartner II*' (162); LG Dortmund, Az. 13 O 55/02 Kart.

[18] W.-H. Roth, in *Frankfurter Kommentar zum Kartellrecht* (2001), § 33 GWB note 53.

[19] Comparison of markets in time (*Zeitliches Vergleichsmarktkonzept*), see W.-H. Roth, in *Frankfurter Kommentar zum Kartellrecht* (2001), § 33 GWB note 160.

reluctance of German courts to allow compensatory claims does not fit together with the tendency to maintain subsequent contracts.

Greece (13)

By fixing the cable sale prices, A, B and C entered into an agreement prohibited by art. 1 of L. 703/1977. The sale contract between A and E is concluded on the basis of such prohibited agreement. As far as the validity of the sale contract is concerned, the following should be noted: the contract is an accessory act of the invalid agreement. Legal doctrine accepts that such accessory contracts are not invalid.[20] Therefore, they may not be attacked on the sole ground that they have been concluded on the basis of a completely invalid agreement that is prohibited by the antitrust law. Legal doctrine supports, for example, that the nullity of the original agreement does not create a right to third parties to terminate an accessory contract of a continuous nature. The accessory contract will be null and void *only* if it incorporates the prohibited agreement in such a way that in its turn it also falls under the scope of application of art. 1 of L. 703/1977 or if it is concluded between the *same* enterprises.[21] In the present case, the sale to E is a contract that is based on a void price agreement between third enterprises (A, B and C). However, it is not void in itself and, therefore, E is not entitled to refuse performance thereof.

Additionally, E does not have the right to attack the said contract on the grounds that he was deceived by A[22] as far as the real value of the products is concerned, since it is accepted that the co-contractor bears the risk of his own possible miscalculations relating to the price to be paid.[23] Therefore, E does not have in principle the right to refuse delivery of the cables and if he chooses to do so he will be a defaulting creditor.[24] In any case, however, E has a compensatory claim for the price difference according to the Civil Code provisions on liability in tort; by this indirect way, the price may be reduced to its normal market value.

[20] A. Liakopoulos (2000) 5 *Industrial Property* 541; L. Kotsiris, *Unfair Competition and Antitrust Law* (2001), p. 481.

[21] Ibid. [22] Art. 142 CC.

[23] Maggivas, in Georgiades- Stathopoulos (ed.), *The Civil Code*, Article 513 (1980); pp. 40–41. In the present case, a 10% increase in the price does not create a substantial deviation from the actual price and therefore the said contract may not be regarded as abusive (art. 179CC).

[24] Art. 349 CC.

Hungary (13)

According to sec. 11(3) HCA the legal consequences of infringement of sec. 11 (1) HCA shall be applied together with those applied by the Civil Code to illegal contracts. According to sec. 200(2) of the HCC contracts in violation of legal regulations and contracts concluded by evading a legal regulation shall be null and void, unless the legal regulation stipulates another legal consequence. A contract shall also be null and void if it is evidently in contravention of good morals. E can refuse to accept the goods and can claim compensatory damages. According to sec. 238(2) HCC a person who has, in good faith, believed in the existence of an invalid contract can demand compensation from the parties for damages that originate from the conclusion of the contract. This means that the contract between A and E is affected and E can claim damages for believing in good faith in the existence of an invalid contract.

Ireland (13)

E could refuse acceptance of the goods, claiming that the contract was null and void on the basis of illegality. If A should sue E for breach of contract, E should be advised to counterclaim for damages for breach of sec. 4 of the Competition Act 2002, given that the price to which E agreed resulted from a price-fixing agreement between A, B and C. E could also complain to the Competition Authority and request them to take a case on his behalf.

Pure antitrust litigation tends to be the exception rather than the rule in Ireland. In many cases, the antitrust argument is only one of a number of grounds pleaded by the plaintiff. More commonly, in situations such as that described above, the claim could be brought as a defence, if for example A tried to take an action against E.

Italy (13)

A, B and C have reached an agreement, which is prohibited by art. 2 of Law 287/90, and thus avoidable. The price (10 per cent higher) that E has to pay gives effect to such an agreement. In order to be able to refuse delivery, E should claim nullity of the contract, for it is consequential on a prohibited agreement. Thus, the crucial issue is whether the nullity of the anti-competitive practice between A, B and C extends to the contract between A and his customer E. Nullity entails absolute invalidity of the contract (not subject to prescription, not remediable, with effect *ex tunc* and *erga omnes*). Nullity could in principle affect all the contracts which have a functional link with the prohibited agreement. However, in antitrust law, scholars and courts disagree as to whether the nullity of an anti-competitive agreement can be extended to contracts between the companies that entered it and third parties.[25] In any event, E can inform the Competition Authority of the anti-competitive agreement and bring a claim for damages before the ordinary courts.

Netherlands (13)

E refuses to accept the goods (and to pay for them) which basically means that he denies the validity of the agreement. However, the agreement of E is not automatically null and void because of the illegal contract between A, B and C. It is not likely that E can refuse to accept and pay for the purchased goods on the sole ground that the price is based on an anti-competitive agreement between providers. Another question is whether the illegal contract between A, B and C leads to legitimate grounds for E to annul his agreement with A based on error or fraud. If E can prove that he has entered into this agreement under influence of an error (or fraud) regarding the price, because he thought that the price was a competitive market price which was not in fact the case,[26] he can claim the annulment of the agreement and claim damages. Furthermore, E may bring claims for damages based on the general rule of 6:162 DCC and/or he may file a complaint with the NCA to take action against the anti-competitive behaviour of A, B and C.

Poland (13)

The direct or indirect imposition of unfair prices shall, in their entirety or in the relevant part, be null and void (art. 8. 3 u.o.k.k.). Therefore, E has the right to refuse to accept the cable. The administrative decision of the President of the OCCP made on the basis of art. 9 u.o.k.k. does not have retroactive effect. However, art. 8.3 u.o.k.k. creates an automatic sanction and considers the illegal actions, entirely or partially null and void. The sanction has the result *ex tunc* i.e. retroactive from the moment the agreement was concluded. Moreover, art. 8.3 u.o.k.k. has direct

25 O.W. Vogelaar, in J. Stuyck/B. L.P. Van Reeken (eds.), *Competition Law in the EU, Its Member States and Switzerland*, 2-I, The Hague, at 396. Some case law has mitigated the effects of invalidity of a prohibited agreement by confining its effects to the parties that have reached it; see M. Tavassi/M. Scuffi, *Diritto Processuale Antitrust, Tutela Giurisdizionale della Concorrenza* (1998), at 298.

26 And if the other conditions of art. 6:228 DCC (error) or art. 3: 44(3) DCC are met.

consequences in private law, and every person having an interest (both the parties to the agreement as well as third parties) can utilize the consequences flowing from the nullity of the agreement. The President of the OCCP is not competent to decide on the nullity of the agreement. The civil court on the basis of art. 189 k.p.c has authority in that respect. Since the actions (here the agreement between A, B and C), which constitute abuse of a dominant position are entirely or partly null and void E can utilize the consequences. Consequently, he has the right to refuse the cable. Furthermore, E can bring a claim under the provisions of art. 84 et seq. u.o.k.k regarding antimonopoly proceedings in cases of anti-competitive practices.

Portugal (13)

The agreement between A, B and C is not valid according to art. 4 Law no. 18/2003, June 11. This invalidity does not extend to the contract between A and E. The necessity of certainty in commercial transactions demands that the contract between A and E be valid. However, if art. 4 Law no. 18/2003, June 11 is considered a rule protective of individual competitors, E could claim for compensation under art. 483°. CC if he has suffered losses.

Spain (13)

The agreement between A, B and C is contrary to what is stated in art. 1 LDC and therefore void. This nullity does not extend to the contract between E and A on account of legal certainty. Nevertheless, E would be legally able to bring an action against A, B and C before the SDC (see Case 9) once he knows about the cartel. In the view of this writer, E cannot ask a court to declare the contract void because his will to enter into the contract has not been affected by the existence of the cartel. One can safely assume that E would have entered the contract even if the price had been lower, which could have been the case in the absence of the cartel. But A cannot get any advantage from his own malfeasance and from violating the law, so a remedy on damages is available to E (the difference between cartel price and market price, art. 13.2 LDC).

Sweden (13)

According to sec. 7 of KL any agreements or decisions prohibited by sec. 6 of the act, i.e. the prohibition of cartels, are automatically void. Sec. 7 is thus a copy of art. 81.2 of the EC Treaty. As a general rule only the part of the agreement, which is prohibited by art. 6, is void. The entire agreement can, however, be declared void if the void part influences other parts of the agreement to a large degree and thereby makes it impossible to separate it from the rest of the agreement. If the agreement is declared void it means that it has never been valid, i.e. it was void the moment it was entered into. Applied to the scenario in Case 13 this means that the agreement between A, B and C is void, since it is in breach of art. 6 of the Swedish Competition Act. The agreement between E and A is, however, not in breach of art. 6 and is thus not void according to art. 7 of KL. Thus, E would not have the right to withdraw from his agreement with E arguing that the agreement is invalid.

Under Swedish private law a buyer may withdraw from an agreement where he can show that the seller has deceived him. It is also possible to have the contract declared void or altered, where circumstances existing at the time of the conclusion of the contract or circumstances occurring later, would make it unfair to enforce the contract with its original terms (Act on Contracts sec. 36). Furthermore, E has a right to compensation for loss suffered as a result of the agreement between A, B and C (see Case 10 above). In this case, it would seem that E could successfully make a claim for a reduction of the price agreed between E and A, due to the fact that it would be unfair to enforce the contract on its original terms.

The preparatory documents to the Swedish Competition Act briefly mention the situation of 'linked' agreements, such as the one between E and A, in connection with the provision on compensation for damages (sec. 33). It is submitted that bid rigging entitles the buyer to compensation for the mark-up that the prohibited agreement resulted in. If the buyer, in accordance with sec. 7 of the act, withdraws from the agreement, he has a right to compensation for all the sunk costs he has incurred due to the quotation process. Judging by this comment it seems the intention is that 'linked' agreements are also to be void under sec. 7. At least that seems to be the case when it comes to vertical agreements that the buyer has entered into with a seller that has engaged in a prohibited horizontal agreement with other sellers. One should, however, keep in mind that the declaration was made in connection with sec. 33 of the Competition Act and not the relevant provision, i.e. sec. 7. The value of it is thus highly uncertain. Recent case law also points in another direction. The Court of Appeal in a judgment delivered in May 2002[27] declared that 'linked' agreements, which are

[27] T 3236-01 *Boliden Mineral AB / Birka Värme Stockholm AB* (2002-05-14).

not as such in breach of sec. 6 of KL are not caught by sec. 7 of the act solely on the basis of the fact that they are results of agreements in breach of sec. 6. This judgment has been appealed to the Supreme Court and it is still uncertain whether a certiorari will be granted or not. Still, as submitted above it would be hard to argue that it would be fair under Swedish contract law to enforce the cartel price against E in the situation described.

As mentioned above sec. 7 of the act only stipulates that agreements contrary to sec. 6 are void. But what about agreements which are in breach of sec. 19 (abuse of dominant position)? Are there reasons to treat these agreements differently? The Court of Appeal held, in the case *Luftfartsverket/SAS*,[28] that certain clauses of a contested agreement, which were considered to constitute an abuse of a dominant position, were in fact void. The court came to the conclusion that the clauses were in conflict with the Competition Act and that the consequences of this had to be judged in the light of both EC law and Swedish law. The court found that this derived from the preparatory documents to sec. 36 of the Act on Contracts, where it is submitted that anti-competitive agreements should be considered void, from a private law perspective. Consequently, the court held that a contract containing two clauses, which constitute abuses of dominant position under Swedish and EC competition law, should be considered void due to the direct effect of art. 82 EC. Since an appeal to the Supreme Court was not granted, the judgment by the Court of Appeal stands. With this in mind one could argue that sec. 36 of the Act on Contracts has the same significance when it comes to agreements under sec. 6 as in respect of agreements constituting abuses under sec. 19 of the Competition Act.

Summary (13)

1. *Outline*

Case 13 builds on Case 12 but goes one step further in that the claimant E is not a mere remotely affected party but rather a direct customer of a cartel member, who on the basis of a price agreement has paid a 10 per cent higher price. The question is whether such a directly affected customer has greater rights than a merely indirectly affected consumer, and if so, what precise rights he has. Will he be able to repudiate the

[28] T 33-00 *Staten genom Luftfartsverket / Scandinavian Airlines Systems* (2001-04-27).

contract with the cartel member, or is he still bound? Is it possible to claim compensation or to reduce the sales price with reference to the unmanipulated market price? The factual pattern of Case 13 is highly significant for the topic of private claims. Competing enterprises often have no interest in proceeding against a cartel of their competitors, for example where a cartel operates throughout a branch, meaning they are themselves involved. In this case only private claims by customers harmed by the cartel remain. Case 13 is intended to demonstrate the extent to which such customers actually have claims against the cartel members.

2. *Validity of subsequent contracts*

With regard to the starting point, the price cartel between the three producers of high-tension cable constitutes a prohibited agreement in all the reporting countries. The prohibition universally results in invalidity of the price agreement. However, the question receives differing answers on the extent of the invalidity. In some countries it is presumed that subsequent contracts, that is contracts between a cartel member and its customers, are also void (Hungary, Poland, and with reservations Austria). In the majority of countries on the contrary it is assumed that subsequent contracts are valid (Denmark, England, Finland, France, Germany, Greece, Ireland, Netherlands, Portugal, Spain, Sweden). This is explained by the fact that the cartel prohibition only refers to the actual cartel agreement and not to contracts with enterprises that are not party to the anti-competitive agreement. In addition the aspect of legal certainty militates towards the effectiveness of subsequent contracts. The customer must be able to rely on the effectiveness of its contracts and that they will not be affected by legal infringements based on an agreement between their seller and a third party. Legal certainty is, however, not put at risk if the customer himself is in a position to decide on the validity of his contract. Against this background it is sometimes discussed whether the customer should have the right to challenge the contract or something similar under general civil law (Denmark, Netherlands). In the absence of case law on this question no definitive answer can be given. In the other jurisdictions, to the extent that this question is discussed at all, the customer is inescapably bound by the contract. This is partly justified on the grounds that he has not acted on the basis of a material mistake; indeed he knows precisely at what price he is buying (Greece). The manner in which this price is arrived at was not relevant to his contractual intention. Subtle considerations can rather lead to a flexible compensatory claim than to the complete termination (rescission) of the legal transaction.

3. *Compensatory claims*

The majority of reports call for the existence of a compensatory claim. Here there is a material difference to Case 12. While in that case the consumer was exposed to the indirect effects of a cartel, in Case 13 E is directly affected as he has purchased at an artificially inflated price from a cartel member. Here in almost all countries a material difference is seen so that the directly affected customer, as opposed to a merely indirectly affected customer, has a compensatory claim. The claim is for the reduction of the sales price to the price which would have been charged without the cartel agreement, that is the cancellation of the 10 per cent surcharge. The problem of passing on of the damage does not arise, since E as an energy producer does not sell the high-tension cables on.[29] So far as can be seen, only the German jurisdiction under the Competition Act in force until 2005 tended towards a negative result for E. With the reform in 2005, German law fell into line with other European legal systems.

4. *Conclusions*

Despite the introduction of leniency programmes, cartels have often been in existence for years. Therefore, in addition to the antitrust authority remedies, private claims should be created, by means of which affected parties could defend themselves in their own right.[30] Such claims should particularly be made available to those who suffer most directly from the cartel. These are the direct customers who pay too high prices because of the cartel. This would not require extensive reform as almost all reporting countries have compensatory claims for direct customers against suppliers that are cartel members. In Case 13 for this reason the greatest degree of convergence between the reporting countries is to be seen.

[29] The problem of passing on will be discussed in the final conclusions.

[30] However, leniency programmes could be jeopardized if self-incriminating statements of 'whistle blowers' could be used against them in civil damage proceedings. In order to avoid this danger, the European Commission has included rules on the confidentiality of corporate statements in its Leniency Notice (OJ C 298/17 of December 8, 2006, no. 31 et seq.).

Case 14 Vertical restraints of competition – resale price maintenance

Company A produces skateboards and sells them under the trade mark 'Flash'. A sells the skateboards through wholesalers who sell them on to retailers. B is one of these wholesalers. In a sales contract A and B agree that B has to sell the skateboards to retailers at a certain minimum price. B experiences marketing difficulties because of the high set price and suffers losses amounting to €300,000. As a result, he starts to sell the skateboards at a lower price.

1. Can A prohibit the sale of the boards at a lower price?
2. What claims does B have against A? Are B's claims influenced by the fact that he participated in the restrictive agreement?

Austria (14)

(1) and (2) Regardless of whether they have entered into a sales agreement, the agreement between A and B constitutes vertical price fixing. § 13 KartG 1988 provided that the cartel which binds one or more members at one or more or all succeeding economic levels to the same price for goods or services constitutes a price-fixing agreement. Price fixing was considered to be an intentional cartel (*Absichtskartell*) pursuant to § 10 para. 1 KartG 1988, which was not allowed to be carried out without approval of the cartel court unless it was a so-called 'bagatelle' cartel pursuant to § 16 KartG 1988, that is a cartel that at the time of its creation serves a market share of less than 5 per cent of the entire domestic market and a share of less than 25 per cent of a domestic local market. This rule was taken over into § 2 para. 2 n. 1 KartG 2005 as one of the legal exceptions.[1] The validity of the agreement between A and B therefore depends on the market share of A (the enterprise imposing the restraint) in the skateboard market. An addition of the market shares of A and B, who in the strict sense are active in different markets (distribution levels), is excluded.[2]

If the price agreement is permissible as a bagatelle cartel, B could terminate the contract already at the end of the first year and after every further half year on two months' notice, or even terminate the agreement prematurely for cause (§ 28 para. 1 and 3 KartG 1988), especially

[1] However, §2 para. 2 n. 1 KartG 2005 uses the term 'geographical sub-market' (*räumlicher Teilmarkt*) instead of 'local sub-market' (*örtlicher Teilmarkt*).

[2] H.-G. Koppensteiner, p. 128.

if continued membership of the cartel, despite B's taking the care expected of a prudent business person, would mean a serious endangering of his commercial activities, which he could not be expected to undergo on an equitable weighing of the competing interests.

The KartG 2005 has entirely abolished the imperative rules on cartel agreements in §§ 28 to 30 KartG 1988 (against the so-called 'internal cartel pressure') which were to a large extent obsolete law, so that the discontinuation of the agreement for cause is only possible according to general civil law. From §§ 1162, 1117 et seq. ABGB the general principle has been derived that continuing obligations may be cancelled at any time for good cause because of the confidence demanded by the parties.[3] The OGH has recognized this reasoning also with respect to distribution agreements.[4] Therefore, B could invoke good cause if an unforeseeable price trend on the skateboard market forced him to deviate from the agreed resale price. In such a case, A could not prevent the sale of the goods at a lower price.

However, B probably has no compensatory claim against A because as a business person he had himself to assess the risk of the agreed price and he could have avoided losses by using in time his right of termination of the contract (see above).

If the cartel between A and B is void, A cannot forbid the sale of the boards at a lower price since B may rely on the invalidity of the agreement. However, in this case B has no compensatory claim against A because he has participated in a void cartel agreement whose invalidity he either was or should have been aware of. The ECJ has nevertheless diluted these consequences.[5] According to the court, art. 81 EC Treaty is contrary to a principle of domestic law according to which a contracting party has no claim to compensation from the performance of a contract in restriction of competition simply because it is a contracting party. Admissible under community law, on the other hand, is a national regulation according to which compensation can be denied in such cases, to the extent that the affected party bears a significant responsibility for the distortion of competition.

Denmark (14)

(1) An agreement on fixed distribution prices will be a violation of CA § 6. The agreement will, furthermore, not be covered by the block

[3] R. Welser in H. Koziol/R. Welser II 8. [4] OGH, 5.5.1987, ÖBl 1987, 152 – Stefanel.
[5] ECJ, 20.9.2001, C-453/99, *Courage Ltd. v. Crehan* [2001] ECR I-6297.

exemption on vertical agreements.[6] Finally, the agreement will not be considered as *de minimis* according to CA § 7, which specifically does not cover agreements including conditions on price fixing. According to CA § 6, sec. 5, the agreement will be invalid *inter partes*, at least in relation to the price condition, and the agreement can therefore not be enforced in relation to this rule. If A with reference to the price condition attempts to refuse delivery, claims that a breach of contract exists or claims compensation from B, then B will successfully be able to counterclaim that the price condition is not enforceable in relation to B. A violation of CA § 6, sec. 1, exists.

(2) A violation of the Competition Act may in principle constitute the basis of liability in a lawsuit on compensation. B is part of an agreement which is contrary to CA § 6, sec. 1. Basically, B will therefore not be able to claim compensation for the loss, which the performance of the agreement has caused for him as B is contributing to the violation of the Competition Act. If B can prove or substantiate that he had no equal negotiating position compared to A it may be assumed that B's damages have to be compensated by A in whole or in part. In evaluating equality of negotiation position the interest B had in the clause/condition on fixing distribution prices will need to be considered.[7]

England (14)

(1) Absolutely not, and the fact that the skateboards are marketed under company A's trade mark 'Flash' does not alter that. This is vertical resale price maintenance, a 'hard-core' restriction under the EC vertical agreements block exemption[8] and under the parallel UK secondary legislation,[9] and is prohibited even if A only has a very small market share.[10]

(2) The effect of the *Crehan* case is that the simple fact that B was a party to the unlawful contract and performed it for a time cannot, of itself, operate so as to deny him a right to damages in respect of the €300,000 (subject to the problems of burden of proof, causation, quantum etc.), but that it remains open to national law to deny him a right to

6 Executive Order issued by the Ministry of Economic and Business Affairs, No. 353 of May 15, 2000.

7 In general on this matter B. von Eyben et al., *Lærebog i Erstatningsret* (4th edn 1999), pp. 58 et seq. and pp. 295 et seq.

8 Commission Regulation 2790/99, art. 4(a) (OJ L336/21 of December 29, 1999); Commission Guidelines on Vertical Restraints, para. 47 (OJ C291/1 of October 13, 2000).

9 Competition Act (Land Agreements Exclusion and Revocation Order) 2004, SI 2004/1260.

10 Commission Notice on Agreements of minor importance, para. 11 (OJ 2001 C368/13).

damages if he bore 'significant responsibility' for the breach.[11] 'Significant responsibility' involves taking account of 'the respective bargaining power and conduct of the two parties to the contract'.[12] Mr Crehan on the facts was found not to have borne 'significant responsibility' for the breach of competition law (the breach being the vertical exclusive purchasing obligation imposed on him by the brewery). In this Case, B must have observed the resale price maintenance for a time, or he would not have suffered the loss. Given the 'hard-core' nature of vertical resale price maintenance (which is anti-competitive by object), one would have thought, on balance, that a court would find that B does bear significant responsibility for the breach, and so would be denied a damages remedy.

Finland (14)

(1) According to sec. 4 of the Finnish Act on Competition Restrictions, agreements, decisions or practices which have as their direct or indirect object the establishment of a fixed or minimum resale price shall be prohibited.[13] The resale price maintenance condition in question breaches sec. 4. According to sec. 18, the resale price maintenance condition must not be applied or implemented. Therefore, A cannot require B to sell the skateboards at the agreed price.

Before the Amendment 318/2004 vertical restraints were mainly dealt with under the principle of abuse in the Finnish Act on Competition Restrictions. Only resale price maintenance was prohibited by the Act. This was one of the main differences between EC and Finnish competition law.

(2) Under secs. 4 and 18, B could require that the resale price maintenance condition should not be applied or implemented. B has suffered losses because of the high set price. B could also make a claim for compensation against A for €300,000 based on sec. 18(a). On the other hand, the concept of contribution is included in the general doctrine of compensation for damage in Finland. When calculating the amount of damages, the contribution of the party suffering the damage should be taken into consideration.[14] If B has intentionally and voluntarily entered into a contract breaching sec. 4, this could affect the amount of damages.

[11] See C-453/99 *Courage Ltd. v. Crehan*, paras. 31–33. [12] Ibid., para. 32.
[13] HE 11/2004 vp, p. 31. [14] J. Pöyhönen, in J. Pöyhönen (ed.), p. 76.

France (14)

(1) The fixing of minimum prices is prohibited by French competition law. Art. L 442-5 of the commercial code prohibits the act of any person to impose, directly or indirectly, a minimum on the resale price of a product or good, on the price of a service provision or on a trading margin. It is punished by a fine of €15,000. It is a criminal provision. It supposes, however, that the contracting parties are different entities. This is not the case when there is a dependant position of the distributor in a legal sense, such as groups, agents or such.[15] This is not the case with distributors. Considering that there is a legal prohibition of minimal price fixing, tribunals consider that fraudulent intention can be presumed.[16] Besides, civil tribunals can annul price-determination clauses or even the entire contract if the clause is a key clause.[17] Alternatively, rescission of the contract can be ordered.[18]

French authorities are extremely attached to the principle of free price fixing, whereas in the literature the harm of minimum price fixing is seen as less important for several economic reasons (protection of reputation and guarantee of a minimum quality of a brand-mark, no prejudice for the consumer, the fact that modern competition passes via service and not price).[19]

(2) Setting aside criminal procedures, A can obtain annulment of the clause or the rescission of the contract. It seems that damages claims in the present situation cannot be made, the main goal being to be liberated from such a contract.[20]

Germany (14)

(1) The agreement with B may entitle A to bring a cease-and-desist claim against B to refrain from selling at a lower price. B has breached the contractual obligation to sell the skateboards at a certain price. Until 2005, German law contained a special interdiction of vertical price fixing in § 14 GWB. Now, following the European model of art. 81(1) EC, § 1 GWB prohibits all horizontal and vertical restraints of competition. § 2 para. 2 GWB declares applicable the European block exemption

[15] M. Malaurie-Vignal, *Droit de la concurrence*, p. 106.
[16] Cour de cassation, chambre criminelle, October 31, 2000 in *Bulletin criminel*, no. 326.
[17] Cour de cassation, chambre commerciale, October 7, 1997, in: *Contrats, concurrence, consommation* (1998), no. 2.
[18] Cour d'appel de Paris, March 10, 1989, in *Petites Affiches 28 April 1989*.
[19] M. Malaurie-Vignal, *Droit de la concurrence*, p. 105. [20] Ibid., p. 108.

regulations, hence Regulation 2790/1999 on vertical agreements. As vertical price fixing is black-listed in the regulation (Art. 4 lit. (a)), the substantive result is the same: the agreement between A and B is void pursuant to § 134 BGB together with § 1 GWB. Thus, A cannot require B to sell the skateboards at the agreed price.

The legal treatment of vertical price fixing has changed in time. Until 1973, resale price maintenance was allowed for branded goods. Since then, it is prohibited with some rare exceptions, for example, for books. Stay allowed non-binding price recommendations. The prohibition of resale price maintenance belongs to the core of German competition law. Scepticism in the US about a *per se* prohibition of resale price maintenance[21] is not shared. On the contrary, the exception for books was under attack by European law and was abolished by the German legislature in 2000 for intra-EU transborder sales. The same is true for the new system of legally fixed prices introduced in 2002.

(2) B could have a compensatory claim against A to an amount of €300,000 under § 33 para. 3 together with § 1 GWB. Until 2005, the protective scope of the prohibition of vertical price fixing had to be explored. Prior to the 6th Cartel Reform 1999 this question was the subject of controversy because it was partly assumed that the bound company was adequately protected by the nullity of the agreement. However, by 1999 at the latest, when the former special rule on vertical price fixing was changed from a norm merely providing for nullity to a true prohibition norm, legal opinion affirming compensatory claims had the better arguments on its side.[22] Because in 2005 private claims were extended to anyone affected by a restriction of competition the partner bound by a vertical price fixing agreement has his own claims. Thus, B not only has the objection of nullity against A but also a compensatory claim to an amount of €300,000 under § 33 para. 3 together with § 1 GWB.

The other problem is if B's own participation in the restrictive contract affects his claims against A. There is no general principle in German law of *ex dolo malo non oritur actio* or *nemo auditur propriam turpitudinem allegans*.[23] However, B's behaviour could be classified as

[21] See L. Sullivan/W. Grimes, *The Law of Antitrust* (2000), pp. 335 et seq.

[22] J. Topel, in Wiedemann, *Handbuch des Kartellrechts* (1999), § 50 note 62; contra (concerning the law before 1999) H.-M. Müller-Laube, *Der private Rechtsschutz gegen unzulässige Beschränkungen des Wettbewerbs und mißbräuchliche Ausübung von Marktmacht im deutschen Kartellrecht* (1980), pp. 37 et seq.

[23] § 817 s. 2 BGB only refers to claims based on unjustified enrichment, and is not applicable to tort law.

contributory negligence in the sense of § 254 BGB diminishing his claim to the extent of his own negligence. If the initiative for the vertical price fixing came exclusively from A the contributory negligence of B would be zero. This is probably the case here because B did not have any economic interest in the vertical price-fixing agreement. Therefore, B's claim is not affected by his participation in the contract.

The question of how participation in a restraint of competition affects own claims will become more prominent after the *Courage* case, where the ECJ dealt with the relationship between private remedies and European competition law.[24] According to English law a party to an illegal agreement was not allowed to claim damages from the other party. The ECJ held that the full effectiveness of art. 81 EC Treaty would be put at risk if it were not open to any individual to claim damages for loss caused to him by a contract in restraint of competition.[25] Therefore, an absolute bar to such actions would not be compatible with art. 81 EC. However, national law may exclude such actions if the party in question bears significant responsibility for the restraint of competition.[26] These principles apply only to cases covered by art. 81 EC. But apparently German competition law follows the same lines.

Greece (14)

(1) The sales contract between manufacturer A and retailer B is a vertical price-fixing agreement. Greek law does not provide for specific rules on vertical agreements, therefore the general prohibition of art. 1 of L. 703/1977 is applicable. The Competition Commission has adopted European community practices in relation to vertical agreement disputes.[27] As a result, the Community interpretative rules are used when applying the Greek antitrust law, thus leading to the indirect application of Commission directives as well as the Commission's regulations and interpretative guidelines.[28] Therefore, if the present case was brought before the Competition Commission or before the national courts as an ancillary issue, the clause by virtue of which the highest sale price for

[24] See J. Drexl, *Do we need 'Courage' for International Antitrust Law?*, in J. Drexl (ed.), *The Future of Transnational Antitrust* (2003), pp. 311 et seq.; G. Mäsch, *Private Ansprüche bei Verstößen gegen das europäische Kartellverbot*, (2003) EuR 825.

[25] ECJ, *Courage*, para. 26. [26] Ibid., para. 31.

[27] D. Tzouganatos, *Exclusive and Selective Distribution Agreements* (2001), p. 2 [in Greek].

[28] See Competition Commission's Information Notice of 19.12.2001 on 'The Application of L. 703/77 to Vertical Agreements and of the Regulation 2790/1999 of the European Commission', *Annual Report* 2001–2002.

resale was set would be declared null. In so doing the Greek authorities would be applying art. 4[29] of the European Commission's block exemption regulation 2790/1999 on vertical agreements[30] (provided that the other conditions set by the Regulation are met). Consequently, A cannot prohibit the sale of skateboards at a lower price, since such a claim would be based on a clause that is null and included in the agreement concluded with B. The nullity is absolute and retroactive and may be put forward by any person having a legal interest therein.

(2) The next question is whether B, being himself a contracting party to the vertical agreement, may raise claims founded on the invalidity of such agreement. As already mentioned, B is entitled to invoke the nullity of the clause and refuse performance thereof. B also has a claim for compensation against A for damages of €300,000, i.e. equal to the damage incurred through his inability to sell the products due to the high price. In fact, any person having suffered losses due to the prohibited agreement is entitled to request damages on the basis of tortious liability, provided the conditions set by art. 914 CC are met.[31] In any case, the courts will take into consideration his involvement in the prohibited agreement, as well as the profit he has already made from selling at the higher price. Relevant compensation may thus be reduced due to B's own fault.[32] In particular, the court will examine whether B's conduct contributed to the damage incurred by him. The issue of whether compensation will be reduced or not will depend on the buying power as between distributor and manufacturer and the degree of the former's dependence on the latter. The court will reach a conclusion as to whether B had the option of refusing the conclusion of the contract and of contacting other manufacturers of skateboards. Additionally, the profit made by B from A's damaging conduct will also be taken into consideration, since the Greek law on compensation is governed by the principle of restitution of the actual damage incurred and thus does not

[29] Art. 4 prohibits 'the restriction of the buyer's ability to determine its sale price, without prejudice to the possibility of the suppliers imposing a maximum sale price or recommending a sale price, provided that they do not amount to a fixed or minimum sale price as a result of pressure from, or incentives offered by, any of the parties'. See also *Competition Commission*, decision 1/1979, Arm (1981) 874 [in Greek], reaching exactly the same conclusion twenty years prior to the enactment of regulation 2790/1999.

[30] OJ EC 1999 L 336, p. 21.

[31] See A. Liakopoulos, The *Economic Freedom as Subject of Protection in Antitrust Law* (1981), p. 305.

[32] M. Stathopoulos, in Georgiades-Stathopoulos (ed.), *The Civil Code II, Article 300* (1979), pp. 106–108.

allow for the damaged party to become unjustly enriched.[33] Therefore, profit from sales effectuated at the higher price during this intermediate stage will be deducted from the compensation amount that B would normally be entitled to.

Hungary (14)

(1) No, according to sec. 11(2)(a) HCA agreements that directly or indirectly fix purchase or selling prices or other business terms and conditions fall under the prohibition of cartels. While in the HCA of 1990 only resale price maintenance was prohibited and other vertical agreements were allowed, this was changed by the HCA of 1996. Now all vertical agreements are prohibited, including resale price maintenance.

(2) According to sec. 238(2) HCC a person who has, in good faith, believed in the validity of a contract that is invalid can demand compensation from the other party to the contract for damages that originate from the conclusion of the contract. Sec. 238(2) HCC also argues that if invalidity of the contract is attributable to the conduct of one of the parties, the court shall not condemn the other party. Therefore, it has to be established whether the setting up of the vertical price fixing could be attributed to B. This is unlikely to be the case here. Thus, B's claim is not affected by his participation in the contract.

Ireland (14)

(1) A cannot prohibit the sale of the boards at a lower price because he has sold them to B, and resale price maintenance of this kind is not permitted under sec. 4 of the Competition Act 2002. In 2000, the Competition Authority took successful criminal actions against Estuary Fuel Ltd. for entering into and implementing an agreement to fix the price at which motor fuels were sold by a filling station in Tralee, a small town in the west of Ireland.

In another case, following an investigation by the Competition Authority into their contracts with retailers, two large newspaper publishers, Irish Times Limited and Independent Newspapers (Ireland) Limited undertook to amend the terms and conditions of their distribution agreements with newspaper retailers. The Authority alleged that the distribution agreements in question contained clauses that imposed resale price maintenance on newspaper distributors. Prior to the conclusion of the Authority's investigation both undertakings undertook,

[33] M. Stathopoulos, ibid., *Articles 297–298*, p. 87.

inter alia, to indicate on the front page of their newspapers that the prices quoted were recommended retail prices.[34] Similarly, the Authority conducted an investigation into possible resale price maintenance by Statoil Ireland Limited, which investigation was closed when Statoil agreed to change its price support scheme which contained a price ceiling and a price floor on retailers party to the agreement.[35]

(2) B could claim against A for breach of sec. 4 of the Competition Act 2002. While B's participation in the agreement might be raised by A in the proceedings, the court is likely to accept that he was the weaker party in the relationship and was forced to comply with A's terms. As resale price maintenance is not a hard-core offence, the court can impose a fine but not a prison sentence.

Italy (14)

(1) B has breached his obligation to sell the skateboards at a set price. However, resale price maintenance falls under the prohibition of art. 2 of Law 287/90 (as long as the agreement consistently affects competition).[36] Vertical price fixing indeed alters the competition mechanism,[37] impeding a natural decrease of the prices to consumers as a consequence of the competition between distributors. Since prohibited agreements are null and void (art. 2 of Law 287/90), A cannot restrain B from selling the boards at a lower price.

(2) B could bring a claim for damages in front of the Court of Appeal, which is competent for the territory. One could argue that since B agreed with A to adopt certain prices, he somehow contributed to causing the damage. Pursuant to art. 1227 cc, if the aggrieved party has partially caused the damage, the amount of damages due is decreased in relation to the relevance of the aggrieved party's fault and the type of consequences that followed. However, the distributor B probably had no choice. B had no special reason for agreeing on a higher price. And, due to the high set price he suffers losses amounting to €300,000.

[34] Competition Authority Press Release December 13, 2003.

[35] Competition Authority Decision no. E/03/001, November 4, 2003.

[36] O.W. Vogelaar, in J. Stuyck/B.L.P. Van Reeken (eds.), *Competition Law in the EU, Its Member States and Switzerland*, 2-I, at p. 384.

[37] See AGCM June 19, 1996, n. 4001, Bollettino n. 25/1996, in which the Authority held that a resale price maintenance agreement constituted infringement of art. 2 of Law 287/90.

Netherlands (14)

(1) According to art. 6(2) DCA the relevant clause in the contract is null and void. Therefore, A cannot claim such a prohibition on the sole ground of this clause in the contract. Of course A can take other types of action against B to prevent him from selling the goods for the lower price. He might for example terminate the contract and stop delivering the goods to B.[38]

(2) In civil proceedings B could claim damages as he suffered losses as a result of the fact that pursuant to the contract he was obliged to sell the goods for a price that appeared to be too high. However, in principle B has chosen to enter into this agreement and therefore he may be, at least partially, regarded as responsible for the infringement and the losses incurred. However, it depends very much on other facts of the case whether such a claim would be successful.

Poland (14)

(1) and (2) The facts of the case do not indicate whether or not A has got a dominant market position. In case A has a dominant position art 8.2 (1 and 6) u.o.k.k will apply. One or more undertakings can abuse a dominant position. Actions by such undertakings that constitute an abuse of a dominant position shall be null and void. In the case when the prices set by A are too high, the act of setting the prices on such a high level is null and void and B can make use of the consequence that stems from that fact. Since every person having an interest (parties to the agreement as well as third parties) can make use of consequences stemming from the nullity of an agreement, B's claims will not be influenced by the fact that he participated in the restrictive agreement.

Besides abuse of a dominant position, the rules on vertical agreements apply. Agreements on minimal resale prices or minimal margins limit distributors' chances to react to market forces and distort

[38] See for an interesting example of such a case: Pres. Civil Court Den Bosch, February 10, 2005, *Albert Heijn – Peijnenburg*, LJ AS5628. In this case Peijnenburg refused to deliver goods to Albert Heijn because of the fact that Albert Heijn sold the goods for a price as a result of which Peijnenburg claimed to suffer losses. Albert Heijn had refused to sell the goods for the price as mentioned by Peijnenburg and therefore Peijnenburg terminated the distribution agreement. Albert Heijn claimed delivery of the goods and stated that it was not bound by the price mentioned by Peijnenburg on the ground that such a statement infringed the cartel provisions. The President ruled that Peijnenburg had a reasonable ground for the termination of the agreement because Peijnenbureg suffered losses as a result of the price strategy of Albert Heijn. Therefore, the court found that Peijnenburg could refuse the delivery of the goods to Albert Heijn.

competition. As a consequence, such practices are recognized as restricting competition. In the case in question, A and B agreed that B has to sell the skateboards at a price which was set too high for the market conditions. B can bring an action before the President of the OCCP to determine that the agreement is one that restricts competition. Subsequently, he can claim the nullity of the agreement (every person having an interest can make use of consequences arising from the nullity of the agreement) and claim damages for the losses he has suffered.

Portugal (14)

(1) According to art. 4 Law no. 18/2003, June 11 this vertical restraint of competition is illegal. The contract between A and B is not valid. Therefore, A cannot prevent B from selling the skateboard at a lower price. There are however legal writers[39] who consider that the antitrust authorities should not interfere with the distribution agreements and the vertical restraints if there are no relevant effects such as a great reduction in competition.

(2) B can claim for compensation against A in an amount of €300,000 under art. 4 Law no. 18/2003, June 11 *ex vi* art. 483 CC. This provision must be considered as a protective rule for B. In fact, this provision is not only a rule providing for nullity, it is also a prohibition rule.[40] The purpose of this provision is the protection of free competition and also individual competitors against any agreements that restrain competition. Concerning the problem of B's own participation in the restrictive agreement made with A, it is possible to admit that the conduct of B was against *bona fides*. B initially consented to the restrictive agreement but afterwards he claims compensation. This kind of behaviour is normally seen as a *venire contra factum proprium* and an abuse of his own position (art. 334 CC).[41] This qualification depends on numerous factors: fault, circumstances of the case and other aspects. In Portuguese law there is also no principle of *ex dolo malo non oritur actio* or *nemo auditur propriam turpitudinem allegans*. Therefore, if B's conduct was not considered against *bona fides*, he could claim compensation. Moreover, the

[39] A. Ferreira Palma, *Das Pequenas e Médias Empresas (maxime, no direito da concorrência)* (2001), p. 239.

[40] A. dos Santos/M.E. Gonçalves/M.M. Leitão Marques, *Direito Económico*, p. 352 defend the application of civil liability and nullity for cases like this one.

[41] Menezes Cordeiro, *Tratado de Direito Civil Português, I, Parte Geral* (2nd edn 2000), p. 250 and Luís Menezes Leitão, *Direito das Obrigações*, vol. I, *Introdução, Constituição das Obrigações* (2nd edn 2002), pp. 281–282.

Courage decision of the ECJ has to be respected, excluding private claims of a party to the agreement only in case of 'significant responsibility'.[42]

Spain (14)

(1) No, A is not able to fix prices in relation to distributors pursuant to the prohibition set up in art. 1 LDC, which forbids and declares void any agreement, decision or practice which have as its object or have or may have as its effect the prevention, restriction or distortion of competition within the whole or a part of the national market, and in particular those which directly or indirectly fix purchase or selling prices or any other trading conditions. Consequently, distributors are free to set up the resale price. This was always the state of Spanish law and is especially true after Spanish legislation established a general application of the EC Regulations on vertical restraints including the complementary guidelines.[43]

(2) B is entitled to bring a claim against A before the SDC asking for a cease-and-desist order as well as for the removal of the effects produced by the forbidden agreement. Although B is part of the restrictive agreement, the TDC has often considered distributors as the weaker party in the agreement and has not found them to be culpable.[44] Once the TDC has resolved that the agreement between A and B contravenes art. 1 LDC and is therefore void, B is legally able to sue A before an ordinary civil judge in order to claim damages (art. 13 LDC).

Sweden (14)

(1) The agreement constitutes a vertical price fixing which is contrary to the prohibition in sec. 6 KL. According to sec. 7 KL the contract is therefore void and its anti-competitive provisions will be declared null by a court. Thus, A cannot claim breach of contract as a result of B selling at lower prices than agreed.

The prohibition of vertical price fixing is at the core of Swedish competition law. The Swedish Competition Authority has contested many wholesale and resale agreements with price fixing components. All provisions fixing certain prices in a subsequent market of trade are *per se* in breach of sec. 6 KL. Still, many cases of price recommendations have been considered to support smaller dealers and thus been deemed,

42 Supra, note 5.
43 Real Decreto 378/2003 de 28-III, Official Gazette, no. 90 of April 15, 2003.
44 E.g. TDC, 30.5.2001, Case 493/00 – *CEPSA*, available on www.tdcompetencia.es.

in a way, to promote competition. The main question according to Swedish law is whether a 'recommended' price in fact leaves the undertaking any real freedom to decide its own prices.

The Market Court has decided that a recommended price that was pre-fixed on books was contrary to sec. 6 KL since the retailers had to take active measures to diverge from the price. Before this the Competition Authority had in many cases dismissed the use of pre-fixed prices on goods such as product catalogues, coupons in advertisement brochures and on price lists for display in stores concerning ice-cream. The decision in the book case is interesting also from another point of view. According to the previous Competition Act, which was in force until 1993, fixing of maximum prices was as a general rule not to be considered contrary to the act. Accordingly, anyone could agree, or enforce agreements that predetermined a highest price. Even though such agreements could often be considered in breach of EC competition law there has been some argument as to the application of the new Swedish Competition Act in this matter. The Competition Authority has consistently contested the use of maximum prices when deciding on exemptions from sec. 6 KL, but has proved somewhat reluctant to pursue these cases on its own initiative as a result of complaints. In fact the authority has in several answers to complaints mentioned that maximum prices may in fact have positive effects on competition. In the case of pre-fixed book prices the Market Court opened the window for evidence showing that the maximum prices had a positive influence on competition but it clearly held that there is no presumption that the fixing of maximum prices eludes the prohibition.

(2) If an undertaking infringes any of the prohibitions in KL, obviously including sec. 6 KL, the undertaking shall, according to sec. 33 KL, compensate the damage inflicted on another undertaking or party to the agreement. Having said this, it is clear that the wording of the provision suggests that a party to an illegal agreement, suffering economic loss, has the right to compensation. However, even though the ultimate subject protected by the KL is the consumer, KL primarily protects competitors and concerned undertakings. In the light of this, the reference to 'the party to the agreement' is most likely a reference merely to the fact that not only undertakings should have the right to compensation for damages stemming from an illegal agreement, rather than a reference to a clear right for the parties to the agreement to have claims for damages. If B has willingly and knowingly entered into an illegal agreement, which turns out to be too hard on him, it would indeed be very difficult to obtain

compensation. However, it should be possible for B to make a claim for a declaratory judgment before an ordinary court, certifying that his contract with A should not include the void price-fixing clause. By bringing such a claim B risks that the court declares the whole sales contract void, thereby depriving B of the possibility of selling any of the 'Flash' skateboards. On the application of Swedish contract law in the context of competition law, see Case 13 above.

The preparatory documents to the Swedish Competition Act, which are of great significance in interpreting the law, exemplify a number of situations where damages can become relevant. Inter alia, it is suggested that a retailer prevented by a supplier to sell at a low price should have the right to compensation for the loss of profits as the result of decreased revenues.[45] This also suggests a right to B for compensation in respect of his loss resulting from the anti-competitive agreement. In our opinion, however, this reference to a right to B is also in doubt. It is not clear what significance the preparatory documents attribute to the fact that the retailer is being 'prevented'. When administrative fines are decided, as a general rule there is an important difference between parties forced into an illegal agreement and parties that freely and by their own will conclude such contracts. As a consequence there is reason to assume that B would have little prospect in getting compensation, being an equal partner in the agreement. The circumstances in the case are not clear. General principles of contract law, such as *culpa in contrahendo*, would suggest that an equal party to an unlawful agreement has limited possibilities of claiming compensation for his involvement in the affairs. Clearly, this would not be the case if B did not enter into the agreement out of free will, but was forced in some way. In this case it also seems clear that B, as a result of the nullity provided for in sec. 7 KL, at no time had any obligation *de facto* or *de jure* to charge the higher price and therefore not even in this respect was forced to suffer loss.

Summary (14)

1. *Vertical price fixing*

Case 14 also concerns price fixing, but this time in a vertical, not in a horizontal, relationship. As the legal remedies should again be the focus

[45] Bill 1992/93:56 p. 97.

of attention, the example taken represents the most intensive form of vertical restraint, that is vertical price fixing. As might be expected vertical price fixing is generally prohibited in all reporting countries. There are, however, certain nuances of difference: the prohibition in most countries applies to the fixing of minimum *and* maximum prices. In other countries by contrast (similar to European antitrust law under art. 4(a) of the block exemption regulation on vertical agreements[46]) only the fixing of minimum prices is prohibited (France, and arguably Sweden). In some countries the *de minimis* rule also applies to vertical price fixing: in Austria, for example, in bagatelle cases, that is where certain market share thresholds are not exceeded, vertical price fixing is permitted. In other countries by contrast (e.g. in Denmark and Germany) vertical price fixing is prohibited even in bagatelle cases. The case in question does not concern the exceptions to the prohibition on vertical price fixing, such as for books or non-binding recommended prices. At the centre of the case are sports products for which none of the reporting countries allows an exception to the price-fixing prohibition. Nevertheless, in some reporting countries it is argued whether strict rules on vertical price fixing continue to make economic sense (e.g. in Finland and Germany). This discussion is based on the development in US-American law in which the influence of the Chicago School allows a more generous approach to vertical price fixing. Restrictions of *intrabrand* competition have been allowed in the interest of an intensification of *interbrand* competition. Nevertheless, even in the USA, vertical minimum price-fixing agreements are still subject to a *per se* prohibition. This is also the status of the discussion in Europe: even if partial relaxations of the distribution cartel law are called for, the prohibition against vertical price fixing continues to enjoy broad acceptance. To an extent it is given central importance for antitrust law (France, Sweden). The securing of *intrabrand* competition is sometimes regarded as equally important as *interbrand* competition (Italy).

2. *Validity of contract*

As the price fixing between A and B violates antitrust law in all countries, it is void. The invalidity does not extend to the rest of the sales agreement.[47] Accordingly, B may retain the skateboards bought from A

[46] See supra note 30.

[47] In Sweden, the risk has been pointed out that the court may declare the entire contract void.

and sell them on. Because of the invalidity of the price-fixing clause A cannot forbid B from selling the goods at a lower price. Thus, antitrust law ensures that B's freedom to trade remains uncurtailed with regard to the fixing of the retail price. Unlimited *intrabrand* competition on the price is thereby possible.

3. *Claims of bound parties*

B may seek a declaration from the court that the price-fixing clause is void, and he can require A no longer to apply the clause. The decisive question consists in whether B is adequately protected under the consequences of invalidity, or whether he has further claims for compensation. This is of particular importance in the present case because B has sustained an actual quantifiable loss due to the price fixing. In the large majority of countries B is entitled in principle to a compensatory claim. A frequent justification is that the prohibition against vertical price fixing is intended primarily to benefit the consumer, in that he should enjoy competitive prices for the same product. On the other hand, however, the bound party should also be protected by the prohibition in that its competitive freedom of trade is upheld regarding the price. Only in one country, that is France, are compensatory claims excluded from the beginning. The invalidity of the price-fixing clause is seen here as an adequate remedy in itself as in France there is a strict penal regulation. In Spain there is the peculiarity mentioned in connection with other cases that civil law claims are only admissible once the antitrust authority has rendered a decision. Thus, there are compensatory claims but they require a prior successful administrative proceeding. In the interests of clarity it must be added that the above presentation reflects valid current law but there is no practical experience of such a case available, for example in the form of court decisions.

4. *Compensation also in the case of own participation in the limiting agreement?*

As we have seen, compensatory claims are possible for B as a matter of principle. Is this conclusion altered by the fact that B himself participated in the agreement which led to the price fixing in violation of antitrust law? In some countries this circumstance is regarded as highly significant, and the complete exclusion of compensatory claims is seen as possible (England, Greece, Sweden). In other countries such participation is considered under the aspect of contributory liability and may lead to a reduction or even complete exclusion of the compensatory claim. The precise calculation of quantum is a matter of the circumstances in the individual case, in particular the degree of responsibility which B bears for the vertical price fixing. If B was pressured, or if he was under duress by A at the time of conclusion of the agreement, then it is reasonable to reduce B's liability. Moreover, it is relevant whether B himself had an interest in the price fixing (Denmark, Italy). If B's responsibility is set low, the reduction of the compensatory claim may not apply at all (Germany, Hungary, Poland, Portugal). Mention must also be made of peculiar aspects of the calculation of quantum. In part the existence of loss is doubted: since the price-fixing agreement was void *ex tunc* (from the beginning) B need not have sold at the fixed price but would from the beginning have been free in the setting of the price (Sweden). A further circumstance which might result in a reduction of the amount of the claim was raised in the Greek report. As B was able to gain higher profit margins on the basis of the higher price, this should be deducted from his compensatory claim.

All countries are influenced by the *Courage* decision of the ECJ. According to this – in the field of application of European antitrust law – compensatory claims for the violation of the cartel prohibition are not excluded simply because the claimant is party to the competition distorting agreement. On the other hand, compensatory claims may be excluded if the claimant 'bears significant responsibility for the distortion of competition'. There is a tendency to apply this rule of European competition law to domestic cases and situations. The principle derived from English law that a party cannot claim compensation from another under an unlawful contract[48] can therefore only be upheld where the claimant who is a party to the contract bears significant responsibility for the violation of competition law.

5. *Conclusions*

Private claims are also conceivable in the context of competition distorting agreements within a vertical relationship. The peculiarity here consists in the fact that the claim is frequently – as in Case 14 – pursued by an enterprise that is itself party to the distorting agreement. This constitutes a significant difference to horizontal distortion of competition, where the legitimacy of cartel members for the filing of a claim is limited. The survey shows that also in this case the overwhelming majority of reporting countries permit compensatory claims in

[48] See ECJ *Courage* note 11 above.

principle. For the field of application of European antitrust law this result is mandatorily determined by the *Courage* decision of the ECJ. But for purely domestic situations too a strong harmonization dynamic will develop. As in the long run it does not seem tenable to allow private claims in the field of application of European antitrust law, but to deny or restrict them to purely domestic cases, a general alignment of private antitrust law will be effected.

Case 15 Selective distribution and refusal to deal

A is the producer of several luxury perfumes which are well known. A has a market share with his perfumes of 15 per cent. The perfumes are only sold to perfumeries which maintain a certain high level in terms of location, interior decoration and presentation. Consumers expect a good perfumery to stock A's products. B operates a perfumery which A has supplied all perfumes ordered over a number of years. When B switches to a low-price policy A stops supplies even though B maintains the required qualitative level. B suffers losses thereby amounting to €300,000.

What claims does B have against A? Is it relevant that A's conduct has been prohibited by order of an antitrust authority?

Austria (15)

In Austria selective distribution fell until 31.12.2005 under § 30a KartG 1988. This was a special rule for vertical restraints of competition which in Austria for technical reasons were excluded from the notion of cartel and were subject to a privileged treatment concerning restrictions of competition connected to the purchase or sale of goods.

Vertical restraints were in principle permissible, but had to be notified by the binding enterprise to the cartel court before they were implemented (§ 30b KartG 1988). Pursuant to § 30c KartG 1988 the cartel court could on application forbid the implementation of a vertical restraint under conditions similar to those applying to the cartel interdiction (§ 23 KartG 1988), which in practice hardly ever happened so that such agreements were mostly exempt in Austria.

Vertical price fixing (§ 13 KartG 1988) was by contrast prohibited and invalid ('intentional cartel', see Case 14). Such an agreement is admittedly not present here. Nevertheless, it could be inferred from the interdiction in § 13 KartG 1988 that the shift of B to a low-price policy in itself did not constitute a legitimate reason for A to cease further deliveries of perfume, provided B continued to fulfil the contractual obligation to uphold the high-value image and luxurious ambience of his business. In this connection the ECJ has declared[1] that arts. 28 and 30 EC are to be so interpreted that where a retailer customarily markets goods of the same type but not necessarily the same quality as protected goods, then the proprietor of the trademark or copyright

[1] ECJ, 4.11.1997, C-337/95 – *Dior/Evora*, ECR 1997, I-6013.

cannot hinder that retailer from using forms of marketing common in his branch and to publicly announce the further marketing of these goods, provided it is not established that the use of these goods significantly harms their reputation in the actual case. As the ECJ relies on a test of significant harm, it could be supposed that the mere loss of image from a low-price policy did not in itself constitute a breach of contract. Accordingly, there was no justifiable ground for A stopping deliveries to B.

According to the new law the result is the same. The KartG 2005 has abolished the privileged treatment of vertical restraints of distribution as from 1.1.2006, but has authorized the minister of justice to order by regulation that certain groups of cartels in the sense of § 2 para. 1 KartG 2005 are exempted from the cartel interdiction (§ 3 para. 1 KartG 2005). It cannot be predicted what exemption regulations the minister of justice will enact. As § 3 para. 1 KartG 2005 provides that such regulations may refer to the the law based on art. 81(3) EC as amended, it can be supposed with high probability that the regulator – as under § 17 para. 1 KartG 1988 and § 30e KartG 1988[2] – will exempt certain selective distribution systems, and that he will (among other things) order the analogous application of EC Regulation 2790/1999 to categories of vertical agreements and concerted practices. For our context, this prediction is not relevant, because the enforcement of a higher resale price under the threat of a supply stop goes beyond a (expressly non-binding) price recommendation. Price fixing (be it only the effect), however, excludes the application of the block exemption regulation on vertical restraints.

B therefore has a compensatory claim against A for the failure to perform a contractual obligation for damages at the level of actual losses incurred. He also has this claim where the conduct of A is not prohibited by an antitrust authority. However, an antitrust interdiction (§ 26 KartG 2005) gives B the advantage that the unlawfulness of refusing deliveries is already expressly or impliedly established, while by contrast for a compensatory claim he first has to prove these preconditions.

Denmark (15)

An agreement on selective distribution is covered by CA § 6, sec. 1, which includes both horizontal and vertical agreements restricting competition. If a selective distribution system only comprises requirements on qualifications, all the qualified companies may be expected to

[2] See the regulation of BMJ, BGBl II 2000/197.

have a right to obtaining deliveries. If a selective distribution system furthermore comprises quantitative restrictions, an interested company may not expect to obtain deliveries. An agreement on binding distribution prices will be included in the prohibition of anti-competitive agreements in CA § 6, sec. 1.[3] Also indirect agreements on binding distribution prices will be included in the ban in CA § 6, sec. 1. Only quite exceptionally - based on the rule under CA § 8 - exemption from the ban in CA § 6, sec. 1, may be granted if an agreement includes provisions on binding distribution prices. A's market share is 15 per cent. The agreement can therefore not be considered as *de minimis* according to CA § 7, and it is, furthermore, explicitly stated in CA § 7, sec. 2, that the *de minimis* rules of CA § 7 do not apply if the agreement includes a provision concerning the prices for the distribution of the goods. According to what is stated in the case one must assume that B's discount policy is the reason for A's refusal to deliver. A decision in the agreement on binding distribution prices will be contrary to CA § 6, sec. 1, and a refusal to deliver based on a customer's price policy will have the same effect as an explicit clause in the agreement binding the distributor's prices. The refusal to deliver may be characterized as an indirect pricing agreement which will be contrary to CA § 6, sec. 1.[4] Refusal to deal in contravention of CA § 6, sec. 1, may provide sufficient basis for liability in a case before the courts with the aim of obtaining damages. If B can prove that his economic loss amounts to €300,000 and that this loss is caused by A's refusal to deliver, the courts can be expected to award damages which will fully compensate B for the loss suffered. It will most certainly be helpful with a view to establishing a basis for liability that an administrative agency, the Competition Council, have prohibited A's behaviour but it is not a requirement in a court case on compensation/damages.

England (15)

With its 15 per cent market share (assuming reasonable market definition), A is manifestly not dominant. On that basis, it is not subject to a dominant business's obligation in principle to deal with any business which wishes to be its customer. A is free to pick and choose its customers in the normal way. A's decision to cease to supply B appears to be

[3] K. Levinsen, *Konkurrenceloven med kommentarer* (2001), pp. 191 et seq. and 238 et seq.; M. Koktvedgaard, *Lærebog i Konkurrenceret* (4th ed 2000), pp. 296 et seq.

[4] K. Levinsen, *Konkurrenceloven med kommentarer* (2001), p. 193.

taken by A entirely unilaterally, i.e. not pursuant to an agreement with any other business (e.g. a competitor or the other dealers in its selective distribution network). There is clear discrimination in the way A treats B as against how it treats other members of the network, based apparently entirely on B's pricing policies.

However, 'unilateral measures taken by private undertakings are subject to restrictions, by virtue of the principles of [the EC competition rules], only if the undertaking in question occupies a dominant position on the market within the meaning of Article [82], which is not the case here'.[5] We would not therefore regard B as having any competition law based claim against A, though it may have a damages claim for breach of contract depending on the terms of its contract. If A's conduct has been prohibited by order of an antitrust authority, that order appears, in the light of *Bayer*, to be ultra vires and should be the subject of an application for annulment by A.

Finland (15)

A evidently does not have a dominant market position because A's market share is quite low (15 per cent). Sec. 6 does not therefore apply in this case.[6] Vertical restraints are dealt with under the principle of prohibition in the Finnish Act on Competition Restrictions. A selective distribution system is acceptable under this act if there are objective economic grounds for its existence.[7] These requirements must be based on the nature of the product. Distributors should be selected only on the basis of objective and open criteria required by the nature of the product, such as training of sales personnel. The selection criteria should be applied uniformly and without discrimination. Refusing to supply a distributor fulfilling the selection criteria and who has switched to a low-price policy may constitute a breach of sec. 4.

Under sec. 13 of the Finnish Act on Competition Restrictions, the Finnish Competition Authority may order that the business undertaking terminate the conduct violating sec. 4 and require the undertaking to deliver a product to another undertaking on similar conditions to those offered by it to other undertakings in a similar position. Sec. 4 is

[5] ECJ, case C-2/01P and C-3/01P *Bayer AG and others v. Commission*, judgment of January 6, 2004, para. 70. The ECJ judgment in *Bayer* has been followed by the Court of Appeal in *Unipart Group Ltd. v. O2(UK) Ltd.* [2004] EWCA Civ 1034.

[6] See generally P. Virtanen, pp. 406–407. [7] Rissanen and Korah, p. 347.

based on the principle of prohibition. B can demand damages based on sec. 18 (a) if A has infringed sec. 4 and A's acts have caused damage to B.[8]

France (15)

Under French law there are three possibilities: first A's denial could constitute a prohibited practice, secondly B could initiate a general civil tort action (arts. 1382 and 1383 of the Civil Code), finally he could claim that there has been anti-competitive behaviour prohibited by art. 420-1 or 2 of the Commercial Code, that is to say a cartel or an abuse of a dominant position.

As a matter of fact there is no general prohibition of the refusal to deal in French competition law.[9] But as has already been pointed out for Case 14 the fixing of a minimum sales price is illegal in French law: art. L 442-5 of the Commercial Code. Therefore, the provision states that it makes no difference if the price is fixed directly or indirectly. Thus, in jurisprudence the act of a producer to refuse to deal with distributors only for the reason that their prices are too low is a prohibited commercial practice.[10] For B in the present case this means that a civil claim based on practices forbidden by art. L 442-5 of the Commercial Code would be successful. Civil courts can either annul the contract clause containing the price determination or even the contract as a whole if the price determination has been decisive for the conclusion of the contract.[11] The court can also declare the rescission of the contract.[12] However, B's interest in the present case is one where he has already suffered substantial losses and supplies have already ceased (and as it has to be supposed the contract as well) and will therefore not be met through a civil action.

Alternatively, art. L 442–5 of the Commercial Code – a criminal provision – provides that any person that directly or indirectly imposes a minimum on the resale price of a product or goods, on a price of a service provision or on a trading margin, shall be punished by a fine of €15,000. A criminal procedure could successfully be intended by B. The difficulty of a criminal procedure consists in the fact that a criminal

[8] See also HE 243/1997 vp, p. 32. [9] M. Malaurie-Vignal, *Droit de la concurrence*, p. 90.

[10] Cour de cassation, chambre criminelle, October 31, 2000, in: *Contrats, concurrence, consommation* (2001), no. 73.

[11] Cour de cassation, chambre commerciale, October 7, 1997 in: *Contrats, concurrence, consommation* (1998), no. 2.

[12] Court of appeal of Paris, March 10, 1989 in: *Petites Affiches of 28.4.1989.*

intention has to be proved.[13] Yet in B's situation a criminal sanction against A does not have any impact on further supply of perfumes.

In the second possibility fault has to be proved for a damages claim, in the sense of an abuse of rights (*abus de droit*). The consequence of such fault would not only be a damages claim but also reparation of the damage and even an injunction forcing the producer to supply the distributor.[14] Nevertheless, such an order for specific performance of the contract is the exception.[15]

For the third option elements of a cartel or the abuse of a dominant position have to be reported. They can be stated either by the Council on Competition itself or established in a civil damage tort action. This signifies that the contract containing restrictive provisions is void: art. L 420-3 of the Commercial Code. In the present case where B has himself been a member of the distribution network he will have to prove that there has been a price cartel (art. L 420-1 of the Commercial Code) directed against him which limited access to the market, impeded free exercise of competition, or amounted to artificial price fixing (no. 1 or 2 of art. L 420-1 of the Commercial Code). B would have to prove, for example, that he was to be shut out of the perfume sector. Otherwise, B could plead under certain circumstances that there is an abuse of a dominant position, for example to the prejudice of an undertaking that is economically dependent such as in cases of linked sales or refusals to sell (art. L 420-2 II of the Commercial Code). Of course, the dominant market position of A has to be proved. As it has been detailed above, the establishment of an illegal cartel or the proof of an abuse of a dominant market position triggers not only administrative sanctions imposed by the Council on Competition, but also the reparation of the damage based on arts. 1382 and 1383 of the civil code (see Case 10 question 1). Thus, the third option seems to be the most favourable one for B.

The refusal to deal was prohibited until the Act of July 1, 1996 where the provision was repealed. Since it can only be sanctioned indirectly when coinciding with other prohibitions as it has just been shown. Under European case law, selective distribution, in the sense that a producer chooses his distributors for reasons of distribution quality

[13] Cour de cassation, chambre criminelle, October 31, 2000, in: *Contrats, concurrence, consommation* (2001), no. 73.

[14] M. Malaurie-Vignal, *Droit de la concurrence*, p. 90.

[15] Cour de cassation, chambre commerciale, January 26, 1999, in: *Bulletin civil IV*, no. 23.

adapted to the reputation of his products, is admitted when the criteria of the choice are objective and not arbitrary, leaving the freedom to the distributor to decide on his distribution policy himself in order not to eliminate from the beginning a particular way of distribution as a whole.[16]

Germany (15)

Absent a dominant market position (the market share of A is only 15 per cent), only claims under § 20 para. 2 GWB (together with § 33 GWB) are possible. § 20 para. 2 GWB provides for a prohibition of unfair hindrance and discrimination in favour of small and medium-sized companies which are in some particular way dependent on other companies. In the present case there is brand-conditioned dependency. In view of customer expectations, all recognized perfumeries have to offer A's goods. In addition, the conflicting interests of A and B must be weighed. The longstanding business relationship is decisive here. A broke off the business relationship with B because of B's low price policy. As B must be free with regard to setting his own prices, the burden of weight of interests falls upon A. Therefore, an unfair hindrance in the sense of § 20 para.2 GWB can be established here.[17] The obligation to cease the non-delivery leads to an obligation to contract (*Kontrahierungszwang*). Thus, pursuant to § 33 together with § 20 para. 2 GWB A is under an obligation to deliver the ordered perfumes to B. A's behaviour is at fault, so that B can also demand damages to an amount of €300,000. An antitrust authority injunction would only be declaratory under German law, so that it would have no effect on private law claims.

Generally, only a dominant market position leads to higher standards of conduct. In German law, the threshold for such higher standards is lowered in § 20 para. 2 GWB: already the fact that other enterprises are dependent creates specific duties for the enterprise they are dependent on. A dominant market position is not necessary. Thus, in the present case a firm with a market share of only 15 per cent is subject to an obligation to contract because its products are supposed to be in every recognized retailer's range of products. § 20 GWB

[16] ECJ, December 16, 1991, *Yves Saint Laurent Parfums*, in Dalloz 1992, 303 (confirmed in this sense by TPICE, decision T 19/92 of December 12, 1996).

[17] See BGH, December 16, 1986, WuWE 2341, 2349 – *Belieferungsunwürdige Verkaufsstätten II*.

is of great practical importance.[18] In Germany, it is the most visible limit to the general freedom of contract. As the provision on abuse of dominant positions became directly applicable only in 1999,[19] a large part of the relevant case law is based on § 20 GWB which has always had direct effect.

Greece (15)

The network through which A distributes perfumes to the consumers is set up upon selection of specific points of sale, based on strict criteria of quality. It is thus a network of selective distribution. Such a network is in compliance with the law, in the sense that it is exempted from the prohibition of art. 1(1) of L. 703/1977, provided that the selection of retailers is conducted by application of objective quality criteria[20] and that such criteria are applied in a uniform manner to all interested retailers.[21] In the present case, although A seems to maintain a lawful distribution network, he unlawfully refuses to supply B with his products when the latter decided to switch to a low-price policy, since B is continuously meeting the criteria for network participation.[22] In fact, by so acting, A applies, towards B, quantitative discriminating criteria regarding the latter's pricing policy. As has been ruled by the Competition Commission, the distributor is in principle free to fix the resale prices, provided that his conduct does not put the existence of the distribution network or the reputation of the relevant products in danger.[23] Besides, the percentage of A (15 per cent) raises, in the present case, the question of the application of the *de minimis* rule.[24] This rule is also applicable in Greek antitrust law. However, even when the percentage of the market share enters into the scope of the *de minimis rule*, the agreement might still be considered as violating art. 1 para. 1

18 The most famous case is *Rossignol*, (1976) 29 NJW 801, where an obligation to contract was ordered against the well-known ski producer. For a recent case see BGH, July 13, 2004, (2004) GRUR 966 – *Chemical Barrel* (reviewed by Heinemann, 2005 ZWeR 198), where the court confirmed compulsory licences on a copyright under § 20 GWB.

19 See supra Case 10 question 2.

20 D. Tzouganatos, *Exclusive and Selective Distribution Agreements* (2001), p. 183 and the references therein.

21 See also *Competition Commission*, decision 142/1994 1 DEE (1995) 176 [in Greek].

22 In Greek antitrust law, there is no general prohibition of the refusal to deal. Such refusal may be prohibited if is related to an unlawful behaviour, as in the present case.

23 Competition Commission, decision 46/96.

24 See Commission Notice on agreements of minor importance which do not appreciably restrict competition under art. 81(1) of the Treaty (*de minimis*), (2001/C 368/07), art. 7 (b).

L. 703/77, if it contains hard-core restrictions, i.e. the direct or indirect imposition of minimum retail prices.

Consequently, it is very probable that the selective distribution agreement, as applied by A towards B, would be considered by the Competition Commission as violating art. 1 para. 1 of L. 703/77.[25] If this was the case, then the Competition Commission would have the authority to impose, inter alia, any measure necessary for the termination of the prohibited behaviour. Indeed, art. 9(1) of the antitrust law allows the Commission to force the enterprises engaged to end the violation and to omit its repetition in the future. Thus, on the basis of the above, B has the following claims against A:

(a) B may lodge a complaint with the Competition Commission. The latter, if it decides that the agreement as applied is prohibited by art. 1 para. 1 of L. 703/77, may not only impose a fine but also order, on the basis of art. 9(1), any adequate measure to cease the violation (i.e. the continuation of supplies).[26]

(b) B may also bring an action before the civil courts claiming damages according to the general provisions of liability from tort. B also has the right to request satisfaction *in natura*,[27] i.e. request the issuance of an order obliging A to continue supplies. It should be noted that civil courts are exclusively competent to award compensation.

As already indicated, the offended party is under no obligation to lodge a complaint first with the Competition Commission before resorting to the civil courts. The courts, even though they do not have jurisdiction to declare the non-compliance of an agreement or concerted practice with art. 1 of law 703/1977 may, according to art. 18(2) of the same law, decide on the incidental issue of the violation of the antitrust law when adjudicating on a dispute raised by an action for reparation. However, while incidentally examining the validity of the agreement, civil courts are bound by decisions of the Competition Commission which are not

[25] The application of art. 2a regarding the *abuse of the economic dependence* could be envisaged; however, this provision is of a little help, because the incriminated conduct falls within the scope of art. 1(1) of L. 703/77. It should be noted that this provision, deleted in 2000, was reintroduced in the L. 703/77 by the recent L. 3373/2005.

[26] Such a measure was ordered in a recent decision of the Commission regarding the application of art. 2 L. 703/77 (Competition Commission, decision 193/III/2001, *Glaxo*, (2001) 7 *DEE* 995 et seq.). In this case the Commission forced the defendant to sell its products to distributors until the final decision was rendered. See Lia I., Athanassiou, *Comments on decision 193/III/2001 of the Competition Commission*, (2001) 52 EEmpD 806 et seq.

[27] See A. Liakopoulos, *The Economic Freedom as Subject of Protection in Antitrust Law* (1981), pp. 305–306.

subject to an appeal.[28] Therefore, if the antitrust authority has already issued a decision on the subject, the civil courts do not have the competence to adjudicate on the validity of A's refusal.[29] In practice, it will in any case be helpful for B to obtain a Commission's decision declaring the prohibition of the examined conduct, as it will be easier for him to establish the basis for tortious liability.

At the same time and irrespective of whether A does or does not hold a dominant position in the market, such behaviour constitutes an act of obstructive unfair competition in the form of refusal of sale. In particular, a manufacturer's refusal to sell specific products (especially when such products have acquired a certain reputation in the market) to another enterprise dealing in similar products, falls under the general prohibition of art. 1 of L. 146/1914, provided that such refusal is ill-founded (unreasonable) and is made with the intent to compete.[30] According to the above, B has a claim for the ending of A's unfair conduct, which in the present case could be A's obligation to supply products, declared by the court in cases of unfair refusal of delivery of goods, since the delivery alone may lift such violation. Additionally, B has a claim for compensation, the size of which is equal to the damages incurred.

Hungary (15)

According to sec. 21(e) HCA, an abuse of a dominant position can be established when an undertaking, without justification, withdraws goods from circulation or withholds them from trade prior to a price increase or with the purpose of causing a price increase or in any other manner which may possibly produce unjustified advantages or to cause competitive disadvantages. There is no market share level set in the HCA above which a firm would automatically be in a dominant position. Sec. 22 HCA has established the so-called 'dominance test' by saying that a dominant position is held by persons in the relevant market according to sec. 22 HCA who are able to pursue their business activities to a large

28 According to art. 18(1) 'Decisions of the Athens Administrative Court of Appeal and Council of State which are delivered, following an appeal in accordance with the present Act, shall have the force of *res judicata*. Decisions of the Competition Commission, as well as of the Minister of Development, which are not appealed within the time limit specified, are only incidentally judged by the Courts as far as their validity is concerned.'

29 See supra Case 9(2).

30 G. Triantafyllakis, 'Article 1', in N. Rokas (ed.), *Unfair Competition* (1996), p. 221.

extent independently of other market participants substantially without the need to take into account the market reactions of their suppliers, competitors, customers and other trading parties when deciding their market conduct. In any event A seems to have an insignificant market share on the market and is therefore unlikely to be in a dominant position.

B only has a claim against A under the rules of civil law if A is in breach of contract. Then on the basis of sec. 313 HCC 'if an obligor repudiates performance without legitimate reason, the obligee shall be entitled to apply the consequences of either default, or subsequent impossibility'. Thus, B can choose between the legal consequences of default and impossibility of performance as A refuses delivery without giving reasonable grounds.

Ireland (15)

If B can prove that the object or effect of the discontinuance of supply is to maintain high retail prices, B may be in a position to claim damages from A under sec. 14 of the Competition Act 2002, on the basis that A is attempting to enforce an illegal system of resale price maintenance contrary to sec. 4 of the Act. Under Irish competition law, the Competition Authority cannot issue an order itself prohibiting A's conduct. As described in Case 9 above, the Irish Competition Authority has no power to issue injunctions/orders or impose fines itself. The fact that A's conduct has been prohibited by order of another antitrust authority in a different jurisdiction is not binding on the court, although it may be of some indirect assistance to B. If B still owes money to A, he could choose not to pay A and defend any court case brought by A with the argument that the contract with A was illegal and therefore void, because it included an element of resale price maintenance.

Such vertical agreements where neither party has market power are not forbidden in Irish law, but resale price maintenance is deemed anticompetitive. The Authority did consider whether or not to allow maximum prices on the grounds frequently put forward in US doctrine, that such pricing can boost sales and protect brands, but chose not to follow that route.

Under art. 34(1) of the Irish Constitution justice is to be administered by the courts. The Competition Authority's function is limited to investigation.[31] However, under art. 30 of the Competition Act 2002, the

[31] *McDonald v. Bord na gCon (No. 2)* [1965] IR 217.

Authority may publish reasoned decisions concerning selected investigations where it has closed a file either because it has found no breach of the Competition Act 2002 or because it has settled the case. These reasoned decisions are equivalent to a type of comfort letter, and are only given in particular circumstances, where the issues are of public interest or raise issues of complexity. Competition litigation is one of the most expensive and lengthy types of litigation for a potential plaintiff. Complex economic evidence is often required. Ireland is a small jurisdiction and many potential plaintiffs and defendants know each other well. This, coupled with the cost of litigation and the fact that Ireland does not have a treble damages award system, may ensure that the number of competition actions in the Irish courts remains small.

Italy (15)

Qualitative selective systems are allowed. Requirements of specific qualitative standards are deemed to contribute to the improvement of distribution and eventually to benefit consumers, without imposing undue restrictions. Italian case law follows the case law of the ECJ, which considers selective distribution not to be against antitrust law as long as the contract goods or services possess a high qualitative and/or technological value. Besides, the choice of distributors must occur on the basis of qualitative criteria, both factual and pre-established, for example, capacity, competence, professionalism, reliance of manpower, location, etc., applied in a uniform manner to any distributor. Only refusals to deal with distributors that do not comply with pre-established qualitative standards are allowed. In the present case, even if B switches to a low-price policy, he still meets the qualitative criteria required.

Unjustified refusals to contract, by a company with a dominant position in the market, constitute violations of art. 3(b) of the Law 287/90. In this specific case though, A only has a 15 per cent market share. And, an agreement would not 'appreciably' affect competition if parties do not own a significant share of the market (which can be determined both at national or regional level).[32] Should the position of A be determined as dominant,[33] then A's refusal would represent an attempt to limit the

[32] O.W. Vogelaar, in J. Stuyck/B.L.P. Van Reeken (eds.), *Competition Law in the EU, Its Member States and Switzerland*, 2-I, at 380.

[33] Assessment of a dominant position entails a complex comparative evaluation. The practice of the Antitrust Authority shows that there are various elements to consider. Among other elements, there are: the market share of the party allegedly infringing competition and that of competing companies, the relevant market, etc. As an

presence of competitors in the market, i.e. B, by impeding purchase of the perfumes.

B could claim that A abused of his state of economic dependence: art. 9 of the Law on the *Subfornitura*, i.e. the discipline of supply agreements in productive activities.[34] A company is economically dependent on another when the latter is in a position to cause an excessive imbalance of the rights and obligations in their business relationship. Refusals to sell and arbitrary interruption of the commercial relationships between the parties are indeed examples of such abuses. Agreements concluded as a result of an abuse of economic dependence are null and void. The economic dependence is assessed by taking into account the possibility of the aggrieved party to find a satisfactory alternative in the market. In the case at hand, B is somehow dependent on A's supply (since consumers expect a good perfumery to stock A's products) and is not ready to face A's sudden refusal to deal. For many years, B has satisfied the quality requirements imposed by A, i.e. the location and interior decoration of the premises and the way products are presented to the public. And, even when switching to a low-cost policy, B still meets such requirements. Art. 9 provides that 'the ordinary courts shall take cognizance of cases of abuse of economic dependence, including the grant of restraining orders and injunctions and the award of damages'. As a result, should the judge find A liable for abuse of economic dependence, he would then condemn him in damages.

Furthermore, the question arises of whether B could claim for an interim measure, which imposes an obligation to contract upon A. Art. 2908 cc reads that judges are empowered 'to constitute, modify or extinguish juridical relationships, when the case is foreseen by the law'. There are several cases in which companies, allegedly victims either of boycotting behaviours or of an abuse of dominant position, have claimed an urgent measure in front of appellate courts forcing the

example, in AGCM July 17, 2003, n. 12232, Bollettino n. 29/2003, the Authority took into account the market shares (Autogrill: 80%, Ristop: 5%, Finifast S.r.l. 4,6%, etc.), the relevant market (the sum of all the local markets), the access to the market (conditioned upon not only economic elements but also administrative ones, i.e. an administrative concession), and the fact that Autogrill was independent both from competitors (unable to exercise any competitive pressure upon Autogrill's practice) and consumers (unable to find valid alternatives on the highways).

[34] The abuse of a state of economic dependence has been regulated by means of (art. 9 of) the Law 18.6.98, n. 192, *Disciplina della subfornitura nelle attività produttive*, Gazzetta Ufficiale of June 22, 1998, n. 143, art. 11, co.2, modified by the Law of March 5, 2001, note 57, published in GU on March 20, 2001, note 66.

other party to deal.[35] In the majority of cases courts have excluded the possibility of adopting such interim measures. At the same time, one wonders whether there is room for analogous application of art. 2597 cc. This article imposes an obligation to contract on legal monopolists, granting equal treatment to any party requesting their goods and services.[36] Art. 2597 cc only refers to those companies, which have a position of monopoly either granted by law or by an administrative permission. Notwithstanding the attempt of some scholars to extend the scope of application of this article to those cases of de facto monopoly positions, the majority of case law excludes such a possibility. The reason is that art. 2597 has an exceptional character since it derogates from the general principle of contractual freedom. Consequently, B cannot refer to art. 2597 *cc*, since no situation of legal monopoly occurs. Finally, as to the issue of whether an Antitrust Authority's injunction would change matters, as previously stated, private and public enforcement follows two independent paths.

Netherlands (15)

In general, selective distribution agreements which are based on purely qualitative selection criteria, i.e. where distributors are selected only on the basis of objective criteria required by the nature of the product, such as training of sales personnel, are generally considered to fall outside the cartel provisions. The selection criteria should be applied uniformly and without discrimination and accordingly no advance limit should be put on the number of authorized distributors. In this case, the selection criteria appear not to be purely qualitative. Therefore, A cannot state that his refusal to supply is based on a selective distribution system. If

[35] M. Tavassi, *Substantive Remedies for the Enforcement of National and EC Antitrust Rules before Italian Courts*, in *European Competition Law Annual 2001: A Community Perspective* (2003), 147–154, at 151. For an overview of case law on this issue see M. Tavassi/M. Scuffi, *Diritto Processuale Antitrust, Tutela Giurisdizionale della Concorrenza* (1998), at 234.

[36] For an overview of scholarship and case law, see M. Tavassi/M. Scuffi, *Diritto Processuale Antitrust, Tutela Giurisdizionale della Concorrenza* (1998), at 12 et seq. Equal treatment means equal conditions for economically equivalent requests. Against a refusal to contract, scholarship is divided with regard to the available remedies. Some believe that art. 2932 cc is applicable. Should a party not comply with his obligation to conclude a contract, the counterparty would be entitled to obtain a sentence, which produces the effects of the contract not concluded. Others only admit the possibility of obtaining damages, and possibly additional measures to penalize the monopolist. Case law asserts that art. 2932 cc only refers to an obligation to conclude a contract that has been voluntarily undertaken by the one party. It does not apply for non-performance of the legal obligation to contract, in which case only damages are available.

A and B still have a delivery contract, B can start civil proceedings claiming performance of this contract and therefore the delivery of the goods. Furthermore, B can claim damages as a result of the fact that A stopped supplies without a valid basis. The amount of damages has to put B in the same financial position it would have been in, absent the infringement. It helps B in his conduct of the case if an antitrust authority has ruled on the facts of his case and found the conduct of A to be an infringement of the DCA.

Poland (15)

A dominant position is defined as the position of an undertaking which allows him to prevent efficient competition on the relevant market, thus enabling him to act to a significant degree independently from competitors, contracting parties and consumers. It is assumed that an undertaking holds a dominant position where his market share exceeds 40 per cent. The question regarding A's actual market position and potential contractual advantage arises. A dominant position gives undertakings a contractual advantage. However, the reverse situation does not necessarily have to be true. An undertaking's strong position can be caused by high demand in the market or by other factors.[37] The threshold of a 40 per cent market share gives rise to a legal presumption that the undertaking has a dominant position. In the discussed case the gap between 15 per cent and 40 per cent is too big to assume A's dominant position. The u.o.k.k does not contain any rule, which *expressis verbis* protects undertakings against an enterprise which has not got a dominant position but on which the other undertaking is dependent.

Portugal (15)

A is not in a dominant position (art°. 6 Law no. 18/2003, June 11), because his market share is only 15 per cent. However, art°. 7 Law no. 18/2003, June 11 also prohibits the abuse of economic dependence. Actually, in this case A discriminates against B who is in a position of relative economic dependence upon A. In fact, as B has a longstanding business relationship, he does not have an equal option and A restrains the distribution to B.[38] This is a tort according to art°. 7 Law no. 18/2003, June 11. Consequently,

[37] E. Modzelewska-Wachal, *Ustawa*, p. 52.

[38] A. dos Santos/M.E. Gonçalves/M.M. Leitão Marques, *Direito Económico*, p. 353, write that there is abuse of economic dependence when the supplier is the main or only one.

B can claim for compensation under art°. 483°/1 CC. According to art. 5°. Law no. 18/2003, June 11, some restrictive practices can be considered justified if they contribute to improved competition. In each case, economic benefits and disadvantages have to be weighed if selective distribution and refusal to deal are to be justified. If the antitrust authority declares that a practice is illegal according to antitrust law in a previous evaluation (art. 5/2 LDC) this administrative decision does not influence the civil court decision. A civil judge must also evaluate all the requirements of civil liability.

Spain (15)

Since its decision in the *Perfumería* case,[39] the TDC considers, following the European Court (e.g. *Metro v. Commission*),[40] that selective distribution systems do not contravene what is established in art. 1 LDC, provided that selective distributors are chosen on the basis of three principles: necessity (the criteria to select the distributors are always qualitative and in accordance to the nature of the goods); proportionality (the supplier must not impose non-proportional requirements related to the object of the system) and non-discrimination (the qualitative criteria must be the same for all the resellers). In this case, A has excluded B from its selective distribution systems due to its price policy, which does not comprise qualitative criteria similar to the technical qualifications of the resellers, the location of its premises or its stock capability (which are obviously met by B, as former member of A's distribution system). This conduct is contrary to art. 1 LDC, which forbids any agreement, decision or practice which has as its object or has or may have as its effect the prevention, restriction or distortion of competition within the whole or a part of the national market, and in particular those which directly or indirectly apply dissimilar conditions to equivalent transactions in commercial or service relationships, thereby placing some competitors at a disadvantageous position compared to others. Moreover, this exclusion has caused a considerable loss to B, as A's products are a must-stock for consumers and B is not able to offer them.

On the other hand, national competition authorities do not prohibit a behaviour in general, but declare that a particular act is contrary to the

[39] TDC, October 14, 1997, Case 380/96, *Perfumería*.

[40] ECJ, October 22, 1986, Case 75/84, *Metro v. Commission*, [1986] ECR 3021.

LDC and ask the liable party to desist from his behaviour. As only the SDC and the TDC are competent in Spain to apply the LDC, a final decision is necessary in order for B to claim before the civil courts the damages he has suffered due to A's conduct (art. 13 LDC).

Sweden (15)

The behaviour of A is not in conflict with the Swedish Competition Act. With a 15 per cent market share A is not in a dominant position and his behaviour can thus not be in breach of art. 19 of the Competition Act. Furthermore, A's decision to stop supplying B is, as outlined, a unilateral decision taken by A without influence from any other undertaking, for example one of B's competitors. Accordingly, B has no claim against A. Under Swedish law a duty to enter into a contract to deliver goods, or to perform in any other way, in a non-contractual relation, is only conferred on undertakings in monopoly positions on the market. That is definitely not the case here. In spite of this, were the behaviour to be prohibited, B would have a claim against A in accordance with sec. 33 (see Case 10 above).

A selective distribution system is normally characterized by the fact that the supplier and the distributor have an agreement, which typically consists of an obligation on the distributor not to sell to unauthorized distributors. From this follows a limitation of intra-brand competition. However, case law shows that selective distribution systems often fall outside the prohibition in sec. 6 of the Swedish Competition Act or at least that they are eligible for an exemption according to sec. 8 (the same as art. 81.3 EC). A supplier undertaking, which is not dominant, is free to choose its distributors according to any rules it chooses. Only when the supplier forbids the authorized dealers to sell to other non-authorized dealers, sec. 6 applies; this of course presupposes that sec. 6 is not applicable on any other grounds, for example because the supplier decides which price the distributors must charge.

However, a selective distribution system, which does not on its face contain any anti-competitive clauses, might still infringe sec. 6 of the Swedish Competition Act if it for example leads to an undesired *rigidity of pricing*. Furthermore, the actual application of the selective distribution system might result in it being in breach of sec. 6. The criteria for admission to the distribution system, for instance, may systematically be applied in a manner, which hinders, for example, low price dealers to enter the system.

Summary (15)

1. *Outline*

At the centre of Case 15 is a 'refusal to deal' in the context of a selective distribution system. What are the rights of a dealer whose deliveries are stopped even though it fulfils the qualitative requirements made on system dealers? As under the principle of contractual freedom an obligation to contract is the rare exception, the case is elaborated by a special circumstance: further deliveries were stopped because B adopts a low-price policy. The delivery stop affects B particularly severely because according to the details of the scenario the consumers expect of a well-stocked perfumery that A's products will be on offer, and because A has supplied B over a number of years. However, the cosmetics producer A with a market share of 15 per cent is not in a dominant position. Two significant questions arise: whether the delivery stop by A infringes competition law or other norms, and if so, whether B has simply a compensatory claim or also a right to further deliveries. Case 15 does not concern a hard-core infringement of antitrust law, as it involves neither the manipulation of price, quantities or territories nor the abuse of a dominant position. It is therefore not surprising that Case 15 throws up the greatest differences between the reporting countries.

2. *Unilateral conduct*

There is general agreement regarding the starting point. As A has a market share of only 15 per cent, there is no dominant position. All country reports come to this result. However, on the next level differences emerge. In the majority of reporting countries there are no further rules on unilateral conduct. In these countries, at least as regards the antitrust law of unilateral behaviour, the conduct of A is allowed (Denmark, England, Finland, France,[41] Hungary, Ireland, Netherlands, Poland, Spain, Sweden). In other countries by contrast there are special rules on unilateral conduct, which already apply below the threshold of market dominance (Austria, Germany, Greece, Italy, Portugal). These rules are partly antitrust rules (Germany, Greece, Portugal), partly special rules *sui generis* (Austria, Italy), or sometimes unfair competition law is applied. Germany, Greece, Italy and Portugal link the special

[41] There was a special rule on refusal to deal in France until 1996.

conduct rules to a state of economic dependence. Enterprises on which certain other enterprises are dependent are subject to special rules of conduct. Limitations of contractual freedom can be the result. Here substantive law is significantly different between the countries with and without such special rules. This difference was recognised by the European Cartel Regulation:[42] pursuant to art. 3 para. 2 sec. 2 Council Regulation 1/2003, Member States are not precluded from adopting and applying on their territory stricter national laws which prohibit or sanction unilateral conduct engaged in by enterprises. Thus, national rules on unilateral conduct may be stricter, even within the field of application of European antitrust law, than the prohibition of the abuse of a dominant position under art. 82 EC.

3. *Bilateral conduct*

As a selective distribution system is involved, the rules on anti-competitive agreements also apply. The antitrust law requirements of such a system are relatively homogeneous in the Member States. For the qualitative selection of system dealers the establishment of general and objective criteria are everywhere required, and have to be applied in practice without discrimination. According to the case scenario A makes particular demands regarding location, interior decoration and presentation. These criteria were judged to be appropriate in all reporting countries. There was a corresponding consensus that in a selective distribution system the prices may not be fixed (see Case 14 above on the prohibition of vertical price fixing). In the actual case here a problem was seen by the majority of reports. Admittedly retail prices between A and B are not directly bound. However, according to the case scenario, A stops deliveries to B because of B's low-price policy. In numerous country reports this is construed as a price-related disciplinary measure and as such an attempt indirectly to fix retail prices. The prohibition on anti-competitive agreements thus applies not only to the legal structure of the agreement but also to its actual operation in practice. Since B still fulfils the qualitative requirements of A's selective marketing scheme, the refusal to deal constitutes an antitrust infringement. Thus, the large majority of reporting countries conclude that there has been an antitrust infringement in terms of the cartel law on selective distribution.

[42] Council Regulation 1/2003 on the implementation of the rules on competition laid down in arts. 81 and 82 of the Treaty (OJ 2003 L 1/1).

4. *Legal consequences*

The remedies flowing from the antitrust violation were not assessed uniformly. In some countries only a damages claim is possible (according to the facts damages in the amount of €300,000 have occurred). In other countries an additional claim for further delivery, that is obligation to contract, was held possible (Denmark, Finland, Germany, Greece). From the theoretical perspective it should be added that the legal consequences can also depend on which antitrust rule has been infringed upon. According to German case law an obligation to contract is possible if the special rule on economic dependency is infringed. If there is only an infringement of the prohibition of anti-competitive agreements, the claim is limited to damages.[43]

5. *Involvement of antitrust authorities*

Case 15 is structured differently to Cases 9(2) and 10(2). It concerns not a horizontal agreement or abuse of a market-dominant position but a vertical anti-competitive agreement. Some legal systems provide for milder regulations on this in that they do not apply the prohibition principle but the misuse principle. This has the consequence that the conduct in question is only prohibited after the decision of an antitrust authority. This is the case, for example, in Spain, where involvement of the antitrust authority is required as a matter of principle. If A's conduct is deemed to constitute indirect price fixing, then the prohibition principle applies also in those countries where in non-price agreements the misuse principle applies. That means no authority decision is required. The same is true of those countries which have special rules for economic dependence under the level of market dominance. Here, too, the enforcement of delivery or damages claims is not dependent on the involvement of the antitrust authority. In these countries, an antitrust authority decision is only significant to the extent that after such a decision the adducing of evidence in court proceedings becomes easier.

6. *Conclusion*

Under the principle of freedom to contract, everyone is at liberty to decide with whom and under what conditions he enters into a contract. Restrictions of contractual freedom may arise out of antitrust law,

[43] BGH, May 12, 1998 (1999) NJW-RR 189 – *Depotkosmetik*. See criticism by Mäsch (1999) ZIP 1507.

e.g. against dominant enterprises. This statement applies to all reporting countries. The differences begin – as in Case 15 – when it is not the conduct of a dominant enterprise that is to be judged, but rather where dependence arises because, as in the present case, the consumer expects that a well-stocked perfume store also sells the products of manufacturer A. There are specific rules for this in only a few countries, which see the cases of dependence as equivalent to those of market dominance. The resulting differences are however blurred because at the same time the rules on selective distribution become applicable. As in the case at issue an inappropriate selective criterion is applied, that of price discipline; perfume producer A comes into conflict with the prohibition against anti-competitive agreements. In all reporting countries this constitutes a violation of antitrust law. In the countries with special rules on unilateral conduct under the level of market dominance, there is an additional violation of precisely these rules. The legal remedy consists mainly of a compensation claim, in certain countries also of an obligation to contract, that is a claim for further delivery. Aside from the relatively large differences between the reporting countries, Case 15 is characterized by the fact that quite a considerable amount of case law exists. It is in the group of cases concerned with claims for delivery or damages for non-delivery that private enforcement has attained the highest level of practical relevance.

D. Conclusions

I. The overall results of the country reports

The country reports allow the conclusion that – although there is everywhere the theoretical possibility to pursue private remedies for antitrust law infringements – this possibility is rarely availed of in practice. Antitrust law is primarily used as a means of defence, for example where contractual claims are contested by relying on the invalidity of contract under antitrust law. However, the active use of antitrust law is only to be seen in individual cases. Examples of the (successful) enforcement of compensatory clams are almost entirely missing. In recent times, however, a change may be observed: in the wake of the particularly blatant vitamin cartel, private compensatory claims have been pursued in certain EU Member States. In addition, the readiness seems to be growing everywhere to undertake private legal action against antitrust infringements.

There is a variety of reasons for this discrepancy between theory and practice. In part there are legal difficulties, for example restrictions on standing or uncertainty regarding the precise requirements of a compensatory claim, for instance the admissibility of the passing-on defence. The most significant causes, however, are of a practical nature, thus difficulties in providing evidence or a lack of incentive to expose oneself to the costs and risks of a private claim. Also of fundamental importance is the competition between private legal remedies and public enforcement. The applicant incurs no costs by involving an antitrust authority. Where the applicant simply wishes that the anticompetitive conduct should not continue in the future, the involvement of the antitrust authority has several advantages, among others its comprehensive investigative powers. The authority can of course refuse to intervene on the basis of the opportunity principle. But then the applicant still has private remedies available to him.

The differences between the Member States have already been summarized individually for each single case of the questionnaire. A picture emerges in which the common factors outweigh the differences. The country reports confirm the suspicion that the weakness of private antitrust remedies is a Europe-wide phenomenon. From the comprehensive material should be identified the features which have a particular value for potential reforms. Here the starting point should be the presumption that a strengthening of the private remedies is a worthwhile objective. This corresponds to the general opinion, according to which administrative and private antitrust law enforcement are not alternatives but rather complement each other. Contrasting opinions which ascribe a higher legitimacy to public antitrust enforcement than to private remedies are only found very rarely.[1] With just cause, the large majority is in favour of strengthening private enforcement. If private legal interests are injured, then a private law remedy must be available. Otherwise, the injured party would be dependent on state initiative, i.e. incapacitated to a doubtful degree. The interplay between administrative supervision and private initiative has been emphasized by the European Court of Justice. In *Van Gend & Loos* it held (in another context) that the 'vigilance of individuals concerned to protect their rights' should complement and support control by the Commission and Member States.[2]

In what follows the question of how we could get closer to the aim of strengthening private enforcement is explored. The experience in the EU Member States examined will be the basis of these reflections.

[1] See W. Wils, *Should Private Antitrust Enforcement Be Encouraged in Europe?* (2003) 26 World Competition 473–488; idem, Community Report, in D. Cahill, J. Cooke, W. Wils (eds.), *The Modernisation of EU Competition Law Enforcement in the European Union – FIDE 2004 National Reports* (2004), p. 688: 'Public Antitrust Enforcement is Inherently Superior to Private Enforcement'; W. Möschel (2006) WuW 115.

[2] ECJ, 5.2.1963, Case 26/62, *Van Gend & Loos* [1963] ECR 1.

II. Measures for the strengthening of private enforcement

1. *General reflections*

a) Legal basis

In all reporting countries private remedies in case of an antitrust violation exist. The legal basis for such remedies varies considerably, though. While in some countries there are special antitrust claims, in others resort is had to general civil law. It may also be the case that unfair competition law is extended to cover antitrust infringements. These differences are of a merely conceptual nature and have no apparent influence on the result (see Case 10 Summary 1) Nevertheless, it would seem advisable to introduce specific antitrust claims. This serves on the one hand the interests of clarity, that is in the sense that such private law claims exist at all. On the other, it will enable the legislator to provide for certain rules which apply specifically to antitrust law, and which accordingly should not to be regulated under general civil law. In the following a number of such peculiarities will be addressed.

b) Prohibition principle and misuse principle

Antitrust claims are only conceivable where antitrust law norms are based on the prohibition principle rather than the misuse principle. Only if a certain form of conduct is prohibited from the start can an infringement give rise to a private claim. Where norms on the other hand derive exclusively from the misuse principle, they are initially admissible at least until an antitrust authority has prohibited the conduct. In the intervening period before the official ruling there is no legal infringement, so that private claims are conceivably excluded. Consequently, a significant measure towards the strengthening of private claims would be to base antitrust rules on the prohibition principle. Case 15 demonstrates what differences may arise if national domestic antitrust laws pursue divergent paths in this question (see in particular Case 15 Summary 5). Obviously, the adoption of an antitrust law prohibition is only possible if the concerned form of conduct can be classified as anti-competitive. If this depends on further requirements, the legislator has in principle the option between two regulatory models: it can opt for a true prohibition with possible exception provisions, or subject the concerned form of conduct to the misuse principle. In the area of vertical restrictions in particular there are currently several developments under way and the situation is changing radically. From the perspective of private remedies, however, the route of the prohibition with exception provisions is to be preferred. Where the requirements for the exception provision are absent, the form of conduct remains prohibited and private remedies are in principle available.

c) Relationship between private remedies and administrative antitrust proceedings

One of the most important questions in connection with private remedies is the determination of the relationship to administrative proceedings. Case 9 leads to the conclusion that in some countries, as far as cessation claims are concerned, there is an alternative relationship between administrative law and private law legal remedies (see Case 9 Summary 5). The restriction of private cessation claims should be reconsidered. It is not in conformity with the principle that everyone should have the right to commence independent proceedings against legal violations. There are no such limitations in the field of compensatory claims because the antitrust authorities are not competent for private compensatory claims.[1] Also in the area of cessation claims the aggrieved party should be given the possibility of proceeding against the infringer independently of an administrative proceeding. This is also particularly important because the work of antitrust authorities follows the opportunity principle; they have a degree of discretion in the question of whether they should intervene against a certain conduct or not. Civil courts in comparison work more rapidly, particularly regarding an application for an injunction. In addition, only the civil proceeding offers the possibility to recover costs. Costs incurred in taking legal advice in connection with a complaint to the antitrust authority on the other hand are not recoverable.

2. *Standing*

The fundamental topic of private remedies is the question of who can enforce a claim. The country reports have made clear that enterprises generally have standing if they are affected as competitors or direct contractual partners, e.g. as suppliers or purchasers by an antitrust infringement. In other configurations there may be restrictions. For example, the legal position is not clear in the case of those enterprises

[1] Spain is the exception, where civil proceedings must always be preceded by antitrust authority proceedings even for compensatory claims.

which are neither competitors nor contractual partners but rather are positioned on a remote level of the market, i.e. in particular the indirect purchaser. Equally diverse is the question of the standing of non-enterprises, i.e. that of the consumer.

a) Direct purchasers

In almost all reporting countries the direct purchaser has standing for a claim of its own if it is adversely affected by a restrictive agreement on the preceding market level. The only exception was Germany (until 2005) where, according to the view of the majority of courts, claims were only possible if the restriction of competition was directly aimed at the purchaser. Such a narrowing of the circle of those entitled to claims is not appropriate as it precludes claims against the most harmful cartels, that is arrangements across a market sector directed not against a particular enterprise but which rather affect all purchasers to the same degree. In 2005 the law changed; direct purchasers now have their own claim without further restrictions on standing.

b) Indirect purchasers and the problem of 'passing on'

The problem of standing for indirect purchasers is more problematic. As Case 12 has shown (Summary 2), the legal position varies considerably between reporting countries. In some countries indirect purchasers are denied standing as a matter of principle regardless of whether they be enterprises or consumers. Other states regard indirect purchaser claims as possible provided an enterprise is concerned. Only a minority of countries extend standing to indirect purchasers within their broadest definition, that is including consumers.

For a more precise analysis it is necessary to examine the historical context. The indirect purchaser rule (that is the exclusion of claims to the prejudice of indirect purchasers) derives from US-American law. The US Supreme Court ruled in 1977 in *Illinois Brick Co. v Illinois* that indirect purchasers have no standing for compensatory claims based on sec. 4 Clayton Act.[2] This was a direct consequence of the decision in *Hanover Shoe, Inc. v. United Shoe Machinery Corp.*[3] Here, the US Supreme Court had decided that the respondent could not defend itself against an antitrust claim on the grounds that the claimant had shifted the

[2] 431 U.S. 720 (1977).

[3] 392 U.S. 481 (1968). For a detailed analysis of these two decisions see F. Bulst, *Schadensersatzansprüche der Marktgegenseite im Kartellrecht* (2006), p. 64 et seq.

overcharge (the increase in price due to the cartel agreement) onto the next market level. Under US-American law the direct victim of an antitrust infringement can thus claim damages even if from a common sense view it is no longer suffering loss, as it has completely passed on the losses to the next market level by selling the products in question at higher prices. In *Illinois Brick* the Supreme Court drew the (negative) conclusion for the standing of indirect purchasers: as the direct purchaser can already claim full compensation, an involvement of the indirect purchaser is no longer possible. Otherwise, there would be a duplicating of the claim. The apportionment of recovery throughout the distribution chain would lead to severe practical difficulties with the result that private claims would become less effective. This conclusion is significant in the European context, in that the exclusion of claims to the prejudice of indirect purchasers is directly connected to the exclusion of the passing on defence to the prejudice of the antitrust violator.[4]

The position in Europe is unclear in comparison and there are (with the exception of the new competition law in Germany[5]) no special rules on the subject. The application of general considerations of compensation law leads rather to a recognition of the passing on defence, that is awarding the direct purchaser only the actual and final loss incurred. If this viewpoint is shared there is a compelling necessity also to admit indirect purchaser claims. Otherwise, there would be serious gaps in the protection offered by private enforcement.[6] Even if the opposing

[4] It must however be added that even for US American law this connection is not inevitable. In their dissenting opinion in *Illinois Brick* three judges of the Supreme Court held it possible to recognize a damages claim on the part of the indirect purchaser, even when recognizing the exclusion of the passing on defence, see Justice Brennan in *Illinois Brick Co. v. Illinois* 97 S. ct. 2071 (1977).

[5] § 33 para. 3 s. 2 GWB 2005 provides: 'If goods or services are bought at an excessive price, the damage is not excluded by the (mere) fact that the goods or services were resold.' The preparatory works show, that this text does not categorically exclude the passing-on defence. It simply clarifies that even in the case of passing-on damage occurs initially. The question if the damages might be compensated by the benefits received is left over to the courts. In any event, the competition law infringer has the burdon of proof that damages were compensated through the resale. See BT-Drs. 15/5049 of 9.3.2005, p. 49. See also BT-Drs. 15/3640, p. 54, and F.W. Bulst, (2004) EWS 62 et seq. For a restrictive interpretation of this provision see Th. Lübbig and M. le Bell (2006) WRP 1209 (1212).

[6] The German monopoly commission points out the danger that the antitrust violators could otherwise escape antitrust responsibility by artifically involving intermediate traders, see Monopolkommission, *Das allgemeine Wettbewerbsrecht in der 7. GWB-Novelle, Sondergutachten* (2004) (available at: http://www.monopolkommission.de/sg_41/text_s41.pdf), note 73.

standpoint is taken, with the tendency to exclude the passing-on defence, it should not be concluded from this that the indirect purchaser has no claim. This would seriously jeopardize the practical effectiveness of private enforcement. Frequently, the direct purchaser has no incentive to file a claim against the cartel members, for example, for the very reason that he was able to shift the loss onto the next commercial level or because it does not wish to harm the business relationship to the supplier. If the direct purchaser waives its own legal action and if indirect purchaser claims are excluded a priori, private antitrust enforcement would be brought to a complete standstill.

From general principles of compensatory law it also follows that if several claimants are possible, then recovery must be apportioned. Otherwise, there would be a multiplied burden on the violator, which would be equivalent to punitive damages.[7] The most satisfactory solution from the theoretical point of view would be to grant everyone compensation for the loss they have actually suffered. It is true that additional difficulties arise from the fragmentation of compensation claims, but these difficulties do not justify negating claims to the disadvantage of whole groups of affected parties. The difficulties from the legal and practical point of view must be addressed in a different way, for example through specific rules on the burden of proof or the possibility of class actions, respectively collective actions taken by associations. If this proves fruitless then in reality indirect purchasers will not avail themselves of their rights. This however reflects the general phenomenon that an aggrieved party will only exercise its rights if there is a favourable balance between the risks and costs of action on the one side against the expected benefit on the other. This calculation should be undertaken independently by every affected party. Under no circumstances should the undeniable difficulties lead to the conclusion that the aggrieved party is to be deprived of its claim a priori.

This conclusion regarding extension of standing to all trading levels is supported by European Community law. While European competition law is inapplicable to purely domestic situations, it is nevertheless desirable to reach equivalent results in cases of violation of national and European antitrust law. In Community law the *effet utile* of European competition laws points towards a broad definition of standing. Entirely along these lines the ECJ in the *Courage* decision has stated that 'the full effectiveness of art. 85 of the Treaty, and in particular, the practical

[7] See on punitive damages infra, sub 3. a).

effect of the prohibition laid down in art. 85(1) would be put at risk if it were not open to *any individual* to claim damages for loss caused to him by a contract or conduct liable to restrict or distort competition'.[8] This ruling is not compatible with denying entire groups of aggrieved parties active legitimation a priori. Thus, the opportunity for recovery should be extended to all aggrieved parties, whereby everyone should only be able to recover its own actually incurred loss. If this principle is observed, compensatory mechanisms between direct and indirect purchasers are rendered unnecessary. Something else applies only when the passing-on defence is excluded, but indirect purchasers still have standing: to avoid multiple burdening, the antitrust violator must be given the possibility of relying on the compensation already paid to another claimant. The compensation awarded would have to be apportioned internally, that is according to the relationship between direct and indirect purchasers.

c) Consumers

The arguments just aired in favour of standing for indirect purchasers apply independently regardless of whether the indirect purchaser is an enterprise or a consumer. As the country reports show, however, consumers ultimately have standing for antitrust infringements in only few countries. In some countries indirect purchasers are generally excluded from standing, in other countries this exclusion is only valid for consumers, while even in countries where the consumer is not excluded a priori, restrictive criteria sometimes exist which eventually have the same effect (see Case 12). This result is paradoxical: although competition is intended to bring about the best results for the consumer in the interest of consumer sovereignty, these very consumers are denied standing. A future reform of antitrust law should concentrate on the strengthening of consumer rights. Those in whose interest competition is created should have standing if the competition mechanism is disturbed or entirely negated by restrictive practices. Consumer standing (own claims) is also important because, as the typical ultimate user, the consumer cannot pass on his losses to a subsequent market level.

The problem with consumers' own claims consists in the fact that the circle of potential claimants can become immeasurably wide. For

[8] ECJ, 20.9.2001, C-453/99, *Courage Ltd. v. Crehan* [2001] ECR I-6297 note 26 (author's emphasis). Confirmed by ECJ, 13.7.2006, Joined Cases C-295/04 to C-298/04, Manfredi, n. 60.

example, almost all consumers were affected adversely by the vitamin cartel as artificial vitamin additives are customary in a large number of products. Is every individual consumer to be granted standing for proceedings against the cartel? This could lead to an impractical flood of claims which would rapidly overstretch the courts. On the other hand it cannot be ignored that this danger is purely theoretical. The reports on unfair competition law have shown that in many reporting countries there is independent standing for consumers without a resulting flood of claims.[9] The incentives for individuals to pursue such claims are simply too small. The problem of lack of practicability is to be countered by extending standing to consumer protection associations.

d) Consumer protection associations

The involvement of consumer protection associations is necessary to resolve an incentive problem; although the macroeconomic harm of cartel arrangements is immense, the resulting harm to the ultimate consumer can be so fragmented that the pursuit of an independent claim is not worthwhile. The consolidation of multiple individual claims is a precondition for the efficient exercise of these rights. The country reports have shown that there are two models available for a consolidated exercise of consumer rights, that is the Ombudsman of Scandinavian provenance and the consumer protection association. The Ombudsman model has been adopted in Poland but has otherwise not been adopted in Europe as a whole. In addition the competence of the Ombudsman is limited with regard to unfair competition law, so that there is no experience of antitrust law in this area. In contrast there are consumer protection associations in all reporting countries. Their competences under antitrust law have hitherto remained wholly underdeveloped. As they are found universally, however, they are strong candidates as vehicles for the collective pursuit of consumer rights.

At the very least, consumer protection associations should have the right to a cessation claim. Until now consumer protection associations have been limited to calling for intervention by the antitrust authorities. The conferring of cessation claims to be enforced through the civil courts would give such associations scope for autonomous action. Beyond this, consumer protection associations should be granted standing for compensatory claims. Because of the diffusion of loss described above the individual consumer will in practice not

[9] See above Part I B II 6.

exercise his right to claim damages for his trivial individual losses. To avoid an unjustifiable relief of liabity for the infringer, consumer protection associations must be given the right to demand compensation. Otherwise, antitrust violators would be immune to any private compensation liability for no substantive reason. According to the opposite view this result is acceptable as the antitrust violator can be deprived of its unlawful profits under administrative law (fines, disgorgement). This contradicts, however, the important role of private claims described above, that is that a party injured by an antitrust law violation should have his own claims under private law. The reference to administrative law sanctions by contrast reflects the (to be denied) viewpoint of the primacy of administrative law.

The recognition of private compensation is also important for the question of who should actually recover payments made under claims brought by the consumer protection association. If the claim in principle belongs to the individual consumer and if the enforcement of claims is only for reasons of practicability assigned to the consumer protection association, then the compensation awarded should eventually reach the aggrieved consumer. The consumer protection associations should (with the exception of a costs award) not be allowed to retain the moneys for themselves and should also not have to surrender them to the state; they should rather directly benefit the consumer.[10] This could be done by means of a registration system in which consumers have to establish the degree to which they have been affected. In order to limit administrative expenses flat-rate amounts should be possible.

In accordance with the principle of complementarity of administrative and private remedies, the consumer protection association should also have standing in administrative proceedings. In this way the problem of 'buying up' of procedural rights could be resolved.[11] This is in the first place significant in connection with merger control. The approval of mergers can be challenged by other enterprises, with the consequence that considerable delays can ensue. Therefore, it happens in practice that the would-be merging parties settle with the claimants:

[10] The solution discussed in Germany during the 7th Cartel Law Reform was different. The associations were supposed to have a claim to profits. However, the money should then be surrendered to the federal budget. The Monopolkommission was rightly critical (above note 6), n. 92, 132: only where distribution to the affected parties is uneconomic, the money should be spent for a similar use. Eventually, the idea of standing for consumer associations was entirely dropped.

[11] Similarly see Monopolkommission (above note 6), notes 106, 137.

in return for payment or the provision of other benefits the claimants withdraw their legal remedies so that the merger can be implemented. Such a practice is problematic because the legality of the merger is not adjudicated on competition-related grounds but rather by an extra-judicial settlement between enterprises frequently from the same sector. If the consumer protection associations had standing in their own right, the basis for such a settlement between the interested enterprises would be withdrawn; even if the competitors withdrew their claims the association could still maintain its objection.

3. *Legal remedies, especially damages*

a) Punitive damages

If all the requirements for a private law claim are fulfilled, the aggrieved party can demand cessation by the violator. If the infringer is additionally at fault then a claim for damages will result. The country reports all assume that the loss to be recovered includes the actual losses (*damnum emergens*) as well as loss of profit (*lucrum cessans*).[12] The recognition of punitive damages is, however, a rare exception in Europe (see exemplary damages in England and Case 10). A form of punitive damages could be achieved if the antitrust violator were deprived of the passing-on defence (which is here denied), while additionally granting a claim to the indirect purchaser. Whether beyond this punitive damages should be introduced generally in Europe for antitrust infringements is highly controversial. The predominant view in Europe rejects punitive damages, as they cannot be reconciled with the compensatory principles of damages claims. The supporters of punitive damages on the other hand point to the possibility of treble damages in the USA and thereby strengthened incentives actually to make use of the theoretical possibility of private enforcement. As a compromise against the background of European circumstances the introduction of double damages has also been suggested.[13]

The question of the desirability of punitive damages will remain controversial for the foreseeable future in Europe. The right to compensation is too firmly established a core component of civil law and thereby an attribute of Member State competence, for a unified regulation

[12] As regards violations of European competition law, this follows from the principle of effectiveness, see ECJ, 13.7.2006, Joined Cases C-295/04 to C-298/04, Manfredi, n. 95.

[13] Monopolkommission (above note 8), notes 75 et seq., notes 126, 131.

to be achieved in this area.[14] In place of the relatively 'aggressive' introduction of multiple damages the general conditions for private claims should be improved. This includes in the first place the already discussed improvement of standing as well as of the rules on the burden of proof.

b) Violator's profits

A conceivable compromise would however be to introduce an easing or alternatives in the calculation of damages (quantum). The country reports have shown that damages can throughout cover only sustained losses, but do not extend to the profits gained by the violator (see Case 10 Summary 2). Difficulties in the calculation of damages could be minimized if the claimant was granted the right to refer to the profits gained by the violator.[15] Information deficits could then be overcome by granting a right to demand discovery in the preparation of compensatory claims.[16] In general all activities are to be welcomed which render the calculation of compensatory claims following antitrust infringements more transparent and effective.[17]

c) Other remedies

Further remedies may be considered which enhance the status of private claims. It has already been pointed out how important it is to extend standing to the consumer protection associations not only for cessation claims but also for compensatory claims. As considerable time may frequently pass before particular anti-competitive conduct is discovered, it would be advisable to introduce a duty to pay interest from the occurrence of the loss-causing event. To counter the threat of limitation of action (statute bar) a special regulation could be introduced regarding the suspension, for example, suspension of the limitation period

[14] Reservations also held by W. van Gerven, *Substantive Remedies for the Private Enforcement of EC Antitrust Rules Before National Courts*, in Ehlermann/Atanasiu (eds.), *European Competition Law Annual 2001: Effective Private Enforcement of EC Antitrust Law* (2003).

[15] Thus the legal situation in Sweden and in Germany.

[16] In addition details of profit accounting are to be established, e.g. the question of which costs of the infringer may be deducted. See the following footnote.

[17] See for example the overview of accounting methods in *Ashurst* (prepared by E. Clark, M. Hughes and D. Wirth), *Study on the Conditions of Claims for Damages in Case of Infringement of EC Competition Rules – Analysis of Economic Models for the Calculation of Damages* (2004), available at: http://europa.eu.int/comm/competition/antitrust/others/private_enforcement/index_en.html.

for private claims from the active involvement of the antitrust authority.[18]

4. *Evidence issues*

The limited status of private claims in Europe is due among other things to the difficulty of producing evidence. The typical requirements for a private claim are (a) the antitrust law violation, (b) the loss, (c) causation of the loss by the legal infringement, as well as (d) fault. All these preconditions have as a rule to be established by the claimant. There are no special obligations of discovery. Only in England and in Ireland are there comprehensive duties of discovery (see Case 10 Summary 5). With regard to the evidence question there is therefore a divide between common law and civil law countries.[19] It would certainly be too simplistic to say that in common law countries the claimant can file a claim in the hope that the evidence will be revealed by the respondent. But there is at least a certain alleviation of the burden of proof in these countries.[20] In civil law countries by contrast the claimant must undertake intensive preparation of his case. He has to research all the evidence himself. If he realises that he will not be able to produce conclusive comprehensive evidence, he is advised not to persist with the claim. As the evidentiary difficulties are often unavoidable and result in an unjustified advantaging of the respondent, consideration should be given to how an appropriate distribution of the burden of proof could be achieved. In this respect one must distinguish between the various preconditions of the claim.

a) Antitrust law violation

As in practice restrictive practices are often carried out in secret, it is extremely difficult for the aggrieved party to prove the existence of the antitrust infringement. This is the principal reason why private actions in Europe are commenced only after the antitrust authority has

[18] Thus, the solution in Germany, see § 33 para. 5 GWB according to the 7th amendment of German competition law 2005. See generally F. Bulst (2004) EWS 62; R. Hempel, (2004) WuW 362.

[19] D. Woods, A. Sinclair, D. Ashton, *Private Enforcement of Community Competition Law: Modernisation and the Road Ahead* (2004) CPN, no. 2, p. 31 (34).

[20] Therefore there is a strong incentive to claim before English courts. See (particularly with regard to the vitamin cartel) F. Bulst (2003) 4 EBOR 623; (2004) EWS 403 (404): This incentive is strengthened by the possibilities for exemplary damages and group actions under English law.

ascertained the antitrust law violation. This factual connection should however not be required as a legal necessity. It is inappropriate to make a private claim dependant on the prior involvement of the antitrust authority (see Case 9 Summary 2; Case 10 Summary 3). At the same time the evidentiary challenge for the claimant could be reduced by binding the civil court to the determinations of the antitrust authority in an administrative proceeding.[21] Additionally, it would be important to apply general rules on easing of the evidentiary burden to the specific needs of antitrust. If, for example, there is no apparent substantive reason for a price increase (e.g. because costs have remained stable), then the respondent or respondents could be placed under an obligation to reveal the circumstances surrounding the price increase. Even if improvements are possible here, it cannot be overlooked that proof of an antitrust infringement is often the greatest hurdle in a private compensatory claim. As a result the involvement of the antitrust authority is frequently indispensable, particularly in proving secret conduct. However, other situations are not excluded from the outset. There is also behaviour, such as abuse of a dominant position, where all material facts are fully known to the victim and susceptible to proof. Private claims are thus dependant on antitrust authority involvement to a widely varying degree.

b) Loss

The injured party has to establish both the existence and also the level of loss it has sustained. Considerable difficulties may arise here due to the complex intertwining of economic factors. The country reports, however, have shown that there is everywhere significant facilitation of the determination of the loss. It can be established that the greatest leeway in evidentiary law exists in the calculation of quantum. All the reporting countries confer discretion in the assessment of the level of loss sustained. Nevertheless even greater flexibility could be achieved if – as suggested here[22] – an alternative form of quantum calculation could be linked to violator profits, and if the injured party could be granted a claim for rendering of accounts by a violator regarding its profits. The evidentiary difficulties with regard to the incurred loss can thus be completely overcome. It should be added that the proof of harm,

[21] Thus, the solution in Germany, see § 33 para. 4 GWB according to the 7th amendment of German competition law.

[22] See supra Part II D. II 3 (b).

causation and liability are significant only for the compensatory claim, but not for a claim merely for cessation.

c) Causation

The antitrust law violator must have caused the established loss. The causal relationship does not result simply from the chronological relationship between a violation and loss (what is *post hoc* is not necessarily *propter hoc*). If the loss, for example, is due not to the restrictive practice but rather to the difficult economic circumstances or to a decision by the injured party, then the requirements for a compensatory claim are not fulfilled.[23] As economic connections are seldom absolutely clear, the evidentiary problems can be very severe at this point. It should therefore suffice to establish the typical characteristic features of the events. The onus should lie on the respondent to show as plausible causation some factor other than the antitrust infringement. Thus a particular easing of the burden of proof is necessary regarding the characteristic indicators of causation.

d) Fault

The concept of liability should be subject to a strict standard. The infringer can only escape liability if it has taken all necessary steps to ensure the legality of its conduct. It will be expected of it as a matter of principle that it obtain competent legal advice and in cases of doubt contact the antitrust authority. The element of liability should thus not present a practical problem for the enforcement of private claims.

[23] D. Woods, A. Sinclair, D. Ashton (above note 19), p. 36.

III. Conflict of laws

In the age of globalization, international integration becomes even more intense. If a restricting behaviour has cross-border effects, the question arises of which national (or supranational) antitrust regime is to be applied.[1]

1. *International administrative law*

In the enforcement of antitrust law by the administrative authority, it is clear from the outset that an antitrust authority can only apply its own national (or supranational) antitrust law. Administrative authorities lack the competence (directly) to apply foreign law. The most important international law problem in international antitrust administrative law is the phenomenon of extra-territoriality. According to the 'effects doctrine' an antitrust authority may apply its own law to all restrictions of competition which affect its own territory, even when they are initiated from outside the territory. Public international law however imposes limits here; the principle of *negative comity* can oblige a country to be cautious in the application of its own law if the interests of another state will be affected.

2. *International private law*

The question also arises under private law of how far the scope of application of domestic law reaches. In private law however – in contrast to public law – it is also possible to apply foreign law. It is recognized world-wide, even if not universally practised, that the court of a country can be called upon to apply foreign law. Conflict of law rules determine which legal regime is applicable in the individual case. In international private antitrust law there are basically two problems. The first – as in international administrative law – is that of territoriality, that is the danger of an excessive application of domestic law. The second problem concerns the question of the conditions under which the courts of a country can be called upon to apply foreign antitrust law.

[1] A further problem concerns international procedural law, i.e. which country's courts have jurisdiction in an international case, see F. Bulst (2004) EWS 403; G. Mäsch (2005) IPRax 509.

a) The reach of domestic antitrust law

The danger also arises under private antitrust law that domestic law is extended too far. In the context of the international vitamin cartel, the American courts had to analyse the question of the extent to which US antitrust law was applicable to loss caused by a cartel operating worldwide. Can triple damages pursuant to art. 4 Clayton Act be claimed for loss which is sustained outside the USA? In the *Empagran* case the US Supreme Court adopted a restrictive stance: if a cartel harms enterprises within and outside the USA 'but the adverse foreign effect is independent of any adverse domestic effect', then no compensation can be claimed on the basis of US law for the loss sustained outside the country.[2] The decision should be welcomed as it ensures an appropriate limitation of the international field of application of national antitrust law. In general a limitation of private law claims should be derived from the antitrust law effects doctrine. A particular legal regime is only applicable *to the extent* to which it has an effect on the domestic territory. Only the losses sustained on the basis of inland effects should therefore be compensated under the domestic antitrust law. To the extent, on the other hand, that restrictions of competition have effects abroad, the losses caused thereby will fall under the corresponding foreign law.

b) Application of foreign antitrust law

According to the general principles of international private law the courts of a country – limited by the *ordre public* – may be called upon to apply foreign private law. This is also true for private antitrust law. Thus, in theory it is unquestionable that a court of a country X may apply the antitrust law of country Y in a civil proceeding where anti-competitive conduct takes effect in country Y. In practice, however, there are almost no court decisions in which a court has applied foreign antitrust law.[3] This is certainly explicable by the fact that the private enforcement of antitrust law is so underdeveloped in Europe. Thus, if courts only very rarely apply their own antitrust law

[2] US Supreme Court, June 14, 2004, *Hoffman-La Roche et al. v. Empagran et al.*, available at: http://a257.g.akamaitech.net/7/257/2422/14june20041300/www.supremecourtus.gov/opinions/03pdf/03-724.pdf. The consequences of this decision are not clear, however, see R. Michaels/D. Zimmer (2004) IPRax 451; J. Shenefield/J. Beninca (2004) WuW 1276.

[3] J. Basedow (2001) 2 EBOR 443, 461; I. Schwartz, J. Basedow, *Restrictions on Competition*, in *International Encyclopedia of Comparative Law*, vol. III (1995), chap. 35 sec. 103, pp. 109, 112.

in a civil proceeding, it is clear why there is almost no case material to be found on the application of foreign antitrust law. This reluctance on the part of the courts in the application of foreign antitrust law is also due to the lack of clear rules on this question. Antitrust law is at the same time both public and private law. The courts are traditionally very cautious regarding the application of foreign public law. In addition antitrust law has for many the image of 'political law', which increases the reserve regarding its application as the courts of a given country are unwilling to implement the economic policy measures of another.

However, these concerns are without foundation. Antitrust law has now attained a high level of precision, not only in Europe but in large parts of the world. While antitrust law pursues economic policy objectives, it is an essentially legal instrument of economic policy. To this extent it is no different from unfair competition law, in which there is no difficulty in applying foreign law.[4] While antitrust law is both public and private law, the discussion of private enforcement raises only the private law aspects of antitrust law, so that an application of foreign antitrust law should be permitted under the general rules of international tort law.[5]

3. *Consequences*

If the role of private enforcement is to increase, precise rules will have to be developed by which national antitrust regimes are applicable in matters with a foreign dimension. On the one hand the antitrust law of the *lex fori* may be applied only to the extent that effects are perceived domestically. On the other hand there must be an increased readiness to apply foreign antitrust law where effects are perceived abroad. There is admittedly as yet no experience of the application of foreign antitrust law. If there is an increase in private enforcement however then issues of international law will arise with increasing frequency, necessitating a precise determination of the applicable law. Only a clear definition of conflict rules can ensure that the claimant does not face even more risks in the pursuit of its claim. Therefore, it is very deplorable that the draft

[4] For the difficulties in case of multistate violations of unfair competition law see N. Dethloff, *Europäisierung des Wettbewerbsrechts* (2001); A. Höder, *Die kollisionsrechtliche Behandlung unteilbarer Multistate-Verstöße* (2002).

[5] See A. Heinemann, *Die Anwendbarkeit ausländischen Kartellrechts* (Mélanges Dutoit 2002), pp. 115 et seq.

'Rome II' Regulation contains no special rule on the application of foreign antitrust law, but only of unfair competition law.[6] A strengthening of private remedies has to be accompanied by a clarification of the corresponding conflict of law rules.

[6] See Art. 5 of the European Commission's Proposal for a Regulation on the Law Applicable to Non-Contractual Obligations ('Rome II), COM(2003) 427 final of 22.7.2003; J. Basedow, *Perspektiven des Kartelldeliktsrechts* (2006) ZWeR 294 (299); Hamburg Group for Private International Law, *Comments on the European Commission's Draft Proposal for a Council Regulation on the Law Applicable to Non-Contractual Obligations* (2003) 67 RabelsZ 1 (18–19); D. Zimmer/A. Leopold, *Private Durchsetzung des Kartellrechts und der Vorschlag zur 'Rom II-VO* (2005) EWS 149.

IV. European harmonization of remedies in antitrust law?

The reform of European antitrust procedural law was justified, inter alia, on the grounds of strengthening the role of private enforcement in European antitrust law. It is, however, doubtful whether the aim can be achieved by Regulation 1/2003.[1] At any rate it seems unsatisfactory to call for strengthened private enforcement but to undertake no concrete measures to further this aim. Walter van Gerven has pointed out the necessity of supplementing the greater importance of national courts through special Community legislation on remedies. For this purpose he has presented the draft of a 'Regulation on the Substantive Law Aspects of Private Remedies before National Courts', which contains precise provisions, for example on nullity, restitution, compensation, interim relief and collective claims.[2] Such an initiative should be supported. Private enforcement in the field of antitrust law is still in its infancy even if in recent times an increase of activity in the direction is to be observed. If the aim of private enforcement is to be taken seriously the national courts must be given a more precisely defined role. Otherwise, the level of legal uncertainties due to the lack of experience is too high. The equivalence principle of the *Courage* decision has not really made for increase in certainty of application. True, the private law claims which result from the violation of European antitrust law may not lag behind what is awarded for a national law violation. As however, there is no body of court decisions worthy of mention, there is no gain for the application of European antitrust law.

Community law should therefore move forwards. It is true that it can regulate only the legal consequences of a Community law violation. The example it sets, however, will be so significant that Member States will harmonize the remedies for infringements of national antitrust law. The content of a European regulation will have to be discussed carefully. The discussion based on the Green Paper on private remedies for EC

[1] See above Part II A III 5. See generally J. Basedow, *Private Enforcement of Article 81 EC: A German View*, in Ehlermann/Atanasiu (eds.), *European Competition Law Annual 2001: Effective Private Enforcement of EC Antitrust Law* (2003), 137.

[2] W. van Gerven, *Substantive Remedies for the Private Enforcement of EC Antitrust Rules Before National Courts*, in Ehlermann/Atanasiu (eds.), *European Competition Law Annual 2001: Effective Private Enforcement of EC Antitrust Law* (2003); id., *Of Rights, Remedies and Procedures* (2000) 37 CMLR 501 et seq.

competition law violations[3] will lead to a comprehensive survey of the available options. Many details will be argued over, for example the topic of exemplary damages.[4] A European regulation taking into account the most important topics (standing, in particular of consumers and consumer protection associations; damages; disgorging of violator profits) could give private enforcement a decisive boost. In this way the promise with regard to private enforcement that was offered by Regulation 1/2003 would be fulfilled.

[3] European Commission, *Green Paper on Damages Actions for Breach of the EC Antitrust Rules*, 19.12.2005, COM(2005) 672 final.

[4] See above Part II D II 3 (a). W. van Gerven proposes exemplary damages for a case of intentional or reckless infringement.

V. Conclusion

This study has given an overview of law and practice of private enforcement of competition law in the reporting countries. Despite all the differences a common core emerges. A particular feature of the antitrust part of this study consists, however, in the way the common core relates more to theory than practical application. In all reporting countries private law claims in cases of antitrust infringements are admittedly recognized in theory. In practice, until now little use has been made of this. Certain descriptive and metalegal formants are responsible. In the first place the overwhelming importance of antitrust authorities in Europe has to be mentioned. Thus, administrative law has pushed private enforcement into the background. Very recently, however, a shift has become apparent. The logic of 'either/or' is being replaced by a more inclusive approach. The view is gaining acceptance that administrative and private law enforcement mechanisms each have their respective rationales and complement each other. Attorneys will rapidly adjust to the fact that there is demand for antitrust consultation not only on the respondent side, but also for the claimant. It is important that private law claims are so structured that appropriate legal enforcement is possible. In particular no artificial hurdles of standing or adducing evidence may be erected. As this study has shown changes in the operative rules, which will be necessary in individual countries, can be oriented towards regulatory models of other European states. An irony of the entire development consists in the fact that progress, which recently may be noted in private enforcement, was provoked by extraordinarily blatant hard-core cartels. It is to be hoped that the imposition of private law sanctions (possibly in addition to the administrative law sanctions) will lead to an ever stronger respect for antitrust law. The EU could make a significant contribution. As European antitrust law is a 'cornerstone' of the European edifice, community harmonization of private enforcement of European antitrust law seems an imminent possibility. In this way private antitrust law could be the pace setter for a European tort law. After decades of insignificance this would be a satisfactory result.

Outlook: the link between unfair competition law and antitrust law

According to a widely held view the legal nature of unfair competition law is more that of private law whereas antitrust law involves primarily public law enforcement mechanisms. The country reports have shown that, while this is an understandable starting point, it inadequately describes the wide variety of regulatory models in Europe. Regarding unfair competition law there is a rich body of private law experience. In the northern states, however, public law enforcement methods are preferred even in the field of unfair competition law. In many other countries there is a mixture of private law, public law and even criminal law enforcement. In antitrust law a pronounced dominance of administrative law enforcement is to be observed in practice. Nevertheless, the at least theoretical possibility of private enforcement is found everywhere, and this potential requires only to be given life. The question arises of the extent to which the rich body of private law experience in unfair competition can be usefully tapped for the field of antitrust law. Before concrete proposals can be made, it is necessary to explore the reasons, that is the question of why private law enforcement works so well for unfair competition in many European countries but by contrast almost not at all for antitrust law.

I. Reasons for the different weight of private enforcement in unfair competition and antitrust law

The following reasons are often cited: Cartels are mostly operated covertly, while unfair competition practices have direct and visible effects on the market. This results in differences in adducing evidence. While the proof of unfair competition is relatively easy (e.g.

presentation of the newspaper containing the unfair advertisements, witness statements from test purchasers, sending of unsolicited goods, etc.), the uncovering of a secret cartel, by contrast, is almost impossible for the private individual. This statement is certainly accurate for the case examples given here. In addition there is the antitrust law on abuse of market dominance. Determination of market dominance requires an identification of the relevant market, entailing in turn considerable expense and economic expertise. As a further step it must be investigated whether the enterprise concerned occupies a dominant position in the market. These questions basically require obtaining conclusive market information from the affected enterprises. However, while antitrust authorities have the necessary investigative power, private claimants in civil proceedings do not, with the exception of discovery rights under English law.

On the other hand there are many groups of cases in which with regard to adducing evidence there is no decisive difference between unfair competition law and antitrust law. Thus, in the law of unfair competition there are also secret measures which may be difficult to prove, e.g. the unfair headhunting of staff, or industrial espionage. On the other hand, there are numerous antitrust law violations which are open to public scrutiny, such as contractual clauses in contravention of antitrust law, refusal to supply, or price exploitation. The difficulties encountered here are not of adducing evidence, but rather of the legal assessment of the facts. This leads to the next presumption regarding the differences between unfair competition law and antitrust law, in that the legal assessment of a particular conduct is frequently more complicated in antitrust law than in unfair competition law. Under what conditions is a refusal to supply, for example, exceptionally unlawful? At what point does the price demanded by a market-dominant enterprise constitute an abuse? Even if complicated legal questions are raised, it cannot be overlooked that considerable difficulties also arise under unfair competition law, which result from the breadth of the general clauses applied and the continual development of new business methods.

Setting aside the difficulties of delimiting markets in antitrust law, the evidentiary problems in the relation of antitrust law and unfair competition law are not fundamentally but only gradually different. The varying practical significance of private enforcement in both fields can therefore not be fully explained in these terms alone. The deeper reason for the overwhelming practical significance of the administrative procedure in antitrust law is rather the historical tradition. Because in Europe – in contrast to the USA[1] – the prosecution of antitrust infringements was entrusted entirely to the public authorities and not at the same time to the private claimant, no private antitrust law culture has developed.[2]

II. Unfair competition law remedies as a model for antitrust law?

As the example of the USA amply shows there is no intrinsic necessity for restricting the enforcement of antitrust law exclusively to the administrative mode. Private claims are not only possible in antitrust law, but entirely desirable by virtue of the advantages of decentralized application. As private enforcement claims in the USA play such a significant role in practice, it seems appropriate to look to America when developing measures to strengthen private enforcement in Europe. This has been done repeatedly at appropriate points in this study. Apart from this, however, there is a second, far too neglected route. With unfair competition law there is a genuinely European body of experience which can be fruitfully tapped for the closely related field of antitrust law. The aim must accordingly be not only a transnational but also multi-disciplinary *circolazione dei modelli*.[3] Rules which have increased the attractiveness of private enforcement in the unfair competition law field must be explored with regard to their application in the antitrust law field. But also those regulatory instruments which have already been applied in unfair competition law without convincing results have their importance. The reasons for their failure must be investigated in order to learn whether such measures can be improved and then applied in antitrust law.

III. Examples

Numerous examples have been explored autonomously in an exclusively antitrust law context. Where regulations that have already been successfully applied in unfair competition law are concerned, or which

1 See. above D. Gerber Part II B.

2 This is supported by a partial result in connection with unfair competition law. In the Nordic countries competitor claims are rare, as the Ombudsman offers an alternative means of enforcement, See above Part I B. II. 4.

3 See. R. Sacco, *Introduzione al diritto comparato* (1997), p. 147 et seq.

are seen there as potential improvements, then there is an additional argument to apply such rules also under antitrust law.

1. *Standing of consumers*

The most important difference between unfair competition and antitrust law is that of standing. In most of the reporting countries (with the exception of England, Germany, Hungary and Poland) the individual consumer has his own claim against an unfair competition law violation,[4] while in antitrust law this is the exception. The reluctance in antitrust law is, among other reasons, based on the fear that standing for consumers could release a flood of litigation, as frequently large numbers of consumers are harmed by a cartel. The experience of unfair competition shows, on the other hand, that such litigation floods are not the reality.[5] The conclusion should be drawn for antitrust law to grant standing to the true injured party, that is the consumer.[6]

2. *Standing of consumer protection associations*

Since experience shows that consumers who are only marginally injured do not tend to take legal action against antitrust law violations, as a second step the consumer protection associations should be granted standing. While such a power is the exception in European antitrust law, it is customary in unfair competition law, sometimes even provided for by European secondary legislation.[7] The national reports on unfair competition law have however revealed that the practical effectiveness of claims by consumer protection associations is limited. The reasons for this are varied and differ considerably between the reporting nations. Reasons given include the limited experience with consumer protection associations, the importance of administrative means of enforcement, the poor financial situation of the associations, or the costs risk associated with a claim.[8] All these factors can be countered by appropriate measures. The most important consists in granting standing to consumer protection associations for not only cessation claims but also compensatory claims. Private procedures would then have the advantage – compared to administrative proceedings – that not only an interdiction of the anti-competitive conduct but also damages could be obtained. The poor financial situation of consumer protection associations is indeed a fundamental problem which must be addressed if their position is to be

[4] See above Part I B. II 5. [5] See above Part I B. II 6. [6] See above Part II D. II 2 (c).
[7] See above Part I B. II 2. [8] Ibid.

strengthened. However, this problem cannot be solved by the granting of compensatory claims as under the proposal made here the damages are to be awarded entirely to the actual injured party, that is the consumer,[9] although the consumer protection associations should definitely be granted a claim for recovery of costs where they successfully prosecute an antitrust claim.

IV. Future prospects

In most European countries the law of unfair competition and antitrust law have developed on entirely different lines. Although they both concern closely interrelated substantive areas,[10] the enforcement mechanisms are markedly different. To an extent in Europe there are administrative law enforcement mechanisms also in unfair competition. Here, unfair competition law gets very close to antitrust law, where enforcement by administrative authorities has until now been in the foreground. In the remaining countries enforcement of unfair competition law is carried out by private law means. Here the following connection can be observed, that if private law enforcement is relied upon, then there is a tendency to grant standing to several claimants so as to render a public authority redundant.[11] The idea may be reversed and then precisely describes enforcement of antitrust law until now. Where well-resourced public authorities are available for legal enforcement, the pool of claimants with standing for civil proceedings will be reduced and the requirements for a successful claim raised. If the aim is pursued of strengthening private enforcement for antitrust law as well, then the experience of unfair competition law has to be more closely followed. The necessary consequences – especially for standing – have just been drawn. In general the question may be posed whether in the long term private law remedies for violations of unfair competition law and of antitrust law should be fused. The present analysis indicates, however, how far there is to go before this can be achieved. As a first step more cautious measures should be sufficient. Nevertheless, the process of convergence begun here could one day lead to a comprehensive harmonization.

9 For criticism of profit disgorgement claims in favour of the state see above note 10.
10 Many modern legal orders in the world combine both fields of law in one statute.
11 Thus the German BGH, 17.1.2002, (2002) NJW 1494 (1495).

Bibliography

I. General

Arminjon, P., Nolde, B. and Wolff, M., *Traité de droit comparé*, 2 vols. (1950)

Ashurst (prepared by D. Waelbroeck, D. Slater and G. Even-Shoshan), *Study on the Conditions of Claims for Damages in Case of Infringement of EC Competition Rules* (2004)[1]

Bar, C. von, *Gemeineuropäisches Deliktsrecht*, 2 vols. (1996/1999)

Bastian, E., *Sanktionssysteme des unlauteren Wettbewerbs*, in G. Schricker/F. Henning-Bodewig (eds.), *Neuordnung des Wettbewerbsrechts* (1998/1999), p. 199

Behrens, P., *EC Competition Rules in National Courts* (1992–2001)

Beier, F., *Entwicklung und gegenwärtiger Stand des Wettbewerbsrechts in der Europäischen Wirtschaftsgemeinschaft* (1984) 32 GRUR Int. 61 (67), translated as: *The Law of Unfair Competition in the European Community its Development and Present Status* (1985) IIC 139

Bulst, F., *Schadensersatzansprüche der Marktgegenseite im Kartellrecht – Zur Schadensabwälzung nach deutschem, europäischem und US-amerikanischem Recht* (2006)

Bultmann, F., Howells, G., Keßler, J., Micklitz, H., Radeideh, M., Reich, N., Stucek, J. and Voigt, D., *The Feasibility of a General Legislative Framework on Fair Trading, Proposal for a General Legislative Framework on Fair Trading, Country reports etc.*, vol. 2 (2000)[2]

Bussani M. and Mattei, U., *The Common Core Approach to European Private Law*, 3 Colum.J.Eur.L. 339 (1997/98)

Bussani, M. and Palmer, V. (eds.), *Pure Economic Loss in Europe* (2003)

Cahill, D., Cooke, J.D. and Wils, W., *The Modernisation of EU Competition Law Enforcement in the European Union – FIDE 2004 National Reports* (Cambridge University Press 2004)

[1] Available at: http://ec.europa.eu/comm/competition/antitrust/others/actions_for_damages/study.html.

[2] Pre-publication version of November 2000, Study of the European Commission – Consumer Affairs (Da Sanco) – (still) unpublished; see www.europa.eu.int/comm/dgs/health_consumer/library/surveys/sur21_vol1_en.pdf. and www.europa.eu.int/comm/dgs/health_consumer/library/survey/sur21_vol2_en.pdf.

Dannecker, G. and Jansen, O. (eds.), *Competition Law Sanctioning in the European Union – The EU-Law Influence on the National Law System of Sanctions in the European Area* (2004)

David, R. and Grasmann, G., *Einführung in die großen Rechtssysteme der Gegenwart*, vol. 1 (2nd edn 1988)

Drexl, J., *Community Legislation Continued: Complete Harmonisation, Framework Legislation or Non-Bindung Measures – Alternative Approaches to European Contract law, Consumer Protection and Unfair Trade Practices* (2002) 6 European Business Law Review 557

Ehlermann, C.-D. and Atanasiu, I. (eds.), *European Competition Law Annual 2001: Effective Private Enforcement of EC Antitrust* (2003)

Ekey, F., Klippel, D., Kotthoff, J., Meckel, A. and Plaß, G., *Heidelberger Kommentar zum Wettbewerbsrecht* (2000)

Gerber, D., *Law and Competition in Twentieth Century Europe – Protecting Prometheus* (1998)

Glenn, P., *Comparative Law and Legal Practice, On Removing the Borders*, 75 Tulane L.Rev. 977 (2001)

Gordley, J. (ed.), *The Enforceability of Promises in European Contract Law* (2001)

Hempel, R., *Privater Rechtsschutz im Kartellrecht – eine rechtsvergleichende Analyse* (2002)

Joerges, C., *Nachmarktkontrollen im amerikanischen Recht*, in Micklitz, H. (ed.), *Post Market Control of Consumer Goods* (1990), p. 155

Joerges, C., Falke, J., Micklitz, M. and Brüggemeier, G., *Die Sicherheit von Konsumgütern und die Entwicklung der Europäischen Gemeinschaft* (1988)

Jones, Clifford, *Private Enforcement of Antitrust Law in the EU, UK and USA* (1999)

Karakostas, G., *Prostasia tu katanalote – N. 2251/1994* (1997)

Kötz, H., *Alte und neue Aufgaben der Rechtsvergleichung*, 57 JZ 257 (2002)

Kötz, H., *Rechtsvereinheitlichung – Nutzen, Kosten, Methoden, Ziele*, 50 RabelsZ 1 (1986)

Lang, C.G., *Die kartellzivilrechtlichen Ansprüche und ihre Durchsetzung nach dem schweizerischen Kartellgesetz* (2000)

Legrand, P., *Le droit comparé* (1999)

Lettl, T., *UWG* (2004)

Mattei, U., *An Opportunity Not to be Missed. The Future of Comparative Law*, 46 Am.J.Comp.L. 709 (1998)

Maxeiner, J. and Schotthöfer, P. (eds.), *Advertising Law in Europe and North America* (2nd edn 1999)

Micklitz, H. and Keßler, J. (eds.), *Marketing Practices Regulation and Consumer Protection in the EC Member States and the US* (2002)

Micklitz, H. and Keßler, J., *Europäisches Lauterkeitsrecht – Dogmatische und ökonomische Aspekte einer Harmonisierung des Wettbewerbsverhaltensrechts im europäischen Binnenmarkt* (2002) 50 GRUR Int. 885

Möllers, T., *Die Rolle des Rechts im Rahmen der europäischen Integration* (1999), translated as *Role of Law in European Integration* (2003)

Neuhaus, P. and Kropholler, J., *Rechtsvereinheitlichung – Rechtsverbesserung*, 45 RabelsZ 73 (1981)

Ogus, A., *Competition Between National Legal Systems. A Contribution of Economic Analysis to Comparative Law*, 48 Int.Comp.L.Q. 405 (1999)
Radeideh, M., *Fair Trading in EC Law* (2005)
Rittner, F., *Das Gemeinschaftsprivatrecht und die europäische Integration* (1995) 50 JZ 849
Sacco, R., *Legal Formants. A Dynamic Approach to Comparative Law*, 39 Am.J.Comp.L. 1 (1991)
Schricker, G. (ed.), *Recht der Werbung in Europa*, vol. 2 (Supp. 1995 et seq.)
Schulze, R. and Schulte-Nölke, H. (eds.), *Analysis of National Fairness Laws Aimed at Protecting Consumers in Relation to Precontractual Commercial Practices and the Handing of Consumer Complaints by Business* (2003)[3]
Stürner, R., *Die Rezeption U.S.-amerikanischen Rechts in der Bundesrepublik Deutschland*, in: FS Rebmann 839 (1989)
Wiegand, W., *The Reception of American Law in Europe*, 39 Am.J.Comp.L. 229 (1991)
Zimmermann, R. and Whittaker, S. (eds.), *Good Faith in European Contract Law* (2000)
Zweigert, K. and Kötz, H., *Einführung in die Rechtsvergleichung* (3rd edn. 1996), translated as *Introduction to Comparative Law* (3rd edn, 1998, translation by Weir, T.)

II. USA

Allen, A., *North Carolina Unfair Business Practice*, 3rd edn Supp. (2004)
Alperin, A. and Chase, R., *Consumer Law. Sales Practices and Credit Regulation*, vol. 2 (1986), Supp. 2004
American Law Institute (ed.), *Restatement (Third) of the Law of Unfair Competition* (1995)
Broder, D., *A Guide to US Antitrust Law* (2005)
Chaffee, Z., *Unfair Competition*, (1940) 53 Harv.L.Rev. 1289
Epstein, D. and Nickles, S., *Consumer Law in a Nutshell* (1981)
Fair, L., *Federal Trade Commission Advertising Enforcement*, in Edelstein, J. (ed.), *Advertising Law in the New Media Age* (2000), pp. 267–308.
Ginsburg, J., Litman, J., Goldberg, D. and Kevlin, M., *Trademark and Unfair Competition Law, Cases and Materials* (1996, Supp. 1998)
Greenfield, M., *Consumer Transactions* (4th edn 2003)
Handler, M., *Unfair Competition* (1936) 21 Iowa Law Review 175
Hovenkamp, H., *Federal Antitrust Policy: The Law of Competition and its Practice* (3rd edn 2005)
Kanwit, S., *Federal Trade Commission*, vol. 2 (Supp. 2003)
Kitch, E. and Perlman, H., *Intellectual Property and Unfair Competition* (5th edn 1998)

[3] Pre-publication version of June 18, 2003, Study of the European Commission – Consumer Affairs (Da Sanco), unpublished; see www.europa.eu.int/comm/consumer/cons_int/safe_shop/fair_bus_pract/green_paper_comm/studies/index_en.htm.

Levine, A., *NAD Case Reports Voluntary Self-Regulation of National Advertising*, in J. Edelstein (edn.), *Advertising Law in the New Media Age* (2000), p. 73
Maxeiner, J. and Kent, F., *United Staates*, in Maxeiner, J. and Schotthöfer, P. (eds.), *Advertising Law in Europe and North America* (2nd edn 1999) p. 513
McCarthy, J., *McCarthy on Trademarks and Unfair Competition*, vol. 6 (4th edn Supp. 2000)
McKenney, C. and Young, G., *Federal Unfair Competition: Lanham Act § 43 (a)* (1990)
McManis, C., *Intellectual Property and Unfair Competition in a Nutshell* (5th edn 2004)
Moore, R., Farrar, R. and Collins, E., *Advertising and Public Relations Law* (1998)
Oppenheim, S., Weston G. and McCarthy, J., *Federal Antitrust Laws* (4th edn 1981), p. 1100
Pattishall, B., Hilliard, D., and Welch, II, J., *Trademarks and Unfair Competition* (4th edn 2000)
Perlman, H., *The Restatement of the Law of Unfair Competition: A work in Progress*, (1990) 80 Trademark Rep. 461
Pitofsky, H., *Beyond Nader: Consumer Protection and the Regulation of Advertising* (1977) 90 Harv. L.Rev. 671 translated as: *Verbraucherschutz und Kontrolle der Werbung in den USA*, (1977) 25 GRUR Int. 304
Pound, R., *Law in Books and Law in Action*, (1910) 44 American Law Review 12
Pridgen, D., *Consumer Protection and the Law* (2003)
Ramsay, I., *Consumer Protection* (1989)
Sacks, L., *Unfair Competition Claims 2003: California Section 17200's Impact on Consumers & Businesses Everywhere* (2003)
Sheldon, J. and Carter, C., *Unfair and Deceptive Acts and Practices* (5th edn 2001; Supp. 2003)
Sheldon, J. and Zweibel, G, *Survey of Consumer Fraud*, by National Institute of Law Enforcement and Criminal Justice (1978)

III. Member States

Austria

AnwZ 1934, 43: *Gutachten des Ausschusses der Rechtsanwaltskammer Wien zum Entwurf einer Verordnung der Bundesregierung über Schiedsstellen für Wettbewerbsstreitigkeiten*
Auer, G. and Urlesberger, F., *Kartellrecht* (5th edn 2003)
Barfuss, W. and Auer, G., *Kartellrecht* (4th edn 1989)
Barfuss, W., Wollman, H. and Tahedl, R., *Österreichisches Kartellrecht* (1996)
Eilmansberger, T. in H.-G. Koppensteiner: *Österreichisches und Europäisches Wirtschaftsprivatrecht Teil6/1: Wettbewerbsrecht-Kartellrecht, Akademie der Wissenschaften* (1998)
Engel, A., *Austria*, in R. Schulze and H. Schulte-Nölke, 2.i)
Fitz, H. and Gamerith, H., *Wettbewerbsrecht* (4th edn 2003)

Gamerith, H., *Neue Herausforderungen für ein europäisches Lauterkeitsrecht*, Research paper on behalf of the Ministry for Economics and Labor (2nd edn 2003) 49 WRP 143
Gamerith, H., *Der Richtlinienvorschlag über unlautere Geschäftspraktiken – Möglichkeiten einer harmonischen Umsetzung* (2005) 51 WRP 391
Gamerith, H., *Wettbewerbsrechtliche Unterlassungsansprüche gegen Gehilfen*, WBl 1991, 305
Gschnitzer, F., *Klang-Kommentar, Band IV/1* (2nd edn 1968)
Gugerbauer, N., *Kommentar zum Kartellgesetz* (1989, 2nd edn 1994)
Hausmaninger, H., *The Austrian Legal System* (3rd edn 2003)
Hoffer, R. and Barbist, J., *Das neue Kartellrecht* (2005)
Kofler, S., *Österreich*, in Maxeiner, J. and Schotthöfer, P. (eds.), *Advertising Law in Europe and North America* (2nd edn 1999) p. 3
Koziol, H., *Haftpflichtrecht* (3rd edn 1997)
Koziol, H. and Welser, R., *Bürgerliches Recht, Band II* (12th edn 2001)
Koppensteiner, H., *Österreichisches und Europäisches Wettbewerbsrecht* (3rd edn 1997)
Kramer E.A. and Mayrhofer H., *Konsumentenschutz im Privat- und Wirtschaftsrecht* (1997)
Loacker, W., *Österreich*, in *Heidelberger Kommentar zum Wettbewerbsrecht* (2000)
Reich-Rohrwig, J. and Zehetner, J., *Kartellrecht I* (2000)
Rüffler, F., in Koppensteiner, H., *Österreichisches und europäisches Wirtschaftsrecht, Teil 6/2: Wettbewerbsrecht – UWG* (Akademie der Wissenschaften 1998)
Rummel, P., *ABGB* (3rd edn 2002/2003/2004)
Rummel, P., in Koziol, H., *Haftpflichtrecht* (2nd edn 1984)
Sack R., *Regierungsentwurf einer UWG-Novelle – Ausgewählte Probleme*, BB 2003, 1073
Schanda, R., *Markenschutzgesetz in der Fassung der Markenrechtsnovelle* (1999)
Stockenhuber, P., *Europäisches Kartellrecht* (1999)
Tahedl, R., *Der Missbrauch marktbeherrschender Stellung im österreichischen Kartellrecht* (1993)
Wiltschek, L., *UWG* (7th edn 2003)
Wiltschek, L. and Reitböck, G., *Wettbewerbs- und Markenrecht in Österreich* (2003) 49 WRP 785

Denmark

Borcher, E. and Bøggild, F., *Markedsføringsloven* (2001)
Bruun, E. et al., *Fogedsager* (2nd edn 2000)
Eyben, B. von, et al., *Karnovs lovssamling* (2001)
Eyben, B. von, et al., *Lærebog i Erstatningsret* (4th edn 1999)
Gomard, B., *Civilprocessen* (5th edn 2000)
Koktvedgaard, M., *Lærebog i Konkurrenceret* (4th edn 2000)
Kristoffersen, S. and Gravesen, K.V., *Forbrugerretten* (2001)
Kur, A. and Schovsbo, J., *Denmark*, in Schricker, G. (eds.), *Recht der Werbung in Europa* (Supp. 1999)

K. Levinsen, *Konkurrenceloven med kommentarer* (2001)
Madsen, P.B., *Markedsret*, vol. 2 (4th edn 2002)
P.B. Madsen, *Markedsret*, vol. 1 (4th edn 2000)
Vinding Kruse, A., *Erstatningsretten* (5th edn 1989)

England

Bellamy and Child, *European Community Law of Competition* (5th edn 2001)
Brömmekamp, B., *Die Pressefreiheit und ihre Grenzen in England und der Bundesrepublik Deutschland* (1997)
Coleman, M. and Grenfell, M., *The Competition Act 1998: Law and Practice* (1999)
Dobson, P., *Sale of Goods and Consumer Credit* (6th edn 2000)
Flynn, J. and Stratford, J., *Competition: Understanding the 1998 Act* (1999)
Freeman, P. and Whish, R., *Butterworths Competition Law* (5-vols., 2005)
Furse, M., *Competition and the Enterprise Act 2002* (2003)
Goyder, D., *EC Competition Law* (4th edn 2003)
Green, N. and Robertson, A., *The Europeanisation of UK Competition Law* (1999)
Harpwood, V., *Principles of Tort Law* (4th edn 2000)
Harvey, B. and Parry D., *The Law of Consumer Protection and Fair Trading* (6th edn 2000)
Jergolla, M., *Die britische Werbeselbstkontrolle anhand des Advertising Code – eine Gegenüberstellung mit der Rechtslage in Deutschland* (2003) 49 WRP p. 431
Jergolla, M., *Der neue British Code of Advertising, Sales Promotion and Direct Marketing* (2003) 49 WRP p. 606
Jones, A., *Restitution and European Community Law* (2000)
Jones, A. and Sufrin, B., *EC Competition Law* (2nd edn 2004)
Jones, M., *Torts* (7th edn 2000)
Kerse, C. and Khan, N., *EC Anti-trust Procedure* (5th edn 2005)
Macleod, J., *Consumer Sales Law* (2002)
Micklitz, H.-W. and Rott, P., *Richtlinie 98/27/EG*, in Grabitz, E., Hilf, M. and Wolf, M. (eds.), *Das Recht der Europäischen Union* (supp. 2005)
Miller, C., Harvey, B. and Parry, D., *Consumer and Trading Law* (1998)
Obermair, S., *Der Schutz des Verbrauchers vor unlauterer Werbung in Deutschland und Großbritannien* (2004)
Ohly, A., *Richterrecht und Generalklausel im Recht des unlauteren Wettbewerbs* (1997)
Oughton, D. and Lowry, J., *Textbook on Consumer Law* (2nd edn 2000)
Parry, D., *Product Quality and the Criminal Law* (2002) 25 JCP p. 439
Ramsay, I., *Consumer Protection* (1989)
Rodger, B. and MacCulloch, A., *The UK Competition Act: A New Era for UK Competition Law* (2000)
Rott, P., *The Protection of Consumers' Interests after the Implementation of the EC Injunctions Directive into German and English Law* (2001) 24 JCP p. 401
Scott, C. and Black, J., *Cranston's Consumer and the Law* (3rd edn 2000)
Torremans, P., *Holyoak and Torremans Intellectual Property Law* (3rd edn 2001)

Ward, T. and Smith, K., *Competition Litigation in the UK* (2005)
Whish, R., *Competition Law* (5th edn 2004)

Finland

Aalto-Setälä, I., Aine, A., Lehto, P., Petäjäniemi, B.A., Stenborg, M. and Virtanen, P., *Kilpailulait ja laki julkisista hankinnoista* (2003)
Aine, A., *Suomen kilpailulainsäädännön mukainen pätemättömyysseuraus* (1999), p. 60, ref. to as *A. Aine 1999a*
Aine, A., *Kilpailunrajoituksella aiheutetun vahingon korvaaminen* (1999), p. 799, ref. to as *A. Aine 1999b*
Aine, A., *Kilpailulainsäädännön vaikutus sopimusten pätevyyteen, toinen, uudistettu painos* (2000), ref. to as *A. Aine 2000*
Kuoppamäki, P., *Kilpailuoikeuden perusteet* (2000), ref. to as *P. Kuoppamäki 2000*
Kuoppamäki, P., *Markkinavoiman sääntely EY:n ja Suomen kilpailuoikeudessa* (2003), ref. to as *P. Kuoppamäki 2003*
Lappalainen, J., *Suomen siviiliprosessioikeus I* (1995), ref. to as *J. Lappalainen 1995*
Lappalainen, J., *Suomen siviiliprosessioikeus II* (2001), ref. to as *J. Lappalainen 2001*
Mentula, A., *Kartellit Suomen ja EY:n kilpailuoikeudessa* (2002)
Pöyhönen, J. (ed.), *An Introduction to Finnish Law* (2002)
Rissanen, Kirsti – Korah, V., *EY:n ja Suomen kilpailuoikeus* (1991)
Tirkkonen, T., *Suomen siviiliprosessioikeus I* (1974)
Virtanen, P., *Määräävän markkina-aseman kontrollointi* (2001)
Wilhelmsson, T., *Konsumentskyddet i Finland* (1989)

Preparatory Documents:

HE 162/1991 vp, *Hallituksen esitys Eduskunnalle laiksi kilpailunrajoituksista*
HE 243/1997 vp, *Hallituksen esitys Eduskunnalle kilpailunrajoituksista annetun lain ja eräiden siihen liittyvien lakien muuttamisesta*
HE 11/2004 vp, *Hallituksen esitys Eduskunnalle laeiksi kilpailunrajoituksista annetun lain ja eräiden siihen liittyvien lakien muuttamisesta.*

France

Calais-Auloy, J. and Steinmetz, F., *Droit de la Consommation* (5th edn 2000)
Guyon, Y., *Droit des affaires*, vol. 2 (11th edn 2001)
Malaurie-Vignal, M., *Droit de la concurrence* (2nd edn 2003)
Pizzio, J.-P., *Code de la consommation commenté* (1995)
Ripert, G. and Roblot, R., under the direction of Germain, M., by Vogel, L., *Traité de droit commercial*, vol. 1 (18th edn 2001)

Manuals and Treatises:

Arhel, P., *La pratique des accords de distribution* (2nd edn 2000), éditions EFE (éd. Formation entreprise)

Azéma, J., *Droit de la concurrence* (2nd edn 2002), éditions Thémis
Blaise, J.-B., *Droit des affaires, Commerçants, concurrence et distribution* (2nd edn 2000), éditions LGDJ, coll. Manuel
Burst, J.-J. and Kovar, R., *Droit de la concurrence* (1981), éditions Economica
Decocq, A. and G., *Droit de la concurrence* (2002), éditions LGDJ coll. Manuel
Ferrier, D., *Droit de la distribution* (2nd edn 2000), éditions Litec
Cl. Lucas de Leyssac and Parléani, G., *Droit du marché* (2002), éditions PUF
Pédamon, M., *Droit commercial* (2nd edn 2000), éditions Dalloy, Précis
Pizzio, J.-P., and Lambert-Badouin, J., *Droit du marché* (1993), éditions Dalloz, coll. Droit usuel
Sélinsky, V. and Mousserons, J.M., *Le droit français nouveau de la concurrence* (1988), éditions Litec, coll. Act. De droit de l'entreprise.

Encyclopedias:

Cas, G. and Bout, R., by Bout, R., Bruschi, M., Poillot-Peruzzetto, Luby, M., *Lamy droit économique Juris-Classeur Concurrence, Consommation*
Répertoire Dalloz de droit commercial
Dictionnaire permanent de droit des affaires, éd. Législatives
Mémento Concurrence - consommation, F. Lefebvre

Germany

Basedow, J., Hopt, K., Kötz, H. and Baetge, D. (eds.), *Die Bündelung gleichgerichteter Interessen im Prozess* (1999)
Bastian, E., *Sanktionssysteme im Recht des unlauteren Wettbewerb*, in Schricker, G. and Henning-Bodewig, F., *Neuordnung des Wettbewerbsrecht* (1999), p. 199
Baumbach, A. and Hefermehl, W., *Wettbewerbsrecht* (22nd edn 2001)
Baumbach, A. and Hefermehl, W., by Köhler, H. and Bornekamm, J., *Wettbewerbsrecht* (23rd edn 2004)
Beater, A., *Unlauterer Wettbewerb* (2002)
Bechtold, R., *GWB* (3rd edn 2002)
Berlit, W., *Wettbewerbsrecht anhand ausgewählter Rechtsprechung* (3rd edn 1998)
Brandmair, L., *Die freiwillige Selbstkontrolle der Werbung* (1978)
Bundeskartellamt, *Private Kartellrechtsdurchsetzung - Stand, Probleme, Perspektiven* (2005), available at: http://www.bundeskartellamt.de/wDeutsch/download/pdf/Diskussionsbeitraege/050926Proftag.pdf
Bunte, H.-J., *Kartellrecht* (2003)
Emmerich, V., *Kartellrecht* (9th edn 2001)
Emmerich V., *Das Recht des unlauteren Wettbewerbs* (6th edn 2002)
Emmerich, V., *Unlauterer Wettbewerb*, in 50 Jahres BGH, Bd. 2, 2000, p. 627
Falckenstein, R. von, *Die Bekämpfung unlauterer Geschäftspraktiken durch Verbraucherverbände* (1977)
Fezer, K. H., *Lauterkeitsrecht* (2005)
Fikentscher, W., *Wirtschaftsrecht*, 2 vols. (1983)

Fritsche, J., *Unterlassungsanspruch und Unterlassungsklage* (2000)
Gamm, O.-F. Frhr. von, *Kartellrecht – Kommentar zum Gesetz gegen Wettbewerbsbeschränkungen und zu Art.85, 86 EWGV* (2nd edn 1990)
Gamm, O. von, *Wettbewerbsrecht*, 2 vols. (5th edn 1987)
Gassner, U.M., *Grundzüge des Kartellrechts* (1999)
Glassen, H. et al. (eds.), *Frankfurter Kommentar zum Kartellrecht* (loose-leaf edition)
Gloy, W. and Loschelder, M. (eds.), *Handbuch des Wettbewerbsrecht* (3rd edn 2005)
Harte-Bavendamm, H. and Henning-Bodewig, F. (eds.), *UWG* (2004)
Hippel, E. von, *Verbraucherschutz* (1974)
Immenga, U./Mestmäcker, E.-J. (eds.), *EG Wettbewerbsrecht*, 2 vols. (1997)
Immenga, Ulrich, Mestmäcker, Ernst-Joachim (eds.), *Gesetz gegen Wettbewerbsbeschränkungen* (3rd edn 2001)
Jacobs, R., Lindacher W. and Teplitzky, O. (eds.), *UWG Großkommentar* (supp. 1991 et seq.)
Keßler, J. and Micklitz, H., *Die Harmonisierung des Lauterkeitsrechts in den Mitgliedstaaten der Europäischen Gemeinschaft und die Reform des UWG* (2003)
Kisseler, M., *Die Werbeselbstkontrolle in Deutschland*, in Festschrift H. Piper (1996), p. 283
Kling, M. and Thomas, S., *Grundkurs Wettbewerbs- und Kartellrecht* (2004)
Köhler, H. and Piper, H., *UWG* (3rd edn 2002)
Langen, Eugen and Bunte, Hermann-Josef, *Kommentar zum deutschen und europäischen Kartellrecht*, (10th edn 2004)
Lettl, T., *Kartellrecht* (2005)
Loewenheim, U., Meessen, K., Riesenkampff, A. (eds.), *Kartellrecht, Band 1 – Europäisches Recht* (2005)
Mestmäcker, E.-J. and Schweitzer, H., *Europäisches Wettbewerbsrecht* (2nd edn 2004)
Monopolkommission, *Das allgemeine Wettbewerbsrecht in der 7. GWB-Novelle*, Sondergutachten (2004)[4]
Möschel, Wernhard, *Recht der Wettbewerbsbeschränkung* (1983)
Müller-Henneberg et al. (eds.), *Gemeinschaftskommentar* (5th edn 1999)
Nieder, M., *Außergerichtliche Konfliktlösung im gewerblichen Rechtsschutz* (1999)
Nordemann, Wilhelm, Nordemann, Axel and Nordemann, Jan, *Wettbewerbs- und Markenrecht* (9th edn 2003)
Pastor, W. and Ahrens, H., *Der Wettbewerbsprozeß* (4th edn 1999)
Piper, H., *Zur wettbewerbsrechtlichen Beurteilung von Werbeanzeigen und redaktionellen Beiträgen werbenden Inhalts insbesondere in der Rechtsprechung des Bundsgerichtshofs*, in Festschrift R. Vieregge (1995), p. 717
Proband, M., *Die Einigungsstelle nach § 27a UWG* (1993)
Rittner, Fritz, *Wettbewerbs- und Kartellrecht* (6th edn 1999)
Schmidt, I., *Wettbewerbspolitik und Kartellrecht* (8th edn 2005)
Schwintowski, H.-P., *Wettbewerbsrecht (GWB/UWG)* (3rd edn 1999)
Teplitzky, O., *Wettbewerbsrechtliche Ansprüche und Verfahren* (8th edn 2002)

[4] www.monopolkommission.de/sg_41/text_s41.pdf.

Wallenberg, G. von, *Kartellrecht* (2nd edn 2002)
Wiedemann, G., *Handbuch des Kartellrechts* (1999)

Greece

Alexandridou, E., *Consumer Protection Law*, vol. 2 (1996)
Antonopoulos, V., *Industrial Property Law* (2002)
Gazetas, K., *Misleading Advertisement* (2002)
Georgiades A.-Stathopoulos M. (ed.), The Civil Code, Article by Article Commentary, vol.II (1979), III (1980), IV (1982)
Karakostas, Y. and Tzouganatos, D., *Consumer Protection: the Law 2251/1994*, 2nd edn (2003)
Kerameus K. and Kozyris Ph., *Introduction to Greek Law*, 2nd edn (1993)
Kerameus K., Kondilis D. G. and Nikas NT, *Code of Civil Procedure, Article-by-Article Commentary*, vol. 2, (2000)
Kotsiris, L., *Unfair Competition and Antitrust Law*, 4th edn (2001)
Koussoulis, S., *Arbitration, Article-by-Article Commentary* (2004)
Liakopoulos, A., *The Economic Freedom as Subject of Protection in Antitrust Law* (1981)
Liakopoulos, A., *Industrial Property*, 5th edn (2000)
Marinos, M.-Th., *Unfair Competition* (2002)
Panayotidou, E., *Comparative Advertisement* (2000)
Papanikolaou P. A.-Roussos Kl., *The New Law of the Seller's Liability* (2003)
Perakis, E., *General Commercial Law* (1999)
Pouliadis A., *Consumers Associations and the Collective Action* (1988)
Rokas N. and Perakis E., *World Law of Competition (Greece)*, Matthew Bender, New York (1983)
Rokas, N. (ed.), *Unfair Competition* (1996)
Rokas, N., *Industrial Property* (2004)
Schinas, I (ed.), *Antitrust Law* (1992)
Stathopoulos, M., *General Law of Obligations*, 4th edn (2004)
Tzouganatos, D., *Exclusive and Selective Distribution Agreements* (2001)

Hungary

Bakardjieva-Engelbrekt, A., *International Treaty Obligations and Legal Developments in Central and Eastern Europe, Towards a Harmonised View on Fair Trading in Europe, Report of the Conference 'Towards a Harmonised View on Fair trading in Europe' held in Stockholm 9–10 March* (2001) p. 19
Boytha, Györgyné, *Competition Act: Act No. LVII of 1996 on the Prohibition of Unfair and Restrictive Market Practices paragraphs 33–9*, in Boytha, Györgyné, Bodócsi, A., Kaszainé Mezey Katalin, Nagy, Z., Pázmándi, K. Vörös, I. and Sárközy, T. (eds.): *Versenyjog, HVG-ORAC, 2001*, p. 228
Boytha, Györgyné, *Versenyjogi ismeretek, Budapest: Szent István Társulat* (1998)
Csépai, B. and Remetei Filep, Á., *Hazai versenyjogunk történeti perspektívában, Jogi Melléklet*, (2001) 6 p. 81

Cseres, K., The *Hungarian Cocktail of Competition Law and Consumer Protection: Should it be Dissolved?* (2004) JCP p. 43

Cseres, K.J., *Competition Law and Consumer Protection*, European Monographs (2005)

Darázs, L., *A honi versenyjog általános kérdései, Cégvezetés* (1995), p. 54

Dietz, A., *Überblick über die Entwicklung des Wettbewerbsrechts in den (ehemals sozialistischen) Ländern Mittel- und Osteuropas*, *in*: Beier, F.K., Bastian, E.M. and Kur, A. (eds.), *Wettbewerbsrecht und Verbraucherschutz in Mittel- und Osteuropa* (1992), p. 179

European Commission, *Regular Report from the Commission on Hungary's progress towards accession* (1998)[5]

Explanatory Memorandum of Act No. LVII of 1996 on the Prohibition of Unfair and Restrictive Market Practices, CD Jogtár 2000, KJK Kerszöv

Fazekas, J., *Fogyasztóvédelmi jog, Miskolc: Novotni Kiadó* (2001)

Freshfields Bruckhaus Deringer, *Recent Changes in Hungarian Competition Law* (October 2005)

Fritsch, M. and Hansen, H. (eds.), *Rules of Competition and East-West Integration* (1997)

Gazdasági Versenyhivatal, *Beszámoló az Országgyűlés részére a Gazdasági Versenyhivatal 1998.évi tevékenységéről* (1999)

Gazdasági Versenyhivatal, *Beszámoló az Országgyűlés részére a Gazdasági Versenyhivatal 2000.évi tevékenységéről* (2001)[6]

Gazdasági Versenyhivatal, *Beszámoló az Országgyűlés számára, a Gazdasági Versenyhivatal 2001. évi tevékenységéről és a versenytörvény alkalmazása során szerzett, a verseny tisztaságának és szabadságának érvényesülésével kapcsolatos tapasztalatokról* (2002)[7]

Kajdiné Suhajda, Zs. Kardos L., *Reklámjogi és reklámetikai kézikönyv* (1998)

Kajdiné Suhajda., Zs., *Development of the Consumer Protection – Related Legislation in Hungary, Conference on Consumer Protection and Market Surveillance 2000*, Budapest, 23–24 February, 2000, Abstracts of the papers, p. 166

Kaszainé Mezey, K. and Miskolczi Bodnár, P., *Versenyjogi Kézikönyv* (1997)

Kaszainé Mezey, K., *Competition Act: Act No. LVII of 1996 on the Prohibition of Unfair and Restrictive Market Practices*, paragraphs 1–10, in Boytha Györgyné, Bodócsi, A., Kaszainé Mezey Katalin, Nagy, Z., Pázmándi, K., Vörös, I. and Sárközy T. (eds.), Versenyjog, HVG-ORAC (2001), p. 49

Kováts, S., *Certain Issues of Vertical Restrictions in the European Union and in Hungary* (1999)[8]

Kozminski, A.K., *Consumers in Transition from the Centrally Planned Economy to Market Economy*, (1991) 14 JCP, p. 351

Kulcsár, A., *A versenytörvény hatálya kiterjed az államra is, Magyar Hírlap* (21.05.) (2001)[9]

NACP (2000a) *Report on the Activities of the NACP between 1997–2000*[10]

[5] europa.eu.int/comm/enlargement/report_11_98/pdf/en/hungary_en.pdf.
[6] www.gvh.hu/index.php?id=105&l=h.
[7] www.gvh.hu/data/pdf/ob2001_vegleges%20teljes%2002%2009%2023.pdf.
[8] www.gvh.hu/index.php?id=2549&l=h.
[9] www.magyarhirlap.hu/Archivumindex.php3?cikk=10000003165&next=0&archi. . ., p. 1.
[10] www.ofe.hu/szerv/bszm2.htm.

NACP (2000b) *Report on the Activities of the NACP in 2000*[11]
Németh, G., *A tisztességtelen piaci magatartás és versenykorlátozás tilalma, Gazdaság és Gazdálkodás*, 11. szám (1996), p. 23
Ojala, M., *The Competition Law of Central and Eastern Europe* (1999)
Office of Economic Competition, *The Competition Policy Position of the Office of Economic Competition – the Key Competition Issues of Large Scale Retail Trade*, (2000) Competition Office Bulletin No.3
OECD, *OECD háttérjelentés a versenypolitika szerepéről a szabályozási reformban Magyarországon* (Background report on the role of competition policy in the regulatory reform), Versenyhivatali füzetek 4.szám, Gazdasági Versenyhivatal (2001)[12]
Pázmándi, K., *Act LVIII of 1997 on Business Advertising Activity* in Boytha Györgyné, Bodócsi, A. Kaszainé Mezey, K., Nagy, Z., Pázmándi, K., Vörös, I. and Sárközy, T. (eds.), *Versenyjog, HVG-ORAC* (2001), p. 502
Ritter, T., *Fogyasztói érdekek érvényesülése a fogyasztási szolgáltatásokban* (1999)[13]
Sárközy, T., *A magyar versenyjog fejlesztéséről, Állam és Jogtudomány*, XXXVI. Évfolyam 1994, (1994) p. 37
Tevan, I., *Titkos szolgák, Heti Világ Gazdaság, 1999.szeptember 18* (1999), p. 134
Várady, T., *The Emergence of Competition Law in the (Former) Socialist Countries*, (1999) 47 The American Journal of Comparative Law, p. 229
Vörös, I., *Länderberichte: Ungarn*, in Beier, F.K., Bastian, E.M. and Kur, E.M. (eds.), *Wettbewerbsrecht und Verbraucherschutz in Mittel- und Osteuropa* (1992), p. 160

Ireland

Consumer Strategy Group Report *Make Consumers Count: A New Direction for Irish Consumers*, April 2005[14]
Doherty B., *EC Competition Law before the Irish Courts. The first 25 years*, (1999) 20 European Competition Law Review p. 78
Forde, M., *Commercial Law* (2nd edn 1997)
Goggin I., *Irish and EU Competition Law*, 13 May 2002[15]
Heusel, W. (ed.), *Community Law in Practice: Including Facets of Consumer Protection Law*, Irish Centre for European Law (2004)
Lucey, M., *The Competition Act 2002* (2003)
Maher, I., *Competition Law Alignment and Reform* (1999)
Massey, P. and O'Hare, P., *Competition Law and Policy in Ireland* (1996)
McMahon and Binchy, W., *Irish Law of Torts* (3rd edn 2000)
O'Connor, T., *Competition Law Source Book*, 2 vols. (1996)
O'Reilly, P., *Commercial and Consumer Law* (2000)
Power, V., *Competition Law and Practice* (2001)
Quill, E., *Torts in Ireland* (2nd edn 2004)

11 www.ofe.hu/szerv/bszm3.htm. 12 www.gvh.hu/index.php?id=168&l=h.
13 www.ofe.hu/elemzesek/fogyszolg.htm.
14 www.ireland.com/newspaper/special/2005/consumer/csg.pdf.
15 www.tca.ie/speeches/lawsoc.pdf.

Global Competition Review: *Private Antitrust Litigation 2005* (2004)
Global Competition Review: *The European Antitrust Review 2005* (2004)

Italy

AA.VV., *Antitrust between EC Law and National Law/Antitrust fra diritto nazionale e diritto comunitario, IV Conference* (Treviso, 13–14 May 1999) (2000)
Ariani, N., Cottino, G. and Ricolfi, M., *Il diritto industriale*, in Tratt. dir. comm. diretto da Cottino (2001)
Ascarelli, T., *Tutela della concorrenza e dei beni immateriali* (3rd edn 1960)
Auteri P., *La concorrenza sleale*, in Tratt. dir. priv. diretto da P. Rescigno, XVIII (1983)
Auteri, A., *I poteri dell'Autorità Garante in materia di pubblicità ingannevole e comparativa*, in (2002) Riv. dir. ind. I, p. 265
Stefano Bastianon, *L'abuso di posizione dominante*, in *Il diritto privato oggi* (2001)
Giampaolo Dalle Vedove, *Concentrazioni e gruppi nel diritto antitrust* (1999)
Lorenzo Delli Priscoli, *Le restrizioni verticali della concorrenza*, in *Quaderni di giurisprudenza commerciale 239* (2002)
Fusi, M. and Testa, P., *Diritto e pubblicità* (1996)
Fusi, M. and Testa, P., *L'autodisciplina pubblicitaria in Italia* (1963)
Fusi, M., Testa, P., and Cottafavi, V., *La pubblicità ingannevole* (1996)
Ghidini, G., *Introduzione allo studio della pubblicità commerciale* (1968)
Ghidini, G., *Della concorrenza sleale*, in *Il codice civile. Commentario diretto da P. Schlesinger* (1991)
Ghidini, G., Libertini, M. and Volpe Putzolu, G., *La concorrenza e i consorsi*, in (1981) Tratt. dir. comm. e dir. pubbl. economia diretto da F. Galgano, IV
Gianvito Giannelli, *Impresa pubblica e privata nella legge* antitrust (2001)
Guglielmetti, G., *La concorrenza e i consorzi*, in Tratt. dir. civ. it. diretto da F. Vassalli, X, 1, 2 (1970)
Käser, C., *Effizienz des Rechtsschutzes im deutschen und italienischen Wettbewerbsrecht* (2003)
Marchetti, P. and Ubertazzi, L.C., *Commentario breve al diritto della concorrenza* (1997)
Meli, V., *La repressione della pubblicità ingannevole* (1994)
Meli V., *I rimedi per la violazione del divieto di pubblicità ingannevole*, in (2000) *Riv. dir. ind.*, I, p. 6
Minervini, G., *Concorrenza e consorzi*, in Tratt. dir. civ. diretto da G. Grosso e F. Santoro Passatelli (2nd edn 1965)
Vito Mangini-Gustavo Olivieri, *Diritto antitrust* (2000)
Rossi, G., *La pubblicità dannosa. Concorrenza sleale, 'diritto a non essere ingannati', diritti della personalità* (2000)

Netherlands

Asser, C. and Hartkamp, A.S. (bew door), *Verbintenissenrecht: De verbintenis in het algemeen* (12th edn 2004)

Dekker, C.T., *Nederlands mededingingsprocesrecht: besluitvormingsprocedures en rechtsbescherming in het kader van de Mededingingswet* (2002)
Hidma, T. R. and Rutgers, G. R., *Het Nederlands burgerlijk recht: bewijs*, (8th edn 2004)
Mok, M.R., *Kartelrecht I: Nederland: De mededingingswet* (5th edn 2004)
Nieuwenhuis, J.H. (ed.), Stolker, C.J.J.M., Valk, W.L., et al., *Burgerlijk wetboek: tekst en commentaar: de tekst van de Boeken 5, 6, 7, en 8 van het BW voorzien van commentaar* (5th edn 2003)
Slot, P.J. Van Reeken, B.L.P. and Drion, C.E., *Mededingingswet: Tekst en Commentaar* (2000)
Stolker C.J.J.M (ed.), *Onrechtmatige Daad* (loose-leaf edn)
Van Gerven, W., Gyselen. L., Maresceau, M. and Stuyck, J., *Kartelrecht II: Europese Gemeenschap* (2nd edn 1997)
Verkade, D.W.F., *Ongeoorloofde mededinging* (3rd edn 1986)
Verkade, D.W.F., *Misleidende reclame* (1992)

Poland

Czachorski, W., *System prawa cywilnego t3* (1981)
DuVall, M., *Dochodzenie roszczen w sprawach o zwalczanie nieuczciwej konkurencji*, in Szymanek, T. (ed.), *Naruszenie praw na dobrach niematerialnych* (2001)
Emmerich V., *Prawo antymonopolowe*, w: *Prawo gospodarcze Unii Europejskiej* Skubisz R. (red wydania polskiego) (1999)
Gornicki, L., *Nieuczciwa konkurencja, w szczegolnosci przez wprowadzajace w blad oznaczenie towarow i uslug, i srodki ochrony w prawie polskim* (1997)
Knypl, T., *Zwalczanie nieuczciwej konkurencji w Polsce i Europie* (1995)
Kraus, A. and Zoll, F., *Polska ustawa o zwalczaniu nieuczciwej konkurencji* (1929) after Nowinska, E. and Du Vall, M., *Komentarz do ustawy o zwalczaniu nieuczciwej konkurencji* (2001)
Letowska, E., *Bezpodstawne wzbogacenie* (2000)
Modzelewska-Wachal E., *Ustawa o ochronie konkurencji i konsumentow. Komentarz*, Warszawa 2002,
Pozniak-Niedzielska, M., *Przeslanka wprowdzenia w blad jako podstawa odpowiedzialnosci z tytulu nieuczciwej konkurencji. Studia Prawa Prywatnego* (1997)
Skubisz, R., *Prawo znakow towarowych. Komentarz* (1997)
Sobczak, J., *Ustawa prawo prasowe. Komentarz* (1999)
Solarz, J., *Ekonomiczne uwarunkowania reklamy* (1995)
Szwaja, J. (ed.), *Ustawa o zwalczaniu nieuczciwej konkurencji, Komentarz* (2000)

Portugal

Ascensão, J., *Concorrência Desleal* (2002)
Ascensão, J., *Direito industrial/APDI* (2001)
Cordeiro, A., *Tratado de Direito Civil Português*, I, Parte Geral (2nd edn 2000)
Ferreira, E.P., *Lições de Direito da Economia*, AAFDL (Lisboa 2001)

Leitão, A., *Imitação servil, concorrência parasitária e concorrência desleal*, in Direito Industrial/APDI (2001)

Leitão, A., *Estudo de Direito Privado sobre a Cláusula Geral de Concorrência Desleal* (2000)

Leitão, A., *Estudo sobre os interesses protegidos e a legitimidade na concorrência desleal*, Revista da Faculdade de Direito da Universidade de Lisboa, vol. XXXYII (1996)

Leitão, L., *Direito das Obrigações*, vol. I, Introdução, Constituição das Obrigações (2nd edn 2002)

Leitão, L., *O enriquecimento sem causa no direito civil português*, CEF (1996)

Möllering, J., *Das Recht des unlauteren Wettbewerbs in Portugal* (1991) 37 WRP p. 634

Olavo, C., *Propriedade Industrial* (1997)

Palma, A. F., *Das Pequenas e Médias Empresas (maxime, no direito da Concorrência)* (2001)

Paz-Ares, C. and Aguila-Real, J., *Ensayo sobre la libertad de empresa*, publicado en el libro Estudios homenaje a L. Diez-Picazo, vol. IV (2003), p. 5971

Pego, J. P. F. M., A *posição dominante relativa no direito da concorrência*, (2001)

Santana, Carlos Alberto Caboz, *O abuso da posição dominante no direito da concorrência*, (1995)

Santos, A. C., Gonçalves, M. E. et al., *Direito Económico* (4th edn 2001)

Schricker, G., *Einführung in das portugiesische Recht des unlauteren Wettbewerbs* (1994) 42 GRUR Int. 819

Serens, M. N. and Maia, P., *Legislação comunitária e nacional de defesa da concorrência*

Silva, P., *Meios de reacção civil à concorrência desleal*, in Concorrência Desleal (1997), p. 116

Spain

Alfaro Aguila-Real, J., *Competencia desleal por infracción de normas* (1991) 202, Revista de Derecho Mercantil, p. 667

Baño León, J.M., *Potestades administrativas y garantías de las empresas en el derecho español de la competencia* (1996)

Bercovitz, Alberto, *Apuntes de derecho mercantil derecho mercantil, derecho de la competencia y propiedad industrial* (2003)

Berg, A., *Das spanische Recht gegen den unlauteren Wettbewerb* (1998)

Cases Pallarés, L., *Derecho administrativo de la defensa de la competencia* (1995)

Díez Estella, F., *La discriminación de precios en el derecho de competencia* (2003)

Fernández-Lerga Garralda, C., *Derecho de la competencia Comunidad Europea y España* (1994)

Freyer, H., *Das neue spanische Gesetz gegen den unlauteren Wettbewerb* (1991) 92 ZVglRWiss p. 96

Gonzalez-Varas Ibañez, S., *La aplicación del derecho de la competencia a los colegios profesionales* (1997)

González-Varas Ibáñez, S., *Los mercados de interés general telecomunicaciones y postales, energéticos y de transportes (privatización, liberalización, regulación pública y derecho de la competencia)* (2001)
Kieninger, E., *Die Verbandsklage in Spanien*, in Basedow, J., Hopt, K., Kötz, H. and Baetge, D. (eds.), *Die Bündelung gleichgerichteter Interessen im Prozeß* (1999) p. 253
Massaguer Fuentes, J., *Comentario a la ley de competencia desleal* (1999)
Menéndez, A., *La competencia desleal* (1988)
Nordemann, W., *Das neue spanische Werbegesetz im Vergleich zum deutschen Werberecht*, in Festschrift für von Gamm, O. (1990), p. 109
Ortells Ramos, M., *Las medidas cautelares en derecho de la competencia La práctica del Tribunal de Defensa de la Competencia y de los Tribunales civiles* (1999)
Ortiz Blanco, L., *Derecho de la competencia europeo y español curso de iniciación* (2002)
Paz-Ares, C. and Alfaro Aguila-Real, J., *Ensayo sobre la libertad de empresa*, publicado en el libro Estudios homenaje a Luis Diez-Picazo, vol. IV (2003) p. 971
Soriano, J.E., *Derecho público de la competencia* (1998)
Tato Plaza, A., *Das neue System zur Selbstkontrolle der Werbung in Spanien* (1999) 47 GRUR Int. p. 853
Väzquez Albert, D., *Derecho de la competencia y ejercicio de las profesiones* (2002)
Wirt, A., *Die Werbeselbstkontrolle in Spanien* (1993) 39 WRP p. 94

Sweden

Bernitz, U., *Marknadsföringslagen* (1997)
Bernitz, U., *Das neue schwedische Marktgesetz – insbesondere der Schutz von Gewerbetreibenden gegen Nachahmung* (1996) 44 GRUR Int. p. 433
Bernitz, U., *Otillbörlig konkurrens mellan näringsidkare – det bortglömda rättsområdet*, in Festskrift till J. Hellner (1984), p. 115
Olsen, L., *Konsumentskyddets former* (1995)
Treis, M., *Recht des unlauteren Wettbewerbs- und Marktvertriebsrecht in Schweden* (1991)

General index

Index by state